MAGNETIC
STORAGE
HANDBOOK

Other McGraw-Hill Reference Books of Interest

Handbooks

Avallone and Baumeister • MARK'S STANDARD HANDBOOK FOR MECHANICAL
  ENGINEERS

Benson • AUDIO ENGINEERING HANDBOOK

Benson • TELEVISION ENGINEERING HANDBOOK

Coombs • PRINTED CIRCUITS HANDBOOK

Coombs • BASIC ELECTRONIC INSTRUMENT HANDBOOK

Croft and Summers • AMERICAN ELECTRICIANS' HANDBOOK

Di Giacomo • VLSI HANDBOOK

Fink and Beaty • STANDARD HANDBOOK FOR ELECTRICAL ENGINEERS

Fink and Christiansen • ELECTRONIC ENGINEERS' HANDBOOK

Harper • HANDBOOK OF ELECTRONIC SYSTEMS DESIGN

Harper • HANDBOOK OF THICK FILM HYBRID MICROELECTRONICS

Harper • HANDBOOK OF WIRING, CABLING, AND INTERCONNECTING FOR ELECTRONICS

Hicks • STANDARD HANDBOOK OF ENGINEERING CALCULATIONS

Inglis • ELECTRONIC COMMUNICATIONS HANDBOOK

Juran and Gryna • JURAN'S QUALITY CONTROL HANDBOOK

Kaufman and Seidman • HANDBOOK OF ELECTRONICS CALCULATIONS

Kurtz • HANDBOOK OF ENGINEERING ECONOMICS

Stout • MICROPROCESSOR APPLICATIONS HANDBOOK

Stout and Kaufman • HANDBOOK OF MICROCIRCUIT DESIGN AND APPLICATION

Stout and Kaufman • HANDBOOK OF OPERATIONAL AMPLIFIER CIRCUIT DESIGN

Tuma • ENGINEERING MATHEMATICS HANDBOOK

Williams • DESIGNER'S HANDBOOK OF INTEGRATED CIRCUITS

Williams and Taylor • ELECTRONIC FILTER DESIGN HANDBOOK

Dictionaries

DICTIONARY OF COMPUTERS

DICTIONARY OF ELECTRICAL AND ELECTRONIC ENGINEERING

DICTIONARY OF ENGINEERING

DICTIONARY OF SCIENTIFIC AND TECHNICAL TERMS

Markus • ELECTRONICS DICTIONARY

Other

Luther • DIGITAL VIDEO IN THE PC ENVIRONMENT

Mee and Daniel • MAGNETIC RECORDING TECHNOLOGY

Philips • COMPACT DISC INTERACTIVE

*To order or receive additional information on these or any other
McGraw-Hill titles, in the United States please call 1-800-822-8158.
In other countries, contact your local McGraw-Hill representative.*   **KEY=WM16XXA**

MAGNETIC STORAGE HANDBOOK

C. Denis Mee Editor

Los Gatos, California

Eric D. Daniel Editor

Redwood City, California

Second Edition

McGRAW-HILL

New York   San Francisco   Washington, D.C.   Auckland   Bogotá
Caracas   Lisbon   London   Madrid   Mexico City   Milan
Montreal   New Delhi   San Juan   Singapore
Sydney   Tokyo   Toronto

Library of Congress Cataloging-in-Publication Data

Magnetic storage handbook / C. Denis Mee, editor : Eric D. Daniel,
   editor. — 2nd ed.
        p.   cm.
   "Revised and updated version of Part II of the Magnetic recording
handbook published in 1990"—Foreword.
   Includes bibliographical references and index.
   ISBN 0-07-041275-8 (hc)
   1. Magnetic recorders and recording—Equipment and supplies.
I. Mee, C. Denis.   II. Daniel, Eric D.   III. Magnetic recording
handbook.
TK7881.6.M257   1996
621.382'34—dc20   96-19057
                                                             CIP

Second edition of Part II of *Magnetic Recording Handbook,* © 1990.

McGraw-Hill

A Division of The McGraw-Hill Companies

*The sponsoring editor for this book was Stephen S. Chapman, and the
production supervisor was Pamela Pelton. It was set in Times Roman by
Huron Valley Graphics, Ann Arbor, Michigan.*

Printed and bound by R. R. Donnelley & Sons Company.

This book is printed on acid-free paper.

McGraw-Hill books are available at special quantity discounts to use as
premiums and sales promotions, or for use in corporate training
programs. For more information, please write to the Director of Special
Sales, McGraw-Hill, 11 West 19th Street, New York, NY 10011. Or
contact your local bookstore.

We would like to dedicate this book to the memory of Katsuya Yokoyama, author of the contribution on Digital Video Recording published in previous editions of this book, who died in October, 1993.

C. Denis Mee
Eric D. Daniel

February, 1996

CONTENTS

Chapter 5. Analog Video Recording   *Hiroshi Sugaya*   5.1

Chapter 6. Digital Video Recording   *Chojuro Yamamitsu*   6.1

Chapter 7. Analog Audio Recording   *Eric D. Daniel*   7.1

Chapter 8. Digital Audio Recording   *John R. Watkinson*   8.1

ABOUT THE EDITORS

C. Denis Mee spent nearly three decades with IBM, where he specialized in advanced storage technologies, magnetooptical storage, bubbles, magnetic recording heads, media, and recording technologies for computer rigid disks. He was appointed an IBM Fellow in 1983. He retired from IBM in 1993.

Eric D. Daniel worked with Memorex Corporation for 17 years on a wide variety of magnetic recording media, including computer, instrumentation, video and audio tapes, computer rigid, and flexible disks. He is a former Fellow of Memorex, and has a total of more than 40 years' experience in magnetic recording research and development.

CONTRIBUTORS

R. Lawrence Comstock *San Jose, California*

Eric D. Daniel *Redwood City, California*

John Heath *Winchester, England*

James U. Lemke *San Diego, California*

C. Denis Mee *Los Gatos, California*

Arvind M. Patel *IBM Corporation, San Jose, California*

S. Robert Perera *Boulder, Colorado*

Richard C. Schneider *Storage Technology Corporation, Louisville, Colorado*

Hiroshi Sugaya *Kansai University, Osaka, Japan*

John R. Watkinson *Watkinson International Communications, Reading, Berkshire, England*

Michael L. Workman *IBM Corporation, San Jose, California*

Chojuro Yamamitsu *Matsushita Electric Industrial Company, Osaka, Japan*

Seiichi Yaskawa *Yaskawa Electric Corporation, Tokyo, Japan*

FOREWORD

The *Magnetic Storage Handbook* is a thoroughly revised and updated version of Part II of the *Magnetic Recording Handbook* published in 1990. A revised version of Part I has recently been published under the title *Magnetic Recording Technology*.

The extent of the revisions and additions made to the various chapters of the *Magnetic Storage Handbook* have been dictated by how rapidly the subject covered has changed since the earlier handbook was written. Revisions vary from relatively minor (10%) updates to complete rewrites and, in some cases, the recruitment of new authors. The chapters receiving the most extensive revisions are the following:

Data Storage on Rigid Disks. This chapter has been extensively updated to reflect the extraordinary achievements made in recent years in producing disk drives combining high capacity, small size, and low cost.

Data Storage on Flexible Disks. The major additions here cover the progress made in developing high-capacity, replaceable-disk drives designed to backup hard-disk files. These drives combine sophisticated servo systems and advanced flexible media design, and have capacities two orders of magnitude greater than regular 3.5-inch floppies.

Data Storage on Tape. This chapter is entirely new. It covers both fixed and rotating-head tape cartridges, and their primary application in providing large-capacity backup for hard-disk data.

Digital Video Recording. Formerly this subject was covered as a part of the chapter on video recording. It now warrants a newly written, greatly expanded, separate chapter. Digital video recording is now firmly established, with digital video tape recorders becoming increasingly available for both professional and consumer applications.

Digital Audio Recording. This chapter has been completely rewritten.

Other chapters of the *Magnetic Storage Handbook* required less extensive revision. However, where significant technological advances have occurred in recent years, these are covered by the inclusion of the relevant new data, descriptive text, and appropriate references.

PREFACE

The *Magnetic Storage Handbook* provides a comprehensive, up-to-date source of reference information on the major applications of magnetic recording technology for storing computer data, and recording video, audio, and instrumentation information in both analog and digital form. The handbook should be useful to the student as a reference book, but its main purpose is to provide the scientists and engineers in industry with a single source of information on the major applications of magnetic recording, and the related storage products that have been developed.

Magnetic Recording Technology, a recently published companion volume, covers the technologies underlying the various applications. It should also be of interest to industry scientists, particularly those engaged in research and advanced development, and will be of particular interest to the students and staff at the various University Storage Research Centers that have been set up in recent years.

It is some six years since the publication of the *Handbook of Magnetic Recording* that forms the foundation of the present work. The preface written at that time remarked on the rapid growth of the information storage industry and the position occupied by magnetic recording as the dominant, nonstatic memory technology. In the intervening years, the industry has grown at an accelerated pace, but magnetic recording still remains ubiquitous as the technology of choice for reversible, low-cost information storage. The versatility of magnetic recording is still unmatched in providing different storage formats—tapes, stripes, cards, flexible disks, as well as hard disks—a capability that makes magnetic recording uniquely adaptable to a wide variety of data, video, and audio applications, both at the business and consumer level.

The book treats each of the major applications in a separate chapter. The first three chapters deal with applications in the computer area, namely the storage of computer data on rigid (hard) disks, on flexible (floppy) disks, and on tape cartridges. The hard disk is the basis of the large-capacity storage files that are now an essential adjunct to all computers, from the personal computers used in the home to the super computers used in scientific laboratories. The advances made in hard-disk files in recent years are truly remarkable. Capacities of a gigabyte or more that required a stack of a dozen 14-inch diameter disks ten years ago are now readily, and inexpensively, obtainable in a package some four inches square by one-half inch thick. This in turn has stimulated the development of higher performance flexible-disk and tape-cartridge files, since a major use of these removable media files is as backup for hard-disk data. For example, over 100 MB can now be recorded on a single, removable 3-1/2 inch flexible disk. Huge data storage capabilities are available from tape cartridges and cartridges with a capacity of over 100 GB are under development.

The next four chapters cover video and audio recording, in both their traditional and still widely used analog forms, and in their increasingly important and, in the long run, probably dominant, digital forms. In view of their rapid development and increasing presence, digital video recording and digital audio recording are now allotted separate, entirely rewritten chapters, covering both professional or business applications and developments aimed at the consumer market. Another chapter is devoted to instrumentation recording which also uses both analog and digital formats.

The final chapter is concerned with signal and error-correction coding, from fundamental and practical viewpoints. This subject becomes of increasingly wide interest as computer storage applications expand, and digital forms of recording take over from the traditional analog techniques in more and more applications.

SI (Système International d'Unités) units are used throughout. Where other units (such as cgs) are widely used, values expressed in these units are listed in parentheses.

A comprehensive treatise of this scope is possible only by combining the knowledge of many talented people. We greatly appreciate the dedicated efforts of the authors who have contributed their reviews of each branch of the subject and have cooperated in producing an in-depth coverage of this multidisciplined field. We are also indebted to a number of others who provided independent reviews of draft chapters or provided special items of information that assisted us to produce a uniform and up-to-date coverage of the subject matter. These include Tom Howell at Phase Metrics Corporation, J. G. McKnight, and David P. Robinson at Magnetic Reference Laboratory.

LIST OF ABBREVIATIONS AND SYMBOLS

Abbreviations

ADC	analog-to-digital	EIA-J	Electronic Industry Association of Japan
ADRC	adaptive dynamic range coding	ELP	extra long play
AGC	automatic gain control	EPR4	extended partial response Class 4
ANSI	American National Standards Institute	EPRML	extended partial response, maximum likelihood
APC	automatic phase control	ERP	error recovery procedures
ATF	automatic track following	FDD	floppy disk drive
AXP	adaptive cross-parity code	FM	frequency modulation
BCH	binary-coded hexadecimal	GCR	group coded recording
CAV	constant angular velocity	GF	Galois field
CCIR	Commité Consultatif Internationale des Radio-Communications	HDA	head-disk assembly
		HDDR	high-density digital recording
CDS	code word digital sum	HDI	head-disk interface
CIRC	cross-interleaved Reed-Solomon code	HIP	hot isostatic pressed
CLV	constant linear velocity	HPF	hot pressed ferrite
CNR	carrier-to-noise ratio	IBC	International Broadcasting Convention
CRC	cyclic redundancy code	I/O	input/output
DAB	digital audio broadcasting	ITI	insert & tracking information
DAC	digital-to-analog converter		
DASD	direct access storage device	IEC	International Electrotechnical Commission
DASH	digital audio stationary head		
DAT	digital audio tape		
DCC	digital compact cassette	IRIG	Inter-Range Instrumental Group
DCT	discrete cosine transform		
DPCM	differential pulse-code modulation	ISI	intersymbol interference
		ISO	International Standards Organization
DR	density ratio		
DRAW	direct read after write	LQR	linear quadratic regulator
DSL	digital simulation language	LRC	longitudinal redundancy code
DSV	digital sum variation		
DTF	dynamic track following	LSB	least significant bit
DVTR	digital VTR	M^2	Miller squared
ECC	error-correction coding	MD	Mini Disc
EDL	edit decision list	ME	metal evaporated

MFM	modified frequency modulation
MO	magnetooptical
MOL	maximum output level
MP	metal powder (particle)
MSB	most significant bit
MSS	mass storage system
MTBF	mean time between failures
MTF	modulation transfer function
MUSE	multiple sub-Nyquist encoding
MZM	modified zero modulation
NEP	noise-equivalent power
NPR	noise-power ratio
NRZ	non-return-to-zero
NRZ-ASE	NRZ code with adapted spectral energy
NRZI	modified non-return-to-zero
NRZI-S	synchronized non-return-to-zero
NTSC	National Television System Committee
ORC	orthogonal rectangular code
PAL	phase alternation line
PAM	pulse amplitude modulation
PBS	polarizing beam splitter
PCM	pulse-code modulation
PE	phase encoding
PES	position error signal
PET	polyethylene teraphthalate
PIN	positive intrinsic negative
PLL	phase-locked loop
PMMA	polymethyl methacrylate
PR IV (PR4)	partial response Class IV (4)
PRML	partial response, maximum likelihood
QAM	quadrature-amplitude modulation
R-DAT	rotating-head digital audio tape recorder
RLL	run-length-limited
S-I-NRZI	scrambled and interleaved NRZI code
SCF	single crystal ferrite
SCSI	small computer standard interface
SECAM	sequential color and memory
SER	soft error rate

SFD	switching field distribution
SNR	signal-to-noise ratio
S-NRZ	scrambled NRZ
SP	standard play
SR	shift register
SSR	stretched surface recording
TBC	time base correction
THD	third harmonic distortion
TMR	track misregistration
VCM	voice coil motor
VCO	voltage controlled oscillator
VCXO	voltage controlled crystal oscillator
VFO	variable frequency oscillator
VHS	video home system
VLC	variable length coding
VRC	vertical redundancy code
VSM	vibrating sample magnetometer
VTR	video tape recorder
XOR	exclusive or
ZM	zero modulation
3PM	three-position modulation

Symbols

A	area; an element of GF (2^8)
a	acceleration; arctangent transition parameter
a_i	first digit of the ith digit-pair
$A_m(t)$	mth bit in track t in set A
$A(x)$	polynomial representation of A
B	magnetic induction (flux density)
b	base-film thickness; bit length; length of burst-error; width of guard band
B_i	written data byte in ith position
$\hat{B}_i$	read data byte in ith position
b_i	second digit of ith digit-pair
B_m	maximum induction (flux density)
$B_m(t)$	mth bit in track t in set B
B_r	remanent induction (flux density)

Symbol	Definition
B_s	saturation induction (flux density)
$B(x)$	data polynomial
C	capacitance; capacity (bytes)
c	accumulated dc charge at any digit position in a binary sequence
C_R	damping constant for rotary actuator
C_r	crosstalk
$C(x)$	check polynomial
D	data rate; delay factor; recording density; delay operator
d	head-drum diameter; head-to-medium spacing; minimum run-length of zeros in a binary sequence; RLL code constraint
D_a	areal density (b/mm^2)
D_c	recording density for maximum resolution
d_{eff}	effective head-to-medium spacing
d_i	data bit in the ith position in a data stream
D_l	linear (bit) density (b/mm)
D_r	recording density (fr/mm)
D_t	track density (t/mm)
D_u	user density (bytes/mm)
d_0	spacing corresponding to nominal "in-contact" conditions
D_{50}	linear density at which the output falls 50%
E	energy; Young's modulus
e	charge of electron; cycle length of modulo-$G(x)$ shift register; exponent of a polynomial $G(x)$; head output voltage
e_b	back emf
E_i	error pattern in ith position
$E(x)$	error polynomial
F	force; system matrix used in servo design; video field frequency
f	frequency; number of data bits in a section
f_c	carrier frequency
F_f	field frequency
f_H	horizontal sync frequency
f_m	maximum frequency
$f_{\max}$	maximum recorded frequency
f_s	signal frequency; sampling frequency
f_{sc}	subcarrier frequency
f_u	color-under subcarrier frequency
$F(\theta)$	particle orientation factor
G	gain
$G(D)$	characteristic polynominal in D
g	gap length
g_{eff}	effective gap length
g_i	ith coefficient in the generator polynomial $G(x)$
$G(x)$	generator polynomial
gb	guard band between tracks
GF(2^m)	Galois field of 2^m elements
H	magnetic field
H_b	bias field
H_c	coercivity
H_d	demagnetizing field
H_g	deep gap field
H_p	print field
H_r	remanence coercivity
i	current
j	$\sqrt{-1}$
k	Boltzmann constant; maximum runlength of zeros in a binary sequence; number of information bits in a code word; number of message symbols in a block; ratio of read-to-write widths (w_r/w_w); RLL code constraint; wave number ($2\pi/\lambda$)
k_b	back emf coefficient
k_d	damping coefficient
k_f	actuator force factor
k_x	position gain constant
L	inductance; inductance of voice coil; length of head poles; length of slider
l_{coil}	coil length (actuator)
L_1, L_2	inductance components of voice coil with shorted turns
$L_{1,2}$	coupling inductance of voice coil with shorted turn

M	magnetization; mass; moving mass of actuator	r	radial coordinate; radius; number of check bits in a code word
m	dipole magnetic moment; mass; mass of electron; number of data bits; particle magnetic moment	r_d	disk radius
		R_m	modulation code rate
M_p	printed magnetization	S	remanence squareness; synchronization pattern
M_r	remanent magnetization (remanence); modulation ratio (b/fr)	s	distance between head and permeable layer; number of message bits in a symbol
M_s	saturation magnetization	S_{MTF}	normalized zero-to-peak signal from an NRZ 1010 . . . pattern
N	number of particles per unit volume; see distance in units of tracks	S_{sat}	zero-to-peak signal from a saturated region
n	index of number of tracks; index of mode of vibration; number of bits in a code word; number of message bits; number of symbols in a block; number of turns; quantization bit number	S_{trans}	normalized zero-to-peak signal from an isolated transition
		S^*	coercivity squareness factor
		$S(x)$	syndrome polynomial
		Sd_m^a	mth cross parity syndrome in Set A
N_d	noise density	Sd_m^b	mth cross parity syndrome in set B
n_e	tracks remaining to target track	Sv_m^a	mth vertical parity syndrome in set A
N_h	number of turns on head	Sv_m^b	mth vertical parity syndrome in set B
N_l	number of turns on coil		
N_s	total number of sectors	T	companion matrix of a polynomial; data period; temperature; tension
N_t	total number of tracks		
P	power; print-to-signal ratio	t	time; total thickness of medium including substrate; track spacing
p	number of parity symbols in a block; location of error in a code word; pole-tip length; pressure; volumetric packing density		
		T_A	multiplier matrix corresponding to element A
p_a	ambient (atmospheric) pressure	t_a	audio track width
		T_c	Curie temperature
p_i	coded bit in the ith position in a data word	t_c	clock window; control track width
P_m	maximum print-to-signal ratio	t_g	guard band track width
		T_{max}	maximum duration between flux changes
p_{25}	pulse width at 25% amplitude		
p_{50}	pulse width at 50% amplitude	T_{min}	minimum duration between flux changes
$P(A)$	look-ahead parity in zero modulation	t_{min}	minimum track spacing
$P(B)$	look-back parity in zero modulation	$TMR_{W,R}$	write-to-read track misregistration
$P(x)$	prime polynomial	$TMR_{W,W}$	write-to-write track misregistration
Q	information bit redundancy; quality factor in servo design	$TMR_{3\sigma}$	3σ value of track misregistration
R	data rate; reluctance; resolution; resistance	t_p	track pitch

t_r	response time of rigid-disk file	α_{OT}	off-track constant
T_s	sampling time	Δw	side fringe width; discrepancy between track and playback head
t_{se}	service time of rigid-disk file		
t_v	video track width	δ	thickness of a magnetic medium
T_W	detection window		
t_w	wait time of rigid-disk file	δ_w	side fringe width of read head
$T_{\{i\}}$	timing window for $\{i\} =$ RLL and $\{i\} =$ NRZ codes	δw_w	side fringe width of write head
V	head-to-medium velocity; output voltage	η	efficiency
v	data word corresponding to a code word w; mean velocity of actuator	Θ	angle of rotary actuator
		θ	angular coordinate; video track inclined angle
V_c	clip level	θ_0	video track inclined angle when tape is stationary
V_m	medium velocity (when different from head-to-medium velocity)	Λ_{trans}	characteristic length of readback from isolated transition
v_{max}	maximum velocity of actuator	λ	wavelength
v_r	velocity of disk	λ_c	critical wavelength for maximum resolution
W	code word; transverse displacement; work	λ_{cutoff}	threshold for modulation transfer function
w	head width; track width; written mark width	λ_m	wavelength for maximum print-through
w_a	audio track width	λ_{min}	minimum recordable wavelength
w_c	control track width		
w_{eff}	effective track width	λ_s	magnetostriction coefficient
w_h	width of head	μ	magnetic permeability
w_r	read track width	μ_0	magnetic permeability of vacuum
w_t	tape width		
w_v	video track width	ρ	resistivity
w_w	write track width	σ	standard diviation
$W(x)$	code-word polynomial	τ	time constant; dibit peak shift
x_d	command to servo		
x_e	position error	$\bar{\tau}$	average access time
x_i	data bit in the ith position in a data word; first digit of the ith group of three digits	τ_{sk}	seek time
		$\bar{\tau}_{sk}$	average seek time
		τ_v	dominant time constant of actuator
x/y	rate of a run-length limited code	$\tau(n)$	time to access n tracks
Y_{coil}	admittance of voice coil	Φ	magnetic flux
y_i	second digit of the ith group of three digits	ϕ	angular coordinate; gap azimuth angle; magnetic flux
Z	impedance		
z_i	third digit of the ith group of three digits	χ	susceptibility
		χ_p	print susceptibility
α_a	coefficient of thermal expansion of arm	ψ	azimuthal angle
		Ω	rotational rate
α_s	turns ratio for shorted turn	ω	angular frequency $(2\pi f)$

CHAPTER 1

INTRODUCTION

C. Denis Mee
Los Gatos, California

Eric D. Daniel
Redwood City, California

Magnetic recording applications can logically be classified in several ways according to the type of signal to be recorded, the geometric shape of the recording medium, or the type of signal encoding used. Another classification recognizes that the interests of those working in the magnetic recording industry fall into certain well-defined categories. Classification by these categories has been the primary guide in organizing the contents of this book.

Chapters 2 through 4 are concerned with the storage of computer data on rigid disks, flexible disks, and tapes. These applications all use binary digital signals and are usually referred to collectively as *digital recording applications.* Chapters 5 through 9 deal with the recording of video, audio, and instrumentation signals. Each of these applications may use frequency modulation or digital encoding, as well as linear analog recording techniques. Nevertheless, they are usually referred to collectively as *analog recording applications* since they ideally provide an output that is an exact replica of the input. A chapter on signal and error-control coding, which is applicable to all digital recording applications, concludes the contents of this book.

Digital and analog applications differ mainly in terms of the requirements placed upon system performance. The primary requirements of a digital application are high data reliability, fast access to stored data, and low cost per bit. The primary requirements of an analog application are high signal-to-noise ratio, low distortion, and low cost per unit of playing time. Of these differences, the most fundamental is with respect to access time because this largely dictates the mechanical systems and media configurations that are used. In analog applications, the signal is usually in the form of large blocks of serial information—a musical composition, a television show, a transmission of data from a satellite. In such cases, a recording system using a medium in the form of a long length of tape is very suitable. However, in the words of Oberlin Smith, one of the early pioneers of magnetic recording, one disadvantage of a tape is "that if some small portion of the record near the middle has to be repeated there is a good deal of unwinding to do to get at it" (Smith, 1888). This difficulty of achieving quick access to stored data rules out tape media for on-line computer usage. Instead, magnetic media are more attractive in such forms as cards, strips, drums, and most importantly, disks.

Despite the differences outlined above, the two types of applications have much in common. The various species of digital and analog systems evolved over the years from the same origin and still share the same underlying technology—the subject matter of the companion book *Magnetic Recording Technology*. Unfortunately, during the course of this evolutionary process, the technical community working in magnetic recording became more firmly divided than seems reasonable in view of their common ground. This book brings together detailed discussions of all the major magnetic recording applications in one work. By so doing, it is hoped that some of the barriers that exist between workers in different areas will be reduced.

The pace of the evolution of storage technologies is strongly affected by the momentum of the applications that use magnetic and optical recording systems. However, other nonmagnetic optical recording techniques have been introduced into very large consumer applications and provide complementary and competitive storage products. Most significant is the domination of consumer audio recording products by the optically read digitally recorded compact disc. Also, this application has been supported more recently by new digital magnetic recording devices that offer recording as well as playback capability. One device is a digitally recorded magnetic tape, compatible with the popular analog tape cassette (Lokhoff, 1991). The other is a miniature magnetooptical disk drive (Yoshida, 1994).

The evolution of storage devices for the personal computer is also influencing the pace of storage technology development. Primarily, it has greatly accelerated the development of small rigid-disk files. Here, the pace of technology advancement, measured by the storage capacity of small drives, has been increased to the highest level of the 40-year history of disk file development. In turn, this is increasing the use of higher capacity programs in PCs and therefore has put pressure on the development of higher capacity program storage devices. High capacity magnetic floppy disks have been developed to meet this requirement. However, the compact disc technology, called CD-ROM, is finding rapidly increasing application for high capacity PC program storage.

The depth of coverage of recording systems for different applications is weighted by the individual experiences of the authors. Nevertheless, in this book there is collectively a detailed description of the generic magnetic storage technologies used in today's products. For instance, the designs of digital recording channels described for rigid disks and tapes are largely applicable to flexible disks and magnetooptical disks. Likewise, the servo technology discussion on rigid disks applies to flexible and magnetooptical disk systems. While signal coding and error correction coding are mentioned in each of the digital recording chapters, the detailed coverage of the subject is relevant to all applications. Thus, it is hoped that readers will profit from studying chapters that are beyond but related to their specific fields of interest.

The following description of magnetic recording systems will serve as an introduction for those not familiar with magnetic recording.

1.1 EVOLUTION OF MAGNETIC RECORDING SYSTEMS

Every magnetic recording system comprises a means for mechanically transporting recording media and heads with respect to each other, together with a package for the recording medium appropriate to the application. Also included is an electronic signal processor to deliver the signal to the recording head in a form suited to the recording method chosen. Another signal processor reconstructs the reproduced signal into an undistorted replica of the original or into a form that retains certain significant characteristics of the original.

The traditional systems using magnetically coated tape, ring heads, and longitudinal magnetization have dominated product applications since the late 1940s. The first major product application was for audio recording, which was founded on, and continues to use, linear analog methods based on ac biasing. Digital audio recording, used in many professional audio recorders, has yet to supplant the analog audio cassette application. Many instrumentation applications have also used ac bias although, here also, the development of digital instrumentation recorders is now emphasized. The requirements for providing high signal-to-noise ratios while increasing recording densities have kept audio and instrumentation applications at the leading edge of high-density magnetic recording technology.

Extensions of tape recording to the storage of digital data were developed using unbiased nonlinear recording over 40 years ago (Harris et al., 1981). New tape-drive devices were required to operate at high tape speeds and provide fast access to the stored data. The requirement for fast access spurred the development of magnetic strips and loops, but these approaches suffered from poor reliability. Magnetic tape-drive systems continue to be the primary mass storage technology for digital data. Attempts to extend stationary-head tape machines to video recording failed because they required excessive tape speed to record the very high frequencies involved. This problem was solved in 1956 with the introduction of a scanning-head machine. This major innovation was initially applied to professional video recording using high-speed transverse scanning of a slowly moving tape. Subsequent evolution of helical scanning techniques expanded the application to lower-cost drives and ushered in the huge consumer video-recording market (Kihara et al., 1976; Shiraishi and Hirota, 1978).

Another significant innovation was the introduction of the rotating rigid disk for digital data storage in 1957 (Lesser and Haanstra, 1957; Noyes and Dickinson, 1957). Using an air bearing to support a read-write head allowed a substantial increase in head-media velocity. Not only did this provide high reliability and high data rate, but it enabled fast radial accessing over the disk. The rigid-disk system has become the ubiquitous design of choice for on-line storage of computer data. The related flexible-disk system using in-contact recording became a major product with the advent of the personal computer (Noble, 1974; Engh, 1981). This inexpensive storage technology uses a single coated plastic disk inside a protective jacket. The removable, lightweight "diskette" became the primary low-cost storage medium for small computers and only recently has been complemented by the much larger capacity CD-ROM.

The success of magnetic recording products in penetrating the markets for data storage and video and audio applications has relied on a sustained upgrading of heads, media and electronics. Improvements in linear recording density resulted from advances in the magnetic and mechanical properties of head and media materials. Areal density has been increased by improvements in both linear and track densities for the major applications of disk and tape recording. There are always some technical factors which limit the relative rates of linear and track density improvement, but the major impediments in some applications are the constraints of standardization. This is particularly true of tape recording where, for example, compatibility requirements in computer data tapes initially prohibited track density advances. The 1985 introduction of an alternative to the nine-track open tape reel provided a break with the data storage standard and has led to substantial advances in linear and track densities. Subsequently, the introduction of narrow width tapes and rotary head drives using a range of tape widths has provided a proliferation of tape storage systems and media cartridges or cassettes for data storage. Backward compatibility for each format is still important, but with many different design approaches in use, the advancement in storage density has proceeded more rapidly. In audio recording, the introduction of digital audio recording was accompanied by very high linear and track densities using either stationary multitrack heads or rotating single-track heads (Nakajima et al., 1983; Mukasa, 1985).

The combination of higher linear density, greater head-medium velocity, and multiple-track recording has provided an increase in the upper limit of recording bandwidth of nine orders of magnitude over the last 40 years. Progress in providing faster access to the stored data has also been impressive particularly in rigid-disk systems. Further improvements in accessing by providing more heads, for example a head per track on a disk, are no longer cost competitive with low-cost large-scale integration (LSI) electronic memories. The combination of high-performance memory and moderate-performance, direct-access disk storage is preferred for on-line data storage.

Some of the difficult challenges for heads and media are circumvented in the emerging optical-beam storage technology (Kryder, 1985). Laser-beam writing and reading on magnetic media provides at once an out-of-contact erasable recording method and the capability for narrow-track operation. This high-density recording technology, using rigid disks, has emerged in PC backup applications as well as large capacity data storage libraries. While the basic concept for reversible recording was demonstrated about 25 years ago, major product implementations have been slow to emerge. The combined performance potential of fast accessing capability and high areal recording density will have to be advanced aggressively to compete with the incumbent storage technology.

1.2 DATA STORAGE SYSTEMS

Binary digital signals are particularly well-suited for magnetic recording. Ideally, they are written by reversals of a head field sufficient to saturate the recording medium. No attempt is made to linearize the writing process, and maximum reproduce head flux is obtained on reading the recorded transitions. In order to reduce errors to a minimum, heads, media, and data channels are designed to write and read the data transitions with minimum shift in the timing of the reproduced pulses. With only two states in binary data recording, it is profitable to apply error detection and correction coding techniques in order to provide many orders of magnitude of error reduction (Peterson et al., 1972). The incorporation of error correction codes decreases the storage density of data on the medium, but the net effect is a substantial improvement in error-free storage density. The primary magnetic recording systems for data storage utilize rigid disks, flexible disks, and tapes.

1.2.1 Rigid-Disk Drives

The main components of a disk drive are illustrated in Fig. 1.1. This part of the storage system contains a stack of disks mounted on a spindle rotating inside an enclosure to minimize internal contamination. Writing and reading are achieved with magnetic heads, each provided with a spring suspension attached to an arm. The head elements are individually mounted on sliders which are loaded against the surface of a disk. A hydrodynamic bearing is generated at the slider-disk interface,

FIGURE 1.1   Rigid-disk drive components (courtesy IBM, San Jose).

which provides a small but stable spacing between the heads and the disk. The head arms are connected to a common spindle which is positioned by an electromagnetic actuator to provide random access of the heads to any desired track on the disk. Usually, one head near the center of the stack reads a control track, and the signal from this head is used to control the swing-arm electromagnetic actuator. In other designs, a linear electromagnetic actuator is used and provides somewhat faster accessing speeds.

The accessing performance of different designs of large and small files varies because of the ranges of the track-seeking time, the disk rotational delay time, and the channel-busy time. Typically, these three times are about equal to each other. Their sum leads to the average time to complete a request for data, known as the *service time*. The total response time comprises the service time plus the data queueing time, which depends on the number of access paths into the data. As storage densities go up, there is a need to increase the number of access arms and heads in order to contain the queueing time within a reasonable fraction of the total response time.

The advances in areal density achieved over the last 40 years have been made possible through a steady introduction of improved design concepts (Harker et al., 1981; Kaneko and Koshimoto, 1982; Bajorek and Mee, 1994). Early files were designed to use removable disk stacks, but these became impractical as closer head-to-media and track spacings were required. Today, heads are permanently dedicated to a disk surface in order to improve the alignment of heads and recorded tracks. For these designs, there is a complex relationship between the tribological behavior of the heads and disks in the various modes of operation of the disk file, that is, during starting and stopping, during accessing of the head, and during the resting period when the heads and disks are in contact. The environment inside the head-disk enclosure, the formation of debris in the enclosure, and the lubricant on the disk all play a part, as do any changes in these factors with usage of the disk file. Magnetic film media with protective film overcoats and lubricants have been developed with adequate durability during starting and stopping, but the layers are required to be progressively thinner in order to improve recording resolution. Thinner layers, in turn, demand defect-free substrates since they are less effective in masking substrate imperfections. Heads have been reduced in size, and the materials and processes used have been improved to produce smaller gaps and narrower tracks. Magnetoresistive film heads have been used in some new disk file designs and are expected to be extended to many future designs as costs are reduced. Detailed descriptions of heads and media and their performance in disk files are given in the companion book *Magnetic Recording Technology.*

1.2.2 Flexible-Disk Drives

The key elements of a flexible-disk drive are shown in Fig. 1.2. The drive is designed for easy insertion and removal of the single flexible disk (diskette) in its enclosing jacket. When mounted in the drive, the disk is clamped at its center and rotated at a relatively low speed while the read-write head accesses the disk through a slot in the jacket. In many designs the accessing arms traverse above and below the disk and with read-write head elements mounted on spring suspensions. When reading and writing take place, the suspensions push the heads together with the double-coated disk interposed. In this way writing and reading can be achieved on both sides of the disk. Since the heads are in contact with the recording surface, high linear densities can be achieved. On the other hand, track densities are relatively low compared with rigid-disk files, because of the poor dimensional stability of the plastic disk substrate, the limited positioning accuracy of the disk clamp, and the lack of a track servo system in a low-cost drive. Head positioning is usually accomplished by a stepping motor whose rotational position is translated to a linear position of the head arm via a steel band as seen in Fig. 1.2. Track position inaccuracy is allowed for by providing an erasing head to erase the regions on either side of the read-write track. This "tunnel erase" design is usually a part of the read-write head. As higher track density systems evolve, servos will be required to follow

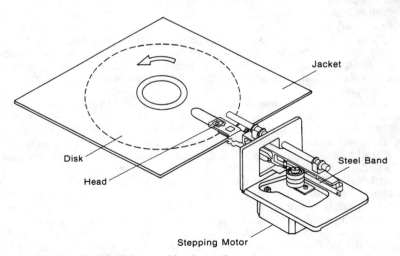

FIGURE 1.2   Flexible diskette and head accessing system.

the tracks. One approach is to intersperse servo information at regular intervals around the track between sectors of data.

The trend in flexible-disk designs has been toward smaller disks, protected by a hard-shell jacket, with no exposed recording surfaces when the disk is not in use (Katoh et al., 1981). The constraints imposed by the removable diskette are the unique limitations of this technology. Otherwise, the recording innovations for higher densities follow those developed for tapes and rigid disks; this includes thinner coatings, higher coercivity media, improved wear characteristics of the media and heads, and improved disk lubrication (Bate et al., 1981). The primary applications of flexible disks have been as inexpensive products with high tolerance to handling damage. The track densities used have lagged the achievements of more expensive rigid-disk applications. More expensive flexible-disk products achieve higher track densities using head servoing technology and faster data rates using high-velocity "flying" disks.

1.2.3 Tape Drives

Data recording on magnetic tape involves the application of 0.5-in-wide or narrower tapes in open-reel and single-reel cartridge, or double-reel cassette formats. In the higher-performance systems, the tape-drive mechanism must be capable of accurately guiding the tape at up to 200 in per second in contact with a multitrack read-write head. A requirement for on-line tape drives is the need for very fast starts and stops in order to minimize the wasted time between blocks of data. This requirement led to the use of low-inertia motors under servo control, together with vacuum columns to mechanically decouple the tape from the tape reels in the region of the read-write head. Subsequently, the need for fast starting and stopping was relieved by electronic buffering of the data stream; this allows lower tape acceleration and deceleration without loss of recording area on the tape. Also, interchanging tapes between different drives is helped by the use of electronic buffers to realign the signals for the different tracks of the multitrack head. Thus, the design of a data tape drive is simplified as illustrated in Fig. 1.3, which is a single-cartridge drive using a stationary multitrack read-

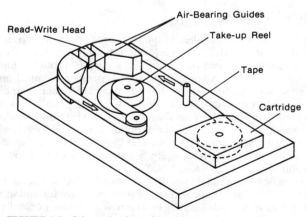

FIGURE 1.3 Schematic of cartridge drive for data recording.

write head. This drive is designed to match the data rate of an on-line data disk file.

The increases in recording density in 0.5-in data tape have resulted from the development of improved magnetic oxides, the introduction of metal particles, reductions in the number of defects in the recording medium, and the introduction of superior head-medium interface designs which maintain a uniformly small spacing between the head and medium with minimum wear. The track density for tape recording is relatively low compared with other data recording drive systems and, therefore, a high signal level is achievable; this allows substantial amplitude equalization to be applied to the recording and reading channels with consequent gains in overall recording density. Complementing the equalization, powerful error correction codes have provided many orders of magnitude reduction in errors which would otherwise increase dramatically as the recording density increases.

Several different tape-drive formats have been developed to complement the mainstream evolution of 0.5-in tape drives. One motivation has been to alleviate the high cost of multitrack heads. A promising contending head design is the rotating single-track head developed for video recording (Newby and Yen, 1983). The ability to scan a relatively wide tape shortens the length of tape required for a given data capacity and thereby improves the access time to a given track. High data rate per track is achieved owing to an increase in the head-medium velocity by about an order of magnitude over the stationary-head, 0.5-in tape drives. This approximately offsets the data rate reduction due to using a single-track head. The scanning head approach has been applied widely in video and instrumentation recording. It now also is firmly entrenched in the computer data storage field.

Very high density digital tape recording has been developed for recording the wide-bandwidth transmissions encountered in certain instrumentation applications. One direction of this area of development involves the use of multitrack heads to achieve the required bandwidth. Rotary-head designs have also been developed with higher recording density capability. Magnetic recording still remains the most cost-effective storage and retrieval technology for this type of data (Kalil, 1982, 1985).

1.3 IMAGE RECORDING SYSTEMS

1.3.1 FM Video Recording

As mentioned earlier, stationary-head tape machines originally proved impractical to record the large bandwidth of video information, which stretches from dc to over 4 MHz. The dc requirement can be overcome by using FM, but the high-frequency requirement leads to either excessive tape speeds or uneconomical multiple-track multiplexing schemes. The breakthrough occurred in 1956 when Ampex introduced the Quadruplex video recorder (Kirk, 1981; Ginsburg, 1986). This uses a head-scanning mechanism in which four heads, mounted on a rotating wheel, scan successively across the width of a 2-in-wide tape at about 40 m/s (1600 in/s), while the tape moves by at a leisurely 38 cm/s (15 in/s). The high head-to-tape speed allows the whole video signal to be recorded using a specially developed low-modulation-index FM (Robinson, 1981; Benson, 1986).

The transverse-scanning machines, in a series of enhanced versions, remained the standard recorders for broadcast use for over two decades and are still in use. The alternative is to scan heads (usually two) across a narrower (usually 1-in or less) tape, forming long tracks at an acute angle to the tape length. This means that the

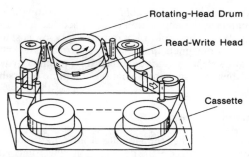

FIGURE 1.4   Helical-scan video recorder.

tape moves in a helical path around a drum containing the rotating heads. A home video tape recorder using a helical-scanning head and a two-reel cassette is shown in Fig. 1.4. The helical-scanning method simplifies the electronics in that a whole video field is recorded by one head scan. Without correction, the time-base stability associated with the long track is inherently insufficient to meet broadcasting standards but may be adequate to meet the requirements of many closed-circuit television applications in industry and other areas. The development of electronic means of time-base correction has allowed the helical-scan method to be developed for broadcasting use where, compared with transverse-scan, it offers economies in equipment and tape costs. The helical-scan method has also become the basis of the huge market for home video recording. Modifications are required in order to make the necessary dramatic reductions in the cost and size of the equipment and in the tape consumption per hour of playing time. First, at some small expense in color picture quality, the high-frequency color carrier is placed at a lower frequency than the luminance signal ("color-under"), thus compressing the overall bandwidth. Second, the guard bands, normally required between successive scans of the tape, are eliminated by using different head gap azimuth angles for adjacent recorded tracks. The consequent misalignment of the recorded signals reduces the pickup of the adjacent-track signal, should the head wander off the desired track. The scheme fits well with the convention, convenient for other reasons, of using two head elements on the rotating drum.

Head improvements have been required to achieve shorter wavelength recording as well as narrower tracking capability. This challenge has been met, for the most part, by improving or modifying ferrite heads. In particular, single-crystal ferrites are used for combined mechanical and magnetic performance reasons. Alloy pole tips are added to provide sufficient recording field for the high-coercivity particles required for very short wavelength recording. Track-following servos have also been introduced to achieve better tracking of the recorded media. Piezoelectric mounting arms for the heads provide up to 100 μin of lateral head motion for tracking purposes.

Additional signal manipulation is being applied to different applications for video recording. In the consumer recorder, for instance, the repetitious nature of the video signal is used to conceal the signal degradation due to imperfect media. When loss of signal occurs, the error is concealed by repeating the previous television field.

8-mm video recorders are now widely used in small, hand-held camera-recorder systems, continuing the preference for magnetic tape as the leading technology for video recording. Perhaps the major challenge for video tape recording is the lack of a fast, low-cost duplication process. Today, copies are made by rerecording at normal operating tape speeds. Replication of disks is a low-cost advantage for high-density, read-only optical disk storage. Recordable versions of compatible storage disks are available and will enhance the application of compact disc technology in both video and audio recording. When the application requires very low cost technology but only limited reversibility, a nonmagnetic phase-change recording technology will compete advantageously. However, magnetooptical recording technology will continue to improve and simplify, thus allowing a combination of infinite reversibility and low cost.

1.3.2 Digital Video Recording

In professional video recording, the significant advantages of digital recording—higher signal-to-noise ratio, no copying degradation, fewer uncorrectable errors and data compression—are receiving increased attention, and international standards are being promulgated. The application of powerful Reed-Solomon error correction plus interpolation of picture elements will allow digital recording densities to be achieved with lower tape consumption than analog recording. Powerful data compression techniques have been applied to video signals allowing compression factors of more than 20 times. This has had a profound effect on the ability of all types of magnetic recording and optical recording technologies to be able to store video signals in extremely small media cartridges. The consequent development of consumer digital video recorders and players is supported with several recording technologies for both disk and tape designs.

1.4 AUDIO RECORDING SYSTEMS

1.4.1 Linear Analog Audio Recording

The recording of audio signals, using linear analog techniques, is the oldest application of magnetic recording. It is also one of the most demanding in terms of signal-to-noise ratio and bandwidth (10 octaves) and the requirements these place upon the properties of the magnetic medium.

The elements of the generic audio recording have changed little since it was discovered that ac bias could be used to linearize the recording process. Separate recording, reproducing, and erasing heads are used on all but the least expensive recorders (Fig. 1.5). The original single-track, quarter-inch tape recorder has been

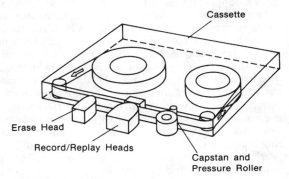

FIGURE 1.5   Audio cassette recorder.

expanded or contracted to form many configurations aimed at meeting the special needs of the recording studio, the home, industry, and school. Thus, at one extreme, there are machines for the professional recording engineer that use up to 32 tracks on 2-in-wide tape for program editing and mastering. At the other extreme, there are machines designed to fulfill special needs such as portable headphone recorders, microcassette dictating machines, and telephone-answering devices.

At the consumer level, the quarter-inch tape recorder has all but disappeared, and the two-reel "compact cassette," has become the worldwide standard. This format uses two pairs of stereo tracks on 3.8-mm-wide tape running at 48 mm/s. Despite the narrow tracks and slow tape speed, a good-quality cassette recording delivers an audio performance that rivals that of its quarter-inch predecessors running at four or more times the speed. This performance has been achieved by making improvements in all the components of the system: record, replay, and erase heads; mechanical drives; magnetic media; and signal processing. Of these, the last two deserve brief mention here.

Traditionally, audio recording, more than any other form of recording, provided the stimulus for exploring new materials for magnetic media. In part, this was because there was always a need to increase signal-to-noise ratio while maintaining (or increasing) bandwidth. Also, the volume of material involved in audio applications is large enough to provide the incentive to the independent manufacturers of such materials. Finally, although governed by strict international standards, the audio recording industry is not loath to try something new, provided the advantages offered are significant. Thus, audio recording has been the proving ground for many new materials—fine-particle oxides, chromium dioxide, cobalt-modified oxides, metal particles, and even evaporated metal—before these materials found application in video or data recording.

Another way of increasing signal-to-noise ratio is to introduce complementary signal-processing techniques into the recording and reproducing channels which have the net effect of reducing the noise that is not already masked by a high signal level (Dolby, 1967). These noise-reduction schemes have had a major impact on audio recording performance, both at the professional and the consumer level.

1.4.2 Digital Audio Recording

Digital audio recording has the potential of producing a high signal-to-noise ratio while avoiding virtually all of the other signal degradations associated with the analog approach. Digital recording is used in producing master tapes for high-quality program duplication when the program production does not demand complex editing and mixing between a large number of channels. When such mixing is required, as it is for much popular music, ac-biased master recording is still employed. In order to record at the approximate data rate of 1 Mb/s per channel, professional mastering recorders use either a stationary-head recorder with the digital audio signal divided between multiple tracks or a modified video helical-scan recorder.

For the consumer, audio recording using either FM pulse code modulation or digital (PCM) encoding is available on the higher quality home video recorders. Also, dedicated digital audio technologies have emerged based, again, on either a multiple-track stationary-head approach (S-DAT) or a rotating-head approach (R-DAT). Both are remarkable for the high track density (12.5 and 73.6 tracks per millimeter) and high linear density (2560 and 2440 fr/mm). Both systems use high-coercivity metal-particle tapes.

1.5 MAGNETOOPTICAL RECORDING SYSTEMS

An alternative type of magnetic-recording system uses an optical-beam read-write device instead of an inductive or flux-sensing head. Writing is achieved via a change in the magnetic properties of the media when heated by the beam. Reading is accomplished with a lower intensity beam using the magnetooptical rotation of the plane of polarization. Very high recording densities are projected. This technology has the major advantage of avoiding close proximity between heads and media, while offering a higher areal density than currently practiced in magnetic recording products.

The rudiments of an optical head and disk are shown in Fig. 1.6. The focusing and tracking lens above the disk can be mechanically accessed with a small electromagnetic actuator of the type used for magnetic recording on disks. Writing is achieved by modulating the beam in the presence of a perpendicular magnetic field applied, for instance, from a current-carrying coil underneath the disk. This magnetic field need not be localized to the recorded track since switching of the magnetization can occur only where the focused spot heats the surface and reduces the coercivity below the applied field magnitude. Recording takes place in physically pregrooved tracks molded into the substrate. Reading of the magnetized track is achieved at reduced beam power and without the field applied. In this mode, the plane of polarization of the reflected beam is changed slightly depending upon the magnetization direction of an element of the recorded track. Detection of this change of polarization is achieved with a polarizing beam splitter and photo detector. Overwriting of a previously recorded track is normally achieved by applying an unmodulated writing beam and resetting the magnetization. The drawback of this simple scheme is that it requires two revolutions of the disk to rewrite a new track. A unique advantage of optical storage media is that the recording layer is protected

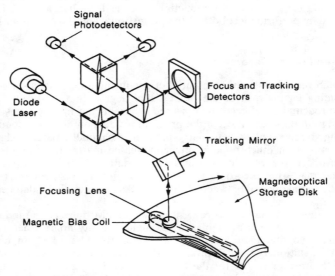

FIGURE 1.6 Components for an optical read-write head for recording on magnetic media.

on one side by the transparent substrate and on the other side by a relatively thick overcoat. Thus the surfaces of the disk can be made insensitive to handling damage since the recording beam is focused on the internal recording layer and not on the medium surface. Therefore, under normal handling conditions, optical disks do not require a protective jacket.

The most successful consumer application for optical recording is the read-only compact audio disk. Although this is a different recording technology to magnetooptical recording, it has demonstrated the practicality of recording at the highest areal densities in a commercial product in normal domestic environments including the poor conditions of audio players in automobiles. Magnetooptical read-write disks have similar environmental behavior, since adequate stability of the recording medium itself has been achieved. At this stage of development, magnetic coatings for conventional magnetic recording have superior intrinsic stability compared with reversible optical media, and they can be designed with either rigid or flexible substrates. Consequently, although magnetooptical recording will find increasing acceptance, the wide range of product applications described in this book is expected to continue for conventional magnetic recording and for new non-magnetic optical recording disks.

1.6 OUTLOOK

The number of applications for magnetic-recording products has increased impressively over the last 40 years and shows every sign of continuing to advance through the remainder of the twentieth century. In contrast to many predictions that the underlying technology would top out, there has been no slowing down of improvements in recording performance. In data storage applications the challenges from solid-state storage or from beam-addressable storage have, so far, had little impact on the domination of this business by magnetic recording products. Successful incursion of these new technologies into the realm of magnetic recording applications will depend on their continued rapid advance and a slowing down of magnetic recording advances. In the near future, developments currently underway to improve magnetic recording components and signal processing and control systems will ensure continued advances in recording density, data rates, and access speeds. This will present the challenging technologies with the same kind of moving target they have seen in the past. Any new technology will have to demonstrate the collected set of attributes that have made magnetic recording such a durable technology—that is, reversibility without degradation, environmental stability, and recording performance at an advantageous product cost. The recent successes of read-only optical storage technology in personal computer applications have spurred an increase in research programs to advance true read-write optical storage. The surge of activity has advanced a number of technologies in this area with magnetooptical and phase change optical recording as leading contenders.

REFERENCES

Bajorek, C. H., and C. D. Mee, "Trends in Storage Technology through the Year 2000," *Data Storage,* **1,** 23 (1994).

Bate, G., G. J. Hampton, and B. J. Latta, "A 5-Megabyte Flexible Disk," *IEEE Trans. Magn.*, **MAG-17,** 1408 (1981).

Benson, K. B. (ed.), *Television Engineering Handbook,* McGraw-Hill, New York, 1986.

Benson, K. B. (ed.), *Audio Engineering Handbook,* McGraw-Hill, New York, 1988.

Dolby, R. M., "An Audio Noise Reduction System," *J. Audio Eng. Soc.,* **15,** 383 (1967).

Engh, J. T., "The IBM Diskette and Diskette Drive," *IBM J. Res. Dev.,* **25,** 701 (1981).

Ginsburg, C. P., "Development of the Videotape Recorder," in *Videotape Recording,* Ampex Corporation, Redwood City, CA, 1986, Chap. 1, p. 3.

Harker, J. M., D. W. Brede, R. E. Pattison, G. R. Santana, and L. G. Taft, "A Quarter Century of Disk File Innovation," *IBM J. Res. Dev.,* **25,** 677 (1981).

Harris, J. P., W. B. Phillips, J. F. Wells, and W. D. Winger, "Innovations in the Design of Magnetic Tape Subsystems," *IBM J. Res. Dev.,* **25,** 691 (1981).

Kalil, F., *Magnetic Tape Recording for the Eighties,* NASA Reference Publication 1075, U.S. Govt. Printing Office, Washington, DC, 1982.

Kalil, F., *High-Density Digital Recording,* NASA Reference Publication 1111, U.S. Govt. Printing Office, Washington, DC, 1985.

Kaneko, R., and Y. Koshimoto, "Technology in Compact and High Recording Density Disk Storage," *IEEE Trans. Magn.,* **MAG-18,** 1221 (1982).

Katoh, Y., M. Nakayama, Y. Tanaka, and K. Takahashi, "Development of a New Compact Floppy Disk Drive System," *IEEE Trans. Magn.,* **MAG-17,** 2742 (1981).

Kihara, N., F. Kohno, and Y. Ishigaki, "Development of a New System of Cassette Tape Consumer VTR," *IEEE Trans. Consum. Electron.,* **22,** 26 (1976).

Kirk, D. (ed.), *25 Years of Video Tape Recording,* 3M United Kingdom Ltd., Bracknell, England, 1981.

Kryder, M., "Magneto-Optic Recording Technology," *J. Appl. Phys.,* **57,** 3913 (1985).

Lesser, M. L., and J. W. Haanstra, "The Random-Access Memory Accounting Machine. I. System Organization of the IBM 305," *IBM J. Res. Dev.,* **1,** 62 (1957).

Lokhoff, G. C. P., "Digital Compact Cassette," *IEEE Trans. Consum. Electron.,* **CE-37,** 702 (1991).

Mukasa, K., "Magnetic Heads," *J. Inst., Telev. Eng. Japan,* **30,** 295 (1985).

Nakajima, H., T. Doi, J. Fukuda, and A. Iga, *Digital Audio Technology,* TAB Books, Blue Ridge Summit, PA, 1983.

Newby, P. S., and J. L. Yen, "High Density Digital Recording Using Videocassette Recorders," *IEEE Trans. Magn.,* **MAG-19,** 2245 (1983).

Noble, D. L., "Some Design Considerations for an Interchangeable Disk File," *IEEE Trans. Magn.,* **MAG-10,** 571 (1974).

Noyes, T., and W. E. Dickinson, "The Random-Access Memory Accounting Machine. II. The Magnetic-Disk, Random-Access Memory," *IBM J. Res. Dev.,* **1,** 72 (1957).

Peterson, W. W., and E. J. Weldon, *Error Correction Codes,* MIT Press, Cambridge, MA, 1972.

Robinson, J. F., *Videotape Recording,* Focal Press, London, 1981.

Shiraishi, Y., and A. Hirota, "Video Cassette Recorder Development for Consumers," *IEEE Trans. Consum. Electron.,* **CE-24,** 468 (1978).

Smith, O., "Some Possible Forms of Phonograph," *The Electrical World,* **9,** 116 (1888).

Yoshida, T., "The Rewritable Minidisc System," *Proc. IEEE,* **82,** 1492 (1994).

CHAPTER 2
DATA STORAGE ON RIGID DISKS

R. Lawrence Comstock
San Jose, California

With sections on head-positioning servomechanism by

Michael L. Workman
IBM Corporation, San Jose, California

2.1 OVERVIEW OF RIGID-DISK FILES

2.1.1 Disk File Technology

Rigid-disk files, or hard disk drives, consist of a single disk, or stack of disks, which have a thin magnetic coating and rotate at a high speed. The disk surfaces are recorded using heads mounted on arms that are moved across the disk surfaces by a high-speed actuator. Information is recorded in circumferential tracks on the disk surfaces. In one disk file architecture the actuator position is measured with respect to a disk surface written with information that can be used to measure relative position with respect to track centerlines. This surface is referred to as the *servo surface,* and in this dedicated-servo file architecture all the heads on a given actuator are maintained in a "cylinder" of tracks that can be accessed in microseconds. In another disk file architecture, the *sector servo* architecture, and low-end disk files, the servo information is embedded in the data tracks as prerecorded sectors. Digital recording is used and information is read back as strings of encoded positive and negative voltage pulses that are detected in a recording channel. The mechanical and electronic systems used in a disk file are shown in Fig. 2.1. They are the head-disk assembly; the data channel, which processes the analog read signals and digital write-current pulses; and the actuator control system, which controls the position of the actuator and the head-arm assembly over the disk surfaces.

Rigid-disk files have been used as the primary device for storage of on-line data in personal computers and workstations to intermediate and high-end computer systems since the early 1960s. Disk files, also known in high-end systems as *direct access storage devices,* have maintained this position because advances in areal

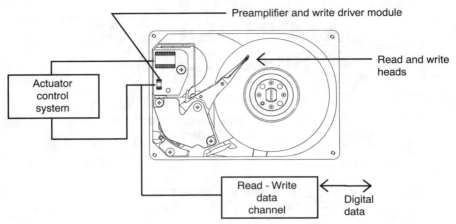

FIGURE 2.1   A rigid-disk file including the head disk assembly consisting of a base plate and the rotating disks and rotary actuator on which is mounted the recording heads. Block diagrams of the actuator control system and the read-write data channel are also shown. The electronic components for the disk file are mounted on a printed circuit board attached to the bottom of the base plate. A sealed cover is attached to protect the magnetic recording components.

recording density have kept pace with the requirements for on-line storage. During the past 15 years, areal density has increased by a factor of about 100 and has resulted in dramatically lower cost of storage. In Fig. 2.2 is shown the progression of areal density in Kbits/mm^2, which is the product of the maximum linear density in b/mm times the track density in tr/mm, since 1985. The historical trend was a compound growth rate of 30% per year until the early 1990s when it increased to 60% per year. The explanation for the rapid increase in areal density over the period since 1990 will be a significant part of the chapter. The underlying recording head technologies that have been used in disk files during this period used the hydrodynamic air bearing which supports the recording head slider close to the disk. Narrow gap recording heads were developed which, starting in the early 1970s, used ferrite cores and since the early 1980s, have increasingly used plated permalloy poles and integrated coils (thin-film heads). Magnetoresistive read heads have greatly accelerated the increase in areal density since the early 1990s, as shown in Fig. 2.2. Initially disk file technology used disks with particulate coatings which, starting in the early 1980s, were oriented along the circumference of the disk. With the advent of smaller disk diameters, thin metallic alloy disk coatings prepared by vacuum sputtering emerged in the late 1980s. In order for the spacing between the head and disk surface to decrease it was necessary to improve the mechanical aspects of the disk surface to control stiction, friction, and wear. The dimensions of the slider have been reduced over time and this has reduced the stiction and friction. The technologies associated with detecting the read-back signals from digital magnetic recording have also contributed to the increase in areal density over this period of time; these improvements are coding of the data recorded on the disk surface, improvements in the technology for detecting the read-back pulses, and error correction of the detected data. In addition, the servo systems which control access to the data tracks and maintain the recording heads on track have improved over time. All of these technologies will be discussed in this chapter.

One key parameter that has been improved during the period shown in Fig. 2.2

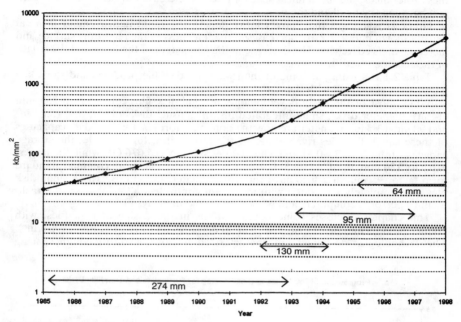

FIGURE 2.2 Trend for the areal density in kb/mm^2 of disk files over time. The projected diameters for the disks to be used are shown superimposed. The rapid increase in the slope of the areal density starting from 1991 is discussed in the text.

is the magnetic spacing (d_m) between the bottom of the gap of the recording head to the center of the recording film. This parameter is key since the dependence of the output signal voltage with spacing and wavelength (λ), which is the spacing loss, is given by

$$L_d \propto \exp\left[-\frac{2\pi d_m}{\lambda}\right]$$

In Fig. 2.3a is shown the reduction in the magnetic head to media spacing over time for particulate and thin-film media. The details of the actual and predicted reduction in the components of the spacing with thin-film recording disk surfaces and thin-film heads since 1993 is shown in Fig. 2.3b and c (Procker, 1993). The total spacing loss is due to several components, the mechanical spacing or "flying height," the lubricant film to reduce wear with start-stop in contact sliders, the overcoat to reduce corrosion and wear, and the thickness of the magnetic film. The texture, placed on the substrate to reduce stiction, also contributes to the spacing but this is much smaller than the contributors listed above. In addition, the recession of the pole tips of the recording heads resulting from lapping of the air bearing surface, contributes to the overall spacing. Another contributor to the overall mechanical spacing is the tolerance of the mechanical spacing, e.g., from the dimensional tolerances of the air bearing, the altitude and temperature tolerances of the air bearing and the mechanical tolerances of the head mounting structure. Given these tolerances, the mechanical spacing must be increased in order to avoid contact between the head and the disk.

Other key changes that have contributed to the rapid improvement in areal density shown in Fig. 2.2 are decreases in the thickness of the recording surface and increases in its coercivity. The decrease in the gap length of the head and the length of the recorded transition is also discussed.

Table 2.1 is a listing of some of the significant disk file products and some key parameters associated with them.

While most of the early developments in rigid-disk files centered on 355 mm (14 in) diameter disks, small-integrated disk files using disks of 130 mm (5.25 in) and 90 mm (3.5 in) diameter are now the dominant form factor. The data capacities of these small disk files rivals those of the larger files; for example, the storage capacity of the IBM 3390 Model 3 head disk assembly is 5.676 GB while the largest capacity 130 mm disk file (1995) is greater than 8 GB. The more common standard form factor 95 mm disk files have capacities greater than 2 GB. These small disk files are completely integrated with intelligent controllers allowing ease of attachment to personal computers and workstations and in arrays of files.

This chapter discusses some considerations in the design of disk files, with emphasis on technologies that lead to areal densities up to 16 Mb/mm^2 (10 Gb/in^2). The technologies described are characterized by low head-to-medium spacing

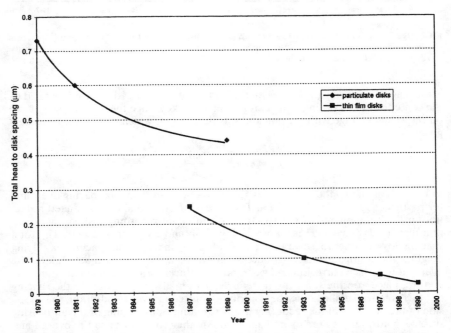

Progression of Total Head to Disk Spacing for Particulate and Thin Film Disks

FIGURE 2.3a Progression over time in the spacing of the head to midpoint of the magnetic recording film spacing in μm for both particulate and thin-film disks.

TABLE 2.1 Disk File Performance Parameters

Year of first customer shipment	Product	Storage capacity MB	Data rate Mb/s	Number of disks	Seek time, avg., ms	Bit density, b/mm	Track density, t/mm	Comments
1957	IBM 350	5m characters	0.07	50	600	3.9	0.8	606 mm (24 in) particulate disks
1963	IBM 1311	3m characters	0.54	6	150	39.4	2.0	355 mm (14 in) particulate disks
1966	IBM 2314	29.2 × 2	2.5	11	60	86.6	3.9	Hydraulic actuator
1971	IBM 3330	100 × 2	6.5	12	30	159	7.6	Servo control of actuator
1973	IBM 3340	70 × 2	7.1	4	25	222	11.8	"Winchester" data module
1974	IBM 3330–11	200 × 2	6.5	12	30	159	15	
1976	IBM 3350	317.5 × 2	9.58	9	25	253	18.8	Nonremovable HDA
1979	IBM 3310	65	8.25	6	27	335.8	17.7	210 mm (8.3 in) particulate disks, rotary actuator
1979	IBM 3370	571	14.9	7	20	478	25	Thin-film heads
1981	IBM 3380	1260 × 2	24	9	16	598	32	Thin-film heads. Two actuators per HDA
1985	IBM 3380E	2520 × 2	24	9	18	598	54.6	Thin-film heads
1987	Conner Peripherals CP-3100	120	10	2	25	915.7	45.3	90 mm (3.5 in) thin-film disks
1987	Maxtor XT8760E	769	15	8	24.8	1244	54.2	133 mm (5.25 in) thin-film disks, thin-film heads
1987	IBM 3380K	3780 × 2	24	9	16	598	82.2	Thin-film heads, digital servo
1989	IBM 3390	3784 × 2	33.6	9	12.5	1100	88.3	274 mm (10.8 in) disk diameter
1989	IBM Lightning	320	32.0	8	12.5	1470	47.3	High capacity 95 mm thin-film disk
1992	IBM Corsair	1044	80	8	9.4R, 11.4W	2317.9	105.7	Magnetoresistive head, PRML
1993	IBM Spitfire	1052	160	3	8.6R, 10.1W	3421.2	160.5	354 Mb/sq.in 1 in high
1993	Seagate Barracuda	1689	80	8	8R, 9W	2054.6	119.9	7200RPM
1993	Maxtor MXL	105	32	2	24.7	2283.4	106.3	48 mm (1.8 in) disk diameter
1996	IBM Travelstar	2160	74.4	3	12	6023.6	338.5	64 mm (2.5 in) disk diameter, MR head, PRML 1.3 Gb/in^2

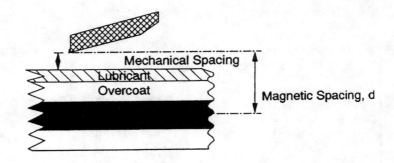

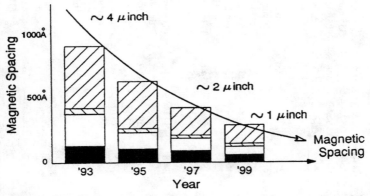

FIGURE 2.3b, c Projection of the decrease over time of the components of the spacing between the recording head and the mid point of the magnetic recording film. *(after Procker et al., 1993)*.

(< 0.4 μm), short head gap (< 0.3 μm), low slider load (≤ 1 g), and metallic film head cores. Disk recording films are high coercivity metal alloy. The actuators are composed of a voice-coil motor drive with closed-loop servo control and dedicated servo surfaces or sector (embedded) servo patterns. Recording channels are characterized by wide bandwidth (≥ 18 MHz) and peak and amplitude detection of the reproduced signal. The emphasis of this chapter will be on developing an understanding of the interplay of the mechanical, magnetic recording, and electronic aspects of a disk file in determining the key factors in disk file design. Following a description of the key elements of a disk file including the head-disk assembly, head-positioning servomechanism, and data channel, the limitations on areal density imposed by mechanical tolerances will be discussed in Sec. 2.5, Component Integration.

2.1.2 Performance Parameters

The disk file performance parameters that are important in the application of a file in a computer system are given below.

1. *Formatted disk file storage capacity.* C = (bytes/track − overhead bytes) (tracks/ data band) (data bands/head-disk assembly). With the data recorded in fixed length blocks, the components of overhead are: interblock gaps to accommodate tolerances in disk rotation and clock circuits, block identification (frequently in the form of Gray code), and synchronization bytes to allow time for clock circuits to synchronize with the data and error correction code bytes.

2. *Seek time.* The actuator seek time $\bar{\tau}$ is given by the sum of the average seek time $\bar{\tau}_{sk}$ and the settling time τ_s. The value of $\bar{\tau}_{sk}$ for random seeks is found to be the time to seek to a distance of 28% of the maximum distance of the tracks per recording band. In file usage, the actuators are found to have significantly shorter seek times than $\bar{\tau}$ since it is common for 50 to 60 percent of all seeks to be of zero length. Moreover, when motions do occur, they tend to be clustered and take less time than $\bar{\tau}$. Values of seek times depend on the type of programs being run, and typical values are in the range of 3 to 6 ms.

3. *Latency.* Latency is defined as one-half of a disk rotation time since, on the average, the desired record is located 180° from the position of the data heads.

4. *Access time.* The total access time is the sum of the seek time and the latency.

5. *Data rate:* D = (bytes/mm) × (velocity of inside track radius, mm/s).

Disk files are developed to standard form factors which are stated in terms of the diameter of the disks: 130 mm (5.25 in), 95 mm (3.5 in), 65 mm (2.5 in) and 48 mm (1.8 in), and even smaller form factors are predicted for the future. In the figure showing the predicted progression of areal density (Fig. 2.2) it was indicated that the form factors of the devices will play a role in the achievement of the areal density. This is the case since data rate from an individual data channel in a disk file is not predicted to increase as fast as the increase in linear density (Wood and Hodges, 1993). Therefore, as the linear density increases to produce increased areal density and hence capacity of the disk file, the trend will be toward smaller form factors. This fact has already put a limit on the rotational speed (RPM) for the largest disk files. Form factor should be listed as one of the key parameters along with head-disk spacing, head gap, and medium thickness and coercivity for the achievement of high areal densities. The high areal densities can be used with the larger form factors but only with reduced RPM (Wood and Hodges, 1993).

2.1.3 Application Parameters

Accesses to data in the disk file from the host are in the form of input/output (I/O) requests, and the response time to these requests has two parts—waiting time and service time. For example, in a mainframe computer the requester asks that a particular program be executed through a specified actuator or device. Executing the program requires that the control unit and storage device both be available. Consequently, the present program will have a wait time t_w. In a heavily accessed system, t_w can be the dominant part of the total response time.

From a model of system performance, the wait time t_w is found to be dependent on the number of requests per second N_r and service time t_{se} by

$$t_w = \frac{N_r t_{se}^2}{1 - N_r t_{se}} \tag{2.1}$$

For example, typical values for the access time $\bar{\tau} = 16$ ms, $D = 3$ MB/s, and the latency is 8.3 ms. The service time consists of (1) the start input/output time, (2) the access time (actuator positioning time), (3) the latency, (4) the search time (delay while programs search for record addresses), and (5) the data transfer time.

For a typical system, the request rate is 10 per second, and for an information management system program, t_{se} is 0.024 s, resulting in $t_w = 0.005$ s, and the total response time to transfer a record of 5120 bytes of data is given by $t_r = t_w + t_{se} = 29$ ms.

The important points to be learned from this compilation of service times are, first, the rotational disk speed is of primary importance because it directly influences the latency, the rotational position sensing miss time, and indirectly influences the data transfer time if the bit density is maintained constant. The percentage of the service time which depends (inversely) on the rotational speed in the above example is 54 percent. Therefore, high rotational speed is essential to short system service time. Second, the actuator access time is significant, but not as significant as would be estimated by the average access time. In the above example, the access time is 21 percent of the total response time. Third, the data rate is of significance to file throughput; in the above example it is 6 percent of the total time.

The small integrated disk files have built-in storage controllers which allow direct attachment to personal computers and minicomputers. These controllers have standard interfaces which allow the disk files manufactured by many vendors to be attached to the host computer. As an example, the small computer systems interface (SCSI-86) allows the attachment of up to eight devices on an 8-bit bus with a maximum data rate of 5 MB/s. SCSI controllers have data buffering and data caching to improve the performance of the data transfer. Data buffering allows data to be transferred from the buffer memory to the host even when the desired record is not under the head in the disk file. The size of data buffers included in the controllers resident in the disk file has increased from 10 KB in 1985 to 1 MB in 1994. The buffer memories are implemented as DRAM integrated circuits. The SCSI interface standard has been improved (SCSI-2) to 8, 16, or 32 bits wide and with a maximum data rate of 10 MB/s.

If the pattern of access to data in the disk file can be inferred, then records which have a high probability of being used in the future can be prefetched into a cache memory. Algorithms which manage the data in the memory can then be used to improve the likelihood that a desired record is in fact located in the memory, e.g., records which are least frequently used can be discarded to make room for new records. Such devices can substantially improve the performance of disk files. In one example, the number of input-output requests was tripled by the use of a cache memory (Wood and Hodges, 1993). In addition, cache memory can be used to implement "read look ahead," in which the data from the track currently being addressed are prefetched anticipating future requests and "immediate write," in which the controller posts "write complete" when all the data are in the buffer. This latter algorithm reduces the time required to write data since the time to physically move the actuator to the track and sector is eliminated. The status of attachment of disk files to hosts has been reviewed (Hospodor and Hoagland, 1993; Wood and Hodges, 1993).

Another technology for utilizing the small integrated disk files as a possible replacement for the larger devices, e.g., the 274 mm (10.8 in) disk files, is the use of arrays of the smaller files (Patterson et al., 1988). With arrays, the data from a number of disk files are presented to the host as a single logical unit, a *redundant array of inexpensive (now independent) devices* or RAID. Data in a RAID system are striped, i.e., the data from an individual head are combined with that from other heads to present a parallel data stream to a buffer. Striping increases the effective data rate from the RAID system. Wood and Hodges report data transfer rates as high as 52 MB/s (416 Mb/s) from a transfer of 150 32 Kblocks of data using a RAID system. Reliability of the disk files is key to the success of arrays since failure of one device with data striping can lead to some interruption of the system, although redundant devices can be used to alleviate this problem. For the small integrated disk files the mean time to failure (MTF) is 150 K hours or more and this will result in a 4% failure rate of a single device in three years.

The capacity of a disk file is reduced by the overheads in a block of data. The efficiency of customer data as a percentage of the total data stored is typically 80–90%. However, it is possible to improve this ratio if intelligent buffers are used to strip part of the overheads from the data before recording but to present the correct image of the data to the host. This process is known as *data compaction.* In addition to compaction it is also possible to increase the amount of data stored on the disk by *data compression.* Data compression refers to a class of algorithms by which the number of bits required to represent the data in storage is reduced. Ratios of 2:1 to 5:1 are possible depending on the data and the algorithms.

2.2 THE HEAD-DISK ASSEMBLY

2.2.1 General Considerations

The head-disk assembly is the closed mechanical structure that contains the rotating disks, the actuator with the head-arm assemblies, and mechanisms for contamination control. In Fig. 2.4 is shown a drawing of a representative 95 mm (3.5 in) head-disk assembly—the Maxtor 345 MB file (Maxtor 7345). This head-disk assembly contains two disks and four heads and a rotary actuator in a small standardized form factor size of 146 × 101.6 × 25.4 mm (5.75 × 4.00 × 1.00 in). The rotary actuator has permanent magnets and a moveable coil assembly and a crash-stop assembly mounted to the back of the actuator arm. The crash-stop is used to absorb the impact of loss of servo control during a seek. Mounted on the bottom of the base casting is a printed circuit board which conforms to the standard form factor size and which contains all of the required electronics to both operate the file and to attach it to a computer. Thus, the file is an integrated unit.

The head-disk assembly mechanical structure has profound effects on the capability of the file to support high track and bit densities. The principal influence of the mechanical design in determining track density is through controlling track misregistration. Track misregistration has two related aspects; the first, referred to as *write-to-read track misregistration,* is the misregistration, for whatever cause, between the centerline of a recorded track and that of the readback head following a seek to a desired record; the second, referred to as *write-to-write track misregistration,* is the misregistration between a recorded track and an adjacent track, resulting in track encroachment or track-to-track "squeeze," depending on the direction of the misregistration on the adjacent recorded track. Among the physical factors that can result in track misregistration of both types are thermal track shift, resulting from misalignment of a data head from the servo head due to thermal effects, including differences in thermal expansion of the arms in a dedicated-servo disk file; incomplete head settling following a track seek; apparent runout of the head-track combination due to spindle bearing and arm vibrations at frequencies outside the capability of the servo system; and errors in the servo position detection circuits. Track misregistration (TMR) is a random variable whose distribution is described by its 3σ value ($\text{TMR}_{3\sigma}$). This is the value such that for 0.997 of the time,

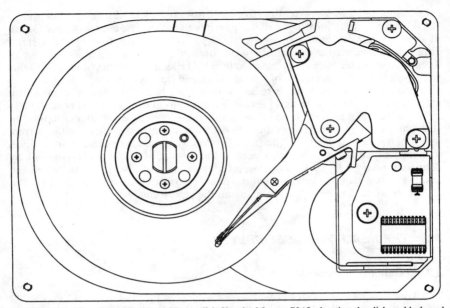

FIGURE 2.4 Top view of a typical 95 mm disk file, the Maxtor 7345, showing the disk and hub and the rotary actuator. Part of the moving coil for the actuator is seen at the back of the top cover which supports the permanent magnet assembly. The slider for the thin-film head is at the end of the suspension over the disk surface. The electronic components are mounted on a printed circuit board on the bottom of the head disk assembly.

TMR is within the range from $m - \text{TMR}_{3\sigma}$ to $m + \text{TMR}_{3\sigma}$, where m is the mean of the TMR. The value 0.997 is the fraction of the time a Gaussian random variable is within 3 standard deviations of its mean. Track misregistration directly limits track density since the data channel will record errors if the read head is more than a certain percentage of a track width off-track. In practice, errors occur if the misregistration is greater than approximately 12 percent of the track width. Thus, the allowable track density D_t is related to the effective 3σ value of the write-to-read track misregistration TMR by

$$D_t \approx \frac{1}{8\text{TMR}_{3\sigma}} \qquad (2.2)$$

To illustrate the definitions of track misregistration, refer to Fig. 2.5. In this figure are shown a recorded track of width w_w, resulting from recording with a write head of physical width w_t somewhat less in width than w_w to account for side fringing on recording, and a read head of width w_r with an explicit side fringe width of δw_r and a guard band between adjacent tracks of width gb. Because of write-to-read track misregistration, the position of the read head is shown reading off-track and in fact reading interference in the guard band (position 1) and from the adjacent track (position 2). Since track misregistration results in a variation in the position of the track center line on track n, and many write operations can have taken place before

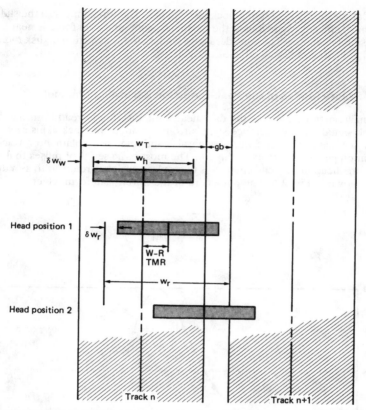

Figure. 2.5 Track and head geometries in a disk file showing definition of write-to-read track misregistration $\mathrm{TMR}_{W,R}$ which increases from head position 1 to head position 2. Write-to-write track misregistration $\mathrm{TMR}_{W,W}$ would occur on track $n + 1$ if the head were used to record while in position 1 or 2. The side writing of the head has magnitude δw_w, and the side reading has magnitude δw_r.

the present read operation, old-information data are present in the "guard band." This old-information noise contributes to data errors. It is noted that if the head in position 2 were recording, then write-to-write track misregistration would result on track $n + 1$. In Sec. 2.5, an analysis is made of the signal-to-noise ratio in the data channel resulting from the readback head reading both signal interference and noise from the desired track and adjacent tracks.

A second influence of the mechanical design of the head-disk assembly on areal density is through the head-to-disk spacing of the read-write head. The spacing of the head is determined by the selection of disk velocity, disk radius, air-bearing surface, suspension load, and the force input to the slider resulting from the motion of the disk perpendicular to its surface—the *perpendicular runout*. Perpendicular runout results from the disk not being perpendicular to the axis of the spindle, not being flat, or locally containing pockets or peaks. The force inputs to the slider can result in significant excursions if the frequency content of the force is near a head-suspension resonance. The considerations leading to the selection of disk radius and angular velocity are discussed in Sec. 2.2.4.

2.2.2   Failure Modes of the Peak-Detection Recording Channel

Track misregistration causes the data heads in a disk file to read both the desired on-track signal and interference signals from the adjacent track. This section will discuss the data channel from a general standpoint to explain how track misregistration generates errors in the file. The most basic series of pulses that is read back in the head in the read channel is two pulses, which is referred to as a dibit. A dibit is shown in Fig. 2.6. The pulses are of the Lorentzian form, given by

$$e(t) = \frac{E_{\max}}{1 + \left(\dfrac{2(t - t_0)}{PW_{50}} \right)^2}$$

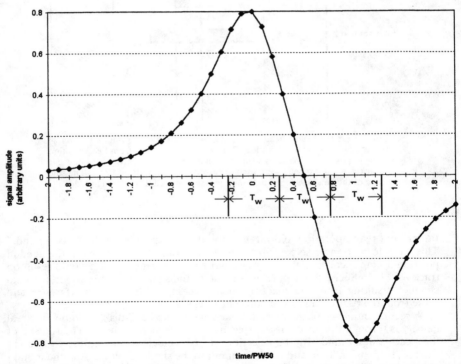

FIGURE 2.6   A dibit read signal. The clock window (T_w) for the (1, 7) data code is shown. The pulses are separated by one clock period.

where t is the time, PW_{50} is the pulse width at the 50% amplitude level and E_{max} is the amplitude of the isolated pulse. In this example, the second pulse is delayed with respect to the first pulse by a time equal to PW_{50}. This delay will be shown in Sec. 2.4.2 to correspond to the (1, 7) run-length limited data code, with the channel data representing adjacent "ones." In Fig. 2.6 is shown the clock window for this data code (T_w), which depends on the data rate, disk velocity and disk diameter, and the pulses are detected by locating the peaks of the pulses within this window. Note that the peaks of the dibit are separated by one clock period. This is the minimum separation allowed by the (1, 7) data code, as will be explained in Sec. 2.4.2. Due to interference between the two signals, the peaks of the two pulses are shifted in time from the isolated pulses, with the peak of the first pulse occuring early in time and the peak of the second pulse occuring later in time. If the pulses were moved even closer together, then the location of the peaks will shift even more. The "peak shift" can be determined by locating the zero crossings of the differentiated signals and in Fig. 2.7 is shown the peak shift for the first pulse as the pulses are moved closer together. This peak shift can cause errors when the location of the peak of the pulse is outside of the clock window.

In order to show the effects of adjacent track signals on peak shift, an interfering signal shifted in time so that the maximum slope of the interfering signal occurs at the peak of the first pulse of the dibit with amplitude equal to 12.5% of the dibit signal is added to the on-track signal. The result is shown in Fig. 2.8. For simplicity the off-track signal is taken to be a sinusoid. It is seen that the signal is distorted and that the position of the peak of the first pulse of the dibit is moved early in time from the location without the interfering signal. The peak shift in this case is -0.1 in units of time/PW_{50}.

In addition to the peak shift resulting from intersymbol interference, peak shift can also arise from incomplete erasure. This peak shift is due to the shift in the location of transitions. Erasure of previously recorded data by new data is quantified as *write-over-modulation* or *overwrite* noise (N_{ow}). In the worst case, in which high frequency data are used to overwrite low-frequency data:

$$N_{ow} = S'_{lf}/S_{lf} \qquad (2.3)$$

Where S_{lf} is the as-recorded low-frequency signal and S'_{lf} is the signal after erasure. The noise is expressed in dB.

The effects of overwrite on peak shift have been analysed in terms of the difference in transition shifts for "hard" and "easy" transitions (Fayling et al., 1984; Roscamp and Curland, 1988; Hoagland and Monson, 1991; Bertram, 1994). The difference between hard and easy transitions is governed by the state of the storage medium as the transition enters the gap region of the head. In the hard transition case, the leading edge of the magnetic field from the head has to reverse the magnetization of the medium and this generates a demagnetizing field that interferes with the transition that is actually recorded at the trailing edge of the head. In the easy transition case the state of the magnetization entering the gap region is such that the leading edge of the magnetic field from the head does not have to

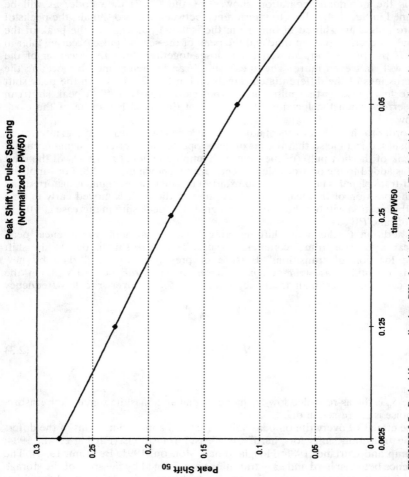

FIGURE 2.7 Peak shift normalized to PW_{50} for the dibit shown in Fig. 2.6 with reduced spacing between the pulses.

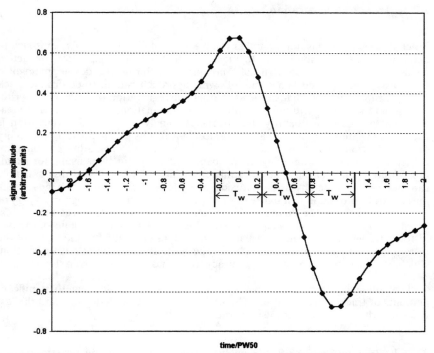

FIGURE 2.8 Dibit signal with an interfering signal due to reading an off-track signal with 12.5% of the dibit amplitude.

reverse the magnetization. The resulting peak shift is given by (Hoagland and Monson, 1991):

$$T_{ow} = \left(\frac{D_{r(min)}}{D_{r(max)}} \right) \frac{1}{\pi v D_{r(max)}} \frac{N_{ow}}{R} \tag{2.4}$$

where D_r is the recording density in flux change per meter (or inch), v is the head to disk velocity in m/s (or in/s), N_{ow} is defined above, and R is the resolution (the ratio of the signal amplitude at $D_{r(max)}$ to that at $D_{r(min)}$. The flux-change densities are dependent on the data code used (Sec. 2.4.2).

This peak shift should be added to that for intersymbol interference to assess the overall peak shift. Another transition shift is due to the nonlinear interaction of transitions (Bertram, 1994). Other contributors to peak shift include disk defects, random noise, and clocking errors.

Another failure mode of disk file technology is loss of adequate signal amplitude which can also result from excessive intersymbol interference, for example when a tribit pattern is recorded and the center bit of the tribit is reduced in amplitude. These errors are referred to as *gate errors,* since the data read channel contains circuits which gate the signal off when the read amplitude is below a specified gate threshold.

2.2.3 Track Misregistration

Track misregistration is not a number but a statistical distribution. An approach to determining the distribution is to measure the track misregistration on actual head-disk assemblies. This is usually not practical during the development of a head-disk assembly, and hence the following approach is used to determine track misregistration. Effects that can lead to track misregistration of both types (write-to-read and write-to-write) are identified, and combinations of modeling and measurement are used to quantify the effects. An analysis of machine operation is used to translate the modeling and measurement results into statistical probability density functions. The total track misregistration of a given head-disk combination is then developed by combining the probability density functions using, for example, Monte Carlo analysis. The track misregistration of a given head-disk assembly can then be developed by using statistical analysis on the assembly of heads. Track misregistration of an individual read or write operation has a histogram of $p(r)$ or $p(w)$ with respect to the theoretical track center line. The write-to-read track misregistration then has a mean equal to the difference between the means of the two histograms, which difference is usually zero, and a sigma equal to the sigma of the histograms (assumed equal) times $\sqrt{2}$. The write-to-write track misregistration, which includes the servowriter accuracy (σ_s), has a sigma given by $\sigma_{w-w} = \sqrt{2\sigma_r^2 + \sigma_s^2}$

The following sections discuss four component effects leading to significant amounts of track misregistration. The first three lead to write-to-read and the last leads to write-to-write track misregistration.

2.2.3.1 *Thermal Track Shift.*

In analyzing the thermal track misregistration in a dedicated-servo head-disk assembly, the assumption is made that the servo head follows the prerecorded servo tracks perfectly. Thermal track shift causes the mean location of a data head from the previously written data track to be different from that for the servo head on the servo disk. This is shown diagrammatically in Fig. 2.9. The track misregistration results from the fact that the data recorded by the head at location k was recorded when the temperature was $T_{w,k}$ and read back when the temperature was $T_{r,k}$. Typical reasons for the temperature difference would be warm-up of the file and ambient temperature changes outside the file which affect the data arm and the servo arm differently and likewise affect the data arm and the data disk differently. The arms in a typical disk file are made from cast aluminum, whereas the disks are machined from cast and rolled aluminum-magnesium alloy, resulting in different thermal expansion coefficients α. Typical values are $\alpha_a = 23.73 \times 10^{-6}$ for cast aluminum arms and $\alpha_d = 23.55 \times 10^{-6}$ for aluminum disks.

An estimate of thermal track misregistration for a three-arm linear actuator (Fig. 2.9) with $L_1 = 56.8$ mm. $L_2 = 90.2$ mm, $L_3 = 132$ mm, $L_4 = 165.4$ mm, $\Delta L = 33.3$ mm, and a temperature change of $\Delta T = 15.5°C$ is

Head position	Estimated TMR
1-2	1.15 μm
1-4	1.76 μm
2-2	0 μm
2-4	0.707 μm

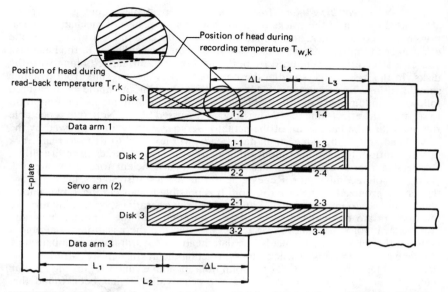

FIGURE 2.9 Disk file geometry used for thermal track misregistration analysis. The three data arms with 10 heads address three disks. The inset shows the thermal track shift observed after recording at temperature $T_{w,k}$ and reading at temperature $T_{r,k}$, where k refers to the head location. The dimensions for the analysis are given in the text.

For example, track misregistration for head 1-4 is given by

$$\text{TMR} = \Delta T \left[\alpha_a \left(L_2 - L_1 \right) + \alpha_d \left(L_3 - L_4 \right) \right]$$

The measured track misregistration may be different from the simplified analysis given above because of the difficulty of assessing the actual temperature distribution in the head-disk assembly, because of the air pumping action of the disks and the presence of the actuator protruding between the disks. Thermal track shift arises because of the operating conditions for the file. First, during warm-up, the track-to-track shift increases, reaches a peak, then approaches a steady-state value. Second, thermal track shift occurs because of head-to-track shift which occurs after warm-up as a result of changes in the ambient temperature. In a typical file operation, the temperature swing is characterized by $\overline{\Delta T} = 25°C$, $\Delta T_\sigma = 2°C$. Track misregistration values are typically 0.2 μm/°C; however, a thermal track shift of a worst-case data head of 0.4 μm for a 60°C ambient swing was reported for a disk file with a closed-loop air system (Mizoshita and Matsuo, 1981).

The thermal track misregistration for the smaller size disk files is reduced in proportion to the length of the actuator arms (proportional to the disk diameter). In addition, most of these small disk files use the embedded servo architecture, which eliminates steady-state track misregistration. In one form of embedded servo architecture one, or a small number, of thermal compensation sectors are recorded on each data disk surface and the misregistration is measured periodically to calibrate the thermal offsets.

2.2.3.2 *Nonrepeatable Runout Track Shift.* Nonrepeatable runout is nonrepeatable radial motion of the tracks or heads and arises because of mechanical vibrations in the actuator, disk, and spindle assembly. In the case of the arm and disk, the effect is due to flutter; resonant modes with motion perpendicular to the head arm and disk structures are induced by buffeting from the air carried along with the disks. In the case of the spindle, the nonrepeatable runout results from dynamic spindle tilting. To correlate with file operation, the runout should be measured following random seeks of different lengths. In these measurements it is important to separate the effects due to servowriting, as discussed below. Note that repeatable runout within the bandwidth of the actuator servo system will be followed by the servo head and, if the same on all data heads, will not lead to write-to-read track misregistration. Repeatable runout will lead to write-to-write track misregistration. Repeatable runout arises from disk slip, due to insufficient torque on the disk clamp, or spindle imbalance. Repeatable runout has a statistical ensemble average that is synchronized to the disk rotation. It is possible to cancel repeatable runout, which will lead to improved arrivals following seek operations, by feeding forward the appropriate coil current to cancel the harmonics of the runout (Chew and Tomizuka, 1990; Workman, 1986; Sacks et al., 1993). If there is differential runout between the servo and data heads, the data head runout will not be compensated. Nonrepeatable runout is measured by subtracting the average misregistration from the ensemble. Typical values for the total nonrepeatable runout following random seeks is $\bar{x} + 3\sigma = 0.5$ to 1.5 μm base-to-peak value. It has been found that nonrepeatable runout varies rapidly with spindle angular velocity. For example, in the IBM 3350 drive, the runout increased by a factor of 1.8 with an increase in angular velocity from 2964 to 3600 rpm. Repeatable and nonrepeatable runout can be amplified by as much as 4 to 10 dB by the closed-loop servo system if the error rejection transfer function $[H_{er}(s)]$ in dB is positive, which can take place at frequencies as low as 200 to 400 Hz (Sec. 2.3).

A significant contribution to nonrepeatable runout is from the spindle bearings. An analysis of the contribution of spindle ball bearings with deformed inner and outer bearings races to nonrepeatable runout in an 11-disk file has been published (Naruse et al., 1983). Figure 2.10a shows the assumed model of the deformation in the inner race. If the rotational speed of the shaft is Ω, the bearing rotation speed is found to be near $0.4\ \Omega$, and hence the relative speed between the inner race and the balls is $0.6\ \Omega$. With the single inner race deformation, which is assumed to result from the bearing or head-disk assembly process, a radial force F_r results, which is F_0 cos $(0.6\Omega zt)$, where z is the number of balls in the bearing. The eigenvalues for the four lowest frequency modes of vibration of the file are shown in Fig. 2.10b along with the frequencies of the bearing forces. It is seen that for an angular velocity of 3600 rpm, a close match exists between the frequencies of mode 4 (in the direction of rotation $+$) shown in Fig. 2.10b and the frequency for the positive inner race mode for $z = 9$. Since there is no relationship between the phases of the bearing forces and the structure modes, the resulting motions are nonrepeatable. To reduce this nonrepeatable vibration, either the spindle or the number z of bearings should be changed.

In the small integrated disk files, the nonrepeatable runout is significantly reduced over that for the larger high-end disk files since the moment arm of the disks to the bearings are proportionately reduced. In addition, some of the smaller disk files use hydrodynamic and self-pumped air bearing spindles. Nonrepeatable run out for 95 mm disk files with ball bearings has been observed to be 0.175 ± 0.05 μm (7 ± 2 μin).

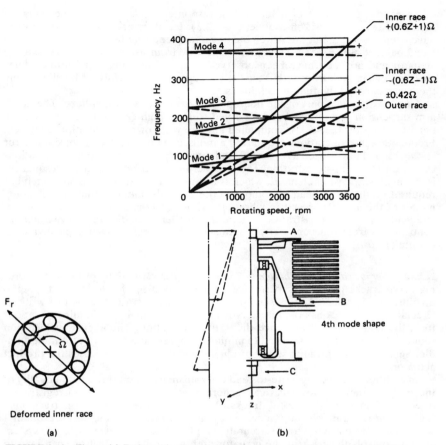

FIGURE 2.10 Figure (*a*) Deformation in spindle ball bearings, leading to nonrepeatable runout; (*b*) modes of vibration of an 11-disk spindle structure with the motions for mode 4 illustrated on the diagram of the structure. The frequencies of the modes of vibration of the rotating spindle with the distortions of the ball bearings shown in (*a*) are superimposed on the spindle-disk-structured modes, showing that the mode frequencies intersect at a rotating speed of 3600 rpm *(Naruse et al., 1983).*

The disk files used in personal computers are subjected to external shock and vibration which can result in track misregistration even after the servo system reduces the effect of the vibration. For example, with a 95 mm (3.5 in) disk file with four disks and an active servo control system, the off-track misregistration is in the range of 0.25 to 0.4 μm (10 to 16 μin), with a sinusoidal vibration of amplitude 0.5 g in the 5-1 kHz range. The range depends on the axis of vibration of the disk file.

Another important dynamic effect observed in disk files subjected to seeks of different lengths is the tuned-seek track misregistration component. Tuned seeks, as the name implies, can be observed when a particular set of conditions arises; these are short seeks (5 to 15 tracks) and a narrow band of delays, typically several milliseconds. The result of a tuned-seek response is a large amplitude signal as measured from the position channel (Sec. 2.3). Head excursions of up to 3.25 μm have been observed, but this is weighted by a frequency of observation estimated at 1 to 2 percent of the seeks. The tuned seeks arise from structural resonances of the actuator and arm and have been observed with different magnitudes in all files. Electronics can be introduced in the file to reduce the effect further by eliminating the occurrences of the tuning conditions.

Head settling is a part of the nonrepeatable runout as defined here. The head-arm-suspension system has been observed to have high Q resonances, which can persist even after the seek is completed and the write or read operation is started. Frequently these operations are started a millisecond or so after the position-error channel signal has crossed a threshold, and thus the persistent servo-head vibrations can lead to track misregistration. The most serious contributor to these resonances is the head suspension element, which is a thin, compliant stainless-steel member required to allow the head to comply to the vertical runout of the disk. Bending modes of the arm also result in vibrations with high Q and hence can also persist and lead to track misregistration. Again, the smaller-sized disk files have a smaller contribution from transient arrivals because of the shorter arms; a typical value is 0.4 μm (16 μin).

2.2.3.3 Servowriting Contribution to Track Misregistration. The process of recording servo tracks on the servo surface, or embedded sectors in the sector servo architecture, is referred to as *servowriting*. Servowriters are designed to write as circular a servo track as possible. Servowriters are designed to minimize vibrations from the floor that will influence the writing operation. The angular velocity on some servowriters is also selected to minimize nonrepeatable runout from the spindle. Servowriters typically use the product spindle, and in most cases the product actuator.

In addition to affecting write-to-read track misregistration through the quality of the written track, servowriters can generate write-to-write track misregistration directly by squeezing adjacent tracks. This track-squeeze effect on track misregistration is minimized in practice by using laser interferometers as sensors in a servo system to place the tracks accurately on the disks. However, the laser system usually controls the back of the actuator and, again, head vibrations can lead to track misregistration. Defects in the servo recording surface can also contribute to servowriting track misregistration since the servo-position demodulation circuits can interpret signals resulting from defects as an indication to move the servo head in file operation. Typical values for write-to-write track misregistration from servowriting with the larger disks are $\bar{x} = 0.75$ μm with $\sigma = 0.35$ μm, while with the smaller disks, $\bar{x} = 0.1$ μm with $\sigma = 0.01$ μm.

2.2.3.4 Track Misregistration with Magnetoresistive Read and Inductive Write Heads. With the introduction of integrated inductive write and magnetoresistive read heads, a unique track misregistration component must be considered, which is due to the spacing between the write and read elements of the head. This effect is shown in Fig. 2.11, in which the write and read head elements are shown superimposed on a band of recorded tracks (Chopra et al., 1992). It is seen that the write head is off-track even when the read head is perfectly aligned. The effect on the recording performance of the write-wide and read-narrow widths of the heads, as shown schematically in Fig. 2.11, and of the separation between the read and write elements, has been quantified (Bonyhard and Lee, 1990; Lee and Bonyhard, 1990;

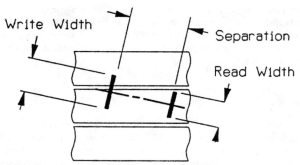

FIGURE 2.11 Magnetoresistive read head separated from inductive write head with three adjacent tracks superimposed, showing the write head being off-track when the read head is on the center track *(after Chopra et al., 1992)*.

Chopra et al., 1992). The assessment of these effects on data-channel error rates will be discussed in Sec. 2.5 on component integration.

2.2.3.5 Track Misregistration Limits. The typical track misregistration components of a dedicated-servo disk file are tabulated in Table 2.2. For simplicity the components were assumed to be normally distributed and combined to a total using the square root of the sum of the squares. Using the $\frac{1}{8}$ rule discussed in Sec. 2.2.1 [Eq. (2.2)], the track density achievable is 116 tr/mm (2946 tr/in). It is of interest to estimate what track misregistration would result from using a sector servo system, in which servo information is recorded in sectors on each data track (Sec. 2.3). An estimate of the achievable track misregistration with a sector servo and a 95 mm head-disk assembly with two to four disks is also shown in Table 2.2. The thermal track misregistration is set to zero because each data head acts as its own servo head. The nonrepeatable runout is reduced because the data heads now can follow part of the nonrepeatable runout on the data surfaces. The transient arrival component is assumed equal to that for the dedicated system. Achievable track densities are 370 tr/mm with these assumptions. The ability of data channels to operate at these high track densities will be discussed in Sec. 2.5. Track densities can, of

TABLE 2.2 Track Misregistration Components in Dedicated-Servo and Sector-Servo Disk Files

Component	Track misregistration, dedicated servo (μm)	Track misregistration, sector servo (μm)
Thermal	1.0	0
Nonrepeatable runout	0.4	0.15
Transient arrival	0.3	0.3
Total (rms sum)	1.08	0.37
Track density	116 tr/mm	370 tr/mm
(with 1/8 TMR$_{3\sigma}$ rule)	(2946 tr/in)	(9500 tr/in)

course, be increased with the dedicated-servo system by reducing the individual track misregistration components. The reduction of nonrepeatable runout is key to achieving ultimate limits of track density since it has a wide bandwidth and hence cannot be followed by the servo system unless very significant increases in servo bandwidth are realized.

2.2.4 Actuators

Previous sections have shown the importance of track misregistration in limiting achievable track density in disk files. This section on actuators and the following section on mechanical design of a head-disk assembly discuss the design considerations that can minimize track misregistration. Actuators are one part of a servo control system (Sec. 2.3) used to control the movement of multiple head-arm assemblies across the disk surface and to maintain the heads on-track to minimize track misregistration during processing of a record.

2.2.4.1 General Considerations.   Modern linear and rotary actuators are driven by voice-coil motors (VCMs) in conjunction with servo systems which sense position information from the disks. These actuators have been developed to have large electromechanical bandwidths (in excess of 1 kHz), and the forces developed from the motors have been adequate to achieve desired access times.

As shown in Fig. 2.1, actuator prime movers are voice-coil motors consisting of a permanent magnet structure and a movable bobbin or coil attached to the comb of arms carrying the read-write heads. With linear actuators the movable assembly is supported on bearings that move on hardened, flat surfaces called *ways*. With rotary actuators compact cylindrical bearings are used. Voice-coil motors have antecedents in the motors used in loudspeaker systems. However, design goals for the two are different because of the long stroke required in the disk file application. Design of a voice-coil motor must start with well-defined performance objectives and identification of key parameters in the movable part of the actuator, for example, mass or inertia and stroke, either linear or angular.

2.2.4.2 Design Goals.   A key performance parameter for disk files is the seek time (Sec. 2.1). Specifications for seek time are shown in Table 2.3. The average total seek time is specified for the worst-case conditions, including lowest power supply voltage, largest movable mass, and highest bias forces. An expression for the average seek time is derived below.

The time to move across n tracks of track pitch t_p assuming constant acceleration and deceleration ($\ddot{x}$) is given by

$$\tau\,(n) = \tau_s + \tau_{\text{sk}} = \tau_s + \left(\frac{t_p}{\ddot{x}}\right)^{1/2} n^{1/2} \tag{2.5}$$

The average time to access the total number of tracks N_t is given by

TABLE 2.3 Seek-Time Parameters

Settling time	τ_s
Time for an average seek	$\overline{\tau}_{\text{sk}}$
Average total seek time	$\overline{\tau} = \tau_s + \overline{\tau}_{\text{sk}}$

$$\bar{\tau} = \frac{\sum\limits_{n=1}^{N_t} P(n)\tau(n)}{\sum\limits_{n=1}^{N_t} P(n)} \qquad (2.6)$$

where $P(n)$ is the number of unique seeks corresponding to a seek length of n. For a random seek pattern with equal probability of being on any cylinder at any time,

$$P(n) = 2(N_t - n) \qquad (2.7)$$

and, for large N_t

$$\sum_{n=1}^{N_t} n^k \approx \frac{N_t^{k+1}}{k+1} \qquad (2.8)$$

giving

$$\bar{\tau} \approx \tau_s + \frac{8}{15}\left(\frac{t_p}{\ddot{x}}\right)^{1/2} N_t^{1/2} \qquad (2.9)$$

The average seek time is the time required for a seek of $(\frac{8}{15})^2 N_t$ tracks or a distance corresponding to 0.284 of the total band. An approximation to this result of $N_t/3$ is frequently encountered. It is convenient in measuring performance of disk files to use the approximate $N_t/3$ relationship and stress the file with worst-case conditions to measure $\bar{\tau}$. Note that $\bar{\tau}$ is not characteristic of the actuator alone but also includes parameters of the servo control system.

Another key performance parameter for a disk file actuator is the ability to follow tracks. This parameter is included as part of the track misregistration. Effects that contribute to imperfect track following are friction, stiction, and response to external force disturbances (like windage force resulting from air flow generated by the disks and by forces resulting from the actuator voice-coil, motor power cable). These effects will be discussed further after an actuator model is developed below.

2.2.4.3 Linear Actuator Model.   The approach is to derive the simplest model of the actuator relating electrical and mechanical parameters, and to add other effects, such as friction, to the model later. Consider the model of the actuator, as shown in Fig. 2.12, to be a voice-coil motor with series resistance and inductance and a total

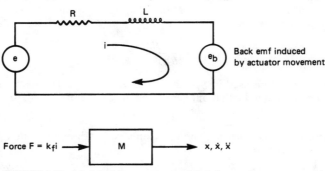

FIGURE 2.12   Model of linear actuator driven by a voltage source with amplitude e, resulting in a force F on the actuator of mass M.

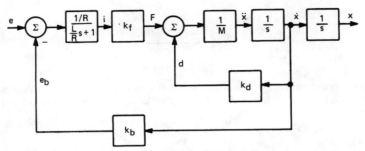

FIGURE 2.13 Block diagram for a linear actuator with viscous friction (coefficient k_d) and back emf (coefficient k_b).

moving mass M with a force acting through the center of gravity. The equations governing the system are

$$e(t) = iR + L\frac{di}{dt} + e_b \tag{2.10}$$

where the back emf (coefficient k_b) is given by

$$e_b = k_b\frac{dx}{dt} \tag{2.11}$$

where the force equation is given in terms of the force factor k_f by

$$F = M\ddot{x} + k_d\dot{x} = k_f i \tag{2.12}$$

and a viscous damping force (coefficient k_d) proportional to velocity has been assumed.[†]
 By application of the Laplace transform (see Fig. 2.13), the following equation results:

$$\frac{\dot{X}(s)}{E(s)} = \frac{k_f/Rk_d}{(\tau_e s + 1)(\tau_1 s + 1) + (k_b k_f/Rk_d)} \tag{2.13}$$

where the electrical time constant $\tau_e = L/R$, and the mechanical or load time constant $\tau_1 = M/k_d$. For many applications, $Lk_d << RM$, and the dominant time constant for the actuator is

$$\tau_v = \frac{RM}{Rk_d + k_b k_f} \tag{2.14}$$

These results will be used in Sec. 2.3 on servo systems. The next discussion is on the design parameters that influence the force factor k_f and the back emf coefficient k_b.

2.2.4.4 Actuator Force Factor. The force on a coil with N_1 turns in a permanent magnetic field is given by

[†]The radial position of the actuator is taken to be x to correspond to standard usage in the servo control field. In Sec. 2.5, which discusses the recording process, x is taken to be parallel to the track.

$$F = B_g l_{coil} N_1 i = k_f i \tag{2.15}$$

where B_g = air gap flux density
    l_{coil} = coil length
     i = coil current
    k_f = force factor

Two extremes of voice-coil motor design for linear actuators have evolved as shown in Fig. 2.14: the long coil and short gap (*a*), and the short coil and long gap (*b*). In general, the long coil and short gap design has a more nonlinear force factor versus position but is easier to cool than the short coil and long gap design.

Hard magnets are used in the magnetic circuit in which soft pole pieces guide the

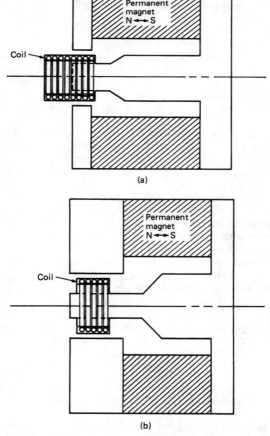

(a)

(b)

FIGURE 2.14 Schematic of voice-coil motors. (*a*) Long coil and short working gap; (*b*) short coil and long working gap.

TABLE 2.4   Magnetic Materials Used in Voice-Coil Motors

	Material		
	Barium Ferrite	$SmCo_5$	$Nd_{15}Fe_{77}B_8$
B_r			
mT	395	950	1150
kG	4.0	9.5	11.5
H_c			
kA/m	175	717	1250
kOe	2.2	9.0	15.7

flux to the air gap containing the coil and return it through the soft center pole as shown in Fig. 2.14. Design of the magnetic structure is accomplished using standard magnetic circuit analysis with a key parameter being the air gap flux density.

A listing of typical hard magnetic materials used in actuators is given in Table 2.4. It is important to magnetize the hard magnetic material above the knee of the demagnetizing curve in order not to have the material demagnetized by the fields from the coil. The fields from the coil with current in one direction aid the magnetic field of the permanent magnet and in the other direction oppose it, which results in a different force factor in the "push" and "pull" directions. This variation in force factor is typically 5%, and the servo must be designed to operate with this variation.

2.2.4.5   Modifications to Actuator Model.
Several important effects are not modeled in the actuator of Fig. 2.13. First the damping effect is assumed to be a force proportional to velocity, whereas in practice the damping is more complex. Examples are Coulomb friction, which depends on the sign of the velocity; stiction, which is a frictional force that exists only at low velocities; and spring forces, which may result from the actuator's moving over contamination on the way rails. Second, complex resonances are associated with the actuator. Figure 2.15 shows the magnitude of the mechanical transfer function of an IBM 3380 actuator. The transfer function is the ratio of the head-to-track error (induced by a disturbance voltage at various frequencies within the closed-loop servo system) to input current. The slope of the curve as predicted by the actuator model would be proportional to $1/s^2$, where in fact above 1 kHz many significant resonances would be observed. These resonances result from bending modes of the arms and tilt of the entire actuator, and large amplitude resonances result from head suspensions.

In order to predict the servo performance, a representation of the resonances is required. In the frequency domain, it is possible to add blocks in series with the force block of the form

$$\frac{s^2 + cs + d}{s^2 + as + b}$$

to represent the resonances and then evaluate the system performance with the resonance terms.

A third change to the basic actuator model is required to take account of windage forces. These forces act in a summing junction together with the force from the current and result from air movement and the voice-coil motor cable. All these modifications are shown in Fig. 2.16. To assess actuator performance in a servo

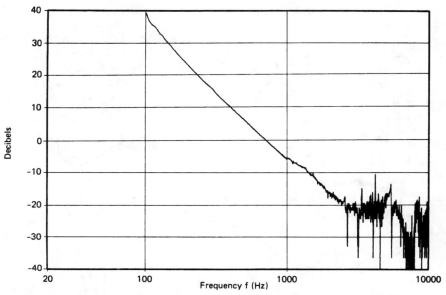

FIGURE 2.15 Mechanical transfer function magnitude as a function of frequency for an IBM 3380 linear actuator. The ideal curve would vary as $1/s^2$, while the actual curve exhibits mechanical resonances beyond 1 kHz.

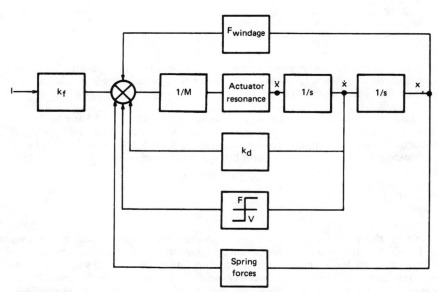

FIGURE 2.16 Model of linear actuator showing modifications to the basic model resulting from Coulomb friction, stiction, spring forces, mechanical resonances, and windage forces.

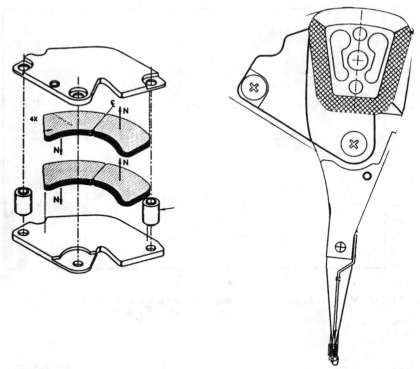

FIGURE 2.17 Components of the rotary actuator from the disk file shown in Fig. 2.4. Shown on the left are the oppositely magnetized magnets and on the right the coil structure mounted to the actuator arm. The axis of rotation is also shown.

system, it is necessary to develop such models of the actuator, together with models of the servo electronics in order to predict head-to-track arrivals, track-following performance, and servo stability.

2.2.4.6 Rotary Actuators. A rotary actuator is shown in Fig. 2.17 and in Fig. 2.4. The two permanent magnets are oppositely magnetized to result in a "push-pull" force on the two sides of the coil, doubling the resulting force. Typical values for the parameters for a rotary actuator with three arms (4 heads) are:

$$J = 4.5 \times 10^{-5} \, Nm^2$$
$$k_t = 0.06 N{-}m/A$$
$$N = 225$$
$$R = 18\Omega \text{ at } 20°C$$

The rotary actuator has found wide usage in the small integrated disk files because of its smaller size. It is also used in some high-performance files. Rotary actuators with dynamic balance are less susceptible than linear actuators to shock and vibration that cause the heads to be forced off track. With linear actuators, radial forces can result in radial motion of the heads, particularly if the frequency of excitation is outside the bandwidth of the servo system.

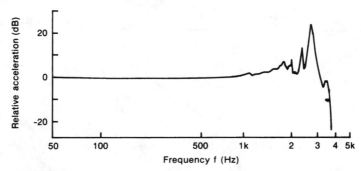

FIGURE 2.18 Acceleration transfer function for a rotary actuator showing the large resonance at 2.53 kHz resulting from the in-plane bending mode of the actuator arm *(Mitsuya et al., 1982).*

The model of a rotary actuator, suitable for use with a servo system, to predict performance is developed below. Torque for a rotary actuator with bearing-to-center-of-force distance r is given by

$$\text{Torque} = B_g l_{\text{coil}} i r = k_t i \tag{2.16}$$

where B_g = gap flux density
l_{coil} = length of coil wire in the gap flux density
i = coil current
k_t = torque constant

The equation of motion for the rotary actuator is given by

$$\text{Torque} = J\ddot{\Theta} + C_R\dot{\Theta} \tag{2.17}$$

Where J is the moment of inertia of the moving member and C_R is a damping coefficient and is seen to be analogous to Eq. (2.12) for linear actuators. An acceleration transfer function for a rotary actuator showing the in-plane resonance from the bending mode of the arm is shown in Fig. 2.18.

A novel design for a rotary actuator using a stationary coil and a moving magnet has been reported (Yamada et al., 1994). A complication with rotary actuators is the fact that the center lines of the spindle motor axis and the actuator pivot point do not coincide. The result of this is shown in Fig. 2.19. In this figure are shown the centers of rotation of the spindle and the actuator, and the actuator arm with the gap of the head at the end of the arm. The decrease in track width (and pitch) on the outside (OD) tracks on the disk compared with the inside (ID) tracks is shown in the figure. In addition, at the OD tracks, considerable skew is developed between the head element and the radial line through the head element. This effect reduces the read signal by the cosine of the skew angle. However, the flying height variation over the total band is reduced by the skew at the outside tracks because the increase in flying height engendered by the increased velocity is approximately balanced by the reduction in efficiency of the air bearing. The practice has evolved of mounting the head suspension on the arm of the actuator to result in the gap of the head element being at right angles to the arm. This produces minimum vibration sensitivity, but introduces skew. With a typical 95 mm disk file, the change in

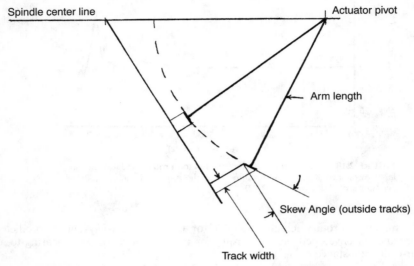

FIGURE 2.19 Schematic diagram of the axis of rotation of a disk spindle and actuator pivot point for a disk file with a rotary actuator. Shown on the end of the actuator arm is the gap length of the head. With rotation of the arm, the gap records smaller tracks at the outside of the disk than at the inside and the skew angle between the gap and a radial line is shown to increase at the outside of the disk.

track pitch can be as large as $\pm 5\%$ from the nominal track pitch, while the skew angles can be as large as $13°$ for the ID tracks and $27°$ for the OD tracks.

2.2.4.7 *Shorted Turn.* To improve the transient response of actuators, it has been found necessary to add a shorted turn. These shorted turns take the form of thin, high-conductivity material (usually copper) placed close to the moving coil in the air gap. The effect of a shorted turn can be modeled by adding a transformer with turns ratio $\alpha_s = N_1/l$ to the electrical model of the actuator, as shown in Fig. 2.20. Note that for this analysis, the coil is stationary and hence there is no back emf. The permeance $dP = \mu \, dA/l$ can be evaluated for the geometry of the coil and magnetic structure. By comparing the circuit in Fig. 2.20 with that in Fig. 2.12, it is seen that the initial time constants arising from a step in voltage would be approximately ($L_{12} \gg L_2$)

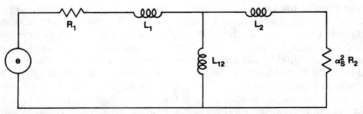

FIGURE 2.20 Model of the coil in a voice-coil motor with a shorted turn.

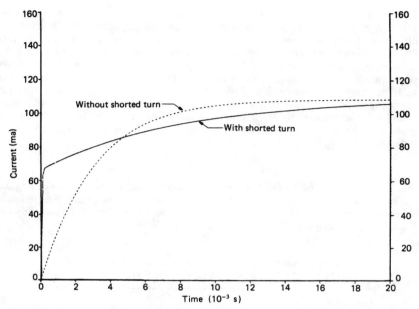

FIGURE 2.21 Simulation of the current response of a voice-coil motor to a step in input voltage with and without shorted turn. Note the reduction in initial current rise time and the small reduction in final current with the shorted turn.

$$\tau_1 \text{ (with shorted turn)} = \frac{L_1 + L_2}{R_1 + \alpha_s^2 R_2} \tag{2.18}$$

and

$$\tau_{12} \text{ (without shorted turn)} = \frac{L_1 + L_{12}}{R_1} \tag{2.19}$$

The objective is to have $\tau_1 \ll \tau_{12}$. Detailed analysis has shown that typically τ_1 may be 300 to 400 μs and $\tau_{12} = 3$ ms. Fig. 2.21 shows a simulation of the equivalent circuit of the coil with and without the shorted turn to illustrate the improvement in initial rise time with the shorted turn. There is a loss of amplitude of the current with the shorted turn during part of the acceleration period, and power dissipation in the shorted turn must be accounted for in actuator cooling. The thickness of the shorted turn should be more than a skin depth.

2.2.5 Head-Disk Assembly Mechanical Design

This section will discuss how the mechanical design of head-disk assemblies influences track misregistration, temperature and contamination control, size, and weight. The discussion is intended to indicate general direction.

2.2.5.1 Disk Diameter.   Disk diameter selection is fundamental to head-disk assembly design. With disk files intended for low-end applications—for example, with personal computers—size is dictated by available space. With high-end disk files, disk diameter selection is a trade-off among the desire for large capacity per head-disk assembly, the desire for lower cost per unit of capacity, and the desire for low granularity of data under a given actuator. The objective of this trade-off is to give large throughput and reduced exposure to loss of data availability. Another issue in the selection of disk diameter is the amount of heat dissipated as a function of diameter and angular velocity. The dependence of power dissipation P on disk angular velocity ω and radius r_d caused by moving the air by the pumping action of the disks is given by

$$P \propto \omega^{2.8}(r_d)^{4.6} \tag{2.20}$$

Table 2.5 gives the relative capacity and heat dissipation for two values of angular velocity for disks of standard diameter. With the 355-mm disks, heat dissipation in the head-disk assembly with nine disks requires external cooling. Disk diameters of selected files are shown in Table 2.1.

TABLE 2.5   Relative Disk Surface Area and Power Dissipation of Selected Standard Disk Diameters and Angular Velocities

Disk diameter		Relative surface area	Power dissipation per disk		
mm	in		3600 RPM	5000 RPM	10 KRPM
355	14	8	85.41	214.27	1492.32
268	10.5	4	23.44	58.81	409.55
203	8	2	6.53	16.38	114.09
135	5.25	1	1.00	2.51	17.47
95	3.5	$\frac{1}{2}$	0.20	0.50	3.49
65	2.5	$\frac{1}{4}$	0.03	0.07	0.52

With the outside diameter of the disk selected, the width of the data recording band must be chosen. It is shown below that there is an optimum value for the width of the recording band if the data rate is constant. The total number of bits on the innermost track with radius r_i and recording density D_l is given by

$$2\pi D_l r_i$$

The total number of tracks in the band is related to the track density D_t and the inner and outer radii (r_i and r_o) by

$$D_t(r_o - r_i)$$

and the total capacity per surface is given by

$$C = 2\pi D_l r_i D_t(r_o - r_i)$$

The optimum value of r_i for maximum capacity is found by setting the derivative of the above equation with respect to r_i equal to zero, resulting in

$$(r_i)_{\text{opt}} = \frac{r_o}{2} \tag{2.21}$$

The capacity per surface with this value of inner radius is

$$C = \tfrac{1}{2}\,\pi r_o^2\, D_l D_t \tag{2.22}$$

It is possible to increase this capacity by dividing the surface into bands with the same bit density on the inner tracks of each band. For example, if there are n bands, each with the same value of linear density D_l on the inner track of the band, then it can be shown that the capacity per surface with banding, C_b is

$$C_b = \frac{\pi D_l D_t\,[(n-1)r_o^2 - (n+1)\,r_i^2 + 2r_o r_i]}{n} \tag{2.23}$$

If no restrictions are placed on the inner radius r_i, then the optimum radius $r_{i(\text{opt})}$ is found by the solution to

$$\frac{dC_b}{dr_i} = 0$$

resulting in

$$r_{i(opt)} = \frac{r_o}{n+1} \tag{2.24}$$

The corresponding capacity is then

$$C_{b(\text{opt})} = \pi D_l D_t\, r_o^2 \left(\frac{n}{n+1} \right) \tag{2.25}$$

The ratio of the optimum capacity with data banding (again with no restriction on the inner radius) to that without data banding is:

$$\frac{C_{b(\text{opt})}}{C} = \frac{2n}{n+1} \tag{2.26}$$

and as n increases to large numbers the percentage increase approaches 100%.

If the inner radius with data banding is restricted to be the same as the optimum value without data banding in order to maintain the space for clamping the same, then the ratio of the capacities is:

$$\frac{C_b}{C} = \frac{3n-1}{2n} \left(r_i = \frac{r_o}{2} \right) \tag{2.27}$$

and as n increases to large numbers the percentage increase in capacity with data banding approaches 50%. With n equal to five, the percentage increase with data banding is 40%.

With data banding and fixed disk RPM the data rates change in each band and the data channel must supply the n clock signals. Disk files with data banding have been made with as many as 16 bands. However, with the data on the disk organized as sectors, which is the case on all of the small size disk files, the number of sectors in each track changes with the bands. In Fig. 2.22 is shown the data organization for four bands. The outside bands carry significantly more data sectors (M) than the

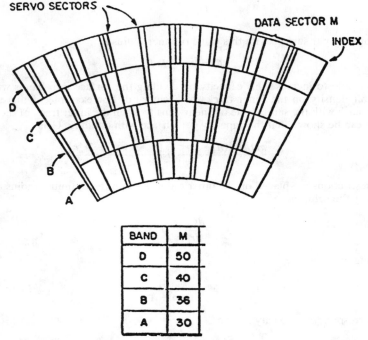

BAND	M
D	50
C	40
B	36
A	30

FIGURE 2.22   Track format for a typical disk file with banded data with embedded or sector servo information encoded within the data fields. Shown are four separate bands (A–D) with the number (*M*) of data sectors in each band shown in the table.

inner bands. Note that with the data organized as shown it is necessary to split the data fields to accommodate the fixed-spaced servo sectors.

Disk thickness is selected by the requirement to avoid disk resonances coincident with the selected value of angular velocity. A disk is stiffer with increased thickness, resulting in lower disk flutter (vertical motion of the disk) that could cause track misregistration through movement of the data tracks with respect to the data heads. Figure 2.23 shows the lowest eigenvalues of a 355-mm disk with thickness of 1.27 mm (0.05 in). The disk is clamped at a 229-mm (9-in) diameter. The normal modes are split because of disk rotation, and the numbers $n = 1, 2, 3$, 4, and 5 refer to the number of nodal diameters. The numbers $m = 1, 2, 3$ refer to the fundamental and first two harmonics of the disk-rotation speed. These modes can be calculated by using the theory of Lamb and Southwell (1921). It is seen that no resonances coincide with a disk speed of 60 rps (3600 rpm), and, hence, the modes should not be excited. Note that at 90 rps, the $n = 4$ and $n = 5$ modes approach zero frequency and could be excited by imbalances in loading forces on the two sides of the disk.

2.2.5.2   *Overall Head-Disk Assembly Configuration.*   Two general designs of head-disk assemblies have evolved. The first is the clamshell configuration, in which the hub structure supporting the disks is mounted on bearings at the top (cover) and

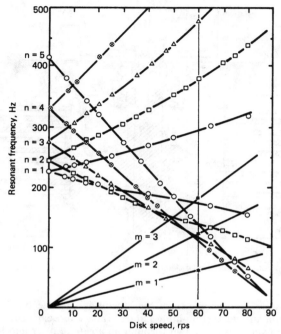

FIGURE 2.23 Frequencies of the modes of vibration of a rotating disk versus the rotational speed. The index n refers to the number of nodal diameters, and the modes are split by the disk rotation. The index m refers to the harmonic of the rotational speed.

bottom (baseplate) of the head-disk assembly. The second is the cantilever construction, in which the hub structure is supported on ball bearings on just the bottom (baseplate) side. Finite element analysis shows that modes of vibration of the cantilever structure are lower in frequency than for a clamshell design with equivalent length and mass. Hence the cantilever design is a less stiff configuration and, in general, should exhibit more nonrepeatable runout than the clamshell design. An example of a head-disk assembly with the clamshell design is shown in Fig. 2.24. Spindle bearings are mounted on the bottom and top of the spindle assembly. To correct for thermal expansion of the shaft, the bearings on the pulley side of the head-disk assembly are preloaded. The small integrated disk files have been made with a cantilevered design but the spindle shafts are short (as was shown in Fig. 2.4) and the increase in nonrepeatable runout due to the absence of the top bearing support is negligible.

2.2.5.3 Temperature and Contamination Control. Because of the power dissipation caused by the moving air dragged along with the spinning disks, some form of cooling is required in order to prevent excessive thermal track misregistration. In addition, it is essential to purge any particles away from the head-disk interface. Two general designs for handling the air flow within the head-disk assembly are considered.

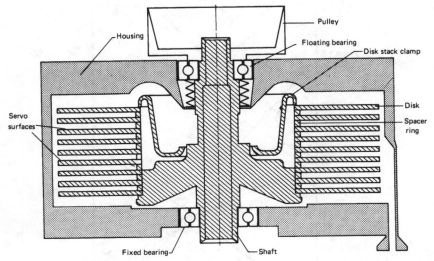

FIGURE 2.24   Spindle structure and disks for a clamshell-type head-disk assembly.

In an open-loop air system, fresh air is supplied to the head-disk assembly through a plenum structure containing flapper valves and exits through the actuators. This system supplies air drawn through an absolute filter and has the advantage that contamination generated within the head-disk assembly can be purged to the outside, but a disadvantage is that contamination generated on the outside can be brought into the head-disk assembly. It is important that the pressure distribution not have points of stagnation or closed flow regions for the open-loop air system to function optimally. This technique is highly effective in carrying away heat generated within the head-disk assembly because of the use of cooling air at ambient temperatures.

The second approach is a closed-loop system with makeup air. In this design, most of the air within the head-disk assembly is recirculated, and only a small percentage of air is supplied through a small breather hole with a filter to the outside. This air makes up for leaks or pressure changes and maintains pressure inside the head-disk assembly at or above ambient pressure.

2.2.5.4   Tools to Aid Mechanical Design.   An objective of the mechanical design of a head-disk assembly is to achieve low vibration levels of the disk and head-arm assemblies. Mechanical design tools that have been found useful in achieving these goals are finite-element, modal, and transfer function analyses.

Finite-element analysis programs were developed originally to aid in the design of aerospace structures (e.g., the NASTRAN program), but they have also found application in disk file design. In finite-element analysis, the structure is broken up into small units which are described by stress-strain relationships and combined with appropriate boundary conditions. An example of the finite-element analysis is shown in Fig. 2.25. Figure 2.25*a* shows an arm which supports the servo head in a rotary actuator with acceleration transfer function shown in Fig. 2.18. The first two in-plane modes of vibration of the arm are illustrated. The program used to predict mode frequencies resulted in predictions of 2.53 kHz for the first mode and

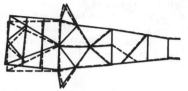

(a) 1st mode Natural frequency : 2.53 kHz

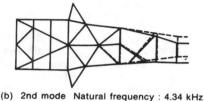

(b) 2nd mode Natural frequency : 4.34 kHz

FIGURE 2.25 Computed mode shapes for the arm from a rotary actuator showing the resonance at 2.53 kHz shown in the acceleration transfer function of Fig. 2.18.

4.34 kHz for the second. Note from Fig. 2.18 that the large resonance observed in the acceleration transfer function is at the frequency of the first mode.

The second example of finite-element analysis is in calculating a mode of vibration of a cantilevered disk-spindle structure. Figure 2.26 shows one mode of vibration of a clamped disk with one nodal diameter (greatly exaggerated) and the tilt of the spindle. The usefulness of finite-element analysis is that a large number of modes can be identified and the structure redesigned to stiffen a particular member and to reduce the motion of a sensitive part. In the present case, the particularly sensitive parts are the disks. The mode shown exhibits radial motion on all disks and would require the servo system to follow the motion; differences in motion of the disks up the disk stack would result in data-head misregistration.

As an adjunct to finite-element analysis, it is useful to determine mode shapes and frequencies by using modal analysis in which the structure is instrumented with accelerometers and struck with a hammer. The measured vibrations are processed in computers designed to display mode shapes and frequencies. The modes observed are processed so that they occur at frequencies that can be observed on the output terminal, and the outputs show clearly what parts of the structure are involved in the mode. Corrective action can be taken to stiffen the member. Modal analysis and finite-element analysis are complementary. Modal analysis has the advantage that mode damping is accurately assessed.

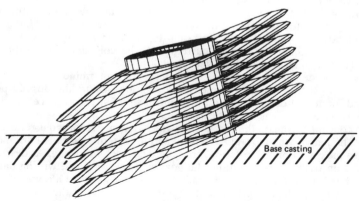

FIGURE 2.26 Mode shape for a cantilevered spindle-disk structure as calculated using the NASTRAN program.

Two transfer functions have been shown earlier. The first is shown in Fig. 2.15 and is a mechanical transfer function for an actuator. The second, shown in Fig. 2.18, is an acceleration transfer function $\ddot{\theta}/i$. Such transfer functions show the impact of mechanical resonances on the function of an actuator or other mechanical structures. More details on how transfer functions are measured will be given in Sec. 2.3.

2.3 HEAD-POSITIONING SERVOMECHANISMS

The following section on the head-position servomechanism is substantially the same as in the earlier edition of this book published in 1989. The most significant advance in servo control of disk file actuators and spindles since that time is the replacement of discrete-time analog control with discrete-time and discrete-amplitude (digital) control. Some of the significant references to work on disk file actuator control are as follows: Cooper, 1988; Miu and Bhat, 1991; Sri-Jayantha et al., 1991; and the book reference Franklin, Powell and Workman, 2nd ed., 1990. In addition to the change to digital control, the actuators used to move recording heads across the disk are largely rotary whereas in the older disk files they were linear. The following analysis is explicitly for linear actuators but can be applied to rotary actuators by changing variables. The linear to rotary actuator conversion is easily obtained by the following substitutions:

$$x = \theta, v = \dot{\theta}, a = \ddot{\theta}, M = J, k_f = k_t, F = T, \text{ or Force} = \text{Torque} = k_t\, I/J.$$

Some parameters for a typical rotary actuator are given in section 2.2.4.6.

2.3.1 Description

The head-positioning servomechanism in a disk file provides a means for locating a set of read-write heads in fixed radial locations over the disk surface and allowing the repositioning of these heads from one radial location to another. A block diagram of a typical head-positioning servo with a rotary voice-coil actuator is shown in Fig. 2.27. The angular position of the heads, and hence the entire moving inertia of the actuator assembly, is denoted by $x(t)$. As seen in Fig. 2.27, the control system plant (plant refers to the subsystem to be controlled) is composed of the actuator, the amplifier that drives current into the coil, and the position error channel (Commander and Taylor, 1980; Oswald, 1980).

The servo system has two primary functions: (1) to determine the position of the actuator and (2) to compare the measured position against the desired position command input and determine the best control signal $u(t)$ to reduce the position error to as close to zero as is practical.

Each concentric ring on the surfaces on which data are recorded is referred to as a *track*. The heads, when located at a fixed and predetermined radial distance with respect to the center of disk rotation, are said to be *track-following*. As described in Sec. 2.2.3 on track misregistration, the goal while reading and writing data is to keep the heads following in the same radial path throughout the lifetime of the disk file. Ideally, this path is a perfect circle, requiring that $x(t)$ of the actuator remain constant in order to track-follow, In practice, disk vibration, spindle vibration, spindle bearing runout, and imperfections in the position measurement reference

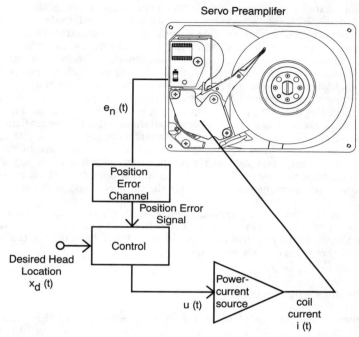

FIGURE 2.27 Block diagram of a typical head-positioning servo system with a rotary actuator.

require a significant control action and motion $x(t)$ to reduce head-position error to near zero.

When the control system is directed to place the read-write heads on a track different from the present track (the command $x_d(t)$ in Fig. 2.27 changes), the servo is said to "seek." Seeking involves larger motions than track-following—up to 50 mm, or 16,000 tracks (at 320 tracks per millimeter) in some disk files. As discussed in Sec. 2.1.2, the access time plays a significant role in file performance and must be minimized within the limits of technologies and the intended cost of the machine. Optimal control techniques are used to provide the minimum seek time with constrained control effort. As will be shown, the seek time is a strong function of the power that can be dissipated in the voice coil.

The actuator position on high-performance files is measured with respect to a disk surface written with position information. Positioning the heads with respect to the baseplate assembly is a less expensive alternative, but motion between the track centerlines and the baseplate makes it less accurate; hence, it is not used in hard disk files. Referring position measurement from the disk surface has two basic implementations. First, the dedicated-servo technique uses one head (servo head) to provide only position information to the system. In this technique the servo disk surface is servowritten with position information at the time of manufacture. The deficiency of this system is that the servo is measuring and thus controlling the position of the servo head, with the underlying assumption that the data heads (those not dedicated to the servo) are accurately positioned over their track centers. The assumption that the data heads follow the servo heads is not perfectly valid as discussed in Sec. 2.2.3. The second implementation is often referred to as embedded servo, because the position information is contained on all data tracks such that each head provides its own position information. There are numerous techniques with which the read-write head can measure its position with respect to the data-track center, the most common of which is called *sector servo*. Sector servo is a time-division multiplex technique: position fields are spaced on every track at regular, even intervals around the entire track circumference. The space between the fields is used for recording data. Thus the sector-servo approach gives rise to a sampled data control system. Depending on the required gap durations and the chosen field length, the servo information can occupy from 5 to 30 percent of the available disk surface. An estimate of reduction in track misregistration for a specific case of dedicated position error signal versus data sector position error signal is given in Sec. 2.2.3 (Table 2.2). Although some products on the market use one or a combination of these two position-measurement schemes, by far the most common is the sector-servo approach.

A discussion focusing on a typical, somewhat idealized position channel for a dedicated servo follows. Once the basic function and characteristics have been described, some of the practical realities will be addressed and used in the description of different types of position channels.

2.3.2 Position Error Channel

The output of the position channel, the position error signal (PES), is a signal proportional to the relative difference of the positions of the center of the servo head and the nearest track center. Thus the position error signal is a periodic function of x for stationary and ideal track centers (Oswald, 1974). The position error signal contains two sources of motion: motion of the actuator and motion of the disk surface itself. A simple mathematical description of the position error signal is given by

$$\text{PES} = k_x x_e = k_x \left\{ \text{MOD} \left[(r - x) + c, w \right] - \frac{w}{2} \right\} \qquad (2.28)$$

where w = track width
r = track center position reference (Fig. 2.27)
c = any constant such that $(r(t) - x(t) + c) > 0$, for all r, x

For clarity the gain k_x will be set to 1 and dropped from further discussion.

Figure 2.28a shows the position error signal as a function of actuator position x, which matches Eq. (2.28) except for slope reversals on every boundary between tracks. The pattern used on the servo surface is designed in concert with a demodulation scheme, such that when read back, the signals infer the head position relative to the nearest track center. The location of the pattern on the surface determines where the track centers will be.

Two basic types of demodulation are employed: peak detection and area detection. Both peak detection and area detection are sensitive to the amplitude of the readback signal from the servo head. Area detection is less sensitive to disk surface defects and noise. Because many parameters affect a wide range of readback signal amplitude, an automatic gain control (AGC) technique is employed to avoid unwanted variations in the position-error signal gain.

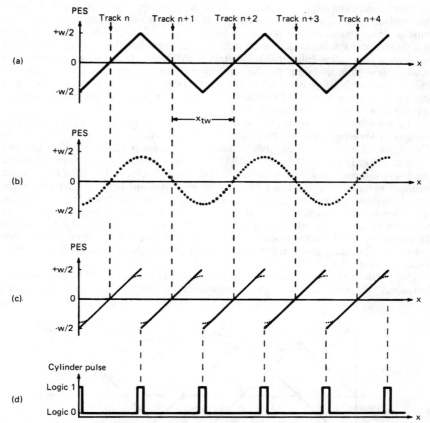

FIGURE 2.28 Output signals of a typical position error channel. (*a*) Ideal triangular output waveform, the zero crossings of which represent track centers; (*b*) actual position error signal (PES) showing rounding of the peaks; (*c*) PES ramps derived from ideal and rounded PES waveforms. PES ramps have a slope with a constant sign; (*d*) cylinder pulses indicate servo head is at half-track point.

All PES channels suffer degradation in performance under nonideal conditions. Figure 2.28*b* illustrates a common defect of most PES channels, nonlinear output/input relationship. A servo head which is narrower than the design value can cause this nonlinearity.

Converting the signals shown in Fig. 2.28*a* or *b* into PES (ramps) yields the signals shown in Fig. 2.28*c*, which in the ideal case matches the description given by Eq. (2.28). To keep track of the absolute position of the actuator, cylinder pulses are generated (Fig. 2.28*d*) which indicate that a track boundary was traversed. Use of the cylinder pulse signal will be described later.

The effect of servo surface irregularities or defects on the PES and hence on servo system performance can be severe. Large track misregistration contributions, excess noise leading to unreliable operation, and nonoptimal seek performance are the most significant effects. In order to improve linearity, and reduce sensitivity to disk surface effects, most position channels employ a quadrature technique, and some use a servo head twice as wide as the desired data-track spacing. The essence of a quadrature system is that two position error signals, often called *normal* and *quadrature,* are demodulated. The signals are derived from two sets of patterns which, when demodulated, produce position error signals that are in space (*x* direction) quadrature to each other. Having two signals allows use of only the most linear part of each. Figure 2.29 illustrates the basic outputs of a quadrature position channel as a function of motion *x*.

The introduction of magnetoresistive read heads as data transducers has also stimulated investigations for their use as servo position error signal transducers (Comstock et al., 1981; Yeh, 1982; Heim, 1988; Lee et al., 1991; Cahalan and Chopra, 1994; Tan et al., 1994). To utilize the magnetoresistive head as both a data and a servo transducer requires embedded servo architecture (Sec. 2.3.8). The most common magnetoresistive head design, the soft adjacent layer (SAL) transverse biased single-stripe head, exhibits nonsymmetrical response from the sides of the head element and this leads to different slopes of the position error signal on the two sides of the head (Cahalan and Chopra, 1994). One solution to this problem is the use of algorithms in the position error channel to linearize the predictable servo gain errors. The dual-stripe magnetoresistive head has a more symmetrical off-track response (Hsu et al., 1995).

The position error channel contains dynamic elements (i.e., filters) of its own; therefore, the position error signal also constitutes part of the system plant. To

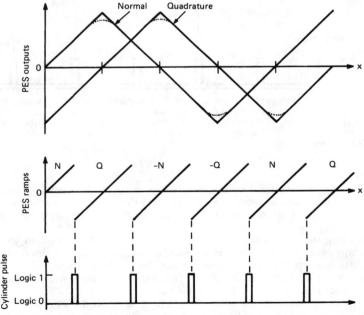

FIGURE 2.29 Normal and quadrature position channel outputs. Note that ramps developed from normal and quadrature outputs are linear even when some rounding is present.

design a control system for the plant shown in Fig. 2.27, it is necessary to understand the form taken by a command to the servo.

2.3.3 Servo Command Inputs

In all normal read-write operations in the disk file, the data heads must be kept as close to their track centers as possible. All the tracks under the data heads are said to form a cylinder of information. When read-write operations in a dedicated-servo disk file involve data in a cylinder, no repositioning of the heads need take place; the only requirement is to select the head. Head-switching operations are very fast (<1 μs), and this mode of operation is often referred to as *cylinder mode*. The cylinder mode of operation is the main reason for the popularity of the dedicated-servo approach. Embedded servo systems are far more common, and these require repositioning time when a new head is selected.

To switch cylinders, the servo must seek, as described earlier. In older disk files, the seek is accomplished through a command passed to the servo indicating the direction to move and the desired length of the movement in units of tracks. Since the servo is only given relative position data, the control logic usually keeps track of the absolute position or cylinder address at which the servo must be track-following. In all recent hard disk drives, the control of the actuator is accomplished by digital control as described later in Sec. 2.3.9. The digital controller is a microprocessor, or a signal processor which keeps track of the actuator location, velocity, and general status, and provides the control signal through a power amplifier to the voice coil. Thus in digital controllers, the disk file system gives absolute positioning instructions to the servo for desired track and head. Since the servo can only read position information from the selected head when the drive is running, initializing any servo (analog or digital) is required. A calibrate (or rezero) operation places the read-write heads over a fixed location on the disk, often denoted cylinder zero. Outside the normal data band of tracks, the position channel detects a change in the pattern indicating that the servo head is outside the normal region of customer operation of the disk file. The regions at both the inner and outer diameter locations adjacent to the normal servo tracks are often called *guard bands*. The position channel usually provides two digital outputs which indicate that the servo head is in either the inner or outer guard band. To carry out the rezero operation, the servo moves the actuator to find the first data track nearest the outer guard band. On some occasions the actuator must come to rest at either the inner or outer crash stops, an operation referred to as "parking" the actuator. As described later in Sec. 2.3.8, sector servo systems are the most commonly used today, and these systems generally have servo samples written in sectors that not only allow demodulation of track position, but also supply absolute track address and circumferential or sector address. This information adds to the robustness of the servo recalibrate algorithms.

On rare occasions, when the data channel is unable to read data off any track, the data head position can be offset (in either direction) from the normal track center in an attempt to recover the information. A data-recovery operation involves an offset command to the servo, in which a desired bias in the position reference is added. Table 2.6 lists these five basic servo functions.

2.3.4 The Plant

In the field of automatic control, the term *plant* refers to the system to be controlled. The pictorial block diagram of Fig. 2.27 illustrates the typical plant compo-

TABLE 2.6 Servo Functions

Command	Function
Track-follow	At any data track, reduce the position error signal to zero.
Seek	Given direction, and number of tracks to move, reposition the heads over new track center and track-follow.
Rezero	Move the heads to a fixed location on the disk as inferred from the written position error signal pattern.
Park	Bring the actuator to rest at either the inside diameter or outside diameter crash stop.
Offset	Track-follow with a position offset from track center (read only).

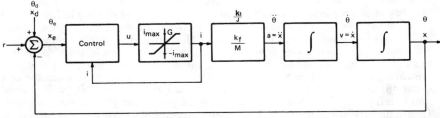

FIGURE 2.30 Simplified block diagram of the head-positioning servo. Note that current is measured and fed back for use in the control function rather than at u because of the saturating nonlinearity. Note the simple change of variables for rotary actuators.

nents for the disk file servo. Figure 2.30 contains a simplified and linearized functional block diagram of this plant (Ogata, 1970). Several basic key assumptions have been made: (1) the position error signal channel has no dynamics of its own, (2) the source producing the current i in the voice coil is ideal except for the saturation characteristic, (3) the force from the voice-coil motor is a linear function of current, (4) the relationship between position x and force f is assumed to be that of a simple inertia with no resonances acted on by a force in the x direction, and (5) there are no disturbance forces on the actuator.

In reality all these assumptions are inaccurate and define an upper bound on the control system performance. Before these realities are discussed, however, it is most instructive to describe the ideal plant model. The state space description of the plant is

$$\begin{bmatrix} \dot{x} \\ \dot{v} \end{bmatrix} = \begin{bmatrix} 0 & 1 \\ 0 & 0 \end{bmatrix} \begin{bmatrix} x \\ v \end{bmatrix} + \begin{bmatrix} 0 \\ Gk_f/M \end{bmatrix} u \qquad (2.29)$$

and

$$|u| \le \frac{i_{max}}{G}$$

where $v = \dot{x}$ = actuator velocity
G = gain of the saturating current source from control input u
i_{max} = maximum current
k_f = actuator force constant
M = mass of the actuator

The measurement provided by the position channel yields

$$\text{PES} = y = (-1 \quad 0) \begin{bmatrix} x \\ v \end{bmatrix} + r \tag{2.30a}$$

for
$$|r - x| < \frac{w}{2} \tag{2.30b}$$

where r represents the motion of any track center.

To account for motions greater than one-half-track in magnitude ($|r - x| > w/2$), the scheme shown in Fig. 2.31 is used. Note that at the target track, the signal x_e is always driven to zero. Thus the seek command loads the desired distance N to the

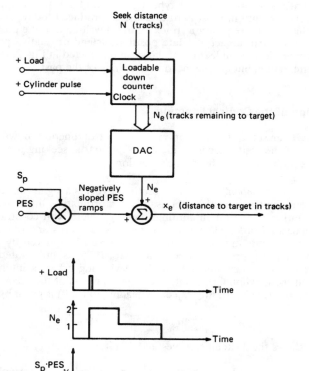

FIGURE 2.31 System used to construct continuous position error x_e, with the signals shown for a two-track seek.

target in units of tracks into the digital down counter, and the position error signal is either added (x increasing) or subtracted (x decreasing) to form x_e as

$$x_e = wN_e + S_p\text{PES} \tag{2.30c}$$

where $S_p = \begin{cases} -1 \text{ reverse motion } (x \text{ decreasing}) \\ +1 \text{ forward motion } (x \text{ increasing}) \end{cases}$ \hfill (2.30d)

and the position error signals and N_e are scaled as shown in Fig. 2.31. The typical waveforms are shown for a two-track seek.

The signals in Fig. 2.31 are important in the circuitry used to implement the control system, but they complicate the analysis of the system. For the forthcoming analysis, the simplified linear system shown in Fig. 2.30 will be used (unsaturated current source) in which the position variables are continuous functions and do not contain discontinuous position error-type signals. In effect, this simplification has become closer to reality in most hard disk drives produced today. Sector systems (Sec. 2.3.8) have absolute position (track address) written into the position sectors and thus the servo can detect absolute position instead of relative position error from track center. The complexities of the system depicted in Fig. 2.31 are instructional and interesting, but quickly becoming a thing of the past.

2.3.5   Design of the Control Function

The stage has been set for the derivation of the control function shown in Fig. 2.30. The function of the controller is divided into two parts, seeking the actuator and regulating its position to a desired track location.

2.3.5.1   The Seek Problem.   A seek operation involves a significant change in x_d, anywhere from one track width to thousands. Unfortunately, linear state feedback is not the solution to the minimum-time move problem with constrained control effort. For a second order plant with no transmission zeros and real eigenvalues, the solution to the minimum-time move problem can be derived by applying the Pontrayagin maximum principle (Bryson and Ho, 1975). Simply stated, the system is accelerated at the maximum rate until a switching curve is intersected, then decelerated at the maximum rate until the target is met. For the second order ($n = 2$) plant given by Eq. (2.29), the trajectory leading to (0, 0) is given by

$$\dot{x} = v = \text{sgn}\,(x_e)\sqrt{2i_{\max}(ki_f/M)|x_e|} \tag{2.31}$$

Figure 2.32 shows the switching curves and resultant trajectory for the final plant state ($x_e = 0$, $v = 0$).

For a plant with friction or back emf (Fig. 2.13) driven by a voltage limited current source, the trajectory is not given by Eq. (2.31). The actual limitation on the current source is output voltage. Hence, when the output voltage is at maximum or minimum value, the voltage generated in the voice coil as it moves with velocity v through the magnetic field in the motor gap directly subtracts from the maximum output voltage (E_{pasat}). The current source model is shown in Fig. 2.33. This is a highly nonlinear model, which is used only in analyzing the nonlinear seek operation of the servo. Important effects such as motor back emf are taken into account, allowing more accurate analysis. The gain A_{ol} of the power amplifier is usually high enough to justify the approximation $i = (-R_2/R_1 R_{\text{sense}})U$. When the

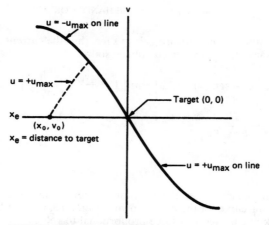

FIGURE 2.32 Velocity trajectories leading to the target position (heavy black lines). Dashed line is an acceleration trajectory.

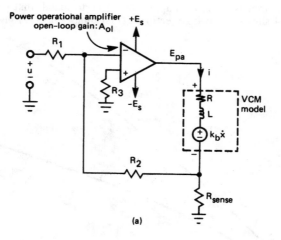

(a)

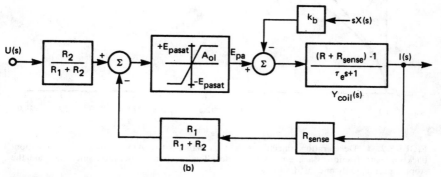

(b)

FIGURE 2.33 (a) Schematic diagram of power-current source implementation; (b) control block diagram of power-current source.

output voltage saturates, the forward gain is zero, thus the current response is that of a voice-coil motor driven by a fixed voltage source.

$$x_e = \text{sgn}(v) \, \tau_v v_{max} \left[-\ln\left(1 - \frac{|v|}{v_{max}}\right) - \frac{|v|}{v_{max}} \right] \qquad (2.32)$$

where $\qquad v_{max} = \dfrac{k_f E_{pasat}}{k_f k_b + R k_d} \qquad\qquad\qquad\qquad (2.33)$

$$\tau_v = \frac{RM}{k_f k_b + R k_d} \qquad\qquad\qquad\qquad (2.34)$$

The dominant time constant τ_v of the actuator was derived in Sec. 2.2.4.3. Equation (2.32) is a switching curve for the plant shown in Fig. 2.13, with both coil-generated voltage feedback and a frictional force proportional to velocity (Kirk, 1970). Note the increase in complexity of Eqs. (2.32) versus (2.31). If the actual coil inductance were added to the model, the plant would become third order, indicating a much more complicated switching *surface* for the optimal-time motion problem. In practical application, most implementations include only a switching curve, rather than a surface, and an attempt is made at shaping the curve to match that given by Eq. (2.32). Figure 2.34 shows the two trajectories (first quadrant only) given by Eqs.

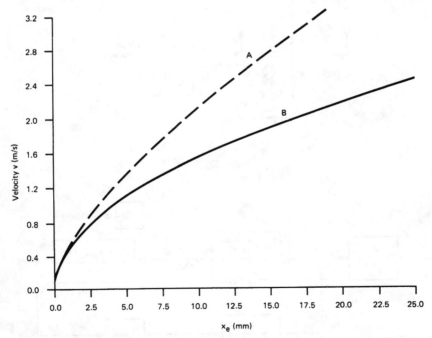

FIGURE 2.34 Deceleration trajectories used for plants (curve *A*) with and (curve *B*) without back emf and friction. Back emf and friction allow steeper deceleration since they aid the stopping force. Only one quadrant is shown.

TABLE 2.7 Actuator Parameters: An Example

Parameter	Nominal value	Units	Tolerance
Mass	0.2	kg	±3%
k_f (force factor)	15.0	N/A	±12%
R	8.0	Ω	±25%
R_{sense} (see Fig. 2.33a)	1.0	Ω	±1%
L	1.0	mH	±15%
First major resonance frequency	5.0	kHz	+20%, −0%
First major resonance amplitude	20	dB (mass line to peak)	±5 dB
k_d (frictional force)	0.5	(N/s)/m	+0%, −30%
k_b (back emf constant)	k_f	V · s/m	tracks k_f

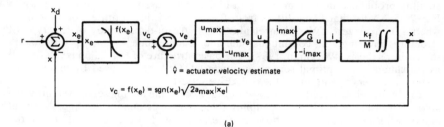

(a)

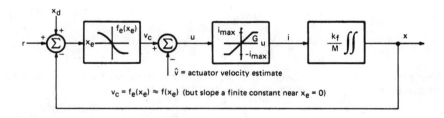

(b)

FIGURE 2.35 (a) Control system implementing time optimal bang-bang control; (b) linearized control system of (a). Linearization includes a finite slope velocity trajectory near target and proportional actuator current control for $|u| < i_{\text{max}}/G$.

(2.31) and (2.32) for comparison, with the voice-coil motor parameters as given in Table 2.7. Equation (2.32) produces a steeper velocity trajectory, yielding higher deceleration as the back emf and the friction aid the decelerating force.

The control system in Fig. 2.35a implements the switching curve given by Eq. (2.31) or (2.32). The distance to the target is the input to the switching function $f(x_e)$. The actual velocity of the actuator v is subtracted from the reference velocity v_e, and the sign of the result determines whether the plant is accelerating or decelerating (Oswald, 1974).

$$u = u_{max} \operatorname{sgn}(v_e - v) \tag{2.35}$$

$$v_e = f(x_e) = \operatorname{sgn}(x_e)\sqrt{2\alpha_{max}|x_e|} \tag{2.36}$$

where $a_{max} = i_{max}k_f/M$, and $u_{max} \geq i_{max}/G$.

Equations (2.35) and (2.36) are often referred to as the "bang-bang" control law for the second-order double integrator plant. Replacing $f(x_e)$ by a new function of x_e as derived from Eq. (2.32) would take into account the actual back emf and friction in the plant.

The nonlinear solution of Fig. 2.35a is inadequate for two reasons. First, as the system followed Eq. (2.32) to the target, the control Eq. (2.35) would "chatter" or switch rapidly between its maximum positive and negative values. Chattering causes large amounts of system noise, and the large $\ddot{x}$ terms excite system resonances. Second, as the position neared the target value (x_e tends to zero), the slope of the function $f(x_e)$ tends toward infinity. An arbitrarily high slope cannot be tolerated from bandwidth and stability considerations. Additionally, the control near the target would still be alternating between the most positive and negative limits, yielding poor track-following results. To linearize the system and eliminate stability problems, the system shown in Fig. 2.35b is used instead of that shown in Fig. 2.35a. Note that $f_e(x_e)$ differs from $f(x_e)$ in that it has a finite, constant slope when x_e is near zero (Workman et al., 1987). An in-depth study of this type of structure, covering both continuous-time and discrete-time systems is contained in the author's thesis (Workman, 1987). The basic structure of Fig. 2.35b is referred to as proximate time-optimal servomechanism (PTOS), and is used by many servo system designers in and out of the disk drive industry.

To obtain velocity feedback shown in Fig. 2.35, some analog servo systems use a velocity transducer, while others employ some type of estimating scheme. A typical analog velocity estimator uses both the filtered integral of the acceleration and the filtered derivative of the position.

$$\hat{V}_x \triangleq sX(s) \tag{2.37}$$

$$\hat{V}_i \triangleq \frac{I(s)k_f}{Ms} \tag{2.38}$$

Using the low-frequency information of $\hat{V}_x$ and the high-frequency information of $\hat{V}_i$ by means of a simple real-pole, all-pass network leads to

$$\hat{V} = \hat{V}_x \frac{\omega_f}{s + \omega_f} + \hat{V}_i \frac{s}{s + \omega_f} \tag{2.39}$$

$$\hat{V} = sX(s) \frac{\omega_f}{s + \omega_f} + \frac{I(s)k_f}{Ms} \frac{s}{s + \omega_f} \tag{2.40}$$

$$\hat{V} = X(s) \frac{s\omega_f}{s + \omega_f} + I(s) \frac{k_f/M}{s + \omega_f} \tag{2.41}$$

$$\hat{V} = \left(X(s)\omega_f s + I(s) \frac{k_f}{M} \right) \frac{1}{s + \omega_f} \tag{2.42}$$

Equations (2.37) through (2.42) show the derivation of the electronic velocity estimator shown in Fig. 2.36. To construct the filtered derivative of x, a circuit that is protected from the discontinuities in the position error signal is employed. Although this estimator was originally designed with an intuitive approach using

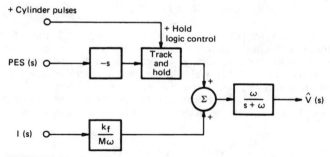

FIGURE 2.36 Open-loop analog velocity estimator. Velocity estimate is based on information in both position and actuator current. Note the use of the negative PES derivative because PES is $(r - x)$.

classical techniques, the result can be duplicated by designing a reduced order state estimator for the double integrator plant. Digital controllers used in today's hard disk drive servos use state estimators to determine velocity. These state estimators require far less art in design relative to their construction because they typically have more information to work with and the advantage of sophisticated nonlinear digital signal processing which would be prohibitively expensive in analog circuitry.

It is important to note that the power dissipated in the voice coil P_E is a strong function of seek time performance. Using the definitions set forth in Table 2.3, the average power dissipated in the voice coil when doing seeks of average length $N_t/3$ is

$$\overline{P}_E \approx \left(\frac{M}{k_f} \right)^2 \left(\frac{4}{3} \right)^2 \frac{x_s^2}{\tau_{sk}^4}$$

where x_s is the total stroke length in meters. Thus, seek time comes at the high cost of power dissipation. The task of the servo designer is to use as much of the capability of the voice-coil motor to withstand high accelerations and that of the head-disk assembly to dissipate heat. If time is allowed to lapse between seeks, the power $\overline{P}_E$ is decreased accordingly.

2.3.5.2 The Regulator Problem.
When the servo head reaches the target near the end of a seek ($|x_e| < w/4$), the control system objective changes from minimum time to minimum variance of position error (subject to constraints). While track-following, the desired track x_d (or "set point") remains constant, and the task of the control system is to reject force disturbances and follow small changes in r, the track position. A system which maintains control of a plant with a constant "set point" is often referred to as a *regulator*.

The solution almost universally chosen for the control structure during state regulation is that of a stabilizing linear compensator acting on x_e and i to produce a control signal u. Another approach which is equivalent to a compensator is that of a state estimator in combination with linear state feedback. Equation (2.43) represents the classical "compensator design" approach to generating the control

$$U(s) = C_x(s)X_e(s) + C_i(s)I(s) \tag{2.43}$$

where $C_i(s)$ could be taken as 0 if desired.

To avoid switching the control function, it is desirable to merge the terminal portion of the seek into linear control

$$U(s) = [k_1 X_e(s) - \hat{V}(s)]C(s) \tag{2.44}$$

where $k_1 = df(x_e)/dx_e$ for $|x_e| < \alpha_w w$; α_w, usually between 0.2 and 0.5, represents such an approach. When the position error is within a fraction of a track, the slope of the velocity-versus-position curve is designed to be a constant k_1. The normal seek loop control structure then yields linear state feedback (position and velocity estimate) in the control signal. In the case of the system shown in Fig. 2.35b, the control is given by Eq. (2.45). Recall that the power current source gain G is a design choice, hence, giving the designer complete control of the state feedback gain

$$U(s) = k_1 X_e(s) - \hat{V}(s) \tag{2.45}$$

If the velocity estimator of Fig. 2.36 is used to generate $\hat{V}(s)$, the complete form of the control is found from Eqs. (2.42) and (2.45).

Whether a compensator $C(s)$ (or $C_x(s)$, $C_i(s)$) is switched in near the target track or the terminal phase of the seek merges to linear control, the designer is faced with the problem of how to choose the exact control function to minimize position error $\dot{x}_e$. It is important at this point to discuss some of the practicalities which must be taken into account in the design of the regulator.

The $1/s^2$ transfer function of the actuator poses no challenge because the gains k_1 and G can be chosen to place the closed-loop system poles in any location. Unfortunately, the transfer function of real actuators always departs significantly from $1/s^2$, exhibiting high-frequency resonant modes which limit the usable bandwidth of the actuator (Oswald, 1980). In Sec. 2.2.4, the mechanical transfer function of a typical linear actuator demonstrates the resonant modes. An important factor is that these resonant modes vary greatly with temperature and time and from one actuator to another. This variation makes it necessary to attenuate the resonances sufficiently so that with the worst-case actuator, the servo remains stable. Attenuation of the plant resonances puts an upper bound on servo bandwidth (the -3 dB point of the $X(s)/R(s)$ transfer function, where $R(s)$ is the input and $X(s)$ the output of the measurement). To provide the necessary attenuation of these resonances, the designer must take them into account when choosing the compensator $C(s)$ or the state feedback gains.

Another important factor is that the actuator is under constant disturbance forces: cooling air, vibration, electrical cabling, and gravity all act on the actuator under varying conditions to accelerate it in one direction or another. Constant forces must not be allowed to offset the heads from the target. The solution to this problem is to construct a type-1 position loop. This is done by integrating x_e while track-following and then feeding the scaled result into the control signal (increasing the order of the compensator or adding a new bias state). Because of the large transient in x_e during any seek, the integrator is held in the reset condition until the servo is very near the target.

2.3.6 Complete System Example

Combining the pieces derived in previous sections yields the block diagram of Fig. 2.37. The design process will be described briefly to illustrate trade-offs and performance measurements for a disk file servo.

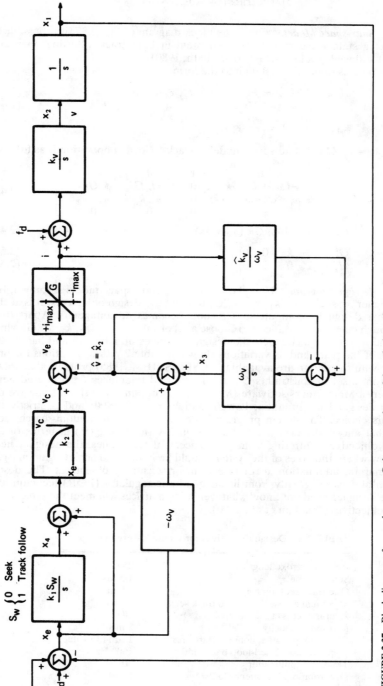

FIGURE 2.37 Block diagram of an analog servo. Only one quadrant of the velocity trajectory is shown. The power amplifier block is a simplified version of that shown in Fig. 2.33.

2.3.6.1 State-space Model. Given the block diagram of Fig. 2.37, it is possible to construct a state-space model for the system in both track-following operation ($S_w = 1$) and while seeking ($S_w = 0$) (Kailath, 1980).

The object is to put the system into the form

$$\dot{x} = Fx + G_r r + G_x x_d + G_f f_d \qquad (2.46)$$
$$y = Hx \qquad (2.47)$$

where $x^\tau = [x_1\, x_2\, x_3\, x_4] = [x\, v\, x_3\, x_4]$

Putting $k_v = k_f/M$ the state-space model in track-following operation is as follows:

$$F = \begin{bmatrix} 0 & 1 & 0 & 0 \\ -(\omega_v + k_2)Gk_v & 0 & -k_vG & k_vGk_2 \\ -\omega_{v-}^2\, k_vG(\omega_v + k_2) & 0 & -\omega_{v-}k_vG & \omega_vGk_2 \\ -k_1 & 0 & 0 & 0 \end{bmatrix} \qquad (2.48)$$

$$G_r^T = G_x^T \quad [0 \quad Gk_v(\omega_v + k_2) \quad \omega_v^2 + Gk_v(\omega_v + k_2) \quad k_1] \qquad (2.49)$$

$$G_f^T = [0 \quad k_v \quad 0 \quad 0] \qquad (2.50)$$
$$H_x = [1 \quad 0 \quad 0 \quad 0] \qquad (2.51)$$

2.3.6.2 Design Program. Now the form of the state-space model is known, but the designer must choose (k_1, k_2, ω_v, G) to meet the design objectives. It is at this point that design by computer-based tools becomes advantageous. Apart from some rough guesses, it is difficult to choose a set of values $P^T = (k_1, k_2, \omega_v, G)$ which will yield a system which meets the design objectives of Table 2.8 and handle the realities of the plant and its variations shown in Table 2.7. Many options for proceeding with the design are available; a DSL/VS (IBM, 1985) program that solves for P from a set of constraints C^0 and normalized tolerances C^* was used here. However, a Math Works software (MATLAB) program was written to derive the systems designed in (Franklin, Powell, and Workman, 1990) and is strictly the designers choice. The design program is an iterative linear random-search technique that allows the designer to build a quality function $Q(P)$ in terms of the desired objectives. Differing from pole-placement techniques, the designer need not know where the poles of the system should be in order to achieve gain margin, phase margin, attenuation, error rejection, or sensitivity objectives. The design program also varies greatly from linear quadratic regulator (LQR) techniques in that the designer need not know what weighting matrices will meet the same set of design objectives (Franklin et al., 1990).

TABLE 2.8   Design Objectives for Example Servo Design

Actuator stroke length x_s	25 mm
Settling time τ_s	1.5 ms
One-track seek time τ_1	2.9 ms
Maximum access time (1250 track seek)	30 ms
Average access time (worst case)	18 ms
Maximum velocity	2 m/s
Closed-loop system nonrepeatable runout	1 μm (3σ value)
Approximate closed-loop bandwidth	1000 Hz
Tracks per millimeter	50
Disk rotational frequency $\omega/2\pi$	60 r/s

Instead, the quality function Q (P) is written directly in terms of the design objectives themselves. The program calculates a system performance in terms of the desired constraints C, weights them in relation to C^*, and either accepts or rejects the system as being better or worse than the present design that comes closest to meeting the constraints. Table 2.9 gives a list of constraints that are explained in the following paragraphs.

Constraint 1 is simply a statement about the basic system frequency response and is perhaps taken care of by the constraints on eigenvalues as well as gains at the disk rotation rate (60 Hz in this example, but frequently as high as 120 Hz and up to 167 Hz in today's higher performance systems) and attenuation at the major resonant frequency, but it is included for completeness. Constraint 2 is included to limit amplification of noise and nonrepeatable runout as well as to limit system sensitivity to parameter tolerances.

Because the base system design does not contain a full resonance model of actuator dynamics, it is important to design the system to handle the mechanical resonances actually present. Constraint 3 provides sufficient gain margin for the system at the primary radial resonance frequency as listed in Table 2.7. The error transfer function is defined as the ratio error/input. Once a base fourth-order design is complete, the system model should be augmented to include resonances and other yet unmodeled phenomena. The reason for leaving these higher-order modes out of the initial design is twofold: first, the designer is able more easily to obtain a feel for the basic system when it is fourth-order than perhaps twelfth, and, second, it is easier for the design program to converge on a set of parameters P that meet the basic design constraints C when the order of the system is smaller. When the full, higher-order model is then put into the design program, the changes required to P will be small (if the constraints C were chosen properly).

As would be expected, nonrepeatable and repeatable runout power spectra are rich in energy at harmonics of the rotational frequency of the disk. The energy almost always diminishes with increasing frequency, except near base-casting or spindle-resonant frequencies. Accordingly, it is imperative that the servo system follow track motion at the rotational frequency with high fidelity or low error, necessitating high open-loop system gain at this frequency. Constraint 4 places the

TABLE 2.9 Design Constraints, Tolerances, and Results with $P_0^T = [764.0\ 3549\ 1009\ 90.20]$

Constraint	C_i^0	C_i^*	Value (at $P = P_0$)
1. Approximate $X(s)/R(s)$ − 3 dB BW	1000 Hz	100 Hz	1012.7 Hz
2. Maximum $|X(s)/R(s)|$	3.5 dB	1 dB	3.53 dB
3. $|X(s)/E(s)|$ at 5000 Hz	−30 dB	3 dB	−30.4 dB
4. $|X(s)/E(s)|$ at 60 Hz	30 dB	2 dB	34.24 dB
5. $\min_{\text{all } i} \cos [\arctan (\omega_i/\sigma_i)]$ for eigenvalues of system $\lambda_i = (\sigma_i + jw_i) = 1$ to 4	0.50	0.10	0.67
6. $\sum_{i=1}^{4} \frac{1}{|\sigma_i|}$(sum of all time constants)	0.003 s	0.0005 s	0.00275 s
7. $\min_{\text{all } i} \{|\sigma_i|\}$ (smallest real part of all roots)	1000 rad/s	250 rad/s	1007 rad/s
8. Eigenvalues	. . .	. . .	$-2879 \pm j315$ -1004 -1006

objective for this system at 30 dB, yielding an error in following the fundamental (rotational frequency) track motion of approximately 1 part in 32.

Closed-loop roots with low damping ratios cause very high system sensitivity to parameter variations. To minimize sensitivity, constraint 5 places a lower bound on the smallest damping ratio (cosine of the angle of the positive frequency pole and the $-\sigma$ axis with respect to the origin of the s-plane). Constraints 6 and 7 place bounds on the closed-loop system time-domain response. The desired values are a function of the objectives for the system settling time. While constraint 7 puts a lower bound on the rate of decay of any eigenmode, constraint 6 prevents a clustering of eigenvalues near the boundary set by constraint 7.

After putting the system matrices F, G_r, and H into the design program, along with the constraints and tolerances C^0, C^*, the following design parameters were chosen:

$$P_0^T = [764.0 \quad 3549 \quad 1009 \quad 90.20]$$

given C^0, C^* from Table 2.9. The resulting system does not meet the requirements exactly; the final system measurements are shown in Table 2.8. Before we discuss the performance of the example design, the measurement of system transfer functions will be described.

2.3.6.3 Transfer Functions.

One of the most common measurements of a disk file servo system is its open- and closed-loop transfer functions. Transfer functions are sinusoidal steady-state output over input ratios (complex numbers), where the output and input are defined as any two points of interest. The signals in the system are bounded by the constraint that the system must remain linear when a transfer function is being measured. When analyzing a transfer function, the system is assumed to be linear (Kailath, 1980). One of the most common transfer functions is defined by Eq. (2.52).

$$H_{xr}(s) = \frac{X_1(s)}{R(s)} \tag{2.52}$$

From the state-space system model,

$$H_{xr}(s) = H_x(sI - F)^{-1}G_r \tag{2.53}$$

The closed-loop transfer function $H_{xr}(s)$ describes the ratio of the actuator position response to a position command. Classical measurements of a feedback system design include gain margin and phase margin. These frequency-domain measurements are calculated by plotting another important transfer function, the open-loop transfer function $H_{xe}(s)$

$$H_{xe}(s) = \frac{X_1(s)}{X_e(s)} \tag{2.54}$$

and

$$H_{xe}(s) = \frac{H_{xr}(s)}{I - H_{xr}(s)} \tag{2.55}$$

Although the closed-loop transfer function $H_{xr}(s)$ is good for obtaining an intuitive feel for the system, it is the servo-error responses during track-following that are of primary importance. Two primary sources of error are known: (1) track motion and (2) force disturbances on the actuator. It is possible to define transfer functions from each input to the position error

$$H_{er}(s) = \frac{X_e(s)}{R(s)} \tag{2.56}$$

but
$$X_e(s) = R(s) - X_1(s) \tag{2.57}$$

$$H_{er}(s) = 1 - H_{xr}(s) \tag{2.58}$$

Another important transfer function is $H_{ef}(s)$, as it relates disturbance forces to positioning error.

$$H_{ef}(s) = \frac{X_1(s)}{F_d(s)} k_{tpm} \tag{2.59}$$

$$H_{ef}(s) = H_x(sI - F)^{-1} G_f k_{tpm} \tag{2.60}$$

where G_f is given by Eq. (2.50), and k_{tpm} is a scale factor that converts the units of H_{ef} from meters per newton to tracks per newton.

$$k_{tpm} = \frac{1}{w} \tag{2.61}$$

where w = width of one track in meters.

2.3.6.4   Performance.   A simulation program using DSL/VS was written to evaluate the system-transfer functions given by Eqs. (2.53), (2.58), and (2.60). The parameters P_0 will be used as the nominal values throughout the following analysis. Figure 2.38 is the Bode (frequency) plot of H_{xr}, H_{er}, and H_{ef}. The frequency range

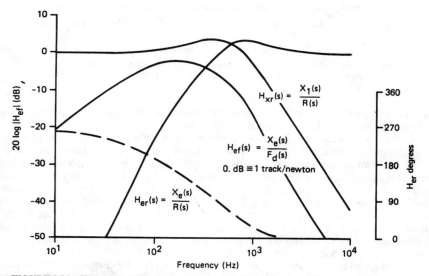

FIGURE 2.38   Three important servo system transfer functions: servo-head position response to command input ($H_{xr}(s)$), servo-head position error in response to a command input ($H_{er}(s)$), and servo-head position with respect to track center in response to a disturbance force input ($H_{ef}(s)$).

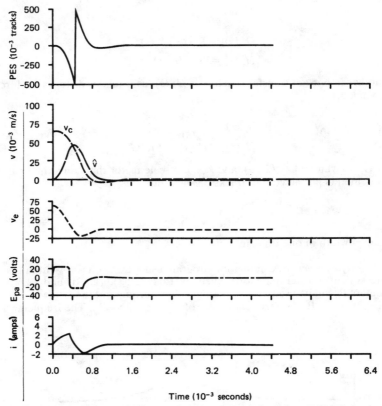

FIGURE 2.39 One-track seek servo waveforms as predicted by a DSL/VS simulation. Position error signal ramps are shown instead of continuous position error x_e.

was chosen to start at 10 Hz and stop at 10,000 Hz. Many of the design criteria satisfied by $P = P_0$ can be observed in Fig. 2.38.

Although the servo designer usually examines many aspects of the time-domain performance of the complete system, we will look only at signals from a short seek (1 track), and an intermediate length seek (417 tracks). Figure 2.39 contains the time-domain response of the system to a one-track move. The position error signal (PES) is used to show position for short seeks. The intermediate-length seek shown in Fig. 2.40 shows position error x_e instead of PES. At high velocities, the position error signal is difficult to plot because of its high frequency components (the fundamental frequency of the sawtooth waveform is 100 kHz at an actuator velocity of 2 m/s). Table 2.10 summarizes the data for the seek lengths in Figs. 2.38 and 2.39 as well as additional seek lengths.

Although all the performance objectives were met for the design, several considerations could force the servo designer to increase the order of the system. System noise (or process noise) and measurement noise can cause operational problems under certain amplitude and power spectral density conditions. An example of an

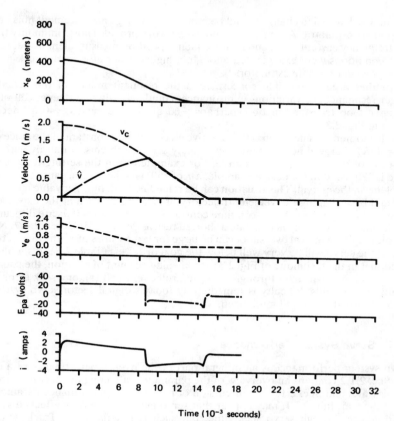

FIGURE 2.40 Nominal length seek (417 tracks) waveforms.

TABLE 2.10 Nominal Seek Data

Seek length, tracks	τ_{move}, ms	τ_{sk}, ms	$\overline{P}_E\ (\tau_d = 0)$, W	$\overline{P}_E\ (\tau_d = 0.002)$, W	See figure
1	0.460	0.720	24.8	6.57	Fig. 2.39
2	0.740	0.980	33.2	10.9	
4	1.14	1.36	38.3	15.5	
10	1.92	2.14	41.3	21.4	
100	6.72	6.94	40.7	31.6	
417	14.4	14.62	35.4	31.1	Fig. 2.40
1250	27.2	27.42	25.4	23.7	

area in which a design change would be motivated by large measurement noise is in the velocity estimator. A single-pole all-pass network provides noise immunity from low-frequency current noise and high-frequency position-measurement noise. If the noise conditions were exaggerated enough, a higher-order all-pass network might be employed, or a state estimator.

Another area of possible concern is in the resonant modes of the actuator. Larger resonances or variations in resonances could necessitate a steeper roll-off in the open-loop transfer function, perhaps -60 dB/decade versus -40 dB/decade shown in Fig. 2.38.

Still another consideration is the effective electrical time constant of the voice coil ($\tau_e = L/R$). Large time constants cause many servo problems, primarily with the response of the power-current source. For example, when the setting time of the servo is 220 μs, as in the design example, a τ_e of 150 μs or larger can cause overshoot problems in the arrival. This situation can be remedied both by eigenvalue modification and by reshaping the velocity trajectory of Eq. (2.32), each at the expense of some performance loss. Voice-coil time constants shorter than 500 μs are difficult to obtain and almost surely necessitate a shorted turn as described in Sec. 2.2.4.7. Note that although the arrival overshoot can be large for large values of τ_e, the final setting time of the servo will be very well below the goal of 1.5 ms (Table 2.8). It should be noted that in the technique of Fig. 2.31 for keeping account of position, the counter logic must not down count through zero (i.e., roll over to all 1s), or a seek error will result. Happily this difficulty is remedied by today's digital sector servo systems, although overshoot is still minimized.

2.3.7   Servo System Performance

Servo system performance is an integral part of the overall performance of a disk file. Sec. 2.1.2 contains an overview of the parameters affecting the performance of the disk file, and Sec. 2.1.3 is a discussion of how certain performance parameters affect the wait time t_w. It may appear that servo performance only affects disk file performance through servo seek time, but such is not the case. Track density, latency, and number of voice-coil motors per head-disk assembly are all functions of servo system performance. Other measures of disk file performance are affected by the servo system as well. Total disk file efficiency (and therefore cost), sensitivity of the disk file to physical disturbances, and data integrity are also functions of servo performance and design.

2.3.7.1   Track Density.   Track misregistration, as discussed in Secs. 2.2.1 and 2.2.3, is of primary consideration in determining the upper bound of the track density of a disk file. The track misregistration is the result of many sources of head-positioning error and, in a dedicated servo (servo head separate from data heads), is affected by the servo performance.

Any nonrepeatable runout that can be acted on by the closed-loop position system is greatly affected by servo bandwidth. A low-frequency motion of the disk stack is tracked well by the servo; however, as the frequency of motion rises, the servo becomes less effective at following the track centers. Both actuator design and servo system architecture and design are important in determining the band-width (lowest frequency at which the error transfer function crosses -6 dB) of the error transfer function. For a given actuator design and its associated resonances (including all tolerances), the servo structure determines the maximum usable band-width. A servo with a roll-off of 40 dB per decade will have a lower error transfer function bandwidth than that of a system with a roll-off of 60 dB per decade. There is a range of frequencies for which the servo does not perform well and, in this range, it would be better if the servo were turned off. The area under a log-linear plot of $H_{er}(jw)$ is zero. (This applies to minimum phase systems. For nonminimum phase systems, the area is actually positive.) That is, for a range of disturbance frequencies, the servo actually increases the mean-squared position error. Fortunately, the disturbances are not white (equal power at all frequencies). The non-repeatable track center motions tend to fall off in magnitude proportional to the square of the reciprocal of the frequency of motion, and sometimes faster. Hence, the power spectrum of the track motion is a low pass function. Since the error transfer function is lowest in the low frequency range, the servo produces a very large net gain in positioning accuracy over an open-loop system.

Although the track motions are bandwidth-limited functions of time, not all lie within the bandwidth of the error transfer function. Spindle and spindle bearings interact to produce large motions at frequencies at which the servo can actually amplify the error. Care must be taken in the choice of the bearings as well as in the amplitude of the error transfer function to minimize this track misregistration component.

Not all nonrepeatable motion is reported to the servo loop in a dedicated-servo system. Disk flutter, dynamic actuator tilt, and data-arm flutter all produce errors between the data heads and track centers that are not measured and therefore cannot be corrected by a dedicated-servo system. Herein lies the advantage of embedded-servo systems (either sector or continuous). The servo plays a much more dominant role in reducing track misregistration in an embedded system because almost all track misregistration components are acted on by the servo system. All mechanical track misregistration components are acted on by the servo, with the exception of very small effects such as surface degradation over time (track centerline shifting due to physical changes in the media). A key benefit of embedded servo is the elimination of all of the low frequency thermal offsets between data and servo heads which occur in a dedicated system.

A portion of the servo nonrepeatable runout is due to the action of disturbance forces on the actuator. Cooling air, air turbulence in the disk enclosure, and gravity all act in varying degrees to produce radial forces on the actuator. Servo structure and design play a large role in the shape and magnitude of $H_{ef}(s)$, the disturbance force-to-error transfer function. A servo design which seeks and track-follows well will not necessarily have good disturbance-force rejection characteristics. As indicated in Sec. 2.3.5.2, position error is often integrated and fed forward to produce a type 1 position loop which is tolerant to biases in force and electronics offsets. However, this type of design is susceptible to residual roots, that is, roots at low frequencies masked by zeros in the position transfer function. Pole-zero "near cancellation" yields responses to position commands with almost undetectable amounts of response of the mode represented by the pole canceled. The important observation about these cancellations is that although poles are the same for any system transfer function, the zeros are not. This implies the mode suppressed in the position input response may not (and probably will not) be suppressed in the force input response. In other words, a pole-zero cancellation in the $H_{ef}(s)$ transfer function does not occur because the zeros are not the same.

A design procedure which penalizes low-frequency or large time constants will prevent the occurrence of residual roots in the design. Control system structures can also be changed to avoid residual roots. A state estimate that includes bias force as a state will aid in improving disturbance force rejection.

The seek action of the servo can cause both nonrepeatable position inputs and force inputs. Reaction forces of the voice-coil motor acting on the head-disk assembly excite bending modes in the structure that supports the spindle bearings. The magnitude of the vibration as seen at the servo head is a function of both the magnitude of the force and the rate of change in force per unit time. Force variation per unit time (dF/dt) is referred to as "jerk." Servo systems can be designed to minimize the jerk that the disk file is subjected to as a result of control actions. For systems with voltage-limited power amplifiers driving an inductive load, the maximum jerk is given by

$$\left(\frac{dF}{dt}\right)_{\max} k_{f\max} \frac{dI}{dt} = \frac{k_f(E_{pa})_{\max}}{L} \tag{2.62}$$

where $(E_{pa})_{\max}$ is the maximum output voltage of the voice-coil driver.

The variables on the right side of Eq. (2.62) cannot be set to achieve a particular value of jerk; therefore, a power amplifier design that limits the output slew rate is often employed. In disk files using an integrating power amplifier, slew-rate limiting of the force is easy to achieve by limiting the size of the input to the integrator (e.g., in the IBM 3380, the value of dI/dt is limited to 16,000 A/s). For a given maximum force dictated by the desired access time, a servo that limits the jerk used during the seek operation improves the performance of the disk file by improving track misregistration and thus increases track density capability.

Another major source of track misregistration can be inconsistent arrivals onto the target track. The last half of a track of motion before the servo head reaches the target track center is commonly referred to as the *arrival*. In the case of a one-track seek, the last half track represents 50% of the total move. In the case of a 1000-track move, the same arrival only represents 0.05% of the total move transient. Because the arrival represents such a large disparity in the fraction of the transient, it is not clear that any control design will result in arrivals which are invariant with seek length, and in fact, most designs will not. The structure of the control system plays a large role in determining the consistency of the arrivals. Consistent arrivals are important in determining a component of track misregistration referred to as *transient arrival*. When a servo is directed to locate or to seek to a track, it is important to determine that it is positively safe to write or read data. Inconsistent arrivals have two important impacts: first, they usually imply variable settling time (time to file ready), yielding poor performance, and second, widely varying arrival characteristics make it difficult to design the "file ready" function.

2.3.7.2 *File Ready Function and Data Integrity.* In all disk files, there exists a block of circuitry and/or logic that determines whether the file is ready to read data, write data, or both. Depending on the exact architecture, there may be just one output of this block called "write inhibit," or there may be more elaborate outputs such as read ready, file ready, and write ready. Other than possible soft read errors, no damage is done by reading early in the arrival onto a track. Such is not the case for writing, however, as writing too far off-track can destroy data on an adjacent track. If arrivals are consistent, the file ready function could be just a time-out after the distance-to-go in a seek less than one-half track. However, if the function were just a time-out, the system would be left open to many different conditions that might prohibit the servo from arriving on target properly. Additionally, while track-following, an electrical or mechanical failure or an accidental impact to the drive could cause the actuator position to wander from the desired track. A loss of system integrity or impending large positioning error must be detected to ensure the integrity of user data, especially true for drives (usually 2.5-in) in portable systems such as laptop computers.

Simply windowing the position error signal after the total position error is less than one-half track is usually not sufficient for several reasons: noise spikes in the position error signal would cause interruption in the writing or reading process, degrading performance; impending disasters would not be caught before they occurred. Filtering can be employed to mitigate the noise problem; however, this yields time lag, which exposes the system to writing on user data. Other system state variables can be used to aid in solving the time lag problem, and a combination of filters, windowing, and additional inputs such as voice-coil voltage and current can be used to provide a file-ready function of extremely high reliability. Use of the voice-coil current improves the time response of the inhibit function, while the power amp voltage protects against open-loop-type failures. Electrical noise disturbance forces, disk defects, and servowriting accuracy all play important roles in determining the bandwidths and window function trip levels used to formulate a write-ready signal. Providing a write inhibit function in a sampled data function is far more thought provoking than in a system with continuous-time signals available. Sampling position error every 100 μsec for example, leaves the servo vulnerable between samples. A shock to the drive (easily pictured in a laptop computer) immediately after a sample time could cause the selected head to *just miss* the inhibit threshold on the following sample but far exceed it on the next. Engineers spend a lot of time protecting written data from just these type of events. Longer sample times of low performance servomechanisms pose the most hazard, especially since low performance systems are not synonymous with low track density as in the past. Indeed, some of the highest aerial density systems being shipped are in smaller 2.5-in form-factor laptop disk drives. Shock sensors, software re-write algorithms, and other more complex techniques are used to provide this critical function.

2.3.7.3 Disk Latency and Servo Performance. The power spectral characteristics of most of the sources of nonrepeatable runout are direct functions of disk velocity. To decrease latency, it is necessary to increase disk velocity. Increasing the rpm of the disks by a factor of α has the effect of shifting the power spectral components of the disturbance functions up in frequency by a factor of α as well. If the servo bandwidth is also scaled by a factor of α, the components of track misregistration will remain the same (actually, they may increase because the phenomena that generate the disturbances are functions of higher powers of frequency). Thus the ability of a disk file to operate at a particular rpm and track density is in part a function of the ability of the servo to correct for the disturbance functions generated by the rotating disks.

2.3.8 Sector Servo

Position-error signal data are written at regular sectors of all data tracks. Since user data cannot be stored in these sectors, there is strong motivation to make the sectors as small as possible without yielding unacceptably large sensitivity to surface irregularities and electrical noise.

The output of the position error signal is sampled position information. Thus the servo control system is a discrete-time system. To minimize data-space loss, it is desirable to have as few position-error signal fields per revolution of the disk as is possible while still obtaining a wide enough bandwidth of position information to accomplish the servo system objectives. Thus, while the servo designer would like a high sampling rate, there is always pressure to lower the space lost to position-error-signal data fields. If the number of sectors written per track is denoted N_s, the

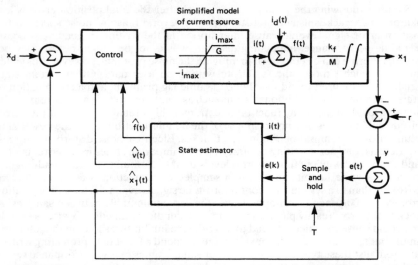

FIGURE 2.41 Sampled data sector servo implemented with an analog-control structure. For clarity, the model producing the PES estimate $\hat{x}$ (t) is not shown. The signal $e(k)$ denotes the kth sample of the signal $e(t)$.

sampling time T_s and frequency f_s become $T_s = 1/f_s$, and $f_s = N_s\Omega$, where Ω is the rotational rate in r/s.

There are many approaches to the design of a sector servo. Figure 2.41 shows the block diagram of an analog sector servo. The essence of this design is the use of a state estimator to obtain continuous position, velocity, and track-crossing pulses. There are many references (Ogata, 1970; Kailath, 1980; Franklin, Powell, and Workman, 1990) from which the estimator theory can be obtained, but implementing a state estimator that can deal with a position error signal as a measurement input is not straightforward. The plant model must contain a model of the continuous-time position error signal with track-crossing pulses (Stephens and Workman, 1986). Once this is established, the estimator error is derived at the sampling intervals by subtracting the model output from the position error signal samples. For simplicity, Fig. 2.41 is shown with only one sample and hold. The actual system would form estimator error $e(kT)$ samples by sampling $y(kT) - \hat{x}_1(t)$.

An important feature that has been added to the estimator shown in Fig. 2.41 is the state $\hat{f}$. Under all conditions, practical actuators contain bias forces (represented in Fig. 2.41 as $i_d(t)$, a disturbance current equivalent) acting on them which must be overcome to track-follow. The resulting nonzero mean voice-coil current does not cause acceleration, and feeding it into a state estimator without a bias-force state estimate would cause a nonzero offset between the estimated and the measured position error signals. Continually estimating this bias force allows the system to be robust with respect to the bias force on the actuator, implying that small and slow changes do not adversely affect system performance.

Although this system has a different architecture, the design procedure is the same. First, a mathematical model of the system of Fig. 2.41 must be derived. Because of the sample and hold, a discrete-time model of the system must be formulated. A key step, the discrete-time state-space model of the system, can be made nearly exact. To construct the discrete-time state-space model, a continuous-time state-space model is constructed with the open-loop system input being that of the output of the sample and hold, as shown by Eqs. (2.63) through (2.66)

$$x^T = [x_1\, x_2\, x_3\, x_4\, x_5\, x_6] \tag{2.63}$$

$$\dot{x} = Fx + G_e e + G_x x_d \tag{2.64}$$

$$y = r - x_1 \tag{2.65}$$

$$e(kT) = x_1(k) - \hat{x}_1(k) - r(k) \tag{2.66}$$

The next step is to convert these differential equations into difference equations describing the open-loop discrete-time plant

$$x^T(k) = [x_1(k)\, x_2(k)\, x_3(k)\, x_4(k)\, x_5(k)\, x_6(k)] \tag{2.67}$$

$$x(k + 1) = \Phi_{ol} x(k) + \Gamma_x\, x_d(k) + \Gamma_e e(k) \tag{2.68}$$

where $x_d(k)$ is assumed to be the output of a fictitious sample and hold of $x_d(t)$.

There are several numerical ways to obtain the discrete-time system matrices Φ_{ol}, Γ_x, and Γ_e (Moler and Van Loan, 1978; Franklin, Powell, and Workman, 1990). The formulas for these matrices are given by Eqs. (2.69) through (2.71)

$$\Phi_{ol} = e^{FT} = I + \Psi FT \tag{2.69}$$

$$\Gamma_x = \Psi G_x T \tag{2.70}$$

$$\Gamma_e = \Psi G_e T \tag{2.71}$$

where
$$\Psi = I + \frac{FT}{2}\left\{ I + \frac{FT}{3}\left[\cdots \frac{FT}{M-1}\left(I + \frac{FT}{M} \right) \right] \cdots \right\} \tag{2.72}$$

and $T = T_s$, the integer M is the number of terms used to evaluate Ψ, and I is the identity matrix.

Once the matrices of Eq. (2.68) are found, an exact† set of equations is at hand to describe the closed-loop system at the sampling instants. The closed-loop discrete-time model is found by using Eq. (2.46).

$$x(k + 1) = \Phi_{cl} x(k) + \Gamma_x x_d(k) + \Gamma_e r(k) \tag{2.73}$$

where
$$\Phi_{cl} = \Phi_{ol} + \Gamma_e H_1 \tag{2.74}$$
$$H_1 = [1\quad 0\quad 0\quad 0\quad 0\quad 0] \tag{2.75}$$

The design procedure for sector servo now parallels that used in the servo design example. The only difference lies in the fact that the frequency-domain analysis is done in the z-plane rather than the s-plane. Another important point is that the estimator and the control law are not designed independently. Although the poles of the estimator are a subset of the poles of the complete closed-loop system, the dynamics of the estimator play an important role in system response when the plant model in the estimator does not match the plant exactly. Various continuous plant disturbances $i_d(t)$ and measurement "noise" $r(t)$ also contribute to estimator errors. Track motion appears as noise to the estimator since there is no way to model this unknown quantity, and it does not reflect actual motion of the actuator mass.

---

†The only approximation lies in the number of terms M used to calculate Ψ in Eq. (2.72). If $F_i T$ is first normalized, 11 terms ($M = 11$) yield accuracies to the 10th significant digit in the entries of Φ_{cl} (Franklin, Powell, and Workman, 1990; App. to Chap. 6).

2.3.9 Digital Control

A long-time goal has been the replacement of all analog control electronics with a programmable digital controller (Rabiner and Gold, 1975; Franklin, Powell, and Workman, 1990). Motivations for this goal include (1) elimination of component drift; (2) ability to integrate into VLSI; (3) increased flexibility of control algorithms; (4) relative ease of adding adaptive control and estimation features (Goodwin and Sin, 1984; Workman, 1987a); (5) ease with which nonmonotonic and nonlinear functions can be added (Workman, 1984); (6) increased testability during manufacture; and (7) improved reliability, availability, and serviceability of the product.

Digital control as shown in Fig. 2.42 for disk file servomechanisms with closed-loop bandwidths in excess of 1 kHz only became feasible in the early 1980s. The first products in the marketplace that rely solely on a processor for algorithmic computation of the control $u(kT)$ were the IBM 3380 models J and K (Workman, 1987b). Although the continuous time analog system is pedagogically the most illustrative, nearly all of today's disk drives are shipped with digital controllers. Both the head positioning servomechanism and the spindle speed controller are done with a digital signal processor and some associated circuitry for obtaining plant measurements and manipulating the prime mover or control input to the plants. In addition, nearly all of today's disk drives utilize sector servo for accuracy in head positioning.

From a design point of view, digital control is very similar in procedure to discrete-time analog control. The similarity is due to the fact that digital control is discrete-time and discrete-amplitude control. Although the discrete-amplitude characteristic must be dealt with, proper scaling and choice of word size usually allow the system-dynamics design and algorithmic computation to be decoupled.

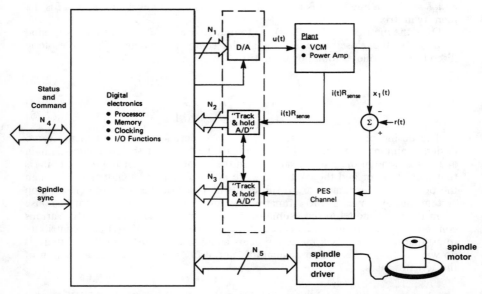

FIGURE 2.42 Typical digital control system for a hard disk drive which includes head positioning and spindle control.

The basic design procedure consists of four parts. First, construct a continuous state-space model for the analog plant from the point of the output of the control digital-to-analog converter as shown in Fig. 2.42 ($u(t)$). Second, construct a discrete-time model of this plant, including a real-time delay λ. The delay λ is used to model the constant delay of the processor in using the samples of i and PES at time kT to output the next control $u(kT + \lambda)$. For best results, in general λ should be minimized. Third, combine the discrete-time plant model and real-time delay λ with the state-space model of the control algorithm executed by the processor. Fourth, place the complete state-space model in a design program, along with the design constraints C and tolerances C^*, and a quality function $Q(P)$. The parameter vector P will consist of programmable gains, used by the processor in calculating the control $u(kT + \lambda)$ via the control equations.

Figure 2.42 a typical block diagram of the digital servo function. Several features are typical beyond those required for data head positioning: 1) The system usually regulates spindle speed and phase (reference to other disk drive spindles to provide synchronization), 2) Digital servos today are usually involved in head selection and the commands from the system process to the DSP include track address, head select, and even sector number for circumferential information.

2.4 DATA CHANNELS

2.4.1 Functional Description

Peak detection has been the primary technology used to recover data in disk files. The components of a peak-detection channel are discussed here with an emphasis on the important functional parameters. Detailed circuit implementation and the details of the logic and microcode used to control the communications from the computer channel to each recording channel and head will not be discussed. A block diagram of one read channel plus analog and digital signals at the different points in the channel are shown as Fig. 2.43. The input to the final "and" gate from the gate path is required to insure that the amplitude of the output from the differentiated signal does not fall below a specified level, for example, from intersymbol interference. The path for write data will be discussed in the following section. The key parameters and design objectives for the parts of the channel are discussed below.

The output signal that is read back from the head with digital recording is composed of alternating pulses, characterized by their amplitude, and pulse width at the 50% amplitude level which is referred to as PW_{50}. In addition, in the case of film heads there are undershoots due to reading from the edges of the poles. A typical isolated pulse from a film head is shown in Fig. 2.44 by the curve labeled "unequalized" (Roscamp, 1992). The amplitude and PW_{50} for a variety of head and media combinations will be analyzed in Sec. 2.5.3. This signal with accompanying noise is then the input signal for the peak detection channel.

Another key attribute of the channel is the user bit density (UBD), defined by

$$\text{UBD} = (\text{number of data bits})/PW_{50},$$

or, in terms of the clock time per bit (T_b),

$$\text{UBD} = PW_{50}/T_b.$$

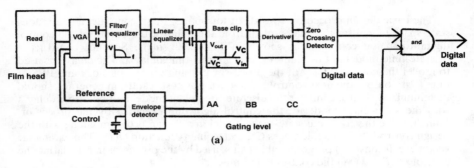

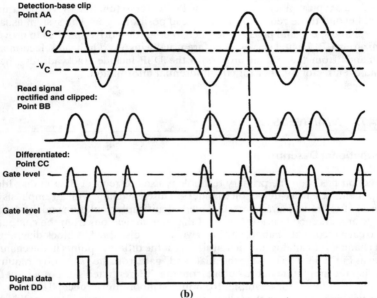

FIGURE 2.43 (*a*) Block diagram of a peak-detection data channel; (*b*) readback signals at key points in the channel.

In terms of the flux change density and the defining parameters of run-length-limited codes (Sec. 2.4.2), the user bit density is

$$\text{UBD} = (m/n)(d + 1)(\text{flux changes}/PW_{50})$$

where D_r is the flux change density. In order to achieve user bit densities greater than unity, pulse slimming equalization is used with the peak detection channel or a channel other than peak detection is used. Both of these approaches are discussed in this section.

2.4.1.1 Read and Write Module. To minimize noise and the inductance of leads, the preamplifier and write-current sources are usually placed near the actuator arms and attached with flexible cable. High levels of semiconductor integration have been

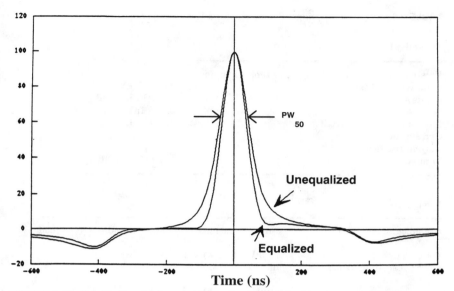

FIGURE 2.44 Read back pulse from a thin-film head and disk with parameters as listed in Table 2.15 (Sec. 2.5.2). Shown in the figure are the pulse as read back from the head unequalized and after electronic equalization *(Roscamp, 1992).*

used in the preamplifiers and write drivers. The modules typically contain selectable read preamplifiers, write drivers, and write-current sources. In addition, the modules contain circuits to detect whether the write current is driven to the selected head and whether the head circuit is open or shorted. Functional parameters for typical read and write modules for use with film heads are listed in Table 2.11. To achieve the listed preamplifier performance, low-noise bipolar or BiCMOS transistors are used. To minimize pulse distortion, it is necessary to maintain linear phase over the bandwidth of the signal.

Noise from the preamplifier is key since this noise will dominate the noise of following amplifiers. Noise of preamplifiers in the read mode is specified as noise spectral density (NSD), in which the noise is assumed to be gaussian and arises from the input resistance of the differential amplifier. This noise is given by Nyquist's Theorem (Nyquist, 1927) for the rms voltage from a resistive source as:

$$v_n = \sqrt{4kTR(NBW)} \tag{2.76}$$

where k is Boltzmann's constant (1.3805×10^{-23} J/°K), T is the absolute temperature (°K) and R is the average resistance (Ω) over the noise bandwidth (NBW) of the amplifier. The NSD is equal to $v_n/\sqrt{NBW}$ and is measured in volts/$\sqrt{Hz}$. To assess the noise voltage over a particular bandwidth the NSD is multiplied by the square root of the bandwidth. To the NSD for the preamplifier must be added the NSD from the input resistance for the head (Sec. 2.5.3). The NSD for a typical preamplifier arising from thermal noise in the base resistance and current shot noise is 0.5 to 2.0 nV/$\sqrt{Hz}$. These noise terms will be discussed again in Sec. 2.5.

The preamplifiers for magnetoresistive heads must not only amplify the input signal with low noise but must also supply the bias and sense currents for the

TABLE 2.11 Typical Functional Parameters for a Read and Write Module (Preamplifier)

Thin Film Head

Voltage gain (worst case over power supply margins)	250
Input voltage from head	300–400 μV
Bandwidth	80 MHz at $-$3dB
Noise spectral density (NSD)	0.5 to 1nV/$\sqrt{Hz}$
Input impedance for read	300–600 Ω
Current source	3–100 mA
Current rise time	$\leq$ 6 ns
Common mode rejection	> 60 dB at 5–10 MHz

Magnetoresistive Head[†]

Architecture	Current bias and current sense with differential read and write
Power supplies	+5.0 V ($\pm$ 10%), $-$1.25 V ($\pm$8%)
Power dissipation modes	idle: 41 mW
	read: 420 mW
	write: 585 mW
Input noise spectral density	0.58 nV/$\sqrt{Hz}$ with R_{mr} = 15 Ω and I_h = 16 mA
Magnetoresistive head resistance range	12 to 25 Ω
Write head current	10 to 30 mA
Magnetoresistive head bias current	10 to 17 mA
Head protection	Excessive magnetoresistive head
	Sense current
	Thermal asperity detection
	Head open
	Head shorted

[†]The specification is for a Texas Instruments TLS21003 module.

magnetoresistive head. The sense circuits for magnetoresistive heads can operate in either a constant voltage or constant current mode, i.e., the average or direct current or voltage does not change with changes in the resistance of the magnetoresistive stripe. With constant current sense (I_s) the sensitivity of the magnetoresistive read head is

$$\Delta I_s = \frac{-\Delta R_{mr}}{R_{mr}} I_s$$

and the figure of merit for the magnetoresistive head is $\Delta R_{mr}/R_{mr}$, where R_{mr} is the resistance of the magnetoresistive head and ΔR_{mr} is the magnetoresistance. The advantage of constant current biasing and sensing, and the analogous constant voltage biasing and sensing, is that the output signal is independent of the stripe height of the sensor and this reduces the effects of the throat height lapping tolerance. Two problems with magnetoresistive heads which have been addressed within the preamplifier are spurious signals from contact of the magnetoresistive head with asperities which can heat the magnetoresistive stripe, and excess current flow through the head when the head is in contact with the disk surface. For the former problem circuits have been developed which use nonlinear filtering to remove the thermally generated voltage spikes. For the latter problem it is found necessary either to use a dual voltage power supply to keep the sensor near zero volts allowing the disks to be grounded, or a single ended amplifier can be used or feedback amplifiers can be used (Klaassen and van Peppen, 1995). Excess current flow through the head is to be avoided since the heads are operated with current levels which approach the electromigration limit. To increase the life of the heads the sense current is switched off when the head is neither reading nor writing. With the sector servo architecture it is not possible to turn the sense current off when the head is in the write mode because thermal time constants do not allow the head to be turned on rapidly to allow reading a sector servo signal. Parameters for a typical preamplifier for magnetoresistive heads are listed in Table 2.11. The subject of preamplifiers has been reviewed (Klaassen, 1991; Klaassen and van Peppen, 1995).

The write drivers for use with film heads have used an H-driver configuration. In this configuration, the film head is the center bar on the H, and logic circuits are used to switch voltages from the vertical members of the H to drive the current in a controlled manner in both directions through the head. Asymmetry less than 100 ps and rise times less than 6 ns are required. In writing the digital data, it is necessary to saturate the recording medium through its entire thickness, and with the film head and longitudinal recording, it is typically found that an mmf of approximately $1/2A \cdot$ turn is required. It is also important that the rise time of the current pulses be fast compared with the clock interval. Adequate writing can be measured by checking the *write-over-modulation noise* (Sec. 2.2.2).

2.4.1.2 *Automatic Gain Circuit.*

An automatic-gain circuit is required to compensate for head-to-head and disk-to-disk tolerances and inside-track-to-outside-track amplitude tolerances. The automatic-gain circuit consists of a variable-gain amplifier and envelope detector with close tracking between the envelope-detection and data-detection clip levels. The requirement of the automatic gain circuit is that the gain-versus-control voltage follows as nearly as possible a linear-logarithmic law.

2.4.1.3 *Filter and Equalizer.*

The low-pass filter is important in achieving desired error rates. A typical filter is a fifth-order Butterworth or Bessel filter with corner frequency selected to cut off high-frequency noise, resulting in a more symmetrical pulse and reduced shift peak. For the IBM 3380, the filter has a magnitude and group delay as shown in Fig. 2.45. The -3 dB corner frequency is seen to be 16 MHz. The resulting isolated pulses at the inside and outside data tracks are shown in Fig. 2.46a and b. The filter is seen to improve the symmetry of the film-head pulse. The improved symmetry can be shown, using pulse-superposition studies as seen in Sec. 2.2.2, to result in less ontrack peak shift. To achieve the minimum pulse width the filter cut-off frequency must pass all of the required bandwidth as used by the channel. In the case of run-length-limited codes, the filter -3 dB bandedge should be near $1/2\,T_{\min}$ (Sec. 2.4.2). To avoid unwanted distortion it is also required to have linear phase response and this can be achieved by cascading unity gain phase equalizers with the filters, or by careful selection of the target response for the filter (DeVeirman and Yamasaki, 1992). Note the narrower pulse shape (in time) at the outside data track compared with that at the inside data track. A factor which can compensate for the reduced pulse width at the outside tracks is the increase in flying height of the heads at the outside diameter tracks due to increased air velocity. In the small disk files with rotary actuators the large skew angle of the heads at the outside diameter tracks tends to maintain the flying height constant and the pulse width at the outside diameter tracks is expected to be smaller than at the inside tracks.

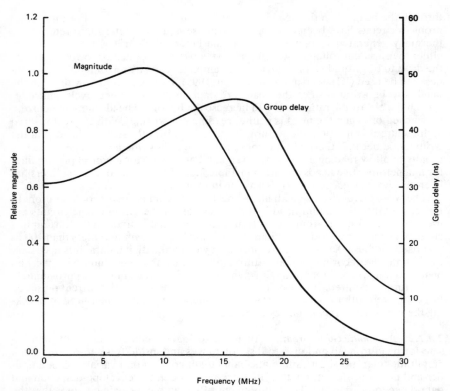

FIGURE 2.45   Magnitude and group delay versus frequency for a Butterworth filter as used in the IBM 3380 recording channel.

Electronic equalization shapes the frequency response of the channel to achieve specific objectives. In the case of the read channel in digital magnetic recording the objective is to slim the isolated pulse to achieve higher linear densities. The procedure is to select a target response and to design a circuit to convert the unequalized response from the head and media into the target response. An example of a target response is the cosine function,

$$H(\omega) = 1 - 2\,k\cos(\omega T_d) \tag{2.77}$$

The term $\cos(\omega T_d)$ results in a peaking of the transfer function at a frequency near the cut-off frequency of the low-pass filter. The magnitude of the combined equalizer and low-pass filter transfer function is shown in Fig. 2.47. To realize this transfer function and to evaluate the pulse narrowing in the frequency domain, the transfer function for the equalizer is derived from adding inverted replica pulses delayed and advanced with respect to the data pulse as shown in Fig. 2.48 (Roscamp, 1992). That this operation results in the cosine transfer function can be derived as follows:

$$H(\omega) = 1 - ke^{j\omega T_d} - ke^{-j\omega T_d} = 1 - 2\,k\cos\omega T_d \tag{2.78}$$

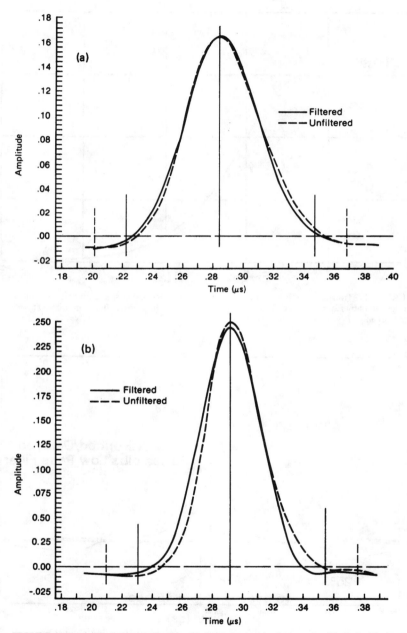

FIGURE 2.46 (*a*) Isolated readback pulse from the inside data track with and without a Butterworth filter (Fig. 2.45); (*b*) isolated readback pulse from the outside data track with and without a Butterworth filter (Fig. 2.45).

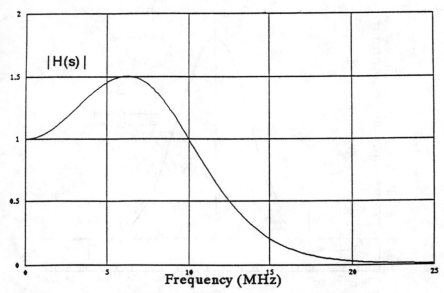

FIGURE 2.47 Transfer function in the frequency domain for the cosine equalizer and a low-pass filter described by Eq. (2.77) with $k = 1/4$. The large peak in the transfer function occurs at $f = 1/2T_d$ *(after Roscamp, 1992).*

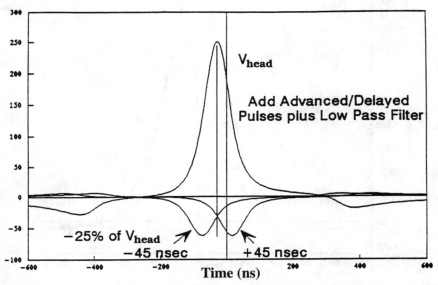

FIGURE 2.48 Read back pulses from the thin-film head and disk shown in Fig. 2.44 shown displaced in time to result in the cosine equalizer response. The displaced pulses are 25% of the amplitude of the center pulse and delayed and advanced by $1/2\ PW_{50}$. The narrowing of the resulting pulse is shown here and in Fig. 2.44 *(after Roscamp, 1992).*

The narrowing of the pulse is determined by the boost near the cut-off frequency of the low-pass filter and the delay time T_d. The slimming of the film-head pulse resulting from cosine equalization is shown in Fig. 2.44 (curve labeled "equalized"). By expanding the delay operator $e^{s\tau}$ in an infinite series and retaining only the first term, it can be shown that the transfer function is equivalent to

$$H(s) = \left[s - \frac{\sqrt{2(1-k)}}{\tau} \right] \times \left[s + \frac{\sqrt{2(1-k)}}{\tau} \right] \qquad (2.79)$$

These are two real-axis zeros in the s-plane and provide slimming of an input pulse. A curve of peak shift as a function of off-track interference with and without an equalizer is shown as Fig. 2.49 and the improvement in performance with the equalizer is clear.

Equalizers for use in disk files with banded recording (Sec. 2.2.5.1) require adjustability and programmability since the data frequencies in the bands vary and the degree of equalization and hence boost required also varies in the different bands. This has been accomplished using filters based on bipolar transconductance–capacitance (g_m-C) circuits. These circuits have many advantages, including digital controllability, high frequency operation, and the absence of inductors which require significant space on the circuit board. In Fig. 2.50 is shown the block diagram of a three-stage g_m-C filter with feed forward to achieve boost and hence equalization (DeVeirman and Yamasaki, 1992). The transfer function for the equalizer is given by:

$$H(\overline{\omega}) = \frac{K(\omega^2 + \omega_0^2)}{\omega_0^2 - \omega^2 + j\dfrac{\omega\omega_0}{Q_0}} \qquad (2.80)$$

The boost is determined by the value of the parameter K and, in one realization, the boost is variable from 0 to 13 dB, and is controlled by a digital input which can be varied to accommodate the changing requirements for equalization of the zones. The 3 dB cut off frequency for the combination of the equalizer and a low-pass filter, which is incorporated on the same semiconductor chip, is also controlled by a fixed resister and a digital input. In Fig. 2.51 is shown the transfer function for the equalizer and low-pass filter combination. It is seen that the boost is varied from 0 to 13 dB and the cut-off frequency is varied from 9 to 27 MHz, which covers a wide range of read channel applications (De Veirman and Yamasaki, 1992).

In Fig. 2.52 is shown the effect of differentiation on the transfer functions of a channel which has had amplitude boost near the edge of the bandpass of the channel to result in pulse slimming (see Fig. 2.51). The increase in bandwidth of the differentiated transfer function is clarified by comparing Figs. 2.51 and 2.52.

Equalization has a negative effect on signal-to-noise ratio since the noise at high frequencies is boosted, and thin-film media transition noise has a rapid increase as the recording density is increased. To estimate this loss in signal-to-noise ratio, the transfer function can be integrated to evaluate the noise bandwidth (NBW),

$$\text{NBW} = \int_0^\infty \frac{|H(\omega)|^2}{4\pi} \, d\omega \qquad (2.81)$$

To estimate the increase in NBW with equalization, the increase in 3 dB bandedge with equalization can be used and, for the g_m-C equalizer/filters, typical increases in

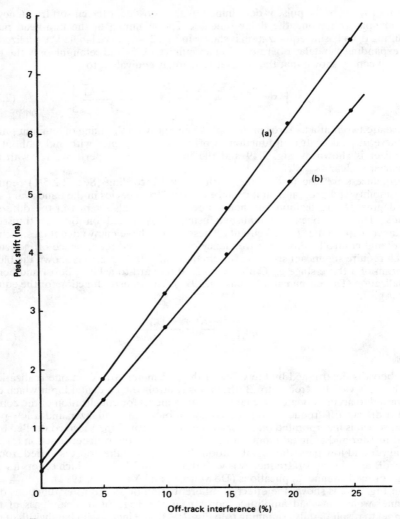

FIGURE 2.49   Peak shift versus percentage off-track noise for a recording channel with a Butterworth filter. (*a*) Without a cosine equalizer; (*b*) with a cosine equalizer. The curves were simulated using a typical film-head pulse (Fig. 2.46*a*).

−3 dB bandwidth are 2.6 times for 9 dB boost. In addition, the equalizers themselves introduce noise, although the percentage increase over noise from heads, media, and the preamplifier is about 3% for a 27 MHz filter with 9 dB boost.

The change in signal-to-noise ratio due to equalization for a peak detection channel has been quantified (Koren, 1991). The input signal-to-noise ratio for both the amplitude qualification or gate channel, and the timing channel containing the

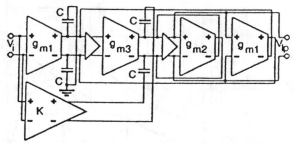

FIGURE 2.50 Schematic diagram for a three-stage tuneable equalizer and low pass filter. The blocks labeled "g_m" are transconductance elements which are voltage controlled current sources. The transfer function for the circuit is given as Eq. (2.80) and the location of the poles responsible for the equalization are adjustable by the gain of the feed-back amplifier (K) *(after DeVeirman and Yamasaki, 1992).*

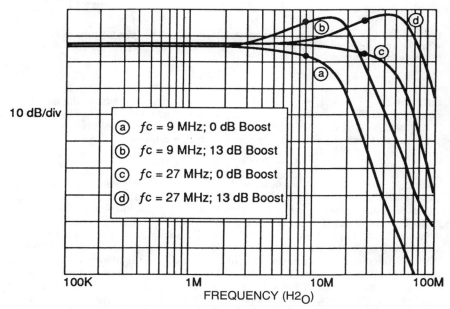

FIGURE 2.51 Transfer function for the tuneable equalizer and low pass filter shown in Fig. 2.50 and described by Eq. (2.80). The significant variation in the location and magnitude of the boost in the transfer function and the cut-off frequency (f_c) are shown *(after DeVeirman and Yamasaki, 1992).*

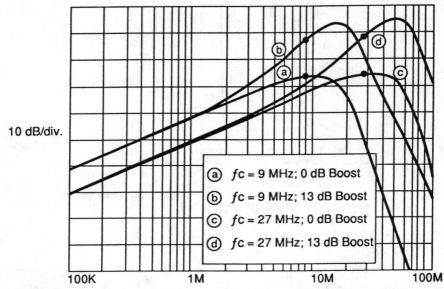

FIGURE 2.52   Transfer function for the tuneable equalizer and low-pass filter shown in Fig. 2.50 with the output differentiated to give zero crossings for the output signal for a peak detection data channel *(after DeVeirman and Yamasaki, 1992).*

differentiation channel, is degraded by an amount that depends on the degree of equalization. For an assumed cosine[4] input function, a rate 2/3 (1, 7) code (Sec. 2.4.2), and a matched filter response, the signal-to-noise ratio loss is shown in Fig. 2.53. In this figure the abscissa is the data slimming ratio defined by

$$S_d = T_d/PW_{50} \text{ (in)} = 1/\text{UBD}$$

where PW_{50} (in) is the 50% pulse width for the input isolated pulse. The data slimming ratio is the inverse of the user bit density (UBD). It is seen that high values for pulse slimming can lead to significant loss in signal-to-noise ratio.

More sophisticated equalizer designs have been developed. One such design uses a procedure which ensures that large fixed percentages of the signal are constrained to the clock window (Barbosa, 1981). The signal-to-noise ratio after equalization is degraded by the increase in noise power due to the high-frequency boost, but increased due to the sharper pulse and hence increased slope of the pulse after differentiation (Tachibana and Ohara, 1977). The presence of the differentiator in the peak-detection part of the channel complicates the analysis of signal-to-noise ratio, since the differentiator itself boosts the high frequencies (Fig. 2.52).

2.4.1.4   Data Detector.   In the base-clip peak-detection channel, data are detected by clipping the signal near the baseline to remove spurious peaks; rectifying, differentiating, and limiting the signal; then triggering logic circuits which give output logic pulses with leading edges aligned with the peaks of the input analog signal. The sequence of operations and the resulting signals are shown in Fig. 2.43*a* and *b*. This process is discussed again in Sec. 2.5. The selection of clip level is a compro-

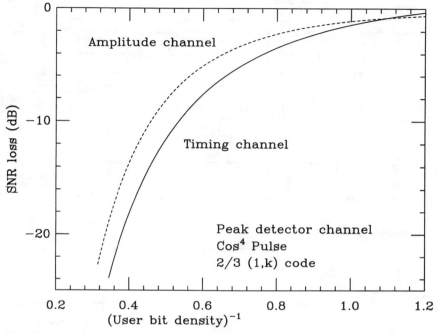

FIGURE 2.53 Loss in signal-to-noise ratio in an equalized channel versus the inverse of the user bit density. The pulse is raised cosine with $n = 4$. The losses for both the amplitude and timing channels are shown *(after Koren, 1991)*.

mise between allowing pulses from disk defects to be detected (clip level $|V_c|$ too low) and not allowing desired pulses to be detected (clip level $|V_c|$ too high).

An alternative data detector can be realized by using the fact that in magnetic recording, the analog pulses always alternate in sign. In the ΔV detector, the amplitude of the analog signal is tracked after a peak, and it is required that in a time interval Δt the output voltage must drop by an amount at least ΔV. The selection of Δt and ΔV depends on the pulse shape and the distribution of disk-defect pulses.

2.4.1.5 *Clocking and Data Synchronization Circuits.* The pulses from the data detector all have the same width, and all are aligned in time with the peaks of the analog signals. The pulses, however, are not located at the correct bit times because of bit shift generated by all the effects discussed in Sec. 2.2 (intersymbol interference, overwrite modulation, off-track interference, and electronics noise). For the data from the disk file to be usable in the computer central processing unit, the data must be standardized so that the digital pulses are all associated with a particular clock cell. Also, disk-speed tolerances make it necessary to synchronize the clock to the read data. Clock circuits are also required to generate the write data.

The clocking system used to generate the clock pulses from the random data is typically a phase-locked loop, as shown in Fig. 2.54. The loop consists of a 180° phase discriminator, an integrator, compensation circuits, and a voltage-controlled oscillator. In this system, the voltage-controlled oscillator and phase discriminator

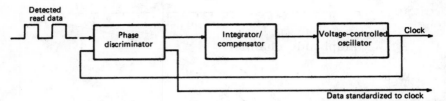

FIGURE 2.54 Phase-locked loop used to generate the clock signals used in the peak-detection channel. The clock is synchronized to the data stream.

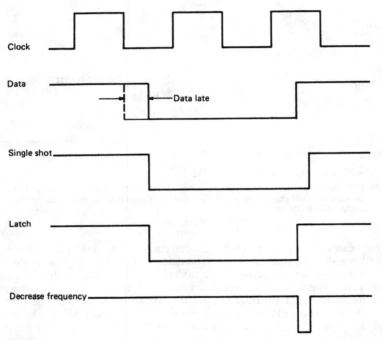

FIGURE 2.55 Output from the phase discriminator to the integrator and compensator circuits in the phase-locked loop, which then drive the voltage-controlled oscillator frequency to a lower value to correct for the data being late with respect to the clock window.

convert frequency to phase (integration), and in the steady state, phase error is approximately zero.

Phase discrimination is achieved by digital means. Signals resulting from data pulses being late with respect to the clock pulse are shown in Fig. 2.55. The pulses, whose durations are proportional to phase difference between data and clock, are then fed to an integrator which integrates the error current, and the output voltage is coupled to a compensation circuit and dc amplifier. The transfer function of the integrator compensator is given by

$$E_0(s) = \frac{I(s)}{cs}\frac{s + \omega_z}{s + \omega_p} \qquad (2.82)$$

where the location of the filter pole ω_p and zero ω_z can be altered to change the synchronization time and bandwidth of the phase-locked loop. This is required since the clock circuit is used to satisfy conflicting demands: first, it must maintain fast synchronization time at the start of a read operation, which implies wide bandwidth; and second, there must be low phase error between data and clock in the presence of jitter on the clock during reading of data, which implies narrow bandwidth.

A crystal oscillator running at a multiple of the data rate is used to establish the clock signals for the encoding and decoding of the run-length limited data codes (Sec. 2.4.2). A voltage controlled oscillator, whose center frequency is set by a frequency synthesizer for each data band, is used. For example, for the rate 2/3 (1, 7) data code, clock signals at three times the data rate are required. The system clock for writing and reading data is then locked with the phase locked loop to the crystal frequency. The total clock system is then formed by feeding the output of the voltage-controlled oscillator back to the phase discriminator.

The clocking system has tolerances that limit achievable recording density. The tolerance components are steady-state error, jitter (open-loop transient response to bit shift), component drift in the clock circuits, frequency deviation, and adjustment errors in the single-shot and variable-frequency oscillator.

2.4.1.6 Write Precompensation. A significant advantage can be achieved by predistorting the write data before they are sent to the write driver. This is referred to as *write precompensation,* and the operation may take place in the device attachment or in the drive itself. As explained in the discussion on peak shift in Sec. 2.2, the worst-case peak shift arises from a 1 (presence of a pulse) isolated by 0s on one or both sides. With write precompensation, peak shift is anticipated, and the write transitions are preshifted to compensate for the intersymbol interference; the net result is less observed peak shift in the detected data. Consider the serial bit pattern allowed by the 2, 7 run-length-limited (RLL) code shown below.

$$b_0\,b_1\,b_2\,b_3\,b_4\,b_5\,b_6\,b_7\,b_8\,b_9\,b_{10}\,b_{11}$$
$$1\ 0\ 0\ 0\ 1\ 0\ 0\ 1\ 0\ 0\ 1\ 0$$

Assume that three or more 0s precede b_0 and three or more 0s follow b_{11}. Bit b_4 is shifted so that the write transition is written late in time, and b_{10} is shifted so that it is written early in time. The algorithm used does not shift bit b_0, since it is not at the highest density allowed by the 2,7 code (it is adjoined by three, and not two, 0s). Write precompensation for peak detection results in moving transitions closer and, in order to compensate for the pulse shifting due to intersymbol interference, a loss in signal amplitude occurs. In addition, if there is significant interaction between transitions during writing, write precompensation is not effective due to partial erasure of the transitions. This limitation is observed when the ratio of the transition spacing (B) to the transition length (a) (Sec. 2.5.2) is less than about 3.5 (Bertram, 1994). For sampled amplitude detection, as for example PRML (Sec. 2.4.3), to reduce nonlinear transition shift write precompensation moves transitions farther apart. More complex algorithms are possible with write precompensation with the added complexity of the logic circuits.

TABLE 2.12 Parameters for Modulation Codes

Code name	d	k	m	n	Code rate (m/n)	Density Ratio DR	T_{min}	T_{max}	T_w	User Bit Density (UBD)
NRZI	0	∞	1	1	1.0	1.0	T	∞	T	1.0
FM	0	1	1	2	0.5	0.5	$0.5\,T$	T	$0.5\,T$	0.5
MFM	1	3	1	2	0.5	1.0	T	$2\,T$	$0.5\,T$	1.0
1, 7	1	7	$\left(\frac{2}{4}\right)$	$\left(\frac{3}{6}\right)$	0.67	1.33	$1.33\,T$	$5.33\,T$	$0.67\,T$	1.33
2, 7	2	7	$\left(\frac{2}{\frac{3}{4}}\right)$	$\left(\frac{4}{\frac{6}{8}}\right)$	0.5	1.5	$1.5\,T$	$4\,T$	$0.5\,T$	1.5
0, 4/4	0	4	8	9	0.89	0.89	T	$4.44\,T$	$0.89\,T$	2.0 to 2.25

$$DR = (m/n)(d + 1)$$
$$T_{min} = (m/n)(d + 1)T$$
$$T_{max} = (m/n)(k + 1)T$$
$$T_w = (m/n)T$$
$$T = \text{data period} = 1/\text{data rate}$$

UBD = data bits/PW_{50} = $(m/n)\,(d + 1)$ (flux changes/PW_{50}). The values for UBD listed assume a conservative value for flux changes/$PW_{50} = 1$ except for the (0, 4/4) code for which flux changes/$PW_{50} = 2.25$ to 2.53 (see Sec. 2.4.1).

2.4.2 Data Codes

The technology for encoding digital data has progressed along with the rest of the disk file technologies. Improvements have been made in finding codes in which customer data are encoded, resulting in less intersymbol interference and improper clocking. Table 2.12 lists a number of codes with variations in the number of 0s between 1s for the coded data; the 1s are separated by at least d 0s, but no more than k 0s. To meet the (d, k) constraint, m bits of customer data are mapped into n bits of channel code. The code rate is m/n and the run length limited codes are specified by m/n (d, k). The density ratio DR is the ratio of bits to recorded transitions and represents the efficiency of the code in utilizing recording space. However, the penalty for increased density rates is the smaller clock window compared with NRZI. The most common data code used is the rate 2/3 (1, 7) code. The numbers before the parenthesis indicate the mappings between customer data and channel data, e.g., for the (1, 7) code two customer bits are encoded as three channel bits.

The increase in linear density resulting from the use of the 2/3 (1, 7) code can be realized by noting that if the minimum spacing between transitions (T_{min}) is kept constant in comparing an uncoded data sequence and a coded one, then the same length of track would require 6 bits of coded data compared with 3 uncoded bits. However, the 6 codes bits actually represents 4 information bits and therefore the information density is improved by a factor of 4/3, but the bit cells are one-half as wide.

The last entry in Table 2.12, the (0, 4, 4) code, will be discussed along with the partial response maximum likelihood (PRML) channel (Sec. 2.4.3).

2.4.3 Sampled Amplitude Detection

Peak detection as discussed in Sec. 2.4.1 suffers a significant loss of signal-to-noise ratio because of the differentiation process required to identify the peaks of the pulses. This decrease in signal-to-noise ratio can best be noted by reference to Fig. 2.52, which shows the output from the differentiator following the equalizer in a peak detection channel. The significant boost at the higher frequencies due to the differentiation will increase the noise. As shown in Sec. 2.5, an estimate of the loss in signal-to-noise ratio is 1.25 dB. Because of this loss of signal-to-noise ratio and to allow operation at a higher user bit density, sampled amplitude detection has been introduced in rigid-disk systems (Howell et al., 1990; Coker et al., 1991). Key to the application of sampled amplitude detection to magnetic recording was the recognition that Class IV partial response signaling for data detection (Lender, 1963; Kretzmer, 1966) is especially suited for the magnetic recording channel (Kobayashi and Tang, 1970; Wood et al., 1984). The application of minimum mean-square error detection to the partial response channel was recognized later (Kobayashi, 1971).

A sampled amplitude channel that has been reduced to practice is the Class IV partial response (PR IV) channel with maximum likelihood detection, which has been referred to as PRML (Coker et al., 1991). A block diagram of this channel is shown as Fig. 2.56. The precoding, equalization and Viterbi detection parts of the system will be discussed in this section. The analog-to-digital converter is used to sample the analog read signal at the clock times and to convert the sampled values to a 6 bit binary word. The recordings used for PR IV are non-return-to-zero (NRZ) in which the 1 data bit is represented by write current in one direction and the 0 bit by current in the opposite direction. For PR IV the channel is equalized in the frequency domain to a sinusoidal response with nulls at zero frequency and at the Nyquist frequency $(1/2T)$† as shown in Fig. 2.57. In this figure (Behrens and Armstrong, 1993) is shown the target equalization sinusoidal response and a measured channel response using a typical film head and thin film disk. In order to utilize the PR IV channel with thin-film heads it is necessary to equalize the total frequency response, including the oscillations caused by the thin-film head undershoots, to the sinusoidal response. With ferrite and magnetorestive heads, which have no undershoots, the equalization has proven less difficult. To match the actual to the target equalization response would require approximately 8 to 10 dB of amplitude boost near one-half the Nyquist frequency. The user bit density with PR IV equalization has been as high as 2.2. This value of user bit density is significantly larger than achievable with peak detection (≈ 1.5) and the increase in linear density achievable with PR IV over peak detection is approximately 30%.

The response of the properly equalized PR IV channel to a pulse of write current $I(t)$ with width equal to the user bit time can be described in the time domain as

$$h(t) = \text{sinc}\left(\frac{\pi t}{T}\right) - \text{sinc}\frac{\pi}{T}(t - 2T) \tag{2.83}$$

This relationship is shown in Fig. 2.58. With this partial response system, the output to the current pulse $I(t)$ is seen to be formed by the combination of the pulse from the present clock period and that from the pulse from two previous clock periods. The two sinc functions have values of zero at all other clock periods and therefore there is no interference with the output from other channel bits. The output has three levels (± 2 and 0) as can be seen by examining Eq. (2.83) and this is compared to peak detection channels which have two levels (± 1). Dividing the total signal into more levels decreases the detection margin, but this is balanced by the larger amount of intersymbol interference that can be tolerated with PR IV. Note

---

†The Nyquist frequency is the lowest frequency at which a band-limited continuous signal can be sampled and allow the signal to be reconstructed and it is equal to twice the highest frequency component in the signal (Lee and Messerschmitt, 1988).

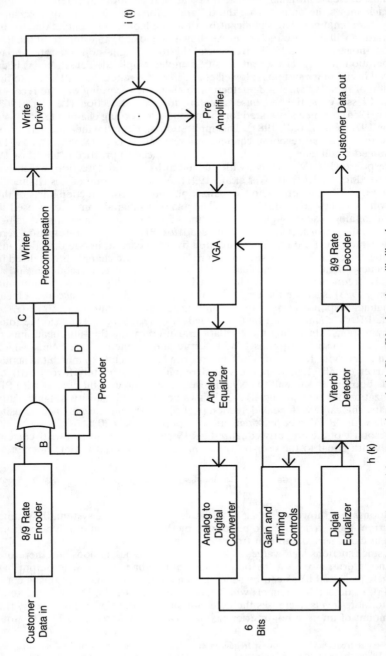

FIGURE 2.56 Block diagram for a partial response channel with Class IV and maximum likelihood (Viterbi) detection (PRML).

2.84

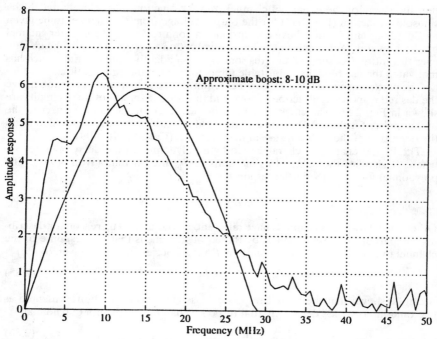

FIGURE 2.57 Theoretical amplitude response for a PR IV channel and measured response using a typical thin-film head and disk. The user bit density is 2.2 *(after Behrens and Armstrong, 1993).*

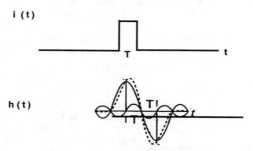

FIGURE 2.58 Input current pulse and output read back signal for a PR IV channel with the sinusoidal frequency response shown in Fig. 2.57. The time domain response is given by Eq. (2.83). Note that there is no response at sampling times other than at $t = 0$ and $t = 2T$, where T is the channel bit time.

that the shape of the equalized channel transfer function must closely match the sinusoidal function (Fig. 2.57) for the output voltage from the channel to be given by Eq. (2.83) and for the above conclusions on noninterference from other channel bits to be valid. Achieving this precise equalization over the range of heads and over the entire disk surface requires some form of adaptive equalization which has motivated the use of digital adjustable filters for part of the equalization.

The partial response Class IV channel requires precise gain and timing to achieve the desired response as described above and the block diagrams of these circuits are shown in Fig. 2.56. The clock cells must be placed accurately with respect to the output pulses for the PR IV system to function as described above. More details on the operation of these circuits are in the reference (Coker et al., 1991).

The PR IV channel is characterized by a polynomial in the delay operator D, where D^i signifies the delay of i time units of T_b, the bit time (Wolf, 1991). The polynomial for Class IV partial response is

$$h(D) = 1 - D^2 \tag{2.84}$$

Other partial response channels have different polynomials. The reason for describing the partial response channels by these polynomials is that the response of the channel to a pulse of current of duration T has a Fourier transform given by

$$h(f) = 1 - e^{-2j\omega T} = h(D) = 1 - D^2 \tag{2.85}$$

It can be shown that the partial response Class IV channel can be represented as two time-interleaved "dicode" partial response channels, each with polynomial

$$h(D) = 1 - D \tag{2.86}$$

The sampled data stream can be broken in two streams, one for the even time intervals and one for the odd time intervals and these channels operate at one-half the user bit rate.

In Fig. 2.57 the upper frequency of the band limited response is shown to be 0.5/T and this is the Nyquist frequency for the channel. This is in contrast with the peak detection channel, in which the reduced code rate of the codes used [2/3 (1, 7) and 1/2 (2, 7)] results in significant response at the Nyquist rate, as shown in Fig. 2.59 (Dolivo, 1989). This figure shows the power spectral density for random data encoded with run length limited (2, 7) and (1, 7) data codes and the horizontal axis is normalized by the data bit time (T). Reduced channel bandwidth and the attendant reduced noise is another advantage of the PR IV channel.

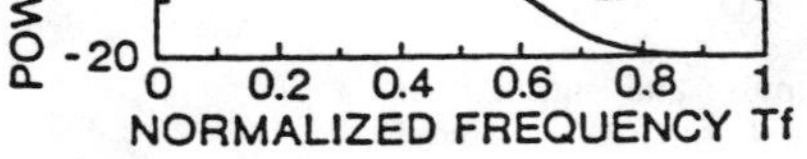

FIGURE 2.59 Power density for a channel with the (2, 7) and (1, 7) run length data codes. The data was taken using a pseudo-random sequence of data and the frequency is normalized to the all-ones customer data frequency ($f_{\text{all-ones}} = 1/T_{\text{in}}$). Note the large response beyond the Nyquist frequency of $1/2T_{\text{in}}$ *(after Dolivo, 1989).*

The code selected for the PR IV channel is a high-rate code—the 8/9 (04/4) code which was described in Table 2.12 (Eggenberger and Patel, 1987; Wolf, 1991). The designation in the parenthesis for the 8/9 (04/4) code is that there are no 0's required between the 1's from the encoder, and there must be no more than four 0's between 1's, which allows adequate clocking. The last symbol 4 indicates that within the interleaved even and odd bit stream detectors there must be no more than four 0's between 1's. This code is a high-rate code and therefore the channel operates at a frequency near that for the incoming data stream,

$$T_{min} = (8/9)T_{data}$$

The channels for the run-length limited codes used for peak detection have somewhat larger values of T_{min} and hence lower values of channel speed, e.g., for the 2/3 (1, 7) code the value of T_{min} is

$$T_{min} = 4/3T_{data}$$

However, a significant disadvantage of the high-rate code is the higher transition density (flux changes per mm) which accentuates the effects of nonlinear transition shift (Howell et al., 1994). Nonlinear transition shift is due to the interaction of the demagnetizing field from a newly recorded transition with the field from the write head resulting in a shift in the following transition. The nonlinear transition shift can be corrected by write precompensation for $B/a > 3.5$, where B is the transition spacing and a is the transition length; however, for $B/a < 3.5$ write precompensation is no longer effective and errors can occur. The approach that has been used is to reduce the transition length (a) from that for a run length limited system by reducing the ratio $M_r\delta/H_c$ for the magnetic recording surface, where M_r is the remanent magnetization, δ is the thickness and H_c is the coercivity (see Sec. 2.5.2).

Detection of the digital data arising from sampling the amplitude $h(t)$, resulting in a sequence $h(k)$, can be accomplished by associating the sampled values with + 2, 0 or − 2. However, as described earlier, the transfer function of the channel has the form $1 − D^2$ and in order to recover the input data it is necessary to divide the output sequence by $1 − D^2$. In order to reduce the propagation of errors, it is preferable to perform the $1 − D^2$ function by precoding using shift registers on the write side of the channel as shown in Fig. 2.56. In this precoding circuit the input data is used as the input to an exclusive-or circuit and the other input is the output of the exclusive-or circuit delayed by two bit times.

$$C(k) = A(k) \oplus C(k-2) = A(k) \oplus B(k)$$

In Fig. 2.60 (Lemke, 1989) is shown how a sequence of data bits is recorded and subsequently detected using a precoded PR IV channel. In this example it is assumed that the initial state has a "1" in each of the shift registers in the precoding circuit. The long periods of positive or negative current are represented as individual pulses of the form of Fig. 2.58 and the resulting readback pulse [Eq. (2.83)]. Since the tails of the readback pulses cancel, only the peaks of the readback pulses are shown as indicated by the arrows. Note that in the coded bit cell times labeled "13" and "14" the individual pulses have nearly merged. Such a pair of pulses would be difficult to detect using peak detection which illustrates the advantage of the PRIV channel. It is seen that the input data sequence could be detected by sampling the data and associating each value above + 1 or below − 1 with a digital "1." Each amplitude value between these threshold levels is detected as a digital "0." The implementation can be simplified by using the dicode channels and precoding with 1-D for the even and odd bit intervals (Coker et al., 1991). In the decode channels it can be shown that a "1" is always followed by a "0."

In the PRML system the digital data are detected using a maximum likelihood or

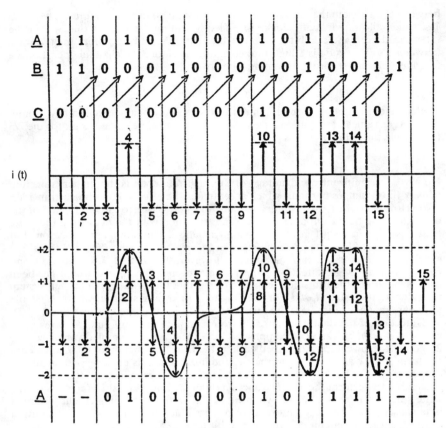

FIGURE 2.60 Response of a PR IV channel as shown in the block diagram of Fig. 2.56 to data encoded with the rate 8/9 (0, 4/4) code (input A) showing the precoding function, the write current and the read back signal after equalization. The arrows show the relationship between the centers of the current pulses and the responses at the encoded bit times and two bit times later resulting from the PR IV channel equalization. The three-level signal is sampled and correctly detected by setting detection levels at +1, 0 and −1 *(after Lemke, 1989)*.

Viterbi detector (Fig. 2.56). In this detector the sequence of binary numbers $\{a(k)\}$ which minimizes the mean-square error

$$\sum [\{h(k)\} - (\{a_k\} - \{a_{k-2}\})]^2 \qquad (2.87)$$

can be determined with a small amount of computation and storage. A convenient way of implementing the Viterbi detector is with a sliding threshold in which a threshold band of width 2 volts is dynamically adjusted to the level of the last sample detected as a $+ 2$ or $- 2$ (Wood, 1990). The sliding threshold algorithm is shown in Fig. 2.61 using a sequence of h (k) given in Table 2.13. Separate but identical computations are carried out for the even and odd numbered samples. The last sample which causes a positive(negative) change in threshold is registered as a

Sliding Threshold Representation of Viterbi Detection

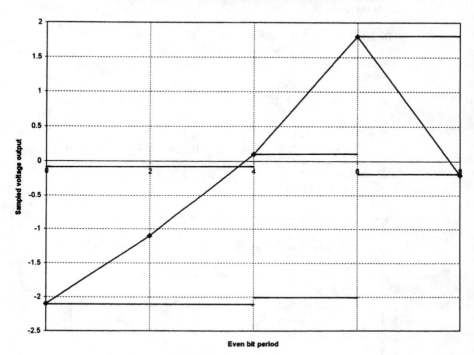

FIGURE 2.61 Sampled digital values are shown at the sampling times from 0 to 8 for a PRIV channel. A maximum likelihood (Viterbi) detector operates on the samples as shown by the sliding threshold with amplitude = 2. The threshold is moved whenever a sample falls outside of the threshold region *(after Wood, 1990)*.

candidate $+ 2(- 2)$ and resets the threshold band. A sample below(above) the threshold band confirms the candidate $+ 2(- 2)$ and becomes a new candidate $- 2(+ 2)$. The threshold band is moved so that its negative(positive) edge is at the new sample value. The sampled values and the decision process are shown for the example sequence in Table 2.13. Note also that the decision for the coded bit in interval 0 is delayed until interval 4.

Other detection algorithms have been developed. A general review of peak detection and the partial response alternatives has been published (Siegel and Wolf, 1991). One alternative channel is the EEPR IV (1, 7) channel which has the polynomial $(1 - D) (1 + D)^3$ (Behrens and Armstrong, 1992). In this channel the data are encoded with the familiar code rate 2/3 (1, 7) data code. The number of levels to be detected with this channel are five as opposed to the three with the PR IV channel. The advantage of this channel over PR IV is that the effects of nonlinearities with the channel, for example, partial erasure (Chap. 3) are reduced because of the reduced ratio of flux-change density to bits with the (1, 7) code as compared with the (0, 4/4) code. In Fig. 2.62 is shown the target frequency response for the EEPR4 (1, 7) channel for a user bit density of 3, together

TABLE 2.13 Example of Sliding Threshold Viterbi Detection for Even Bit Intervals

Bit interval	0	2	4	6	8
Sampled values	−2.1	−1.1	0.1	1.8	−.2
Decision alternatives	(−2, 0)				
	(−2, 0)	0			
	−2	0	(+2, 0)		
	−2	0	0	(+2, 0)	
	−2	0	0	+2	(−2, 0)

SOURCE: Wolf, 1992

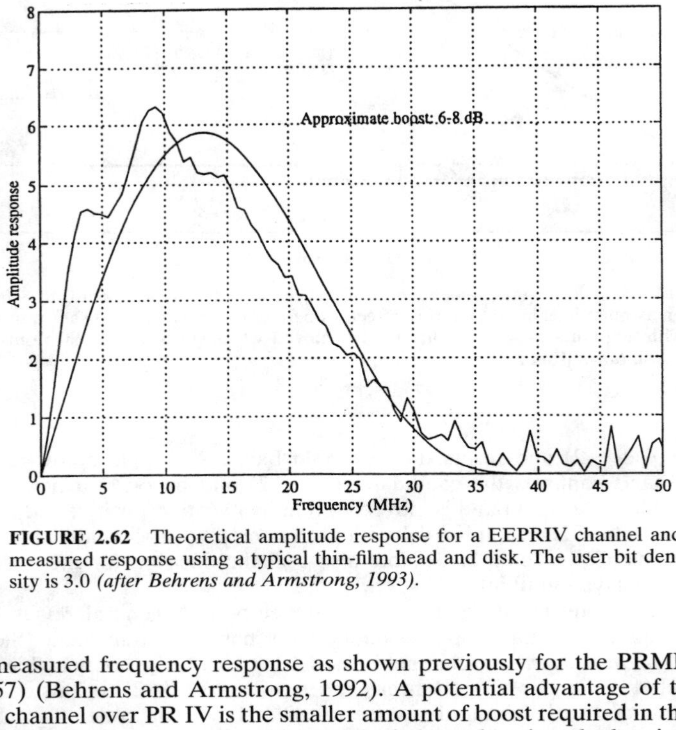

FIGURE 2.62 Theoretical amplitude response for a EEPRIV channel and measured response using a typical thin-film head and disk. The user bit density is 3.0 *(after Behrens and Armstrong, 1993)*.

with a measured frequency response as shown previously for the PRML channel (Fig. 2.57) (Behrens and Armstrong, 1992). A potential advantage of the EEPR IV(1, 7) channel over PR IV is the smaller amount of boost required in the channel to match the target response but this must be balanced against the loss in signal-to-noise ratio because of the smaller detection level associated with the 5 versus 3 levels.

Another alternative channel is the EPR IV channel with a partial response polynomial of $(1 - D)(1 + D)^2$ (Thapar and Patel, 1987; Patel, 1991). This channel also uses the reduced code rate 2/3 (1, 7) code and also has five levels. However, the EPR IV channel retains the write path and the gain control and timing recovery circuits from the peak detector channel. This channel is discussed in detail in the chapter on Signal and Error-Control Coding.

Decision feedback equalization (DFE) is another channel alternative which has found application in communications and has been proposed for magnetic recording channels (Bergmans, 1986, Fisher et al., 1989; Abbott et al., 1991; Fisher et al., 1991). With DFE, a threshold detector is used together with a decision feedback filter and a two-state detector. In an analysis of the above alternatives, DFE with a maximum likelihood detector has been shown to be superior to all the other alternatives for user bit densities greater than 2.4 (Howell et al., 1994). One novel technique for detecting decision feedback equalized signals is the fixed-delay tree search algorithm (Moon and Carley, 1991). This paper also discusses the relative performance of a number of the channels discussed above. A book on the topic of sequence detection for storage has been published (Moon and Carley, 1992).

2.4.4 Data Handling Problems Arising from Disk Defects

The channel impairments discussed so far include intersymbol interference, off-track interference, and amplifier noise. To this list must be added disk defects. Disk defects manifest themselves in two ways. First, there is noise associated with the random nature of the disk surface without defects. This noise can be separated from the rest of the noise in the channel by measuring the noise from the preamplifier with the head flying over the disk and then unloaded from the disk. The difference is the disk noise. Typical signal-to-noise ratios (base-to-peak signal to wide-band rms noise) for a variety of disks is shown in Table 2.14.

Media noise spectra increase faster than $1/\lambda$ with reduction in wavelength, and the noise varies as the square root of the track width (Mallinson, 1974). All other dependencies can be combined in a noise-signal density $N_d(\text{BW})$ which depends on the electrical bandwidth of the channel used to detect the signal (and noise).

Disk defects also manifest themselves as missing bits or extra bits. Missing bits are reductions in the amplitude of the envelope of the signal, usually over a small number of bits (one to four), such that the amplitude falls below the channel-detector gating level. The number of missing bits observed depends on the setting of the clip level in the data channel (Fig. 2.43). A certain number of defects per track can be skipped by a process known as *surface analysis*. The penalty paid for defects is decreased head-disk assembly yield and lost capacity. For satisfactory head-disk assembly yields, it is necessary for the average number of defects found

TABLE 2.14 Signal-to-Noise Ratio for Particulate and Thin-Film Disks

Disk type	S/N, dB
20% γ-Fe_2O_3 particulate + Al_2O_3 particles	20–25
20% γ-Fe_2O_3 particulate	20–30
Sputtered γ-Fe_2O_3 film	30–40
Metallic thin film	30–40

per track to be less than 10% of the maximum for a reasonable expectation that
all tracks on all disk surfaces will satisfy the skip criterion. If the clip level is
lowered to decrease the number of missing bits, then the number of file errors
logged because of noise in the channel will increase. Therefore the clip-level
setting, typically 50 to 60%, is a compromise between head-disk assembly yield
and data integrity.

2.4.5 Error-Correction Codes

As an additional safeguard for data integrity, disk files use error-detection and
error-correction codes (ECCs). For example, disk defects have been found to exhibit a degree of softness, that is, the size of a given defect is observed to change
depending on exactly how the defect and the recorded transition defining the bit are
related. To find hard defects, it is necessary to record the bits many times to observe
the number of times the defect appears and to define an algorithm to indicate if the
defect should be skipped. To protect against soft defects causing errors in data
detection, error-correction codes are used. The typical error detection and correction (ECC) logic used in small disk files is part of the controller module. Advanced
implementations of ECC utilize Reed-Solomon codes. An example of the capability of such codes is as follows:

number of bytes added at the end of a 512 byte data field for error detection	38 bytes
correctable error burst spans	
1 burst error	113 bits
2 burst span	41 bits
3 burst span	17 bits
probability of uncorrectable errors (10^{-7} input error rate)	8.8×10^{-16}

More details on the capability and the implementation of ECC codes are in the
chapter on Signal and Error-Control Coding.

If a given error is not corrected by error-correction codes, additional safeguards
for data integrity are frequently used. For example, the data heads can be deliberately shifted off-track in controlled amounts by shifting the servo head in an effort to
achieve error-free recovery. This is known as the *head-shift error-recovery procedure.*

2.5 COMPONENT INTEGRATION

2.5.1 General Comments

Up to this point, the discussion on the data channel in disk files has focused on track
misregistration, intersymbol interference, noise, and their effect in limiting the
performance of the data channels. What have not been discussed are methods for
calculating or measuring the error rates in disk files resulting from channel impairments. The most significant measure of file performance is the number of errors
generated in a record; data on track misregistration, peak shift, disk defects, and

noise are only intermediaries to this measure. It is also important to understand how robust the design is or, stated another way, how large a margin exists between the nominal error rate and that which would be observed in a stressed environment (noise-reduced voltage margin, mechanical vibration, high altitude and high temperature). The objective of assessing error rates is also to determine specifications for head, disk, and channel parameters and for track misregistration.

The methodology for assessing error rates and margins in disk files is known as *component integration,* and several approaches have emerged. The first approach consists of selecting a population of heads, disks, and channels covering an expected range in manufacturing and measuring the off-track performance. This is the ability of the components to record and read back data with random or worst-case patterns with the heads moved off track center in a controlled and measurable way. Precision, low-vibration test stands with a single head and disk are used, and the resulting data showing the dependence of error rate on misregistration are frequently plotted in the form of a "bathtub" curve, as shown in Fig. 2.63. This is a curve of the error rate of a given head disk and data channel with a specified data pattern (pseudo-random sequences are frequently used) as a function of the amount of displacement off-track and squeeze or track encroachment of adjacent tracks. The data are shown for two values of squeeze, or write-to-write track misregistration, and it is evident that a large increase in error rate occurs for 10 to 15 percent off-track measured as a percentage of the magnetic core width of the head. The bathtub-shaped curve gives the probability of error if the head is off-track by a certain amount. To determine error rate, it is necessary to build up distributions of bathtub curves over the population of heads, disks, and channels anticipated and to multiply these distributions by the distributions of the probability of a particular head being off-track in the course of a seek to a record (the track-misregistration distribution for the given head).

To determine soft-error rate, the bathtub curve $P_E (\mathrm{TMR}_{W,R}, \mathrm{TMR}_{W,W})$ is multiplied by the track misregistration TMR distribution point-by-point as shown in Fig. 2.64. This results in a sum of errors per byte for the given parameters. More generally, the soft-error rate SER is given by:

$$\mathrm{SER} = \int d(\mathrm{TMR}_{W,R}) \, d(\mathrm{TMR}_{W,W}) \, P_{\mathrm{TMR}} P_E \qquad (2.88)$$

To do a complete assessment of soft-error rate, it is necessary to have evaluated or modeled the bathtub curves at all values of write-to-read and write-to-write track misregistration.

Another approach to assessing error rates is by stressing (reducing) the clock window and measuring error rates. By decreasing the window, curves of error rate versus window length can be generated and, by extrapolation to the unstressed window, the robustness of the channel and error rates at file operating conditions can be assessed. This technique is known as *phase margin* testing.

The approach to be discussed here in more detail is an analytical model of disk file error rate based on a signal-to-noise assessment of the data channel.

2.5.2 Specification of Head and Disk Parameters for High-Density Recording

Before the error rates of the data channel can be evaluated it is necessary to discuss the specification of head and disk parameters for high density recording. The

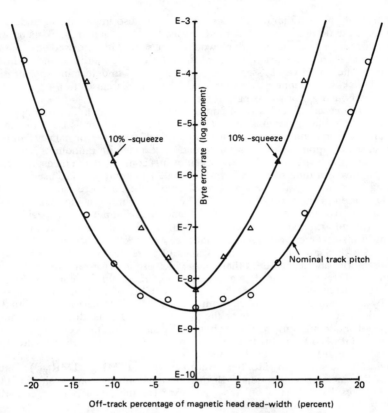

FIGURE 2.63 Error rate in a typical peak-detection recording channel versus the off-track position as a percentage of the magnetic core width—the "bathtub" curve. The error-rate curve is shown for two values of spacing of the adjacent track: nominal, and a 10 percent reduction or "squeeze" in spacing.

emphasis will be on thin-film media and both thin-film heads and magnetoresistive heads will be discussed. To investigate the design parameters for heads, disks, and head-disk spacing, it is desirable to use an analytical model of saturation magnetic recording. It is assumed that the transitions are arctangent shaped.

$$M(x) = -\frac{2M_r}{\pi}\tan^{-1}\frac{x}{a} \qquad (2.89)$$

where M_r is the remanent magnetization, and the x direction is along the track. The transition parameter depends on the magnetic properties of the medium, the dimensions of the head, and head-to-disk spacing. A useful approximation is given by Williams and Comstock (1971):

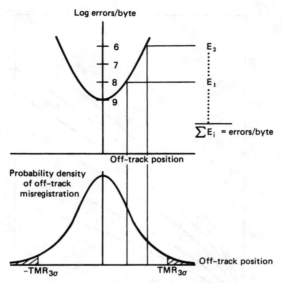

FIGURE 2.64 Formation of the error rate by multiplying point-by-point the "bathtub" curve by the track-misregistration probability-density curve.

$$a = \frac{a_1}{2r} + \left[\left(\frac{a_1}{2r} \right)^2 + \frac{2\pi\chi\delta a_1}{r} \right]^{1/2} \tag{2.90}$$

with
$$\frac{a_1}{r} = d\frac{1 - S^*}{\pi Q} + \left[\left(d\frac{1 - S^*}{\pi Q} \right)^2 + \frac{2M_r\delta}{H_c} \left(\frac{2d}{Qr} \right) \right]^{1/2} \tag{2.91}$$

where $r = 1 - (1 - S^*)\chi H_c/M_r$
  χ = remagnetization susceptibility $\approx M_r/4H_c$ (found experimentally)
  δ = thickness of medium
  Q = parameter characterizing the slope of the head field
  S^* = coercivity squareness
  d = distance from pole face of the head to the recording medium

Values of a found from these equations are in good agreement with those found with more exact computer simulations of the write process. Curves of a/g versus $M_r\delta/H_c g$ where g is gap length, with effective spacing d_{eff} as a parameter, are shown in Figs. 2.65 and 2.66 for two values of S^*. The parameter Q has an optimum value of about 0.84 for a ratio of the deep gap field to coercivity of about 3.75 for a typical value of $d_{\text{eff}}/g = 0.25$ (Bertram, 1994).

An effective flying height approximation is used in which the medium of remanent magnetization M_r and thickness δ, whose top surface is a distance d from the air-bearing surface of the head, can be approximated by an infinitesimally thin layer of the same $M_r\delta$ product at a distance d_{eff} from the head, where

$$d_{\text{eff}} = \sqrt{d(d + \delta)} \tag{2.92}$$

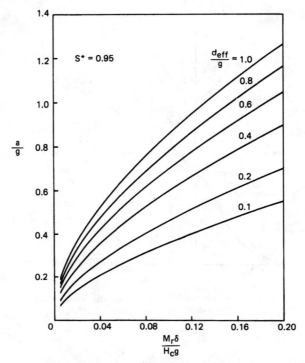

FIGURE 2.65 Arctangent transition parameter a/g versus $M_r \delta H_c g$ with variable d_{eff}/g for $S^* = 0.95$, which is characteristic of metallic film media.

Purely longitudinal recording is considered and only the x component of the head-sensitivity function is required. Use is made of the head-sensitivity functions for an N_h-turn film head (Szczech, 1979; Bertero et al., 1993). The parameters characterizing the head are:

$$P_{1,2} = \text{pole dimensions of head}$$
$$g = \text{gap dimension of head}$$
$$N_h = \text{number of turns on head}$$
$$H_g = \text{maximum gap field at } y = 0$$

The field characterizing the strength of the film-head field is $H_x(y = 0) = H_g$ and is assumed to be given by

$$H_g = \frac{\eta N_h I}{g}$$

where η = head efficiency
N_h = number of turns
I = current
g = gap length

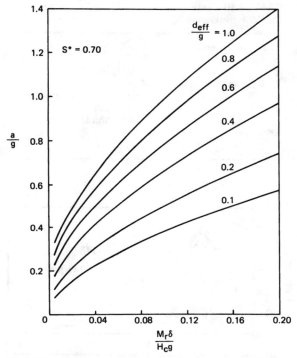

FIGURE 2.66 Arctangent transition parameter a/g versus $M_r \delta H_c g$ with variable d_{eff}/g for $S^* = 0.70$, which is characteristic of oriented particulate media.

A typical value for η for a film head is 0.7.

Applying the reciprocity principle, the output voltage of the isolated pulse from the head is given by

$$e(\bar{x}) = \frac{2N_h \eta v_r w_r u_0 M_r \delta H_x(\bar{x}, d + a)}{H_g g} \tag{2.93}$$

where $e(\bar{x})$ is the output voltage from the head, N_h is the number of turns on the head, v_r is the velocity of the media with respect to the head, w_r is the width of the read head, g is the head gap and $H_x(\bar{x}, d + a)$ is the head field at the plane of the recording media with remanent magnetization M_r and thickness δ and $\bar{x} = v_r t$ (Bertram, 1994). This important result indicates that in the case of the arctangent transition, the output voltage is only dependent on the sum of $a + d$, and d is taken to be equal to d_{eff}.

Recent work with thin film media and thin film write heads has shown that the assumption of hyperbolic tangent form for the transition shape improves the fit to experimental data. A transition shape of an error function has been used in an analysis similar to that outlined above (Tsang et al., 1990).

Thin-film heads designed for particulate media had pole dimensions that were

TABLE 2.15 Thin-Film Head and Disk Parameters
for Pulse Evaluation

Head parameters	
$p_1 = p_2$	3.0 μm
g	0.40 μm
Disk parameters	
M_r	637 kA/m (637 emu/cm³)
δ	0.058 μm
H_c	107 kA/m (1350 Oe)
$S\star$	0.95
d	0.125 μm

Source: After Roscamp, 1992

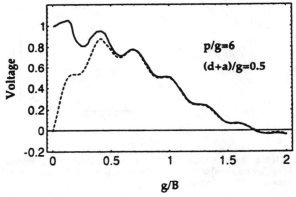

FIGURE 2.67 Pulse amplitude for reduced pulse spacing (roll-off curve) for a thin-film head with pole-to-gap ratio (p/g) = 6 and $(d + a)/g = 0.5$ as a function of g/B. B is the channel bit length and a is the arctangent transition length. The envelope of the fundamental component of the roll-off curve is also shown (dashed line) *(after Bertero et al., 1994)*.

significantly smaller than are used with thin-film media. This is the case since the coercive fields for the particulate media were smaller than for thin-film media and less field from the head was required to saturate the recording film. The following analysis applies only to the thick-pole design which has supplanted the thin-pole design. The poles of thick-pole heads are typically 3 to 4 microns thick.

An isolated pulse from a thick-pole thin-film head and thin-film media with parameters as given in Table 2.15 is shown in Fig. 2.44 in Sec. 2.4 (curve labeled "unequalized") (Roscamp, 1992). The undershoots are the result of reading from the tips of the poles. The pulse width at the 50% amplitude point is found to be close to that from a Karlqvist-type head with the same gap (g),

$$PW_{50} = \sqrt{g^2 + 4(d + a)(d + a + \delta)} \tag{2.94}$$

The response of the head to an alternating series of square waves of current with resulting increasing flux reversal density is given by superimposing an alternating series of these pulses with the result shown in Fig. 2.67 (Bertero et al., 1993). In this curve the output voltage from the head is plotted versus the product of the head gap length and the inverse of the coded or channel bit period spacing (B). This curve is referred to as a "roll-off" curve and represents the output of the head to "all-ones" input data. It is observed that there are multiple humps in amplitude in this curve and it must be determined where the recordings on the disk will be located with respect to the humps. Operation over the full radius on the disk will result in a variation in flux-change density. A separate roll-off curve must be constructed for each band on the disk (data banding makes the roll-off curves approximately constant over the radius of the disk). With the rate 2/3 (1, 7) data code the range of flux change density is 4:1 (see Table 2.12) and some distortion of the data is expected due to the distorted roll-off curve in each band. As a first approximation the roll-off curve for a Karlqvist head can be used and the result for an arctangent transition with a negligible gap (Comstock and Williams, 1973):

$$\frac{E(B)}{A} = \frac{\pi PW_{50} / 2B}{\sinh\left(\pi PW_{50} / 2B\right)} \qquad (2.95)$$

where B is the spacing between transitions, A is the amplitude of the isolated pulse and $E(B)$ is the output voltage as a function of B. For $E(B)$ equal to 50% of the isolated pulse amplitude it is found that the spacing B_{50} and its reciprocal density D_{50} are:

$$1/B_{50} = D_{50} = 1.39/PW_{50} \qquad (2.96)$$

For $E(B)$ 70% of the isolated pulse amplitude, it is found that

$$1/B_{70} = D_{70} = 0.97/PW_{50} \qquad (2.97)$$

If the analysis from Bertero, Bertram and Barnett is used, then the result for D_{50} and D_{25} varies in a periodic fashion versus the ratio of pole to gap dimensions as shown in Fig. 2.68. This curve was calculated for a value of $(d+a)/g = 0.5$ and the medium thickness was assumed to be zero. As the ratio of p/g increases, the value of D_{50} approaches a value of 0.95 for the selected value of $(d+a)/g = 0.5$; whereas, for the same parameters, the value predicted from Eq. (2.96) for a negligible medium thickness and a Karlqvist-type head is 0.80. It is seen from this result that it is possible to choose a particular value for p/g to optimize the value of D_{50}, e.g., a choice of p/g of 4 instead of p/g of 3 results in an increase in D_{50} of approximately 22%. The equations in the Bertero, Bertram and Barnett paper for the Fourier transform of the head field with other values of the parameters of the recording system can be used to evaluate D_{50}.

Two approaches have evolved to eliminate or reduce the effects of the undershoots on the read back signal from thin-film heads. First, modifications have been introduced to the pole tips of the thin-film heads on the air bearing surface which reduce the sharpness of the edge of the poles and thereby reduces the size of the undershoot signals (Yoshida et al., 1993). This approach adds some complexity and cost to the thin-film heads. The second approach is to use a "horizontal" thin-film head design, in which the poles of the head are wide with respect to the transition spacing and the head is similar to a ferrite head with no undershoot signals (Lazzari et al., 1989). This type of head has been fabricated using silicon substrates and, to

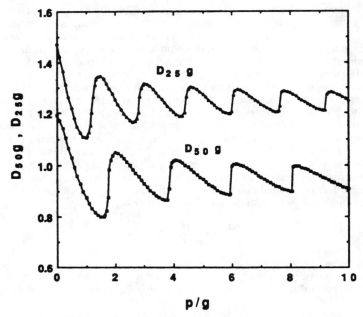

FIGURE 2.68   Plot of recording density for 50% and 25% of the isolated pulse amplitude for pulses read back at reduced spacing (D_{50} and D_{25}) versus p/g for $(d + a)/g = 0.5$ *(after Bertero et al., 1994)*.

attempt to achieve the required durability, the air bearing surface has been oxidized to SiO_2 (Bhushan et al., 1992).

   To achieve a target linear density the first parameter that must be chosen is the head-disk spacing (d in the above equations). The head-disk spacing is composed of the mechanical spacing between the head gap and the surface of the disk medium (the "flying height") and overcoats (sees Fig. 2.3b). This parameter is limited by the ability of the head-disk mechanical parameters to achieve a satisfactory number of start-stop cycles of the file, with the head initially in contact with the disk, in the presence of stiction and friction. (Sec. 2.6). In order to qualify a particular head and disk combination for the ability to sustain flying heights of a particular value, a test of the "glide-height" is used. In this test a head instrumented to record contacts with the disk surface is flown over the disk surface at a flying height lower than that for the product head. In Fig. 2.69 is shown a curve of the progression of flying height versus glide height for thin-film heads and disks (Chen, 1993). A projection for flying height has been shown in Fig. 2.3a (Sec. 2.1.1). The present limit for glide height is near 0.0125 μm (0.5 μin) and the resulting flying height is near 0.025 μm (1 μin) and for heights below this value the head will have significant contact with the disk, resulting in a regime of "proximity recording" (Williams, 1993). With proximity recording the slider for the head is made small and the load is reduced so that the potential for damage to the head or disk is minimized. The head gap length (g) is limited by the ability to record on media with high values of coercive field (H_c). This limit is given by

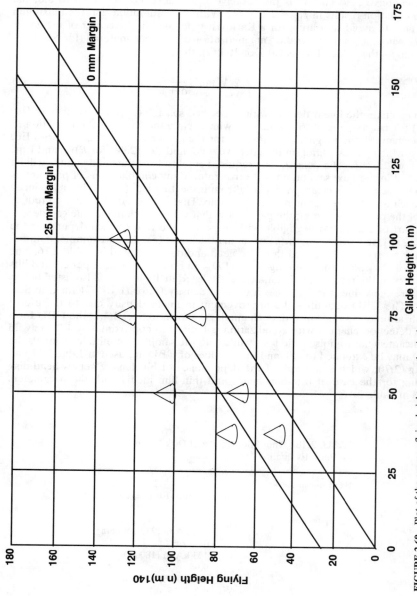

FIGURE 2.69 Plot of the average flying height or mechanical spacing versus the glide height with two values of margin between the flying and glide heights for thin-film media *(after Chen, 1993)*.

2.101

$$H_h \geq [1.3 + 4\,(1 - S^*)]\,H_c, \tag{2.98}$$

where H_h is the value of the head field at the lower surface of the recording film, H_c is the coercive field and S^* is the coercive squareness. For S^* equal to 0.8, the above equation results in $H_h \geq 2.1 \times H_c$. With the assumption that the maximum head field to avoid saturation for a Karlqvist-type head in the center of the gap is $0.8\,M_s$, where M_s is the saturation magnetization of the head material (for $Ni_{80}Fe_{20}$-permalloy—the value of M_s is 1.0 T or 10 kG), the result is

$$H_{(c)max} = 0.2\,M_s \tan^{-1}\frac{g}{d + a} \tag{2.99}$$

To evaluate the linear density with a specified spacing (d_{eff}), use is made of Eq. (2.91) (or charts—Figs. 2.65 and 2.66), which relate the width of the transition to the mechanical and magnetic parameters for the head and disk, together with Eq. (2.99), which places a limit on the coercive field, and Eq. (2.94) for PW_{50} and Eqs. (2.96) or (2.97) for the density. The required amplitude of the head voltage will be discussed in the next section on soft error rate. Many combinations of parameters are possible and it is clear, particularly from inspecting Eq. (2.94), that a balanced approach to selecting parameters is desirable. That is, it is not desirable to reduce one of the parameters, e.g., the gap, below that value which makes the gap dependent part of Eq. (2.94) negligible with respect to the terms which depend on the spacing (d), transition length (a) or media thickness (δ). As an example, parameters for a very closely spaced thin-film head and disk are listed in Table 2.16. The values of PW_{50}, and the resulting D_{50} and D_{70}, in both flux changes per cm and bits per cm with the rate 2/3 (1, 7) data code are listed in Table 2.17. Also listed in this table are the values for D_{70} times a user bit density factor (UBD) defined in Sec. 2.4.1. The UBD quantifies the improvement in linear density due to the use of equalization or an improved data channel. As shown in Sec. 2.4.1, the UBD for a peak detection channel with equalization is limited to approximately 1.3 to avoid significant signal-to-noise ratio loss, while with the sampled amplitude channels the UBD may be extended to 2.0, and these values of UBD are used in Table 2.17 and in Fig. 2.70, which is a graph of the dependence of bit density versus head-disk spacing for the case of thin-film heads and thin-film media with the parameters listed in Table 2.16.

TABLE 2.16 Thin-Film Head and Disk Parameters for Pulse Evaluation

Head parameters	
$p_1 = p_2$	3.5 μm (for reference)
g	0.25 μm
Disk parameters	
M_r	233 kA/m (233 emu/cm³)
δ	0.03 μm
H_c	143 kA/m (1800 Oe)
S^*	0.95
d	0.10, 0.05, 0.025 μm
a	0.2, 0.15, 0.1 μm

TABLE 2.17 Recording Density for Thin-Film Head and Thin-Film Disk (parameters from Table 2.16)

Head-disk spacing (d)		0.1 μm	0.05 μm	0.025 μm
PW_{50}	μm	0.677	0.500	0.374
	(μin)	(27.08)	(19.86)	(15.00)
D_{50}	fc/cm	20,531	27,800	37,166
	(fc/in)	(52,148)	(70,000)	(92,873)
D_{50} with 2/3(1, 7) code	fc/cm	27,375	37,070	49,554
	(fc/in)	(69,530)	(93,310)	(123,800)
D_{70}	fc/cm	14,327	19,400	25,936
	(fc/in)	(36,391)	(48,849)	(64810)
D_{70} with 2/3 (1, 7)code	bits/cm	19,103	25,870	34,581
	(bits/in)	(48,521)	(65,115)	(86392)
$D_{70} \times$ (UBD = 1.3)	bits/cm	24,840	33,631	44,955
2/3 (1, 7) code	(bits/in)	(63,077)	(84,650)	(112,310)
$D_{70} \times$ (UBD = 2)	bits/cm	38,206	51,740	69,162
2/3 (1, 7) code	(bits/in)	(97,042)	(130,230)	(172,784)

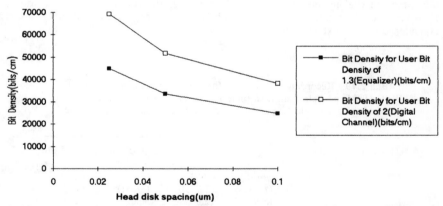

FIGURE 2.70 Bit density (D_{70}) plotted against head-to-disk spacing for a thin-film head and disk with an equalized channel (user bit density of 1.3) and a partial response or digital channel (user bit density of 2). The parameters for the thin-film head and disk are given in Table 2.16.

Magnetoresistive heads more closely follow the above analysis for linear density than do thin-film heads because of the absence of undershoots in the read-back signal. Magnetoresistive heads have additional films between the shields and this will limit the physical shield-to-shield spacing; however, the value of "g" to be used in the above equations lies between 0.5 and 0.7 times the physical shield-to-shield spacing.

Since the write head, associated with the magnetoresistive read head, can be separately optimized, it can write media with a larger value of coercive field (H_c) than can a single-element inductive head and hence the transition can be made sharper than with an inductive head. The read-back amplitudes from the magnetoresistive read head are higher than for the inductive thin-film head and hence the signal-to-noise ratio with magnetoresistive heads is expected to be higher than for inductive heads. This will be discussed in the next section on soft error rates. For magnetoresistive read heads it is required to carefully select the media parameters to reduce the flux and hence avoid saturation of the magnetoresistive stripe. Typically the ratio of $M_r\delta/H_c$ is adjusted to about 35% of that for thin-film heads. In addition, to reduce the nonlinear peak shift with high transition density codes as used with PR IV, the above ratio is also selected in changing from peak detection with the (1, 7) code (Howell et al., 1994).

To compare the linear density performance of a magnetoresistive read head together with an inductive write head with the thin-film read and write head, the assumption is made that the inductive write head and the recording medium have the same parameters as in Table 2.16 and that the shield-to-shield spacing (gap) of the magnetoresistive head is the same as that for the inductive head. Therefore the transition parameter (a) is the same as in Table 2.16. The 50% pulse width is modified by using an effective gap length of the magnetoresistive head 70% of the physical length. The linear densities for the magnetoresistive read and inductive write head with the above assumption are shown in Table 2.18.

The linear recording density (D_{70}) versus head-disk spacing for both the thin-film head and the magnetoresistive read head are shown in Fig. 2.71. The significant advantage of the magnetoresistive read head over the thin-film head is evident; however, the advantage will be shown to be even larger when the soft error rate is considered in the next section.

TABLE 2.18 Recording Density for Magnetoresistive Read and Inductive Write Head and Thin-Film Disk (parameters for the write head from Table 2.15 and the gap of the magnetoresistive read head is the same as for the inductive head)

Head-disk spacing (d)		0.1 μm	0.05 μm	0.025 μm
PW_{50}	μm	0.623	0.463	0.328
	(μin)	(26.12)	(18.52)	(13.12)
D_{50}	fc/cm	22,063	30,021	42,378
	(fc/in)	(56,041)	(76,255)	(107,640)
D_{50} with 2/3 (1, 7) code	bits/cm	29,417	40,029	56,504
	(bits/in)	(74,722)	(101,673)	(143,520)
D_{70}	fc/cm	15,396	20,951	29,573
	(fc/in)	(39,108)	(53,214)	(75,116)
D_{70} with 2/3 (1, 7) code	bits/cm	20,528	27,934	39,431
	(bits/in)	(52,144)	(70,952)	(100,154)
$D_{70} \times$ (UBD = 1.3)	bits/cm	26,686	36,314	51,260
2/3 (1, 7) code	(bits/in)	(67,787)	(92,238)	(130,200)
$D_{70} \times$ (UBD = 2)	bits/cm	41,056	55,868	78,862
2/3 (1, 7) code	(bits/in)	(104,288)	(141,904)	(200,308)

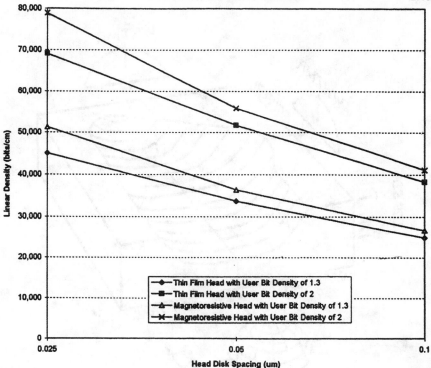

FIGURE 2.71 Linear bit density for a channel with a (1, 7) code versus head to disk spacing for a thin film and a magnetoresistive head and thin-film disk. Two values of user bit density are used: 1.3 and 2.0. The parameters for the recording components are given in Table 2.16 and in the text.

2.5.3 Soft Error Rate Assessment

In this section the soft error rate of the peak detection channel with thin-film media and both thin-film inductive and magnetoresistive heads, as described in Sec. 2.5.2, will be discussed.

The soft error rate of the data channel depends on both the off-track misregistration and the adjacent-track pitch of the head and the error rate is properly shown as a three-dimensional surface as shown in Fig. 2.72 (Hardy and Malone, 1991). In this figure the logarithm of the soft error rate is plotted on the vertical axis and the off-track distance or off-track capability, i.e., the distance that the head can be moved off track before the error rate increases to a specified level, e.g., one error per sector or 10^{-4} errors per byte, is plotted on one horizontal axis and the adjacent track pitch is plotted on the other horizontal axes. It is noted that the curve for a constant error rate has the appearance of the nose and cockpit of the Boeing 747 aircraft. This curve is referred to as the "747" curve and has found extensive use in assessing the error rates of disk files (Cunningham and Palmer, 1988).

The variation in track pitch which results in the 747 curve is shown in Fig. 2.73 (Vea and Howell, 1995). The desired signal is recorded over "old information noise" which was previously recorded on the desired track and this noise is within the frequency band of the data. For the case of the adjacent track far removed from

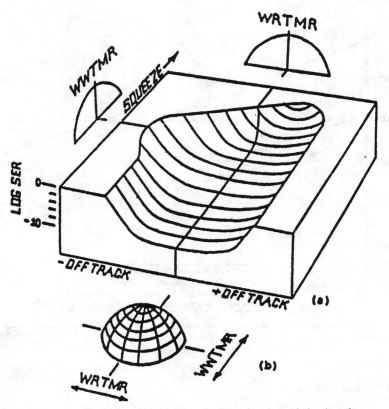

FIGURE 2.72 (*a*). Three dimensional surface showing the variation in soft error rate versus adjacent track pitch or "squeeze" and off-track capability (labeled "off track"). The curve at a given error rate is referred to as the 747 curve because of the resemblance to the front end of that aircraft. (*b*) The three dimensional surface of write-to-read track misregistration (labeled "WRTMR") and write-to-write track misregistration labeled (WWTMR). The error rate is the integration of the two surfaces *(after Hardy and Malone, 1991)*.

the desired track (no "squeeze"), the off-track capability is at the nominal value determined by noise sources within the data channel. Starting from the right side of the desired track (below the "detected track" in Fig. 2.73), as the recording from the adjacent track moves closer to the desired track, the off-track distance actually increases and reaches a maximum. This is the case since the erase band at the side of the head erases the old information noise and breaks the interference into subbands. As the adjacent track encroaches even farther into the desired track, that track is partially erased and the off-track distance decreases until the the head can no longer be moved off-track and maintain the specified error rate. This latter adjacent track spacing is referred to as the "track-pitch-to failure." To complete the 747 curve, the adjacent track squeeze is reduced and the off-track distance is measured in the "negative" direction by moving to the left of the desired track,

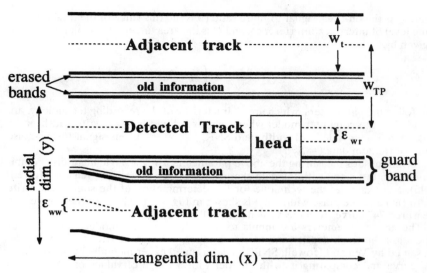

FIGURE 2.73 Definition of parameters characterizing a recording head and the detected and adjacent tracks *(after Vea and Howell, 1995).*

resulting in the nominal off-track distance. The 747 curve can be used to assess the ability of a given recording channel, including the head and disk technology, to meet the soft error rate goals. The write-to-read track misregistration must be less than the vertical extent of the 747 curve (the negative "off-track" part of Fig. 2.72) and therefore can be larger when the adjacent track is such that the operation is in the "cockpit" region. The track pitch is selected such that the nominal value of the adjacent track pitch minus the write-to-write track misregistration, which results in a variation in the track spacing, does not result in operation too far to the left (large value of "squeeze" in Fig. 2.72) of the cockpit region. By overlaying a two dimensional plot of the write-to-read and write-to-write track misregistrations on the 747 curve it is possible to estimate the optimum track pitch for any head disk combination. For small values of write-to-write track misregistration operation near the peak of the cockpit region is optimum. As the write-to-write track misregistration increases, the optimum track pitch moves to the right to ensure that the operation does not move to the left of the "nose" where hard errors are of concern. Moving to the right in the 747 curve reduces the track density and hence data capacity. It is possible to measure the write width plus erase width of the given write head by measuring the track pitch where the off-track distance to the left hand side of the cockpit is equal to that for large values of adjacent track pitch. This adjacent track pitch is equal to $w_t + w_e$, where w_t = write width, and w_e = erase width.

An analytical model of the 747 curve has been developed (Vea and Howell, 1995). The parameters for the track spacings and head parameters are defined in Fig. 2.73. In this model the probability of error is given in terms of the signal-to-noise ratios in the channel with variable amounts of adjacent track interference.

$$P(e|y_p,y_r,i) = Q\left[\frac{S_o}{\sigma} \left(\frac{S}{S_o} - \frac{i}{S_o} \right) \right] \qquad (2.100)$$

where $\frac{S_0}{\sigma}$ is the on-track signal-to-noise ratio (σ is the rms value of the total noise), i is the level of intertrack interference, and Q is the area under a Gaussian tail, which is given by,

$$Q(x) = \frac{1}{\sqrt{2\pi}} \int_x^\infty e^{-t^2/2}dt \qquad (2.101)$$

The following parameters, which are characteristic of the recording technology, are included in the computer model where w_r = read width, w_t = write width, w_e = erase band, w_s = side read width, and SNR_{eff} = on-track rms-signal-to-rms-noise ratio for random data ($= S_0/\sigma$).

Techniques for measuring the above parameters using a single head-disk combination on a test stand with the data channel have been described (Vea and Howell, 1995). For example, the technique for the determination of the sum of the write width (w_t) and the erase width (w_e) is shown in Fig. 2.74, which is an example of a measured 747 curve from the Vea and Howell model.

The above parameters are inputs to the soft error rate model and the other inputs are the track density and the track misregistration ($TMR_{3\sigma}$). In the model presented by Vea and Howell, SNR_{eff} is determined experimentally by measuring a 747 curve and comparing it to the model with a range of values of SNR_{eff}, and

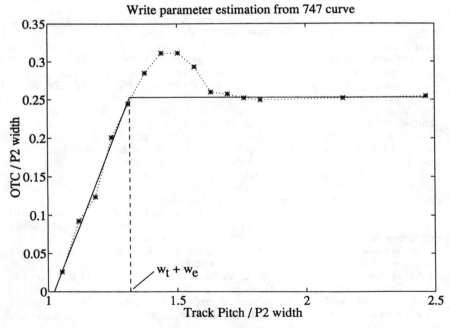

FIGURE 2.74 An experimental 747 curve which is a plot of the off-track capability (OTC) of a thin-film head versus adjacent track pitch at a constant error rate. The axes are normalized to the width of the narrower pole (P2) of the thin-film head. Also shown is the experimental determination of the sum of the write width and erase width *(after Vea and Howell, 1995)*.

TABLE 2.19 Head Read and Write
Parameters [inside diameter of 95 mm disk
at the high frequency for the (1, 7) code]

Head parameter	(μm)
w_r (read width)	9.74
w_s (side reading width)[†]	1.31
w_f (write width)	8.43
w_e (erase width)	1.31

[†]The value of the side reading width was
reduced by one-half from that reported by Vea
and Howell to reflect the projected improvement in thin-film head side reading, e.g., from
pole tip trimming (Wu and Peske, 1994).
SOURCE: From Vea and Howell, 1995

selecting the value which most closely matches the experimental curve. With a thin-film head and disk with the following dimensions: track width = 7.73 μm, gap thickness = 0.35 μm, flying height = 0.15 μm, and the value of SNR_{eff} was found to be 15.5 dB. With the above recording head and disk parameters of the values of the head width parameters were found to be as given in Table 2.19. It is clear from these values that thin-film heads with different values of the widths of the top and bottom poles exhibit the undesirable feature of "write-narrow and read-wide" and the impact of this on channel performance will be discussed in Sec. 2.5.3.1. A similar approach to the determination of the head width parameters uses a 747 curve and a dc-erased adjacent track (Huang et al., 1994). Also, it is found that the write width and erase width change with flux change density and that thin-film heads with symmetrical poles exhibit less change in erase width with increasing flux-change density than with heads with asymmetric poles (Wu and Peske, 1994).

In another model of the soft error rate performance of a digital magnetic recording peak detection channel the effects of the qualification threshold or gate level is clearly established (Sobey et al., 1994). In this model the probability of error is shown to depend on the qualification threshold (q), which is the amplitude qualification threshold as a percentage of the isolated pulse amplitude (see Sec. 2.4.1).

$$\text{Probability (error/}q) = Q\left\{\left|\frac{\dot{V}_{max}}{\dot{N}}\right|\right\} + Q\left\{\left|\frac{\dot{V}_{min}}{\dot{N}}\right|\right\}, \qquad (2.102)$$

where Q was given previously [Eq. (2.101)] and V_{max} and V_{min} are the maximum and minimum values of the signal during the clock interval, respectively. In this model the noise (N) and signal (V) both pass through the differentiator channel as shown in Fig. 2.75 (Sobey et al., 1994) and this is indicated by the differentiation notation in Eq. (2.102). In this figure the clock interval is shown on the horizontal axis and the differentiated signal and noise signals are shown passing through zero somewhere in the clock interval. If the noise is excessive or the intersymbol interference is high or the qualification threshold is set incorrectly, then it is possible for the total differentiated signal not to pass through zero (the pulse peak does not fall within the clock window) because either the total signal is too low or too high as shown in the cross-hatched tails of the Gaussian distribution. The model described by Sobey et al., calculates the above probability of error using as input pulse shapes

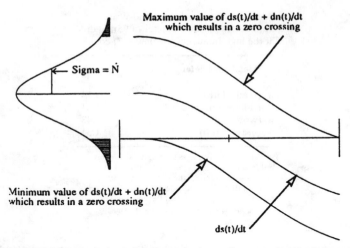

FIGURE 2.75   A clock window (between the two larger vertical bars) showing the differentiated signal and noise signals. For proper detection the total
differentiated signal plus noise must pass through zero within the window
duration. Also shown are the limits of the total differentiated signal plus noise
which will not pass through zero within the window. The differentiated noise
is assumed to be contained within the tails of the gaussian distribution *(after
Sobey et al., 1994).*

determined theoretically or experimentally and noise signals determined by evaluating the total noise from head, media, and electronics.

The results of the Sobey et al. model, which evaluates Eq. (2.102), is shown for a
particular case as Fig. 2.76. In this figure the variation of the logarithm of the bit
error rate versus the qualification threshold is shown. It is seen that too low a
threshold will cause errors because the channel will pass extra or "drop-in" bits,
whereas too large a threshold will reject desired pulses as "drop-out" bits. In Fig.
2.77 is shown a three-dimensional plot of the variation of logarithm of the bit error
rate versus threshold (q) and thin-film head gap length. In both the Vea and Howell, and Sobey et al. models, the signal-to-noise ratio is key, and the factors which
comprise the signal-to-noise ratio will be discussed in the following sections.

2.5.3.1   *Soft Error Rate.*   The soft error rate (SER) into the differentiator in a peak
detection channel is given in terms of the signal-to-noise ratio (SNR) by (Hughes and
Schmidt, 1976; Katz and Campbell, 1979; Hoagland and Monson, 1991):

$$\text{SER} = \text{erfc}\left[\frac{SNR \sqrt{2}\,(T_w - T_{isi} - T_{wo})}{PW_{50}} \right] = \text{erfc}(z) \qquad (2.103)$$

where erfc(z) is the complementary error function $[1 - \text{erf}(z)]$, SER is the soft
error rate in bits in error/bits transferred, and SNR is the signal voltage (peak) to
noise (RMS) ratio before differentiation. The effect of differentiation for the peak
detection channel will be included in the analysis by modifying the value of the

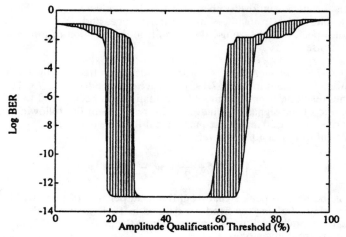

FIGURE 2.76 Logarithm of the bit error rate in a peak detection channel versus the amplitude qualification threshold as a percentage of the isolated pulse amplitude. Too high a threshold will result in excess errors due to missing bits and too low a threshold will result in excess errors due to extra bits (*after Sobey et al., 1994*).

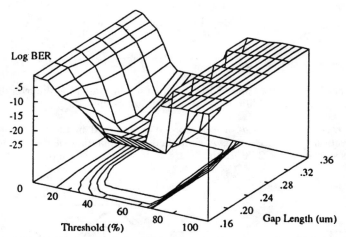

FIGURE 2.77 Three dimensional plot of the bit error rate in a peak detection channel versus the amplitude qualification threshold and the gap length of a thin-film head (*after Sobey et al., 1994*).

SNR. T_w is the clock window for the particular data code used, T_{isi} is the shift in the peak of a data pulse from intersymbol interference, and T_{wo} is the shift in the position of a peak of a data pulse due to shift in the position of a transition from write-over noise.

2.5.3.2 Old-Information Noise. In order to assess the effects on the soft error rate of the parameters listed in Table 2.19, reference is made to Fig. 2.73. The noise in the channel resulting from reading old information has been found to be given by the rms value of the signal (Williams, 1992), resulting in the following rms noise voltage terms to be used in a subsequent signal-to-noise evaluation.

The old-information noise is given by

$$v_{old} = \frac{v_s}{\sqrt{2}} \left[TMR + \frac{w_r}{2} + w_s - \left(\frac{w_t}{2} + w_e \right) \right] \qquad (2.104)$$

where v_s is the base-to-peak signal from the head per unit of track width, and the parameters characterizing the head are defined in Table 2.19. For the special case where the track pitch is adjusted for operation at the peak of the 747 curve the old-information noise is given by

$$v_{old} = \frac{v_s}{\sqrt{2}} \left[TMR + \frac{w_r}{2} + w_s - \left(\frac{w_t}{2} + 2 w_e \right) \right] \qquad (2.105)$$

since at the peak of the 747 curve the erase bands of the desired and interfering tracks are adjacent to each other. The desired signal in the above cases of reading old-information noise is given by

$$v_{\text{signal (base to peak)}} = v_s \left(\frac{w_t}{2} + \frac{w_t}{2} \right) \text{ for } TMR < \frac{w_r}{2} + w_s - \frac{w_t}{2} \qquad (2.106)$$

$$v_{\text{signal (base to peak)}} = v_s \left(\frac{w_r}{2} + w_s + \frac{w_t}{2} - TMR \right) \text{ for } TMR > \frac{w_r}{2} + w_s - \frac{w_t}{2} \qquad (2.107)$$

The results of Eqs. (2.106) and (2.107) will be used in evaluating the overall signal-to-noise ratio after the additional noise sources are discussed.

2.5.3.3. On-Track Signal-to-Noise Ratio. It is assumed in the following that a peak detection channel is used. A simplified block diagram of a peak detection channel is shown as Fig. 2.78. In this figure is shown the essence of peak detection:

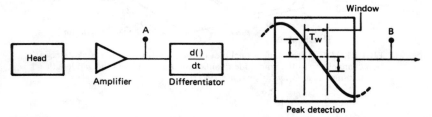

FIGURE 2.78 Simplified block diagram of a peak-detection channel showing the key points (*A* and *B*) in the channel for signal-to-noise determination. The differentiated signal is detected in the clock window of net width T_w.

the differentiator and the clock window with the differentiated signal passing through zero at the center of the window. The required signal-to-noise ratio at the output of the head terminals will be determined by first evaluating all of the relevant noise sources, including the head itself, the preamplifier, the media and losses in differentiation and reduction in amplitude at the edges of the clock window.

   a. Head Noise. A general treatment of the noise from metal-in-gap ferrite, thin-film and magnetoresistive heads has been presented (Williams, 1992). The approximation is made that a lumped element equivalent circuit for all these heads attached to a preamplifier can be used as shown in Fig. 2.79 where L is the head coil and lead inductance, R_h is the DC resistance of the coil, C is the shunt capacitance of the element, R_s is the equivalent resistance for damping within the head element, R_1 is the input resistance of the preamplifier, and C_s is the input capacitance of the preamplifier. The resistance R_s is a representation of the losses in the head element, e.g., losses due to domain wall motion in a thin-film head. (Klaassen and van Peppen, 1992; Corb, 1994).

   In Table 2.20 are listed measured values for the head parameters without the loading from a preamplifier (Williams, 1993). The noise from the head is represented by the real part of the complex impedance $\{Re[Z]\}$ at the terminals shown in Fig. 2.79 without R_1 and C_s from the preamplifier. The noise voltage resulting from $Re[Z]$ is given by the Nyquist equation [Eq. (2.76)].

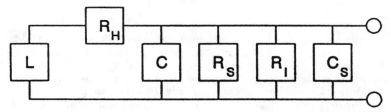

FIGURE 2.79 Lumped constant equivalent circuit for a head attached to a preamplifier. The inductance L and resistance R_H are associated with the head and the capacitance C with the leads attaching the head to the preamplifier with input resistance R_1 and capacitance C_s. *(after Williams, 1992).*

TABLE 2.20 Electrical Properties of Head Elements

Head type	R_h (Ω)	R_s (Ω)	$L(nH)$	$C(pF)$	$F_r(MHz)$
Thin film (30 turn)	31.0	292	475	5.2	101.3
Thin film (42 turn)	45.0	417	825	5.0	78.4
MIG (34 turn)	4.4	2805	1580	5.0	56.8
Mini-composite	6.0	3410	4200	5.2	33.9
Mini-monolithic	6.0	5410	14000	6.0	17.4
Magnetoresistive read head (300 Å thick, 5 μm wide and 2.5 μm high NiFe stripe)	16 Ω (head element) + 3 Ω (twisted pair)		~100	4.0	>200

SOURCE: E. M. Williams, 1992.

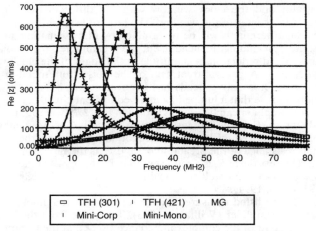

FIGURE 2.80   The real part of the impedance of thin-film (TFH) and metal-in-gap, mini-monolithic and mini-composite ferrite heads versus frequency. The coil turns for the thin-film heads are in parenthesis. The large peaks for the ferrite heads is due to the loss part of the complex permeability for ferrites and the much higher frequency and lower magnitude for the loss peak for thin-film heads is noted *(after Williams, 1992)*.

At frequencies approaching the resonant frequency (F_r) determined by L and C the read back signal will be distorted resulting in additional peak shift, and this frequency represents an upper limit for the operation of the head. The significant advantage of the magnetoresistive head with regard to noise is evident since it has both low resistance and low inductance. In Fig. 2.80 is shown the frequency dependence of the $Re[Z]$ for the inductive heads. Since all of the data codes used in digital magnetic recording channels have significant response at the lower frequencies (see Fig. 2.59), the noise from the large peaks from the ferrite heads will contribute significantly to the head noise as compared with the thin-film heads. For a forty-two turn thin-film head the equivalent noise spectral density is approximately $0.87 nV/\sqrt{Hz}$.

b. Preamplifier Noise.   Preamplifier noise has been discussed in Sec. 2.4.1. The noise spectral density was found to be approximately 0.5 to 2.0 $nV/\sqrt{Hz}$.

c. Media Noise.   Noise from thin-film media exhibits a supra-linear characteristic in which the noise voltage rises at a rate faster than linear versus recording density (Arnoldussen and Nunnelley, 1992). This rapid increase in noise is due to the percolation of magnetization domains across the "zig-zag" transition wall resulting in excess noise from the transitions. Media noise is not statistically stationary as is the noise from electronics and the head but rather is correlated with the transitions (Fitzpatrick et al., 1994). For the analysis presented in this section this effect is not considered and the noise is treated as the other sources as being statistically stationary. Noise from transitions has been shown to depend on the transition density (Arnoldussen and Nunnelley, 1992). Measurements of media noise from a typical CoCrTa thin-film media as measured with a thin-film head with a 5 μm head width are shown as Fig. 2.81 (Miura, 1993). In this figure the rms value of the noise is shown plotted versus recording density in kfc/in with a fixed 20 MHz bandwidth. Also shown in the figure are the noise characteristics of a double-layer medium for longitudinal recording and a medium with perpendicular anisotropy to be used with

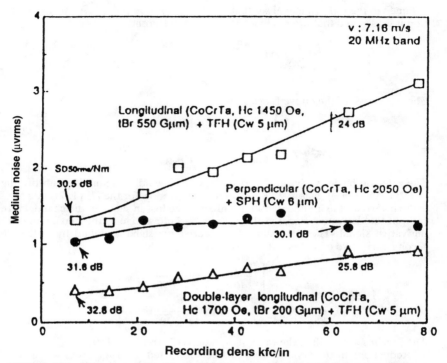

FIGURE 2.81   Noise as measured from thin-film media, including single-layer media for longitudinal recording, double-layer media for longitudinal recording and media with perpendicular anisotropy as used for perpendicular recording. The data was taken with a linear velocity of 7.16 m/s and a bandwidth of 20 MHz. The signal-to-noise ratio in dB is also shown *(after Miura, 1993).*

perpendicular recording. The noise from the double-layer medium is significantly reduced and may find application in the future. For the single-layer medium the noise spectral density at 60 kfc/in (23.62 kfc/cm) can be approximated by

$$NSD = \frac{v_{rms}}{\sqrt{bandwidth(Hz)}} = \frac{2.65 \ \mu V}{\sqrt{20 \times 10^6}} = 0.6 \ nV/\sqrt{Hz}$$

This noise spectral density also varies with the square root of trackwidth. So at the above recording density the overall noise spectral density from the example recording medium is given by

$$NSD = \frac{0.6x\sqrt{w(\mu m)}}{\sqrt{5}} = 0.268\sqrt{w(\mu m)} \ nV/\sqrt{Hz}$$

where w is the trackwidth.

   d.   Reduction in Signal at Clock Window Edge.   As shown in Fig. 2.78, the amplitude of the read-back signal at the edge of the clock cell is reduced from the peak amplitude and this results in additional losses in the channel. The width of the clock window depends on the data rate and the data code used, and it is assumed in the following analysis that the 2/3 (1, 7) code is used. As an approximation it is assumed that the readback pulse has the Lorentzian form

$$v(t) = \frac{V_0}{1 + \left(\dfrac{2t}{PW_{50}}\right)^2} \tag{2.108}$$

The derivative of the above function is given by

$$\frac{dv(t)}{dt} = \frac{8V_0 t/PW_{50}^2}{\left[1 + \left(\dfrac{2t}{PW_{50}}\right)^2\right]^2} \tag{2.109}$$

The value of the derivative at the edge of the clock window is found by substituting $t = 1/2(T_w) = 1/2(\frac{2T}{3})$, where T_w is the total clock window for the 2/3 (1, 7) code and T is the inverse of the input data rate (in bits/s). The loss in signal in the channel is the ratio of the derivative signal at the net clock window edge to the maximum of the derivative signal. The maximum of the derivative signal is found by setting the second derivative of $v(t)$ equal to zero, resulting in

$$\left[\frac{dv(t)}{dt}\right]_{\text{max}} = \frac{1.3 \, V_0}{PW_{50}}$$

$$\text{at } t = \frac{PW_{50}}{\sqrt{12}} \tag{2.110}$$

The loss in signal is then the ratio of equations (2.109) to (2.110).

Reductions in the window width to be subtracted from the gross width ($2T/3$) include tolerances in the clock circuit itself due to incorrect setting of the center frequency of the voltage controlled oscillator and jitter in the clock signal.

e. Loss of Signal-to-Noise Ratio Due to Differentiation in the Peak Detection Channel. If it is assumed that the readback wave form from a closely spaced alternating series of pulses is sinusoidal, then the signal-to-noise ratio into the differentiator is given by

$$\frac{signal \ (base\text{-}to\text{-}peak)}{noise \ (\text{rms})} = \frac{V_s}{V_{noise}(\text{rms})} e^{j\omega t} \tag{2.111}$$

The noise is assumed to be white with noise spectral density NSD_{diff}, where the noise into the differentiator is assumed to have a bandwidth equal to 1.5 times the highest frequency (f_m) allowed by the data code (see Sec. 2.4.3). Then the above value of signal to noise is given by

$$\left(\frac{signal}{noise}\right)_{in} = \frac{V_s e^{j\omega t}}{NSD \sqrt{1.5 f_m}} \tag{2.112}$$

After differentiation the signal-to-noise ratio is given by

$$\left(\frac{signal}{noise}\right)_{out} = V_s \frac{2\pi f_m}{\sqrt{\displaystyle\int_0^{f_{co}} (NSD)^2 df}} = \frac{V_s \sqrt{3}}{1.5 \, NSD \sqrt{1.5 f_m}} \tag{2.113}$$

The loss in signal-to-noise ratio due to differentiation is then

$$\frac{\dfrac{V_s\sqrt{3}}{NSD1.5\sqrt{1.5f_m}}}{\dfrac{V_s}{NSD\sqrt{1.5f_m}}} = \frac{\sqrt{3}}{1.5} = 1.25 \text{ dB} \tag{2.114}$$

This factor will be used in the subsequent evaluation of the signal-to-noise ratio at the data detector.

f. Window Loss Due to Imperfect Overwrite. Another loss in the channel which has an effect on the channel performance is that due to imperfect erasure of previously recorded data. The most severe case is where data at the lowest frequency allowed by the data code is erased by the data at the highest frequency allowed by the data code. This effect was quantified in Sec. 2.2.2. As an approximation the shift in transition position due to imperfect overwrite will be subtracted from the clock window width.

g. Intersymbol Interference. The last channel loss term that will be discussed is the loss due to the fact that with intersymbol interference the peak of the signal is not located in the center of the clock window. The peak shift for a thin-film head dipulse (two adjacent thin-film head pulses) with each pulse as shown in Fig. 2.44 has been evaluated by a self-consistent analysis and is shown as Fig. 2.82 (Roscamp, 1992). The initial peak of the dipulse is shifted early and the following pulse is

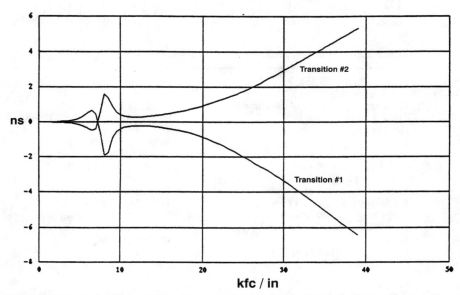

FIGURE 2.82 Peak shift for the two pulses of a dibit as calculated for a thin-film head and media versus the recording density in flux changes per in. The effects of the undershoots for the isolated pulse from a thin-film head are clearly shown *(after Roscamp, 1992).*

shifted late with respect to the position of the pulses without intersymbol interference. It has been shown that when a pseudo-random pattern of pulses is recorded the peak shift is a probability distribution with the range of shifts approximately limited by the above values of dibit peak shift (Williams, 1992). With equalization the effects of intersymbol interference can be minimized but with some loss of signal-to-noise ratio (Sec. 2.4.1). In the following analysis the peak shift for the dipulse shown in Fig. 2.82 will be evaluated at the particular value of bit density used.

In order to quantify the performance of the peak detection channel two examples will be discussed.

2.5.3.4. Thin-Film Head and Thin-Film Disk. The parameters assumed are for the head and disk described in Table 2.15 with resulting isolated readback pulse shown in Fig. 2.44 and peakshift resulting from pulse superposition shown in Fig. 2.82. The read and write widths of the head are assumed to be the same as listed in Table 2.19. The value of the readback signal amplitude was evaluated using the Roscamp model (Roscamp, 1992).

With the parameters from Table 2.21 the noise contributions are listed in Table 2.22. With these noise parameters the signal-to-noise ratio and hence the soft error rate can be calculated. The overall equation for signal-to-noise ratio (SNR) for the case where the two erase bands from adjacent tracks just touch, which is the peak of the 747 curve, is given by:

$$SNR = \frac{\left(\frac{V_p}{\mu m}\right)(w_t)}{\left[v_h^2 + v_a^2 + v_m^2 + 0.5\left(\frac{V_p}{\mu m}\right)^2\left[TMR + \frac{w_r}{2} + w_s - \left(\frac{w_t}{2} + 2w_e\right)\right]^2\right]^{1/2}} \qquad (2.115)$$

TABLE 2.21 Pulse Parameters for Signal-to-Noise Evaluation

Thin-film head and disk isolated pulse	Fig. 2.44 and Table 2.15
Track spacing for peak of 747 curve [$w_t + 2w_8$]	11.05 μm
Track density	90.5 tracks/mm (2262 t/in)
Head turns	42
PW_{50}	92 ns at 0.88 in (ID) and 3600 RPM
Isolated pulse amplitude (base to peak)	251 × (w_r/9 μm) μv (ID)
Pulse amplitude per unit of track width	28 μv/ μm (ID)
Bit density 2/3 (1, 7 data code)	1.771 Kb/mm (45 Kb/in)
Flux-change density (maximum)	1.328 fc/mm (33.750 Kfc/in)
Flux-change density (minimum)	.332 fc/mm (8.43 Kfc/in)
Data rate	15 Mb/s (ID)
Data period (1/data rate) (T)	67 ns (ID)
Channel bandwidth $\left(\frac{data - rate}{4/3}\right) \times 1/2 \times 1.5$	8.44 MHz (ID)
Clock window $\left(\frac{2T}{3}\right)$	44.67 ns (ID)

TABLE 2.22 Noise Sources and Signal Reduction Terms in Peak Detection Channel for Thin-Film Head and Thin-Film Disk

Noise or signal reduction term	Value (using parameters from Table 2.21) in μvolts or dB
Head noise Eq.(2.76) and Table 2.20	2.53 μv
Preamplifier noise (Sec. 2.5.3.3b)	1.45 μv
Media noise (Sec. 2.5.3.3c)	1.55 μv
Reduction in signal-to-noise ratio due to differentiation (Sec. 2.5.3.3e)	1.25 dB
Loss of clock window due to peak shift (from Fig. 2.82)	worst case for dibit: 4.5 ns assumed as average: 2.0 ns
Signal-to-noise loss at edge of clock window (including effects of peak shift) (Sec. 2.5.3.3d)	0.19 dB
Signal to noise loss due to imperfect over-write (Sec. 2.5.3.3f)	0 dB (loss is small if overwrite is greater than 28dB)

TABLE 2.23 Signal-to-Noise Ratio and Soft Error Rate from Inductive Head and Thin-Film Disk

TMR (μm)	SNR (dB) ID track	ID track $z = \dfrac{SNR \sqrt{2}(T_w - T_{isi} - T_{ow})}{PW_{50}}$	ID log soft error rate at specified TMR (errors/bit)	ID log soft error rate times probability of being at the 3σ TMR value (errors/bit)
1	28.51	8.75	negligible	negligible
1.5	21.43	3.86	−7.18	−10.18
1.9	18.14	2.64	−3.5	−6.5

With the parameters listed in Tables 2.21 and 2.22, the value of the signal-to-noise ratio for the two cases of track misregistration and the resulting soft error rate from Eq. (2.115) is given in Table 2.23. To arrive at the error rate given the value of z, use is made of Eq. (2.103) which is plotted as Fig. 2.83.

The last column in Table 2.23 is the soft error rate when the head is at the 3σ value of TMR times the probability of the head being at the 3σ value of TMR, which is approximately 10^{-3}. In a more exact analysis the product of the probability density function for the track misregistration times the probability function for the error rate would be integrated to determine the average soft error rate. The soft error rate for inductive heads is plotted versus track misregistration (TMR) in Fig. 2.84. It is seen from this analysis that the effects of "write narrow and read wide" on error rates are significant. The limit on soft error rate is near 10^{-5} since error rates higher than this are difficult to correct with conventional error correction codes.

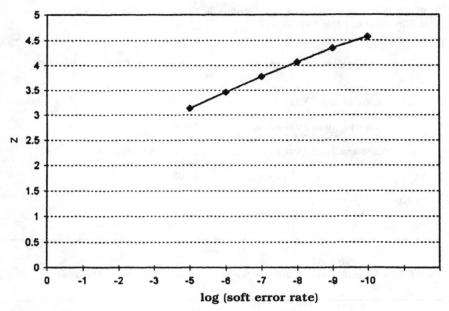

FIGURE 2.83   Logarithm of the soft error rate versus the parameter $z = [SNR \sqrt{2}(T_w - T_{isi} - T_{ow})]/PW_{50}$.

2.5.3.5 *Magnetoresistive Read and Inductive Write Heads.*

The limitation on off-track performance with inductive thin-film heads due to their "write narrow read wide" characteristic is improved by using a dual head consisting of a magnetoresistive read element and an inductive write element. With these heads the read element can be made narrower than the write element and track misregistration can take place before the read element reaches the edge of the track. In addition, the magnetoresistive read head has less resistance and inductance than the inductive thin-film head (Table 2.20). The parameters assumed for the magnetoresistive read and inductive write head are shown as Table 2.24. The pulse width for the magnetoresistive head is assumed to be the same as for the inductive head and the amplitude per unit track width is taken to be 100 $\mu v/\mu m$. The values for the resulting noise sources in the peak detection channel are listed in Table 2.25.

In this analysis the preamplifier and media noise are maintained the same as for the inductive head case. The media noise with magnetoresistive heads may be made smaller since the magnetization for the media associated with the magnetoresistive head can be reduced and this factor will tend to decrease the following error rates. The noise due to the resistance of the magnetoresistive element is reduced from that for the inductive head. The loss in clock window due to intersymbol interference from peak shift is reduced to 1 ns for the magnetoresistive head since there are no undershoots in the isolated pulse. All other loss terms were maintained equal to those for the inductive head. The summary of soft error rates is given in Table 2.26.

The total soft error rates for the thin-film inductive head and for the magnetoresistive read and inductive write head both with thin-film media versus track

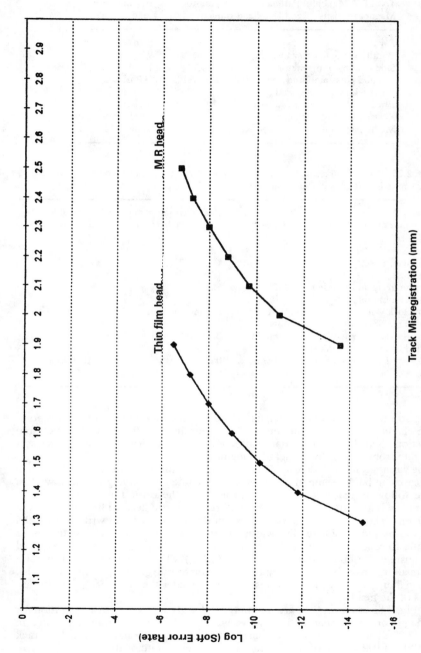

FIGURE 2.84 Logarithm of the soft error rate versus track misregistration for recording systems using peak detection with thin-film and magnetoresistive heads and thin-film media.

TABLE 2.24 Pulse Parameters for Signal-to-Noise Evaluation for
Magneto-resistive Read Head and Inductive Write Head

PW_{50}	92 ns at 0.88 in
Width of magnetoresistive read element	9.5 μm
Side reading of magnetoresistive stripe (w_s)	1 μm
Isolated pulse amplitude per unit of track width	100 μv/μm
Write width of write head (w_t)	8.43 μm
Erase width of write head (w_e)	1.31 μm
Resistance of read element	19 Ω (Table 2.20)
Media parameters	Table 2.15

TABLE 2.25 Noise Sources and Signal Reduction Terms in Peak Detection Channel for
Magnetoresistive Head and Thin-Film Disk

Noise or signal reduction term	Value (using parameters from Table 2.24) in μvolts or dB
Head noise	1.59 μv
Preamplifier noise	1.45 μv
Media noise	1.55 μv
Reduction in signal-to-noise ratio due to differentiation	1.25 dB
Loss of clock window due to peak shift (from Fig. 2.82 with no undershoots)	assumed as average: 1.0 ns
Signal-to-noise loss at edge of clock window (including effects of peak shift)	0.19 dB
Signal-to-noise loss due to imperfect over-write	0 dB (loss is small if overwrite is greater than 28 dB)

misregistration are shown as Fig. 2.84. The error rate that is allowable at this point
in the channel (after the data detector) is determined by the error detection and
correction code (ECC) in the data path controller. A typical improvement in soft
error rate from ECC is five orders of magnitude.

The variation in track density with track misregistration for the magnetoresistive
head case can be determined by fixing the error rate and varying the head widths.
In the following example, shown as Table 2.27, the error rate with track misregistration is fixed at 10^{-5} and the magnetoresistive read head width is varied from
2 to 7 μm. The values for the differences between the read and write widths, the
erase widths and the side reading widths are reduced from those shown in the above
example to reflect the expected improvements in these parameters. The required
track misregistration is evaluated from Eq. (2.115) with the value of signal-to-noise
ratio resulting from the assumption of the 10^{-5} error rate given by 18.21 dB or 8.14.
Even higher track densities are possible by reducing the side reading and erase
widths of the head.

In Fig. 2.85 is shown the variation in track density with track misregistration for
the magnetoresistive read and inductive write head with the parameters listed in
Table 2.27. These values of track misregistration are equivalent to the "off-track
capability" for the peak of the 747 curve with an error rate of 10^{-5}.

A more detailed analysis of the variation in track density with track mis-

TABLE 2.26 Signal-to-Noise Ratio and Soft Error Rate from a Magnetoresistive Head and Thin-Film Disk

TMR (μm)	SNR (dB) ID track	ID track $z = \dfrac{SNR\sqrt{2}(T_w - T_{isi} - T_{ow})}{PW_{50}}$	ID log soft error rate (errors/bit)	ID log soft error rate times probability of being at the 3σ TMR value (errors/bit)
1.9	22.94	4.70	−10.57	−13.57
2.2	20.21	3.43	−6	−9
2.4	18.77	2.91	−4.5	−7.5

TABLE 2.27 Parameters for Evaluation of Track Density and Required Track Misregistration

Write width minus read width ($w_t - w_r$)	0.5 μm			
Erase width (w_e)	0.25 μm			
Side reading width (w_s)	0.5 μm			
Read width (w_r) (μm)	track pitch ($w_t + 2w_r$) (μm)	track density (tracks/cm)	track density (tracks/in)	track misregistration (μm)
2	3	3333	8467	0.59
3	4	2500	6350	0.77
4	5	2000	5080	0.94
5	6	1667	4233	1.12
6	7	1429	3629	1.29
7	8	1250	3175	1.46

registration for a magnetoresistive read head has been published (Jensen et al., 1990). This analysis was applied to a system with an areal density of 77.5 Mbits/cm² (500 Mbits per in²) with a flying height of 0.0625 μm (2.5 μin), a total head disk separation of 0.102 μm and a head read gap of 0.4 μm. In Fig. 2.86 (Jensen et al., 1990) is shown the variation in the track density with track misregistration for an error rate of 10^{-6} errors per byte or approximately 10^{-7} errors per bit.

A treatment of the off-track capability of magnetoresistive read and inductive write heads has been published (Bonyhard and Lee, 1990; Lee and Bonyhard, 1990). The underlying assumption of this analysis is that the noise read from old information and the adjacent track dominates the signal-to-noise ratio and hence the error rate. This assumption is often valid but the analysis which considers all noise sources is more general. In the Bonyhard and Lee analysis the off-track performance is characterized by a parameter k, which is related to the maximum off-track distance (x) for a specified error rate by

$$x_{max} = 0.5(w_t - w_r) + kw_r \qquad (2.116)$$

where the notation used is changed from that in the references.

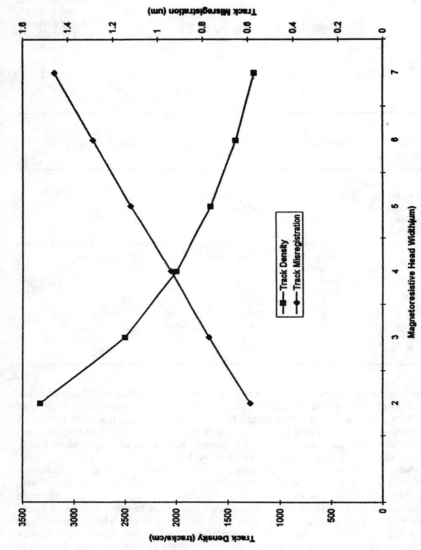

FIGURE 2.85 Track density and track misregistration versus head width for a recording system using a magnetoresistive head and thin-film media. The soft error rate is fixed at 10^{-5}.

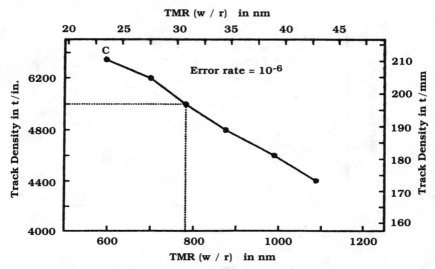

FIGURE 2.86 Track density versus write-to-read track misregistration for a recording system using a peak detection channel with an error rate of 10^{-6} with a magnetoresistive head and a thin-film media *(after Jensen et al., 1990).*

The first term is due to the write wide and read narrow characteristic of the dual-element heads and the second term characterizes the ability of the head and disk technology to read off-track at the specified error rate, which is the off-track capability. A tabulation of the parameter k for a wide range of magnetoresistive head track widths showed that the following empirical result applies for narrow track heads using patterned exchange longitudinal bias and soft adjacent transverse bias.

$$k = 0.0787w_r - 0.301 \text{ for } w_r < 5.5 \ \mu\text{m} \qquad (2.117)$$

More recent data on narrower track and hence higher areal density magneto-resistive read heads have a value of k of 0.18 for a read head width of 3.6 μm (Jensen et al., 1990).

Using the above values for the slope of the off-track performance parameter (k), the "off-track capability" (head track misregistration for a specified error rate) can be related to the parameters k, w_t, w_r, w_e and the displacement (d) between the read element and write element due to photolithographic tolerances. For example, the off-track capability (OTC) in the region where the adjacent track is far away from the track to be read and the read head reads desired signal and old-information noise but not noise from the adjacent track is

$$\text{OTC(I)} = 0.5(w_t - w_r) + k_0 w_r + (0.5 - k_0)w_e \pm d_{r\text{-}w} \qquad (2.118)$$

where

k_0 is the value of the parameter k with no erase band, and $d_{r\text{-}w}$ is the displacement of read from write element.

The entire 747 curve can be developed using the above approach. The off-track capability versus adjacent track pitch space was divided into five regions and the

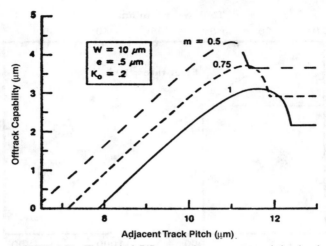

FIGURE 2.87 Theoretical 747 curves for a magnetoresistive head with varying ratio (m) of read-to-write track width. The nominal read width is 10 μm and the erase width is 0.5 μm and K_0 is the off-track capability with no erase band at large values of adjacent track pitch *(after Lee and Bonyhard, 1990).*

peak of the 747 curve depends on the parameters k_0, w_r, w_t, w_r/w_t and the track pitch. In Fig. 2.87 is shown the variation in the 747 curve with changes in the ratio of the read to write width ($m = w_r/w_t$). It is seen in this figure that there is a significant improvement in the amplitude of the 747 curve with reduction in the read-to-write width ratio at all values of adjacent track pitch.

In another model of the off-track performance of the combined magnetoresistive read and inductive write head the effects of the skew between the head gaps and the tangent to the track direction with rotary actuators and the separation between the magnetoresistive read and inductive write elements is explicitly discussed (Chopra et al., 1992). The effects of track skew and element separation with these heads on the track misregistration has been discussed in Sec. 2.2.3.4 (Fig. 2.11). The analysis of Chopra et al., assumed that the dominant noise source is the old-information noise as with Bonyhard and Lee. The nominal parameters for the Chopra et al. analysis are listed in Table 2.28.

In Fig. 2.88 is shown the prediction of track width versus $\mathrm{TMR}_{w-r,3\sigma}$ from the Chopra et al. analysis. The parameters used were as listed in Table 2.28. The effects of the separation of the read and write elements and track skew limit the achievable track width to values somewhat lower than predicted by the signal-to-noise analysis given in Sec. 2.5.3.5. The loss in achievable track density with separation of the read and write elements has motivated the reduction in this spacing. In the "merged" head design, the top shield of the magnetoresistive read head is merged with the lower pole of the write head. If it is assumed that the read head is held on-track by the servo system during a read operation, then the write head is moved to be on-track before a write operation can be performed. The amount of movement required depends on the track location on the disk, and frequently a look-up table of calculated movements is used. This single-track seek operation identified in Fig. 2.88 as "systems solution" (also referred to as a micro-jog) takes time (at least several hundred microseconds) and can result in a lost revolution. This loss of time in switching between a read and a write operation can have a negative impact on data throughout. However,

TABLE 2.28 Parameters for Track Density Analysis of
Magnetoresistive Read and Inductive Write Heads

Read-write separation	4.00 μm
Read-write separation tolerance (1σ)	0.25 μm
Effective read width	3.5 μm
Read width tolerance (1σ)	0.25 μm
Write width tolerance (1σ)	0.25 μm
Read-write separation tolerance (1σ)	0.10 μm
Erase width	0.50 μm
Off-track capability factor (k)	0.20
Actuator skew	12°
$TMR_{w-r,3\sigma}$	1.02 μm (40 μin)

(Chopra et al., 1992).

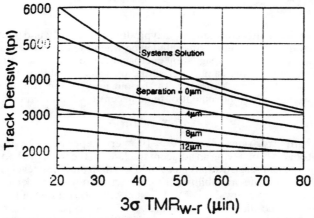

FIGURE 2.88 Theoretical variation in track density versus the 3 sigma
value of write-to-read track misregistration for a magnetoresistive head
with varying spacing between the read and write elements. A value of
head skew angle of 12° is assumed. The "systems solution" refers to
moving the write head to align with the recorded track following a read
operation (see Fig. 2.11) *(after Chopra et al., 1992).*

improvements in caching algorithms in data controllers has reduced the impact of
this overhead.

An alternative analysis of the performance of magnetoresistive heads and thin-
film recording media in a peak detection channel is to use a timing jitter model
which evaluates the uncertainty of "jitter" in the location of the peak due to noise in
the location of the transition due to media noise and head and electronic noise.
Again the model predicts the importance of media noise in the case of magnetoresistive read heads (Tsang, 1991).

2.5.4 Hard Error-Rate Limits to Track Density

The analysis carried out in Sec. 2.5.3.3 deals with soft errors, that is, errors that
result from noise which is statistical and would be expected to change from one

reading of the data to another. As discussed in Sec. 2.2, it is possible for data to be unrecoverable on multiple rereads if data from an adjacent track encroaches too closely on the desired track because of write-to-write track misregistration. Adjacent track encroachment of a magnitude large enough to cause such *hard errors* are represented on the 747 curve by the linear region which intersects the off-track capability axis at $w_t - \text{OTC}_\infty$, where OTC_∞ corresponds to the off-track capability for large track pitch. Such track encroachment places an upper bound on the track density, which could be smaller than the results predicted in Sec. 2.5.3.3. It is the purpose here to estimate the track density achievable under conditions that result in low probability of hard errors.

Curves illustrating the variation of soft error rate due to movement of the readback head into old information recorded on the same track were given earlier (Fig. 2.84). Movement of the head by an amount that results in a high error rate—for example, a probability of 10^{-5} of having one or more bits in error—defines the "off-track" capability x_{OTC}. This is proportional to the head core width w_r, given that the failure mechanism is loss of signal-to-noise ratio. That is

$$x_{\text{OTC}} = \alpha_{\text{OT}} w_r \qquad (2.119)$$

where the proportionality constant α_{OT} is typically between 0.12 and 0.2. In the case of hard errors, the errors can be generated even when the head is on-track because of erasure of part of the track signal by encroachment of an adjacent track. If the hard error rate reaches the same level as the off-track capability, the amount of noise readback will be the same as with the old information condition, and the "track pitch to failure" x_{pf} movement of the adjacent track is given by

$$x_{\text{pf}} = w_r - x_{\text{OTC}} \qquad (2.120)$$

Satisfactory hard error rates are near 2×10^{-12} errors per byte. To ensure a sufficiently low probability of having an adjacent track reach the track pitch to failure, the write-to-write track misregistration can be held less than the 5.88σ level. That is, with a normal distribution, the probability of having a write-to-write track misregistration value greater than the 5.88σ value is 2×10^{-9}, and with an error rate of 10^{-5} errors/bit, the hard error rate specification of less than 2×10^{-12} errors per byte can be achieved. The track pitch to failure x_{pf} is then given in terms of the track pitch by

$$x_{\text{pf}} = x_p - (\text{TMR}_{W,W})_{5.88\sigma} \qquad (2.121)$$

By combining Eqs. (2.119), (2.120), and (2.121), the following equation for the track pitch as limited by the hard error rate criteria results:

$$x_p = w_r(1 - \alpha_{\text{OT}}) + (\text{TMR}_{W,W})_{5.88\sigma} \qquad (2.122)$$

From the previous results on soft error rate, it was observed that higher track densities would be achieved if the read width were narrower than the track width, resulting in a final equation for the hard error rate limit, with k_h = read head width/track pitch.

$$x_p = \frac{(\text{TMR}_{W,W})_{5.88\sigma}}{1 - k_h(1 - \alpha_{\text{OT}})} \qquad (2.123)$$

The write-to-write track misregistration values are always larger than the write-to-read track misregistration values because they include servowriter tolerances, which cause track encroachment. Track density limits resulting from the hard error criteria are tabulated in Table 2.29 for values of $(\text{TMR}_{W,W})_{5.88\sigma}$ ranging from 0.5 to

TABLE 2.29 Hard Error Rate Limits on Track Density

$TMR_{w\text{-}w}$	k_h	α	Tracks/cm	Tracks/in
0.5	0.8	0.15	6400	16256
1.0	0.8	0.15	3200	8128
1.5	0.8	0.15	2133	5418
2.0	0.8	0.15	1600	4064
0.5	0.8	0.20	7200	18288
1.0	0.8	0.20	3600	9144
1.5	0.8	0.20	2400	6096
2.0	0.8	0.20	1800	4572
0.5	1.0	0.20	4000	10160
1.0	1.0	0.20	1818	4618
1.5	1.0	0.20	1333	3387
2.0	1.0	0.20	1000	2540

2.0 μm and values of α_{OT} from 0.15 to 0.2 and values of k_h of 0.8 and 1.0. The conclusions are that the hard error limits on track density can be less than the track density limits resulting from a specified soft error rate.

As expected, smaller read-head widths are favored to reduce hard errors. For write-to-read track misregistration values less than 2.0 μm, the track density limits predicted here are somewhat larger than those for the soft error rate limits. Both limits should be evaluated in disk file development.

2.5.5 Projections for Areal Density

The results of the analysis in Secs. 2.5.2 and 2.5.3 have shown the significant advantage of magnetoresistive heads over thin-film inductive heads in achieving both higher linear and track densities. Two disadvantages with the magnetoresistive head are the undesirable spacing between the read and write elements and the potential difficulty with reading encoded position error signals due to the unequal response from the sides of the magnetoresistive head. The former problem is at least partially alleviated by the "systems solution" described in Sec. 2.5.3.5 and the latter problem is addressed by suitable algorithms in the position error channel. The lower noise introduced into the recording channel by use of the magnetoresistive head can be further reduced by improvements in the noise from media and by improved track misregistration tolerances. An areal density of 155 Mb/cm^2 (1 Gb/in^2) has already been demonstrated using a closely-spaced magnetoresistive head and a partial response maximum likelihood channel (Howell et al., 1990; Tsang et al., 1990). An areal density of 310 Mb/cm^2 (2 Gb/in^2) has been demonstrated using sub-micron width magnetoresistive heads together with a laminated iron film write head with ion-milled pole tips, a head-to-disk spacing of 0.05 μm, a low-noise laminated magnetic recording film and an extended partial response (EPR IV) maximum likelihood data channel together with servo technology consisting of an optical transducer mounted on the side of the slider, a recording surface with etched pits for track following and a two-stage actuator (Futamoto et al., 1991). An areal density of 3 Gb/in^2 has been demonstrated with a 2 μm wide magnetoresistive read head and a write head with ion-milled pole tips (Tsang et al., 1995). The key parameters for the read and write

TABLE 2.30 Components of Areal Density for 3 Gb/in² Technology Demonstration

Write head	
turns	10(8)
pole thickness	3 μm (electroplated Permalloy) (4 μm)
gap thickness	0.25 μm (0.4 μm)
top pole width (P2W)	1.3 μm (ion-milled) (2.5–3.5 μm)
Read head	
transverse bias technology	soft adjacent layer
shield thickness	3 μm (top shield shared as bottom pole of write head)
gap (shield to shield)	0.2 μm (0.25 μm)
track width	1.1 μm (2.0 μm)
magnetoresistive film thickness	120Å (150Å)
Recording film	
alloy	quaternary (CoCrPtX)(ternary alloy of CoPtCr)
$M_t\delta$	0.53 memu/cm² (0.7 memu/cm²)
H_c	2 kOe (1.75 kOe)
S^*	0.68 (0.8)
Mechanical spacing	1.5 μin (similar to 1 Gb/in²)
Data channel	PRML
data rate	5 MB/s (3.5 MB/s)
off-track distance (max)	±0.35 μm
track pitch for maximum of 747 curve	1.5–1.6 μm
Linear density	180 kb/in (118 kb/in)
Track density	16.7 ktracks/in (8.5 ktracks/in)

SOURCE: Tsang et al., 1995.

heads and the components of areal density for this demonstration are shown in Table 2.30. Also in this table are shown in parenthesis the parameters for the 1 Gb/in² demonstration (Tsang et al, 1990). It is seen that the emphasis in the 3 Gb/in² demonstration is for a larger percentage change in track density than for linear density. The advantage of stressing high track density is that the magnetic spacing can be maintained nearly constant in moving from the 1 Gb/in² regime.

A recent development which offers promise of extending the recording densities even further is the giant magnetoresistive (GMR) technology (see *Magnetic Recording Technology*). With the GMR technology the magnetoresistive parameter $\Delta R_{mr}/R_{mr}$ is increased from the value for $Ni_{80}Fe_{20}$, which is approximately 2%. The output signal is increased in proportion to this ratio. This increase is the result of laminating the magnetoresistive films with 20 to 40 Å thick nonmagnetic spacing layers and values as high as $\Delta R_{mr}/R_{mr}$ of 4 to 6% have been achieved in thin films of NiFe/Ag annealed at 315°C and with low values of magnetic field (Hylton et al., 1992). In addition, the implementation of the GMR effect in the spin-valve system (Dieny et al., 1991; Tsang et al., 1994) has resulted in the linearized response, which does not require a transverse bias, given by

$$V_{out} \propto \Delta R \propto \sin(\theta_1) = H_y H_k \tag{2.119}$$

where θ_1 is the angle of the magnetization in one of the two GMR films and hence reverses sign and the response is linear in H_y, where H_y is the field from the disk and H_k is the anisotropy field for small excursions of angle (Dieny et al., 1994). The second GMR film is pinned to a fixed angle ($\pi/2$) by another magnetic film. Peak output signals as high as 500 $\mu V/\mu m$ have been achieved with heads as narrow as 2 μm (Tsang et al., 1994). This is significantly larger than reported for anisotropic magnetoresistive heads (the value for signal per unit of track width used in the analysis of Sec. 2.5.3.5 was 100 $\mu V/\mu m$). The recording density at 50% of the roll-off for all-ones recording was 4200 fc/mm (106,680 fc/in).

A review of the directions required to allow a continued increase of areal density of 60% per year has been published (Grochowski and Thompson, 1994). It is concluded for areal densities greater than approximately 7750 Mb/cm^2 (0.5×10^5 Mb/in^2) that near-contact recording (spacing between head and disk surface of less than 10 nm) is required. One key technology to achieving these high areal densities is the use of small sliders for reduced stiction and low spacing tolerances or for in-contact recording. A technology for reduced spacing is the "tri-pad" head with a small footprint and light head-load (3.5 gm) which uses horizontal recording in a "proximity recording" mode (Williams, 1993). With the latter technology the areal density achieved using a thin-film head as the transducer was 62 Mb/cm^2 (400 Mb/in^2) with a peak detection channel and with a partial response channel with a user bit density improvement of 1.5, an areal density of 77.5–93 Mb/cm^2 (500–600 Mb/in^2) is predicted.

Recording films for densities higher than 1.55 Gb/cm^2 (10 Gb/in^2) must have high coercivity (> 3000 Oe), high coercive squareness (~ 0.9) and small grain size (~ 100 Å) (Murdock et al., 1992). This has proven difficult in practice and multilayered films may be required (Murdoch et al., 1990). Care must be taken to avoid thermal instability due to superparamagnetism of very fine grains in thin-film media and multilayer media at these areal densities (Charap and Lu, 1994).

2.6 TRIBOLOGY IN RIGID-DISK FILES

Tribology has been a major concern for the heads and disks in rigid-disk files since their inception. The concern has heightened since the early 1970s because of the development of the start and stop in-contact technology, in which the heads are normally in contact with the disk surface and "take-off" and "fly" when the disk starts to spin and "lands" when the disk stops. This start-stop technology was initially used with particulate disks but the technology has been found to be more robust with thin-film disks. Robustness refers to the ability to achieve many thousands of start stop cycles, as is required with small computers, without damage to the surfaces of the heads or the disks. In this section the emphasis will be on the presentation of data on the start-stop performance and the initial stiction peak observed on lubricated disk surfaces. The details on the undercoat texturing, overcoat, and lubrication required to achieve the required tribological performance are in the companion volume *Magnetic Recording Technology*. The subject of tribology for storage devices has been reviewed (Bushan, 1990; Bhushan and Gupta, 1991).

2.6.1 Start-Stop In-Contact Data

A key mechanical performance measure for rigid-disk files is the ability of the file to start rotation of the disks after repeated start-stop cycles. This performance is made

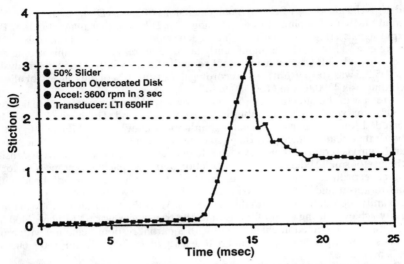

FIGURE 2.89 Measured stiction peak on a typical rotary actuator with a thin-film disk and head with a "50%" slider *(after Lipton et al., 1994).*

even more difficult in small portable disk files in which dc power supplies are limited in capacity and the rotation of the file is frequently stopped to conserve power. The impediments to starting of the file are the intermolecular attraction force between the two materials from which the slider and disk surface are made, typically Al_2O_3-TiC and amorphous carbon, respectively and the friction force of the disk surface and the sliding or viscous forces associated with the lubricant, resulting in "stiction." Stiction is the static frictional force which acts on the head before there is motion of the interface. In Fig. 2.89 is shown a typical measurement of the tangential force on a rotary actuator as disk rotation starts (Lipton et al., 1994). The actuator is instrumented with a strain gauge and an amplifier with an electrical bandwidth sufficient to pass the high frequencies required to record a short time duration stiction event. These data were taken on a "50%" slider (dimensions approximately 50% of those for the IBM 3380 slider) on a carbon overcoated disk. It is seen that large forces can exist between the interface and if these forces are large enough the disk may not start rotating. Following the stiction event the force on the actuator rises for a few seconds before the head flies above the disk surface and the friction force reaches a minimum value associated with the asperity height and frequency distribution. The variation in the friction force with time for one start and stop cycle is shown in Fig. 2.90 (Lipton et al., 1994). In addition, the number of contact start and stop cycles has an effect on the stiction and this is shown in Fig. 2.91 (Lipton et al., 1994). Two different disks were used in this experiment and for the data labeled "Mfg 1," the increase in stiction peak is small over the range of 5000 contact start and stop cycles. The increase in stiction with the number of start and stop cycles is believed to be due to the burnishing of the disk surface and the increase in the attractive intermolecular forces between the head and the disk surfaces. Some of the factors which affect stiction are: rest time, humidity and temperature, lubricant type and thickness, surface roughness of both the head and disk overcoat, head slider area and load force, and acceleration of the disk. The principal technology for reducing stiction is texturing of the disk surface

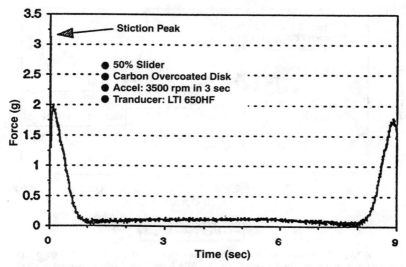

FIGURE 2.90 Variation in friction force for one start and stop cycle for the same conditions as in Fig. 2.89 *(after Lipton et al., 1994)*.

in which the disk substrate is roughened in a controlled manner. Texturing results in some modulation of the read signal and contributes to the head to disk spacing. A possible approach to having a smooth surface for recording and the textured region for reduced stiction is "zoned texture," in which the textured region is located near the inside diameter of the disk away from the recording band (Miura, 1994). A concern with this latter technology is the possibility of head crashes when the head traverses the texture boundary.

Even after the head is flying, frictional forces are found between the head and disk. The friction associated with the flying head is characteristic of the average surfaces of the head and disk, in contrast with stiction, which is characteristic of a single point on the disk. As the number of start and stop cycles increases the dynamic friction can increase. The increase in dynamic friction is believed to be due to the burnishing of the asperities on the disk surface by the flying head and some accumulation of debris on the slider and by wear of the carbon overcoat. Hard slider materials like the frequently used Al_2O_3-TiC (Knoop hardness of 2300 Kg/mm²) can burnish the asperities more readily than softer materials like ferrites (Knoop hardness of 600 Kg/mm²). Wear of the disk overcoat material can be described by Archard's law (Bhushan, 1990), which states that the real area of contact between two mating surfaces is given by

$$A_{real} = \text{constant} \left(\frac{load}{hardness} \right)^c \tag{2.124}$$

where $4/5 < c < 44/45$. The friction and wear can be minimized by minimizing the ratio of the real area of contact to the apparent area of contact, e.g., the slider area. For an elastic interface, the following relationship has been derived (Bhushan, 1990)

$$A_{real} \sim \frac{3.2 P_a A_a}{E_c (\delta_p / R_p)^{1/2}} \tag{2.125}$$

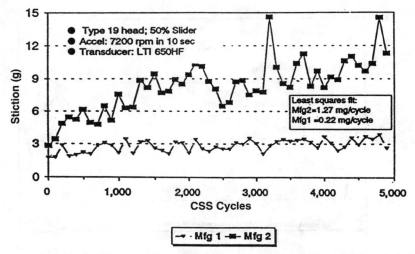

FIGURE 2.91 Variation in stiction peak versus contact start and stop cycles for a typical thin-film disk and head. Two disks are shown: Mfg 1 and Mfg 2 *(after Lipton et al., 1994)*.

where P_a = applied load, A_a = apparent area of contact, E_c composite Young's modulus between the two materials, δ_p = standard deviation of the peak height distribution, and R_p = asperity peak curvature.

This expression can be used to guide the selection of materials for both head sliders and overcoats. For example, materials with large values of Young's modulus and a narrow distribution of asperity heights are desired.

The addition of liquid lubricants, e.g., perfluorpolyethers can greatly improve the durability of the disk surface. The effect of the lubricant is to reduce the friction and wear and to maintain the flying characteristics of the mechanical system, which is referred to as "flyability" (Bhushan, 1990).

REFERENCES

Abbott, W. L., J. M. Cioffi, and H. K. Thapar, "Performance of Digital Magnetic Recording with Equalization and Offtrack Interference," *IEEE Trans. Magn.,* **MAG-27,** 705 (1991).

Arnoldussen, T. C., and L. L. Nunnelley (eds.), *Noise in Digital Magnetic Recording,* World Scientific Publishing Co. Pte. Ltd., Singapore, 1992.

Bajorek, C. H., S. Krongelb, L. T. Romankiw, and D. A. Thompson, "An Integrated Magnetoresistive Read, Inductive Write High Density Recording Head," *AIP Conf. Proc., Magn. Magn. Mater.,* **24,** 548 (1974).

Barbosa, L. C., "Minimum Noise Pulse Slimmer," *IEEE Trans. Magn.,* **MAG-17,** 3340 (1981).

Behrens, R. T., and A. J. Armstrong, "An Advanced Read/Write Channel for Magnetic Disk Storage," *Proc. 26th Asilomar Conf. on Signals, Systems and Computers, IEEE Comput. Soc.,* 1992.

Bergmans, J. W., "Density Improvement in Digital Magnetic Recording by Decision Feedback Equalization," *IEEE Trans. Magn.,* **MAG-22,** 157 (1986).

Bertero, G. A., N. H. Bertram, and D. M. Burnett, "Fields and Transforms for Thin Film Heads," *IEEE Trans. Magn.*, **MAG-29,** 67 (1993).

Bertram, H. N., *Theory of Magnetic Recording,* Cambridge University Press, Cambridge, England, 1994.

Bhushan, B., *Tribology and Mechanics of Magnetic Storage Devices,* Springer-Verlag, New York, 1990.

Bhushan, B., and B. K. Gupta, *Handbook of Tribology,* McGraw-Hill, New York, 1991.

Bhushan, B., M. Dominiak, and J. P. Lazzari, "Contact Start-Stop Studies with Silicon Planar Head Sliders Against Thin Film Disks," *IEEE Trans. Magn.*, **MAG-28,** 2874 (1992).

Bonyhard, P. I., and J. K. Lee, "Magnetoresistive Read Magnetic Recording Head Offtrack Assessment," *IEEE Trans. Magn.*, **MAG-26,** 2448 (1990).

Bryson, A., Jr., and Y. Ho, *Applied Optimal Control,* Hemisphere, Washington, DC, 1975.

Cahalan, D., and K. Chopra, "Effects of MR Head Track Profile Characteristics on Servo Performance," *IEEE Trans. Magn.*, **MAG-30,** 4203 (1994).

Charap, S., and P. L. Lu, "Thermal Instability at 10 Gbit/in^2 Magnetic Recording," *IEEE Trans. Magn.*, **MAG-30,** 4230 (1994).

Chen, T., "Virtual Contact Recording," *Head/Media Tech. Rev.,* Peripheral Research Corporation, Santa Barbara, California, 1993.

Chew, K., and M. Tomizuka, "Digital Control of Repetitive Errors in Disk Drive Systems," *IEEE Control Sys. Mag.,* **10,** 16 (1990).

Chopra, K., G. M. Grammens, and R. E. Weinstein, "Track Density Constraints in the Application of MR Head Technology," *IEEE Trans. Magn.*, **MAG-28,** 2730 (1992).

Coker, J. D., R. L. Galbraith, G. J. Kerwin, J. W. Rae, and P. A. Ziperovich, "Implementation of PRML in a Rigid Disk Drive," *IEEE Trans. Magn.*, **MAG-27,** 4538 (1991).

Commander, R. D., and J. R. Taylor, "Servo Design for an Eight-Inch Disk File," Disk File Technology, No. GA 26-1665-0, 90, IBM, 1980.

Comstock, R. L., and M. L. Williams, "Frequency Response in Digital Magnetic Recording," *IEEE Trans. Magn.*, **MAG-9,** 342 (1973).

Comstock, R. L., C. C. Lin, and G. E. Mauersberger, "A 2000 Track/Inch Disk File Servo System Using a Magnetoresistive Head," *IEEE Trans. Magn.*, **MAG-17,** 2739 (1981).

Cooper, E. S., "Minimizing Power Dissipation in a Disk File Actuator," *IEEE Trans. Magn.*, **MAG-24,** 2081 (1988).

Corb, B., "High Frequency Head and Playback Model for Thin-Film Recording Heads," *IEEE Trans. Magn.*, **MAG-30,** 394 (1994).

Cunningham, E. A., and D. C. Palmer, "A Model for the Prediction of Disk File Performance from Basic Component Capabilities," paper JE-3, *Magn. Magn. Mater. Conf.,* 1988.

DeVeirman, G. A., and R. G. Yamasaki, "Design of a Bipolar 10 Mhz Programmable Continuous-Time 0.05° Equiripple Linear Phase Filter," *IEEE J. Solid-State Circuits,* **27,** 324 (1992).

Dieny, B., V. S. Speriosu, S. Metin, S. S. P. Parkin, B. R. Wilhot, and D. Marui, "Giant Magnetoresistance in Soft Ferromagnetic Multilayers," *Phy. Rev. B,* **43,** 1297 (1991).

Dolivo, F., "Signal Processing for High-Density Digital Magnetic Recording," *Proc. COMPEURO* **89** (1989).

Eggenberger, J., and A. M. Patel, "Method and Apparatus for Implementing Optimum PRML Codes," U.S. Patent 4,707,681, 1987.

Fayling, R. E., T. J. Szezech, and E. F. Wollack, "A Model for Overwrite Modulation in Longitudinal Recording," *IEEE Trans. Magn.*, **MAG-20,** 718 (1984).

Fisher, K., J. Cioffi, and C. Melas, "An Adaptive DFE for Storage Channels Suffering from Nonlinear ISI," *IEEE Int. Conf. Comm.,* Boston, MA, 1638, 1989.

Fisher, K., J. Cioffi, W. Abbott, P. Bednarz, and C. M. Melas, "An Adaptive RAM-DFE for Storage Channels," *IEEE Trans. Magn.*, **MAG-29,** 1559 (1991).

Fitzpatrick, J., H. N. Bertram, X. Che, L. C. Barbosa, and G. H. Lin, "The Relationship of Medium Noise to System Error Rate in a PRML Channel," *IEEE Trans. Magn.,* **MAG-30,** 3990 (1994).

Franklin, G. F., D. Powell, and M. L. Workman, *Digital Control of Dynamic Systems,* Addison-Wesley, Reading, MA, 1990.

Futamota, M., F. Kugiya, M. Suzuki, H. Takano, Y. Matsuda, N. Inabe, Y. Miyamura, K. Ahagi, T. Nakao, and H. Sawaguchi, "Investigation of 2 Gb/in^2 Magnetic Recording at a Track Density of 17 ktpi," *IEEE Trans. Magn.,* **MAG-27,** 5280 (1991).

Goodwin, G. C., and K. S. Sin, *Adaptive Filtering, Prediction, and Control,* Prentice-Hall, Englewood Cliffs, NJ, 1984.

Grochowski, E., and D. A. Thompson, "Outlook for Maintaining Areal Density Growth in Magnetic Recording," *IEEE Trans. Magn.,* **MAG-30,** 3797 (1994).

Hamilton, H., R. Anderson, and K. Goodson, "Contact Perpendicular Recording on Rigid Media," *IEEE Trans. Magn.,* **MAG-27,** 4921 (1991).

Hardy, P., and D. J. Malone, "Evolution of the Soft Error Rate Model," *IEEE Trans. Magn.,* **MAG-27,** 5313 (1991).

Heim, D. E., "The Track-Edge Bias Profile in Shunt Biased Magnetoresistive Heads," *J. Appl. Phys.,* **63,** 4026 (1988).

Hoagland, A. S., and J. E. Monson, *Digital Magnetic Recording,* Second Ed., John Wiley & Sons, New York, 1991.

Hospodor, A. D., and A. S. Hoagland, "The Changing Nature of Disk Controllers," *Proc. IEEE,* **81,** 586 (1993).

Howell, T. T., D. P. McCown, T. A. Diola, T. Yow-Shing, K. R. Hense, and R. L. Gee, "Error Rate Performance of Experimental Gigabit per Square Inch Recording Components," *IEEE Trans. Magn.,* **MAG-26,** 2298 (1990).

Howell, T. D., W. L. Abbott, and K. D. Fisher, "Advanced Head Channels for Magnetic Disk Drives," *IEEE Trans. Magn.,* **MAG-30,** 3807 (1994).

Hsu, Y., C. C. Han, H. Chang, G. Ching, D. Hernandez, M. M. Chen, K. Ju, C. Che, and J. Fitzpatrick, "Dual-Stripe MR Heads for One Gigabit per Inch Square Recording Density," *IEEE Trans. Magn.,* **MAG-31,** 2621 (1995).

Hughes, G. F., and R. K. Schmidt, "On Noise in Digital Recording," *IEEE Trans. Magn.,* **MAG-12,** 752 (1976).

Huang, M., R. Chu, Y.-T. Hsia, and T. Tran, "Determination of the Narrow Read Width of Thin Film Magnetic Recording Heads Using an Error Rate Model," *IEEE Trans. Magn.,* **MAG-30,** 4251 (1994).

Hylton, T., K. Coffey, M. Parker, and J. Howard, "Giant Magnetoresistance at Low Fields in Discontinuous NiFe-Ag Multilayer Thin Films," *Science,* **261,** 1021 (1993).

Ichiyama, Y., "Reproducing Characteristics of Thin Film Heads," *IEEE Trans. Magn.,* **MAG-11,** 1203 (1975).

Jensen, R. A., J. Mortelmans, and R. Hauswitzer, "Demonstration of 500 Megabits per Square Inch with Digital Magnetic Recording," *IEEE Trans. Magn.,* **MAG-26,** 2169 (1990).

Kaileth, T., *Linear Systems,* Prentice-Hall, Englewood Cliffs, NJ, 1980.

Kakehi, A., M. Oshiki, T. Aikawa, M. Sasaki, and T. Kozai, "A Thin Film Head for High Density Recording," *IEEE Trans. Magn.,* **MAG-18,** 1131 (1982).

Kaneko, R., and Y. Koshimoto, "Technology in Compact and High Recording Density Disk Storage," *IEEE Trans. Magn.,* **MAG-18,** 1221 (1982).

Katz, E., and T. Campbell, "Effect of Bitshift Distribution on Error Rate in Magnetic Recording," *IEEE Trans. Magn.,* **MAG-15,** 1050 (1979).

Kelley, G. V., J. Freeman, H. Copenhaver, R. A. Ketcham, and E. P. Valstyn, "High-Track-Density Coupled-Film Magnetoresistive Head," *IEEE Trans. Magn.,* **MAG-17,** 2890 (1981).

Kirk, D. E., *Optimal Control Theory—An Introduction,* Prentice-Hall, Englewood Cliffs, NJ, 1970.

Klaassen, K. B., "Magnetic Recording Channel Front-Ends," *IEEE Trans. Magn.,* **MAG-27,** 4503 (1991).

Klaassen, K. B., and J. C. L. van Peppen, "Noise in Thin-Film Inductive Heads," *IEEE Trans. Magn.,* **MAG-28,** 2097 (1992).

Klaassen, K. B., and J. C. L. van Peppen, "Read/Write Amplifier Design Considerations for MR Heads," *IEEE Trans. Magn.,* **MAG-31,** 1056 (1995).

Kobayashi, H., "Application of Probabilistic Decoding to Digital Magnetic Recording," *IBM J. Res. Dev.,* **15,** 69 (1971).

Kobayashi, H., and D. T. Tang, "Application of Partial Response Channel Coding to Magnetic Recording Systems," *IBM J. Res. Dev.,* **14,** 368 (1970).

Koren N. L., "Matched Filter Limits and Code Performance in Digital Magnetic Recording," *IEEE Trans. Magn.,* **MAG-27,** 4594 (1991).

Kretzmer, E. R., "Generalization of a Technique for Binary Data Communication," *IEEE Trans. Comm. Tech.,* **COM-14,** 67 (1966).

Kryder, M. H., and W-Y Lai, "Modeling of Narrow Track Thin Film Write Head Fields," *IEEE Trans. Magn.,* **MAG-30,** 3873 (1994).

Lamb, H., and R. V. Southwell, "The Vibrations of a Spinning Disk," *Proc. R. Soc.,* **A99,** 272 (1921).

Lazzari, J. P., and P. Deroux-Dauphin, "A New Thin Film Head Generation IC Head," *IEEE Trans. Magn.,* **MAG-25,** 3190 (1989).

Lee, E. A., and D. G. Messerschmitt, *Digital Communications,* Kluwer Academic Publications, Boston, MA, 1988.

Lee, K. J., and P. I. Bonyhard, "A Track Density Model for Magnetoresistive Heads Considering Erase Bands," *IEEE Trans. Magn.,* **MAG-26,** 2448 (1990).

Lee, K. J., A. Wallash, and A. L. Poon, "Effects of Read/Write Misalignment and Asymmetric Side Reading on Magnetoresistive Head Off-Track Performance," *J. Appl. Phys.,* **69,** 5399 (1991).

Lemke, J. U., "Magnetic Recording of Digital Audio," *Proc. AES 7th Intl. Conf.,* 21 (1989).

Lender, A., "The Duobinary Technique for High-Speed Data Transmission," *IEEE Trans. Comm.,* **82,** 214 (1963).

Lipton, L. T., D. C. Stark, and S. Romine, "Advances in Contact Start/Stop Testing," *1994 DISCON Conference sponsored by the International Disk Equipment and Materials Association (IDEMA).*

Mallinson, J. C., "On Extremely High Density Digital Recording," *IEEE Trans. Magn.,* **MAG-10,** 368 (1974).

Maruyama, E., K. Yamada, H. Tanaka, S. Ito, H. Urai, and H. Kaneko, "A Yoke Magnetoresistive Head for High Track Density Recording," *IEEE Trans. Magn.,* **MAG-23,** 2403 (1987).

Mee, C. D. and E. D. Daniel (eds.), *Magnetic Recording Handbook,* McGraw-Hill, New York, 1989.

Mee, C. D., and E. D. Daniel (eds.), *Magnetic Recording Technology,* McGraw-Hill, New York, 1996.

Melas, C. M., P. Arnett, I. Beardsley, and D. Palmer, "Nonlinear Superposition in Saturation Recording of Disk Media," *IEEE Trans. Magn.,* **MAG-23,** 2079 (1987).

Mitsuya, Y., K. Kogure, and S. Oguchi, "Mechanisms for 3.2 GByte Multi-Device Disk Storage," *Rev. Elect. Comm. Labs,* **30,** 46 (1982).

Mitsuya, Y., and S. Takanami, "Technologies for High Recording Density in Large-Capacity Fast-Access Magnetic Disk Storage," *IEEE Trans. Magn.,* **MAG-23,** 2674 (1987).

Miu, D. K., and P. Bhat, "Minimum Power and Minimum Jerk Position Control and Its Application in Computer Disk Drives," *IEEE Trans. Magn.,* **MAG-27,** 4471 (1991).

Miura, Y., "Advances in Magnetic Disk Storage Technology," R. F. C. Farrow et al. (eds.), *Magnetism and Structure in Systems of Reduced Dimension,* Plenum Press, New York, 1993.

Mizoshita, Y., and N. Matsuo, "Mechanical and Servo Design of a 10-Inch Disk Drive," *IEEE Trans. Magn.*, **MAG-17**, 1387 (1981).

Moler, C. B., and C. F. Van Loan, "19 Dubious Ways to Calculate the Exponent of a Matrix," *SIAM Rev.*, **20**, 801 (1978).

Moon, J., and L. R. Carley, "Performance Comparison of Detection Methods in Magnetic Recording," *IEEE Trans. Magn.*, **MAG-26**, 3155 (1991).

Moon, J., and L. R. Carley, *Sequence Detection for High-Density Storage Channels*, Kluwer Academic Publishers, Boston MA, 1992.

Murdock, E. S., B. R. Natarajan, and R. G. Walmsley, "Noise Properties of Multilayered Co-Alloy Magnetic Recording Media," *IEEE Trans. Magn.*, **MAG-26**, 2700 (1990).

Murdock, E. S., R. F. Simmons, and R. Davidson, "Roadmap for 10 Gbit/in^2 Media: Challenges," *IEEE Trans. Magn.*, **MAG-28**, 3078 (1992).

Naruse, J., M. Tsutsumi, T. Tamura, Y. Hirano, T. Haysuma, and O. Matsushita, "Design of a Large Capacity Disk Drive with Two Actuators," *IEEE Trans. Magn.*, **MAG-19**, 1695 (1983).

Nyquist, H., "Thermal Agitation of Electronic Charge in Conductors," *Phys. Rev.*, **29**, 614 (1927).

Ogata, K., *Modern Control Engineering*, Prentice-Hall, Englewood Cliffs, NJ, 1970.

Oswald, R. K., "Design of a Disk-File Head-Positioning Servo," *IBM J. Res. Dev.*, **18**, 506 (1974).

Oswald, R. K., "The IBM 3370 Head-Positioning Control System," Disk File Technology, No. GA 26-1665-0, 41, IBM, 1980.

Patel, A. M., "A New Digital Signal Processing Channel for Storage Products," *IEEE Trans. Magn.*, **MAG-27**, 4579 (1991).

Patterson, D. A., G. Gibson, and R. H. Katz, "A Case for Redundant Arrays of Inexpensive Disks," *ACM SIGMOD Conf., 109, Chicago, June, 1988.*

Procker, L., I. Sanders, and V. Veswanathan, "Media Technology Evolution or Revolution," *Head/Media Tech. Rev.*, Peripheral Research Corporation, Santa Barbara, CA, 1993.

Rabiner, L. R., and B. Gold, *Theory and Application of Digital Signal Processing*, Prentice-Hall, Englewood Cliffs, NJ, 1975.

Roscamp, T. A., "Recording Process Simulation," Woodland Park, CO, 1992.

Roscamp, T. A., and N. Curland, "A Self-Consistent Model for Overwrite Modulation in Thin Film Recording Media," *IEEE Trans. Magn.*, **MAG-24**, 3090 (1988).

Sacks, A., M. Bodson, and P. Khosla, "Experimental Results of Adaptive Periodic Disturbance Cancellation in a High Performance Disk Drive," *Proc. Amer. Control Conf.*, San Francisco, CA, June, 1993.

Schneider, R. C., "An Improved Pulse-Slimming Method for Magnetic Recording," *IEEE Trans. Magn.*, **MAG-11**, 1240 (1975).

Schwartz, T. A., "A Statistical Model for Determining the Error Rate of the Recording Channel," *IEEE Trans. Magn.*, **MAG-16**, 634 (1980).

Siegel, P. H., "Applications of a Peak Detection Channel Model," *IEEE Trans. Magn.*, **MAG-18**, 1250 (1982).

Siegel, P. H., and J. K. Wolf, "Modulation and Coding for Information Storage," *IEEE Trans. Magn.*, **MAG-29**, (1991).

Simonds, J. L., "U.S. Digital Recording Industry," NSIC, San Diego, California, 1995.

Simmons, R., G. Jackson, M. Covault, C. Wacken, and J. Rausch, "Design and Peak Shift Characterization of a Magnetoresistive Head Thin Film Media System," *IEEE Trans. Magn.*, **MAG-19**, 1737 (1983).

Singh, A., and P. G. Bischoff, "Optimization of Thin Film Heads for Resolution, Peak Shift and Overwrite," *IEEE Trans. Magn.*, **MAG-21**, 1572 (1985).

Sri-Jayantha, M., T. J. Chainer, and D. H. Brown, "Digital Servo Control of a Novel Disk Actuator," *IEEE Trans. Magn.*, **MAG-27**, 4476 (1991).

Sobey, C. H., R. M. Lansky, and T. Perkins, "A Drive-Level Error Rate Model for Component Design and System Evaluation," *IEEE Trans. Magn.,* **MAG-30,** 269 (1994).

Stephens, H. C., and M. L. Workman, "Position Error Signal Modulator/Demodulator," U.S. Patent 4,575,776, 1986.

Szczech, T. J., "Analytic Expressions for Field Components of Nonsymmetrical Finite Pole Tip Length Magnetic Head Based on Measurements on Large Scale Model," *IEEE Trans. Magn.,* **MAG-15,** 1319 (1979).

Szczech, T. J., D. M. Perry, and K. E. Palmquist, "Improved Field Equation for Ring Heads," *IEEE Trans. Magn.,* **MAG-19,** 1740 (1983).

Tachibana, M., and M. Ohara, "Optimum Waveform Design and Its Effect on the Peak Shift Compensation," *IEEE Trans. Magn.,* **MAG-13,** 1199 (1977).

Tahara, Y., H. Takagi, and Y. Ikeda, "Optimum Design of Channel Filters for Digital Magnetic Recording," *IEEE Trans. Magn.,* **MAG-12,** 749 (1976).

Tan, B., G. Pan, and D. J. Mapps, "A New MR Head Track Following Method for Submicron Track Servo on Rigid Disks," *IEEE Trans. Magn.,* **MAG-30,** 4206 (1994).

Thompson, D. A., "Magnetoresistive Transducers in High-Density Magnetic Recording," *AIP Conf. Proc., Magn. Magn. Mater.,* **24,** 528 (1974).

Thapar, H. K., and A. M. Patel, "A Class of Partial Response Systems for Increased Storage Density in Magnetic Recording," *IEEE Trans. Magn.,* **MAG-23,** 3666 (1987).

Tsang, C. "Design and Performance Considerations in High Areal Density Longitudinal Recording," *J. Appl. Phys.,* **69,** 5393 (1991).

Tsang, C., M. Chen, T. Yogi, and K. Ju. "Gigabit Density Recording Using Dual-Element MR/Inductive Heads on Thin-Film Disks," *IEEE Trans. Magn.,* **MAG-26,** 1689 (1990).

Tsang, C., R. Fontana, T. Lin, D. E. Heim, U. S. Speriosu, B. A. Gurney, and M. L. Williams, "Design, Fabrication and Testing of Spin-Valve Read Heads for High Density Recording," *IEEE Trans. Magn.,* **MAG-30,** 3801 (1994).

Tsang, C., D. McCowen, H. A. Santini, J. Lo, and R. E. Lee, "3 Gb/in^2 Recording Demonstration with Dual Element Heads and Thin Film Disks," *IEEE Trans. Magn.,* **MAG-32,** 7 (1996).

Vea, M. P., and T. D. Howell, "A Soft Error Rate Model for Predicting Off-Track Performance," *IEEE Trans. Magn.,* **MAG-31,** 820 (1995).

Williams, E. M., "Recording Systems Considerations of Noise and Interference," Chap. 7 in T. C. Arnoldussen and L. L. Nunnelley (eds.), *Noise in Digital Magnetic Recording,* World Scientific Publishing Co., Singapore, 1992.

Williams, E. M., "Proximity Recording," *Head/Media Tech. Rev.,* Peripheral Research Corporation, Santa Barbara, CA, 1993.

Williams, M. L., and R. L. Comstock, "An Analytical Model of the Write Process in Digital Magnetic Recording," *AIP Conf. Proc.,* **5,** 738 (1971).

Wolf, J. K., "A Survey of Codes for Partial Response Channels," *IEEE Trans. Magn.,* **MAG-27,** 4585 (1991).

Wolf, J. K., "Digital Magnetic Recording Channels: from Peak Detection to PRL/DFE/FDTS," notes from course, 1992.

Wood, C., and P. Hodges, "DASD Trends: Cost, Performance and Form Factor," *Proc. IEEE,* **81,** 573 (1993).

Wood, R., "Magnetic Megabits," *IEEE Spectrum,* 32, May (1990).

Wood, R., S. Ahlgrim, K. Hollarmask, and R. Stenerson, "An Experimental 8-Inch Disk Drive with 100 Megabytes per Surface," *IEEE Trans. Magn.,* **MAG-20,** 698 (1984).

Workman, M. L., "Sliding Mask Variable Resolution Velocity Trajectory for Track Following Servo," U.S. Patent 4,486,797 (1984).

Workman, M. L., "Disk File Servo Control System with Fast Reduction of Repeatable Head Position Error," U.S. Patent 4,616,276 (1986).

Workman, M. L., "Adaptive Proximate Time-Optimal Servomechanisms," Ph.D. thesis, Stanford University, Stanford, CA, 1987.

Workman, M. L., "Digital Control System for a Data Recording Disk File," U.S. Patent 4,679,103, 1987.

Workman, M. L., R. Kosut, and G. F. Franklin, "Adaptive Proximate Time-Optical Servomechanisms: Continuous-Time Case," *Proc. Auto. Conf.,* **1,** 859 (1987).

Wu, E. Y., and J. V. Peske, "Edge Effects in Narrow Track Recording Using Symmetric and Asymmetric Write Pole Geometries," *IEEE Trans. Magn.,* **MAG-30,** 4254 (1994).

Yamada, T., S. Koganezawa, K. Aruga, and Y. Mizoshita, "A High Performance and Low-Profile Moving Magnet Actuator for Disk Drives," *IEEE Trans. Magn.,* **MAG-30,** 4227 (1994).

Yeh, N. H., "Asymmetric Crosstalk of Magnetoresistive Heads," *IEEE Trans. Magn.,* **MAG-18,** 1155 (1982).

Yoshida, M., M. Sakai, K. Fukuda, N. Yananaka, T. Koyanagi, and M. Matsuzaki, "Edge Eliminated Head," *IEEE Trans. Magn.,* **MAG-29,** 3037 (1993).

CHAPTER 3
DATA STORAGE ON FLEXIBLE DISKS

Seiichi Yaskawa
Yaskawa Electric Corporation, Tokyo, Japan

S. Robert Perera
Boulder, Colorado

John Heath
Winchester, England

The *flexible disk,* also called a *floppy disk* or *diskette,* is a magnetic recording medium which is physically a thin and pliable disk and functionally a removable, random-access cartridge. The flexible-disk drive is a mechanism with electronics which writes transmitted data onto a flexible disk and reads back the recorded data from the disk.

The material of a flexible disk is similar to that of a magnetic tape and is subject to anisotropic, hygroscopic, and thermal expansion and contraction. The read-write head is usually in contact with the disk and, in this respect, is like a magnetic tape and different from a rigid disk. The drive mechanism is basically the same as in a moving-head, removable rigid-disk drive. These factors characterize and limit the performance of the flexible disk and its drive as a magnetic recording device.

Since the introduction of the 203-mm (8-in) disk drive in 1970, flexible disks and drives have grown rapidly in variety and range of application. The initial 203-mm-diameter disks were followed in 1976 by 133-mm (5.25-in) disks and in the early 1980s by 88.9-mm (3.5-in) disks. The 3.5-in floppy disks are universally accepted as standard interchange media and 3.5-in floppy disk drives are found in almost all word processors, microcomputers, and personal computers. The disks are removable and inexpensive and require only very small space as an off-line storage medium; the drives are very low cost. The majority of floppy disk drives shipped today are 2 MB (1.44-MB formatted) 3.5-in drives and have obsolete performance and capacity but are widely used because no alternate standard exists. Drives and disks with much higher capacity and performance have been developed, and storage capacities up to 230 MB are available.

3.1   DRIVE DESIGN EVOLUTION

3.1.1   Early Developments

The first flexible-disk drive was developed in 1960, using flexible magnetic-oxide-coated, polyester disks. In order to stabilize the disk motion, the device used a stationary backplate (Bernoulli plate), and the head was designed to be in close proximity but not in contact with the disk. A capacity of 12.5 kB per disk was achieved using 40 tracks per disk and rotational speeds of 1800 to 8000 rpm. This flexible-disk drive system did not find wide product application, but the development provided basic analyses of the dynamics of flexible, magnetic media (Pearson, 1961). It took ten years for the flexible-disk drive, in today's sense, to come to the scene.

In 1970 a flexible-disk drive was used as a read-only device to load an initial program into a mainframe computer, or a diagnostic program into a large fixed-disk drive controller. The disk diameter chosen was 203 mm (8-in), and the substrate was coated with magnetic oxide on both sides to promote flatness. The formatted storage capacity was initially 65 to 81.6 kB with a linear density of 43.3 to 62.8 bits per millimeter (1100 to 1594 bits per inch) and a track density of 1.26 tracks per millimeter (32 tracks per inch), and the data were written onto one side of the disk only. A leadscrew accessing mechanism, turned by a rotary solenoid, was used to move the head across the disk to any selected position, or track. In addition, a second solenoid loaded the head into contact with the disk. This permitted the disk to rotate continuously while the head was loaded or unloaded from the disk, thus minimizing wear on the head and disk and eliminating rotational start-up time before data could be read.

The disk was permanently enclosed in a flexible but adequately stiff plastic jacket. This eliminated the need for any supporting pad or plate such as used on earlier flexible-disk drive systems. The inside of the jacket was lined with a non-woven fabric which protected the disk from abrasion and served as a wiping surface to clean the disk. The adoption of this enclosure was key in the widespread acceptance of the flexible disk and its drive. It provided the ease of handling and protection that are essential in the variety of applications that emerged.

Track registration, or radial alignment of the head on the disk, is a function of drive and disk materials, component and adjustment tolerances, and operating environment. Since the production unit could be rather tightly controlled for alignment, a write-wide and read-narrow system was adopted to allow for the differences that could be expected between the write unit in the factory and the read unit in the field. This disk and drive system formed the basis for most of the future, higher-performance flexible disks and drives.

3.1.2   Eight-Inch Drives

Flexible disk drives with 8-in-diameter disks were developed, mass produced, and used in a variety of applications during the 1970s (Engh, 1981).

3.1.2.1   Single-Head 8-in Drive.   A flexible 8-in disk drive, which eventually set a standard in the flexible-disk and drive industry, was announced in 1971 and shipped in 1973, incorporated in a key-to-flexible-disk data entry system. The formatted storage capacity was 243 kB with inner track linear density of 129 bits per millimeter (3268 bits per inch) and a track density of 1.89 tracks per millimeter (48 tracks per inch). The drive was a readwrite unit with improvements in nearly all functional parameters from the predecessor described above. The basic flexible disk was not changed, but its recording area was enlarged, and the recording density was heightened by increasing both linear bit density and radial track density. The increase in linear bit density was achieved by a reduction of coating thickness to 2.5 micrometers and improvements in the surface finish of the coating and substrate. A lubricant was applied to the disk to reduce wear on the medium and the head.

The disk had a single index hole located inside the innermost track. When the index hole was detected, it indicated the beginning of a track. Individual sectors were located at uniform angular positions from the index position and were identified by markers (address marks) recorded in the same way but with a special unique pattern as were data on the track. The use of the sector holes used on the early floppies is called *hard sectoring*. The use of the address marks, called *soft sectoring*, allows the user to vary the record length.

Once the flexible-disk drive system was used as a read-write device, media interchangeability became one of the most important performance requirements. Media interchangeability could be degraded by head-track misalignment caused by tolerances from parts, adjustments, and environmental effects. A tunnel-erase head was adopted to absorb these variations. The new track was written wide and trimmed narrow with tunnel erase gaps which erased either side of the track to clean out unwanted information. Figure 3.1 illustrates the structure of the tunnel-erase head.

A lead-screw mechanism was again used. In order to satisfy the required head-positioning accuracy, a Geneva mechanism, which is a mechanical conversion from continuous to intermittent rotary motion, was used to couple the lead screw to a low-cost 90° stepping motor instead of driving the screw directly by a rotary solenoid.

3.1.2.2 Dual-Head 8-in Drive. Replacing the pressure pad on the single-head drive with another recording head was a logical step in order to double the data

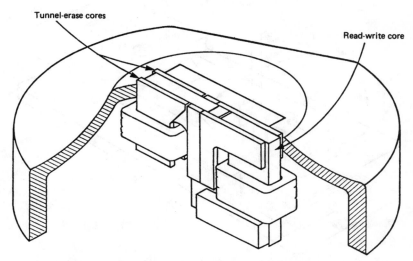

FIGURE 3.1 Construction of a tunnel-erase head for a single-head drive *(Engh, 1981)*.

storage capacity, and a new drive was announced and shipped in 1976. The formatted capacity was 568 kB with an inner track bit density of 134 bits per millimeter
(3408 bits per inch) and a track density of 1.89 tracks per millimeter (48 tracks per
inch). A new head and suspension technology similar to that of rigid disk drives was
developed to avoid media wear and to achieve satisfactory head-to-disk compliance. The downward compatibility which allowed the new drive to read and write
the existing one-sided flexible disk was kept, and the new disk dimensions were
identical to those of the previous type, except that the new disk jacket had the index
hole window at a different location to distinguish the two types.

Simply replacing the felt pad on the single-head drive with another recording
head did not satisfy head-to-disk compliance and caused wear of the medium. Both
the head carriage and the head contact surface were modified to solve the problem.
The head contact surface was like a catamaran in that it had a pair of flat surfaces
with a central relief between them. The relief dimensions and edges of the flat
surfaces were designed to maintain a proper air bearing beneath the head to provide signal stability and good wear performance and to prevent damage to the disk
during head loading. To avoid magnetic coupling through the disk, the read-write
cores were radially offset from each other by four tracks.

The head carriage had to maintain accurate head position and azimuth alignment, to control the pitch and roll accelerations contributed by the disk, to provide
high stiffness in the radial, tangential, and yaw directions, and to allow the heads to
be separated by at least 1.5 mm to remove the flexible disk. The carriage also had to
control head-bounce during load and unload cycles so that the disk was not damaged and so that uniform signals could be quickly established. Figure 3.2 illustrates
the suspension and load-spring structure. The head cores were the same as on the
single head drive.

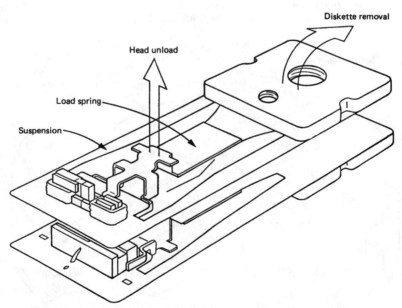

FIGURE 3.2   Head suspension and load spring for a dual-head drive *(Engh, 1981)*.

TABLE 3.1 Specifications of an 8-in Dual-Head Double-Density Drive

Unformatted disk capacity	1604 kB
Formatted disk capacity	1212 kB
Heads	2
Read-write gap length, width	1.9 μm, 330 μm
Erase gap length, width	3.0 μ, 170 μm
Read-write to erase span	850 μm
Data transfer rate	500 kb/s
Inner-track bit density	268 b/m (6816 b/in)
Track density	1.89 t/m (48 t/in)
Tracks	154
Encoding	MFM
Rotational speed	360 rpm
Access time	8.2 ms track-to-track
Accessing mechanism	Guide rods and band-capstan stepping motor
Actuator	Stepping motor

3.1.2.3. Dual-Head Double-Density 8-in Drive.   A year after the announcement of the dual-head drive, a new drive doubled the capacity by using modified-frequency-modulation encoding (MFM) instead of frequency-modulation encoding (FM). The formatted capacity was 1.2 MB with the doubled linear density of 268 bits per millimeter (6816 bits per inch) and the same track density of 1.89 tracks per millimeter (48 tracks per inch).

Improvements in encoding were coupled with improvements in heads and read electronics. The erase core gaps were deliberately not parallel to the read-write core gap to minimize the coupling of adjacent-track magnetic transitions into the read-write core. The read-write core gap was reduced to 1.9 μm in order to record the smaller flux transition at this higher bit density.

The use of modified frequency modulation doubled the data rate to 500 kb/s, thereby reducing the bit cell duration to 2 μs. The main issue was how to cope with peak-shift problems caused by a pair of closely packed adjacent bits. There are two ways to compensate for the peak shift: write precompensation and read post-compensation (Harman, 1981). The latter is a peaking filter technique which was adopted on the drive to compensate for loss in recording channel bandwidth due to head and medium effects. The filter consisted of an underdamped, second-order, low-pass stage with a resonance frequency above that of the recording channel. This provided a high-frequency boost in the channel response, resulting in broader bandwidth and reduced peak shift. The filter was switched on only for the inner tracks, where the bit density is higher. The specifications for 8-in dual-head double-density drive are shown in Table 3.1.

3.1.3 Five-and-One-Quarter-Inch Drives

In 1976, a 5.25-in flexible-disk drive was announced with the aim of achieving the compactness of a cassette tape recorder and the performance of a conventional disk drive. This size became very widely used, keeping pace with and helping the growth of personal computers.

3.1.3.1   Single-Head 5.25-in Drive.   The track density adopted was the same 1.89 tracks per millimeter as the larger diameter drives. The rotational speed was reduced from 360 to 300 rpm, and the transfer data rate was halved to 125 kb/s in order to lower the inner-track bit density. This density had been increased, compared with the 8-in disk, because of the small diameter of the new drive. The adopted bit density of 102 bits per millimeter (2581 bits per inch) was lower than the 129 bits per millimeter of the 8-in single-head drive, resulting in an 81 kB formatted data storage capacity. A low-cost spiral cam mechanism was used to position the head (Sec. 3.2.2), an easier task for the 5.25-in drive because of the decreased hygroscopic dimensional change of the smaller diameter disk.

3.1.3.2   Dual-Head 5.25-in Drive.   As in the case of the 8-in drive, the formatted capacity of the 5.25-in drive was increased to 328 kB by adding another head, doubling the bit density with modified frequency modulation encoding, and increasing the number of cylinders from 35 to 40. The down head on a 5.25-in dual-head drive was usually fixed rigidly, or with small gimbals, to the head carriage, instead of using the flexible mounting of the 8-in dual-head drives. This configuration had fewer components and adjustments and gave a higher yield of head-carriage assembly, but still provided enough head-to-disk compliance because of the improved dynamic stability of the smaller diameter disk.

3.1.3.3   High-Track-Density Drive.   The absolute hygroscopic and thermal expansion of a 5.25-in disk is smaller than that of an 8-in disk. This allows an increase in the track density, while using a low-cost stepping motor without a closed-loop servo. After several drives were developed with track densities of 3.94, 5.67, and 3.78-tracks-per-millimeter (100, 144, and 96 tracks per inch), the last track density became popular because the drive could also read a disk recorded on a 1.89 tracks-per-millimeter drive (Brar, 1981; Hashimoto and Yaskawa, 1982).

3.1.3.4   High-Linear-Density 5.25-in Drive.   In 1981, a new 5.25-in flexible-disk drive was developed having the same performance as an 8-in dual-head double-density drive (Adachi and Yano, 1983). The track density was increased to 3.78-track-per-millimeter (80 cylinders). The rotational speed was increased from 300 to 360 rpm and the data transfer rate from 250 to 500 kb/s. As a result, the inner-track linear density had to be raised from 233 to 380 bits per millimeter (5922 to 9646 bits per inch). The high linear density was achieved mainly by a reduction of coating thickness to 1.2 μm and a change of coating material to cobalt-modified ferric oxide, which has higher coercivity. Table 3.2 shows the differences between the high density 5.25-in disk and the conventional one. The height of the high-density drive was reduced to 40 mm (1.6 in). Using this drive, the user could put more data in a small box and use resources already developed for 8-in drives, including software and controllers. In addition to these attributes, the drive could be made compatible with a conventional 5.25-in drive by changing the write current and either the spindle motor speed or the transfer rate. Table 3.3 shows the specifications of typical 5.25-in flexible-disk drives.

3.1.4   Three-and-One-Half-Inch Disk Drives

In the early 1980s several different drives were developed to use small diameter disks. The only surviving diameter is 3.5 in, but other diameters of 2.0, 2.5, 2.8, 3.25, and 4.0 in were explored. The 3.5-in drive was announced in 1980 and,

TABLE 3.2 Comparison of 5.25-in High-Density Disk and Conventional Disks

	High density	Conventional
Material	$Co-\gamma\text{-}Fe_2O_3$	γFe_2O_3
Coating thickness, μm	1.2	2.5
Coercivity, kA/m	50	21
(Oe)	(630)	(270)
Residual flux density, mWb/m^2	76	69
(G)	(760)	(690)
Squareness ratio	0.6	0.6
Half pulse width, μm	3.1	4.3
Saturation current, mA	12	7
Output amplitude, mV	1.7	1.2
Resolution, %	82	57
Overwrite, dB	-34	-34

SOURCE: Adachi and Yano (1983).

TABLE 3.3 Specifications of 5.25-in Flexible-Disk Drives

	Single head, single density	Dual head, double density	Dual head, double density, double track density	Dual head, high density, double track density
Capacity, kB/disk[†]				
Unformatted	109.4	500	1000	1604
Formatted	80.6	327.6	655	1262
Sectors/track	18	16	16	8
Transfer rate, kb/s	125	250	250	500
Bit density, b/m (b/in)	102 (2581)	231 (5876)	233 (5922)	380 (9646)
Track density, t/m (t/in)	1.89 (48)	1.89 (48)	3.78 (96)	3.78 (96)
Cylinders	35	40	80	77
Tracks	35	80	160	154
Encoding	FM	MFM	MFM	MFM
Rotational speed, rpm	300	300	300	360
Access time track-to-track, ms	40	5	3	3

[†]The formatted capacity varies depending upon the format and the number of sectors per track.

although it was a single-head drive, the formatted data storage capacity was 322 kB, close to that of a 5.25-in dual-head double-density drive (Katoh et al., 1981). The small diameter and the use of a metal hub allowed a high track density of 5.31 tracks per millimeter (135 tracks per inch) and 70 tracks on one side of the disk. The disk was encased in a hard plastic jacket which did not bend like the 8-in and 5.25-in soft jackets and incorporated a shutter to protect the disk surface, as shown in Fig. 3.3. As the product evolved, the rotational speed was changed from 600 to 300 rpm, the transfer rate was reduced from 500 to 250 kb/s, a dual-head drive was added, and the number of tracks was increased to 80 for a capacity of 1 MB (740-kB formatted).

The next step in 3.5-in drive development was that the inner-track linear density

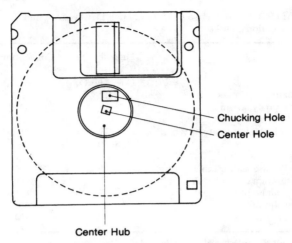

Chucking Hole
Center Hole

Center Hub

FIGURE 3.3 Hard plastic 3.5-in disk cartridge showing shutter that closes over the head-accessing window to protect the
disk surface.

was increased to 558 bits per millimeter (14,183 bits per inch), which was achieved
on a disk coated to a thickness of 1 μm with high-coercivity particles. This disk
format, with a capacity of 1.6 MB (1.2-MB formatted) is a standard floppy format
for Japanese personal computers. A further density increase to 685 b/mm (17.4 kb/
in) proved possible with this medium which resulted in a drive and cartridge with 2-
MB (1.44-MB formatted) capacity. The 2 MB drive and cartridge became the
interchangeable media standard and most of the floppy disk drives today can read
and write the 1 MB and 2 MB disk formats.

3.1.5   Other 3.5-in Developments

A 3.5-in disk drive using barium ferrite (BaFe) disks was developed and started
shipping in 1990. With a metal-in-gap (MIG) head, a bit density of 1372 kb/mm (34.8
kb/in.) was achieved, giving a capacity of 4 MB (2.88-MB formatted). The head in
this drive has an additional metal layer in the gap with low-saturation magnetization.
This gives the small effective gap needed for reading high-density media but, when
writing, the metal saturates providing the larger effective gap needed to write the
thicker low-density media. In combination with improved equalization, this has
enabled a series of drive improvements with full read and write compatibility between capacities of 4, 2, and 1 MB. The drive has not been not well accepted because
of its higher cost. The acceptance of any higher capacity products based on the
standard 3.5-in cartridge for widespread use will remain uncertain until cost expecta-
tions and industry-wide standards are determined. Specifications for the 1, 1.6, 2,
and 4 MB drives and formats are shown in Table 3.4

3.1.5.1   Other 3.5-in Formats.   A drive based on the original 3.5-in double-headed
mechanism, but with a variable-speed spindle motor to keep constant linear density, and using a GCR RLL (0,2; 4, 5) modulation code, was developed for use in
Apple® computers in the early 80s. This format stores 800 kB (formatted).

TABLE 3.4 Specifications of 3.5-in Flexible-Disk Drives

	Extra High Density (ED)	High Density (HD)	High Density (HD)	Normal Density (DD)
Capacity, kB/disk				
Unformatted	4,000	2,000	1,600	1,000
Formatted[†]	2,881	1,475	1,229	737
Data transfer rate (kb/s)	1,000	500	500	250
Innermost track bit density	1,373	686	572	343
b/mm (bpi)	(34,868)	(17,434)	(14,528)	(8,717)
Rotation speed (rpm)	300	300	360	300
Tracks/disk	160	160	160	160
Track density, t/mm (tpi)	5.31	5.31	5.31	5.31
	(135)	(135)	(135)	(135)
Average seek time (ms) (includes settling time)	94	94	94	94
Track-to-track time	3	3	3	3
Settling time (ms)	15	15	15	15

[†]Formatted capacity varies depending upon the format and the number of sectors per track.

3.1.6 High-Capacity Floppy Drive Developments

Many other development efforts have concentrated on upgrading the capacity and performance of floppy drives, and some have resulted in commercially successful products. High-coercivity media, closed-loop servo head positioning, RLL codes, sampled read channels, advanced error-correction codes, Bernoulli stabilization of media, magnetic heads and suspensions copied from hard-disk drives, head and cartridge designs allowing increases in rotational speed, have all contributed to several generations of high-capacity and high-performance flexible disk drives. Those developments are discussed in detail in Sec. 3.7.

3.1.7 Summary of Floppy Drive Evolution

There have been three trends in the evolution of the flexible-disk drive: smaller size, lower cost, and higher storage density. The drive size has been shrunk in both width and height along with the disk diameter, as shown in Table 3.5. The lower height and the reduced footprint have been made possible by evolving more compact mechanisms, including the head-carriage assembly, actuator, spindle motor, head loading and disk clamping mechanisms, and head-carriage-actuator coupling. Drive unit cost

TABLE 3.5 Shrinking Drive Size

Disk size	Drive height
8 in (203 mm)	114 → 57 mm
5.25 in (130 mm)	82.6 → 53 → 41 → 33.5 → 28.5 mm
3.5 in (89 mm)	51 → 41 → 35 → 25 mm → 15 mm

declined from a few hundred dollars for early 5.25-in drives to less than $20 for 3.5-in drives. Because of the concentration of engineering effort on cost reduction, and the need to maintain downward compatibility with previous drives, storage capacity has been increased very slowly from the 65 kB (formatted) of an early (1970) 8-in drive to the 2.88 MB (formatted) of the 3.5-in drive in 1989.

All the flexible-disk drives described above and in use today use essentially the same principle of design as the 8-in single- and dual-head drives of the 1970s. The track density is limited mainly because of anisotropic thermal and hygroscopic expansion and contraction of the polyethylene terephthalate substrate, in conjunction with open-loop head positioning using low-cost stepping motors. The rotational speed and, hence, the data transfer rate are much slower compared with those of rigid-disk drives owing to the in-contact head-disk interface and the method of supporting the rotating medium. The magnetic media used in floppy disks has also not changed since the early 1980s, the exception being the barium ferrite media used in the 4 MB (2.88 MB formatted) 3.5-in drives. The bulk of the industry development efforts have been dedicated to reducing the cost and size of drives.

3.2   DRIVE MECHANISM

The elements of a flexible-disk drive can be classified into the following categories: heads and head-supporting mechanisms, head-positioning mechanisms, disk spindle mechanisms, head-loading mechanisms, disk protection mechanisms, data and control electronics, and status sensors.

3.2.1   Heads and Head-Supporting Mechanisms

Most floppy drives do not use a head positioning servo to locate a magnetic head on the desired track. When magnetic disks written in such open-loop drives are used for read-write exchange, a part of the old data may not be erased during the recording of new data if there is significant head-to-track misalignment. This offtrack condition is caused by several factors, including disk expansion and contraction. Without some compensation, the remnant of the old data would interfere with reading; a variety of head designs can be used to alleviate the problem, including write-wide and read-narrow, erase-wide and read-and-write-narrow, and erase-fringe; these are shown in Fig. 3.4a, b, and c. The erase-fringe system is the most popular for flexible-disk drives. Two types of erase-fringe systems, tunnel erase and straddle erase, are used on commercial flexible-disk drives. The core and gap configurations of these systems are shown in Fig. 3.5.

The tunnel-erase gaps are located at a distance of 600 to 900 μm from the read-write gap along the track, whereas the straddle-erase gaps are located on both sides of the read-write gap. The tunnel-erase gaps have less mutual inductance with the read-write gaps than do the straddle erase gaps and generate smaller unwanted signals when an offtrack causes them to pass over a recorded track. Therefore the tunnel-erase head has an advantage in signal-to-noise ratio. On the other hand, the straddle-erase head allows a shorter space between sectors and hence a higher data storage capacity because the erase current can be switched at the same time as the write current. The tunnel-erase head requires a delay in turning off the erase current after writing a sector, and this delay cuts down the effective data storage area.

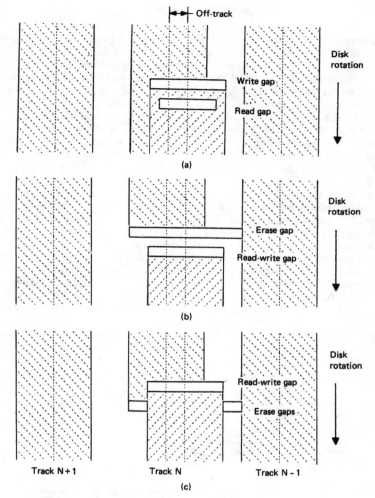

FIGURE 3.4 Types of head design. (*a*) Write-wide and read-narrow; (*b*) erase-wide, write-narrow, and read-narrow; (*c*) erase-fringe.

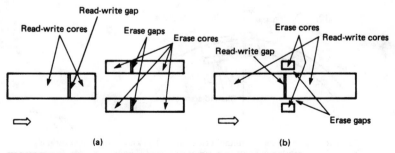

FIGURE 3.5 Head core and gap configuration for (*a*) a tunnel-erase head and (*b*) a straddle-erase head. Arrows indicate direction of medium motion.

The tunnel-erase head has become the dominant form and provides better signal-to-noise ratio at lower cost, especially with high track density or narrow-track heads. Two mechanical improvements can be incorporated with this type of head. The first, the azimuth head, has both the read-write gap and the erase gaps placed along the circular track. As shown in Fig. 3.6a, the inner side of a track is erased too much and the outer side is not erased enough with a conventional tunnel-erase head. The second improvement is the skewed erase gaps, which have some small angle with the read-write gap as shown in Fig. 3.6b. Each portion of these skewed erase gaps generates a signal with a different phase so that the combined current in the erase coils is small because of the cancellation effect. As a result, the mutually induced current in the read-write coil is also reduced.

As the track width became narrower, a ferrite head with similar construction to a video head was used, especially on a sub-5.25-in drive. The conventional laminated alloy head is difficult to manufacture for very narrow track widths. Using video head techniques, a wide ferrite tip is narrowed at the gap to make the necessary gap width as shown in Fig. 3.7. A read-write core and erase cores are molded in a button-shape body or a T-shape body and finished in a spherical surface for use in a single-head drive. A felt pad is pushed against the disk and the spherical head surface to keep them in contact, as shown in Fig. 3.8. In a dual-head configuration, a magnetic core assembly is molded in a ceramic slider, and the surface is finished flat as shown in Fig. 3.9. The up-head slider and the down-head slider are assembled so that the read-write cores are radially offset from each other by a few tracks to avoid magnetic coupling through the disk. The displacement is usually four

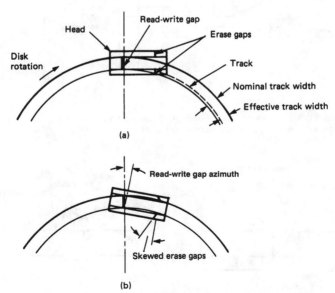

FIGURE 3.6 Types of tunnel-erase head tracking. (*a*) Conventional head; (*b*) azimuth head with skewed erase gaps (*Takahashi, 1984*).

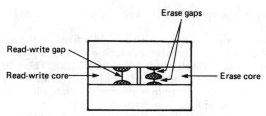

FIGURE 3.7 Ferrite tunnel-erase head core and gap configuration, showing how the core is narrowed at the gaps to provide the required widths for read-write and erase.

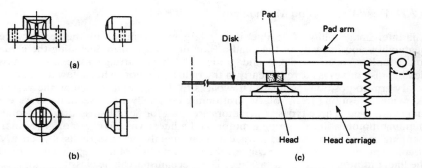

FIGURE 3.8 Single-head slider and carriage. (*a*) T-shaped body; (*b*) button-shaped body; (*c*) felt pad and arm used to promote head-disk contact *(Takahashi, 1984)*.

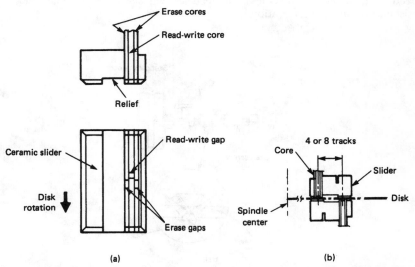

FIGURE 3.9 Dual-head slider. (*a*) Construction showing position of head; (*b*) disposition of sliders on opposite sides of a disk *(Tatsumi and Sakai, 1979)*.

tracks for relatively low track density and eight tracks for high track density as shown in Fig. 3.9.

The head slider of a single-head drive is rigidly fixed to the head carriage. The up-head slider of a dual-head drive is mounted on a gimbal spring suspension which allows tangential motion as well as pitching and rolling. There are three types of suspension for the down-head slider of a dual-head drive: a fully flexible suspension like the up head, a partially flexible suspension which allows only pitching and rolling, and a rigid suspension as in a single-head drive. The first configuration has better compliance with a disk than others and causes less wear owing to a low loading force of 5 to 10 g. However it is more expensive because of complexity and difficulty in adjustment.

3.2.2   Head-Positioning Mechanism

The interchangeability of flexible disks is largely determined by the accuracy, repeatability, and linearity of the head-positioning mechanism, including the actuator, coupling, head carriage, and guide. The head-carriage assembly of most flexible-disk drives is moved linearly in the radial direction, while a few drives use a rotary arm to position the head. Drawbacks to the rotary arm include the varying skew angle resulting from rotary positioning, especially when separate erase elements are used. Three types of actuators are used for flexible-disk drives: a rotary stepping motor, a linear stepping motor, and a linear voice-coil motor. The rotary stepping motor is by far the most common, mainly because of its low cost. A coupling mechanism is used to convert the rotary motion of the stepping motor into the linear motion of the head carriage. The mechanisms can be classified into three types: lead screw, band capstan, and spiral cam. Figures 3.10 through 3.13 illustrate these mechanisms. The spiral cam has a slight advantage in cost, but it is slow. The band capstan, especially the split-band capstan, coupling is widely used for its high speed, accuracy and compactness. The lead screw has advantages in accuracy and resistance to shock and vibration.

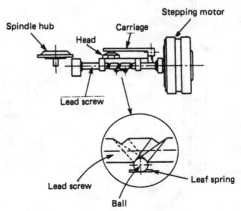

FIGURE 3.10   Lead-screw and ball-positioning mechanism *(Takahashi, 1984).*

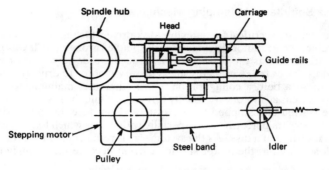

FIGURE 3.11 Loop-band-positioning mechanism *(Takahashi, 1984).*

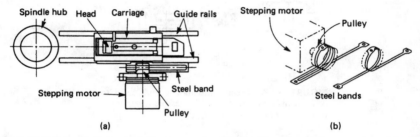

(a)

(b)

FIGURE 3.12 Split-band-positioning mechanism. (*a*) Plan view; (*b*) types of steel bands *(Takahashi, 1984).*

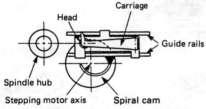

FIGURE 3.13 Spiral-cam-positioning mechanism *(Takahashi, 1984).*

3.2.3 Head-Loading Mechanism

Since the flexible disk is a removable medium and the head-disk contact limits its life, a head loading and unloading mechanism is necessary. There are two ways to load two heads, or a head and a pad, against a disk: immediate loading on disk insertion and independent loading by an actuator. The latter method usually uses a solenoid as an actuator which causes the heads to load onto a disk only when reading or writing data, thus prolonging disk life. Most low-cost drives load the heads immediately when a disk is inserted and clamped, thus eliminating the cost and heat of a solenoid. The spindle motor is turned off to minimize the disk wear when the drive is not in read-write operation. Although independent loading has an advantage in having a loading time of 30 to 50 ms compared with motor start time of 200 ms to 2 s, the speed profile of loading and unloading must be carefully designed to avoid excessive disk wear.

3.2.4 Disk Spindle and Clamping Mechanism

Disk speed stability is critical for a flexible-disk drive which uses frequency modulation recording. An ac motor driving the disk spindle through a belt was popular on early 8-in drives, but as the drive size was reduced, a dc servo motor was widely applied. Most drives today use a brushless dc servo motor to drive the disk spindle directly without a belt, a configuration which eliminates maintenance of brushes and belts. Whereas ac motors are usually turned on while the system power is on, dc motors are started and stopped by the system. Therefore, dc motor start time is important for system performance, especially with drives which load heads immediately upon insertion of a disk. As the system size is reduced, the reduction of power consumption as well as the motor starting current become increasingly important.

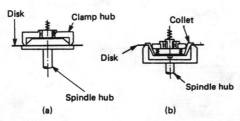

FIGURE 3.14 Direct clamping methods used to connect (*a*) 8-in and (*b*) 5.25-in flexible disks to the drive shaft *(Takahashi, 1984)*.

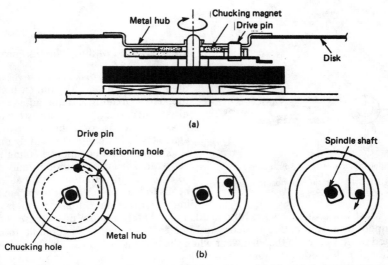

FIGURE 3.15 Magnet chucking used in 3.5-in drives. (*a*) Metal hub and chucking magnet; (*b*) process of positioning a disk *(Takahashi, 1984)*.

Disk clamping, accuracy, and security are additional factors in achieving disk interchangeability. Drives for 8-in or 5.25-in disks clamp the center hole of a disk between a metal spindle hub and a metal clamp hub or a plastic collet as shown in Fig. 3.14. Most sub-5.25-in flexible disks are incorporated with a metal or plastic hub at the center. Drives for these disks have a thin spindle pin and a self-indexing pin to chuck and rotate the disk hub instead of a wide center hole. Although this center hole represents a low-cost system, it is subject to damage, and it is difficult to keep the eccentricity error within 10 μm. To minimize these problems, clamping speed must be slow and clamping travel must be long despite the restriction of ever-shrinking drive height. Two possible improvements are to use absolute vertical clamping instead of rotary motion, and to rotate the collet or the hub during clamping. The 3.5-in flexible disk has a hard metal hub at the center of the disk which is captured by the spindle with a magnet as shown in Fig. 3.15. In this way stress against the disk is avoided.

3.3 HEADS

The magnetic design of a head for a flexible-disk drive is no different in principle from that of other digital recording and reproducing heads. What characterizes the flexible-disk drive head is its in-contact head-disk interface.

3.3.1 Head Design Configurations

Most flexible-disk head cores are of the ring type, although in practice they are made in two or three pieces as shown in Fig. 3.16. These pieces are usually bonded with glass, which fills in the read, write, or erase gap. The same single core is used for both read and write functions on most flexible-disk drives. The reasons why separate sets of read cores and write cores are not used as on magnetic tape drives are as follows: (1) a single core lowers cost, (2) read-after-write verification can be done within 200 ms because of the circular tracks, and (3) there is difficulty in keeping two gaps aligned at a high track density.

3.3.1.1 Tunnel-Erase Head. Two erase gaps are located 600 to 900 μm downstream of the read-write gap so that they trim the written track fringe and a part of any unwanted data which was not overwritten by the write flux. The distance

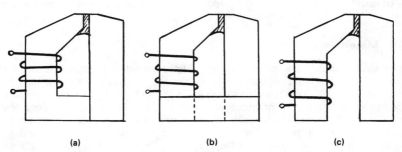

(a)   (b)   (c)

FIGURE 3.16 Types of head core structure. (*a*) Butt-joint; (*b*) overlap; (*c*) open.

decreases the mutual inductance between the erase gaps and the read-write gap and reduces the interference from the erase gaps, which would impair the read signal. On the other hand, this distance requires a longer sector gap, which separates sectors and absorbs sector length variations. As a result, the effective, or formatted, data storage capacity is sacrificed.

The erase gaps may cause asymmetry on the read signal owing to their dc magnetic induction. With an off-track condition, the erase gaps may also degrade the signal-to-noise ratio because of mutually induced signals in the read-write coil caused by the erase gaps picking up flux from an adjacent recorded track. This effect can be reduced by skewed erase gaps.

Thin cores are usually laminated to make a set of flexible-disk drive head cores and gaps. As the track width narrows, especially on sub-5.25-in drives, the width becomes as thin as 120 μm for read-write cores and 60 μm for erase cores. A new bulk-type core, similar to that used on video heads, has resolved the yield and low-voltage output problem of the laminated head. A wide ferrite tip is narrowed at the gap position to make the necessary gap width of the bulk-type head.

3.3.1.2 Straddle-Erase Head. In this configuration, two erase poles are laid out at each side of a read-write core. As the erasing flux goes from one pole to the other at right angles to the writing flux, the distance between the read-write gap and the erase pole tips can be made close to zero. The delay for turning off the erase current after the write current can therefore be minimized. On the other hand, this configuration does not erase the track fringe as sharply as the tunnel-erase head, and the erasing flux through the read-write core may degrade the recording resolution and cause asymmetry.

3.3.2 Pole-Tip Geometry

The read-write gap length governs the field distribution in the writing process and limits the resolution in the reading process. The read-write gap width governs the width of the recorded track. The erase gap width together with the read-write gap width govern the track pitch. Assuming that the read circuit is able to detect recorded signals down to half-track width with enough signal-to-noise ratio, the most effective gap width distribution is two-thirds of the track pitch for the read-write gap and one third for each erase gap. This configuration allows an off-track condition up to one-third of the track pitch from the recorded track center, and is shown in Fig. 3.17 for typical track pitches. The read-write gap length is usually chosen to be comparable with the disk coating thickness and about one-half of the flux transition length. The erase gap length is comparable with the read-write gap.

3.3.3 Materials

A core material for a disk drive head should have the following characteristics: high permeability at high frequencies; high saturation magnetization; low coercivity; high resistivity; high resistance to wear, shock, and chipping; and easy processing.

Manganese-zinc ferrite or nickel-zinc ferrite are usually used for flexible-disk head cores. These materials have higher permeability at high frequencies and higher resistance to wear than permalloy. As the recording density on the flexible-disk increases, manganese-zinc ferrite has replaced nickel-zinc ferrite, which is easy to process but inferior in overall magnetic characteristics. The magnetic cores on

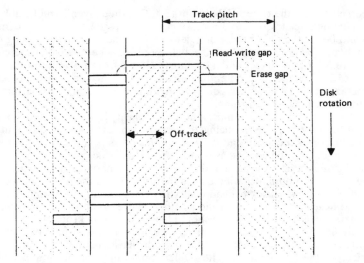

FIGURE 3.17 Track geometry resulting from a tunnel-erase head in which the width of the read-write gap is two-thirds and the width of each erase gap is one-third of the track pitch.

sub-5.25-in flexible-disk drives require very fine processing because of the narrow track width; here, single-crystal manganese-zinc ferrite, in place of polycrystalline ferrite, has the advantage of easier mechanical processing.

The head core is molded in a ceramic body, or slider, which supports the core and forms an adequate mechanical head-disk interface. A slider material should have wear properties and a thermal expansion coefficient similar to those of the magnetic core material.

3.4 MEDIA

The recording medium has played the most important role in the success of the flexible-disk drive system and has evolved to satisfy the following demands from the small-system user: data storage capacity, reliability, rewriting capability, durability, cost, and convenience (Bate et al., 1981, 1983).

3.4.1 Coating

The coating determines the magnetic properties and the in-contact interface with the head. Particulate coatings are widely used, although continuous magnetic films are expected to be an alternative for higher recording density, subject to solving problems such as poor reproducibility of the film, poor wear resistance, and corrosion resistance.

Particulate coatings consist of magnetic particles held in a polymer binder. The most popular magnetic particle is γ-Fe_2O_3, as in all other magnetic recording media.

The coercivity is on the order of 24 kA/m (300 Oe) on conventional flexible disks, and the coating thickness is 2 to 3 μm. These two factors determine the demagnetization and hence the linear recording density. High-density media storing greater than 350 b/mm (9 kb/in) normally use cobalt-modified γ-Fe_2O_3, with a coercivity on the order of 50 A/m (630 Oe) and a coating thickness from 1.5 μm down to 0.9 μm for the 2-MB 3.5-in media. Contending media designs include very-high coercivity oxide media and metal particle media for longitudinal recording, and barium ferrite media for perpendicular recording.

The other factor which determines the linear density is the head-disk separation. Increasing density requires reducing the separation, otherwise the output signal amplitude becomes too small and the resolution suffers.

The roughness of the coating as well as the head surface plays one of the major roles in the separation; the higher the density, the smoother the coating surface must be. Yet too smooth a coating makes the friction and the torque unacceptably high and eventually causes a head-disk stiction problem, especially with drives which load heads into a disk regardless of read-write operation. These conflicting requirements mean that the surface should have a controlled roughness.

The binder holds lubricants as well as magnetic particles. The lubricants give a longer life to both disks and heads and may be dispersed in the binder or applied to the surface of the finished disk. The binder should not only have a capability of dispersing particles and lubricants, but also provide adhesive bonding to the substrate, otherwise a local adhesive failure will lead rapidly to massive failure. Improvements in such factors have given a remarkably long life to flexible disks which were originally seen as just an input medium with limited durability.

3.4.2 Substrate

Almost all flexible disk substrates are 76 μm thick films of polyethylene terephthalate (PET). This material has a nominal thermal expansion coefficient of 17×10^{-6}/°C and a nominal hygroscopic expansion coefficient of 6×10^{-6}/% relative humidity. The mistracking caused by thermal expansion may be compensated with proper mechanical components and design, but the hygroscopic expansion cannot. The anisotropy of these properties makes compensation impossible without a track-following servo. The achievable number of tracks on a flexible disk are thus on the order of 80 tracks per surface. The track densities are 1.89 tracks per millimeter for 8-in disks, 3.78 tracks per millimeter for 5.25-in disks, and 5.31 tracks per millimeter for 3.5-in disks. The maximum data storage capacity with an open-loop positioning system is in the same range regardless of the disk size provided the magnetic recording system is designed to increase linear density as the diameter gets smaller. The anisotropy of the substrate comes not so much from the nature of the material but from the roll stretching during the manufacture of the film.

3.4.3 Jacket and Cartridge

The disk in the form of a double-coated substrate is encased in a soft jacket or a hard cartridge with liners between the coating surfaces and the inner surfaces of the container. The jacket or the cartridge with the liners perform the following functions: disk protection, rotation stabilization, disk cleaning and handling convenience.

Flexible disks of 8-in and 5.25-in diameters are enclosed in a soft jacket, whereas most of the sub-5.25-in flexible disks, including 3.5-in disks, are encased in a hard cartridge, The soft jacket made of polyvinyl chloride is inexpensive, but it is easily bent, and the disk surface and center hole are subject to damage during handling. The hard cartridge gives better protection along with a metal or plastic window shutter and a metal or plastic hub. These cartridges are provided with a write-protection notch at the edge or corner to indicate to the system whether the disk is write-protected. The liner is nonwoven fabric (polyester, rayon, or nylon), which cleans the disk surface and prevents contact between the disk and the harder jacket or cartridge. The soft jacket near the data window is pressed with a sponge pad to create a slight friction and hence stabilize the disk motion under the heads. The hard cartridge is provided with an internal plastic leaf spring for the same purpose.

3.5 DATA CHANNEL

3.5.1 Encoding

The most popular encoding scheme for flexible-disk drive systems is modified frequency modulation, except for early systems and low-cost systems, which use frequency modulation. Some advanced systems use the 2, 7 run-length-limited code for 50% more data storage capacity with the same flux reversal density.

The reasons for the popularity of modified frequency modulation are self-clocking capability, higher data density, and relatively simple encoding and decoding circuits. The frequency-modulation encoding scheme assigns 1s and bit cell boundaries (clock) to flux reversals, while 0s indicate no flux reversals. As each bit cell contains at least one flux reversal, self clocking is easy. The modified encoding is the same except that flux reversals occur at bit cell boundaries only when two adjacent bit cells contain 0s. As a result, the minimum time between flux reversals is twice as wide and the linear data storage density can be doubled without increasing flux reversal density on the disk. Also, the advantage of easy self clocking is maintained. Figure 3.18 shows these encoding schemes.

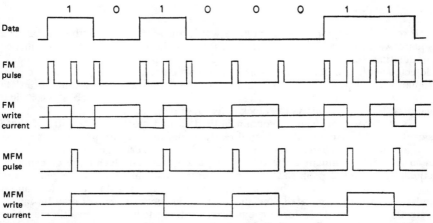

FIGURE 3.18 Comparison of frequency modulation (FM) and modified frequency modulation (MFM) encoding schemes.

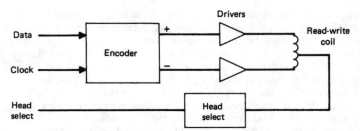

FIGURE 3.19　Basic block diagram of a write channel.

3.5.2 Writing

Data to be written on a flexible disk are usually coded in modified frequency modulation by the controller. The coded signal is transmitted to the write channel of a flexible-disk drive, where it energizes the head coils and creates reversals of the flux in the head core and, ultimately, of the remanent flux of the magnetic coating. Figure 3.19 shows the block diagram of a write channel.

Peak shift, which is caused by a pair of closely packed adjacent bits, is one of the major problems in high linear density recording. Peak shift is more critical to modified frequency modulation than to frequency modulation, because not every bit cell of the former contains a clock signal.

Two techniques are used to minimize peak shift: write-current adjustment and write precompensation. The peak shift occurs because of the superposition of the skirts of packed pulses. The effect of these skirts depends on the magnitude of the write current, which is usually reduced at inner tracks where the linear recording density is high. The directions of peak shifts are predictable from the data train, and write-precompensation techniques shift two adjacent bits in opposite directions to reduce the peak shifts when they are read.

3.5.3 Reading

The read channel converts the voltage waveform of the head output signal to a square waveform which should be the same as the original modified frequency modulation signal. The head output signal is amplified, equalized, and peak-detected with a differentiator and a zero-volt comparator to produce a digital signal, which is transmitted to a controller. The controller usually contains a data separator which separates data signals from clock signals by establishing a time window. Figure 3.20 shows the block diagram of a read channel.

As the read-write signals contain both data and clocks, peak shifts of these signals from their nominal position directly hinder data separation, or data recovery, and increase the error rate. Therefore, the equalizer is a critical factor in the read channel to minimize the effects of peak shifts. The technique of using an equalizer to reduce peak shift is also known as postcompensation, or *pulse* slimming. At the outer tracks the linear recording density is so low that the readout pulses are widely separated, and the zero-output between pulses may be falsely detected as a peak. Therefore the equalizer gain, or the filter bandwidth, may have to be switched according to track locations.

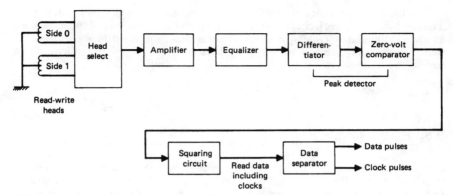

FIGURE 3.20 Basic block diagram of a read channel.

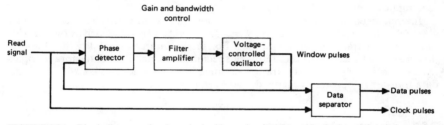

FIGURE 3.21 Block diagram of a phase-locked loop circuit to separate clock and data information.

As clock and data information are combined in bit streams in the flexible-disk coding system, they have to be separated to reproduce data streams. The separation is done by generating window pulses from the readout digital signals. A phase-locked loop (PLL) circuit is usually used to establish synchronization with sync bytes at the beginning of a data block and then to continue to generate window pulses. Figure 3.21 shows a block diagram of data separation using such a scheme. The phase-locked loop should have a rather high frequency response when establishing synchronization, but a lower frequency response when reading subsequent data in order to make itself immune to instantaneous bit phase variations such as peak shifts, asymmetries, and noises.

3.5.4 Error Detection

A cyclic redundancy check (CRC) is the typical error-detecting system for flexible-disk drive systems. The parity check is not practical for flexible disks because most errors are a burst type due to disk surface defects, rotational speed variation, and other causes. Error-correcting codes are not practical for low-cost flexible-disk drive systems, but if the error is a soft error, the data should be recovered at the subsequent reread, usually the next revolution.

The bit stream in a data block to be written on a disk is divided by a polynomial. The residual two bytes from the division are appended at the end of the data block as cyclic redundancy codes. In readback operation, the controller performs the same division and compares the check codes with the recorded two-byte check codes. The usual polynomial used with flexible-disk drive systems is

$$P(X) = X^{16} + X^{12} + X^5 + 1$$

3.6 PERFORMANCE

Data storage capacity on a disk and data read-write speed are the major performance characteristics of a flexible-disk drive system. The required data storage capacity and the chosen disk diameter determine the necessary areal density, which is the product of linear density and track density. The data read-write speed is determined by the track-positioning time, the disk rotational speed and the data transfer rate. Error rate and disk durability are also major performance criteria in real applications.

Interchangeability of disks is another important performance characteristic since a flexible-disk drive must read and write disks written by other drives over a wide range of temperatures and humidities. For media interchangeability, flexible-disk drives are well standardized in terms of specifications including data storage capacity, bit density, track density, track locations, index position, disk size, drive size, data transfer rate, rotational speed, and even error rate and access time.

3.6.1 Recording Performance

The recording performance of a flexible-disk drive is usually specified in terms of linear density, track density, and error rate. Typical densities and track densities are shown in Table 3.6. Error rate includes read-and-seek error rates. A typical read-error rate specification is one soft error per 10^9 bits read and one hard error per 10^{12} bits read. A *soft error* is an error recoverable by a reread operation. A *hard error* is

TABLE 3.6 Typical Recording Densities

Type	Linear density,[†] b/mm (b/in)	Track density, t/mm (t/in)
8 in	268 (6816)	1.89 (48)
5.25 in	231 (5876)	1.89 (48)
	233 (5922)	3.78 (96)
5.25 in, high density	379 (9646)	3.78 (96)
3.5 in	343 (8717)	5.31 (135)
3.5 in, high density	685 (17434)	5.31 (135)
3.5 in, extra high density	1378 (34868)	5.31 (135)

[†]Bit densities are for dual-sided double-density drives at their innermost track.

a permanent error caused by a disk surface defect. A typical seek-error rate specification is one per 10^6 seeks.

Although recording performance can be expressed by such specifications, quite a few parameters affect performance characteristics: amplitude, overwrite, resolution, peak shift, asymmetry, modulation, and window margin. The output amplitude from a head depends on the writing current once the head and other designs are fixed. The writing current is chosen at an optimum value which will produce high signal output (> 0.5 mV) and low peak shift over the recording frequency range and the disk coercivity range. On some drives the write current is switched to be lower at inner tracks where the density is higher and the pulses are crowded.

As flexible-disk drives have neither full-track erase heads nor a separate erase pass, old data must be overwritten with new data. Since it is easier to overwrite a high-frequency recorded signal with a low-frequency signal than the other way around, overwrite performance is specified as the level of the 1F (lowest recording frequency) signal remaining after overwriting with the 2F (highest recording frequency). The remaining signal level should be at least 30 dB below its original level on the innermost track where the density at 2F is the highest.

The *resolution* is defined as the ratio of the 2F to the 1F amplitude on the same track, usually the innermost track where the linear density is the highest. The resolution is optimized by means of an equalizer circuit in the read channel. The usual resolution (2F/1F amplitudes) is more than 80%.

When two adjacent readback pulses are close to each other not only is the amplitude reduced, but the timing of the peak is displaced as shown in Fig. 3.22. If the displacement, or peak shift, were as large as half the shortest nominal bit period, the peak would not be decoded correctly. Two techniques are used to reduce the peak shift: write precompensation and read postcompensation as described before. More fundamentally, the pulse width should be reduced, or in other words, the resolution should be increased. The maximum peak shift occurs in modified frequency modulation recording when the bit stream is a repetition of binary 110. Consequently, the

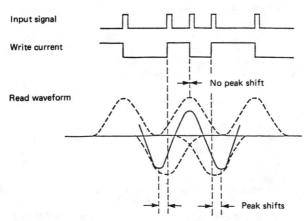

FIGURE 3.22 Illustrating peak shift, the displacement in time of closely spaced readback pulses.

hexadecimal 6DB6 which is binary 0110110110110110 is the worst-case pattern and is used to test for peak shift.

When a bit stream with an even period like a repetition of hexadecimal 0 or F is recorded on a flexible disk, the readback signal waveform should be symmetrical to the zero axis. An actual waveform might be distorted, and hence the digitized signal might have two adjacent pulses with uneven periods. This asymmetry is caused by distorted or unbalanced head coils, head cores, writing current, flux interference, and read channels (Lopez et al., 1981). This phenomenon degrades the window margin in a way which will be described later.

The readback signal envelope of an evenly recorded bit stream may have an amplitude fluctuation or modulation. The frequency of the modulation is lower than that of the recorded signal and is caused by undesirable magnetic particle orientation in the coating, disk-clamping eccentricity, head-disk spacing variation, and disk-speed fluctuation. Such modulation degrades the read-error rate.

As the read-write signal of flexible-disk drive systems contains both clock pulses and data pulses, the readback signal must be gated to produce separate clock signals and data signals. The gating signal is a square wave with a nominal pulse width (or window) which is 50% of the bit cell period. The data pulse or clock pulse should appear ideally at the middle of each window pulse. The data window or clock window (the inverted data window) is generated from the readback signal using a clock counter circuit or a phase-locked loop circuit.

The readback pulses may be early or late from their nominal position because of peak shift, asymmetry, noise, disk-speed variation, and other distortions in the read-write channels. Such pulse jitters will degrade the decoding capability of the flexible-disk drive system. The window margin is defined as the time left in the window after pulse jitter is accounted for. When the bit cell is 2 μs (data rate, 500 Kb/s), the nominal window width is 1 μs, and the window margin should be more than 0.3 μs to have a sufficiently low read-error rate.

3.6.2 Accessing Performance

The access time and data transfer rate determine the read and write speed of a flexible-disk drive system. The access time includes head-positioning time, head-settling time, head-loading time, and latency. The head-positioning time, or the seek time, is expressed in three ways: track-to-track, average and maximum. The track-to-track seek time, typically 3 to 10 ms, is the time for the head-positioning mechanism to move one track pitch. The average and maximum seek times are usually a multiple of the track-to-track time since most of the actuators are stepping motors driven at a fixed rate. The theoretical average of the number of cylinders for random seek is close to one-third of the total cylinder number. The maximum seek time is the track-to-track time multiplied by the total cylinder number minus one.

The head-settling time, and the head-load time if the head is loaded by a separate actuator, has to be accommodated before starting read-write operations. Even after the head is positioned completely at a track, it takes an average of half a disk revolution (latency) for the head to find the desired data. The data transfer rate is the speed at which a flexible disk drive system can transfer information, typically 250 and 500 kb/s. These rates are much slower than those of rigid-disk drives because of the lower rotational speed of flexible-disk drives.

3.6.3 Interchangeability

Interchangeability of disks is an important feature of the flexible-disk drive system. Interchangeability is affected by the track-positioning accuracy, the head-azimuth angle, and the index-positioning accuracy. On top of these factors, the recording formats and data layout on a track must be the same.

The track-positioning accuracy is indicated by offtrack errors which are caused by misalignment of the read-write heads, inaccuracies and backlash in the head-positioning mechanism, disk-clamping errors, thermal expansion or contraction of the drive and disk, and hygroscopic expansion or contraction of the disk. The capability to read a track with offtrack errors is a measure of the off-track window margin. Even on a precisely positioned track the interchangeability may be lost if the readinghead azimuth angle is too much different from that of the recording head. The index signal which shows the starting point of a track, or a sector on a hard-sectored disk, also plays an important role in interchangeability. When the index-positioning accuracy is low, there should be a longer allowance between the index timing and the first data.

3.7 ADVANCED DESIGN DEVELOPMENTS[†]

This section covers the advanced designs used to increase capacity and performance of floppy disk drives and media far beyond the capacity and performance of the standard 2 MB 3.5-in floppy disk. The technology used to increase the capacity and performance falls into four major categories: advanced flexible media, high performance head-to-disk interfaces (HDI), high density servos, and advanced recording channels.

3.7.1 Advanced Flexible Media

The areal density of a 2 MB 3.5-in disk is 2.35 Mbits/in^2. Flexible media supporting disk densities in excess of 100 Mbits/in^2 (Inaba et al., 1993) have been described in literature and are being used in a 100 MB 3.5-in floppy drive (Briggs, 1995).

Increasing the coercivity and decreasing the thickness of the recording layer are both effective ways to increase recording densities. Thinner magnetic coatings are desirable in combination with high coercivity because of smaller demagnetization, improved output at higher frequencies, and better overwrite characteristics. Low demagnetization due to thin layers allows for direct overwrite and simple single-gap magnetic heads. Double coating technology provides a solution to the problem of having a thinner active layer and at the same time solves the problem of increased head/media spacing caused by surface finish roughness of the thin magnetic coating. Figure 3.23 shows the cross-sectional views comparing conventional metal-particle media with double-coated thin metal-particle media. Thin-layer particulate recording media with a nonmagnetic smoothing layer have been developed using both metal and barium ferrite particles. While barium ferrite (BaFe) has a saturation magnetization of 0.2T(2000 G), about half of the saturation magnetization 0.4T(4000 G) of metal particle media, both produce about the same output at densities above

---

[†]Some material in this section and Figs. 3.26, 3.27 and 3.28 used with permission of Dr. John C. Briggs (Briggs, 1995).

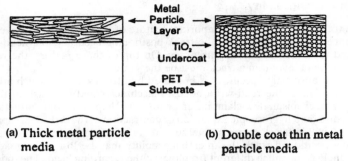

(a) Thick metal particle media

(b) Double coat thin metal particle media

FIGURE 3.23   Cross-sectional views comparing conventional metal particle media and double coated thin metal particle media.

3540 b/mm (90 Kbpi) (Saitoh et al., 1995). Advanced flexible disk recording is currently dominated by metal-particle (MP) media with particle lengths of 180 nm, a particle aspect ratio of 12, and a coercivity of approximately 120 kA/m (1500) Oe. Advanced MP++ and BaFe++ media that support areal densities of 300 Mbits/in^2 have been proposed (Speliotis, 1995). Metal evaporated tape (ME) which is commercially available for video tapes is not currently used in floppy disks due to poor tribological properties (Hashimoto et al., 1992).

3.7.2. High Performance Head/Disk Interface

As described in Sec. 3.2.1, in standard floppy drives, opposing heads clamp floppy media with relatively large force (up to 20 g). The heads have an area of approximately 4 × 6 mm and the large loading force, combined with relatively large head surface area, can cause media wear at high disk rotation speeds. The plastic jacket with liner, adopted for conventional flexible diskettes, may limit the speed at which the disk can be rotated because a frictional drag occurs when the speed is increased (Noble, 1974). In order to solve this problem two practical solutions have been implemented; media flying above the head (Bernoulli stabilization), and heads flying above stabilized centered rotating media (Briggs, 1995).

3.7.2.1 Bernoulli Stabilization for Flexible Disks.   The Bernoulli plate provides one way of overcoming frictional drag limitations and permits rotational velocities comparable with rigid-disk drives. When a flexible disk is rotated in proximity to a rigid, fixed surface, with ventilation provided at the disk hub, the disk adopts a stable form, flying at a separation from the plate that decreases toward the outside diameter. The case of a continuous flat plate has been analyzed (Pearson, 1961; Charbonnier, 1976). The basic mechanism is that the disk forms a vaneless impeller accelerating the air between disk and plate tangentially. For large initial separation, there is a reduction of pressure in the trapped volume through centrifugal pumping action, which moves the disk closer to the plate. Local stability is reached as the radial component of viscous drag increases with the narrowing gap and balances the local pressure gradient because of centripetal acceleration. The total flow of air, and hence the gap at any radius, is determined principally by the axial position of the hub with respect to the plate and the stiffness of the disk near the hub (Fig.

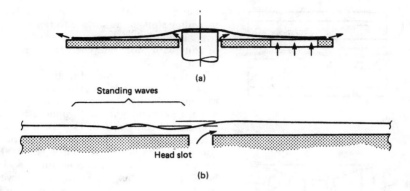

(a)

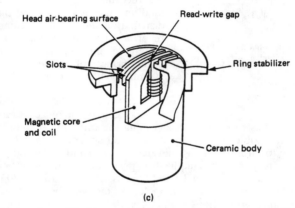

(c)

FIGURE 3.24 Bernoulli disk system. (*a*) The form taken by the medium over the Bernoulli plate with head removed, section through head slot; (*b*) same as (*a*) using annular section; (*c*) construction of the slotted head with ring stabilizer.

3.24*a*). Gaps of 0.15 mm are typical. The local separation is dominated by local viscous drag and is highly stable. Flow between disk and plate for all reasonable configurations is entirely laminar. The disk will follow any simple curvature of the plate provided bending of the disk at any point is limited to one direction.

In one practical application, a slot is cut in the plate through which the read-write head protrudes, and the slot provides an opportunity for additional air to be entrained and carried under the disk. The extra separation that results decays over one revolution of the disk and, at the approach side to the slot, standing waves are formed (Fig. 3.24*b*). The Bernoulli disk configuration has the potential to operate over a wide range of conditions. With a 14-in-diameter disk, rotational speeds of at least 3000 rpm are possible. In two products made using this concept with 8-in and 5.25-in disks, spindle speeds were 1500 and 1964 rpm, respectively. Conventional flexible-disk heads are not suitable for the high media velocities possible with the Bernoulli plate, because the formation of an air bearing on the surface gives excessive separation of the head from the medium. The separation can be reduced by

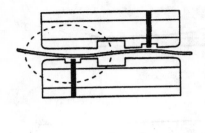

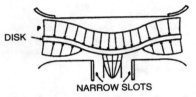

FIGURE 3.25 Double-head configuration with slotted air bearings.

increasing the curvature of the head, or by providing slots in the surface to relieve positive air-bearing pressures. A combination of slots with moderate curvature has been found to have advantages in reduced rates of wear and ease of manufacture.

Different methods for providing the force to couple the head to the disk without the use of a Bernoulli plate for primary stabilization have been devised. One of the more interesting is described here because of its commercial exploitation (White, 1990). By the use of slotted air bearings on opposing head sides the flexible medium is curved, creating a precise flying height relative to the recording gap. Figure 3.25 shows the medium, the head, and the pressure force distribution above the recording gap. At the recording gap, the medium flies approximately 75 nm (3 μin) above the gap. All other surfaces of the head are about 150—300 nm (6–12 μin) from the head.

3.7.2.2 Media Stabilization Using Centered Disks.
One of the biggest drawbacks of using flexible media has to do with overcoming the mechanical stability problems. When spinning a flexible disk, there is a critical speed, above which waves and resonances begin to form on the disk surface (Benson and Takahashi, 1991). Traditional floppies overcome media stabilization problems by operating below the critical speed. The critical speed for a 3.5-in floppy is estimated to be 770 rpm.

The nature of the vibration of spinning flexible disks has been extensively studied but is still poorly understood (Benson and Cole, 1991). The problem is generally overcome in disk drive products by providing some means to stabilize the rotating disk. An extreme example of this is stretched surface recording (SSR) (Benson and Takahashi, 1991). In SSR, two pieces of flexible media are stretched over a rigid frame and bonded in place. The membrane stresses on the disk cause the disk to be quite flat. However, this technique is fairly expensive and has never been commercialized.

Another media stabilization technique was found to simplify the development of the head-disk interface. The technique is called "centered disk stabilization," and is illustrated in Fig. 3.26. In this technique, the spinning disk is centered between two stationary plates. With the airflow pattern generated in this structure, the disk flies stably through the head access slot area of the cartridge. Furthermore, the mechanical operating window for the head/disk interface (HDI) can be made much larger than with the Bernoulli plate technique (Briggs, 1995). The size of the head access slot is critical to the stability of the disk. With certain head access slot geometries, the disk exhibits bistable, and "snapping" modes of behavior (Ma and Jones, 1995). Additionally, the slot geometry affects the tendency of the disk to be attracted to the suspensions. With the combination of centered disk stabilization and a small head access slot, the disk is found to be quite stable up to at least 3000 rpm.

3.7.2.3 Using Winchester Heads and Suspensions.
Early attempts to use Winchester heads and suspensions with flexible media had proven them to be an unreliable

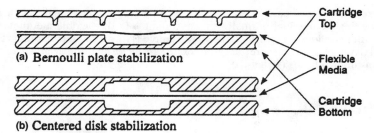

(a) Bernoulli plate stabilization

(b) Centered disk stabilization

Cartridge Top

Flexible Media

Cartridge Bottom

FIGURE 3.26 Bernoulli plate stabilization compared with centered-disk stabilization. These cross-sectional views of the cartridge show that the media tends to dip down into the head access slot with the Bernoulli plate technique.

combination. It was difficult to get good signals from both heads at the same time and maintain good head/disk contact. This is because flexible media tend to have more vertical runout than could be accommodated by hard-disk heads and suspensions. The breakthrough came when nano-sliders (50% sliders) and suspensions, developed for the hard-disk industry, were modified to work on flexible media. The small size (2.00 × 1.60 × 0.46 mm) and light weight of the nanosliders allowed them to track the vertical runout of flexible disks while maintaining good signals from both heads. Taper/flat two-rail composite sliders were found to work well with flexible media. The sliders were designed to fly at about 100 nm above the surface of a hard disk. A cross-cut in the rails brings the slider down into contact with the flexible disk surface, at least at the trailing edge of the rails. The resulting flying-height is about 40 nm, as shown in Fig. 3.27.

To get good signals from both heads, the nanosliders must be properly oriented

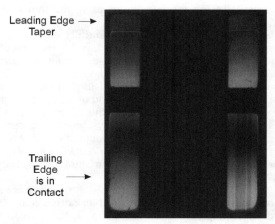

Leading Edge →
Taper

Trailing
Edge
is in →
Contact

FIGURE 3.27 White light image of a nanoslider "flying" on a medium at 3000 rpm.

and directly opposite each other. The air bearing created by a single slider flying over the flexible medium normally creates a dimple in the flexible medium. However, with two sliders properly oriented, no dimple is formed in the medium. Thus a critical parameter for this interface to operate satisfactorily is the accuracy of alignment of the two heads (Briggs, 1995).

3.7.3 High-Density Servos

Anisotropic expansion of a polyester substrate when subjected to changes of temperature and humidity is the principal limitation of track density in flexible-disk devices (Greenberg et al., 1977). Track-following servos can be applied to flexible disks to compensate for expansion and distortion, as commonly used in rigid-disk drives. By this means it is practical to increase the track density up to 100 t/mm (2500 t/in), limited only by servo performance and read signal-to-noise ratio. Several methods of encoding the track position on the medium have been developed. These include magnetically recorded servo information (Matsukawa et al., 1991; Yoshiura et al., 1991; Seo et al., 1994), and embossed grooves between the tracks detected by an optical sensor (Farnsworth et al., 1992).

Three different types of servo systems have made their way into commercial high-capacity flexible-disk drives: buried servo, optical servo and sector servo. Buried servos work by writing continuous low-frequency tones on each disk before it is shipped from the factory. The phase information from the two different sides of the disk are used to create a position error signal (PES). The PES is then used to move the heads onto the desired track. This servo technique has the advantage of providing a continuous PES signal. This, in principle, makes it possible to design a higher-bandwidth servo compared with sector servo systems. One of the drawbacks to the buried servo method is that a separate servo head is used. This adds cost to the read/write heads and necessitates the drive periodically checking the relative alignment of the servo head and the read/write head to correct for thermal expansion in the head. Furthermore, the low-frequency signals used for the servo information require thick magnetic coatings. This makes it more difficult to capitalize on the benefits of using the thin coatings that were discussed in Sec. 3.7.1.

Optical servos use a laser to "read" mechanically embossed grooves in the surface of the floppy disk. These grooves are produced during manufacturing either by using a mechanical embossing process or a laser cutting process. The drive uses the difference in reflection between the grooved and ungrooved areas of the disk to create a PES signal, as shown in Fig. 3.28a. Optically servoed drives are burdened with the additional cost, weight, and complication of an optical system in addition to the magnetic system. As is the case with the buried servo, periodic realignment between the magnetic heads and the optical system is necessary. Optical servo drives have been designed to be downward compatible with low-capacity 3.5-in drives by adding a separate gap to read and write 720 kB/1.44 MB floppies. Also a linear optical scale is needed to find the tracks on these low-capacity cartridges, as shown in Fig. 3.28a.

Sector servo techniques used in high-capacity floppy drives are identical to the sectored (or embedded) servos used in small hard-disk drives and a typical layout of servo fields used for sector servo is shown in Fig. 3.28b,c. As in the case of the buried servo, the media must be servo-written at the factory.

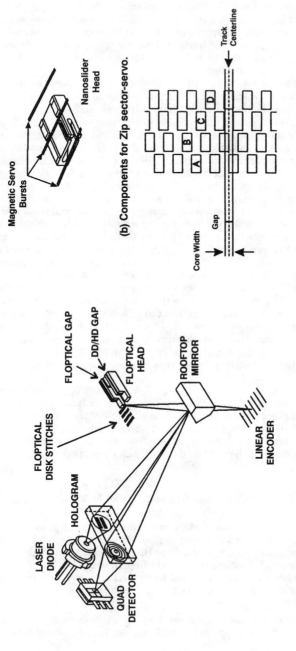

Magnetic Servo Bursts

Nanoslider Head

(b) Components for Zip sector-servo.

Core Width

Gap

A B C D

Track Centerline

(c) Norm and quad field used in magnetic servo-bursts.

FLOPTICAL GAP

DD/HD GAP

FLOPTICAL HEAD

ROOFTOP MIRROR

LINEAR ENCODER

FLOPTICAL DISK STITCHES

HOLOGRAM

LASER DIODE

QUAD DETECTOR

(a) Components for Floptical laser Holographic Optical Tracking servo.

FIGURE 3.28 High-density floppy disk servo designs.

3.7.3.1 Runout Reduction Methods for High Performance Servos on Floppy Disks.
The servo system design for a flexible-disk drive is subject not only to the constraints described in the chapter on rigid disks, but it must also compensate for the
ovality of tracks caused by medium anisotropy, and for eccentricity associated with
the mounting of removable disks. Although these disturbances are at relatively low
frequencies, the servo is not able to reduce the following error to zero because the
gain of the servo loop is not infinite.

Two approaches to solving this problem have been pursued: achieving very high
loop gain, and feeding forward an image of the form of the track. A high loop gain
enables reduction of the residual error at the ovality and runout frequencies. Vibra-
tional resonances of the structure normally limit the maximum loop gain that can be
stably used, and normal practice is to design the structure for the highest possible
resonance frequency. An alternative is to tune the resonant mode to coincide in
frequency with the sector sample rate (Bauck, 1981), or 1.5 times that frequency. In
the first case, instability cannot occur since the loop can deliver no energy at the
sampling frequency. In the second case, the alias of the resonant frequency will be
at half the sampling frequency, the highest alias frequency possible. Since ovality
and eccentricity are the same from one revolution to another and similar from one
track to another, a considerable benefit is gained from using a system that estimates
the form of the track, stores this information, and uses it to make the movement of
the head anticipate the movement of the track. This is called *feed forward* and can
be achieved in several ways. Several simple implementations have been described
(Jacques and Halfhill, 1977). It is possible to make a more accurate prediction of
the form of the track by subtracting the position error from the head position, the
latter being estimated by twice integrating the head drive current. The result twice
differentiated is the current which is required to follow the track. A transformation
of this arrangement is preferable, however, in which the stored quantity represents
the current profile needed to follow the track, since then no integrations are required (Wallis, 1984). This feed-forward approach can also be viewed as a problem
in predictor filter design, in which terms representing eccentricity and ovality are
determined.

With servo gains limited by the mechanical resonances of practical structures,
the tracking error due to ovality and eccentricity can be reduced by a factor of 10–
20 at 1500 rpm, and more at lower speeds. The addition of feed forward can reduce
the error by a further factor of three. It must be remembered that the functional
requirement of the servo is not necessarily to follow servo sectors accurately but
rather to follow the same path over the data on each revolution of the disk.

3.7.4 Recording Channels for High-Capacity Flexible Media

High-capacity flexible drives record data at areal densities that are 2 orders of
magnitude higher than the areal densities used in standard flexible media. Thus the
channels for high capacity flexible media must be designed to deal with much lower
signal-to-noise ratios, higher defect rates, and worse intersymbol interference (ISI).
Methods that have been designed for read/write channels used in hard disk drives
are used to improve the reliability of flexible-media channels.

3.7.4.1 Modulation and Error Correction Codes. High-capacity flexible media
drives currently use a peak-detection channel and run length limited codes (RLL),

with (d, k) of (1, 7), (1, 8) or (2, 7). It is very likely that, just as in hard disk drives, sampled read channels will be used as the density increases from 100 Mb/in^2 to 1000 Mb/in^2. The error detection codes used in low-end flexible drives are not adequate, and high-capacity flexible disk drives use the same standard Reed-Solomon codes (88 bits or 144 bits) as used in hard-disk drives.

3.7.4.2 Write Equalization. Equalization on the read side of the flexible magnetic recording channel, and write compensation on the write side that moves the transition location to offset for ISI induced peak shift, has been described in Sec. 3.5. In addition to those methods, some high-capacity flexible disk drives use a technique which adds pulses to the write waveform for each zero to be recorded. By providing high frequency boost on the write side, write equalization reduces the amount of high frequency noise at the detector. This method has also been used in open-reel tape drives and in 3480-cartridge tape drives (Schneider, 1985). Write data with equalization pulse insertion, used in 20 MB and 128 MB floppy drives with optical tracking, is shown in Fig. 3.29.

3.7.5 High-Capacity Flexible Disk Drive Products

Table 3.7 shows some current and past high-capacity flexible drives. Of the drives listed in the table, only one (the Iomega Benoulli 230) uses 5.25-in diameter media. The remaining drives use 3.5-in media. Some drives use a dual-gap magnetic head to provide compatibility with 2 MB 3.5-in disks.

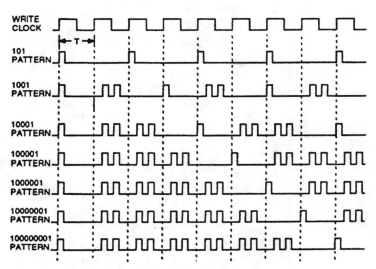

FIGURE 3.29 Write data with equalization pulses inserted.

TABLE 3.7 Comparison of High-Capacity Floppy Disk Drives

Company name	First ship	Model name	User capacity	Media type	tr/mm (tr/in)	Speed RPM	Average seek	Servo type	Actuator type
NEC	1988	FD 1331	9.4 MB	Metal particle	15.98 (406)	360		Sectored servo	linear stepper motor
Toshiba	1989	PD-401	16 MB	Barium ferrite	21.34 (542)	1500	50 ms	Sectored servo	voice coil
Panasonic	1989	JU-3511	16 MB	Metal particle	21.34 (542)	750	50 ms	Sectored servo	
Citizen	1990	IFDD	20.6 MB	Metal particle	21.26 (540)		50 ms		voice coil
Brier	1987	BR-3225	21.4 MB	Barium ferrite	30.59 (777)	720	35 ms	Buried servo	voice coil
Insite	1991	I-325	20.8 MB	Barium ferrite	49.21 (1250)	720	80 ms	Optical servo	stepper and voice coil
Iomega	1994	Bernoulli 230	230 MB	Metal particle	92.52 (2350)	2438	18 ms	Sectored servo	voice coil
Iomega	1995	Zip 100[†]	107 MB	Metal particle	83.33 (2117)	3000	29 ms	Sectored servo	voice coil
Swan	1996	UHC 130	130 MB	Metal particle	87.8 (2230)	3600	18 ms	Sectored servo	voice coil
MKE/Com-paq/3M	1996	LS-120	120 MB	Metal particle	98.43 (2500)	720	65 ms	Optical servo	voice coil

[†]Zip (TM) is a registered trademark of Iomega Corporation.

REFERENCES

Adachi, O., and N. Yano, "A New High-Density Mini Flexible Disk Drive System," *IEEE Trans. Magn.,* **MAG-19,** 1704 (1983).

Bate, G., "The Future of Flexible Disks," *Proc. Symp. Magn. Media Mfg. Meth.,* MMIS, Honolulu, HI, 1983.

Bate, G., G. J. Hampton, and B. J. Latta, "A 5 Megabyte Flexible Disk," *IEEE Trans. Magn.,* **MAG-17,** 1408 (1981).

Bauck, R. C., "Method of Avoiding Resonance in Servo Controlled Apparatus," U.S. Patent 4,398,228, 1981.

Benson, C. R., and T. T. Takahashi, "Mechanics of Flexible Disks in Magnetic Recording," *Adv. Info. Storage Syst.,* **1,** 1991, pp. 15–35.

Benson, R. C., and K. A. Cole, "Transverse Runout of a Nonflat Spinning Disk," *STLE Trib. Trans.,* **34** (1991).

Brar, D., "High Density Magnetic Recording on a Mini Flexible Disk Drive," *IEEE Trans. Magn.,* **MAG-17,** 1423 (1981).

Briggs, J. C, "Enabling Technologies for a 100 MB 3.5-in Floppy (ZIP™) Disk Drive," *SPIE Proc.,* 2604 (1995).

Charbonnier, P. P., "Flight of Flexible Disks over Recording Heads," *IEEE Trans. Magn.,* **MAG-12,** 728 (1976).

Engh, J. T., "The IBM Diskette and Diskette Drive," *IBM J. Res. Dev.,* **25,** 701 (1981).

Farnsworth, S. W., S. D. Wilson, and B. Cohn, "Diffractive Optical System for Tracking on Floptical Disks," *SPIE Vol. 1690 Design of Optical Instruments,* 72 (1992).

Greenberg, H. J., "Flexible Disk: Read/Write Head Interface," *IEEE Trans. Magn.,* **MAG-14,** 336 (1978).

Greenberg, H. J., R. L. Stephens, and F. E. Talke, "Dimensional Stability of Floppy Disks," *IEEE Trans. Magn.,* **MAG-13,** 1397 (1977).

Harman, J. H., "Read Compensation in Flexible Disk Drives," *IEEE Trans. Magn.,* **MAG-17,** 1414 (1981).

Hashimoto, K., and S. Yaskawa, "Coping with Off-track Errors," *Mini-Micro Syst.,* February 1982.

Hashimoto, M, Suzuki, T., Osawa, R., and Funaki, H., "Development of 2-in Diameter Co-Cr Video Floppy Disk," *IEEE Trans. J. Magn., Japan,* **7,** 735 (1992).

Inaba, H., K. Ejiri, N. Abe, and K. Masaki, "On the Thin Layer Metal Particulate Media," *IEEE Trans. Magn.,* **29,** 3607 (1993).

Jacques, J. O., and M. O. Halfhill, "Utilization of Stored Run-Out Information in a Track Following Servo System," U.S. Patent 4,135,217, 1977.

Katoh, Y., M. Nakayama, Y. Tanaka, and K. Takahashi, "Development of a New Compact Floppy Disk Drive System," *IEEE Trans. Magn.,* **MAG-17,** 2742 (1981).

Lopez, O., T. Lam, and R. Stromsta, "Effects of Magnetic Fields on Flexible Disk Drive Performance," *IEEE Trans. Magn.,* **MAG-17,** 1417 (1981).

Ma, Y., and D. E. Jones, "A Qualitative Experimental Investigation of Flexible Media Dynamics," *ASME Winter Conf. Proc.,* 1995.

Matsukawa, S., N. Yoshiura, and N. Wakabayashi, "An Advanced Sector Servo Using a Learning, Estimating, and Over-Sampling Method for a 3.5-in 28 MB FDD," *IEEE Trans. Magn.,* **MAG-27,** 4484 (1991).

Noble, D. L., "Some Design Considerations for an Interchangeable Disk File," *IEEE Trans. Magn.,* **MAG-10,** 571 (1974).

Pearson, R. T., "The Development of the Flexible-Disk Magnetic Recorder," *Proc. IRE,* **49,** 164 (1961).

Saitoh, S.,Inaba H., and Kashiwagi, A., "Development and Advances in Thin Layer Particulate Recording Media," *IEEE Trans. Magn.,* **MAG-31,** 2859 (1995).

Schneider, R. C., "Write Equalization in High-linear-density Magnetic Recording," *IBM J. Res. Dev.,* **29,** 563 (1985).

Seo, Y., T. Yoshiyama, T. Kuriyama, and H. Ikeda, "New Servo System for Large Capacity Floppy Disk," *IEEE Trans. J. Magn., Japan,* **9,** 73 (1994).

Speliotis, D. E., "Performance of MP++ and BaFe++ Tapes in High Density Recording Applications," *IEEE Trans. Magn.,* **MAG-31,** 2877 (1995).

Takahashi, S., *The Latest Floppy Disk Drives and Their Application Know-how* (Japanese), CQ Publishing Co., Tokyo, 1984.

Tatsumi, J., and J. Sakai, *Practical Floppy Disk Drive Guide* (Japanese), Sampo Publishing Co., Tokyo, 1979.

Wallis, C. N., "Track Following Servo System for a Disk File," U.S. Patent 4,594,622, 1984.

White, J. W., and A. K. Migam, "Non Contact Magnetic Head Assembly for a Flexible Disk Drive," U.S. Patent 4, 974, 106 (1990).

Yamamori, K., R. Nishikawa, T. Muraoka, and T. Suzuki, "Perpendicular Magnetic Recording Floppy Disk Drive," *IEEE Trans. Magn.,* **MAG-19,** 1701 (1983).

Yoshiura, T., S. Yoshida, and N. Wakabayashi, "Tracking Servo for High Density FDD," *IEEE Trans. J. Magn., Japan,* **6,** 240 (1991).

CHAPTER 4
DATA STORAGE ON TAPE

Richard C. Schneider
Storage Technology Corporation,
Louisville, Colorado

This chapter describes digital recording on magnetic tape for use as computer data storage. Other magnetic tape applications such as audio and video are covered elsewhere in this book. It will be shown that many of the technical challenges of recording on magnetic tape are shared by particulate hard and flexible magnetic disks. This includes the design of the write/read heads, the selection of particles for the magnetic coating, and the design or the recording channel electronics.

Magnetic tape is distinguished from other storage media as being the lowest cost alternative when compared with solid-state, hard-disks or flexible disks. It is a removable form of storage, whereas solid-state and hard-disk forms of storage are, in general, not. Flexible disks are also removable, but they hold less data than magnetic tapes. Today, a standard $3\frac{1}{2}$-in flexible disk holds only 1.44 MB of data, but capacities up to 100 MB have been achieved. This compares with 800 MB on a standard 3490-style $\frac{1}{2}$-in magnetic tape cartridge.

4.1 OVERVIEW

4.1.1 Computer Tape Drive Applications

A principal reason that computer tape storage has continued to grow is that every five to ten years a new application has been initiated. The first application of magnetic computer tape was as a replacement for punched cards, and this remained true from its inception until approximately 1965. This was followed by the handling of sort and merge applications such as payroll generation. In 1975, a third application of computer tape emerged; this was the attended backup of data from hard disk files. In the mid-1980s, automated tape libraries came into wide use. This enabled the backup of data automatically during off-hours without the need for human intervention. Data backup is the principal use of magnetic tape at the present time. In the decade of the 1990s we are seeing tape used as an important part of Hierarchical Storage Management. Under software control, data are migrated from solid-state to hard disks to magnetic tape as the use of this data becomes less frequent.

Overlaying the above applications are the uses of magnetic tape as an interchange medium between computer systems, and as an archive storage medium.
Both of these last two applications require accepted national and international
standards regarding media packaging and data format. In this way, the same tape
can be written or read by machines from a variety of manufacturers.

4.1.2　History of Computer Tape Drives

In the early 1950s, IBM announced what was to be the first commercially successful
magnetic tape drive, the IBM 727. It was about the size of a home refrigerator. A
considerable amount of the read/write electronics, formatting, and host interface
circuitry was contained in a separate box of comparable size called the tape control
unit. The control unit acted as the interface between the host system and one or
more tape drives. The electronic circuits were implemented with vacuum tubes.
The use of transistors did not come until some five years later, with small-scale
integrated circuits arriving ten years later. The areal density was low by today's
standards; seven parallel tracks across a half-inch wide tape, and a linear density of
100 bits per inch yielded only 1,400 bits per square inch. Today, standard half-inch
computer tape has 36 tracks and 22,000 bits per inch, giving an areal density of 1.6
million bits per square inch. A typical 13 GB quarter-inch cartridge format has 144
tracks on quarter-inch tape and 67,733 bits per inch. This yields an areal density of
39 million bits per square inch. In a strange evolution of technology, the lower-cost
quarter-inch, 8 mm, and 4 mm devices operate today at much higher linear and
track densities than the more expensive half-inch tape drives.

The original refrigerator-sized tape drives had large vacuum columns that served
as a mechanical buffer between the rollers that were accelerating the tape, and the
large high-inertia reel motors. The vacuum columns allowed the initial acceleration
to be applied only to the mass of the tape in the column, allowing the tape to start
and stop within the space between data records. Today, this mechanical and physically large solution has been replaced by lower acceleration drives that stream the
data at constant velocity to and from the drive. Large capacity solid-state memory
in the drive electrically buffers the data in a manner that masks out the operation of
tape "backhitch" whereby the tape is stopped and repositioned in front of the next
record to be read or written.

4.1.3　Modern Computer Tape Drives

Today, computer tape drives come in a variety of sizes, capacities, and data-rates.
There are two basic types of tape transports in use: helical-scan and longitudinal.
Helical-scan drives use a technology very similar to a home video cassette recorder
(VCR). The read/write head is mounted on a rotor or scanner, and the tape is
wrapped around the rotor in a helical fashion so that the head traces a linear path
that is at a small angle (typically 4.9 degrees) to the edge of the tape. Usually, only
one head is reading or writing at one time. Higher data-rate machines have two or
more heads active simultaneously, at the expense of higher cost. The other drive
transport type is longitudinal. This is the basic format of the original tape drives, in
which tracks are written down the tape length parallel to the tape edges. Lower
cost, lower data-rate devices write and read only a single track at a time, while
higher data-rate, higher-cost drives read and write multiple tracks at a time. For

example, the Storage Tek 4490 and the IBM 3490 read and write eighteen tracks at once.

4.1.4 Computer Tape Drive Technology

There are four technology areas that are vital to the design and performance of a computer tape drive. These are: the tape transport, the magnetic tape and container, the read/write head, and the recording channel electronics. These areas will be covered in detail in the following sections.

4.2 THE TAPE TRANSPORT

The tape transport is the mechanism that moves the tape past the read/write head. The read/write head is stationary during reading and writing in a longitudinal recording drive, while the read/write heads are rotating at a constant angular velocity in a helical-scan drive. In both cases, the function of the tape transport mechanism is to keep the tape moving past the read/write head at a constant linear velocity and at a constant tension. The tape must also be accelerated and decelerated in a rapid but gentle manner. There may also be a requirement to move the tape at a higher than normal speed to search for a specific data block, or to rewind the tape back into its cartridge after the read/write operations are completed.

4.2.1 Vacuum Columns and Tension Arms

The early drives used large vacuum columns that were over three feet in length (Fig. 4.1). The vacuum columns served two purposes. The first was to maintain a constant tension on the tape. This tension had to be high enough so that the tape made intimate contact with the read/write head, but not so high that the wear of the tape and head was excessive. The second function performed by the vacuum columns was to decouple the acceleration and deceleration of the large tape reels from the almost instantaneous acceleration of the tape at the read/write head. When spooling tape from the right reel to the left reel, initially tape would be moved from the right vacuum past the head and into the left vacuum head column. In this way, only the tape in the vacuum columns would be accelerating. This gave time for the high-inertia reels and reel motors to come up to speed. Acceleration to the desired tape velocity could be achieved in one or two milliseconds by tape drives in the late 1960s. Vacuum columns perform their assigned tasks very well, but do have drawbacks. The vacuum columns and the vacuum pump take up space, and the pump uses high power and can be noisy. Noise can be a particular problem, especially in an office environment. Spring loaded tension arms avoid the use of vacuum while providing a constant tension on the tape. However, at high accelerations tension arms induce significant tension transients due to the inertia of the arms and the spring load. Therefore, tension arms tended to be used on lower-performance drives, and where smaller size and low noise were important.

Both the vacuum column and tension arm drives were designed to handle tape that was wound on a reel with a typical diameter of ten and one-half inches. In the early drives, the end of the tape had to be manually threaded through the tape path and wound onto the take-up reel. Most high-end drives provided automatic thread-

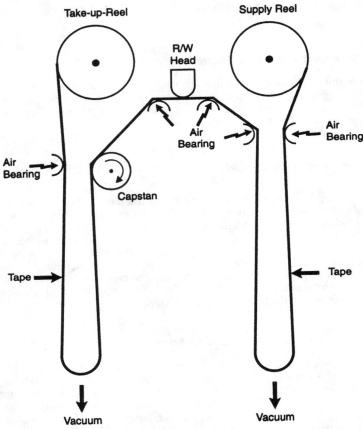

FIGURE 4.1   Vacuum-column tape drive simplified diagram.

ing by the early 1970s. However, the reel still had to be manually mounted onto the drive.

4.2.2 Reel-to-Reel Drives

In the early 1970s a new technology developed that still plays an important part in digital computer tape drives. This technology was reel-to-reel control (Fig. 4.2). Prior to that time, only single closed-loop control was used. The use of new state-space notation in describing control system parameters, enabled the control of two reel motors simultaneously. Six reference variables were defined: tape tension, the derivative of tension, position, velocity, acceleration, and jerk (the derivative of acceleration). The two-motor system could operate open loop if the system parameters such as friction, mass, etc., were known. Closed-loop control could then be invoked to fine-tune the performance. Rather than have a separate tension transducer, motor current could be measured as an indicator of tension. Tension within a few percent of that desired can be achieved using these methods. A tension trans-

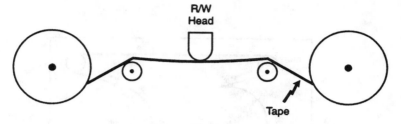

FIGURE 4.2   Simplified reel-to-reel tape path.

ducer is used to achieve greater tension control accuracy, or in situations where drive parameters are changing, or not well known.

Given the new control methods outlined above, there remained a significant problem to overcome. Without vacuum columns or tension arms, large tape reels and the associated reel motors had to be accelerated. Two solutions were used to solve and to mask this problem. First, the ability to pack bits closer together on tape improved with better heads and media. This enabled the number of tracks to be doubled, and the linear density to be tripled. Thus, six times the areal density was now possible, enabling the same amount of data to be stored on a much smaller reel. The reel diameter was reduced from ten and one-half inches to only four inches. This alone was not enough to achieve small interblock spacing, because the inertia of even the small reel was still much greater than the inertia of just the tape in vacuum columns. Therefore, after being given a stop command following a read or write operation, it was necessary to stop the tape and then back up to a point well before the next record was to be read or written. In this way, a much lower acceleration could be used resulting in both lower power and gentler tape handling. To mask this "backhitch" operation during read, the drive would read several records following the last read, and store the data in memory in the drive. The records stored in the drive memory were the next ones likely to be requested by the host to be read. Therefore, the initial read could be done out of memory while the drive was slowly accelerating the tape up to speed. Similarly, during write, the data from the host would be stored in memory during acceleration and be ready to be written when the tape was at the desired velocity. In this manner, the host would see what appeared to be an instantaneous response, while the drive was able to accelerate the tape gently without the need for either vacuum columns or tension arms. High-density recording and low-cost electronic storage enabled the replacement of mechanical complexity.

Reel-to-reel technology is the basis of the IBM 3480/90 and the compatible StorageTek 4480/90 tape drives. These drives record 18 and thirty-six tracks respectively on half-inch chromium-dioxide tape, wound in a cartridge approximately four inches by five inches on a side. These drives have essentially replaced the old ten and one-half inch reel machines.

4.2.3   Belt-Driven Designs

The belt-driven data cartridge was introduced by the 3M company in 1972. The first versions of this cartridge held only 3 MB of data and moved tape at 30 in/s (0.8 m/s). Typically, the cartridge capacity is 13 GB and tape is moved at 120 in/s (3.2 m/s).

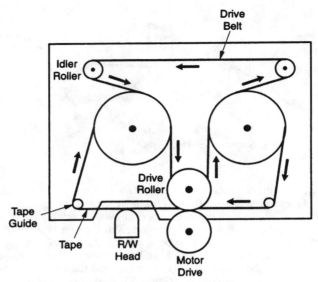

FIGURE 4.3   Simplified tape path belt driven drive.

The arrangement of the tape and belt paths is shown in Fig. 4.3. The motor drive puck and read/write head are part of the drive, otherwise the entire tape path is inside the cassette. This, plus the fact that a threading mechanism is not required, significantly lowers the cost of the drive. The drive operation is straightforward. A single drive motor rotates the motor drive puck at a constant rpm producing a constant linear velocity at the puck circumference. The puck, in turn, rotates the drive roller inside the cassette. The linear velocity at the circumference of the drive roller is ideally identical to the velocity of the puck. The rotating drive roller moves the belt which is wrapped around the drive roller, both cassette reels and two idler rollers. Assuming no slippage between the belt and the tape, the tape velocity should be the same as the belt velocity. The belt is in contact with the tape at three places: at the drive roller and at each of the two reels. At first sight, this drive concept seems to be simplicity itself. However, as drive speeds increase, along with linear and track densities, it is increasingly important to control the belt tension in a variety of environments as the tape is spooled from one reel to the other. Another challenge is the relaxation of the belt tension over time. The belt must also be centered in the tape path, which is accomplished by accurate alignment of the tape path components, and also by slightly crowning the rollers to provide a centering force.

Typically, the state of the art is the QIC-139 cassette which contains 144 data tracks and 24 servo tracks on a quarter-inch tape recorded at 67,733 b/in (2667 b/mm). This results in a cassette capacity of 13 GB. Extensions to over 100 GB capacity appear feasible in the future.

4.2.4 Helical-Scan Drives

The development of helical-scan drives began in the 1950s. A major application was in the television broadcast industry where time-zone differences called for the

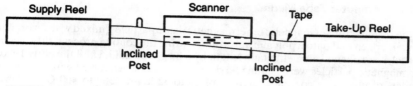

FIGURE 4.4 Simplified helical-scan tape drive.

delayed broadcast of prime-time shows. A second application was the desire for video news gathering. More recently, there has been an explosion in the use of video cassette recorders (VCRs) for consumer use. The above applications all originally used some form of analog recording.

During the past few years, the digital recording of both audio and video tape has evolved. A significant advantage of recording with either the video or audio formats is the possibility that the component prices will be drastically reduced by their use in consumer products that are sold in large quantities. A logical extension of this technology is to use the same or similar recording components and formats to record digital data. Both audio and video recording use elaborate data interleaving and error correction to eliminate errors caused by debris, tape defects or tape damage. When the size or frequency of the errors exceeds the power of the error correction, the errors are masked by techniques such as muting, averaging, repeating the last information, and so forth. Naturally, these methods cannot be used if digital computer data are recorded. It would be very chancy if your paycheck were the average of the person before you and the person after you in the payroll list. Hence additional error correction is used to reduce the bit error rate from 10^7 bits between errors to better than 10^{14} bits between errors.

The basic configuration of a helical-scan drive is shown in Fig. 4.4. The tape is wrapped around the rotating drum in a slanted path, so that the take-up and supply reels must be on different levels. The angle that the tape makes with the rotor is 4.9 degrees in a D-3 digital video recorder. The track angle is a function of both tape angle and relative tape speed. Details on helical-scan recorders are given in the video recording chapters of this book. Track density in a helical-scan machine can be made higher than that of a stationary head machine. One reason for this is that adjacent tracks are placed at an angle to each other such that little signal is read from adjacent tracks. Thus, higher cassette data storage capacity is a principal reason that helical-scan machines will continue to be used for data storage.

4.3 MAGNETIC TAPE

Magnetic tape is made today in a very similar manner to the way tape was made forty years ago for the first computer tape machines. Today, however, the magnetic coatings are smoother, with fewer and smaller defects, and the magnetic particles are smaller and have higher coercivity. For detailed discussions of magnetic media in all forms for tape as well as rigid and flexible disks, see the relevant chapters in *Magnetic Recording Technology*.

4.3.1 Computer Tape Media

In the manufacture of magnetic tape, magnetic oxide particles, mixed with an organic binder, are coated onto a polymer substrate. During the coating process, the acicular particles are aligned along the tape length by a magnetic field. Until the early 1980s, the magnetic particles were gamma ferric oxide which, when mixed with an organic binder, resulted in a coating coercivity of 24 to 32 kA/m (300 to 400 Oe). Newer particles have been commercially introduced during the last ten to fifteen years, including chromium-dioxide, cobalt-doped iron oxide, barium-ferrite and metal (iron)-particles. The general trend is toward higher coercivity and smaller particle size. Metal particle media are now being developed with coercivities above 160 kA/m (2000 Oe). Higher coercivity particles are capable of supporting higher linear densities, resulting in higher data rates and more data stored on the same length of tape.

A second trend in tape media is the use of thinner substrates. This enables more media to be wound into a fixed cartridge or cassette size, with consequent increases in volumetric storage efficiency. In recent years, tape substrate thicknesses have been reduced from 23 microns to 14 microns, and future substrate thicknesses of 5 or 6 microns are possible. Thinner tapes tend to buckle more easily under the guiding forces, a problem which is alleviated by the use of gentler guiding methods, and the introduction of servo tracks where the read/write head follows the media. The thinner longer tape will result in an increase in the length of time that it takes to spool down to the end of tape to read or write data. This time increase can be offset by the use of tape search speeds which are higher than the normal read or write velocity.

4.3.2 Tape Irregularities

A principal objective in the manufacture of computer tape media is low cost. As a result, tape surface irregularities are tolerated that would be rejected in hard-disk media. These irregularities include: asperities, coating clumps, coating voids, edge debris, and foreign particles. Asperities are often protrusions from the substrate through the magnetic coating. Clumps and voids are due to localized coating nonuniformity. Edge debris can come from two sources: First, there may be residual debris from the tape slitter operation, where the tape is slit into the desired widths. Second, debris can be generated from the edges rubbing on guides or flanges in the tape path. Foreign particles can be imbedded in the media surface when they are wound up in the tape reel under tension. Debris can also be generated by rubbing the recording surface, or the backside, over components in the tape path. An obvious potential source of debris is the rubbing of the recording surface on the read/write head, but tape head contours are designed to withstand tens of thousands of passes over the same area of an individual tape section without degradation of the recording surface. The backside of the tape may also be coated to create a more durable surface with designed roughness and resistivity.

The combined effect of the various sources of debris is that tape recording surface defects may cause error events that are hundreds or even thousands of bits long. This compares with hard-disk error events that are typically only one or two bits in length. Various strategies have been developed to mask these error occurrences. The first is to skip over large error events during the write operation and rewrite the data "downstream" from the error event. A second defense is the use of very powerful error-correction codes. More information on these strategies is given in Sec. 4.5.9.

4.4   THE READ/WRITE HEAD

The classic read/write head for computer tape drives performs three functions: erase, write, and read. In drives built before 1980, it was typical for a dc-erase function to occur before writing to remove residual old data, and the erase function on multitrack machines was across the entire tape width. If the tape is recorded in serpentine fashion, then full-width erase cannot be used; instead, an individual erase head for each write element is required. In this case the erase head width is equal to the track pitch. More recently, the erase function is accomplished simply by overwriting the old data. The unerased old data appears as one form of un-wanted noise during the detection process. The worst case situation is where low-density old data written with high write-current amplitude must be overwritten with high-density data written with low write-current amplitude. A typical requirement might be that the residual old data signal strength be only five percent of (26 dB lower than) the new data read signal. Residual old data can be minimized by choosing run-length codes (see Sec. 4.5.3) that restrict the lowest densities that can be written. The use of write equalization has also been an effective method of reducing the low density content (see Sec. 4.5.5).

The write head continues to be an inductive head structure as it was in the original tape drives. What has changed significantly are the materials used and the methods of manufacture. The materials have changed from laminated alloys to ferrite (both NiZn and MnZn) and, finally, to thin films. There may also be composite heads where the bulk of the head is ferrite with metal pole tips to handle the high flux density necessary for recording on high-coercivity media.

An inductive head can be used as a read head as well as a write head, but the read head does not have the requirement to handle high flux densities as does the write head. The low-level read signal from an inductive read head is proportional to the derivative of the read flux with respect to time. In practice, the read element is physically separated from the write element. In this way, the written data can be read back and verified at the time of writing. This eliminates the need to make a second pass over the media to perform the write verify operation. Having separate read and write elements enables each component to be individu-ally optimized for its specific function. The read gap is made smaller than the write gap to better read high-density information. In addition, in longitudinal recording, the read element width is made narrower than the write element width, which this allows some lateral relative motion between the read element and the recorded track without reading information from an adjacent track. There is, however, a tradeoff to be made: the narrower the read element, the lower the likelihood of reading adjacent track information, but the read signal-to-noise ratio will be lower. Computer simulation is often used to model the contributions of the physical tolerances such as element width, tape width, guiding accuracy, dimen-sional changes with temperature and humidity, etc., to determine the optimum read head element width.

In 1983, the magneto-resistive (MR) read element was introduced in commercial tape drives. The advantage was a larger read signal at high linear densities when compared with an inductive read head. The MR head is a flux-sensitive head, so the output does not depend on tape speed. Nevertheless, there is still a derivative action. The read signal is proportional to the spatial derivative of the flux with respect to distance.

4.4.1 Technology Trends in Computer Tape Heads

There exists today a definite trend in longitudinal computer tape drives toward thin-film write heads used in conjunction with MR read heads. This trend includes both high-end drives as well as low-end models. The erase function is often accomplished by overwriting the existing data. More details on the subject of read and write heads is given in *Magnetic Recording Technology*.

4.5 THE RECORDING CHANNEL

The recording channel block diagram for a magnetic tape drive is similar to that for both hard and flexible magnetic disks and also optical disks. More generally, it can be viewed as a form of data communications channel. The write and read side of the recording channel is shown in Fig. 4.5. A brief description of the major functions is given below.

4.5.1 Data Compression

Data compression is used today in virtually all storage devices. It is a method of removing redundancy from the data so that the information can be stored using fewer recorded bits. There are two types of data compression: lossy and lossless. Lossy compression is typically used with image or audio data. For example, video images do not change substantially from one frame to the next, and parts of the

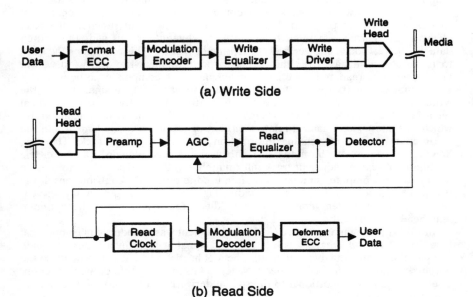

(a) Write Side

(b) Read Side

FIGURE 4.5   Recording channel block diagram.

background may not change at all. By considering what part of the image is changing, by looking at motion of the edges of objects, and by eliminating detail that cannot be perceived by the human eye, compression factors of over 100 can be achieved. In digital recording of data, lossless compression must be used, a method of reducing the redundancy where all the information content is preserved. Compression factors with lossless compression depend on the data set and are typically two or three to one. Factors of five to ten are achievable, but only with selected data sets. As part of the write operation, user data is compressed before any formatting, ECC, or modulation codes are introduced. There is a block that decompresses the data as a last step in the signal processing on the read side, before the data are returned to the user. Today, data compression algorithms are well understood. (Ziv and Lemple, 1977).

4.5.2 Format/ECC

This block determines the spatial arrangement of the data, the error correction code (ECC), and other special bits. For example, along a recorded track, the data are typically preceded by a burst of all-ones for a (0, k) code, 101010 . . . for a (1, k) code, or 1001001 . . . for a (2, k) code. This preamble is used to lock in the read phase-lock clock to the read data frequency. There then must be some bit sequence to let the drive know that the preamble (often called start burst) has ended. The length and frequency of the preamble, and the length and contents of the bit sequence, are features that are determined in the Format/ECC block. Today, Reed-Solomon ECC codes are used in most tape drives. As an example, consider the IBM 3490 or compatible StorageTek 4490 tape drive that records 36 tracks across a half-inch tape. Eighteen of these tracks are written and read simultaneously, first in the forward direction and then in the backward direction. The Reed-Solomon code word is composed of eighteen bytes, one for each track. There are fourteen data bytes, and four ECC bytes. If the code words were written adjacent to each other along a track, it is likely that a single defect could affect two or more bytes. Interleaving the bytes along the track could help. However, a single long defect or scratch could cause the read clock to lose lock, thus making all the data on that track unreadable after the defect. Instead, the code word is spread across each of the eighteen tracks as a defense against long duration single-track errors. Up to four tracks in error can be corrected with this arrangement. Again, the generation of the Reed-Solomon ECC bytes, and their placement on the media is done in the Format/ECC block. A detailed overview of ECC methods is given in Chapter 10 of this book. There is a corresponding block on the read side that strips out the added format features and passes the resulting data through the error-correction circuits.

4.5.3 Modulation Codes

Modulation codes transform the input binary data sequence into an output sequence that the machine designer believes to have more desirable properties. In general, the output sequence could be nonbinary. However, only binary output sequences are considered in this chapter. Further, only non-return-to-zero (NRZ) writing methods are considered, where the media magnetization is either positive or negative, but not zero. Desirable properties may include: maximum or minimum linear density, spectral properties such as zero dc content, or elimination of some "worst case" sequences.

The first code used in a commercial tape drive was called non-return-to-zero-invert (NRZI). Rather than a ONE being an up level and a ZERO a down level, a ONE is a transition from negative to positive current, or a transition from positive to negative current. A ZERO is no transition. Thus, the write current "inverts" for a ONE, and does not "invert" for a ZERO.

The flux in the media will be an approximation of the write current, but modified by high-frequency losses associated with a finite transition width, finite write-gap length, and other effects. The read signal from an inductive head will be the time derivative of the flux. The read signal for an MR head will be the spatial derivative of the flux. Thus, the inductive head read signal will increase or decrease with tape (or head) velocity. The MR read signal will remain at a constant amplitude with velocity. The readback signal in both cases is a pulse for each write current transition (ONE). There will be a positive pulse for a positive write current transition, and a negative pulse for a negative transition as shown in Fig. 4.6.

The first computer tape drives, developed by IBM, wrote one byte, simultaneously, on seven tracks across the tape width. At that time, the standard byte length in IBM computers was six bits. There were six data tracks and one odd parity track. Thus, there was always at least a single ONE across the tape width. During the read operation, the first ONE in each byte was used for clocking. However, as linear densities increased, it was no longer possible to use clock information from neighboring tracks. Each track had to contain its own clocking information. Clocking information had to come from transitions since there is no readback signal if there are no transitions. There was no limit to the number of sequential bits without transitions with NRZI, therefore, a new modulation code was required.

The first idea was to insert ONES periodically. For example, let every fifth bit always be a ONE. This can be viewed as mapping four data bits into five code bits where the first four bits are data, and the fifth bit is a ONE. Later in this section it will be seen that there is a better mapping strategy than this straightforward method. In the early 1960s, tape drives began to use phase encoding (PE, Manchester Code). Hard-disk drives began to use the similar frequency modulation (FM) code. The write currents for these codes are shown in Fig. 4.7 along with the write current for NRZI as a comparison. In PE, a positive current transition in the

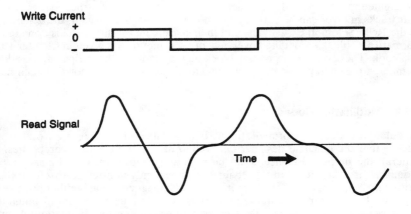

FIGURE 4.6   Write current and resulting read signal.

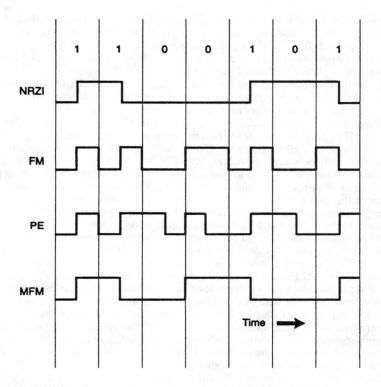

FIGURE 4.7 Write current for NRZI, FM, PE and MFM.

center of the bit cell indicates a ONE. A negative current transition indicates a ZERO. There are transitions at the bit cell edge between consecutive ONES or consecutive ZEROS to insure the correct transition polarity at the bit cell center. In FM, there is a transition in the center of the bit cell for a ONE. This transition can be either positive or negative. There always are transitions at the bit cell edges. These edge transitions can be viewed as clock transitions. The name frequency modulation comes from the observation that a high frequency is being written for a ONE, and half that frequency is written for a ZERO. Both PE and FM require a maximum flux change density that is two times the bit density, and a minimum flux change density that is equal to the bit density. Clearly, the PE and FM waveforms are similar and just differ in interpretation. PE can be detected by looking at the read pulse polarity at the bit cell center. It could also be detected by observing that the ONES signal and the ZEROS signal have different polarity over the entire bit cell. This second method is a bit-by-bit, maximum-likelihood approach. If PE is detected in this way, the shift of a transition of up to 50% of a bit cell is possible before an error occurs. FM can be detected by setting up a gate about the bit cell center and detecting the presence or absence of a transition (read pulse). For example, the gate could open from 25% of a bit cell to the 75% point. Notice that either the clock transition or the data transition can only shift by ± 25% of a bit cell before an error will occur. The gate width can be less than 50% of a bit cell since there will be little peak-shift in the ONES pulse because it is always surrounded on each side by clock transitions. The reduced gate width about the bit cell center will allow for more shift in the clock pulses at the edge of the bit cell.

The next evolutionary step in modulation codes was the introduction of modified frequency modulation (MFM). The write current for MFM is also given in Fig. 4.7. MFM was derived from FM and lowered the required linear density by a factor of two. FM had clock transitions at the edge of every bit regardless of whether they were required or not. For example, if there was a string of ONES, the clock transitions are not required since there would still be one transition per bit. The rules for MFM are: there is a transition in the center of the bit cell for a ONE, and no transition for a ZERO, just like NRZI and FM; and there is a transition at the bit cell edge only between consecutive ZEROS. The MFM linear density is at most one transition per bit, and the lowest density is half that of the maximum density. There is also an in-between density of two-thirds the maximum density that can act to smooth the change from the maximum to the minimum density. Like FM, MFM can only tolerate a ± 25% of a bit cell shift before an error occurs.

In the early 1970s, the first run-length codes were introduced. These can be viewed as generalizations of all the codes that we have considered so far. In run-length codes, a group of m data bits is mapped into a somewhat larger group of n code bits. This group of n code bits is often called a code word. The code words are recorded using NRZI rules: a transition for a ONE and no transition for a ZERO. One example was given above where four user bits were mapped into five code bits. The first four bits were data bits and the fifth bit was always a ONE used for read clock synchronization. Consider a better mapping of four bits into five bits. Since there are four data bits, 2^4 or 16 unique code words are needed at the output of the run-length encoder. If the output consists of five bit code words, then there are 2^5 or 32 possible code words. The designer should pick "the best" sixteen code words. The following rules are used for a code called group coded recording (GCR). First, ONES can exist in adjacent bit cells, that is, there does not have to be any ZEROS between ONES. Second, there can be at most two consecutive ZEROS within a code word. Finally, there can be at most one consecutive ZERO at the start or at the end of a code word so that any code word can follow any other code word, and there still will be no more than two consecutive ZEROS between ONES. Table 4.1 shows that there are seventeen code words of the thirty-two possible code words that meet the GCR constraints. Only sixteen code words are needed to encode all possible four bit sequences.

To encode GCR, five code bits must be squeezed into the space of four data or user bits. This means that the code bits must be recorded at 1.25 (5/4) times the data linear density. Recall that the code bits will be recorded as NRZI; a transition for a ONE and no transition for a ZERO. The readback signal will be a pulse for each transition. The amount of peakshift that can exist before an error occurs is ±50% of a code bit. However, the code bits are only 80% of a data bit in length, so the allowable peakshift is ±40% of a data bit. The longest time between ONE transitions is three code bits or 2.4 data bits. The wavelength ratio of maximum time between ONES to minimum time between ONES is 3:1. Table 4.2 gives a comparison of the important parameters for NRZI, MFM, and GCR.

Compared with MFM, GCR is recorded at a 25% higher code bit density, but it can tolerate 60% more peakshift (40/25). The 60% increase in peakshift tolerance more than offsets the 25% increase required in linear density. GCR was the code of choice for tape drives introduced in the early 1970s. The GCR restrictions on ZEROS can be described by two parameters commonly called the d and k parameters. The d parameter indicates the minimum number of ZEROS that must exist

TABLE 4.1 All Possible
Combinations of Five Bits

00000	10000
00001	10001
00010	†10010
00011	†10011
00100	10100
00101	†10101
00110	†10110
00111	†10111
01000	11000
†01001	†11001
†01010	†11010
†01011	†11011
01100	11100
†01101	†11101
†01110	†11110
†01111	†11111

†These obey GCR constraints.

TABLE 4.2 Comparison of Parameters for NRZI, MFM,
and GCR

Code	bpi	fci	Window	Wavelength ratio
NRZI	10,000	10,000	±0.50T	—
MFM	10,000	10,000	±0.25T	2:1
GCR	10,000	12,500	±0.40T	3:1

between ONES and, in the case of GCR, d is 0. The k parameter is the maximum number of consecutive ZEROS that are allowed between ONES and in the case of GCR, k is 2. The GCR code is therefore called a (0, 2) run-length code. Another important parameter is the code rate. The code rate is defined as the ratio of input data bits divided by the number of code bits. The GCR code rate is therefore 4/5. Initially, GCR referred to this specific (0, 2) code. However, it is now common to use the term GCR to refer to a code where a group of user bits is mapped into a unique and somewhat larger group of code bits.

For a given set of (d, k) constraints, the highest code rate is desired in order to minimize the maximum flux change density required. The k constraint is usually the least important of the (d, k) constraints. The k constraint insures that there will be no more than $k + 1$ code bits between transitions. This restriction means that there will be periodic information to keep the read clock locked in frequency and phase to the data. As a rule of thumb, longer code words will yield either higher data rates or better (d, k) constraints. Consider encoding eight data bits at a time into nine code bits. This would result in a code rate of 8/9 which is higher than the 4/5 code rate for GCR. The number of code words needed to encode the eight data bits is 2^8 or 256. There are 2^9 possible nine bit code words. Are there 256 code words that will meet the GCR (0, 2) constraints? Unfortunately, there are not enough code

TABLE 4.3 Comparison of Parameters for NRZI, MFM, GCR (4/5), and GCR (8/9) Code

Code	bpi	fci	Window	Wavelength ratio
NRZI	10,000	10,000	±0.50T	—
MFM	10,000	10,000	±0.25T	2:1
GCR (4/5)	10,000	12,500	±0.40T	3:1
GCR (8/9)	10,000	11,250	±0.44T	4:1

words to meet the GCR (d, k) constraints. However, there are 297 code words that meet $(0, 3)$ constraints. Table 4.3 compares the parameters of the codes that have been discussed so far.

The higher GCR (8/9) code rate resulted in both a lower maximum flux-change density and a higher allowable peak shift when compared with GCR (4/5). This became the code of choice for the IBM 3480/90 and the StorageTek 4480/90 tape drives.

Codes where the d parameter is greater than 0 will now be described. The discussion is given as if these are block codes where there is a one-to-one mapping between input code word and output code word as with the $(0, 2)$ and $(0, 3)$ codes described above. This is not strictly true, since these codes are generated with shift register logic. However, the concepts presented are true, and it is easier to gain an intuitive feel of the tradeoffs involved.

From the codes that were outlined above, we get the idea that the more bits in the code word, the more choices we have for choosing interesting properties. Consider then mapping 8 user bits into a 16-bit code word. If the d constraint were still 0, then we would have to record at a flux-change density that was twice the bit density. However, with a 16 bit code word there are 2^{16}, or 65,536 possible code words from which to choose the best 2^8, or 256. The $(2, 7)$ code has the restriction that there must be at least two ZEROS between each ONE, and no more than seven ZEROS between each ONE. With $d = 2$, we can achieve a code where the maximum flux change density is lower than the bit density.

Two code bits are being squeezed into the space of each user bit (or 16 code bits into 8 user bits) with the $(2, 7)$ code. Therefore, if the length of a user bit is T, the code bit interval is only $T/2$. However, with the requirement that there must be two ZEROS (at least) between each ONE, then the minimum time between transitions is $3 \times T/2$, or 1.5 T. This means that the $(2, 7)$ flux-change density will be $1/1.5$ or $2/3$ of the bit density. Since the $(2, 7)$ code bit length is $T/2$, then the window will be: $1/2 \times T/2$, or 0.25 T, which is 25% of a user bit.

In describing the $(2, 7)$ code where $d = 2$, it is clear that codes with $d = 1$ were skipped over. This was done because historically hard disk files used the $(2, 7)$ code before they tried and used the $(1, 7)$ code. With slightly more complexity in the encoder and decoder a $(1, 6)$ code can be generated at the same two-thirds code rate. The $(1, 7)$ is described in more detail because of its popularity, and minimum benefit in reducing the k constraint from 7 to 6.

In the $(1, 7)$ code, 8 user bits are mapped into 12 code bits. As before, the best 256 sequences are selected from the 2^{12} or 4096 possible 12 bit code words. This number of possibilities is much more than the required 256, but much less than the 65,536 possible 16 bit sequences that exist for the $(2, 7)$ code. It should be expected that there will not be quite as much flexibility in choosing code word parameters from the 4096 possible code words. There are not enough code words to achieve the

TABLE 4.4 Comparison of Parameters for NRZI, (0, 3), (1, 7) and (2, 7) Codes

Code	bpi	fci	Window	Wavelength ratio
NRZI	10,000	10,000	±0.50T	—
(0, 3),(8/9)	10,000	11,250	±0.44T	4:1
(1, 7),(8/12)	10,000	7,500	±0.33T	4:1
(2, 7),(8/16)	10,000	6,666	±0.25T	2.67:1

restriction of a minimum of two consecutive ZEROS between ONES, but the restriction of a minimum of one ZERO between ONES can be achieved. The further restriction is that a maximum of seven ZEROS between ONES is allowed.

Since 12 code bits must be squeezed into the space of 8 user bits, a code bit is only 2/3T (8/12) long. But because of the $d = 1$ constraint, transitions cannot be spaced closer than every other code bit. Thus, the minimum time between transitions is 2×2 T/3, or 1.33T. The flux-change density is 1/1.33, or 3/4 of the bit density. The window is half of the code bit period, or $1/2 \times 2$ T/3 = T/3. Table 4.4 compares the (8/9) code, the (2, 7), and the (1, 7) codes.

This table shows that 8 user bits can be mapped into longer and longer code words to achieve $d = 3, 4$, and so forth. As d increases, the code bit period becomes smaller and, therefore, the window (half the code bit period) gets smaller. The required maximum linear density also decreases. In the limit, the window becomes infinitely small, and the linear density approaches zero. In theory, we could have only one transition on the tape, but we need to know exactly where it is.

Table 4.4 shows that the (1, 7) code has a linear density and window that is in between those of the (0, 3) code and the (2, 7) code. It is possible to deduce that it is a good compromise among the three codes. First, compare (1, 7) with (2, 7). The (1, 7) linear density is 7500/6666 or 1.125 times that of the (2, 7), but the (1, 7) window is 0.33/0.25 or 1.33 times that of the (2, 7). The (1, 7) code promises a much larger window increase (33.3%) compared with a small (12.5%) linear density increase. Now compare the (0, 3) code with the (1, 7). The (0, 3) linear density is 11,250/7500, or 1.5 times the linear density of the (1, 7) code. However, the (0, 3) window is only 0.44/0.33 or 1.33 times that of the (1, 7) code. This analysis would seem to indicate that the (1, 7) code is the best choice among the three codes. Further, if this is so, it implies that further increases of d beyond 2 are probably not fruitful. The fact that the hard-disk files have switched to (1, 7) indicates that the manufacturers have found that the (1, 7) code is somewhat better, although the choice may also depend on the recording channel parameters. For example, a magneto-optic channel transfer function (magnitude response vs. frequency) rolls off much more rapidly than that of a magnetic recording channel. The linear density increases of (1, 7) over (2, 7) has a much more severe effect, so that (2, 7) might be a better choice for a magnetooptical disk file.

There is logic on the read side of the recording channel that will take the detected code bits and do an inverse mapping to obtain the corresponding user bits.

4.5.4 Write Precompensation

Write precompensation writes transitions offset from their nominal time to compensate for expected residual peak shift at the data detector input. For example, a transition would be written early in time if the read pulse due to that transition were expected to be late in time due to intersymbol interference from surrounding pulses. Similarly, a transition would be written late in time if the corresponding read pulse peak were expected early in time. The measure as to whether a read pulse peak is expected to arrive early or late is made at the detector input after all read and write equalization (see next section) has been accounted for. Theoretically, peak shift can be removed or minimized using only read equalization. However, the necessary read equalization may boost high-frequency noise, be too costly, or take up too much space. Write equalization is an effective peak shift reduction alternative. Many commercially available read channel chips also contain write precompensation hardware. Therefore, write precompensation may often be done with negligible cost. One possible drawback in using write precompensation is that transitions are written in the wrong place on the tape. Improvements in read components might make read reliability worse if the write precompensation were done to make up for read head or read circuit limitations.

4.5.5 Write Equalization

Figure 4.8 shows a plot of read-signal amplitude vs. linear density. The highest linear density for computer tape drives is often well beyond the break point. The highest linear density is the 111111 . . . pattern for the (0, 3) code, the 101010 . . . pattern for the (1, 7) code, and the 100100 . . . pattern for the (2, 7) code. Table 4.1 shows that the lowest density for these codes can be as much as four times lower than the highest density. The lowest density will typically be on the flat portion of the rolloff curve. This results in a low resolution, defined as the ratio of the high-density read-signal amplitude to the lowest-density read-signal amplitude. Resolutions between 0.33 to 0.25 are common. The high-amplitude low-density signals could saturate an MR read head. A way needs to be found to reduce the low-

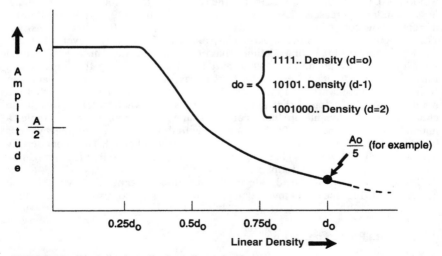

FIGURE 4.8   Read signal amplitude vs. linear density.

density read-signal amplitude without changing the highest-density read-signal amplitude. That way is write equalization.

Write equalization is used in the IBM 3480/90, the StorageTek 4480/90, and the QIC 13 GB drives. Write equalization is a method of adding high frequency pulses to the write current. The pulses are added in such a way that the resulting write current continues to be a two-level signal (Veillard, 1984; Schneider, 1985). Although there is a two-level signal input, and a two-level signal out of the write equalizer, it can be shown that the equalizer has a linear transfer function. A principal advantage of write equalization is that there are no long wavelengths since high-frequency pulses are written in place of the ZEROS. Thus, all read signals will be close to the same amplitude, and it is therefore easier to stay in the linear bias region of an MR read head which was a desired goal. Also, overwrite is easier because of the elimination of the long wavelengths. In general, some amount of high-frequency boost is added to the write side of the recording channel. This reduces the required high-frequency boost in the read equalizer, and thus reduces the amount of high-frequency noise at the read detector. Thus, the signal-to-noise ratio at the read detector is often improved when compared with normal NRZI recording. This is true even though the low-density read signal amplitudes are reduced.

Write equalization is not the same as write precompensation. Write precompensation is a nonlinear operation, and does not add high-frequency boost, amplitude equalize, or diminish overwrite problems as does write equalization. Write equalization is also not the same as write amplitude compensation, where higher current is used at the transition to compensate for current losses in wiring and stray capacitance.

An important property of write equalization is that it has a linear transfer function. Once the transfer function is derived, the magnitude and phase response of the write equalizer can be calculated and graphed. Many different transfer functions are possible depending on the position and width of the added high-frequency pulses. The designer of a new recording channel has some flexibility as to how much equalization to place on the write side and how much to place on the read side. It will be shown that write equalization has a linear transfer function by demonstrating that the desired output can be generated by a set of linear digital-filter building blocks. Please note that the system designer does not have to implement the design using these same building blocks. If the same output is achieved for each input by an alternate implementation, then the transfer function will also be the same.

Figure 4.9 shows the write current for a typical NRZI signal for a (0, 3) code. The concept to be described is valid for any k constraint of two or more. Also shown in Fig. 4.9 is a write-equalized waveform where high-frequency pulses one-half-bit wide have been added to each ZERO. Note that for the special case of the pulses being one-half bit wide, the write-equalized waveform is dc-balanced without the need for any special modulation code. The ONES alternate in polarity, and the ZEROS are either positive in the first half of the bit cell and negative in the second half or vice versa. The one penalty is that write pulses must be written that are one half the width of that required for normal NRZI.

The timing diagram of Fig. 4.10 shows that the write-equalized output can be obtained given the NRZI input using linear digital-filter building blocks. The waveforms shown are the outputs of the linear digital-filter building blocks as shown in Fig. 4.11. The delay operator, D, will always be set to the width of the added high-frequency pulses. In this case, $D = T/2$, where T is the code bit time interval, and the timing diagram of Fig. 4.10 corresponds to the case where $Q = 0$.

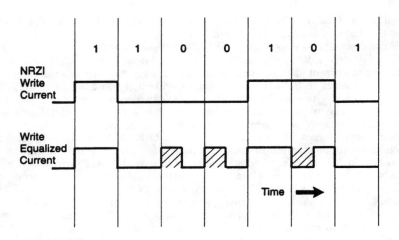

FIGURE 4.9   Write equalization.

The 1-D block delays the NRZI input by an amount D ($T/2$) and subtracts the delayed signal from the original input. The output as shown in line (b) of Fig. 4.10 is a series of alternating polarity pulses, positive following the NRZI positive transitions, and negative following the negative transitions. The next block is $1 + D^2$, meaning the input (line b) is delayed by two Ds (D^n means a delay of $n \times D$ intervals). The delayed line (b) is added to the input line b which produces the output shown in line (c). Line (c) is then fed to the $1/(1-D^2)$ block known as a digital resonator. With a pulse input, the block will continue to produce the same pulse output every D^2 forever, unless fed with an equal pulse input of opposite polarity, when the output ceases until the next input. The resonator output is shown in line (d), and these are the pulses that will be subtracted from the NRZI input. There is a delay block D^Q to offset the pulse positions relative to the NRZI but, in this case, $Q = 0$, so there is no delay. The transfer function can be found by simply multiplying together each of the individual filter blocks.

$$G_1(D) = 1 - (1 - D)(1 + D^2)/(1 - D^2)$$
$$= D(1 - D)/(1 + D) \tag{4.1}$$

Since the first D is just a delay, this becomes:

$$G_1(D) = (1 - D)/(1 + D) \tag{4.2}$$

To get this in the frequency domain, we substitute $e^{-j\omega T/2}$ for D to give

$$G_1(\omega) = (1 - e^{-j\omega T/2})/(1 + e^{-j\omega T/2})$$
$$= j \tan(\omega T/4). \tag{4.3}$$

This transfer function has a constant 90 degree phase due to the j. The magnitude response is shown in Fig. 4.12. Also shown is the magnitude plot for two other transfer functions which have the following parameters.

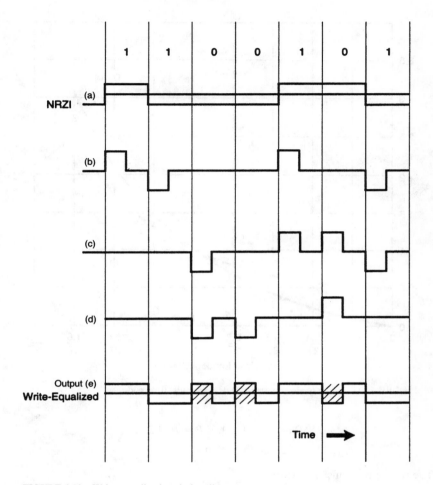

FIGURE 4.10 Write-equalization timing diagram.

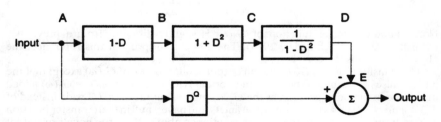

FIGURE 4.11 Write-equalization block diagram.

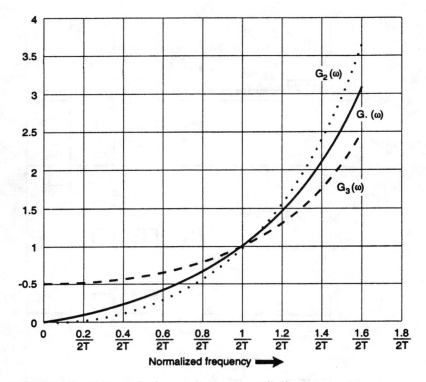

FIGURE 4.12 Write-equalization magnitude responses $(0, k)$ code.

$$G_2(\omega): \quad D = T/2; Q = 1/2; P = R = 2$$

$$G_3(\omega): \quad D = T/4; Q = 0; P = R = 4$$

The respective transfer functions are

$$G_2(\omega) = \frac{(2 \sin(\omega T/8) \sin(3\omega T/8)}{\cos(\omega T/4)} \tag{4.4}$$

$$G_3(\omega) = 1 - \frac{\cos(\omega T/2)}{2 \cos(\omega T/4)} + \frac{j(\tan(\omega T/8) \cos(\omega T/2))}{2 \cos(\omega T/4)} \tag{4.5}$$

Note that the transfer function of $G_3(\omega)$ is slightly different from a previously published version (Schneider, 1985). There was a misprint in this reference; the above equation is the correct one.

The transfer function $G_2(\omega)$ has an output similar to that of $G_1(\omega)$ except that the added pulses are centered between the normal NRZI transitions. The $G_3(\omega)$ added pulses are in the same position as the $G_1(\omega)$ pulses, but they are $T/4$ wide instead of $T/2$. Figure 4.12 shows that both $G_1(\omega)$ and $G_2(\omega)$ have a null in their transfer function at zero frequency. That is because, as mentioned above, the write equalizer output will be dc-balanced regardless of the modulation code used. Note that the

$G_3(\omega)$ transfer function has an amplitude of one-half at dc, and less high-frequency boost when compared with $G_1(\omega)$ or $G_3(\omega)$. As the added pulse width becomes narrower, the resulting transfer function will pivot clockwise about the point at which the amplitude $= 1$, and $\omega = 1$. The high-frequency gain will decrease, and the low-frequency gain will increase. In the limit, the added pulses will have zero width, and the transfer function will be flat, with unity amplitude at all frequencies.

Now let us consider (d, k) modulation codes where $d > 0$. Recall that, for the $(0, 3)$ code, pulses were added for each ZERO. The shortest wavelengths were not affected since this occurred when the code bits were 1, 1, 1 . . . and no ZEROS were involved. The objective is to do the same for other (d, k) codes, namely to avoid adding pulses to the shortest wavelength. Consider a $(1, 7)$ code as an example (Schneider, 1988b). In this code, the shortest wavelength occurs when the code bits are: 1,0,1,0,1, . . . If pulses are not added for these shortest wavelength ZE-ROS, but pulses are added for ZEROS in other data patterns, it would seem that a pattern dependent transfer function would result. Fortunately, intuition is wrong in this case.

It can be shown that write equalization for arbitrary (d, k) codes can be performed by the same type of building blocks that were used for the $d = 0$ codes. There will be no pulses added to the shortest wavelength, therefore the transfer function at this frequency will be unity. Instead of adding pulses for every ZERO, N-d pulses are added between the normal NRZI transitions, where N is the number of ZEROS between ONES for that particular wavelength, and d is from the run length constraints of the code that we are using. For the special case where $d = 0$, we just add N pulses, in other words, a pulse for each ZERO as was done for the $(0, 3)$ code.

With a $(1, 7)$ code and code bit pattern 101001000100001 . . . , there are respectively, 1,2,3,4 ZEROS between ONES. In this case, we would add 0,1,2,3 pulses to that pattern. Three examples are given in Fig. 4.13. These waveforms can be

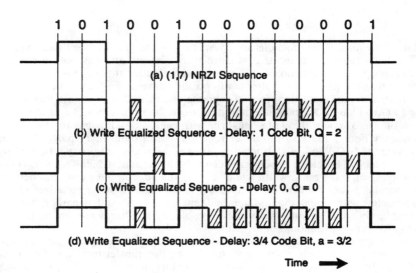

FIGURE 4.13   Write-current waveforms.

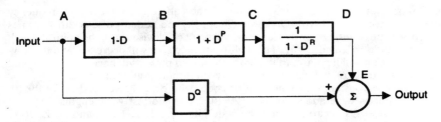

FIGURE 4.14   Block diagram of general write equalizer.

generated by the linear digital filter blocks of Fig. 4.14. A timing diagram for one of the three cases is shown in Fig. 4.15. The added pulses of all three of these wave-forms are one-half-bit wide. Therefore, they are dc-balanced. The parameters and transfer functions of these waveforms are as follows.

$$G_4(\omega): \quad Q = 2; D = T/2; P = 4; R = 2$$

$$G_4(\omega) = (1 - \cos(2\omega T)) - j(\tan(\omega T/2)\cos(2\,\omega T)) \tag{4.6}$$

$$G_5(\omega): \quad Q = 0; D = T/2; P = 4; R = 2$$

$$G_5(\omega) = \frac{j\,(\sin(3\omega T/2))}{\cos(\omega T/2)} \tag{4.7}$$

$$G_6(\omega): \quad Q = 3/2; D = T/2; P = 4; R = 2$$

$$G_6(\omega) = 1 - \frac{\cos(2\omega T)}{\cos(\omega T/2)} \tag{4.8}$$

Plots of the magnitude functions are given in Fig. 4.16. The transfer function $G_4(\omega)$ has a high-frequency boost that is close to maximum, and has both a real and imaginary part. The function $G_5(\omega)$ has the added pulses at the right-most position and, as with the $(0, 3)$ code, pulses in this position have a transfer function with only an imaginary part equivalent to a 90 degree phase shift. The equalizer correspond-ing to $G_6(\omega)$ has added pulses centered between the normal NRZI transitions. As with the $(0, 3)$ code, the write equalizer with centered pulses has the most high-frequency boost, and also a transfer function with no imaginary part. The write equalizer of $G_6(\omega)$ adds high frequency boost without any imaginary term that will change phase. Therefore, the designer can vary the amount of high-frequency boost by varying only the pulse width while keeping the added pulses centered between the normal NRZI transitions. It has been shown that a write equalizer can be constructed with linear digital-filter building blocks. As stated earlier, that the actual hardware does not have to use these blocks; any hardware that adds in the pulses in identical fashion is equivalent.

Referring back to Fig. 1.1, the block diagram of a recording channel, let $W(\omega)$ be the write equalizer transfer function, $C(\omega)$ be the transfer function of the chan-nel itself from write current input to read amplifier output, and $R(\omega)$ be the read equalizer transfer function. Now, assume that for a step input we want a particular pulse shape, at the "target pulse," the read equalizer output, which is also the

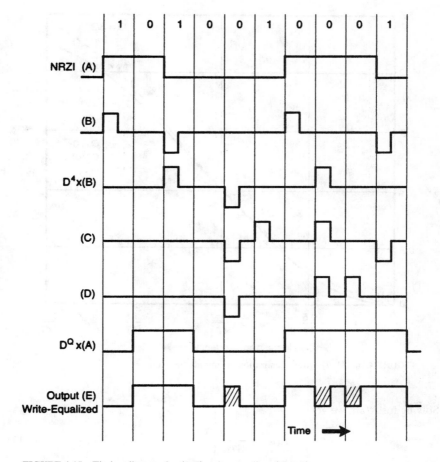

FIGURE 4.15 Timing diagram for $(1, 7)$ write equalizer ($Q = 2$).

detector input. In the next section, target pulses will be discussed in more detail. For now, assume that the target pulse is the Lorentzian pulse

$$V_{out}(\omega) = \frac{1}{1 + (2t/P_{50})^2} \qquad (4.9)$$

where P_{50} is the pulse width at 50% amplitude.

A plot of this pulse is given in Fig. 4.17. The input will be a step represented by $V_{in}(\omega) = 1/j\omega$. Call $D(\omega)$ the overall desired transfer function from step input to Lorentzian pulse output. Then,

$$(V_{out}(\omega)/V_{in}(\omega)) = D(\omega) = W(\omega)C(\omega)R(\omega) \qquad (4.10)$$

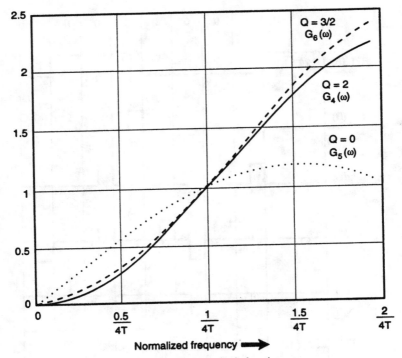

FIGURE 4.16   (1, 7) Write-equalization magnitude functions.

Solving for $R(\omega)$, we get

$$R(\omega) = \frac{D(\omega)}{W(\omega)C(\omega)}$$ (4.11)

Thus, given any write-equalizer transfer function, W_1, W_2, W_3, etc., we can in principle design a read equalizer, R_1, R_2, R_3, etc., to get the desired pulse shape for a step input. How can the best write equalizer be chosen from among the set of practical write equalizers? A few possible approaches are given below.

1. The write equalizer may be defined in a recorded media standard. For example, the IBM 3480/90 and StorageTek 4480/90 write equalizer $G_1(\omega)$ is defined by Eq. (4.8). There is no choice but to use the defined recording method, and to design a corresponding read equalizer $R_1(\omega)$ to give the desired signal at the detector.

2. Assuming comparable cost/complexity, the write/read equalizer combination that gives the highest SNR at the detector input should be chosen. This will depend on the measured spectrum of the total noise at the read equalizer input, including medium noise, thermal spikes, electronic noise, and so forth.

3. There may be a combination that gives lowest cost. For example those transfer functions that are purely imaginary, approximate differentiator. For some systems, a read equalizer may not be required.

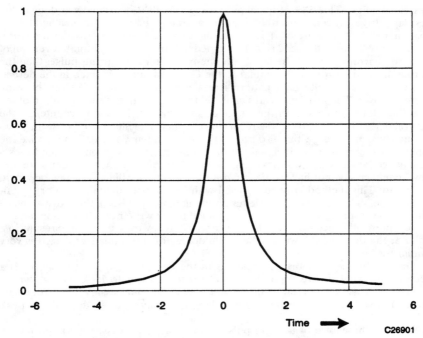

FIGURE 4.17   Lorentzian pulse ($P_{50} = 1$).

4. Any of the write equalizers that use half-bit-wide pulses will have a dc-balanced output and therefore, are suitable for use in rotary-head devices.

4.5.6   Read Equalization

Read equalization was first used in high-density data recording in the mid-1970s on IBM's 3850 Mass Storage helical-scan tape drive (Schneider, 1975). Before that, little more than linear low-pass filters were used to reduce high-frequency noise. Today, read equalization is a major part of the recording channel in both tape and hard disk drives. To this end, semiconductor suppliers have designed digitally controlled analog filters for use as read equalizers. These programmable filters are based on transconductance amplifier technology (Geiger and Sanchez-Sinencio, 1985).

The goal of any read equalizer is to transform the signal at the read amplifier output to some more desirable signal at the detector input. There are two methods currently in use. In the first, a ONE is defined to be a step change in write-current polarity. The read signal is then a Gaussian or Lorentzian-shaped pulse, and is a band-limited version of the time-derivative of the write-current step. For this reason, the method is often called a derivative channel. The write data pattern is made up of sequences of positive and negative transitions, and the read signal will be the linear superposition of the resulting positive and negative pulses, as was shown in Fig. 4.6. The pulses are then further shaped and narrowed in a manner to be described below. This type of signal processing is very close to what was done in the first tape drives. It continues to be used today in high-end one-half inch and lower-cost quarter-inch tape drives. The second method is called write-waveform restoration. In this method, the read signal is shaped to look like a band-limited version of the write-current itself. If the input is a one-bit-wide write-current pulse, then the output at the detector will be similar to the Gaussian pulse obtained in the derivative channel. The write data pattern is made up of a sequence of one-bit-wide current pulses. The resulting read signal will then be the linear superposition of the resulting Gaussian pulses. In this method, an integrator is used to counteract the natural derivative property of the recording channel. The integrator boosts the low-frequency signal energy, but also boosts the low-frequency noise. To minimize the integrator requirement of high gain at low frequencies, this second method uses a dc-balanced code which will have negligible low-frequency energy. Therefore, the low frequencies do not have to be integrated, since there will be no signal energy in this band. This method is typically used with helical-scan digital audio or digital-video drives. The dc-balanced code requirement already exists in these drives, since the write-current signal is transformer coupled to the write head. The remainder of this chapter will concentrate on the first case, where a write-current step results in a pulse at the detector. However, the methodology of read equalizer design is very similar for both cases.

One of the most important questions in the design of any read equalizer is a decision on what do we want the signal at the detector to look like. A wrong choice, such as too narrow a pulse, may result in unnecessary high-frequency noise. Too wide a pulse, or a pulse with long tails may result in undesirable peak shift.

Usually, the choice of a target pulse is an iterative process. Several promising candidates are tried and the resultant high-frequency noise and data reliability measured. More high-frequency boost is needed in a dropout or media defect region, than in a nominal condition. Modern read equalizers often increase the high-frequency boost over what is nominally required, so as to give better performance during conditions of signal loss. With the advent of digitally controlled designs, it is possible to increase high-frequency boost as an error recovery procedure (ERP). Many manufacturers also tune the read equalizer response at the time of manufacture to compensate for read/write head and other machine parameter variations. In the case of nonremovable hard disks, the media parameters can be compensated for as well.

One excellent starting point in the choice of a target pulse is to choose one that nominally does not have any intersymbol interference (ISI) in the center of the bit cell. Several candidates and their strengths and weaknesses will be considered. This will give a good idea of how to choose a target pulse for an actual product.

Consider first the "raised cosine" pulse shown in Fig. 4.18, along with its frequency domain representation (Lathi, 1983). The name raised cosine comes from the shape of the frequency representation. It is assumed for the following discussion that the design is for a system using a $(0, k)$ modulation code. The extension to other codes is straightforward, and will be discussed at the end of this section.

The pulse is chosen to have peak amplitude at the center of its bit cell. The pulse amplitude at the center of the two adjacent bit cells is exactly zero. It is also exactly zero at the centers of all other bits. Thus, there is no amplitude ISI at the bit-cell centers. This is an ideal response if a sampling detector is used in which the signal is sampled by the read clock at the center of each bit cell to determine if the signal is above or below an amplitude threshold.

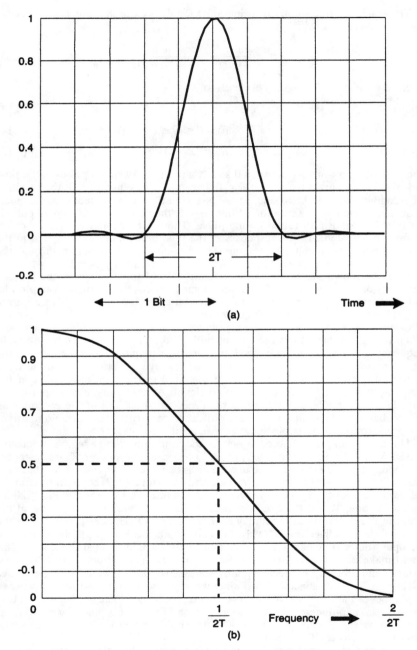

FIGURE 4.18   Raised cosine pulse (a) time domain (b) frequency domain.

The equations for the raised cosine pulse family in both the time and frequency domain is given below.

$$p(t) = \frac{\sin(\pi t/T)}{\pi t/T} \frac{\cos(\pi \alpha \, t/T)}{1 - (2\alpha \, t/T)^2} \tag{4.12}$$

where T is the bit/cell length. This leads to

$$P(\omega) = T \qquad\qquad 0 \leq \omega \leq (1 - \alpha) \, 2\pi/T \tag{4.13}$$

$$P(\omega) = T/2 \left[1 - \sin \frac{T|\omega| - \pi}{2b} \right] (1 - b)\pi/T \leq \omega \leq (1 + \alpha)\pi/T \tag{4.14}$$

$$P(\omega) = 0 \qquad\qquad (1 + \alpha)\pi/T < \omega \tag{4.15}$$

The parameter α can vary between 0 and 1, and Fig. 4.19 shows pulses in the time and frequency domain for $\alpha = 0$, $\alpha = 0.5$, and $\alpha = 1$. When $\alpha = 0$, the resulting time-domain pulse is the "sinc" pulse associated with a perfectly rectangular-frequency domain representation. When, $\alpha = 1$, the resulting time domain pulse is the true full-bandwidth raised cosine pulse. There are an infinite number of responses in between. All the responses in the time domain are exactly zero in the center of adjacent bit cells. All responses in the frequency domain pass through the 50% point at $\omega = \pi/T$. Note that the "ALL ONES" frequency is π/T.

It can be shown that any pulse spectrum that is symmetrical about the Nyquist frequency of $\omega = \pi/T$ will satisfy the time-domain criterion of being zero amplitude, and thus zero ISI, at the centers of adjacent bit cells (Lathi, 1983). This criterion zero ISI is known as Nyquist's first criterion.

Considering the raised cosine family of pulses, we can see tradeoffs can be made. When $\alpha = 1$, we have the widest bandwidth, and therefore will need more high-frequency response, which may result in more high-frequency noise. However, the time-domain pulse has the least ripples, and the eye pattern will be more open horizontally. Hence, more jitter can be tolerated in the relative location of the sampling pulse and the peak of the read signal. As the α parameter approaches zero, less high-frequency response is required, but the width of the eye opening approaches zero. In addition, it is very difficult to construct the very rapid rolloff as α approaches zero, and impossible to construct if α equals zero.

The above pulse shapes were chosen for the condition where a sampling detector is used. When $d > 0$, as in the (1, 7) or (2, 7) codes, a different set of circumstances exist and a peak detector must be used. This is because the equalized isolated read pulse will span 4 code bits for a (1, 7) code and 6 bits for a (2, 7) code. In general the pulse will be $2 \times (d + 1)$ code-bits wide at its baseline. This is shown in Fig. 4.20 for the (1, 7) code. This is the case where the pulse is at about zero amplitude at the center of the closest bit cell that may contain another ONE. Note however that the amplitude in the adjacent ZEROS is about 50% of the peak value. Thus, in order for a sampling detector to be used, the threshold would have to be set at about 75%. This would make detection vulnerable to small changes in amplitude, due to defects, surface nonuniformity, nonideal equalization, and so forth. In addition, the effective SNR would be cut by a factor of two, since we would be trying to distinguish between amplitudes of 1 and 0.5, and 0.5 and 0, rather than between 1 and 0. That is why (1, 7) systems use amplitude-qualified peak-detection. To detect a pulse for a ONE requires both a signal above a nominal 50% threshold, and the derivative of the signal crossing the zero amplitude point.

The raised cosine pulse is designed for a sampling detector. If used in a peak detector, it will have about 4.5% peak shift for a (0, k) code where the pulse is two

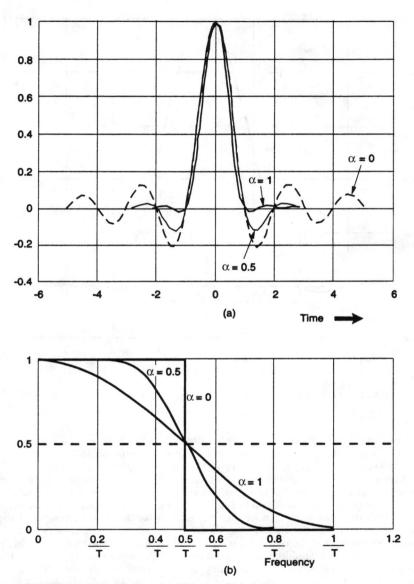

FIGURE 4.19 Raised cosine pulse (a) in time (b) in frequency.

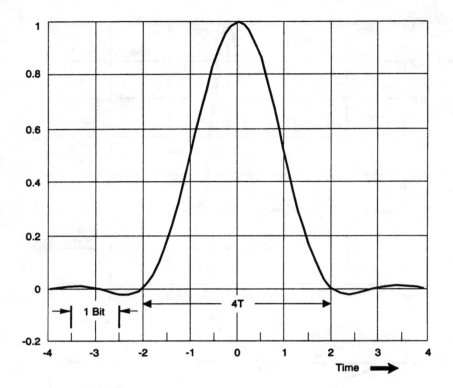

FIGURE 4.20   Raised cosine pulse with (1, 7) code.

code-bits wide, and will cause 9.0% peak shift in a $(1, k)$ code where the pulse is four code-bits wide. This is best-case with an ideal raised cosine pulse. Because of increased baseline ripple, other members of this family will give even more peak shift.

Therefore, what is desired for peak detection (in the absence of noise) is a pulse whose derivative is zero at the center of the closest bit cells where a ONE could be written. This pulse shape is shown in Fig. 4.21 along with the raised cosine pulse. It is seen that the shapes are similar, but the pulse with the zero derivative at the center of the cell with the closest possible ONE, is slightly narrower. Figure 4.22a shows a comparison of the two pulse spectra, while Fig. 4.22b shows the extra high-frequency boost that would be required to convert the raised cosine pulse into the newly desired pulse shape. The frequency axis is normalized so that unity represents the "ALL ONES" frequency for a $d = 0$ code, or the 1010 . . . frequency for a $d = 1$ code. The extra boost really becomes great after this frequency, with twice the extra boost necessary at 1.5 times, a fourfold boost required at 1.75 times this frequency.

The extra high-frequency boost required to obtain a perfect pulse shape may not be worth the resulting increase in high-frequency noise. The resulting pulse will not be ideal if the read equalizer does not provide the ideal extra boost. It will be distorted, and this can be looked on as a form of noise. As the high-frequency boost

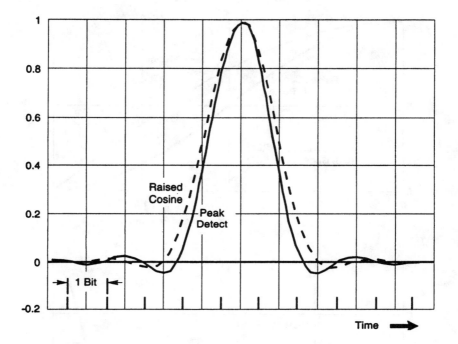

FIGURE 4.21 Raised cosine pulse and peak detector pulse.

is lowered, there is greater signal distortion but, as a tradeoff, there is less high-frequency noise. What is desired is to minimize the sum of both signal distortion and noise (Lathi, 1989).

Once several target pulses have been selected, a read equalizer can be designed. The desired read equalizer is the quotient of the target signal spectrum divided by the read signal spectrum. The target signal is obtained by convolving the target pulse with the data signal constructed with alternating polarity impulses for each ONE in the selected data pattern. A good choice for a data pattern is a pseudo-random pattern (Haynes, 1977).

4.5.7 Data Detection

There are two general classes of detection to be considered. The first is bit-by-bit detection, where the read signal is in some way sampled during each bit cell. A decision is made that the data is either a ONE or a ZERO based solely on the information in that bit cell. The second type of detection is sequence detection or maximum likelihood detection. In this case, information from a sequence or group of bits is examined before a decision is made as to whether a ONE or a ZERO has been read. The vast majority, if not all, tape drives today use bit-by-bit detection. However, hard disk files are now going to some form of maximum likelihood detection in order to achieve higher areal densities. Therefore, it is prudent to consider these methods for the tape environment. It is not clear that tape drives can

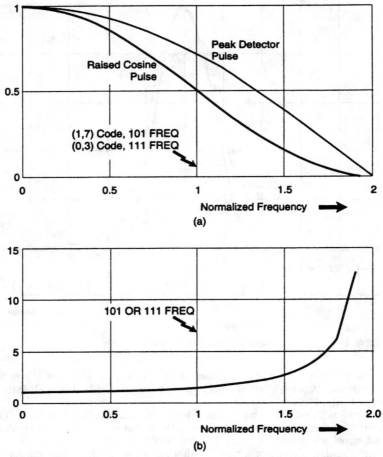

FIGURE 4.22 (*a*) Spectra of raised cosine pulse and peak-detect pulse (*b*) high-frequency boost to convert raised cosine to peak-detect pulse.

realize the full potential of these maximum likelihood methods. Error events in hard-disk drives tend to be only one or two bits in length. These errors can often be avoided by considering the information from a small group of bits in the region of the error event. Error events in tape drives can be hundreds even thousands of bits long. Such error events can, at best, be shortened somewhat or be corrected for short intervals during these long events.

Bit-by-bit detection today is similar to that done with the early tape drives. Several enhancements have been made to improve data detection reliability. Consider first NRZI recording with $(0, k)$ codes. With NRZI writing the readback signal is a pulse for a ONE and no pulse or no signal for a ZERO. The first tape drives simply full-wave rectified the read signal, and decided that a ONE was read when the rectified read signal exceeded an amplitude threshold. The time of occurrence for the ONE was the time when the signal crossed the threshold. The time that the read signal exceeded the threshold was dependent on the signal amplitude. As linear densities increased, a more accurate method of determining the time of a ONE was required. It was found that the time of the zero crossing of the derivative of the read signal was a very accurate indicator of the time of the peak read pulse signal amplitude. Since the derivative could also be zero during ZERO time, the amplitude threshold was used to gate or qualify the derivative signal. The new detection algorithm was then: a ONE is detected when the derivative of the read signal crosses zero amplitude, and the read signal amplitude is above a threshold value.

Further improvements followed. Automatic gain control (AGC) was added to keep the read-signal amplitude more constant over all head and tape combinations. The fixed threshold was changed to a tracking threshold whose value would be a percentage of the average peak signal amplitude. This enabled proper detection even during long defects where the read signal amplitude would only be 10–20% of nominal. This is how bit-by-bit detection is done today. A peak detector is used following an AGC circuit. A ONE is defined to occur when the read signal is above a tracking threshold and the derivative of the read signal passes through zero. A final improvement is to use the fact that the read pulses should alternate in polarity. There are two possible strategies that can be used if two consecutive pulses of the same polarity are detected. The first is to ignore the second pulse of the same polarity. The second is to use the same polarity pulses to be a pointer to the ECC. Pointers are discussed in Sec. 4.5.9.

The use of the derivative signal in detecting ONES has the drawback that the derivative operation accentuates high-frequency noise. Purely in the case of $(0, k)$ codes, it is possible to use the derivative generated pulses only to keep the read clock in phase lock with the read data. These pulses can periodically be missed, or there can be added pulses without disturbing the overall clock performance. Then the read clock itself is used to sample the read signal amplitude to determine if it is above the tracking threshold. This type of detector is known as a sampling detector. Theoretically, the sampling detector should give more reliable operation than the classic peak detector (Schneider, 1988a). However, a sampling detector is only practical with a $(0, k)$ code. For example, in the case of a $(1, k)$ code, the read signal amplitude for a ZERO can be 50% of the peak value, and this is about where a tracking threshold is set. In summary, most tape drives today use some form of peak detection. A sampling detector may be used if a $(0, k)$ code is being used.

At the present time, detection using information from a sequence of bits employs some form of partial response maximum likelihood detection. Partial response and maximum likelihood detection are really two separate signal-processing functions. Partial response is a way of shaping the signal that reduces the required bandwidth. Maximum likelihood decoding is a way of detecting the data by using information from several different bit cells rather than detecting one bit at a time. When they are used together in a particular way, it is called PRML. As will be shown, they do not have to be used together.

As described earlier, when (d, k) run length codes are used with $d > 0$, the recorded transitions could be spaced farther apart so that the resulting read pulses do not interfere, or interfere less with neighboring pulses. As d gets larger, 1,2,3, . . . the recorded density gets lower, but the timing window narrows. From the discussion on modulation codes, it was concluded that a value of $d > 2$ was impractical. In fact, for magnetic recording, $d = 1$ appears to be the best choice among $d = 1$, 2, or 3.

Partial response approaches the problem from another direction. Instead of spreading the pulses apart, partial response allows interference to occur. However, the amount of interference is known and controlled. There are many types of partial response depending on the amount and extent of interference, and also depending on whether the channel can pass dc or not. For example, a magnetic recording channel cannot pass dc because of the differentiation inherent in an inductive read sensor. An optical channel such as that used in data storage or CD audio does pass dc. The classic paper on partial response numbered the different types of partial response into Class 1, Class 2, and so forth (Kabal and Pasupathy, 1975). The discussion will begin with Class 4 partial response. This is a type of partial response that is applicable to magnetic recording, and in fact it is the one used in PRML. We will then look at extensions to partial response Class 4 (also called PR4) as they might apply to magnetic recording.

Figure 4.23 shows the response to a single step of write current in a Class 4 partial response channel. This type of channel is typically used with $(0, k)$ codes. It could be used with other codes (Schneider, 1988a), but that is not where its potential lies. PR4 will be considered only with $(0, k)$ codes in this chapter. Note that the pulse is three-bits wide at the baseline. In Fig. 4.23, each bit is one unit wide, and the pulse width at the baseline goes from -1 to $+2$, or three bits. The channel samples the signal values at the edge of the bit cell rather than the center. From the figure we see that the pulse value at $t = 0$ and $t = 1$ is unity, and the pulse value at all other bit cell edges is exactly zero.

If a second pulse is read one bit later, it will be negative, and appear as shown in Fig. 4.24. Note that the second pulse has a nonzero value of -1 at $t = 1$ and $t = 2$. It is exactly zero at all other bit-cell edges. The sum of these two pulses is shown in Fig. 4.25. The resulting dipulse has values of 1 at $t = 0$; 0 at $t = 1$; and -1 at $t = 2$. Note that at $t = 1$, the value of $+1$ from the first pulse and -1 from the second pulse exactly cancel to give a value of 0. Thus, ideally there are only three possible sample values of $+1$, 0, and -1. This is a three level signal just as in conventional magnetic recording. There is nonzero interference between pulses. However, the

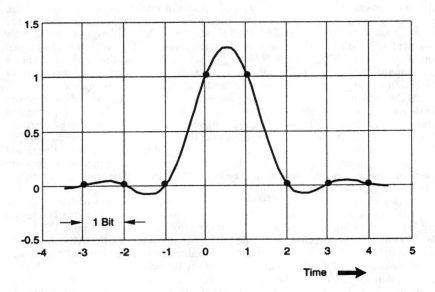

FIGURE 4.23   Partial-response Class 4 (PR4) pulse.

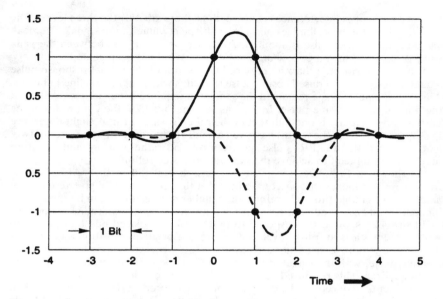

FIGURE 4.24 Two successive PR4 pulses.

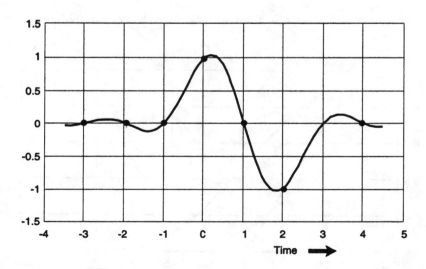

FIGURE 4.25 Sum of two successive PR4 pulses.

type and amount of interference is known, thus, there are only the three levels. The sampling is at the bit-cell edges and not at the peak value of the signal. The peak value of the isolated pulse is about 1.27, so there is a 2 dB loss between the peak value of 1.27 and the bit edge sample value of 1. What has been gained?

It might be expected that the required bandwidth of the partial response pulse would be less than the raised cosine pulse since it is wider at the baseline (3 bits vs. 2 bits). If the pulse shape remained the same, the required bandwidth would be $\frac{2}{3}$ of the normal raised cosine pulse. In fact, as seen in Fig. 4.26, the bandwidth of the partial response pulse is one-half that of the raised cosine pulse. A slight difference in shapes (aside from the width) has given a bandwidth reduction by a factor of two. Note however, that the PR4 pulse spectrum rolls off rather sharply, and therefore may be more difficult to achieve than the raised cosine rolloff.

As shown in Fig. 4.26, the pulse response has a null at the "ALL ONES" frequency. This means that successive pulses at this frequency will give zero output amplitude at sample time. Therefore, the number of pulses that can be spaced one bit apart must be limited in order to insure a nonzero signal amplitude for clocking.

Figure 4.25 showed the response to two transitions placed one bit apart. The write current starts at a low level, then there is a positive transition and, one-bit period later, there is a negative transition. The write current is a one-bit-wide positive pulse, with the waveform of Fig. 4.25 as the desired response out of the read equalizer. This equalized read signal has sample values of $+1$, 0, and -1.

Consider the concept of the delay operator. If 1 occurs at the present time, then the notation $1\ D$ stands for a 1 delayed by the amount D. Let D equal one bit (code bit) period. The notation D^N means a delay in time of $N \times D$. Using this notation, we can write the three sample values of Fig. 4.25 as $1 + 0\ D - 1\ D^2$, which simplifies to $1 - D^2$. For this reason the Class 4 partial response channel (PR4) is also often called a $1 - D^2$ channel. Other partial response channels have their own characteristic polynomial in D. (Strictly speaking, the $1 - D^2$ response should refer to the impulse response, rather than the pulse response).

In summary, partial response Class 4, (PR4) has a characteristic polynomial of:

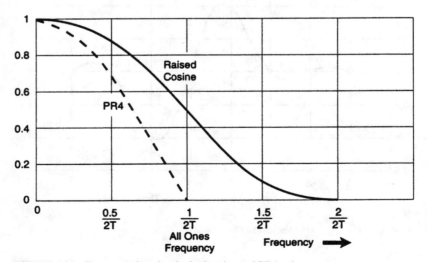

FIGURE 4.26   Frequency domain of raised cosine and PR4 pulses.

$1 - D^2$. There is a known amount of nonzero intersymbol interference with neighboring pulses. Sampling is done at the bit cell edges, which results in SNR loss of 1/1.27 or 2 dB. However, with a wider pulse and slightly different pulse shape, the resultant pulse bandwidth at the equalizer output is one-half that required by the conventional raised cosine pulse.

Now, consider the pulse shown in Fig. 4.27a. It has in fact a raised cosine shape, but it spans 4 bits instead of the conventional 2 bits at the baseline. Therefore, it has

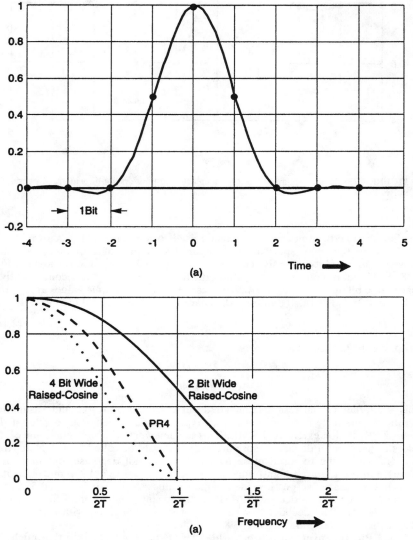

FIGURE 4.27 (*a*) 4-bit-wide raised cosine pulse (*b*) spectra of PR4 and 2- and 4-bit-wide raised cosine pulses.

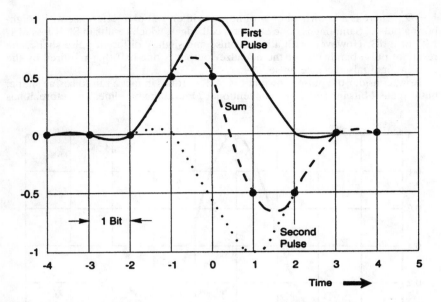

FIGURE 4.28 Pulse response of EPR4 channel step-response is a 4-bit-wide raised cosine pulse.

one half the bandwidth of a conventional raised cosine pulse. This is shown in Fig. 4.27b where the pulse spectrum is compared with that of PR4 pulse, and the conventional two-bit-wide raised cosine pulse. The pulse response is shown in Fig. 4.28. The input is a pulse-two transition, the first positive, and the second negative, spaced one bit apart. From Fig. 4.28, we can see that the sample values are: $+ 1/2$, $+ 1/2$, $- 1/2$, and $- 1/2$. Therefore, the characteristic polynomial in D is

$$G(D) = 0.5(1 + D - D^2 - D^3) \qquad (4.16)$$

Dropping the 0.5 scale factor gives

$$G(D) = 1 + D - D^2 - D^3$$
$$= (1 - D^2) \times (1 + D) \qquad (4.17)$$

This is another partial response included but unnamed by Kabal and Pasupathy. Several papers have been written on this type of channel. They have given it the name EPRML for extended PRML. This is somewhat of a misnomer since ML refers to the type of decoder. More properly it should be called EPR4. Note from Fig. 4.27b that the required pulse bandwidth does not decrease, but there is a decrease in the required high-frequency response. From Fig. 4.27a and 4.28, it is seen that there are five possible ideal sample values: $+ 1$, $+ 0.5$, 0, $- 0.5$, and $- 1$. The ML decoder to decode EPRML is significantly more complicated than to decode PRML. The decoder has six or eight states compared with only two for PR4. EPRML is used in the IBM 3390 disk file.

The EPRML waveform is 4 bits wide. This is the kind of shape that might be considered for peak detection with a (1, 7) code. Because of the $d = 1$ restriction, not all sequences are allowed in (1, 7). This will reduce the complexity of a maximum likelihood decoder from 8 states to only 6 states. Detection becomes more reliable as well, since by design, certain forbidden sequences can never be decoded by the detector.

Some recent papers have discussed EEPRML, or E²PRML. The latter is a natural extension where the original PR4 response is multiplied by $(1 + D)^2$. In general, we can envision transfer functions of this type:

$$G(D) = (1 - D^2) \times (1 + D)^N \tag{4.18}$$

As N increases, less high-frequency boost is required, but the number of signal levels increases, and detection becomes exponentially more complicated. As N goes from 0 to 1 to 2 . . . , the pulse width at the baseline goes from 3 to 4 to 5 bits. The number of detector states goes from 4 to 8 to 16. A special property will allow an interleaved 2-state decoder to be used for PRML rather than a 4-state decoder.

What follows is a heuristic explanation of how a maximum-likelihood detector works. Included is a list of what a maximum-likelihood decoder can and cannot do. A maximum likelihood detector will make errors, but it should make fewer errors than if bit-by-bit detection is used. It does this by using information that can be extracted from read signal dependencies from one bit to the next. An example of this dependency is that the read signal pulses for ONES must alternate in polarity. Therefore, if a positive pulse has been detected, the next detected pulse should be negative. Referring to Fig. 4.29, there is one positive pulse that does not exceed the positive threshold. This is between two negative pulses that exceed the negative threshold. Bit-by-bit detection would decode a ZERO in bit position 320. A maximum-likelihood detector would conclude that there must be a positive pulse between the negative pulse at bit position 260 and the second negative pulse in bit position 400. The positive pulse must occur somewhere between the two negative pulses. The positive pulse is most likely at bit position 320, since that bit position has the most positive amplitude. Although the maximum likelihood detector will decide on the most likely sequence, errors can still be made if the noise or other signal impairments are large enough.

The use of partial response signaling will further increase the amount of bit-to-bit dependency. PR4 pulses have nonzero values at two sample times; EPR4 and E²PR4 pulses have nonzero values at three and four sample times respectively. The use of run-length codes will also restrict the allowable bit sequences. For example, the sequence 101100 is not allowed by a (1, 7) code, and this knowledge can be used in the maximum-likelihood detector design. Sequences with adjacent ONES or more than seven consecutive ZEROS will not be allowed.

It can be seen that the dependencies discussed above affect small groups of bits. The maximum-likelihood detector is a defense against media defects, noise, or off-track signal interference that only affect a small number of bits. A signal dropout greater than ten bits in length would most likely produce an error even if a maximum-likelihood detector were being used. The detector might correct small errors at the start or end of the dropout as the signal amplitude gradually decreased or increased. It might correct marginal errors within the dropout as well. However a maximum likelihood detector will have the most benefit in a hard-disk environment where its correction power more closely matches the length of the typical error events. Further, in a high-end tape drive where eighteen tracks are read in parallel, an analog-to-digital converter and a maximum-likelihood detector would be required for each track.

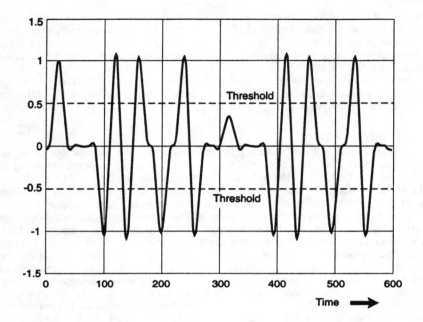

FIGURE 4.29 Read signal with error condition.

Several semiconductor manufacturers have developed off-the-shelf designs for PRML systems. Efforts are now being directed at lowering power consumption, increasing data rate, and lowering package size and cost.

4.5.8 Clocking

It is necessary to phase and frequency lock a read clock to the read signals because the velocity of the tape moving past the head can vary as much as ten to fifteen percent. If the tape is written at a speed faster than nominal velocity, and then read on a drive going slower than nominal, the actual frequency change can double.

The read clock is normally frequency and phase locked to the write clock before reading is to begin. At the read command, the read clock will start in phase with the detected ONES data pulses. A data pulse arriving late in a bit cell is an indication that the read frequency is lower than nominal. Conversely, a data pulse arriving early in the bit cell is an indication that the read frequency is higher than nominal. An error signal is generated that is proportional to the amount of time that the data pulse arrives either early or late. This error signal is filtered and then sent to a voltage controlled oscillator (VCO). The VCO will change frequency in the direction that will minimize the data pulse arrival-time error.

Tape drives that read several tracks in parallel will have a VCO for each track. It is possible to share frequency information among groups of tracks as an error prevention measure. Data pulses may be prevented from supplying error signals to the VCO if a track is experiencing a long error event. The track's VCO will be kept in frequency lock by the other tracks in its group until the error event has passed. The track in error will then only have to phase lock to its read data.

Partial response systems sample the signal amplitude at specific points. There may be a large amount of peak shift even in an ideal partial response signal. Therefore, peak detected pulses are not used to generate error signals for the VCO. Differences in amplitude samples can be used in partial response systems. The read clock VCO is part of all the PRML chip sets that are currently available.

4.5.9 Error Correction and Prevention

One of the easiest ways to avoid errors is to avoid poor or marginal portions of tape. This is called write skipping. It is very common both in magnetic tape and disk drives to somehow stress the channel during read verify-while-write. This will insure that the recorded signals are robust, and will be easily read during a subsequent read operation when the stress is removed.

An early example of this was to raise the qualifying threshold level during read-while-write. For example, the threshold could be set at 40% during read-while-write and 25% during normal read only. There is an obvious tradeoff here between having too many write skips because the threshold is too high, and having poor subsequent read reliability because the threshold during write was too low, and marginal signals were written and allowed to pass.

The write and/or read threshold can also be raised during manufacturing test. This may prevent the shipment of marginal machines. The read threshold can also be lowered or raised during an error recovery procedure (ERP). Typically the threshold on all tracks is changed in the same way during a read ERP. However, conceptually the threshold could be changed one track at a time, or one track group at a time. This would be done as a last resort before posting a permanent read error. The list of ERPs is normally ordered so that the most effective procedures are done first. Last on the list are procedures that have only a small probability of success.

Another procedure that is built into commercially available read-channel chips is to offset or narrow the clocking window. This procedure is sometimes called "phase stress." Like raising the qualifying threshold, this is done as a stress during read-while-write. It is also often employed during manufacturing test to select out marginal machines. Offsetting the clock window can also be done as an ERP during read.

Injecting noise is another way of stressing the channel that could be used in both the development phase of a machine as well as a part of a manufacturing test. The noise could be either bandlimited white noise, or white noise that has been frequency shaped to match the channel frequency response. Whether threshold or window or noise is varied, the ability to change these parameters must be part of the channel design. In the case of noise, there must be a place that the noise can be injected either from an external generator, or from a test circuit built into the read/write card(s).

The use of Reed-Solomon error correction codes is now commonplace. For a given amount of redundancy, these codes offer the most error-correction power compared with alternate codes. The advent of low cost VLSI logic has made it possible to routinely use these codes. The use of Reed-Solomon codes typically operate on the byte level. Data bytes and ECC bytes are grouped into code words. The Reed-Solomon code can correct the number of bytes in error within a code word equal to the number of ECC bytes in the code word. It can do this if the bytes that are in error can be "pointed to." If there are no pointers, then the Reed-Solomon code will only correct half the number of errors. So there is great motivation to have and to use reliable pointers. For example, if a byte contains a modulation code violation such as four zeros in a row in a $(0, 3)$ code, then we know for certain that an error has occurred in that byte. This is known as a "digital pointer" since analog information is not used. Alternatively, one could use an "analog pointer" which would be signals that had marginal amplitude above or below the threshold, or data pulses that were marginally inside the bit cell. The problem with analog pointers is that they usually cannot definitely point to an error, but only to a marginal signal. A strategy of using only digital pointers first, and then employing analog pointers as part of an ERP may be a good compromise strategy.

As mentioned above, a Reed-Solomon code can correct the number of bytes in error equal to the number of ECC bytes in a code word if the error location is pointed to. It requires two ECC bytes per byte in error if the errors are not pointed to. Essentially, one ECC byte is used to identify the error location, and the second ECC byte is used to correct the byte in error. What if some errors are pointed to, and others are not? In general, the number of errors correctable in a Reed-Solomon code word is given by:

$$P + 2E \leq B$$

Where P is the number of errors with pointers, E is the number of errors without pointers, and B is the number of Reed-Solomon ECC bytes within a code word. The bytes are normally spatially spaced apart in order to reduce the probability that multiple bytes are in error within a code word. Bytes are spread among tracks in multitrack machines. The Reed-Solomon code words contain eighteen bytes in eighteen track tape drives. One byte is placed in each track. There are fourteen data bytes and four ECC bytes. Up to four tracks in error can be corrected with pointers. Bytes are spread out along the tape in a serial track format.

For many years cyclic redundancy check (CRC) bytes were added to the track or record to check for errors. If there are N check bits, then the probability of missing an error is $1/2^N$, thus, if a single 8 bit CRC byte is used, the possibility of missing an error is $1/2^8$. There is an error for certain if an error is detected. For a small amount of redundancy, the possibility of missing an error can be made arbitrarily small by increasing the number of CRC bits. A single CRC byte can be used as a digital pointer along a track to point to an error that occurs in a group of bytes. The larger the group of bytes, the lower the redundancy. However, the larger the group of bytes, the less certainty we will have as to where the error occurred. Multiple CRC bytes are often used at the end of a record or sector to insure that there are no remaining errors after ECC. This prevents any miscorrections from being sent to the host as good data. As seen above, the probability of missing an error can be made arbitrarily small.

The combination of write skipping over poor sections of media, the use of error correction codes, and exhaustive error recovery procedures enable error rates of 10^{14} bytes between permanent error to be achieved.

4.6   FUTURE OUTLOOK

Magnetic tape drive development will continue to be robust well into the next century. Longitudinal tape drives will have hundreds of tracks on both quarter and half-inch tapes. There will be dedicated servo tracks or imbedded servo information so that the read and write heads can move to follow the tape media. Helical-scan drives will continue to benefit from technical advances in the consumer audio and video market to produce high-capacity and low-cost devices. Areal densities for longitudinal machines may approach one gigabit per square inch before the end of this decade. Helical-scan devices have the potential to have somewhat higher areal densities, but the areal density differences between longitudinal and helical formats should shrink as servo track following techniques are added to longitudinal machines. Helical formats will continue to benefit from azimuth recording which minimizes the effect of reading offtrack.

REFERENCES

Eige, J. J., A. M. Patel, S. D. Roberts and D. Stedman, "Tape Motion Control for Reel to Reel Drive," U.S. Patent 4,125,881 (1978).

Forney, G. D. Jr., "Maximum Likelihood Sequence Detection in the Presence of Intersymbol Interference," *IEEE Trans. Info. Theory,* **IT-13,** 363 (1972).

Forney, G. D. Jr., "The Viterbi Algorithm," *Proc. IEEE,* **61,** 268 (1973).

Geiger, R., and E. Sanchez-Sinencio, "Active Filter Design Using Operational Trans-conductance Amplifiers: A Tutorial," *IEEE Cir. Dev. Mag.,* **3,** 20, (1985).

Harris, J. P., W. B. Phillips, J. F. Wells and W. D. Winger. "Innovations in the Design of Magnetic Tape Subsystems," *IBM J. Res. Dev.,* **25,** 691 (1981).

Haynes, M. K., "Experimental Determination of the Loss and Phase Functions of a Magnetic Recording Channel," *IEEE Trans. Magn.,* **MAG-13,** 1284 (1977).

Howell, T., D. P. McCown, T. A. Diola, Y. Tang, K. R. Hense, and R. L. Gee, "Error Rate Performance of Experimental Gigabit per Square Inch Recording Components," *IEEE Trans. Magn.,* **MAG-26,** 2298 (1990).

Jorgensen, F., *The Complete Handbook of Magnetic Recording,* Fourth Ed., TAB Books Inc., New York, 1995.

Kabal, P., and S. Pasupathy, "Partial-Response Signaling," *IEEE Trans. Comm.,* **COM-23,** 9 (1975).

Kobayashi, H., and D. T. Tang, "Application of Partial-Response Channel Coding to Magnetic Recording Systems," *IBM J. Res. Dev.,* **14,** 368 (1970).

Lathi, B. P., *Modern Digital and Analog Communication Systems,* Holt, Rinehart and Winston, New York, 1989.

Mallinson, J. C., "A Unified View of High Density Digital Recording Theory," *IEEE Trans. Magn.,* **MAG-11,** 1166 (1975).

Mee, C. D., and E. D. Daniel, *Magnetic Recording* (eds.), Vol. II, 4, 210, McGraw-Hill, New York, 1988. *Magnetic Recording Handbook,* Part 2, Chap. 4, 852, McGraw-Hill, New York, 1990.

Moon, J. J., and L. R. Carley, "Performance Comparison of Detection Methods in Magnetic Recording," *IEEE Trans. Magn.,* **MAG-26,** 3155 (1990).

Schneider, R. C., "An Improved Pulse Slimming Method for Magnetic Recording," *IEEE Trans. Magn.,* **MAG-11,** 302 (1975).

Schneider, R. C., "Write Equalization in High-Linear-Density Magnetic Recording," *IBM J. Res. Dev.,* **29,** 563 (1985).

Schneider, R. C., "Sequence (Viterbi-Equivalent) Decoding," *IEEE Trans. Magn.,* **MAG-24,** 2539 (1988*a*).

Schneider, R. C., "Write Equalization for Generalized (d, k) Codes," *IEEE Trans. Magn.,* **MAG-24,** 2533 (1988*b*).

Shelledy, F. B., and G. W. Brock, "A Linear Self-Biased Magnetoresistive Head," *IEEE Trans. Magn.,* **MAG-11,** 1206 (1975).

Siegel, P., "Applications of a Peak Detection Channel Model," *IEEE Trans. Magn.,* **MAG-18,** 1250 (1984).

Siegel, P., "Recording Codes for Digital Magnetic Storage," *IEEE Trans. Magn.,* **MAG-21,** 1366 (1985).

Thapar, H. K., N. P. Sands, W. L. Abbott, and J. M. Cioffi. "Spectral Shaping for Peak Detection Equalization," *IEEE Trans. Magn.,* **MAG-26,** 2309 (1990).

Veillard, D. H., "Compact Spectrum Recording, a New Binary Process Maximizing the Use of a Recording Channel," *IEEE Trans. Magn.,* **MAG-20,** 891 (1984).

Watkinson, J., *The Art of Data Audio,* Focal Press, Boston, 1994.

Watkinson, J., *The D-3 Digital Video Recorder,* Focal Press, Boston, 1992.

Ziv, J., and A. Lemple, "A Universal Algorithm for Sequential Data Compression," *IEEE Trans. Info. Theory,* **IT-23,** 337 (1977).

CHAPTER 5
ANALOG VIDEO RECORDING

Hiroshi Sugaya
Kansai University, Osaka, Japan

5.1 HISTORICAL DEVELOPMENT AND BACKGROUND[†]

5.1.1 Television Systems

In terms of its impact on our day-to-day lives, television is without a doubt the single most important invention of this century. With the successful advent of high-quality color television, the magnitude of this impact has increased several times over; at the present time there are a great many different color television systems on the market (Pritchard and Gibson, 1980).

To understand the problems inherent in video tape recording (VTR), it is helpful to compare the recording and playback systems used in films and in television broadcasts. In motion pictures, the illusion of continuous motion is created by projecting a series of still-frame pictures onto a screen at such a rate that the eye cannot differentiate between the frames. Owing to the after image phenomenon in the human eye, the segmented pictures are observed as a continuous picture. After a great deal of experimentation, a single international motion picture standard was eventually established: 24 illuminated frames per second, with darkness between each frame.

In order to send a picture as a television signal, the picture is first reconstructed as a series of small dots. In monochrome television, dots of different tone are used—black, white, and gray. The arrangement of these dots constitutes the details of the picture. Although the image is actually constructed from dots, these dots themselves are so small that the human eye blends the individual dots together into an integrated image and perceives them as a complete picture. The definition of the picture will depend upon the total number of lines (series of dots), and the contrast will depend on the number of shades of gray between black and white. The picture is scanned by a television camera, transmitted to the viewer, and displayed on a cathode-ray tube. The camera and the television receiver must be constantly synchronized so that the order in which the camera scans the picture is exactly the same as that on the television display. The camera scans the picture one line at a time

[†]Important historical developments are summarized in the Appendix, Table 5.7.

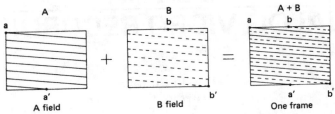

FIGURE 5.1 Interlace principle and composition of a television picture.

and, as each line is completed, a synchronizing pulse is added to the waveform to cause the cathode-ray tube to begin to scan a new line. This continues until the last line of the picture is scanned, at which point a different synchronizing signal is added to the waveform to indicate that not only a new line but a new picture is beginning.

In order to reduce the flicker, which is inherent in a transmission system of this sort, interlace scanning is used in all present-day television systems. As shown in Fig. 5.1, the scanning beam moves from line *a* vertically down the tube, scanning the odd lines to the middle of the bottom line, *a'*; this is called a *field*. Then the beam traces the even lines beginning at line *b*, making another field. The two different fields constitute a complete scene, which is called a *frame* in the United States and a *picture* in Europe.

Initially, it was necessary for television transmission equipment to be synchronized with the main power frequency. In countries such as the United States and Canada, 30 frames are transmitted each second at the vertical scanning rate of 60 Hz, while 25 frames are transmitted each second in Europe, Australia, China, and other 50-Hz countries. Japan has both 50- and 60-Hz systems. Obviously, the greater the number of frames transmitted per second, the more convincing the picture will appear to the human eye, and 25 frames per second is close to the minimum number that the eye will accept as a continuous picture without flicker. This is the source of a serious dilemma in television broadcasting because this frame rate should be kept as low as possible in order to keep the bandwidth narrow.

The number of horizontal lines determines the bandwidth of the television signal as well as the vertical definition of the television picture. There is a lengthy history behind the selection of the number of horizontal lines. In the United Kingdom, at the very beginning stages of television broadcasting, a standard of 405 lines and 50 fields per second was established. A standard of 819 lines and 50 fields per second was established for monochrome in France and Belgium; eventually a unified standard of 625 lines and 50 fields per second was established for western European color transmission, including that of the United Kingdom. Meanwhile, the United States, Japan and other countries using 60 Hz power frequency adopted 525 lines. Thus, countries with a 60-Hz electrical standard use 525 horizontal lines and most areas with a 50-Hz standard use 625 lines.

In color television systems, the dots are formed from a trio of the three primary colors, red (R), green (G), and blue (B). In order for color transmission to be compatible with monochrome transmission, color transmission systems broadcast the basic monochrome signal, which is called the *luminance* signal, plus a *chrominance* signal. Color television systems can be classified into three main types: NTSC (National Television System Committee), PAL (phase alternation line), SECAM (sequential color and memory). A unified worldwide standard for color transmission has not yet been achieved, and at the present time there are some thirteen subsystems of these three major standard systems. The major differences among these various NTSC, PAL, and SECAM subsystems are in the specific modulation processes used for encoding and transmitting the chrominance signal (Table 5.1).

5.1.1.1 NTSC. The basic idea of color television derives from the NTSC system developed by RCA. The standard was established in 1953; it has been used in the United States since 1954 and in Japan since 1960. In order to transmit the three primary R, G, B color signals, a frequency bandwidth three times wider than that necessary for monochrome TV signals is required. The NTSC system, however, can transmit the luminance signal Y and the chrominance signals C within the same frequency band as monochrome and is thus perfectly compatible with monochrome TV signals. This composite system uses two carriers of the same frequency (3.58 MHz), having a phase displacement of 90°, amplitude-modulated by color-component signals. These two color signals are represented by two vector signals I and Q having bandwidths of 1.5 and 0.5 MHz. Color hue (tone) is determined by the phase of the combined color subcarrier signal, and color saturation (intensity) is determined by the amplitude of the color subcarrier signal. A color reference signal (color burst signal) is inserted in a horizontal blanking period to synchronize the subcarrier frequency and phase (Fig. 5.2). In color television, therefore, the phase characteristics of the transmission system are critical. This has more important implications when recording magnetically on tape, which has an intrinsic time-base instability due to its flexibility.

5.1.1.2 PAL. The PAL system, developed by Telefunken in 1962, is similar to the NTSC system, with the exception that the color-difference signals are represented by U and V, which have equal bandwidths and are transmitted on a 4.43-MHz subcarrier, with the V signal reversing in phase on alternate lines. In the NTSC system, phase distortion (color-quadrature distortion) causes an incorrect color transmission, but in the PAL system the V color-difference signal reverses in phase every other line. Thus, the reproduced color signal phase distortion on any two adjacent lines will be in the opposite direction from the true color, and color distortion can be averaged out by means of a single-horizontal-line delay line. Simpler receivers rely on the eye averaging the error on alternate lines.

5.1.1.3 SECAM. The SECAM system was first developed in France in 1967. In this system, the color transmission method is quite different from the NTSC and PAL system. Color-difference signals (R—Y, B—Y) are transformed into frequency modulation signals with different subcarriers and transmitted successively on alternate lines (line sequential transmission). Simultaneous color-difference signals are reproduced using a horizontal scanning period delay line in the TV receiver. This system is, therefore, not influenced by phase distortion in transmitted color signals.

5.1.1.4 High-Definition Television Systems. With the present-day rapid advances in electronic and television technology (including satellite broadcasting), a higher-definition picture quality can be anticipated for many future applications such as broadcasting systems, movie production (including electronic movie theaters), and a variety of industrial information transmission systems. Moreover,

TABLE 5.1 Typical Color Television Systems

	NTSC	PAL	SECAM	High definition[†]
Fields, per second	60	50	50	60
No. of horizontal lines	525	625	625	1125
Aspect ratio	4:3	4:3	4:3	16:9
Subcarrier, MHz	3.58	4.43	4.25 4.40	
Luminance bandwidth Y, MHz	4.2	5.0	6.0	20
Chrominance bandwidth C, MHz	I: 1.3 Q: 0.4	U: 1.3 V: 1.3	D_R: 1.3 D_B: 1.3	C_W: 7.0 C_N: 5.5
Color system	AM by two-color signals having 90° phase displacement	(Similar to NTSC) U and V color-difference signals reverse in phase on alternate lines	Color-difference signals (R—Y and B—Y) are transmitted by FM on alternate lines	Color-difference signals (C_W and C_N) are processed by component

[†]Comité Consultatif International des Radio Communications Proposal, 1986.

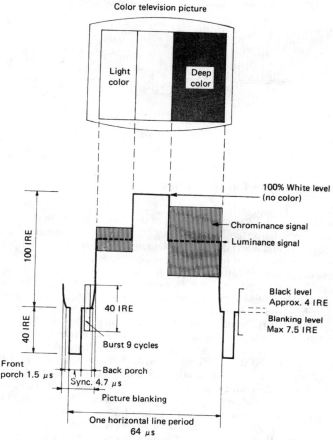

FIGURE 5.2 One horizontal line of an NTSC color television signal.

the amount of information which can be transmitted over the TV screen has increased dramatically in recent years. Future needs will dictate the necessity for pictures of higher definition than the present capabilities of the NTSC, PAL, and SECAM systems.

The development of high-definition television has been guided by studies of the relationships among three main parameters: picture size, number of scanning lines, and visual impact. Both a film simulation method and a real television system have been used (Hayashi, 1981). One proposed future system uses 1125 scanning lines, 60 fields per second, and an aspect ratio of 16:9. The bandwidth of the color-component signal of this 1125-line system is more than 5 MHz, and no recognizable deterioration in line-sequential transmission of R—Y or B—Y is noted. The signals C_W and C_N are obtained by slightly amending R—Y and B—Y, and are used as color-component signals (Fujio, 1978). The major characteristics are listed in Table 5.1.

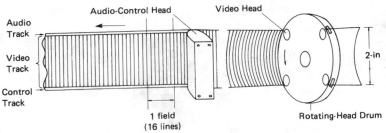

FIGURE 5.3   Quadruplex rotating-head video recorder and transverse recording format.

5.1.2 Broadcast Video Tape Recorders[†]

As the television networks in the United States expanded, the handling of time differences from the east to the west coast of the American continent emerged as a serious problem (Stanton and Stanton, 1987). The development of a television recording device would alleviate this problem, and several such developments were undertaken using fixed-head mechanisms in the 1950s (Abramgon, 1973; Sugaya, 1986). These development activities were directed specifically toward the recording of video signals using a type of tape-transport mechanism similar to that used in audio tape recorders but with faster tape speeds (Axon, 1958). Multichannel recording was used in order to reduce the recorded frequencies to as low a range as possible (Mullin, 1954). None of these methods produced significant results because the immature technology at that time resulted in a recorded signal that had both too short a wavelength and severe time-base instability; it also had an unrealistically short recording time of at most 15 min (Olson et al., 1954, 1956).

In 1956, Ampex Corporation announced their newly developed rotating head video recorder using 2-in-wide tape (Ginsburg, 1956; Snyder, 1956). Rotating-head technology afforded a high head-to-tape speed of about 38 m/s (1500 in/s), which made it possible to record sufficient bandwidth of the video signal by FM. A longer recording time (over 1 h) was achieved while keeping the tape speed at 38 cm/s (15 in/s), which was the same as that of audio recorders then in broadcast use.

The rotary-head recorder employed a transverse format in which recording was done by four heads mounted on a rotating drum; this was also called the *quadruplex head* (see Fig. 5.3). The original quadruplex system recorded only monochrome. In order to introduce color, it was necessary to shift the FM carrier frequency to a higher range without changing the recorded format on the tape. This became possible with the further development of magnetic recording technology and yielded high-band recording in 1964 and super-high-band recording in 1971.

The quadruplex (or quad) system was a significant innovation in recording technology, but this system as developed at the time was still far from ideal. Each transverse track on the magnetic tape could record only one-sixteenth of one field, and complicated switching was required to reassemble a complete field. Any amplitude of phase differences between the picture segments produced an effect called *banding,* to which the eye is especially sensitive. Moreover, tape consumption was high so that the tape cost per hour, as well as tape storage cost, was correspondingly high (Kazama and Itoh, 1979). The quadruplex system was essentially a method to

---

[†]For specifications, see the Appendix, Table 5.8.

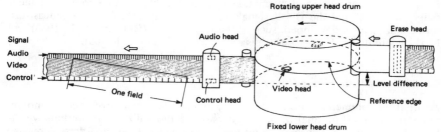

FIGURE 5.4   Two-head helical-scan video recorder and recording format.

record the NTSC signal with broadcast quality at a time when time-base correction using large-scale integrated circuits was unavailable.

In order to record one field continuously on the tape, it is necessary to lengthen the video track; one way to do this is to record the video track on the tape diagonally. To achieve this, the tape must be physically wrapped around the rotating-head drum in a helical-shaped tape path (Fig. 5.4). This *helical-scan* recording method can record one complete field on a single track, with the result that each field can be switched in during the vertical blanking period without the necessity for any complicated circuitry. When helical-scan recording was first introduced, the technology of magnetic recording was still primitive, and the helical-scan method needed a head drum of overly large diameter (Sawazaki et al., 1960). In addition, if a helical-scan recorder designed for the PAL or SECAM system (50 Hz) was adapted for use with the NTSC color system (60 Hz), the head drum diameter had to be increased by 20 percent to achieve the same head-to-tape speed. To solve this problem, the segment sequential-recording format was developed in 1966. In this format, one-fifth of one field of the NTSC signal and one-sixth of one field of the PAL signal (both of which are approximately 52 horizontal lines) are recorded on a single segmented slant track on the tape, without changing the head drum diameter and the tape speed. Thus the head drum rotating speed could be kept constant in order to achieve the same relative head-to-tape speed and could be synchronized to the field rate. This segmented recording method was developed for industrial use with 1-in-wide tape, and the same idea was marketed in 1976 for broadcast use (type B recorders) (Zahn, 1979). A similar principle was used in the first commercial digital video recorder (D-1) developed in the 1980s (Remley, 1985).

Nonsegmented helical-scan recorders were first used exclusively for industrial and institutional applications but, in 1978, a 1-in-wide tape system for broadcast use was developed with the aid of time base correction (type C recorders) (Alden, 1977). Magnetic recording technology is continuously increasing the recording density and it is now possible to record the PAL and SECAM signals on type C machines without changing the head drum diameter and also to use considerably smaller-diameter head drums and smaller reels.

All commercially marketed recorders used a single track for the video signal until 1982, when the M format was introduced (Arimura and Sadashige, 1983). This uses two video tracks (one for the Y signal and the other for the I and Q signals of NTSC), with the same diameter of head drum and cassette as the $\frac{1}{2}$-in format now in wide use throughout the world (video home system, or VHS). A similar development, known as the L format, also uses two video tracks (one for the Y and one for the R—Y and B—Y signals) and the cassette is mechanically compatible with the

Beta half-inch format. The L format, using digital technology, compresses sequentially the R—Y and the B—Y signals to half their length. Other broadcast-use formats have been developed, such as the Quartercam (Reimers et al., 1985) and M-II (Sekimoto et al., 1986) which is replacing the 19 mm U format.

5.1.3 Home Video Tape Recorders[†]

Apart from commercial broadcast needs, market demands developed for home, industrial, and institutional video recorders that could utilize narrower bandwidths than those required in broadcasting use. Home video tape recorders were also originally designed on a stationary-head basis, but the recording time, time-base instability, and video bandwidth proved to be insufficient (Fisher, 1963). Endless-loop systems were also tried but without commercial success (Sawazaki et al., 1979; Sadashige, 1980). As a result, rotating-head methods also became the standard in recording television signals for the home.

The history of home video recording has witnessed a series of significant reductions in both head drum diameter and tape width (Sugaya, 1992). In 1964, $\frac{1}{2}$-in-wide tape was first used to record a 1-h program on a 7-in-reel tape recorder with a two-head helical-scan method. The particular method used was not commercially acceptable since it relied on the "field-skip" process, which records one field, skips the next field, and then plays back the same field picture twice using the two heads. Even though it was possible with this method to record a full 1-h program, the picture quality deteriorated owing to a staccato picture effect during fast motion. Shortly after this a $\frac{1}{2}$-in recorder was developed that could record a complete-frame picture, although the recording time was limited to 40 min.

In order to solve the playing-time problem, azimuth recording was developed (Okamura, 1964; Sugaya et al., 1979). This technique involves the use of two heads with differently inclined gaps ($\pm\phi$), as indicated in Fig. 5.5. When head A cross-tracks into B, the resultant difference in angle is 14° (2ϕ). This produces an azimuth loss of sufficient magnitude to enable guard bands between tracks to be eliminated. A black-and-white video recorder using the azimuth-recording technique was first developed by Matsushita/Panasonic in 1968 and provided a 90-min playing time on a 7-in reel. The azimuth recording method has been a key element in the growth of home video tape recording.

The Beta format, which utilizes the azimuth recording method and a small cassette, was introduced by Sony in 1975 (Kihara et al., 1976), followed a year later by the VHS format of JVC (Shiraishi and Hirota, 1978), also using an azimuth-

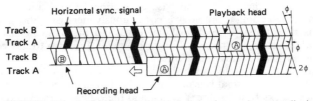

FIGURE 5.5 Azimuth recording principle (overwrite recording) *(Sugaya, 1986).*

[†]For specifications, see the Appendix, Table 5.9 (NTSC) and Table 5.10 (PAL/SECAM).

recording cassette system. In 1980, a fourth azimuth recording format, the V-2000, was introduced by Philips mainly for use in the European market (Kirk, 1979) but was discontinued in 1984. A fifth azimuth recording format, the 8-mm video format, was established by international agreement at the 1984 "8-mm Video Conference" (IEC, 1987).

Based on innovations in magnetic recording technology, which have mainly affected recording heads and recording media, the Beta and VHS formats have been able to double and triple recording time by reducing the video-track pitch to one-half and one-third (Iijima et al., 1977). As a result, the tape cost of video recording per hour has become slightly less than that of audio recording on tape. The development of new recording media and improved heads have led to still higher recording densities; these in turn will make possible still smaller recorders approaching the size and weight of the modern 8-mm movie camera (Morio et al., 1981; Mohri et al., 1981).

5.1.4 Continued Increases in Recording Density

Accompanying innovations and improvements in magnetic tape and heads, the areal recording density has increased and the tape consumption per hour has decreased exponentially over a 35-year period, as shown in Figs. 5.6 and 5.7 (Sugaya, 1982, 1992). Tape consumption is calculated simply from tape width and speed, and so includes audio and other signal tracks as well as video. The areal recording density of video disks is shown in Fig. 5.6 for comparison purposes. The 2-in quadruplex recorder was the first successful machine. The major trend of development has been toward helical-scan recorders, first for industrial and institutional use, later for home use. Currently "camera video" captures a portion of the 8-mm movie market. In broadcast recording, type C and type B helical-scan recorders, which have almost the same picture quality as quadruplex super-high-band recorders, have greatly improved tape consumption and are used widely throughout the world today. Quadruplex production stopped in 1980. The M and L formats were developed to meet the requirements of electronic news gathering.

Figure 5.7 shows that, since 1968, azimuth recording has strongly contributed to decreasing the video track pitch. The development of such recording media as higher-coercivity cobalt-absorbed oxide tape and alloy tape has played a significant role in reducing the minimum recordable wavelength. These trends, revised many times since 1973, have been important in forecasting the future of video recording. The commercially successful video recorders are always located on the trend line.

5.2 PRINCIPLES OF VIDEO RECORDING

5.2.1 Problems in Video Tape Recording

The primary difference between video and audio signals is in the highest frequency required, as shown in Fig. 5.8. Video requires more than 100 times the highest frequency of audio. The other significant difference is the continuity of the signal. An audio signal is continuous, while the video signal is segmented into separate fields similar to movie film. In order to record a television signal on tape, it is necessary to achieve continuous recording of at least a single picture field with sufficient bandwidth and time-base stability.

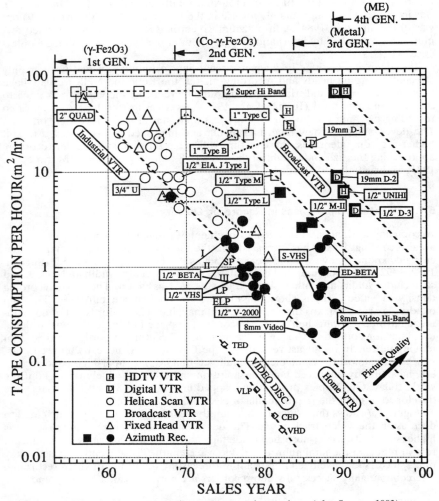

FIGURE 5.6   Historical improvement in tape consumption per hour *(after Sugaya, 1992).*

The transverse rotating-head recording method was developed to achieve sufficient relative head-to-tape velocity without increasing the tape speed itself (Marzocchi, 1941). The inertia of the rotating-head drum also alleviates time-base instability problems. The helical-scan rotating-head method is a more attractive approach because it records an entire-field picture signal on tape (Masterson, 1956). There are, however, some specific advantages to the transverse-type rotating-head recording method: the higher rotating speed of the head drum results in less instability; the track pass is shorter so that the recording is affected less by tape flexibility; finally, the tape is supported in a cupped arc by a rigid tape guide, resulting in considerably improved stability and reduction of errors.

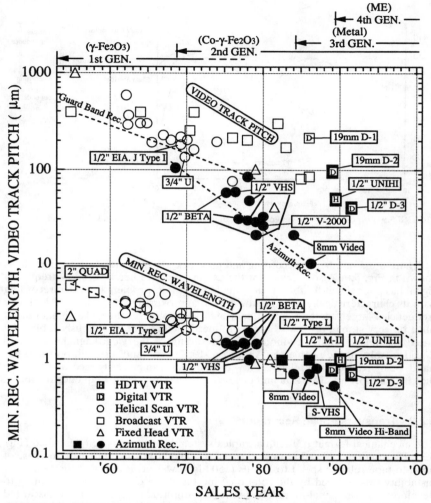

FIGURE 5.7 Historical trend in minimum recording wavelength and track pitch *(after Sugaya, 1992)*.

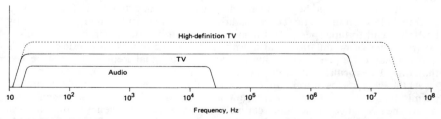

FIGURE 5.8 Frequency bandwidths of audio, regular television, and high-definition television signals.

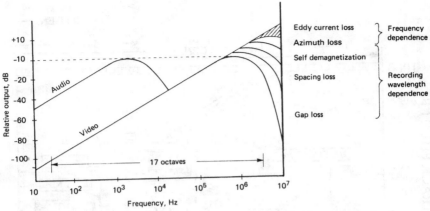

FIGURE 5.9   Types of losses in magnetic recording and playback with an inductive head.

There are a number of recording and playback losses related to wave-length, as shown in Fig. 5.9. Also, because of the use of inductive heads, the low-frequency signal has poor signal-to-noise ratio, which is a serious problem for video recording with its characteristically wide bandwidths of approximately 17 octaves. The lower frequencies largely determine the contrast of the picture; thus, the signal output must be very stable, otherwise the reproduced picture will be seriously spoiled by streaking noise. Frequency-modulation recording of the video signal was introduced to solve these problems (Anderson, 1957). The audio signal, on the other hand, being restricted to relatively low frequencies, can be easily recorded using ac bias with almost no distortion and can be equalized into a flat frequency response.

5.2.2   Transverse-Scan Recorders

The mechanical format of the quadruplex system has already been described (Fig. 5.3). By rotating the head drum at a speed of 14,400 rpm, an immediate increase of head-to-tape relative speed to 38 m/s (1500 in/s) was achieved, and the time-base instability was reduced by the rotational inertia of the drum. It then remained to develop a suitable signal-modulation scheme. Amplitude modulation was discarded because of large amounts of low-frequency noise. Frequency modulation proved successful because it does not have the same sensitivity to low-frequency noise effects. According to the traditional understanding of frequency modulation, the carrier frequency should be set at a much higher frequency than that of the signal to be transmitted. In magnetic recording, however, the highest frequency is limited by both the head-to-tape speed and the minimum recording wavelength, and the highest frequency of modulation is also limited. Thus, the modulation index, which is the modulated frequency deviation divided by the signal frequency, must be less than one. This is called *low-index FM recording* (Anderson, 1957).

At the early stages of transverse-scan recording, the technology available did not permit the recording of the higher frequencies necessary for a FM video signal. As a result, the FM range was located relatively far down in the frequency scale. This was called *low band* and was used until about 1964 (Fig. 5.10). Later, it became possible

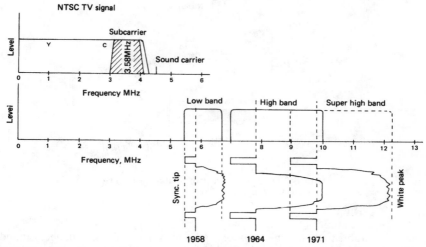

FIGURE 5.10   FM recording spectrum for NTSC broadcast quadruplex recorders.

to realize sufficient FM deviation in higher frequency ranges. This technique, known as *high band,* was responsible for considerable improvement of picture quality. Improvements in head and tape technology and in head drum air-bearing construction, which reduced the high-frequency jitter component, resulted in *super high band* which was introduced in 1971. This made it possible to obtain sufficient deviation without moiré at still higher frequency bands, and a picture of nearly perfect quality could now be recorded.

5.2.3   Helical-Scan Recording for Broadcast Use

Experience with the transverse-scanning recording system revealed some difficulties because the process involves splitting a single field into sixteen segments and stringing them out in a line to record them on the magnetic tape. Thus, when the video signal is reproduced, it is essential to keep switching in the horizontal synchronization period so that there is no switching noise in the reproduced picture (Dolby, 1957). It also proved necessary to readjust the distorted picture in order to compensate both for wear on the video heads and for distortion caused by tape interchange (Benson, 1960). On the other hand, if a single-field image is recorded in a single scan, the circuitry can be greatly simplified. As a consequence, helical-scan systems were proposed and developed in the 1950s (Schüller, 1954; Sawazaki, 1955; Masterson, 1956; Sawazaki et al., 1960).

In the beginning stages, the helical-scan technique was conceived of as using a single video head in the head drum and wrapping the tape around the drum in such a manner that the signal is recorded in a slanted or diagonal locus on the surface of the tape. However, since this locus spans the tape surface from edge to edge, no space remains for the recording of the necessary audio and control signals. The two-head helical-scan system (Fig. 5.4) was devised to compensate for this defect (Tomita, 1961). Since the early helical-scan prototypes were intended for broadcast use, they employed a large head drum in order to obtain a head-to-tape relative

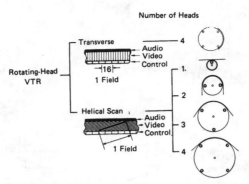

FIGURE 5.11 Various types of rotating-head video tape recorders *(Sugaya, 1986)*.

speed comparable to that of the transverse-scan recorder. This, is turn, necessitated running the flexible magnetic tape in such a long and complex path that an unacceptable degree of time-base instability and tape skew resulted. Consequently, this system proved not to be competitive with the quadruplex system, which had already firmly established itself in the market.

It is characteristic of the helical-scan system that the diameter of the head drum must be increased in proportion to the number of heads in the drum in order to maintain the same head-to-tape relative speed, as is shown in Fig. 5.11. For this reason, it was generally not considered feasible to increase the number of heads for broadcast use because of the high head-to-tape speed required to ensure sufficient picture quality. In response to this, the 1.5-head system was invented; in this system an auxiliary head is used exclusively to record the synchronizing signal on the extreme edge of the tape (Fig. 5.12). This compensates for the portion formerly lost on both edges of the tape, which was the basic drawback of the single-head system. This 1.5-head system was introduced in 1962 in a 2-in tape format for industrial use (Kihara, 1963; Suzuki et al., 1979). Subsequently, further advances in magnetic recording technology, especially in the area of higher-coercivity tape, made it possible, without any loss in broadcast picture quality, to develop a 1-in tape recorder using this principle; it needed less than one-third the amount of tape that was required in the 2-in transverse-scan recorders.

Advances in semiconductor and large-scale integration (LSI) technology have led to video recording equipment reduced in both size and weight, with a picture quality and time-base stability sufficient for broadcast purposes. As an example, the $\frac{3}{4}$-in U-format recorder began to replace movie film as the medium for electronic news gathering in about 1974. A much smaller and more easily portable recorder, the M-format, which uses VHS cassettes, was developed in 1982 for the same purpose. The U-format transforms the NTSC color subcarrier to low frequencies on the order of 700 kHz by the color-under system (see Sec. 5.3.3). The M-format (component recording) has a two-channel track: one channel is used for the FM recording of the luminance signal Y; the other is for the FM recording of the chrominance signals I and Q (Fig. 5.13). In this way, not only can an adequate frequency band be assigned to the color signal, but the Y signal can be recorded separately with no disturbance of the chrominance signal. In a variation of the M-format, one track provides for FM recording of the Y signal, and the other employs

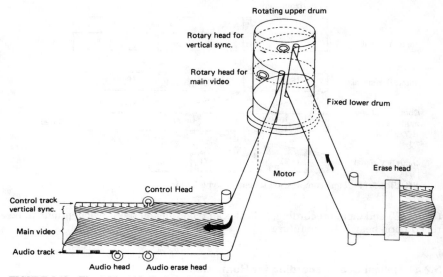

FIGURE 5.12   The 1.5-head helical-scan video recorder and recording format.

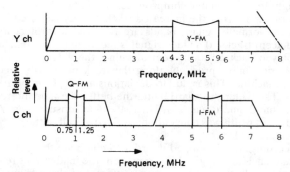

FIGURE 5.13   Frequency allocation of the M-format recorder for electronic news gathering.

a system for alternately recording the R—Y and B—Y signals by compressing the frequency band. This system achieves both high resolution and a high signal-to-noise ratio by providing sufficient FM modulation. A comparable recorder, the L-format, which uses Beta cassettes, was introduced in 1983, and the M-II format appeared in 1985 (Fig. 5.14). With the M or L formats, the television camera and recorder can be combined into a single unit, ideal for electronic news gathering.

In summary, the helical-scan format has become the mainstream format for broadcasting use. It is anticipated that, even though there will doubtless be further significant advances in signal-recording methods, such as two-channel recording

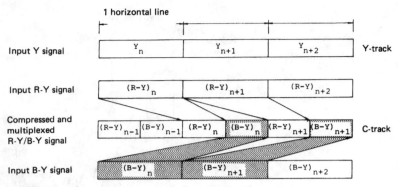

FIGURE 5.14   Time compression scheme of type L video recorders.

(Y and C) and digital recording, helical-scan recording methods will continue to be relied upon heavily in the future.

5.2.4   Helical-Scan Recording for Home Use

One of the most important points to consider in the development of consumer video recorders is that the trade-off between picture quality and tape consumption should be brought to a reasonable compromise. A significant step in decreasing the tape consumption came from the increased track density achieved by eliminating the guard bands. Normally, guard bands are required to protect against disturbances from adjacent tracks. If a video signal is recorded by one machine, and then subsequently played back on a different machine, the video head upon playback does not necessarily follow precisely along the track previously recorded on the tape by the first machine. This is due to deviations arising from both machine and tape tolerances. The wider the guard band, the better the tape interchangeability; but on the other hand, guard bands will increase tape consumption. As a compromise, the guard-band width was conventionally fixed at half of the video track width on all helical-scan recorders.

Azimuth recording was developed in order to eliminate the guard band in two-head helical-scan machines (Fig. 5.15). To prevent the inadvertent reading of adjacent tracks on playback, the head gaps have different angles ($90° \pm \phi$ with respect to the track), such that the azimuth loss is given by

$$L_{az} = 20 \log_{10} \frac{(\pi\omega/\lambda) \tan 2\phi}{\sin [(\pi\omega/\lambda) \tan 2\phi]} \quad \text{dB} \tag{5.1}$$

where λ = recorded wavelength
ω = video track width
2ϕ = the angular difference between the gaps

When the discrepancy between the video track and playback head is $\Delta\omega$, the ratio between the crosstalk C and the signal S is as follows:

$$\frac{C}{S} = 20 \log_{10} \left\{ \frac{\sin [(\pi \Delta\omega/\lambda) \tan 2\phi]}{(\pi \Delta\omega/\lambda) \tan 2\phi} \frac{\Delta\omega}{\omega - \Delta\omega} \right\} \quad \text{dB} \tag{5.2}$$

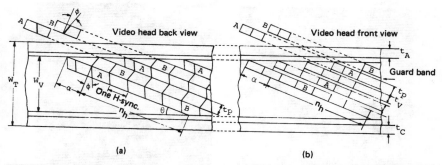

FIGURE 5.15   Two-head helical-scan tape format. (*a*) Without guard bands (azimuth recording); (*b*) with guard bands.

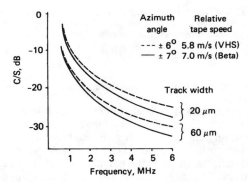

FIGURE 5.16   Frequency characteristics of crosstalk caused by azimuth loss in the azimuth recording method (VHS and Beta).

The dependence of crosstalk on frequency for typical values of tape speed, track width, and azimuth angle is shown in Fig. 5.16.

When the first azimuth recording system was developed in 1968, the minimum recordable wavelength was about 2.5 μm, and the azimuth angle was 30°. When ϕ is large, the effective head gap length will increase by 1/cos ϕ, and the reproduced output will naturally decrease. Moreover, the reproduced signal from the video head will have a time discrepancy of $\Delta\omega \tan \phi$ if the video head deviates by $\Delta\omega$ from the previously recorded video track, and the upper part of each picture played back will be distorted. As the minimum recordable wavelength becomes shorter, smaller azimuth angles can be used, and both sufficient separation and a tolerably low level of crosstalk will still be achieved. Azimuth angles of ±6° are used in VHS recorders. With angles this small, the main disadvantage of azimuth recording is eliminated. Additionally, the azimuth recording method easily allows both recording and playback at one-half or one-third speed without the necessity of changing the heads. This is achieved by means of overwrite recording, in which recording by a wider head partly erases the adjacent track (Fig. 5.5). This was not possible with previous guard-band recording methods.

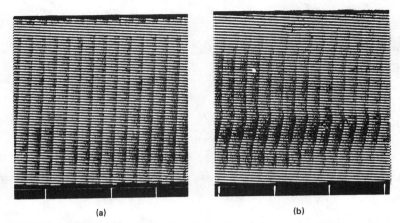

(a)   (b)

FIGURE 5.17 EIA-J type I (fixed-head drum) tape format and the jitter pattern displayed visually by means of fine iron powder. (*a*) Recorded by a standard-alignment tape recorder (small jitter component); (*b*) recorded by a conventional VTR (significant jitter component).

5.2.5 Design Principles of Helical-Scan Recorders

Since the recorded video track of helical-scan machines is much longer than that of transverse-track machines, the playback head may inadvertently trace not only the original track but also an adjacent track at the same time. This is particularly true if there is any nonlinearity in the video track, as may occur when the record and playback machines are different or if the playback video head has shifted position from the original track. The horizontal synchronization signal of adjacent tracks thus needs to be aligned in order to eliminate the influence of any interference between the two adjacent tracks. This is called *horizontal sync pulse alignment* and is illustrated diagrammatically in Fig. 5.15. Figure 5.17 shows the recorded tape pattern, made visible by applying very fine, colloidal iron powder directly to the recorded video tape with a special solvent and then evaporating the solvent.

Horizontal sync pulse lineup requires a special relationship between the tape speed V_m, the head-to-tape speed V_h (which sets the drum diameter d), and the helix angle θ_0. The tape speed is given by

$$V_m = \frac{\pi d}{2} \frac{\alpha}{(n_h \pm \alpha)} \frac{F}{\cos \theta_0} \tag{5.3}$$

where F = field frequency (60 or 50 Hz)
      n_h = number of horizontal sync pulses on one video track
      α = number of horizontal sync pulses between the discrepancy of two adjacent track edges

The term n_h is 262.5 for NTSC and 312.5 for PAL and SECAM. The term α is expressed by an integer plus 0.5 of the horizontal sync, as shown in Fig. 5.15.

When the tape is moved, the recorded video track angle θ is the resultant of both head and tape movements:

$$\sin \theta = \frac{\sin \theta_0}{\sqrt{1 \pm 2 \, (2V_m/\pi Fd) \cos \theta_0 + (2V_m/\pi Fd)^2}} \tag{5.4}$$

(Note: If both the rotating head and the tape run in the same direction, $-$ is used; $+$ is used for opposing direction.)

These design principles can be used to establish the tape format. In practice, standard-alignment tapes are required to ensure interchangeability among mass-produced machines (Sugaya et al., 1974).

5.3 VIDEO RECORDING TECHNOLOGY

5.3.1 Drive Mechanisms

5.3.1.1 Helical-Scan Mechanisms. The main design difference between video and audio tape recorders is in the use of a rotary head in the video recorders. The essential points to be considered in the mechanical system are thus the construction of the rotary head and the manner in which the tape is wound around the head drum when it is mounted on the machine. As shown in Fig. 5.11, one to four heads are used in rotary-head designs; since there are actually no fundamental differences between any of the various competing systems, the description here will concentrate on the most commonly used two-head system. The signal is recorded on the tape at a small angle by the rotary head and, to achieve this, the tape must be wound at a slant to the head motion around the rotary-head drum. Wrapping the tape in a slanted path means that the takeup and supply reels must be on different levels with respect to the head, as shown in Fig. 5.4. This level difference requirement complicates the construction of the tape-transport mechanism. There are three main types of head drum construction (Fig. 5.18). With the fixed drum shown in Fig. 5.18*a* there is considerable tape friction, however the tape movement is stable and if alignment of the bottom reference edge of the tape is necessary, a tape

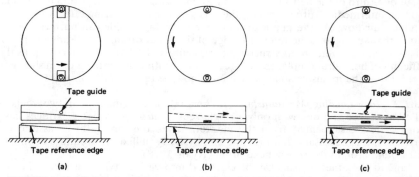

FIGURE 5.18 Various head drum configurations. (*a*) Fixed-head drum; (*b*) rotating upper head drum; (*c*) rotating intermediate head drum.

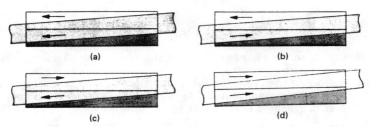

FIGURE 5.19   Types of upper drum rotation. (*a*) A type ($\frac{3}{4}$-in U, $\frac{1}{2}$-in VHS, $\frac{1}{2}$-in V-2000, and 8-mm video formats); (*b*) B type; (*c*) C type; (*d*) D type ($\frac{1}{2}$-in Philips tandem reel).

guide can be attached to the upper part of the drum. Recently, tape surfaces have become smoother, providing better short-wavelength recording; unfortunately, this often worsens tape-running characteristics (stickslip), causing tape-running jitter with the fixed drum. The rotating upper drum shown in Fig. 5.18*b* drags in air, forming an air bearing between the tape and half of the upper drum; thus the friction coefficient becomes very low and is unaffected by tape surface characteristics. However, starting up with this format is difficult when the tape is already in the wound condition. Also, if the tape or drum surface is dirty or damp, the tape tends to stick to the drum. This can result in jerking and other problems at high speed.

For the rotating upper drum, the four possible combinations of tape-running direction and the drum-rotating direction are shown in Fig. 5.19. Normally, the type in Fig. 5.19*a* permits the lightest tape transport. The tape tension in the horizontal direction here is regulated so that the tape runs along the lower fixed-drum reference edge, but this places stress on the tape. In the types in Fig. 5.19*c* and *d*, the air intake between the tape and drum tends to be insufficient to cause the necessary tape float, requiring that a fine groove be undercut into the rotating drum surface.

In all versions of the rotating-upper-drum method, it is comparatively difficult to push the tape with precision from the upper to the lower drum reference edge because the upper drum is rotating. A better system is the rotating intermediate drum shown in Fig. 5.18*c*, which combines the best of both the fixed-drum and rotating-drum types. This system is used in both the type B and Beta formats. Since about one-third of the half-inch tape is in contact with the rotating drum in the Beta rotating-intermediate-drum system, there is sufficient air-bearing effect due to the resultant air flow. As the upper drum is fixed, the tape guide can push the upper end of the tape against the reference edge of the lower drum. The disadvantages of this system, however, are its structural complexity and relatively high cost, plus the difficulty of head drum replacement. Today, the rotating upper head drum shown in Fig. 5.18*b* is the mainstream approach in video tape recorders.

5.3.1.2 Tape-Loading Mechanisms.   In general, a container with two reels is called a *cassette* and one with only a single reel, a *cartridge;* video cartridges have more or less disappeared from the market. When the tape is in a cassette (or cartridge), it is necessary that the tape be physically pulled out from the container and wound around the rotary-head drum (Ryan, 1978).

Tape-loading mechanisms can be classified into various types, as shown in Fig. 5.20. In the early years, the large tape reel size prohibited having two reels in a single container. Initially, the one-reel cartridge was used not only for professional but also for home recorders. The two disadvantages of the cartridge are that the

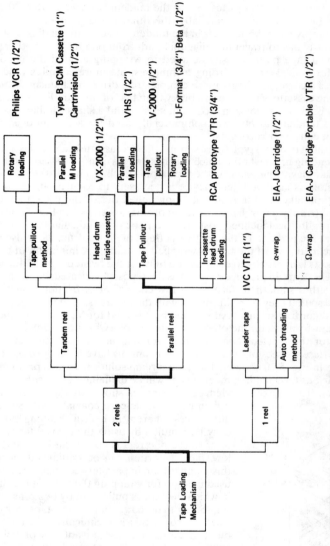

FIGURE 5.20 Classification of various helical-scan tape-loading methods. (Numbers in parentheses indicate tape widths.)

tape cannot be removed from the machine until the rewind is completed, and there is a risk of damaging the exposed end of the tape.

As magnetic recording technology developed, reel size diminished, and two reels could be put into a single container. Thus the cassette gradually came into use. There are two types of cassettes: one is the tandem cassette in which the two reels are stacked over each other coaxially; the other is the parallel two-reel cassette. Since the supply and take-up reels in the tandem cassette are on different levels, the tape obviously has to travel in a diagonal path from one reel to another. Although this diagonal tape path is easily adapted to wrapping around the head drum, as required for helical-scan recording techniques, the more complex tape path here necessitates a correspondingly more complex reel drive mechanism. Moreover, the shape of the cassette is rather more bulky than that of the parallel two-reel cassette, which can be manufactured in a convenient size and a shape similar to an ordinary book. The tandem cassette was commercially used for a few models, but is now obsolete in consumer recorders.

The parallel two-reel type (here simply called a cassette) can be classified into two types depending upon whether each reel has flanges or not. The double-flanged reel is somewhat bigger but protects the tape from shock or undue stress. Whichever of these versions is used, a special device is necessary to compensate for the complex path the tape takes as the result of being pulled out of the cassette and wrapped around the head drum in helical-scan recording. As shown in Fig. 5.21, this device consists of cylindrical inclined posts aligned to be perpendicular to the tape-running direction at the position of the posts. In effect, the head drum itself also serves as a kind of inclined post as the tape is wrapped around it. A minimum of two of these inclined posts is necessary to compensate fully for the twisted tape of the helical-scan method. These are in practice realized as fixed posts fabricated from a nonmagnetic material with a smooth surface and a low coefficient of friction. Ideally, they are positioned so that they come in contact with the reverse side of the tape, not with the magnetic recording surface. An inclined post is used for VHS parallel loading. The U- and Beta-formats, on the other hand, use a rotary loading mechanism that compensates for the twisted tape path in a gradual manner by using inclined posts. Several different types of tape-loading mechanisms have been developed. Note the heavy line in Fig. 5.20 showing the main-stream solutions to this problem.

The various tape-loading mechanisms will be explained using concrete examples (Fig. 5.22). The coaxial tandem-reel system is shown in Fig. 5.22a. The reel is driven by a double-core coaxial shaft. Since the level differences inherent in helical scanning can automatically be handled by using the coaxial tandem-reel system, where one reel is above the head and one is below, tape distortion can be minimized more easily in this manner than in parallel-reel types. Another widely used method for wrapping the tape on the drum is that in which the tape is pulled out by two pins, as shown in Fig. 5.22b. The correction of the tape twist in such a small space as this is technically difficult to achieve, but this design has the advantages of being able to produce a machine of very small size and of being able to load the tape from the cassette quickly. The rotary-loading methods shown in Fig. 5.22c have a longer tape pull-out length; therefore, it is possible to correct any tape twisting, which inevitably accompanies the slanted scanning format, gradually and with no abrupt

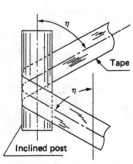

FIGURE 5.21 Inclined-post tape guide.

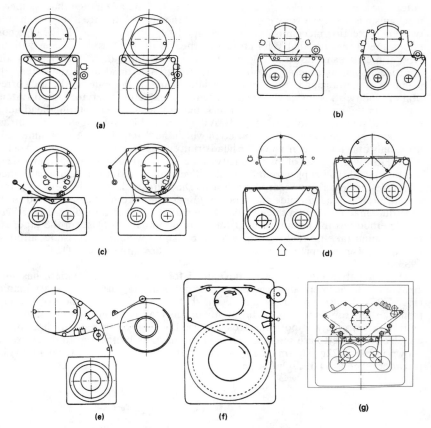

FIGURE 5.22 Various examples of tape-loading mechanisms using cassettes or cartridges. (*a*) Rotary loading with two tandem reels; (*b*) parallel loading with two parallel reels; (*c*) rotary loading with two parallel reels; (*d*) loading of in-cassette head drum using a cassette with two parallel reels; (*e*) α-wrap leader-tape loading with a single-reel cartridge; (*f*) in-cassette single-head-drum loading with two tandem reels; (*g*) three different sizes of cassette are accommodated on a single drive by moving the reel spindles.

bends that might place undue stress on the tape. The tape, however, is pulled out to a considerable length from the container in this method; various problems in tape handling can therefore arise, such as requirements for an overly large loading space or slow loading speed. From this point of view, the parallel loading system shown in Fig. 5.22*b* is a good compromise with respect to tape loading, and the tape-transport unit can be very compact. Sudden bends around the two pins may cause some difficulties during tape transport in the system.

Because of such problems as these, which arise from pulling the tape out of the container and winding it on the drum, various methods for loading the tape on the head drum while it is still in the container have been considered. One of these is the method shown in Fig. 5.22*d*. To facilitate tape loading, four heads of a large drum are used. The tape wrapping angle is small, therefore the degree to which the head enters the container is also small. Such a system has the advantage that no special mechanism is necessary for winding the tape of the drum, but since it requires a tape-twisting correction mechanism to correct tape level differences inside the tape container, the distance available for correcting the end is even less than is true with the type of mechanism shown in Fig. 5.22*b*. There are still many difficulties with this approach, such as accuracy problems (due to greater head drum diameter), the problem of minimizing the functional deviations among the four heads, and correction of tape twisting inside the small space of the cassette. Therefore, such systems are not on the market as video recorders, but are available as rotating-head audio recorders, such as digital audio tape (DAT) (Dare and Katsumi, 1987). In contrast, methods have been variously proposed in which the drum diameter is minimized by using only one head and in which the head drum enters the container, as shown in Fig. 5.22*f*. However, in spite of the simplicity of the one-head design, the container size is too bulky and tape consumption is prohibitively high, and it has been abandoned.

Single-reel cartridge recorders use a method in which only the reel with tape wound on it is placed inside the tape container; the take-up reel is located in the recording machine, and a thick leader tape is used for auto-threading (Fig. 5.22*e*). This method has the advantage that there are no unnatural twists in the tape, and the optimum take-up-reel location suited to slanted winding is possible, although the mechanism is dimensionally complex and rather large in size (IEC standard, 1983).

An innovative video cassette, developed for use with 8-mm video, has sufficient space to accommodate the guide pins necessary in parallel or rotary loading (Fig. 5.23). It also uses a special design that affords full protection of the tape from the environment, a particularly important feature when high-density tapes, with their extremely smooth surfaces, are used. Using the same idea, three different sizes of cassette are mounted on a single machine by moving the reel axes as shown in Fig. 5.22*g* (Heitman, 1988). This method is used mainly for digital video recorders such as D-1, D-2, D-3, and D-5.

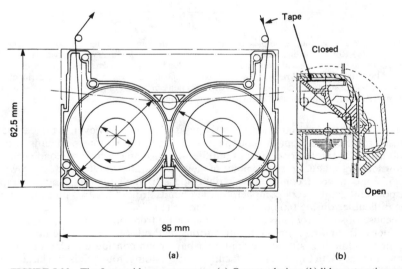

(a)   (b)

FIGURE 5.23   The 8-mm video tape cassette. (*a*) Cassette design; (*b*) lid construction.

In summary, there are two fundamentally different methods of designing a tape transport: one method in which the tape container itself is relatively simple and all of the necessary mechanisms are located on the recorder unit (Fig. 5.23), and another in which the recorder unit has been simplified by including some of the main parts of the mechanism in the tape container itself (Fig. 5.22d). In general, the first of these types, having the relatively simple cassette and the correspondingly more complex recorder unit, appears to be more suited for mass production.

5.3.1.3 *Miniaturization Techniques.*

An exponential decrease in size and weight of consumer recording machines has occurred without change in the basic design, but new features (such as an anti–vibration system, a high zoom ratio, etc.) increase the weight. The weight has now more or less reached a limit, and will not have any further dramatic decrease until a completely new recording system is invented. (Fig. 5.24). Miniaturization of the head drum is the key problem, since head drum interchangeability must be maintained at all costs. One possible solution to this problem, shown in Fig. 5.25a, is the approach taken by the Beta movie recorder, which uses a double-azimuth head unit (see Fig. 5.43f) with a 300° wrap (Sato et al., 1983). The two heads with different azimuth gap angles are mounted in line. This arrangement reduces the head drum diameter by three-fifths (the ratio of 180°/300°). A drawback to this solution, however, is that recorders based on this principle can record only signals generated by a special television camera designed for this purpose, although tapes recorded with this method can be played back on any regular Beta recorder.

Another approach is the four-head, 270°-wrap method used in the VHS movie recorder (Fig. 5.25b). This device has the advantage of being able to record and

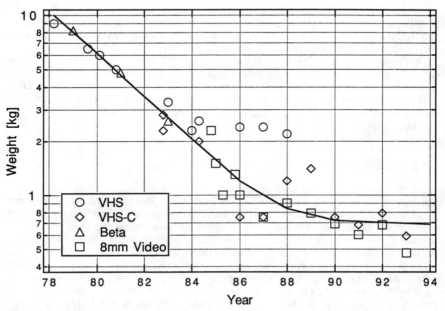

FIGURE 5.24 Historical decreases in the weight of video recorders (weight of battery included).

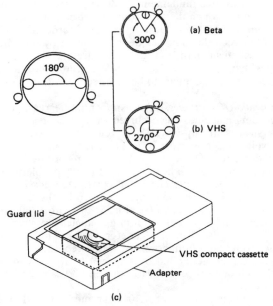

FIGURE 5.25 Mechanisms for miniaturization: (*a*) Beta-movie; (*b*) VHS-movie; (*c*) VHS-C cassette and adapter.

play back any type of standard video signal. The construction of the head drum is relatively complex, however, and requires quite fine tolerances. With this method, the head drum diameter can be reduced by a ratio of 180°/270° or two-thirds.

Yet another miniaturization is the one used in the VHS compact (VHS-C) cassette. This method maintains the interchangeability of the original cassette, which can be used with a standard VHS machine, by means of a simple adapter (Fig. 5.25*c*). The VHS-C cassette can record and play back a 20-min program (standard mode) or a 60-min program (extra-long-play mode) on VHS-C recorders (or on VHS equipment with an adapter.).

5.3.2 Tracking Techniques

With the older transverse-scan recorders, the problems arising from machine-to-machine interchangeability are different from those encountered in helical-scan machines, particularly with respect to head-tip projection (Benson, 1960). The mainstream of video recording research has already shifted to the helical-scan format. For this reason, the tracking techniques discussed in this chapter are limited to those of the nonsegmental type of helical-scan machines.

In NTSC helical-scan recorders, it is necessary to record 60 tracks per second, each containing one field of the video signal. Each of these tracks must be preceded by a vertical synchronization (sync) signal; at the same time, a control signal is recorded on the edge of the tape by a separate stationary head (Fig. 5.4). The control signal is a reference signal used to locate the video head at the proper

TABLE 5.2 Tracking-Servo Methods

	Drum servo	Drum-Capstan servo
Tape speed	Constant (record and playback)	Variable, according to servo (playback only)
Head drum rotational speed	Variable, according to servo	Constant, according to servo
Jitter (picture)	Slight at low frequency	Small
Wow and flutter (sound)	Small	Slightly less than drum servo
Method	1. Servo directly coupled to head 2. Servo by belt extension 3. Servo by stepless speed change	1. Separate servos directly coupled to each motor
Tracking	Adjusted by head drum rotation	Adjusted by tape speed
Features	• Single motor possible • Low cost • Picture unstable during starting • Belt absorbs excessive motor rotation	• Two motors necessary • High-accuracy tracking • Compact (dc motor) • Intersync possible • Electronic editing possible • Small jitter

position on the tape; it is similar in function to the perforations in movie film. When a video tape is played back, the rotary-head timing is locked to the reference signal, and the tracking position is adjusted by using the recorded control signal as reference. These functions form the tracking servo system. Tracking servo systems can be classified into two types, shown in Table 5.2: drum servo systems and drum-capstan servo systems. Each of these has its own particular advantages.

5.3.2.1 Drum Servo Systems.   Early systems used a single motor drive to both the capstan and the head drum (Fig. 5.26). Because the unloaded drum speed was slightly higher than the operational one, a brake could be used to provide first frequency and then phase locking. During recording, the drum was locked to an external vertical sync; in playback, the drum and control-track signals were phase-compared. These systems were inexpensive but were limited in performance and could run at only one speed and are therefore now abandoned.

5.3.2.2 Drum-Capstan Servo Systems.   As video recorders become more and more miniaturized and are designed to perform an increasing variety of specialized

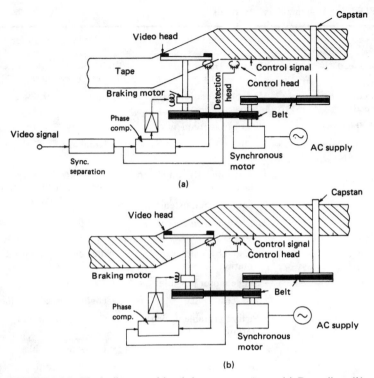

FIGURE 5.26 Block diagram of head drum servo system. (*a*) Recording; (*b*) playback.

functions, it is increasingly necessary to design more-precise servo systems to compensate for the lack of inertia of the numerous small motors used. Brushless dc motors and semiconductor devices are better adapted to miniaturization of high-performance recording equipment, especially for such features as perfect still pictures and variable-speed playback; these are becoming comparatively inexpensive.

The drum-capstan servo system has been used in all helical-scan broadcast recorders since about 1971. At present, most consumer video recorders use this type of tracking servo. In this system, the rotating phase is first detected by a pulse generator, which is similar to a detection transducer, and is adjusted so that the switching position in the picture is located at the front of the vertical sync signal (six to eight horizontal lines advanced position) (Fig. 5.27*a*). Then the signal from the frequency generator mounted on the capstan motor is counted and compared with the phase of the vertical sync signal. This causes the capstan motor to rotate at a constant speed. The control signal (30 Hz), which is separated from the vertical sync, is recorded on the edge of the tape, which is in turn driven by the capstan. During playback, the reference sync signal, generated by means of a countdown process from a crystal generator, and the pulse signal of the drum rotation are compared in phase and controlled so that the head drum rotates at a constant speed and in proper phase (Fig. 5.27*b*). At the same time, in order to trace the video head along on the recorded track

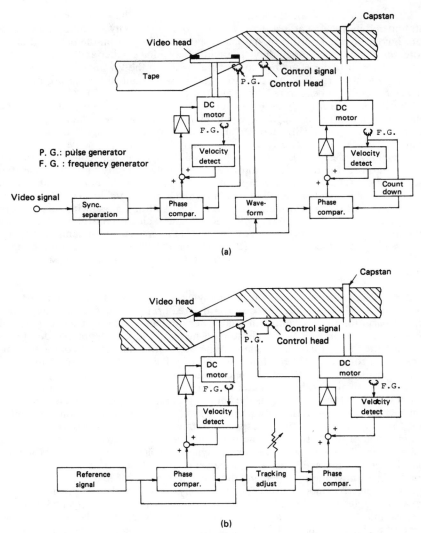

FIGURE 5.27 Block diagram of head drum-capstan servo system. (*a*) Recording; (*b*) playback.

with no deviation, the reference sync signal and the control signal are compared in phase so that the tape speed is controlled. The phase difference can be adjusted (tracking adjust) to within a very few milliseconds with the important result that machine-to-machine compatibility can be made reliable. Drum-capstan servos are widely used in video recorders both to effect high-performance miniaturization and to increase such special-effect functions as variable-speed play-back, quick search, and still pictures.

The original role of the tracking servo was mainly in phase control of the drum rotation and in tracking adjustment; velocity control was only a supplemental function. Increasing miniaturization has had a significant impact on the design of drum motors and capstan motors—they are rapidly becoming smaller and lighter. Flutter and wow are, therefore, tending to increase owing to the low inertia of these new miniaturized motors. To solve this problem, velocity control by the use of a frequency generator is becoming vital in video recording. (Fig. 5.27).

There are several methods for generating a frequency directly related to the rotation mode. One of the most common methods uses a magnetic head as a detector and a magnetically recorded signal on the rotor. The higher the generated frequency, the more precisely the rotation may be controlled; however, a higher frequency increases production costs. In order to apply velocity control effectively for this purpose, the respective motor must be coupled directly to both the capstan and the drum. This direct-drive capstan, in conjunction with velocity control by a frequency generator, has the additional advantage of being able to produce multi-function devices (stills, slow- and quick-search capabilities, along with good picture quality) as well as being highly reliable and durable. Velocity control by a frequency generator has the following three advantages: (1) improvement of damping characteristics in the phase-control servo, (2) control of rotating speed within pull-in range of the phase-control servo, (3) control of rotating speeds of the motors, the head drum, and the capstan.

5.3.2.3 Digital Servo Systems.

Accompanying the increase in the numerous functions demanded of the video recorder is the requirement for a great many component parts for the conventional analog servo. This increase in the number of component parts, as well as the adjustments necessary to keep them in order, tends to inhibit the reliability of the machine. With appropriate application of the innovations in semiconductor devices, however, it is possible to realize such digital-process functions as velocity detection, phase comparison, and mono-multi using the clock signal in conjunction with the counter memory (Table 5.3). The fundamental operation of the digital servo process is the counting of a clock signal which is generated from a crystal generator; therefore, there is neither functional deviation nor change over time. Velocity detection is especially effective in digital servo systems. The pull-in range of the horizontal sync signal of television receivers is rather narrow (± 2 percent) although that of the vertical sync signal is somewhat wider. When the recorded picture is played back with a special function (such as still, slow, or quick-search), the drum rotating speed and the capstan rotating speed have to be adjusted so that the head-to-tape relative speed is always constant. This is possible with a digital servo system. The digital servo system was first used only in broadcast systems, but it has since been used in the consumer field, owing both to the rapid progress and cost reductions in LSIs and to the increasing demands for special functions. The quick-search function, especially, is now considered a basic function of home video recorders.

5.3.2.4 Pilot-Signal Tracking Servos.

The control signal discussed so far is recorded on the tape edge by a fixed head which is normally located in the same housing as the audio head, as shown in Fig. 5.4. Instead of this control signal, four pilot signals, recorded on the video track along with the video signal, can be used for a tracking servo (Sanderson, 1981). In 8-mm video, these pilot signals are recorded by the video head, and the signals are located in the lower range of the color-under signal (see Fig. 5.38a). The four pilot signals are these: $f_1 = 102.5 \text{ kHz}$, $f_2 = 119.0 \text{ kHz}$,

TABLE 5.3 Comparison of Digital and Analog Servos

Functions	Digital servo	Analog servo
Velocity detection	Pulse interval measured by clock pulse (no adjustment necessary)	Phase comparison with one-cycle delayed pulse (needs adjustment)
Phase comparison	Phase-difference-signal interval counted by clock pulse	Phase-difference signal stored in a capacitance
Mono-multi	Pulse generated by means of digital counter	Conventional mono-multi by means of RC circuit
Pull-in time	Fast	Slow
Stability	High, no drift	Low
Number of circuit elements	Many	Few
Circuitry	Complicated but flexible	Simple but limited
Influence of environment	Small	Large (power voltage, temperature, and running time)

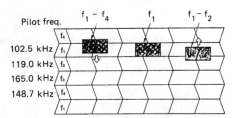

FIGURE 5.28 Pilot-signal tracking servo for 8-mm video recorder. (See Fig. 5.38 for frequency allocation.)

$f_3 = 165.2$ kHz, and $f_4 = 148.7$ kHz. These values provide the following difference frequencies: $f_2 - f_1 = f_3 - f_4 = 16.5$ kHz, and $f_4 - f_1 = f_3 - f_2 = 46.2$ kHz.

As shown in Fig. 5.28, if the video head on track f_1 plays back the signal accurately, only the signal f_1 (102.5 kHz) is reproduced. If the video head deviates to the f_4 track, it will pick up both signals f_1 and f_4 (148.7 kHz). The difference between these two signals $f_4 - f_1$ will give an error signal Δf (46.2 kHz), causing the video head to be moved back to the f_1 track immediately. If the video head shifts to the f_2 track, another error signal, $f_2 - f_1$ (16.5 kHz), will be produced, and the video head will be moved back to the proper f_1 track. Thus, the video head can be made to follow accurately a previously recorded track. This tracking servo has many features: dynamic tracking is easily carried out; no special head is necessary for the tracking signal; a conventional control track can be used for any other signals such

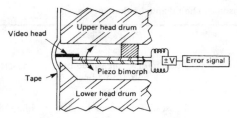

FIGURE 5.29   Dynamic tracking mechanism.

as cueing, additional audio, or time-code signals; and finally, no separate fixed audio head is required if the audio signal is also recorded by FM or pulse-code modulation.

If the video head can move rapidly, it can follow a track of any curvature; in other words, with this servo system, equipment can be manufactured having complete machine-to-machine compatibility. In order to ensure that the video head follows very quickly on the track during play-back, it is mounted on a piezoelectric bimorph element capable of deviating in shape by a predictable degree corresponding to the (high) voltage of the error signal, as shown in Fig. 5.29. With this dynamic tracking servo, the recorder can play back at any tape speed (even during quick search) with no picture degradation because the video head follows a complete track at all times. However, when the quick-search function is used, a characteristic distortion occurs between tracks in the form of a horizontal visual noise bar, as discussed in Sec. 5.3.2.5. This can be avoided by using a combination of the dynamic track-following method with the digital servo. This results in excellent picture quality and the ability to adjust the picture speed continuously from slow to fast without any of the noise-bar characteristics typical of the digital-servo quick search.

5.3.2.5   *Special Effects.*   Special effects, such as slow motion, stills, reverse motion, and high speed (quick search), have been developed primarily for use in helical-scan home recording. The techniques of special effects can be classified into three generations.

The first generation consists of helical-scan machines with guard bands. Slow-motion pictures were obtained by reducing the video tape speed, and still pictures were obtained by stopping the tape movement. These pictures suffered from noise bars caused by the video head crossing the guard bands. A rather primitive mechanism using two subsidiary heads was developed to solve this problem. The two main heads for recording and reproduction and the two subheads are mounted in a staggered position on the rotary-head drum. In slow motion or still reproduction, the higher of the reproducing signal levels from the main or subheads is selected in each field. Thus, a perfect slow-motion effect or still picture can be obtained without any noise bar.

The second generation refers to the azimuth recording method. If a wider-track, double-azimuth video head is used for recording and play-back, as shown in Fig. 5.30*a*, a complete video track of a still frame, a slow frame, or a double-speed frame can be played back. As shown in Fig. 5.30*b*, the locus of the head does not cross other tracks between reverse and triple speed, thus a noiseless picture can be played back. At quadruple and higher speeds, other tracks are crossed and horizontal noise still exists at these speeds when the head crosses from one track to another.

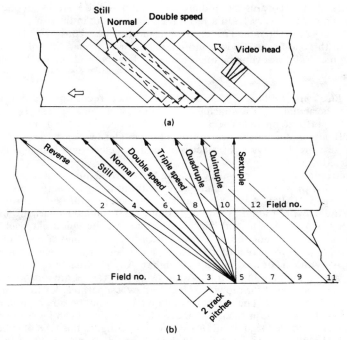

FIGURE 5.30 Video track loci of special effects using the azimuth recording format. (*a*) Overwrite recording and playback by wider-track double-azimuth video head; (*b*) video track loci.

Both still frame and slow motion have considerable flicker in the playback picture owing to temporal error when the picture moves quickly (a two-field picture is reproduced alternately). This flicker motion can be eliminated by the reproduction of a single-field picture instead of a single-frame picture with the aid of an extra video head having the same azimuth angle as the head used to record this particular field. As long-play recorders developed, including the 6-h-mode VHS, this quick-search capability became a very important feature—so important, in fact, that the occurrence of several noise bars in the picture is acceptable. When quick-search speeds surpass quadruple speed, it is inevitable that several horizontal noise bars occur, as shown in Fig. 5.30*b*. On the other hand, certain special-effect techniques that yield pictures free from noise bars (such as going directly from reverse motion to triple speed) have been developed where the noise bar is shifted into the vertical blanking area of the reproduced pictures.

The third generation design takes advantage of the dynamic-tracking method already discussed (Fig. 5.29). Since a piezoelectric actuator has several nonlinear characteristics, a closed looped system is used in order to reject these and to obtain perfect track-following. One of the interesting applications of these special effects is time-lapse recording, which is used effectively in security operations involving banks or warehouses. Recording can take place for an extremely long time (the maximum recording time is, for instance, 480 h) at a very low tape speed, either continuously or at intervals, using a conventional video cassette. Two different approaches to the recording method are used in time-lapse systems. In one of these one field is recorded every 1 s in a 120-h recording mode; in the other one frame is recorded every 2 s in the same 120-h recording mode. The recording and reproducing circuitry of the one-frame mode is more straightforward than that of the one-field recording method; however, the one-field recording method avoids the blurring of motion.

5.3.2.6 *Electronic Editing.*   With quadruplex video recording, editing was performed by the actual physical splicing of the tape. Mechanical splicing is particularly difficult to perform on helical-scan systems. Electronic editing, has, therefore, completely supplanted mechanical editing in the modern video industry (Anderson, 1969). There are two types of electronic editing: electronic splicing and insert electronic editing.

In electronic splicing, a new program can be recorded immediately after a previously recorded program, on the same tape, without any gaps between the two, as shown in Fig. 5.31. Part *A* is the previously recorded program on recorder A, and part *B* is the new program on recorder B that is to be added to part *A* on recorder A. As soon as part *A* is played back on recorder A, the video playback head of recorder A begins to function as a video recording head, and records the output signal (program *B*) from recorder B. Recorder B is operating synchronously with recorder A by means of a common sync signal. Any previously recorded video or audio signals on the tape in recorder A following program *A* are erased in advance by a rotating erase head for the video track and by a separately located audio erase head for the audio track. The control signal on tape A, on the other hand, has been recorded by the saturation recording method; a new signal can be overwritten on the previously recorded signal without any prior erasing. In this type of splicing, the matching of both the control signals and the video signals of *A* and *B* on recorder A

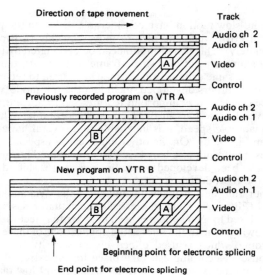

FIGURE 5.31   Electronic splicing.

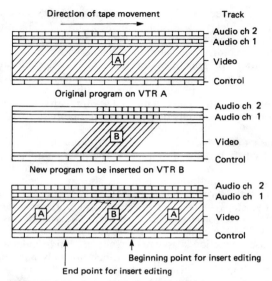

FIGURE 5.32 Insert-type electronic editing.

is done with perfect timing, again as shown in Fig. 5.31. Thus, the program in part *B* from recorder B can be spliced onto program *A* on recorder A with perfect synchronization. The tracking on both recorder A and recorder B is done by the head drum-capstan servo method.

In insert-type editing, the new program (part *B*) on recorder B can be recorded in the middle of the previously recorded program (part *A*) on recorder A without interruption (Fig. 5.32). In insert-type editing, the video signal of part *B* (plus the audio signal if necessary), without the control signal, is re-recorded onto the previously recorded program *A* on recorder A. Thus, the control signal of recorder A, which comes from the previously recorded program (part *A*), is used for the new program (part *B*) as well. All other conditions are similar to those employed in electronic splicing.

Both of these electronic editing methods, electronic splicing and insert-type editing, represent highly sophisticated applications of tracking techniques.

5.3.3 FM Video Recording Methods

5.3.3.1 Direct FM Recording.   As discussed earlier, solving the problem of recording the video signal through frequency modulation was one of the major breakthroughs in video recording technology. In broadcast equipment, picture quality is more important than tape economy, so the FM carrier is located at a high frequency with sufficient deviation so that the NTSC, PAL, or SECAM composite color signals can be recorded directly by FM (see Fig. 5.10).

NTSC and PAL color television signals are extremely sensitive to timing errors; as little as 4 ns can be visually perceived and 20 ns gives a serious change in hue. This is an accuracy impossible to meet in any electromechanical system. Two distinct methods of hue correction are used. The first is to feed the signal through an electronically variable delay as described in Sec. 5.3.3.2. The alternative is the heterodyne process in the color-under method, described later in Sec. 5.3.3.3. During playback, the color signals are heterodyned with the local oscillator signal having the same jitter component as the reproduced color subcarrier. The time "jitter" on the luminance is uncorrected but is visually acceptable. Early quad systems with their high-inertia drums produced relatively small errors (0.5 μs). The helical systems, especially the type C with its 420-mm scan length, had much larger errors that could be corrected only by using digital time-base correctors.

5.3.3.2 Time-Base Correction.   In broadcast equipment, the video signal to be played back must satisfy broadcast standards. The jitter component of the quadruplex recorder, for example, was originally as much as 0.5 μs (Harris, 1961). In order to decrease this jitter to one-hundredth of this amount, a level necessary to meet broadcast standards, the direct color process (Fig. 5.33) was developed. Correction was achieved in two steps—a coarse correction using horizontal sync as reference, followed by a fine correction using the subcarrier. The system was purely analog, with varicaps providing the control (Coleman, 1971).

Digital time-base correction is now universally used in broadcast quality helical-scan recorders (such as type B or type C), which not only have jitter (time-base error) but also skew (time-base discontinuity), a combination which is impossible to correct by analog means. The principles of digital time-base correction are shown in Fig. 5.34. First, the analog play-back signal is converted into a digital signal (8 bits or more) with a sampling (clock) frequency of $3f_{sc}$ or $4f_{sc}$ (f_{sc} is the color subcarrier frequency) derived from the color-burst signal; this converted digital signal is then written into the random-access memory (RAM). A stable read-out clock removes the influence of the jitter. One of the most important features of this method is that the error-correction range can be expanded simply by increasing the random-access memory (RAM) capacity. Another important point is that there is absolutely no picture deterioration.

Digital time-base correction is at present limited in use to broadcasting or other professional applications. If an inexpensive type is realized, it will also be used in consumer applications, and home video recording methods will become very much different from what they have been.

5.3.3.3 Color-Under Method.   In designing video recorders for home (or industrial) use, both the relative head-to-tape speed and the actual transport speed of the tape itself should be kept as low as is feasible. Under these conditions, direct color

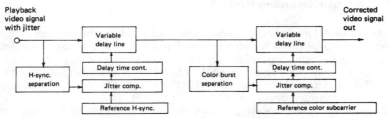

FIGURE 5.33 Block diagram of direct color process. (*a*) Video signal phase correction (Amtec); (*b*) color phase correction (Colortec).

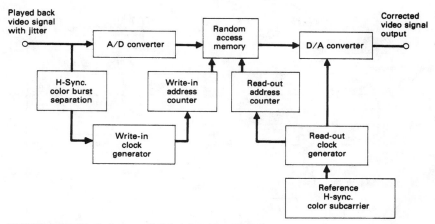

FIGURE 5.34 Block diagram of digital time-base correction.

recording is almost impossible, and the color-under system was developed as a solution (Johnson, 1960; Tajiri et al., 1968; Numakura, 1974).

When the color signal having a color subcarrier f_{sc} (f_{sc} = 3.58 MHz) is separated from the NTSC composite signal, and converted to the color-under signal (frequency f_u between 630 and 780 kHz), the signal can be recorded easily even with lower head-to-tape speeds. In addition, the jitter component of the color signal will also decrease in accordance with the ratio of the frequency conversion (approximately 5:1). This method, where the color signal is moved to the lower area of the frequency range, is called the *color-under method* and is used throughout the consumer field (e.g., VHS and Beta formats) (Arimura and Taniguchi, 1973). The color-under signal is recorded using frequency division multiplex with the FM luminance signal having carrier frequency 3.4 to 5.4 MHz. Video recording by the color-under method is shown in Fig. 5.35. The frequency allocation of the important points is shown in the figure from (*A*) to (*I*). The high-frequency FM luminance signal acts as an ac bias for the low-frequency, low-level chrominance signal (Yokoyama, 1969). The color-under signal f_u can, therefore, be directly recorded on the tape even at low levels with little distortion. When the video signal is played back, the upper sideband of the FM luminance signal is attenuated by the characteristics of the tape and head. The FM deviation of the luminance signal is determined by making an optimum balance of the picture resolution (which requires high-frequency recording) and the signal-to-noise ratio (which requires more output at the carrier frequency). From the reproduced color-under signal, with a substantial jitter component Δf, the color-burst signal is then separated and compared with a reference subcarrier frequency which is, in turn, produced by a crystal oscillator. Thus, an error signal is produced and compensates for the jitter component of the color (chrominance) signal. The color-under frequency f_u is also chosen so that the visibility of undesirable interference beats with the luminance signal is minimized by interleaving them with multiples of the line frequency (Fujita, 1973).

$$f_u = \tfrac{1}{4}(2n + 1)f_H \tag{5.5}$$

where f_H is the horizontal sync frequency and n is an integer.

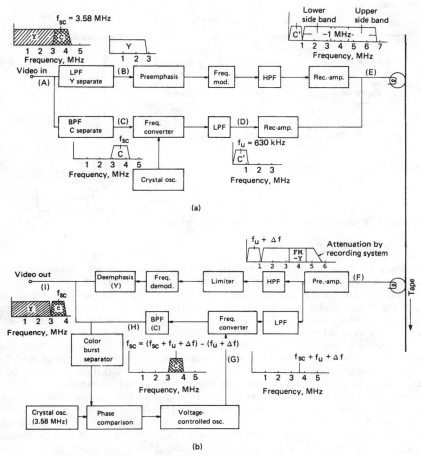

FIGURE 5.35 Block diagram and spectrum allocations of the automatic phase-control process in the color-under method. (*a*) recording; (*b*) playback.

5.3.3.4 Color-Under Method for Azimuth Recording. In azimuth recording, the FM luminance signal, which has a relatively short wavelength, suffers negligible crosstalk from adjacent video tracks. As the color-under signal has a relatively long wavelength, however, the crosstalk signal from the adjacent video track is not eliminated by the azimuth effect; it spoils the reproduced picture quality by producing beat interference. In order to eliminate this crosstalk component, two methods known as the *phase-invert* (PI) and *phase-shift* (PS) methods were introduced (Amari, 1977; Hirota, 1981).

In the phase-invert method, the phase of the color subcarrier on the *A* track is inverted 180° every horizontal sync period, but the *B* track is recorded without phase inversion (Fig. 5.36). When the *A* track is played back, there is a certain amount of crosstalk from the *B* track. In order to eliminate this crosstalk component on the *A* track, the phase is reconverted to its original form (thus inverting by

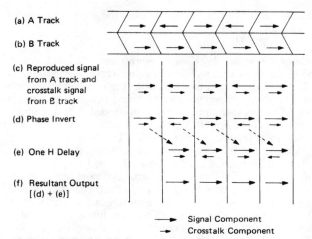

(a) A Track

(b) B Track

(c) Reproduced signal from A track and crosstalk signal from B track

(d) Phase Invert

(e) One H Delay

(f) Resultant Output [(d) + (e)]

⟶ Signal Component
→ Crosstalk Component

FIGURE 5.36 Elimination of crosstalk in azimuth recording by the phase-invert method.

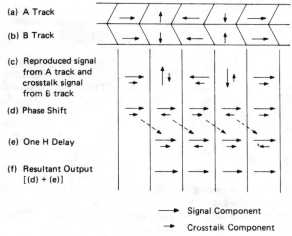

(a) A Track

(b) B Track

(c) Reproduced signal from A track and crosstalk signal from B track

(d) Phase Shift

(e) One H Delay

(f) Resultant Output [(d) + (e)]

⟶ Signal Component
→ Crosstalk Component

FIGURE 5.37 Elimination of cross-talk in azimuth recording by phase shift method.

180° the crosstalk from the *B* track). A new signal is created with a single delayed horizontal-scanning period which allows the crosstalk to be eliminated.

In the phase-shift method, the phase of the color subcarrier on the *A* track is shifted by 90° for every horizontal sync period, and on the *B* track the color phase is also shifted by 90°, but inversely (Fig. 5.37). When the *A* track is played back with the crosstalk component from the *B* track, the phase is inversely rotated for every single horizontal sync period back to its original form, and the resultant output has no crosstalk component. Thus, the crosstalk from the adjacent *B* track is eliminated by means of line interrelation.

5.3.3.5 *Baseband Recording by Time Compression.*

The color-under recording method is one of the most successful color-signal recording methods for consumer recording. It is quite effective in handling both the relatively narrow band and the poor time-base instability characteristics of home equipment. Even so, there are some problems with streaking noise in the reproduced color picture caused by the AM recording of the color signal. Another new color-recording method has been proposed in relation to the 8-mm video format. This is termed *baseband recording by time compression* and has been made possible by the rapid development of digital technology and semiconductor devices (Dieter, 1978).

This new method, as used in the type L format, compresses the color-component signals (R—Y, B—Y) into one horizontal line and records them on a separate track (see Fig. 5.14). This type of two-channel recording is too expensive for consumer use and is too wasteful of tape. In an alternative method, the chrominance and luminance signals are recorded on a single track by recording the color-component signals (R—Y, B—Y) sequentially on two horizontal line periods using digital time-compression (Fig. 5.38). The luminance signal is also compressed and recorded along with the color-component signal. When the total signal is reproduced as is, the color-signal pattern is on the left side of the screen and the monochrome picture is on the right side, somewhat compressed. The color-component signal and the luminance signal are then separated and expanded to their original form by digital means. The color-component signals, which are sequentially recorded on two horizontal lines, are formed into a complete color signal by using a single horizontal line delay.

This baseband recording method is an interesting method for recording color signals without any significant deterioration. The jitter component in baseband recording is, however, not reduced as it is in the color-under recording, and commercial use awaits the development of inexpensive LSI circuits, including a digital means for time-base correction.

5.3.4 Audio Recording

5.3.4.1 *Linear-Track Recording.*

When the rotating-head recording method is used for video signals, the tape speed is similar to that of an audio tape recorder. As described earlier, there is also enough space left to record an audio signal on the edge of the tape. In these cases, the audio recording in a video recorder is the same in principle as it is in conventional audio tape recorders (Chap. 7). There are, however, some special problems. One problem is caused by the rotating head, which hits the surface of the tape as it rotates and causes flutter in the reproduced sound. This problem has been nearly overcome by reductions in the head drum diameter and by the solution of relevant head-to-tape interface problems. Other problems arise because the tape speed has become very slow (the tape speed of VHS in the extra-long-play mode is, for instance, only 11.1 mm/s), and the space for audio tracks is limited, especially for two-channel audio recording (stereo or bilingual recording). The resulting signal-to-noise ratio is poor, and it is necessary to apply noise-reduction methods to these audio recordings (Dolby, 1967). Also, when the tape speed is as slow as this, the rotating speed of the capstan is correspondingly low, and flutter and wow increase owing to the insufficient flywheel

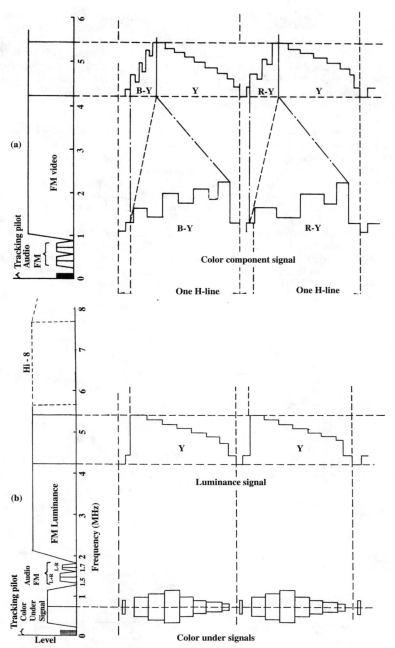

FIGURE 5.38 Frequency allocation in 8-mm video. (*a*) Proposed baseband recording by time compression; (*b*) standardized color-under recording with stereo and high band Hi-8 *(Sugaya, 1986)*.

effect of the capstan and the motor, even if a separate drive motor is used. For these reasons, FM audio and pulse-code modulation (PCM) audio recording methods have been developed for consumer applications. In broadcast video recorders, the tape speeds are sufficient to record the audio signal at broadcasting standards (the quadruplex recorder uses 381 mm/s; type B, 245 mm/s; type C, 244 mm/s; and types L and M, 118 and 105 mm/s). Therefore, at the present time, most research and development activities to improve the audio characteristics of video recordings are being carried out in the consumer field.

5.3.4.2   FM Audio Recording.   In order to improve the audio quality, while maintaining interchangeability with older machines, the rotating head can be used for audio recording. There are two different approaches: frequency-division multiple recording and double-component multiple recording.

Frequency-Division Multiple Recording.   In the frequency allocation of the signals which as recorded by the video head, some usable space can be created for the carrier frequencies of an FM audio signal between the color-under chrominance signal and the FM luminance signals (Fig. 5.39a). In the Beta format, FM audio was developed after the conventional machine using linear audio recording on a separate track was marketed, and space for the new FM audio carrier was created by shifting the FM video range to a 400-kHz higher position. This is believed to be the maximum shift possible while still maintaining interchangeability with conventional machines (Kono, 1983). In order to record the FM audio carrier signal along with

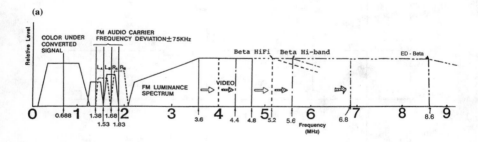

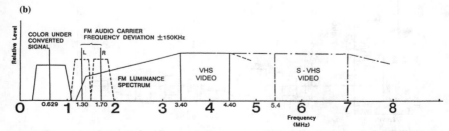

FIGURE 5.39   FM audio recording using a rotary head. (*a*) Frequency-division multiple recording; (*b*) double-component overwrite recording *(Sugaya, 1986).*

the video signal without any interference, an interleaving relation between the video signal and the FM audio frequency needs to be determined. The FM audio carrier frequency for track A and track B (f_A and f_B) must be such that

$$f_A = (n - \tfrac{1}{4})f_H \tag{5.6}$$

$$f_B = (n - \tfrac{3}{4})f_H \tag{5.7}$$

where f_H is the horizontal sync frequency (15,734 Hz for NTSC) and n is an integer.

When the FM audio signal is recorded by the video rotating head using the azimuth recording method, the crosstalk from the adjacent track is a serious problem owing to the relatively low frequency range (i.e., relatively long wavelength), and no line interrelation effects can be used to reduce crosstalk as can be done with the chrominance signal. In the Beta format, this problem is solved by making the FM audio have different carrier frequencies in adjacent tracks, so that the crosstalk can be eliminated by bandpass filters. Two carrier frequencies for each two-channel audio signal are alternately recorded on each video track. Thus, four different carrier frequencies (L_A, L_B, R_A, and R_B), each having a ±75-kHz frequency deviation, are used for FM audio recording and are selected as shown in Fig. 5.39a. In order to avoid interference between the audio and video FM carriers, the audio carrier signal is at a lower level than the video carrier signal.

In 8-mm video, the FM audio signal is limited to a single channel in order to save enough space for the video signal. Use of both a large azimuth angle ($\pm10°$) and noise reduction assures that there is little crosstalk between the two tracks in the 8-mm video system (Sugaya, 1986). A single FM audio carrier frequency is therefore used (1.5 MHz), as shown in Fig. 5.38b, but recently a subcarrier frequency of 1.7 MHz has become standardized for stereo in conjunction with the high-band version (Hi 8).

When the lower sideband of the FM video spectrum is replaced by the FM audio spectrum in frequency-division multiple recording, the high-frequency portion of the video spectrum will be eliminated, resulting in a natural decrease in the resolution of the video signal as well. Otherwise, the carrier frequency of FM video has to be shifted to a still higher region. In the frequency-division recording method, a compromise must be made between FM audio (sound quality) and FM video (picture quality). In practice, the FM video signal has been shifted to a range 400 kHz higher in order to maintain interchangeability with previously marketed equipment and tapes; even so, resolution power has been substantially decreased. Thus, the new Hi-Band Beta Hi-Fi has been developed to improve the picture quality by shifting the FM video carrier frequency an additional 800 kHz over the conventional Beta format to 5.6 MHz for peak white frequency. This sacrifices interchangeability, however, and has not been accepted for prerecorded tape use. If the interchangeability is sacrificed, ED-Beta is still a better approach for picture quality.

Double-Component Overwrite Recording. The double-component overwrite recording method was developed to improve the sound quality without sacrificing video characteristics while at the same time maintaining interchangeability with conventional equipment (Hitotsumachi, 1983). In this method, the FM audio signal is recorded using a pair of audio rotary heads with a large azimuth angle of $\pm30°$ in conjunction with a pair of video heads. This azimuth angle is sufficient to eliminate crosstalk of the audio FM signals of 1.3 and 1.7 MHz. The FM audio signal, having a relatively longer wavelength, is recorded first by a rotating audio head with both a large gap length and a large azimuth gap angle. The FM video signal, having a relatively shorter wavelength, is then recorded directly over the same track with a different azimuth angle. This recording is thus called *double-component overwrite recording.*

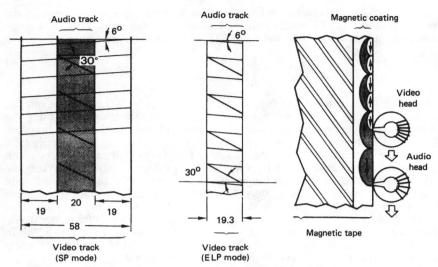

FIGURE 5.40 Double-component overwrite recording of the audio signal by a rotary head *(Sugaya, 1986).*

The principles of double-component overwrite recording are shown in Fig. 5.40. The longer-wavelength audio signal can be recorded in a deeper portion of the magnetic coating, so the shorter-wavelength video signal can be recorded on the shallower portions of the previously recorded long-wavelength audio signal with a different azimuth angle. The FM audio signal is actually erased to a certain degree (approximately 13 dB in VHS FM audio recording); even so, 30 dB of carrier-to-noise ratio can be maintained. In this recording method, FM audio carrier signals do not disturb the FM video signal, thus the video characteristics are not affected and a wider frequency deviation (±150 kHz) for FM audio—i.e., a better signal-to-noise ratio—can be obtained. The principle of this overwrite recording is not simple (Sugaya et al., 1993). In order to use this FM audio recording method for both standard play and extra-long play, the audio track width needs to be very narrow, as shown in Fig. 5.40, and thus the interchangeability of the FM audio signal is difficult unless the tape transport mechanism is exceptionally rigid. The frequency allocation of the recorded signals of the VHS and S-VHS FM audio system is shown in Fig. 5.39*b.*

The inertia effect of the rotary-head recording process considerably reduces the flutter and wow components. The FM audio recording process further improves the frequency response, the signal-to-noise ratio, the dynamic range and the channel separation; dubbing is not possible, however. The frequency-division multiple recording method is used at present only for the NTSC Beta format and the 8-mm video format. The double-component multiple recording method is used for PAL/SECAM Beta format and for all VHS formats.

5.3.4.3 *Pulse-Code-Modulation (PCM) Recording.*

Recording audio signals using pulse-code modulation has become more attractive both technically and economically, following recent developments in digital and semiconductor technologies. One of the advantages of digital processing is that the signal is written into a buffer memory and later can be retrieved from the memory with no deterioration. Thus,

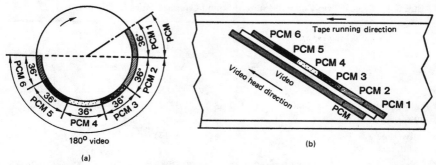

FIGURE 5.41 PCM audio recording for 8-mm video (video plus PCM audio or 6-channel PCM audio (*a*) 8-mm video PCM allocation; (*b*) 8-mm video PCM tape format (*Sugaya,* 1986).

sound quality shows no deterioration even after many duplications. The digital process, in other words, permits a discrete, incremental recording of the continuous audio signal.

Track-Division Multiple Recording. In two-head helical-scan recording, the tape must be wrapped around the head slightly more than 180°. In track-division multiple recording, the tape is wrapped an additional 36°, as shown in Fig. 5.41, and the segmented, time-compressed audio signal is written in this region. If the time-base compression rate is high, the recording density and the recording bit frequency will also become high, so that both dropouts and the error rate will increase.

The sampling frequency f_s for PCM recording is determined by the maximum recordable frequency f_{max} ($f_s > 2f_{max}$) and is also related to the video signal ($f_s = nf_H$). In the 8-mm video format $f_s = 2f_H = 31.5$ kHz, and the quantization bit number M is 10 bits. In simple terms, the dynamic range D is

$$D = 6M + 1.78 \quad \text{dB} \tag{5.8}$$

Eight bits therefore gives approximately 50 dB of dynamic range, which is insufficient even for home entertainment use. Ten bits are used for analog-to-digital conversion; these are then translated to 8 bits by a nonlinear conversion process. As a result, the dynamic range of 8-mm video PCM audio is approximately 62 dB, increasing to 85 dB with noise reduction. The upper recordable frequency limit is 14 kHz, which is just sufficient for consumer applications (Nakano et al., 1982, and Table 5.4). The most important feature of track-division multiple PCM recording is the possibility of overwrite-recording (dubbing), which FM audio recording does not have. Error compensation of the PCM code in 8-mm video is always completed in each block in order to permit the re-recording of edited signals. (The details of error compensation are discussed in the following section.) Another important feature is simplicity—a single pair of video heads can record both the video signal and the audio signal.

If recording is confined to audio only, another five different channels of PCM audio signal can be recorded by shifting the PCM recording phase (Fig. 5.41). That is, a 12-h signal (2 h × 6) can be recorded on a small 8-mm video cassette, which is almost the same size as an audio compact cassette.

PCM Encoder-Decoder. Video tape recording technology makes available an extremely large memory capacity. Thus, if an audio signal is encoded onto a compos-

TABLE 5.4 Typical Two-Channel (Stereo) Sound Characteristics (NTSC)†

	Linear track		FM VHS (Beta)	PCM 8-mm video	PCM VHS + EIA-J processor
	SP	ELP			
Tape speed, cm/s	3.33–4.00	1.11–1.33	3.33–(4)	1.43	3.33
Relative tape speed, m/s			5.8–(7)	3.75	5.8
Frequency response, Hz	50–12,000	50–6000	20–20,000	20–14,000	20–20,000
Dynamic range, dB	55‡	55‡	80‡	85‡	86 (linear) 96 (linear)
Distortion, %	< 1.5	< 1.5	< 0.3	< 0.3	< 0.01
Wow/flutter, %	0.08–0.12	0.22–0.28	< 0.005	< 0.005	0.005
Quantization bits				8 (10/8 conv.)	14 (linear) 16 (linear)
Sampling frequency, kHz				31.5	44.1

†SP = Standard Play. ELP = Extra Long Play. EIAJ = Electronic Industry Association of Japan.
‡With noise reduction.

ite signal (any of NTSC, PAL, or SECAM) by PCM, the recorder can record the PCM audio signal as an FM video signal without any modification. In this case, only the encoder-decoder (or PCM adapter) has to be standardized. The recordable upper limits of data are approximately 3 Mb/s for both Beta and VHS format recorders. In order to record up to 20 kHz of audio signal, the sampling frequency should be $f_S = 44.1$ kHz. Fourteen bits of linear quantization (dynamic range 86 dB) have been determined to be optimum for a PCM encoder-decoder (see Table 5.4).

Error compensation is one of the most important aspects of the technology of digital magnetic recording, which has intrinsic errors due to dropout and head-to-tape interface problems. Generally, error compensation is accomplished by a combination of four methods: (1) interleaving, in which information is distributed so that the error does not destroy important information; (2) error detection, using a cyclic redundancy check code (CRCC); (3) error correction, using a code such as the Reed-Solomon (Reed and Solomon, 1960); and (4) error concealment, in which missing information is estimated by means of a previous word or by adjacent sequential words. With these error compensation methods, audible errors can be effectively eliminated. A comprehensive discussion of error detection and correction methods is given in Chap. 10.

5.4 THE VIDEO HEAD

5.4.1 Development of the Video Head

The video head is one of the most important components in video recording. If an analogy is made with the principles of photography, the video tape corresponds to the photographic film and the video head to the lens. The minimum recordable wavelength will be determined both by the head gap length and by the particle size of the magnetic pigment in the magnetic coating. The corresponding optical properties are the degree of resolution of the lens in a camera and the grain size of the emulsion of the photographic film. One significant difference between the magnetic and optical systems is that there is actual physical contact between the recording medium and the magnetic head, while there is no contact between the film and the lens in a camera. As a consequence, the relationship between the magnetic head and the tape is a more complex one than that between the camera lens and the film (Sugaya, 1985).

The length of the gap is a crucial factor in the design of the video head. In the playback process, the gap length should be less than the minimum recordable wavelength. Theoretically, for maximum output, the gap length should be one-half the signal wavelength. In practice, however, a gap length of one-third the wavelength is preferred to reduce gap loss to a more acceptable level. With modern recording techniques, the recordable wavelength is becoming shorter and shorter, necessitating correspondingly smaller gap lengths. This in turn results in another problem where, if the gap length becomes too small, the main portion of the magnetic flux will be shunted past the gap and insufficient flux will be induced in the core. This is a dilemma which seriously affects the design of the modern video head.

An equally serious problem is that of maintaining the original gap tolerances and the original shape of the gap. The gap dimensions and the shape of the gap itself both tend to be affected adversely over time as the head is subjected to wear from the tape. If the head material is not of sufficient hardness, the head material (as well as the gap material) at the surface can actually be drawn in the direction of the tape movement, resulting in a distortion of the gap shape. This phenomenon of the head and gap material actually moving is called *head-gap smearing;* examples of this are shown in Fig. 5.42.

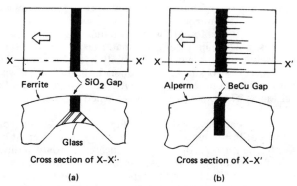

FIGURE 5.42   Metal-head-gap smearing after passage of tape. (*a*) Typical ferrite head with SiO_2 gap and no smearing; (*b*) typical alloy head with Be-Cu gap and smearing.

Alloy materials are relatively soft and are susceptible to this smearing phenomenon. For this reason, head cores and gap materials, which were originally formed from metal alloys, are now mostly formed from ferrite and glass. The adoption of new high-coercivity tapes may present difficulties, in that the limits of magnetic saturation in the poles of the ferrite head are approached. Such developments may demand reversion to the use of metal for the head pole material or to the use of newly developed amorphous materials. The magnetic materials used in the video head must meet a number of essential criteria:

1. Durable physical properties (low porosity, resistance to chipping and wearing) in conjunction with good machinability (necessary for slicing, forming, finishing, and lapping)

2. High permeability and saturation induction in the MHz range (high specific resistivity)

3. Low coercivity, in order to keep the residual magnetization of the head tip as small as possible

4. Low magnetostriction coefficient, to keep the magnetostriction noise as low as possible (i.e., $\lambda_s \rightarrow 0$)

5. Stability of both magnetic and physical properties after long periods of use in various environments

6. Resistance to possible deterioration of mechanical properties due to assembly processes (e.g., bonding) or machining techniques

7. Reasonable cost

If we consider the conditions imposed by these criteria, ferrite appears to be the optimum material available at present. Ferrite is suited for use in video heads because of its low loss at high frequency and its hardness. On the other hand, ferrite has a rather granular and brittle texture; until the late 1950s it was impossible either to make very fine gaps or to maintain the head surface in good condition (Chynoweth, 1955).

The heads in the first video machines were derived directly from audio-head technology and were constructed out of laminated Permalloy, the standard design at the time. In order to record the very high frequencies necessary for video (3.5 MHz), three strips of extremely thin (50 μm) Permalloy were used as shown in Fig. 5.43a, and a rather primitive butt joint was used to form the gap (Olson et al., 1956). Later, as shown in Fig. 5.43b, it was found that a combination of metal alloy and ferrite brought out the desirable qualities of both materials; the alloy could be used to produce an extremely fine gap, and a ferrite body had low loss in the MHz range (Kornei, 1956). Alperm (also known as Alfenol) in 60-μm strips was used as the alloy in the early combination heads because it is much harder than Permalloy and has a higher resistance. The gap of 0.5 μm was formed by silicon monoxide vacuum deposition.

In the quadruplex head design shown in Fig. 5.43c, a similar combination of alloy and ferrite was utilized, but the design was somewhat different because of the narrow track width (250 μm). A copper spacer, located not only in the Alperm head tips but also in the ferrite core gap, was used as an attempt to enhance the magnetic-flux leakage from the gap. The life of this type of head was extremely short (on the order of 200 h) and it had comparatively poor recording characteristics owing to gap smearing (Sugaya, 1968).

Sendust is another alloy that was considered at an early date for use as a video

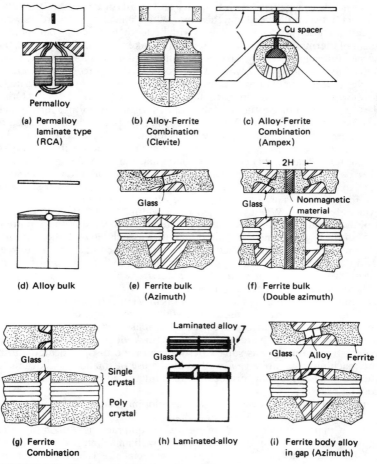

FIGURE 5.43   Various video head configurations.

head material because of its superior physical properties. Sendust is an extremely durable magnetic material, but it is also so brittle that it is not possible to produce it in sheets by rolling (Matsumoto and Yamamoto, 1937). In the early stages of magnetic head development, it was generally believed that the head could not be constructed of a solid block of metal but had to be formed from laminated sheets to reduce eddy currents. In fact, it was subsequently discovered that it was possible to use alloys in bulk form for video heads. This is because eddy currents do not affect the flux at the surface of the head core, thus it is possible to use nonlaminated alloy cores with some loss in efficiency (Sugaya, 1964; Bertram and Mallinson, 1976). Thus bulk-alloy heads made of Sendust were eventually developed (Fig. 5.43*d*). This design is still used for quadruplex machines because the extremely heavy contact between the heads and the tape does not permit the use of ferrite heads, owing to their fragility and susceptibility to noise induced by mechanical stress.

Ferrite heads can be used with helical-scan recorders because of the relatively light contact between the head and the tape. When helical-scan recorders were first introduced, high-density ferrite was used with bonded glass spacers having the same coefficient of thermal expansion as the ferrite (Duinker, 1960). This type of head was used successfully in audio and instrumentation recorders, but its response proved to be insufficient for video use owing to the porosity (0.1 percent) of the material.

In order to improve the physical properties of ferrite, hot-pressed ferrite (HPF) was developed and successfully used for video heads (Sugaya, 1968). Other approaches taken to improve the porosity characteristics of normal ferrite included the use of single-crystal ferrite (Mizushima, 1971), and hot-isostatic-pressed ferrite (HIP) (Takama and Ito, 1979). Also, various ferrite compositions were tried in the development of the video head. Ni-Zn ferrite was first used for its high resistivity, but Mn-Zn ferrite has now become a common material for video heads because of its higher permeability μ, higher saturation induction B_s, and lower coercivity H_c.

Heads made of hot-pressed ferrite have a certain advantage over single-crystal heads in that the grains are of a uniform size, the minimum mean value of which is approximately 10 μm. When the video track width is wider than 40 μm, several grains of the magnetic hot-pressed ferrite material are located in the gap area. The existence of these grains and the grain boundaries associated with them in sufficient quantity prevents the magnetostriction noise caused by contact shock between the head and the tape (Torii et al., 1980; Kimura et al., 1980). Hot-pressed ferrite is also cheaper to produce than is single-crystal ferrite, which is normally produced by the Bridgeman method (Sugimoto, 1966).

When the track width is less than 20 μm (as in VHS extra-long-play mode), hot-pressed ferrite can no longer be used successfully because only one or two grains are actually located in the head gap area. For this reason, single-crystal ferrite came into general use as a head material for narrow-track video recording. The problem of magnetostriction noise was solved by the use of more-sophisticated and more-accurate machining technology, as well as by the use of smaller head drums, which permitted a smaller head-tip projection, resulting in an extremely light head-to-tape contact pressure.

The problem of high cost was solved by developing techniques to produce ferrite in large ingots of approximately 10 cm in diameter (Torii, 1979). The most common material now in use for video heads in consumer equipment is Mn-Zn single-crystal ferrite. A typical example of such a video head with an azimuth angle gap is shown in Fig. 5.43e. The double-azimuth gap head for special effects and for other applications (such as Beta movies) is an example of extremely sophisticated fabrication techniques (Fig. 5.43 f).

In broadcast equipment, on the other hand, the head track width is still quite large (120 μm for type-C recorders), and the contact pressure between the head and the tape is high owing to the large diameter of the head drum and the higher head-to-tape relative speed. Thus, a combination single-crystal and polycrystalline ferrite head was developed for this equipment to take advantage of the strong points of both these materials, as shown in Fig. 5.43g (Camras, 1963a; Tanimura et al., 1983).

With the introduction of alloy magnetic tape, which has a coercivity higher than 80 kA/m (1000 Oe), the low saturation magnetization of ferrite becomes a serious problem, particularly concerning the gap portion of the head where the magnetic flux is concentrated. As a consequence, metal alloy materials, such as Sendust, are once again being investigated as magnetic materials for the video head (Yasuda et al., 1981). Amorphous materials, which have superior physical properties, as shown in Table 5.5, are also used for recording on alloy metal tape (Matsuura et al., 1983).

TABLE 5.5 Physical Properties of Video Head Materials

	Permalloy	Alfenol (Alperm)	Sendust (Alfesil)	Amorphous	High-density ferrite	Hot-pressed ferrite	Single-crystal ferrite	Units
Composition	Ni 79 wt % Mo 4 Fe 17	Al 16 wt % Fe 84	Al 5.4 wt % Si 9.6 Fe 85.0	Fe 4.5 wt % Co 70.5 Si 10 B 15	NiO 1 mol % ZnO 22 Fe_2O_3 67	MnO 28 mol % ZnO 19 Fe_2O_3 53	MnO 29 mol % ZnO 17.5 Fe_2O_3 53.5	
μ/μ_0[†]								
1 kHz	20000	3000	30000	10000	850	12000	10000	
1 MHz	40	30	60			2100	1540	
10 MHz					550	700	720	
Saturation induction B_s	690 (8700)	1430 (18000)	880 (11000)	680 (8500)	310 (3900)	400 (5000)	400 (5000)	kA/m (G)
Coercivity H_c	4 (0.05)	3 (0.04)	4 (0.05)	1.6 (0.02)	32 (0.4)	3 (0.04)	2.4 (0.03)	A/m (Oe)
Resistivity ρ	55×10^{-8}	140×10^{-8}	80×10^{-8}	150×10^{-8}	10^5	$>5 \times 10^{-2}$	$>10^{-3}$	$\Omega \cdot m$
Curie temp. T_c	460	400	500	420	125	150	167	°C
Vickers hardness	130	350	530	900	600	650	650	
Porosity	0	0	0	0	<1	<0.1	0	%

[†] μ/μ_0 = relative permeability.
SOURCE: Sugaya (1986).

In conventional ferrite heads, the gap portion of the head, which is in direct contact with the tape, should be wider than the track width in order to prolong head life as much as possible; this is shown in Fig. 5.43e, f, and g. When an alloy material is used for the video head, a construction similar to that used in ferrite heads cannot be used; instead, the alloy head core needs to be reinforced by a stiff nonmagnetic material, such as crystallized glass, for the tape contact portion, as shown in Fig. 5.43h (Shibaya and Fukuda, 1977). With the development of vacuum-deposited-alloy technology, lamination of alloys is being reconsidered as a means of minimizing the eddy-current loss. Laminated alloy-glass-ferrite head construction is, however, very complicated and is used mainly for broadcast applications. The production of laminated amorphous material is a highly sophisticated application of vacuum-deposition technology; the thickness of the amorphous alloy is 17 nm and the thickness of the nitrogen insulator is only 4 nm (Kaminaka et al., 1990). Therefore the metal-in-gap head of the type shown in Fig. 5.43i was developed; in it the gap portion is reinforced by a metal, such as Sendust or amorphous alloy, with high saturation magnetization (Kobayashi et al., 1985).

5.4.2 Magnetic Materials for Video Heads

The magnetic materials used in video heads change in the wake of any increase in the recording density of magnetic tape. Gamma ferric oxide of coercivity around 26 kA/m (300 Oe) was used in the early stages of video recording development. The main problem concerning the magnetic material centered on maintaining the head gap in good condition and preventing head wear over time. As a result, as durable a material as possible was desirable for head construction. Sendust was selected as the most suitable alloy material, after experiments with Permalloy and Alfenol (Table 5.5).

The fact that ferrite has a higher resistivity than the alloy materials reduces eddy-current loss and provides a high permeability in the video frequency range; this is an especially important consideration in playback. Figure 5.44 shows the efficiency of the playback head (the ratio of the flux from the magnetic tape to the induced flux in the head coil) as a function of core permeability. Another very important feature of ferrite material is its superior mechanical properties. Ferrite is a much harder material than conventional metal alloys, yet it is more easily machinable using modern techniques, and machining does not degrade the magnetic properties as it does with alloys.

As mentioned above, single-crystal ferrite is now the most common video head material for consumer equipment, but it does have the drawback of a strong anisotropy, both magnetically and mechanically (Hirota et al., 1984). Several single-crystal orientations have been tried for use in video head construction, as shown in Fig. 5.45. Type A in this figure is resistant to wear; types B and C are the best selections for output quality.

The first cobalt-modified iron oxide and chromium dioxide video tapes had a coercivity of approximately 40 kA/m (500 Oe), which could be recorded with conventional ferrite heads without saturation. Since then, the coercivity of oxide tapes has increased to around 56 kA/m (700 Oe). Further potential increases in coercivity will be limited by the saturation flux density of the ferrite head material in consumer-oriented equipment, such as VHS and Beta format, which must maintain interchangeability between older equipment and new models. Theoretically, a further increase up to 120 kA/m (1500 Oe) in coercivity is possible if the contact between the head and tape can be made extremely close. In practice, it is physically

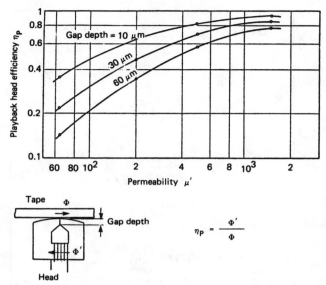

FIGURE 5.44 Relationship between the playback head efficiency η_p and the permeability μ of the head core.

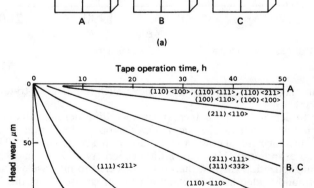

FIGURE 5.45 Use of single-crystal ferrite for video heads. (*a*) Crystal orientations; (*b*) accelerated wear characteristics. [*Reprinted with permission from Hirota (1984). Copyright 1984 American Chemical Society.*]

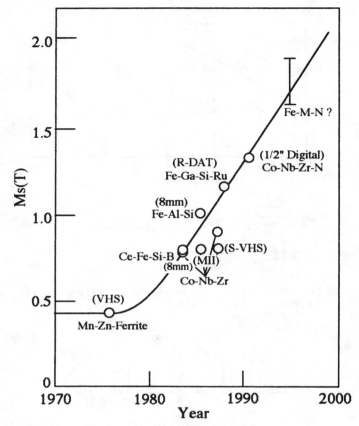

FIGURE 5.46   Development of high M_s head materials.

possible but magnetically difficult to achieve such small head-to-tape spacings (Sugaya, 1985).

In order to achieve a major increase in recording density, a completely new recording medium, such as the metal tapes adopted for 8-mm video, will be needed—for instance, metal powder (MP) tape with a coercivity of 120 kA/m (1500 Oe), or metal-evaporated (ME) tape with a coercivity of 72 kA/m (900 Oe). The saturation magnetization (M_s) is, therefore, expected to increase as shown in Fig. 5.46. Modern alloy video-head development has progressed from this background (Morio et al., 1981). Sendust is still being used, but new amorphous materials are now being seriously considered because of their durability and superior magnetic performance (Makino et al., 1980). There are two different processes for the production of amorphous metals. One is the liquid-quench method, where the molten magnetic material is quenched suddenly on a roller and is thus cooled before crystallization can take place (Fujimori et al., 1977). The other method is the vacuum-deposition method in which the magnetic material is sputtered or evaporated on a nonmagnetic substrate (Shimada, 1983). In this method, magnetic and nonmagnetic

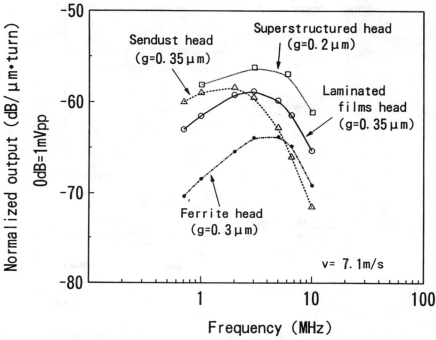

FIGURE 5.47 Frequency responses of various types of video heads using MP tape. (*Takahashi, 1987*).

materials are deposited alternately, so that the high-frequency efficiency is considerably enhanced, even at relatively wide track widths (Fig. 5.47) (Takahashi et al., 1987). The head design is similar, as shown in Fig. 5.43h. This is another example of an earlier technology reemerging in the development of video recording.

5.4.3 Video Head Design

All video heads in use at the present time are of the ring type with a very narrow gap and a small coil. So far, eddy current losses have not been so important (see Fig. 5.9) although, as shown in Fig. 5.48, the recording frequency is increasing every year. The experimental relationship between head gap length and head output is shown in Fig. 5.49; typically, the head gap length is chosen to be one-third of the shortest recordable wavelength. The observed gap length as measured through a microscope is shorter than the effective gap length obtained by measuring the null point (the point at which the effective gap length equals the recorded wavelength). Part of this difference is fundamental; the remainder is the result of what is called the *worked layer* (or the *Beilby layer*). This is a thin, nonmagnetic layer caused by mechanical work or by chemical reaction between the gap surface of the head core and the gap material. In the early stages of ferrite head design, a glass-bonding technique was used to create a strong gap (Duinker, 1960), but this high-temperature bonding

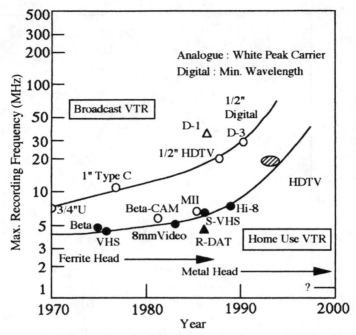

FIGURE 5.48 Trends of the maximum recording frequency of audio-video equipment.

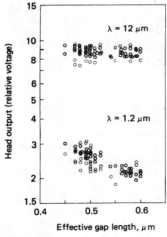

FIGURE 5.49 Experimental relationship between head output and head gap length.

process relied on a chemical reaction between the head core and the spacer material to achieve a strong bond. The nonmagnetic portion that was created by the chemical reaction was of no concern when the minimum recordable wavelength was relatively long (longer than 2 μm, for example). In high-density recording, however, the minimum recordable wavelength becomes less than 1 μm, dictating an effective gap length of 0.3 μm. When the effective gap length becomes this small, the presence of this worked layer is no longer negligible. As a consequence, the glass-bonding technique has recently been replaced by the vacuum-sputtering of nonmagnetic materials.

The worked layer on the single-crystal ferrite can be detected by means of x-ray diffraction analysis methods (Sugaya, 1978, 1985). When the surface of a damage-free single-crystal ferrite is observed by x-rays, a regular lattice x-ray diffraction pattern is evident. If there is a worked layer present, this regular lattice pattern will disappear. The pattern will reappear if the worked layer is removed by chemical etching, for example. Use of x-ray diffraction analysis has led to the development of various damage-free lapping techniques as well as to the improvement of the short-wavelength recording performance of video heads. With alloy magnetic materials, the worked layer can be detected by means of the skin effect at frequencies in the MHz range (Sugaya, 1964, 1985). If there is a worked layer present, the magnetic flux, which is concentrated on the surface of the alloy, is disturbed by the nonmagnetic worked layer, and the permeability of the alloy will be decreased. When the worked layer is removed by chemical etching, the original permeability is recovered. In this way, the thickness of the worked layer can be measured; this may lead to the development of improved damage-free lapping techniques.

One of the most important features of the ferrite head is its suitability to mass production techniques. Figure 5.50 shows a typical example of the video head production process. Ferrite heads are normally produced together in core units of several dozen pieces each and are then separated into the individual head units.

Following the increase in video tape coercivity, the saturation flux density of the head material is becoming a critical limitation. There is at present some activity to develop a high-saturation ferrite material, but there are finite upper limits to this, owing to the crystal characteristics of ferrite. The theoretical limit for ferrite is on the order of 480 kA/m (6000 G), while that for alloy materials is far higher, as shown in Fig. 5.46. For this reason, alloy materials are coming into use once again for video heads. The most serious problems to be faced in the use of alloy materials derive from the complicated design and construction techniques dictated by the nature of the material. These problems can be solved by using multilayered films of nitride alloys which are prepared by nitrogen-reactive rf sputtering (Kaminaka et al., 1990). The various video heads discussed in this section are fabricated mainly through the use of slicing, grinding, and lapping techniques. In the future, however, radically new techniques, such as rf sputtering and laser cutting, will be adopted and will, in turn, trigger new designs and construction methods for video heads.

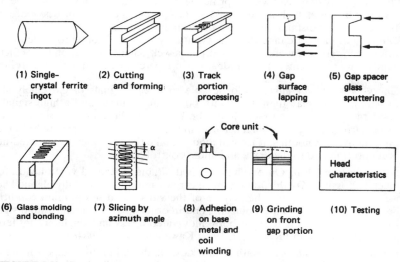

(1) Single-crystal ferrite ingot
(2) Cutting and forming
(3) Track portion processing
(4) Gap surface lapping
(5) Gap spacer glass sputtering

Core unit

(6) Glass molding and bonding
(7) Slicing by azimuth angle
(8) Adhesion on base metal and coil winding
(9) Grinding on front gap portion
(10) Testing

Head characteristics

FIGURE 5.50 Production process for typical ferrite heads shown in Fig. 5.43*e*.

5.5 VIDEO TAPE

5.5.1 Development of Video Tape

As discussed above, the important advances in video recording have centered around the increase of recording density, including the decrease of the minimum recordable wavelength. These advances are strongly dependent on the improvement of magnetic tape materials (Jacobs, 1979).

In the early stages of development, standard audio tape was used for the recording of video signals. When video recording subsequently became commercially feasible through the introduction of the quadruplex format, it became necessary to develop a special video tape. Standard audio tape was not well adapted either to the high relative head-to-tape speed of rotary-head equipment (38 m/s) or to the necessity of recording short-wavelength signals on an extremely narrow track. A tape designed especially for video use was thus needed to solve these and other conflicting problems; in particular it was necessary to devise a very smooth tape surface in order to maintain the requisite precise contact between the video head and the tape. This must be achieved without undue wear to either the tape surface or the head and without any sacrifice in the tape runability around the head drum.

When further developments led to the adoption of helical scan as the industrywide format, increasingly stringent conditions were added to the requirements of video tape. With helical-scan recording, it now became necessary for this extremely smooth-surfaced tape to be transported smoothly, not only around the rotating head drum, but also through the very complex tape path required to compensate for the angling of the tape as it is wrapped around the drum (more than 180° in the case of a two-head machine). This tape path became even more complex with the use of miniaturized cassette-loading mechanisms. As helical-scan equipment has become more sophisticated, the conditions to which the video tape is subjected have become correspondingly more severe. For example, in the process of playing back a still picture, the video head will, in principle, trace the same track on the tape over and over at a rate as high as 3600 passes per minute; the tape must be extremely well designed to withstand this sort of punishment.

The type of magnetic tape that has eventually been developed for video use is, therefore, the result of many compromises—a well-balanced solution to conflicting demands. The requirements of an ideal video tape can be summarized as follows:

1. *Smoothness of tape surface.* To be able to record signals of extremely short wavelength and play them back with both a high output and a high signal-to-noise ratio, the tape surface should be both very flat and very smooth, with surface irregularities less than 0.1 μm, in order to minimize spacing loss. However, an overly smooth surface will tend to make the tape stick to the fixed-head drum portion and to the erase and audio-control heads.

2. *Optimum head wear.* On one hand, it is desirable to extend video head life as much as possible. On the other hand, a certain amount of carefully planned head wear is vital to maintain the surface of the video head in optimum condition, both magnetically and mechanically, and in order to yield the maximum signal-to-noise ratio. This is true for both alloy video heads and single-crystal ferrite heads (Potgiesser and Koorneef, 1973; Kawamata et al., 1984a).

3. *Hardness of tape surface.* Both a hard tape binder and a hard tape surface are durable and will be resistant to scratches and dropout; the drawback of too hard

a tape is that it will cause excessive wear of the video head (Kawamata et al., 1984*b*).

4. *Coercivity and magnetic flux density.* Both higher coercivity H_c and higher maximum induction B_m are necessary to yield higher output, especially at very short wavelengths; there are limitations to this, however, depending on the saturation magnetization of the head core material.

5. *Tape thickness.* For maximum recording time, the tape should, of course, be as thin as possible; however, very thin tape backings, such as tensilized polyester film, are unstable at high temperatures, in addition to being quite fragile mechanically, particularly on the edge portion of the tape (the stiffness of the tape is proportional to the cube of the tape thickness).

It can be seen, then, that the magnetic requirements for the video tape tend to be in direct conflict with the mechanical requirements for a good video recording; the optimum solution therefore becomes a compromise among a number of competing factors. Moreover, in most cases, the video tape is used not only to record the video signal but also to record the audio signal by high-frequency bias recording and to record the control signal by means of saturation recording at the edge of the tape. The magnetic tape for video recording, as a consequence, must meet and satisfy recording conditions which are more stringent and varied than those encountered in magnetic recording of any other form.

The tape width has been decreasing, along with an exponential decrease in tape consumption. Figure 5.51 shows the optimum balance between tape width and tape thickness; this balance also contributes to the decrease in the overall volume of a reel of video cassette tape. The necessity of maintaining sufficient error-free machine-to-machine compatibility has also contributed to very close tape toler-

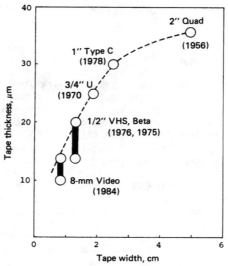

FIGURE 5.51 Historical relationship between tape thickness and width.

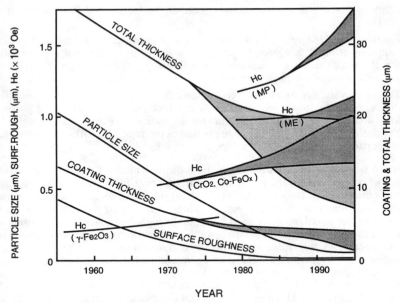

FIGURE 5.52   Historical development of video tape parameters.

ances in modern equipment; this is especially true of machines with extremely narrow-track recording, such as the Beta III and the VHS 6-h mode, where the tape width tolerance is within $\pm$ 10 μm.

A summary of 30 years of progress in improvement of the properties of video tape is shown in Fig. 5.52.

5.5.2   Video Tape Materials

In the beginning stages of video recording, gamma ferric oxide (γ-Fe_2O_3), the same material then used in audio recording, was used as the magnetic pigment in the recording tape. Later, a decrease was made in the particle size of the magnetic pigment in order to improve the signal-to-noise ratio while, at the same time, increasing the coercivity from 20 kA/m (250 Oe) to 28 kA/m (350 Oe) (Fig. 5.52). Due to the shape anisotropy of γ-Fe_2O_3, this pigment was a stable and inexpensive magnetic material, but there was an upper limit to the recording density which could be obtained.

Chromium dioxide pigment (CrO_2) was developed and first used for audio magnetic tape in 1961 (Swoboda et al., 1961); subsequently, it was applied to video use in 1970 in the $\frac{3}{4}$-in U-format recorder. Chromium dioxide tape demonstrated improved performance at short wavelengths (i.e., less than 5 μm) owing to its high coercivity of 36 kA/m (450 Oe) and greater acicularity (Darnell, 1961); however, it was both more abrasive and more expensive than the conventional γ-Fe_2O_3 tape (Table 5.6).

The coercivity of a magnetic recording medium can be increased by cobalt dop-

TABLE 5.6 Video Tape Materials

| | γ-Fe$_2$O$_3$ | CrO$_2$ | Co-γ-Fe$_2$O$_3$ | Ba-ferrite† | Metal | | Units |
					Fe-Co particle	Co-Ni evap.	
H_c	20–35	36–60	40–80	48–160	56–175	70–100	kA/m (4π Oe)
B_r	80–120	100–130	80–120	70–115	150–260	300–360	kA/m (emu/cm^3)
B_m	110–140	130–150	100–145	120–145	220–300	450	kA/M (emu/cm^3)
S	0.7–0.85	0.8–0.87	0.7–0.85	0.6–0.9	0.7–0.85	0.65–0.8	—
Particle size	0.2–0.8	0.3–0.5	0.2–0.6	0.05–0.1	0.1–0.3	—	μm
T_c	675	125	520	340	770	1000	°C
Crystal structure	Spinel	Rutile	Spinel	Hexagonal	Body-centered cubic	Hexagonal	—
Shape	Acicular	Acicular	Acicular	Platelet	Acicular	Thin film	—

†Co-Ti modified.
SOURCE: Sugaya (1986).

ing of the γ-Fe_2O_3 particle, utilizing the strong crystal anisotropy of cobalt. However, the increased coercivity induced in this way by crystal anisotropy is sensitive to the high temperatures and mechanical stresses which are inevitably generated in a video recorder. Eventually, after a great deal of research in this area, cobalt-adsorbed gamma ferric oxide tape (Co-γ-Fe_2O_3) was successfully developed (Umeki et al., 1974). This new tape material combined the crystal anisotropy induced by cobalt with the shape anisotropy of acicular γ-Fe_2O_3. The coercivity can be controlled from 45 kA/m (550 Oe) to 135 kA/m (1700 Oe) with Co-γ-Fe_2O_3 tape; this tape also has the advantage of lower production costs than that of CrO tape and is, at present, the most commonly used material for video tape.

Barium ferrite particles have been developed to effect an increase in the recording density without reference to the coercivity (Fujiwara et al., 1982). Since barium ferrite has a hexagonal-platelet crystal structure and a preferred magnetization along the C axis, it affords, when properly oriented, an optimum axis for magnetization perpendicular to the surface of the coating. There are still unknown areas to be explored in the use of this material, but it appears quite possible that barium ferrite tape may well be situated midway between Co-γ-Fe_2O_3 tape and metal tape.

A coated tape using metal pigment as the recording medium was first reported more than 25 years ago (Nagai, 1961). At that time, however, there was no market demand for such a high-coercivity recording tape, and ferric oxide tapes continued to be dominant in the video recording field for the next 20 years (Sugaya and Tomago, 1983). There are, in addition, other reasons why metal tapes were not readily adopted for practical use; these include chemical instability, noise problems, cost, and incompatibility. Metal tape was first introduced commercially in the new tape format of the 8-mm video; that is, an entirely new video recording system was devised to make use of this new tape. There are two types of metal tapes: metal-powder (MP) and metal-evaporated (ME) tape. The metal-powder tape is a coated tape in which the ferric oxide particles are replaced by particles of an acicular alloy, such as Fe-Ni-Co (Kawasaki and Higuchi, 1972; Chubachi and Tamagawa, 1984). The metal-evaporated tape uses an entirely different coating process, shown in Fig. 5.53, based

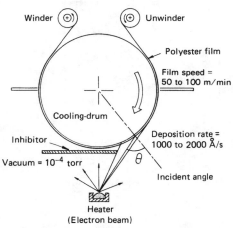

FIGURE 5.53 Mechanism for continuous vacuum deposition with oblique incidence for metal-evaporated (ME) tape.

on vacuum evaporation directly onto the surface of the tape substrate (Maesawa et al., 1982). This results in an anisotropic columnar grain structure which is formed by controlling the angle of incidence and the rate of deposition. The resulting grain structure yields different recording characteristics with different head running directions; it has no influence on either friction or the life of a still frame (Shinohara et al., 1984). Metal-evaporated tape has the following advantages:

1. Higher output at short wavelengths due to the very thin magnetic layer (0.1 μm) and the obliquely inclined crystal structure.

2. Very high saturation magnetization, the result of direct deposition of the Co-Ni magnetic layer without a binder.

Metal-evaporated tape also has some drawbacks. The manufacturing process tape requires an overly long time for the evaporation of the magnetic layer, resulting in low productivity, and the layer thus produced is mechanically fragile and susceptible to cracks. The tape also requires a thin (< 0.02 μm) protective oxidized layer and suffers from the problem of lubrication common to all hard metals. The surface of the evaporated metal alloy material therefore needs to be treated, by various methods, with special lubricants (Iijima and Hanafusa, 1984).

5.5.3 Video Tape Characteristics

5.5.3.1 Signal Output and Noise.   In order to increase the signal output at short wavelengths, both the coercivity and the magnetization of the magnetic recording layer are increased. When the coercivity of the video tape is changed, the optimum recording current is also changed, as shown in Fig. 5.54. Because the video signal is recorded without bias, the replay signal goes through a maximum when the recording current is increased; this is due to the recording demagnetization effect and is especially pronounced at high frequencies.

Most video signals are recorded by frequency modulation; thus, the carrier-to-noise ratio C/N is one of the most important factors in determining picture quality. Noise induced by the tape itself is classified into two main types: erase noise and modulation noise. In particulate tape, erase noise (the noise remaining after a tape is erased) can be determined by the degree of uniformity of dispersion of the magnetic particles and the surface smoothness of the magnetic layer. Modulation noise is a crucial factor in video recording since a carrier frequency signal is always recorded even if the video signal is zero. Modulation noise is caused by recorded-signal amplitude and frequency deviations attributable mainly to irregularities in the coating and on the tape surface (Fig. 5.55). Modulation noise is also induced by frequency modulation associated with time-base instability resulting from "creaking" (a phenomenon similar to stick-slip, but higher in frequency) between the head and the tape. There are three essential conditions that must be met to reduce modulation noise: (1) maximum physical and magnetic uniformity of magnetic particles to give increased packing density, (2) maximally uniform particle dispersion, and (3) maximum smoothness of the tape surface.

The carrier-to-noise ratio of video tape has been improving steadily, at a rate of approximately 1 dB per year for the conventional Co-γ-Fe_2O_3 tapes and at an anticipated rate of several decibels per year for the new generation of tapes. It is expected that the next generation of recording media will be based on metal-evaporated tape, particularly for digital video recording. Doubtless, however, the

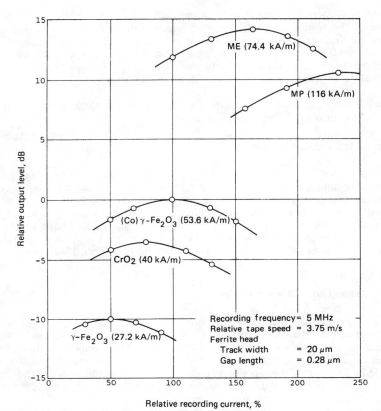

FIGURE 5.54 Relative output versus relative recording current for various video tapes (noise level: -39 dB).

introduction of this new type of tape will engender new problems to be overcome before it matures as the next standard recording medium.

5.5.3.2 Demagnetization of the Recorded Video Signal.   The video signal recorded on tape can be adversely demagnetized as the result of a number of factors: magnetic contamination, head-tip magnetization, mechanical stress, and thermal stress.

Magnetic Contamination.   Many components of the machine which contact the tape can be contaminated by magnetized material from the tape; this contamination can erase the signal that has been recorded on that part of the tape. In order to eliminate demagnetization by this type of magnetic contamination, the tape binder should be made resistant to heavy contact. In addition, the tape transport mechanism should be sufficiently smooth to avoid scratching the tape; in particular, the video head tip must be finished to as smooth as surface as possible.

Magnetization of the Video Head Tip.   A magnetized head tip can erase a recorded signal during playback. To prevent such erasure, the coercivity of the video head core should be as low as possible. Figure 5.56 shows the demagnetiza-

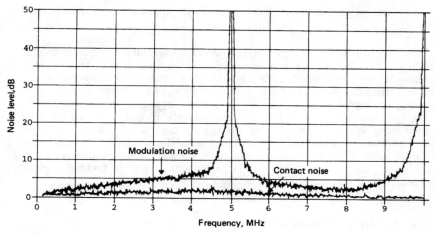

FIGURE 5.55 Typical modulation-noise spectrum of a video tape (amplifier noise = 0 dB).

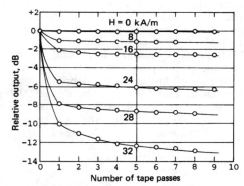

FIGURE 5.56 Demagnetization of a signal ($\lambda = 5$ μm) recorded on Co-γ-Fe$_2$O$_3$ tape after repeatedly applied magnetic fields of different strengths.

tion of a recorded tape by magnetic fields caused by either magnetic contamination or by magnetization of the video head tip.

Mechanical Stress. Mechanical stress on the tape can result from a number of causes, such as pinch-roller pressure and contact with either the video head or small-radius tape guides. Depending upon the magnetic properties of the tape, this mechanical stress can cause magnetostrictive demagnetization. The demagnetization caused by repeated passes of the tape will be accelerated if the acicularity (the ratio between the long axis and the short axis) of the magnetic particles is low. Different acicularities are obtained by different types of magnetic pigment; the highest acicularity is obtained in chromium dioxide, the lowest is obtained by granular-shaped (cubic) cobalt-doped ferric oxide. The gamma ferric oxide widely used at present in video tape has an acicularity approaching that of chromium dioxide.

Thermal Stress. Heavy, prolonged contact between the video tape and either the head tip or the rotary-head drum portion will produce heat by friction, demagnetizing the signal recorded on the tape. In theory, the rate of demagnetization by thermal stress can be determined in the main by the temperature dependencies of crystal anisotropy and magnetization, and second, by the Curie temperature (T_c) of the magnetic pigment (see Table 5.6). The magnetic properties of nonacicular Co-doped ferric oxide are strongly affected by both mechanical and thermal stresses. This has proved to be a fundamental defect in Co-doped ferric oxide and caused it to be abandoned as a material for video tape. Chromium dioxide tape, which has a very low T_c (120°C), is not subject to large demagnetization by thermal stress since the coercivity is relatively constant below T_c.

5.5.4 Head-Tape Interface Problems

5.5.4.1 Dropouts. A dropout is the disappearance, temporary or otherwise, of the recorded signal on playback. Dropouts may be caused by physical peeling of the recorded portion, by spacing loss caused by asperities on the tape surface, or by debris on the head or tape (Geddes, 1965). The dropout rate increases when the recorded wavelength is very short. For broadcast use, a typical maximum acceptable dropout rate is 5 dropouts per minute; for consumer use a typical maximum rate is 15 dropouts per minute. In general, the dropout rate will decrease during the first one or two passes of the tape, as the video head polishes the tape, removing particles of dust and other debris from the tape surface. The dropout rate will then remain fairly steady during the next 300 passes, increasing gradually thereafter. Tape life, as calculated by the maximum acceptable rate of dropouts, is approximately 300 passes when the tape transport mechanism is in good working order; this value may, however, be greatly affected by poor environmental conditions. In the absence of adverse environmental conditions, the dropout rate may be minimized by several means, including careful control of the tape production process, use of a conductive backcoating, use of a durable binder formulation, and cleanly slit tape edges. The video head surface should be both smooth and durable. Soft metal material will be damaged by tape friction; conversely, a rough head surface will damage the tape surface. Finally, greater head-tip projection is desired to ensure minimum dropouts (this is particularly important for quadruplex recorders).

All of the above factors need to be taken into consideration, but each of these measures by itself can have negative influences on other areas of the recording process. Thus the design of the video tape and recorder mechanism must be based on a series of compromises carefully chosen to optimize all aspects of the video recording process.

5.5.4.2 Head Clogging. *Head clogging* refers to the accumulation of debris or contamination from the tape coating on the surface of the video head. Head clogging interferes with both the recording of a signal and the playback of a recorded signal in the short-wavelength range. This occurs as the result of the large spacing loss created by the clogging and is an extremely serious problem in video recording. Head clogging may occur under several conditions. Contamination of the tape surface may cause a clog and is most frequently encountered in the form of finger-prints or dust on the tape. The use of a cassette or cartridge tape container is essential for the prevention of head clogging. Heavy friction between the head and the tape may also cause a clog. Friction is a particularly serious problem when both metal tapes and metal heads are used. Also, the binder formulation and the surface treatment of metal tape is crucial. Environmental conditions are important, the major problems being extremes of low or high humidity and dust in the air. Professional machines are normally used in a controlled environment, but most consumer equipment must be operated in ambient temperature and humidity.

Finally, the composition and formulation of the binder are the most important factors in the prevention of head clogging. The binder must meet two conflicting conditions: on the one hand, it must act as a lubricant; on the other, it must serve as an abrasive to clean the contaminated head surface as well as to polish the head surface appropriately to keep it in good condition.

5.5.4.3 *Brown Stain.* When alloy magnetic materials (such as Sendust) or amorphous materials are used for the tip portion of the video head, another type of head-to-tape interface problem can occur; this is particularly evident in conjunction with the use of metal-powder tapes.

The friction between the tape and the head can affect the surface of the video head tip, turning it into a brown-colored coating. This "brown stain" is an extremely thin nonmagnetic coating caused by a chemical reaction that occurs as the result of the friction. This stain can be the cause of a substantial spacing loss.

The moisture in the air tends to act as a natural lubricant, and when the relative humidity is low (e.g., less than 10 percent), the formation of the brown coating is accelerated. Although a solution to this problem has yet to be discovered, a tape binder with abrasive properties can be used to remove the brown stain once it has formed. The use of metal-evaporated tape, which has no binder, will necessitate a different type of solution which does not rely on the use of a tape binder. We can anticipate that the special treatment of tape surfaces will constitute an important part of the future technology of video recording.

5.6 DUPLICATION OF VIDEO TAPE

5.6.1 Development of Video Tape Duplication

Originally, the video tape recorder was used primarily for time-shift purposes, both for broadcast and home use. Only later did video recording come to be used extensively for the playback of professionally recorded (prerecorded) programs.

In the production of prerecorded audio cassette tapes, the dubbing speed may be as high as 64 times normal playback speed. An increase of this extent translates the audio frequencies up to approximately 1.3 MHz, which may be effectively recorded on specially designed high-speed master and slave tape recorders. At this speed, if the master tape recorder is connected to 10 slave tape recorders, the tape duplication efficiency will be 640 times that of simple copying from machine to machine in real time.

The typical consumer-use video tape recorder, on the other hand, operates at high frequencies of almost 7 MHz, and it is very difficult, if not impossible, to increase the head-to-tape speed for duplication purposes. Consequently, video tape duplication is carried out at present by the rather primitive means of connecting a series of slave recorders to the master video recorder and recording a program played back from the master recorder in real time.

There is, however, an attractive alternative in the contact duplication of magnetic tape by either anhysteretic or thermal magnetization mechanisms. In the contact duplication method, a copy can be made directly from the magnetically recorded master tape to blank slave tapes, in much the same way that contact prints can be made from photographic film. The negative film is analogous to the master tape, which is recorded in a mirror-image pattern; the photographic paper is analogous to the slave tape on which the magnetically recorded signal is transferred; the light corresponds either to the magnetic transfer field in the anhysteretic transfer method or to heat in the thermal transfer method.

The original concept of contact duplication by the anhysteretic method is rather old (Mueller-Ernesti, 1941), and was applied quite early to audio tape duplication (Herr, 1949; Camras and Herr, 1949). The audio signal on tape is, however, distributed over a very wide range of wavelengths from a few micrometers up to several thousand micrometers. The contact duplication efficiency of the lower frequency (longer wavelength) signals is lower than that of the higher frequency (shorter wavelength) signals, as shown in Fig. 5.57 (Sugaya, 1973). As a consequence, contact duplication of audio signals was actually applied only for rather specialized institutional equipment. The FM video recorded signal is, however, concentrated mainly in the short-wavelength range. Thus, the major problem to be faced in contact duplication of a frequency-modulated video signal centers around the increase in the transfer efficiency of very short-wavelength signals (Sugaya et al., 1969). Later, the development of chromium dioxide video tape, which has a very low Curie temperature (125°C), made it possible to consider the use of a thermal

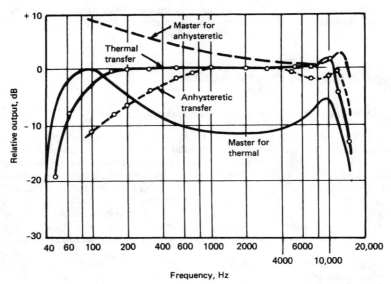

FIGURE 5.57 Comparison between thermal and anhysteretic transfer methods at audio frequencies (relatively long wavelengths). The tape speed is 19 cm/s.

transfer method of contact duplication (Hendershot, 1970). Reports of this possibility stimulated further development of the contact duplication process for video tape (Van den Berg, 1969; Ginsburg, 1970). At the same time, theoretical investigations and analyses of contact duplication were begun (Hokkyo and Ito, 1970; Kobayashi and Sugaya, 1971a, 1971b, Tjaden and Rijckaert, 1971; Mallinson et al., 1971).

In spite of the concerted efforts of numerous researchers into both the theory and feasibility of contact duplication, its practical implementation has been delayed. This delay is attributed partly to technical difficulties, such as the slow development and availability of suitable master tape. Perhaps more important is the fact that direct machine-to-machine duplication has actually proved to be sufficient to handle the demand for tape copying. This has become particularly true as mass production techniques have resulted in a sharp decrease in the price of recorders, along with improved reliability; these can then be economically used in quantity as slave machines in copying. The rapid growth of the prerecorded video tape business may, however, eventually render direct machine-to-machine video copying obsolete and spur further efforts into the development of the contact duplication process.

5.6.2 Head-to-Head Duplication Method

In this method, both the video and the audio signals from the master recorder are sent, via a distribution amplifier, to a series of recorders operating in real time. At large duplication houses, several hundred such slave recorders may be connected in parallel in order to gain duplication efficiency. The decreased price of video cassette recorders, accompanied with comparable increases in both reliability and head life, has enabled the head-to-head method to become the most effective and inexpensive way of duplicating video tapes. This is in spite of the necessity for replacement by hand of the video cassettes in the slave recorders and for the maintenance of the extremely large number of slave recorders.

The head-to-head method provides the following advantages:

1. *A high degree of flexibility.* Any desired quantity of duplication can be done efficiently by simply changing the number of slaves used in the duplication process, and inexpensive consumer recorders can be used with only slight modification.

2. *Excellent picture and sound quality.* Modern mass-produced recorders are sufficiently reliable and of high enough quality to give good results in both sound and picture quality.

There are, however, some disadvantages to the head-to-head duplication:

1. *Manual cassette changing.* This is a laborious process, particularly in the duplication of shorter tapes, such as music and instructional programs, which have an average playing time of about 30 min.

2. *Labor-intensive quality assurance.* Since video recordings are still subject to such problems as head-clogging during the recording process, duplicated tapes must be thoroughly checked by the human eye. Unfortunately, it has proven impossible thus far to develop a practical automated procedure for quality control. Instead, quality problems have been minimized by improvements in tape and system reliability.

As a solution to some of these problems, extremely long video tapes (for example, 5 km, or some 20 times the length of the 250-m VHS cassette tape) on flangeless open reels ("pancakes") are used on the slave recorders instead of the standard cassettes. The long tape on these open reels is run continuously without stopping, thus recording the material from a series of several master programs back-to-back. Either a pair of master recorders is used to switch the source-program cassettes back and forth continuously, or an endless tape in a special bin is used as a continuous program source. This sequential duplicating procedure using a long, open-reel tape can greatly decrease the necessity for changing tapes. Quality-inspection time is also shortened, since most of the problems occur predictably during the starting and stopping of the tape and not while it is continuously running. This duplication method is most effective when the recorded program is a short one, such as a 30-min music program. Once a series of these programs are duplicated sequentially on the long tape, they can be cut to length and loaded into cassettes by an automatic tape-loading machine, which can be operated independently, off-line from the duplication process. The next improvement anticipated in the head-to-head duplication process is the doubling or tripling of the speed of both the head drum and the tape, provided the cost can be kept commercially feasible.

Although the head-to-head duplication method is quite primitive in concept, it has proved to be the most practical method of video tape duplication thus far; and with the modifications discussed here, it is still the main method for commercial video tape duplication.

5.6.3 Contact Duplication Methods

5.6.3.1 The Anhysteretic Process.   In this process, the video signal, along with the audio and control signals, is recorded on a special master tape with approximately three times the coercivity of the slave tape. These signals are recorded by a specially designed master recorder in a format that results in a mirror-image recording of the original signals. The magnetically coated surfaces of both the master and the slave tapes are then placed in direct contact with each other while an alternating magnetic transfer field of carefully adjusted intensity is applied. This instantaneously causes the magnetic field of the master tape to be printed anhysteretically onto the slave tape. Two types of anhysteretic contact duplication have been developed: the parallel-running method and the bifilar-winding method (Fig. 5.58).

The parallel-running method, in principle, can be applied to the continuous (sequential) duplication process described above, as well as to a type of double or triple duplication process which makes use of a single master tape and two or three duplication stations (Crum and Town, 1971). The greatest problem encountered in this method has been the decrease of the duplicated output of short-wavelength signals as the result of slippage between the master and slave tapes during the duplication or transfer process. A compressed-air drum technique was developed to reduce this problem (Kihara et al., 1983).

An alternative is to use a bifilar-winding method to eliminate the slippage problem entirely. In this method, the master and slave tapes are first wound together on a separate reel hub, using a pressure roller to squeeze out any air which is trapped between the two tapes; then the magnetic transfer field is applied. Tape slippage is zero, eliminating any error from this source, and the quality of the output of the transfer-recorded signal, as well as the reliability, is higher than that of the parallel-running method. After this transfer-recording procedure, both the transferred slave tape and the master tape are rewound back onto their respective reels. The drawbacks to the bifilar-winding method arise mainly from this winding and rewinding

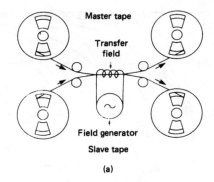

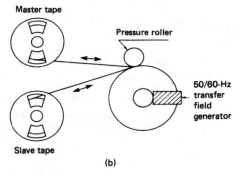

FIGURE 5.58 Principle of anhysteretic tape transfer. (*a*) Tape running in contact; (*b*) bifilar winding.

process. The necessity for rewinding limits the length of both the master and slave tapes. Also, audio print-through of the longer wavelengths occurs as the result of the tapes being tightly wound together during the magnetic transfer process. Separate audio recording is needed to avoid this print-through. This type of video duplication in its present state of development is not suitable for mass duplication; however, its flexibility should make it well-suited to medium-quantity duplication needs.

5.6.3.2 Characteristics of the Master Tape.   In audio tape recording with a high-frequency bias field, the magnetic signal field decreases at the same rate as the bias field in the recording process. In the anhysteretic transfer process, on the other hand, the signal field which is supplied from the master tape surface remains constant, and only the bias, or transfer, field decreases. This is known as the *ideal anhysteretic magnetization process*. The anhysteretic susceptibility of the slave tape increases in proportion to the intensity of the transfer field, as shown in Fig. 5.59. The transfer field for contact duplication should, therefore, be at least 1.5 times higher than that of the slave-tape coercivity; at the same time, however, the bias field will tend to erase the recorded signal on the master tape, as shown in Fig. 5.60. Under optimum conditions, however, the master-tape signal should not be erased by more than 1 dB at the first duplication, and further erasure should be negligible.

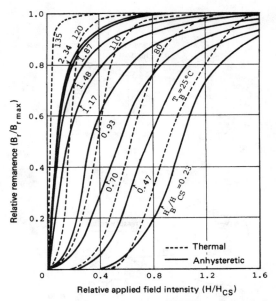

FIGURE 5.59 Remanent magnetization versus applied field curves for various values of transfer field H_B or transfer temperature T_B using CrO_2 tape. The anhysteretic curves are computer-simulated. H_{cs} is the coercivity of the slave tape.

Thus, the slave tape's output signal produced by contact duplication can be maintained at a constant level even after thousands of duplications.

According to both theoretical and experimental results, the coercivity of the master tape should be at least 2.5 times higher than that of the slave tape. The coercivity will, however, be limited by other factors, such as the availability of suitable magnetic materials for the master tape and video head saturation. The coercivity of the master tape required for VHS or Beta tape duplication is, for example, at least 120 kA/m (1500 Oe). The magnetic material used for such a master tape was originally high-coercivity, cobalt-modified iron oxide, but this has begun to be phased out in favor of metal particles with both a higher coercivity of 154 kA/m (1930 Oe) and a higher magnetic remanence of 250 kA/m (emu/cm^3) (Chubachi and Tamagawa, 1984).

In order to obtain a higher transfer efficiency for signals of long wavelengths, the remanent magnetization and the coating thickness of both the master tape and the slave tape should be as great as possible. For short-wavelength signals, the surface roughness of both tapes should be as small as possible. The signal deterioration at short wavelengths, in dB, in general follows the spacing-loss formula 54.6 d/λ, where d, in this case, is the sum of the surface roughness of both tapes. In practice, these conditions for master tapes are not easily satisfied, and problems still exist stemming from head clogging, head wearing, and dropouts.

5.6.3.3 *Contact Duplication by the Thermal Process.* At present, chromium dioxide is the only available material suitable for use as a slave tape in the thermal

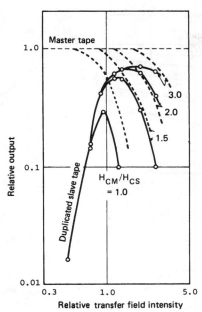

FIGURE 5.60 Recorded master-tape output and duplicated slave-tape output for different transfer fields (H_{cm} and H_{cs} are the coercivities of the master and slave tapes) *(Sugaya, 1973).*

duplication process. The thermal characteristics of CrO_2 tape are shown in Fig. 5.61. In order to minimize the demagnetization effect during the cooling process, H_c should recover faster than B_r does. The apparent susceptibility of CrO_2 tape achieved by thermal transfer is higher than that achieved by anhysteretic means (Fig. 5.59); thus the recording efficiency of thermal transfer is higher than that of the anhysteretic method.

In the thermal duplication process, the characteristics of the slave tape are more important than those of the master tape. In principle, any video tape can be used for the master tape in this process provided it has a high Curie temperature, although a higher magnetic field from the recorded signal will yield better results, as shown in Fig. 5.62. In practice, high-coercivity tape, such as $(Co)FeO_x$ or metal tape, is used for the master tape in thermal duplication. In carrying out a duplication, a CrO_2 slave tape is heated up to the Curie temperature and then cooled by placing the master tape in contact with the surface of the heated slave tape. In this cooling process, the magnetic moment acquired by the slave tape will be fixed in accordance with the magnetic pattern on the master tape. Cooling

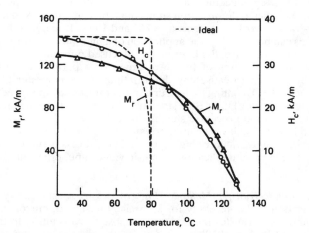

FIGURE 5.61 Temperature dependence of remanent magnetization M, and coercivity H_c of CrO_2. Dashed lines, ideal thermal characteristics.

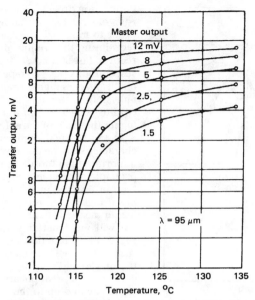

FIGURE 5.62 Temperature dependence of the thermal transfer of CrO_2 slave tape from γ-Fe_2O_3 master tapes having different outputs.

can be very rapid; therefore, the slippage between the master tape and the slave tape is not as critical as it is in the anhysteretic transfer process.

The main problem encountered in the thermal duplication process is the thermal deformation of the tape-backing material (polyester film has 2 to 3 percent shrinkage at 150°C). Significant deformation spoils the tape compatibility, particularly for such narrow-track recording systems as VHS and Beta. It appears, however, that these problems can be solved by the application of a high-power laser beam (Cole et al., 1984). In this procedure, the laser beam is focused onto the CrO_2 coating from behind, through the backing of the slave tape, for a period of 2 ms; this brief exposure is insufficient to cause any deformation of the polyester film, but it is enough to heat the CrO_2 coating to the Curie temperature at a tape speed of 1.65 m/s, which is nearly 50 times VHS or Beta standard-play tape speed. The maximum tape speed in this duplication process is steadily increasing along with developments in high-powered lasers. The laser-beam thermal-duplication process makes it possible to duplicate video signals at very high speeds. This process is successfully applied, for example, to the mass duplication of music video tape, especially for the high-band version.

5.6.3.4 The Double-Transfer Method. One of the least satisfactory features of contact duplication is the necessity for a specially designed, mirror-image master recorder. The double transfer method was proposed as a solution to this (Nelson, 1970; Dickens and Jordan, 1970).

As shown in Fig. 5.63, the first step entails the transfer, by thermal means, of the

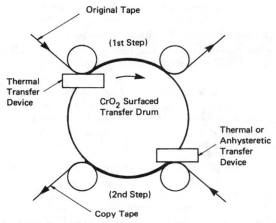

Original Tape

(1st Step)

Thermal
Transfer
Device

CrO$_2$ Surfaced
Transfer Drum

Thermal or
Anhysteretic
Transfer
Device

(2nd Step)

Copy Tape

FIGURE 5.63 Principle of the double-transfer method.

original (master) tape, which has the same tape format as the slave tape, onto a CrO$_2$-surfaced transfer drum. Then this transferred signal, which now exists as a mirror image on the surface of the transfer drum, is duplicated, either by anhysteretic or thermal means. In this manner, the original tape signal can be transferred onto the slave tape without the necessity of either a special master tape or a mirror-imaging master recorder. If the thermal-transfer method is used in the second step, the slave tape should be CrO$_2$ tape; if the anhysteretic method is used, any tape can be used for the slave tape, provided the coercivity on the transfer drum is at least 2.5 times higher than that of the slave tape.

5.6.4 The Future of Video Tape Duplication

In the modern "information era," people are becoming more and more dependent on information transmitted by television. Both cable television networks and direct broadcast by satellite have become extremely important means of information transmission, particularly in the United States. It is expected, however, that the development of inexpensive video recording equipment and software rental will bring about drastic changes in this situation.

Information broadcast over the air waves is limited in terms of both transmission time and the number of programs. Recorded video software, on the other hand, permits the viewer to see whatever he or she wants at any time, and the number of programs is virtually unlimited. Consequently, prerecorded video tape media now occupy a significant share of the information market. Tape duplication is a highly specialized enterprise, with the choice of methodology depending on the application or purpose of the duplicated tape, more or less as follows:

1. *Mass duplication of long programs (e.g., movies).* The head-to-head method, using many slave recorders, will continue to be the main approach. Tape systems will eventually shift from tape-cassette format to the use of pancake tape.

2. *Mass duplication of short programs (e.g., music).* A similar trend is envisioned; the shift from cassettes to pancake tape, however, will be accelerated. Thermal transfer will be used where quick delivery is necessary.

3. *Duplication of medium-sized lots.* The head-to-head approach will continue to be used for the time being; contact duplication may be used more extensively in the future.

4. *Duplication of many kinds of small-sized lots.* Both the head-to-head method and the automatic contact-duplication method will be used. If the double-transfer machine can be commercially developed, then the copying of video tape will become as common an everyday process as xerography and other plain-paper, dry-copying methods.

It can be anticipated that should extra-long-play (ELP) video software begin to be commercially successful, and if the price drops sufficiently (e.g., by contact duplication), then consumers will find it advantageous to purchase video software outright rather than rent it. This phenomenon would have the effect of increasing the actual number of prerecorded video tapes produced and would result in an increase in the extent of the mass production techniques involved in the tape-duplication industry. Accompanying this trend would be the usual benefits accruing from the introduction of wide-scale mass production—increases in quality and standardization, accompanied by even further decreases in price.

5.7 FUTURE PROSPECTS

Continued increases in recording density will soon make feasible such new possibilities as the video disk recorder, wideband signal recording (using high-definition television recorders and digital video recorders), and advanced recording processes (for example, perpendicular magnetic recording and nonmechanically scanned recording).

5.7.1 Video Disk Recording

The video tape recording formats which have been discussed so far in this text have all used longitudinally wound tape. These formats are volumetrically efficient in terms of the amount of information that can be stored; they do have the drawback, however, of a comparatively long access time for the retrieval of data recorded on the tape. For quick retrieval in television broadcasts, limited use is being made at present of video disks to record selected portions of the video signals in a program. The shortened access time afforded by this procedure is used, particularly in sports and news broadcasts, for instant replay, for slow motion, and for inserts of still pictures as an overlay on the main video picture. Figure 5.64 shows the original principle behind this type of slow-motion recording. In order to be able to record and erase continuously without interruption, two plated rigid disks (with a total of four recording surfaces) and four heads are used alternatively in the record-erase-move process shown in Fig. 5.64. A complete single field of the video signal is recorded in a concentric circle on the disk; this requires a very high recording density. To reproduce a recording in slow motion, the video head makes multiple passes over the same concentric track. Conventional helical-scan recorders can also

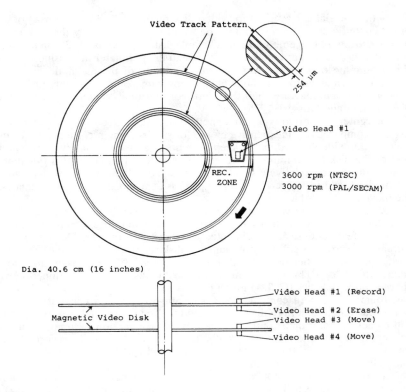

Video Head	1st Step	2nd Step	3rd Step	4th Step
#1	Recording	Moving	Moving	Erasing
#2	Erasing	Recording	Moving	Moving
#3	Moving	Erasing	Recording	Moving
#4	Moving	Moving	Erasing	Recording

FIGURE 5.64 Principle of slow-motion video disk recorder using hard disk.

be used for slow-motion and still-picture playback, but the paths of the head when recording and then playing back in slow motion are not identical, as shown in Fig. 5.30. Hence, with helical-scan recorders, it is difficult to achieve either precise random access of the desired portion of the program or slow-motion and still pictures of perfect quality.

More advanced slow-motion video recorders use a digital signal, with the result that the single video field can be broken up, stored in RAM, and recorded on several tracks instead of on one concentric track, as is done in analog recording. This type of recording allows a lower recording density, thus permitting the use of a conventional coated rigid disk which is today less expensive than the plated disk.

In order to decrease the cost of disk recording media even further, flexible magnetic material can be used for video disk recording. This can consist of unoriented coated video tape material in the web form, provided by the manufacturer before slitting. In one embodiment, a flexible disk approximately 30 cm in diameter is used; this is kept taut by clamping it around the perimeter in a fashion similar to the membrane of a drum. The resulting flexibility of the magnetic sheet in this mounting format yields excellent head-to-medium contact but this disk is more expensive to manufacture than the more conventional, center-supported flexible disk (Kihara and Odagiri, 1975).

The center-supported type of magnetic disk first came into use in video recording as a comparatively inexpensive means for single-frame recording and for use in slow-motion video recorders. To keep both the size (approximately 20 cm) and the cost of the disk to a minimum, the recording time is limited to 10 s (yielding 600 field pictures); this relatively small memory capacity limits its use to such areas as the medical field (x-ray recording) and professional sports (on-the-spot analysis of the movements of athletes).

As more advanced types of recording media (such as metal powder) become available for use in video disks, it will prove feasible to utilize extremely small disks of only a few centimeters in diameter to record still images. Devices using this format are known as still picture magnetic disk recorders. Figure 5.65a shows the design of a 47-mm flexible video disk with sufficient storage capacity to record 25 frames (50 fields). This type of miniature flexible disk, used in conjunction with a charge-coupled device (CCD) miniature television camera, can form the basis of an electronic still camera comparable in size and weight to a conventional 35-mm single-lens reflex camera (Kihara et al., 1981). The picture quality of the electronic still camera is inferior to that produced by the conventional camera; but unlike conventional film, the video disk can be used repeatedly, and the recorded picture can be viewed enlarged on a television screen and can be transmitted over a telephone line by a simple encoding.

The resolution of a still picture needs to be higher than that of a moving picture. Taking the specifications of the 8-mm video format (f_{max} = 5.4 MHz) as a standard for moving video pictures, the recordable frequency in an electronic still camera should therefore be higher than 5.4 MHz. The head drum diameter of 8-mm video is 20 mm for single-head helical-scan recording or 40 mm for the two-head type. It has been found that to achieve the same minimum recordable wavelength in the two-dimensional format of the video floppy, a disk diameter of 47 mm (slightly less than 2 in) is the minimum size. A video disk of this size can therefore be used to record a frequency of 7.5 MHz with a single video head. This is a sufficient amount higher than the 5.4 MHz of the 8-mm video format for use in the video recording of still pictures. In order to achieve improved color quality, the color signal in this format is recorded sequentially as a frequency-modulated color-component signal (R—Y, B—Y). The proposed frequency allocation is shown in Fig. 5.65b.

It is expected that many more applications of the video flexible disk will be found in the future. This will be the result of advances in both hardware and supporting software. Advances in hardware will consist of technological improvements and decreases in prices of materials and components used in the flexible disk format. Advances in software will include the development of new businesses, such as the production of new types of color photo albums, together with facilities for displaying customers' photos on television screens. Also, the development of new methods of taking and processing pictures will be possible, such as the ability to take many pictures rapidly of the same scene using the same disk and then select the best picture by projecting them on a television screen for inspection.

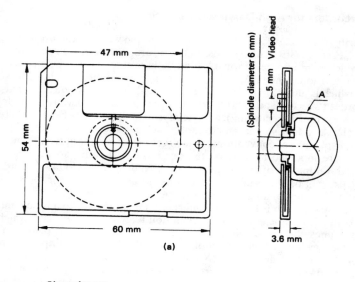

(a)

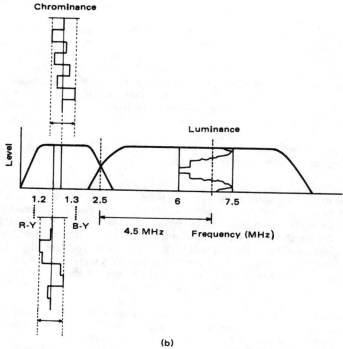

(b)

FIGURE 5.65 Still picture magnetic disk recording. (*a*) Video flexible disk with jacket; (*b*) video signal frequency allocation.

5.7.2   Recorders for High-Definition Television

The majority of the television systems throughout the world at the present time use the NTSC, PAL, or SECAM systems. In the future, however, we can look forward to the development of a new format—high-definition television. One type of high-definition television is shown in Table 5.1. This system requires a bandwidth of 20 to 30 MHz, which is almost five times wider than that needed for conventional television. In order to record such a wide frequency range (from 50 MHz up to approximately 70 MHz for FM recording), a single-crystal Mn-Zn ferrite head could be used (Abe, 1981). As a first step in an attempt to achieve the necessary rotation speed (double or triple that of conventional video recorders), standard type B and type C recorders were modified to increase the head-to-tape relative speed. The second step in the development of high-definition baseband-signal video tape recording for broadcast use will be the establishment of broadcast standards for the worldwide exchange of programs among television studios.

Satellite transmission is limited by international agreement to a base bandwidth of 8 MHz; this is insufficient for high-definition television broadcasts, which need up to four times this bandwidth. To solve this problem and to provide for the satellite broadcasting of high-definition signals, the MUSE (multiple sub-nyquist encoding) system was developed (Ninomiya et al., 1987). This compresses the frequency bandwidth to one-quarter of its original width. This system makes it possible to transmit the high-definition signal through the conventional satellite bandwidth.

The third step will be the development of consumer-type recorders for high-definition television signals. Consumer-use recorders must be able to record both satellite broadcast signals and prerecorded programs. The tape format must be both reasonably priced and in a convenient cassette form. This will necessitate even greater advances in the recording density to be able to produce high-quality recordings over such a wide frequency band while maintaining a compact cassette size comparable to that of present-day cassettes. However, future consumer video recording is expected to develop using digital recording techniques (see Chap. 6).

5.7.3   Digital-Process Analog Recorders

In the audio field, recording technology is rapidly shifting from analog to digital recording in the consumer area, and the optically recorded compact disk is becoming an increasingly popular audio recording medium. The same trend toward an emphasis on digital technology can be expected in the video field as well. However, as we have seen, the video signal bandwidth is more than 100 times wider than that of the audio signal. From the point of view of recording efficiency, digital recording needs several times the area of tape that is required by conventional analog recording. Today, digital techniques are limited to studio use, which must have a minimum of deterioration in picture quality after multiple generations of duplication for editing.

On the other hand, very large digital circuitry can now be integrated into a small silicon chip, and digital processing has been introduced successfully in the consumer color television set. In the same way, modulation and demodulation for video recording are processed by digital means in conjunction with many very precisely tuned digital filters. Thus, conventional video circuitry can be integrated into two chips, an analog-to-digital and digital-to-analog converter, and a digital-process video circuit

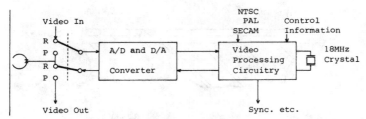

FIGURE 5.66 Digital signal processing for a video tape recorder using two LSI circuits.

(Mehrgardt, 1985). This is referred to as the *digital-process analog recording method* (Fig. 5.66). With this method, a conventional video tape format, such as VHS, can be used with complete compatibility. Furthermore, any television standard such as NTSC, PAL, or SECAM can be operated with the same circuitry simply by changing the software. Many other new functions, such as noise reduction using field-picture relationships, enhancement of a deteriorated picture, and compensation for drop-outs and crosstalk, can be introduced in conjunction with digital memory devices. In summary, the digital-process analog recording method is a very attractive approach for analog consumer video recorders.

5.7.4 Advanced Recording Processes

The longitudinal format is beginning to reach its practical limits in terms of recording loss through self-demagnetization. The minimum recordable wavelength in commercially available video recorders is 0.49 μm at present (for 8-mm video Hi-8); extrapolating from the historical trend line (Fig. 5.7), a minimum wavelength of less than 0.3 μm can be anticipated. This has already been achieved in the research laboratory and will become commercially available in approximately 1996. At such very short wavelengths, three main losses affect video recording. First, the gap loss at short wavelengths will demand very narrow gaps, on the order of 0.1 μm. This can be achieved by special lapping techniques to eliminate the worked layer on the head core material; however, a gap depth shallow enough to achieve a sufficiently high output signal can be created only at a substantial sacrifice of head life (Sugaya, 1985). Next, spacing losses will emphasize the need to solve head-to-tape interface problems as tape surfaces become even smoother. Finally, self-demagnetization losses will increase as the recorded wavelength becomes shorter. Two methods have been developed to minimize self-demagnetization loss, as shown in Fig. 5.67: (1) the use of magnetic tape with extremely thin magnetic coatings (e.g., metal-evaporated tape with a coating thickness on the order of only 0.1 μm) can substantially reduce self-demagnetization loss (Mallinson, 1985); (2) self-demagnetization loss can, in principle, be eliminated by using the perpendicular vector component in the recording process, instead of the conventional longitudinal vector component (Iwasaki, 1980, 1984). Perpendicular recording may be accomplished by the use of a specially designed recording medium, such as Co-Cr film—which favors recording perpendicular to the tape surface—used in conjunction with a perpendicular head (Iwasaki et al., 1980). This process will permit the recording of signals with

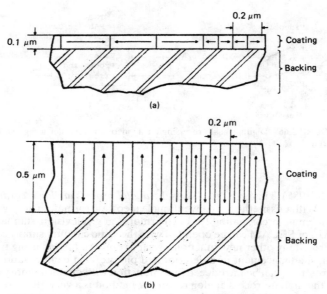

FIGURE 5.67 Typical example of very short-wavelength signal recording. (*a*) Longitudinal recording media; (*b*) perpendicular recording media.

wavelengths even shorter than 0.4 μm. The technology underlying perpendicular recording (*Magnetic Recording Technology*) yields other benefits applicable to the improvement of the recording density, particularly when video information is recorded digitally.

One traditional method of decreasing tape consumption is to decrease the track to very narrow widths. A magnetoresistive head can be used to play back extremely narrow tracks (2 μm) with sufficient output (Kanai et al., 1975). However, 5 μm is the minimum requirement to achieve adequate machine-to-machine compatibility according to the present state of the art. Another possibility for narrow-track recording is to use magnetooptical recording, which is described in detail in *Magnetic Recording Technology*. Magnetooptical recording technology will be effective for video disks as well as for tape recording, provided high-power lasers, semiconductor devices, and commercially viable, high-sensitivity (high signal-to-noise ratio) magnetooptical recording media are successfully developed for this purpose. The combination and mutual reinforcement of the applications of these various advanced recording techniques will yield even higher recording densities in the future.

5.7.5 Nonmechanically Scanned Recording

The video recording techniques discussed so far in this chapter have been limited mainly to rotating-head formats. In video recording technology, it is possible in principle that the rotating-head mechanism will eventually be supplanted by a nonmechanically scanned device. Many schemes for such nonmechanically scanned recording formats have been proposed (see, for example, Camras, 1963*b*; Peters, 1964), but so far these have not yet been made commercially practical. In this section, we review some nonmechanically scanned magnetic tape recording methods and discuss their future prospects.

5.7.5.1 Magnetically Scanned Recording.

Several schemes have been proposed to modulate the permeability of a single wide-track recording gap so that only a small zone of the total head has high enough permeability to allow recording to take place. This high-permeability zone is then scanned along the gap to produce transverse recording on a slowly moving tape (Fig. 5.68). One approach to achieving control of the permeability is to saturate a portion of the head in one direction and another portion in the opposite direction (Peters, 1964). If these two portions each correspond to one-half the head width, there will be an unsaturated zone between them that can, in theory, be used for recording from a coil wound around the complete head. The position of this small recording zone (Fig. 5.68*e*) can then be moved by increasing the width of one saturated portion with respect to the other. Difficulties with this type of scanning head lie in the requirement that certain portions of the head core be saturated without inadvertently producing a field from that portion of the head. The development of the requisite magnetic material, together with a room temperature superconductive material, might make this approach feasible. Another magnetic reluctance scanning head, which does not rely on balanced magnetic circuits, is used to drive a sonic pulse along the direction of the head gap (Johnson, 1962). By choice of a magnetic core material with the correct magneto-

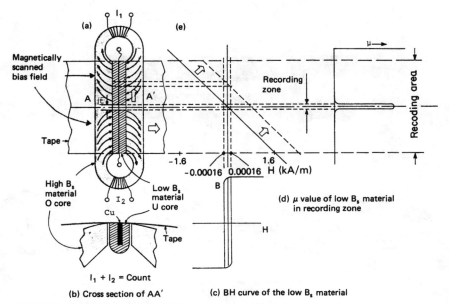

FIGURE 5.68 Principle of magnetically scanned recording.

striction, the narrow sonic pulse can, in principle, produce a narrow zone of high permeability. This ingenious scheme suffers from the lack of control of the speed of the sonic pulse. For most practical schemes, the pulse travels too quickly and only a portion of a television line is recorded each scan. While the examples cited have exhibited problems in development, the advantage of avoiding high-speed head-to-medium interfaces is still desirable, and efforts to produce a workable magnetic scanning head are still worthwhile. Material development will be the key to the realization of any magnetic scanning devices.

5.7.5.2   *Thermomagnetic Direct-Image Recording.*   The forms of video recording described in this chapter have been concerned with the recording and reproduction of a television signal, in which a visual image is encoded as a series of dots and scanning lines. It could be argued, however, that the ultimate objective of video recording should be to record images directly from the image source onto the tape. If an image could be recorded directly, as a photograph is, without the need for any special intervening encoding, new possibilities for video recording would be opened

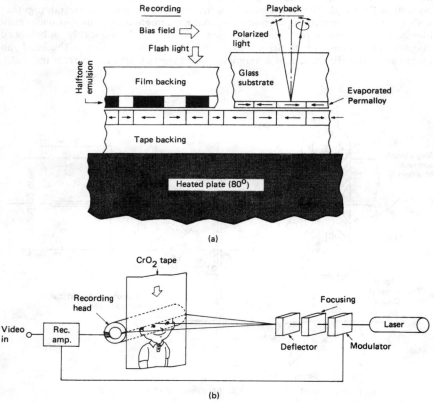

FIGURE 5.69   Principle of thermomagnetic recording. (*a*) Half-tone film, and (*b*) thermomagnetic recording with magnetic head. (The image can be made visible by magnetic powder development.)

up (Waring, 1971). The advantage of direct-image recording is that it would be compatible with any type of television system, whereas conventional types of mechanical-scanning recorders need to be set for a specified rotating speed of the head drum as well as a specified tape speed, according to the frame rate. Direct-image recording would, therefore, be an attractive format for prerecorded video information. A single-format tape could be used throughout the world without the need for adjustment to the various differing types of television systems. A successful direct-image recording scheme would have to compete with conventional video recording in terms of tape consumption.

One possibility of direct-image recording is by thermomagnetic means using a chromium dioxide medium. As discussed previously (Sec. 5.6.3), chromium dioxide has a relatively low Curie temperature (120° C) near which the apparent susceptibility becomes very high, and magnetization of the tape becomes possible in a weak magnetic field. Figure 5.69a shows how this property can be used to record directly from a half-tone photographic image. A chromium dioxide tape is used which is magnetized in a direction opposite to that of the bias field. The tape is pre-heated by a heated plate and subjected to a weak bias field which is not strong enough to change the polarity and thus cannot erase the premagnetized flux. Then, when the preheated coating is exposed to a flash from a powerful light source through the half-tone film, the light will further heat up the chromium dioxide through the transparent part of the film to the Curie temperature and switch the direction of the magnetization of the tape to that of the bias field. Thus, a black-and-white image can be recorded in this way as a magnetized pattern. A possible technique for playing back this magnetically recorded image pattern is shown in Fig. 5.69a. A thin magnetic film, such as Permalloy evaporated on a glass substrate, is placed in proximity to the recorded tape. The magnetization of this film corresponds to the recorded pattern on the tape, and reproduction can be effected using a polarized-light beam and detecting the magnetization by the Kerr effect. When a color image is required, the chrominance signal can be recorded separately using compression.

5.7.5.3 Thermomagnetic Laser-Beam Recording.   Another possibility for thermomagnetic recording uses a high-power laser, as shown diagrammatically in Fig. 5.69b. The laser beam heats up a portion of the tape to the Curie temperature so that a video signal can be easily recorded at the spot where the laser beam is focused (Nomura and Yokoyama, 1979).

To record a complete image directly on the tape by means of this technique, the laser beam must be deflected back and forth transversely on the tape, as indicated in the figure.

APPENDIX

Important historical developments and technical data are summarized in Tables 5.7 to 5.11 and Figs. 5.70 to 5.72.

TABLE 5.7 Milestones of Video Tape Recorder Developments (Mainly NTSC)

Year	Country	New product	Number of video heads	Tape width	Lin. tape speed (cm/s)	Max. rec. time	Recording mode
1953	U.S.A.	Fixed-head color VTR (RCA)	F 4	$\frac{1}{2}$ in	914	$\frac{1}{3}$ h	D + FM
1954	U.S.A.	Fixed-head multitrack VTR (Bing Crosby Enterprises and GE)	F 10	$\frac{1}{2}$ in	254	$\frac{1}{4}$ h	D
1956	U.S.A.	†The first rotary-head broadcasting QUAD VTR (Ampex)	R 4	2 in	38.1	1 h	FM
1956	U.S.A.	Fixed-head color home VTR (RCA)	F 2	$\frac{1}{4}$ in	305	$\frac{1}{4}$ h	D + FM
1957	U.S.A.	†Broadcasting color QUAD VTR (RCA, Ampex)	R 4	2 in	38.1	1 h	FM
1958	Japan	Broadcasting VTR trial model (NHK, Matsushita)	R 8	2 in	38.1	1 h	FM
1958	U.K.	Broadcasting VTR trial model—VERA—(BBC)	F 2	$\frac{1}{2}$ in	508	$\frac{1}{4}$ h	D + FM
1959	Japan	The first 1-head helical-scan broadcasting (Toshiba)	R 1	2 in	38.1	1 h	FM
1960	Japan	The first 2-head helical-scan broadcasting (JVC)	R 2	2 in	38.1	1 h	FM
1961	Japan	†Helical-scan industrial VTR (Matsushita)	R 2	1 in	27.9	1 h	FM
1961	U.S.A.	†α-lap helical-scan industrial VTR (Ampex)	R 1	2 in	12.7	3 h	FM
1962	Japan	†Ω-lap helical-scan industrial VTR (Sony)	R 1.5	2 in	14.4	1 h	FM
1963	U.K.	Simplified fixed-head VTR (Telcan)	F 1	$\frac{1}{4}$ in	305	$\frac{1}{6}$ h	D
1964	Holland	Ω-lap helical-scan industrial VTR (Philips)	R 1	1 in	19.1	$\frac{3}{4}$ h	FM

Year	Country	VTR	Heads	Width (in)	(mm)	Time	System
1964	U.S.A.	†HiBand color QUAD VTR (Ampex)	R 4	2 in	38.1	2 h	FM
1964	Japan	†Field skip VTR (Sony)	R 2	$\frac{1}{2}$ in	19.1	1 h	FM, FS
1965	Japan	†Small-size VTR (Matsushita)	R 2	$1\frac{1}{2}$ in	25.4	$\frac{2}{3}$ h	FM
1965	Japan	Small-size VTR (Ikegami)	R 2	$\frac{2}{3}$ in	30.5	$\frac{3}{4}$ h	FM
1966	Japan	RGB sequential camera and VTR (Matsushita)	R 2	$\frac{1}{2}$ in	6.4	$\frac{1}{3}$ h	FM
1966	Japan	Magnetic-sheet spiral recorder "VIDEO MAT" (Sony)	1	$10\,\phi$ in	—	30 s	FM
1966	U.S.A.	†The first segment sequential VTR (Westel)	R 2	1 in	25.4	1 h	FM
1966	U.S.A.	Newell sys. fixed-head VTR	F 1	$\frac{1}{4}$ in	305	1 h	FM
1966	U.S.A.	†α-lap small VTR (3M)	R 1	$\frac{1}{2}$ in	19.1	1 h	D
1967	Japan	Magnetic-sheet concentric recorder "VSR" (Matsushita)	1	$10\,\phi$ in	—	20 s	FM
1967	U.S.A.	†α-lap helical-scan industrial VTR (IVC)	R 1	1 in	17.5	1 h	FM
1968	Japan	†The first azimuth recording VTR (Matsushita)	R 2	$\frac{1}{2}$ in	12.7	1.5 h	FM, AZ
1969	Japan	†The first video-tape contact printer (VTP) (Matsushita)	—	$\frac{1}{2}$ in	—	—	AT
1969	Japan	†CP-504, unified standards for small VTR (EIA-J)	R 2	$\frac{1}{2}$ in	19.1	1 h	FM
1969	Japan	Cassette VTR (sometimes called magazine VTR) (Matsushita)	R 2	CS $\frac{1}{2}$ in	19.1	$\frac{1}{2}$ h	FM
1969	Japan	Cassette VTR (Sony)	R 2	CS $\frac{3}{4}$ in	9.5	1 h	FM
1970	U.S.A.	†VTR mainly for recorded-tape playback (CTI)	R 3	CS $\frac{1}{2}$ in	9.6	2 h	FM, FS
1970	Japan	Broadcasting video-tapes contact printer (VTP) (Matsushita)	—	2 in	—	—	AT
1970	Holland	†Tandem cassette home VTR (Philips)	R 2	CS $1\frac{1}{2}$ in	14.2	$\frac{2}{3}$ h	FM
1970	U.S.A.	†Segment sequential broadcasting VTR (IVC)	R 2	2 in	20.3	1–2 h	FM

TABLE 5.7 (*Continued*)

Year	Country	New product	Number of video heads	Tape width	Lin. tape speed (cm/s)	Max. rec. time	Recording mode
1971	Japan	†U-Format VTR (Sony, Matsushita, JVC)	R 2	CS $\frac{3}{4}$ in	9.5	1 h	FM
1971	Japan	†Color VTP by anhysteretic transfer (Matsushita)	—	$\frac{1}{2}$ in	—	—	AT
1971	U.S.A.	Color VTP by thermal transfer (CVS)	—	$\frac{1}{2}$–$\frac{3}{4}$ in	—	—	TT
1971	Japan	†CP-507, unified standards for small color VTR (EIA-J)	R 2	$\frac{1}{2}$ in	19.1	1 h	FM
1971	Japan	Small cartridge VTR (Matsushita)	R 2	CT $\frac{1}{4}$ in	19.1	$\frac{1}{2}$ h	FM
1971	U.S.A.	†Super HiBand QUAD VTR (Ampex)	R 4	2 in	38	1–2 h	FM
1972	Japan	†CP-508, unified standards for small cartridge VTR (EIA-J)	R 2	CT $\frac{1}{2}$ in	19.1	$\frac{1}{2}$ h	FM
1972	Japan	Standard-alignment tape recorder for EIA-J Type I (Matsushita)	R 2	$\frac{1}{2}$ in	19.1	2 h	FM
1972	Japan	Color still-picture cassette player (Matsushita)	R 3	3.81 mm	4.8	$\frac{1}{2}\times2$ h	FM
1973	Japan	†Small broadcasting QUAD VTR (Asaka)	R 4	1 in	25.4	1 h	FM
1973	U.S.A.	Thermal/anhysteretic transfer (3M)	—	$\frac{1}{2},\frac{3}{4},$ 1 in	—	—	TT, AT
1974	Japan	†Cartridge color video tape printer (Matsushita)	—	$\frac{1}{2}$ in	—	—	AT
1974	Japan	Magnetic-sheet recorder "MAVICA" (Sony)	R 2	6.5 × 8.5 in	—	$\frac{1}{6}$ h	Phase mod.
1974	Japan	†Cassette VTR V-Cord (Sanyo, Toshiba)	R 2	CS $\frac{1}{2}$ in	13.4	$\frac{1}{2}$ h	FM

Year	Country	Description		Size		Time	Modulation
				8 in ϕ	—	20 s	FM
1975	Japan	Magnetic-sheet recorder "Panaslow" (Matsushita)	R 2	8 in ϕ	—	20 s	FM
1975	Japan	†Azimuth recording color VTR "Betamax" (Sony)	R 2	CS $\frac{1}{2}$ in	4.0	1 h	FM, AZ
1976	Japan	Long-play VTR V-Cord by FS (Sanyo, Toshiba)	R 3	CS $\frac{1}{2}$ in	6.7	1 h	FM, FS
1976	Japan	†1-head tandem cassette VTR (Matsushita)	R 1	CS $\frac{1}{2}$ in	5.2	1.5 h	FM
1976	Japan	†Azimuth recording color VTR "VHS" (JVC)	R 2	CS $\frac{1}{2}$ in	3.3	2 h	FM, AZ
1976	Germany	†Type B segment sequential-broadcast VTR (Bosch)	R 2	1 in	24.5	3 h	FM
1977	Japan	†2-h Beta-format VTR with overlap recording (Sony)	R 2	CS $\frac{1}{2}$ in	2.0	2 h	FM, AZ
1977	Japan	†4-h VHS-format VTR with overlap recording (Matsushita)	R 2	CS $\frac{1}{2}$ in	1.7	4 h	FM, AZ
1978	Japan, U.S.A.	†Type C VTR (Sony, Ampex)	R 1.5	1 in	24.4	3 h	FM
1979	Germany	Newell-type fixed-head VTR (BASF)	F 1	CT $\frac{1}{4}$ in	305	3 h	FM
1979	Japan	†6-h VHS format VTR (VHS Group)	R 2	CS $\frac{1}{2}$ in	1.1	6 h	FM, AZ
1980	Holland	†2×4-h V-2000 VTR for PAL (Philips)	R 2	CS $\frac{1}{2}$ in	2.4	8 h	FM, AZ
1980	Japan	Video movie (Sony)	R 2	CS 8 mm	2.0	$\frac{1}{3}$ h	FM, AZ
1980	Japan	MAG VIDEO (Hitachi)	R 2	CS $\frac{1}{4}$ in	1.6	2 h	FM, AZ
1981	Japan	Microvideo (Matsushita)	R 2	CS 7 mm	1.4	2 h	FM, AZ
1981	Japan, U.S.A.	†Type-M ENG VTR using 2-track with VHS cassette (Matsushita/RCA)	R 4	CS $\frac{1}{2}$ in	6.8	$\frac{1}{3}$ h	FM AZ I/Q
1981	Japan	†Type-L ENG VTR using 2-track with Beta cassette (Sony)	R 4	CS $\frac{1}{2}$ in	11.9	$\frac{1}{3}$ h	FM, Y, R−Y/B−Y Timeplex
1981	Japan	Endless-tape fixed-head VTR (Toshiba)	F 1	CS $\frac{1}{2}$ in	610	2 h	FM

TABLE 5.7 (*Continued*)

Year	Country	New product	Number of video heads	Tape width	Lin. tape speed (cm/s)	Max. rec. time	Recording mode
1981	Japan	Electronic still camera "Mavica" (Sony)	F 1	CT 50 mm ϕ	—	50 fields	FM Y&C
1984	Japan	†8-mm-video format (8 mm video conference)	R 2	CS 8 mm	1.4/0.7	2 h/4 h	FM, AZ
1984	Germany	†Quartercam ENG VTR using 2-track (Bosch)	R 4	CS $\frac{1}{4}$ in	12	$\frac{1}{3}$ h	FM, AZ Timeplex
1985	Japan	†M-II Broadcast VTR using 2-track (Matsushita)	R 4	CS $\frac{1}{2}$ in	6.8	1.5 h	Y FM AZ (R−Y/B−Y) Timeplex
1986	Japan, U.S.A.	D-1 component VTR (Sony, Ampex)	R 4	CS 19 mm	28.66	1.5 h	Scrambled NRZ (RDR 227 Mbps)
1989	Japan, U.S.A.	D-2 Composite VTR (Sony, Ampex)	R 4	CS 19 mm	13.17	4.5 h	AZ M^z (RDR 127 Mbps)
1991	Japan	D-3 Composite VTR (NHK, Matsushita)	R 4	CS $\frac{1}{2}$ in	8.388	4 h	AZ Optimal 8-14 (RDR 125 Mbps)
1993	Japan	Digital Beta-cam (Sony)	R 4	CS $\frac{1}{2}$ in	9.67	2 h	AZ 2:1 compression (RDR 127 Mbps)
1994	Japan	D-5 Component VTR (Matsushita)	R 8	CS $\frac{1}{2}$ in	16.723	2 h	AZ Optimal 8-14 (RDR 303 Mbps)

†Put on the market. NOTE: Only the new systems are listed.

ABBREVIATIONS: R = Rotary-head type; F = Fixed-head type; CS = Cassette (2-reel); CT = Cartridge (1-reel); ϕ = Disk diameter; FM = Freq. modulation; D = Direct; FS = Field skip; AZ = Azimuth; AT = Anhysteretic transfer; TT = Thermal transfer; RDR = Recording Data Rate.

TABLE 5.8 Characteristics of Typical Broadcast Video Tape Recorders (NTSC)[a]

	Tape width, name						
	2 in, QUAD	1 in, type C	1 in, type B	3/4 in, U format	1/2 in, type M	1/2 in, type L	1/2 in, M II
Recording time, min	120 (14 in reel)	90 (10.5 in reel)	90 (10.5 in reel)	60	20	20 (90)[b,c,d]	90 (20)[d]
Tape/speed, mm/s	381	244	245	95.3	204.5	118.6	67.7
Cassette size, mm	—	—	—	221W×140D×32H	188W×104D×25H	156W×96D×25H×(254W×145D×25H)[b,c]	188W×106D×25H (130W×87D×25H)
Relative tape speed, m/s	39.6	25.59	24.08	10.26	5.6	6.9	7.1
Head drum, diameter, mm	52.5	134.6	50.33	110	62.0	74.487	76.0
Drum, rotation, r/s	240	60	150	30	30	30	30
Tape lap angle, degrees	90	150	180	180	180	180	180+30
Video track pitch, μm	250+125[e]	130+52[e]	(160+42)×5[e]	85+52[e]	175+21+65+21[f]	86+1+73+1[f]	44+2.25+36+2.25[f]

TABLE 5.8 (Continued)

				Tape width, name			
	2 in, QUAD	1 in, type C	1 in, type B	3/4 in, U format	1/2 in, type M	1/2 in, type L	1/2 in, M II
Azimuth, degrees	0	0	0	0	0	±15	±15
Format (one field)	4-head transverse (segment)	1.5-head helical (nonsegment)	2-head helical (segment)	4-head helical (nonsegment)	4-head helical (nonsegment)	4-head helical (nonsegment)	
Signal channel	1	1	1	1			
Color recording method	Direct FM	Direct FM	Direct FM	Color-under	2(Y+C) Y: FM C: FM (I,Q)	2(Y+C) Y: FM C: TIMEPLEX (R−Y,B−Y)	2(Y+C) Y: FM C: TIMEPLEX (R−Y, B−Y)
Y FM deviation, MHz	9–12.5	7–10	7–10	3.8–5.4 (5–6.6)c	4.3–5.9	4.4–6.4 (5.7-7.7)b,c	5.6-7.7

aSee Fig. 5.70 for head and track formats.
bMP tape.
cHiBnad model.
dDifferent cassette size.
eY/C+G (G is guard band).
fY+G+C+G.

TABLE 5.9 Characteristics of Typical Home Video Tape Recorders (NTSC)†

	VHS			Beta			8-mm video	
	SP	LP	ELP	β-I	β-II	β-III	SP	LP
Recording time, min	120	240	360	60	120	180	120	240
Tape speed, mm/s	33.3	16.7	11.1	40	20	13.3	14.3	7.2
Track pitch, μm	58	29	19	58	29	19	20	10
H-Alignment difference (α_H)	1.5H	0.75H	0.5H	1.5H	0.75H	0.5H	1.0H	0.5H
Head drum diameter, mm	62			75			40	
Luminance FM carrier, MHz	3.4–4.4 (5.4–7.0)§			3.6–4.8 4.0–5.2‡ (6.8–8.6)§			4.2–5.4 (5.9–7.6)§	
Color-under carrier, MHz	0.63			0.69			0.74	
Cassette dimensions, mm	25H×188W×104D			25H×156W×96D			15H×95W ×62.5D	
Tape length, m	240			150			108	
Tape thickness, μm	20			20			10	
Relative tape speed, m/s	5.8			7.0			3.8	
Tracking method	Control signal by fixed head			Control signal by fixed head			4 Freq. pilot signals by rotating heads	
Azimuth, degrees	±6			±7			±10	
Track angle (running)	5°58′9.9″			5°01′42″			4°54′13.2″	
Fixed-head audio channels	1 or 2			1 or 2			1 (AUX.)	
Audio track width, mm	1.00 or 0.35×2			1.05 or 0.35×2			0.6 (AUX.)	
Rotary-head audio channels	FM 2			FM 2			FM 1 (stereo)	
Recording method	(Double component) Overwrite by different azimuth angle heads			(Freq. division) Record between color-under and FM Y by rotating video heads			(Freq. division) PCM 2 (8-bit with noise reduction) on the extended video track	

†See Figure 5.70 for head and track formats.
‡Audio VM model.
§HiBand model.

TABLE 5.10 Characteristics of Typical Home Video Tape Recorders (PAL/SECAM)†

	VHS	Beta	V-2000	8-mm video
Recording time, min	180/360	130	360 (both ways)	90/180
Tape speed, mm/s	23.4/11.7	18.7	24.4	20/10
Cassette size, mm	25H×188W×104D	25H×156W×96D	26H×183W×62D	15 H×95W×105D
Head drum diameter, mm	62	75	65	40
Luminance FM carrier, MHz	3.8–4.8	3.8–5.2	3.3–4.7	4.2–5.4
Color-under carrier MHz	0.63	0.69	0.63	0.74
SECAM color-recording method	Color-under	Color-under	Color-under	PAL/SECAM Trans Coder
Tape length, m	258	150	260	108
Tape thickness, μm	20	20	15	10
Track pitch, μm	49/24.5	33	23	34/17
H-alignment difference (α_H)	1.5H/0.75H	1.5H±0.5H	1.5H	2H/1H
Relative tape speed, m/s	4.8	5.8	5.0	3.1
Tracking method	Control signal	Control Signal	4 freq. pilot	4 freq. pilot
Azimuth, degrees	±6	±7	±15	±10
Track angle (running)	5°57'50.3"	5°00'58"	2°63'50"	4°54'58.8"
Fixed-head audio channels	1 or 2	1 or 2	1 or 2	1
Audio track width, mm	1.00 or 0.35×2	1.05 or 0.35×2	0.65 or 0.25×2	0.6
Rotary-head audio channels	FM2 (double component)	FM 2 (double component)	…	FM 1 (freq. division) PCM 2 (8-bit with noise reduction)

†See Figure 5.70 for head and track formats.

TABLE 5.11 Proposed Digital Video Tape Recorder Specifications (SMPTE/EBU)

	525/60 System	625/50 System
Coded signals	Y, R−Y, B−Y	
Sampling frequency:		
Y	13.5 MHz	
R−Y, B−Y	6.75 MHz	
Coding form	8-bit linear quantization	
Number of samples per total line:		
Y	858	864
R−Y, B−Y	429	432
Number of samples per active line:		
Y	720	
R−Y, B−Y	360	
Number of recorded lines per field	250	300
Number of tracks per field	10	12
Cassette type	D1-S (11 min), D1-M (34 min), D1-L (94 min)	
Tape material	Improved metal oxide	
Tape width	19.01 mm	
Tape thickness	16 μm (13 μm for long-play)	
Linear tape speed	286.6 mm/s	286.9 mm/s
Helical-track total length	170/1.001 mm	170 mm
Track width	40 μm	
Channel coding	Scrambled NRZ	
Error protection system	Reed-Solomon product code	
Inner code	(64,60) Reed-Solomon code	
Outer code	(32,30) Reed-Solomon code	

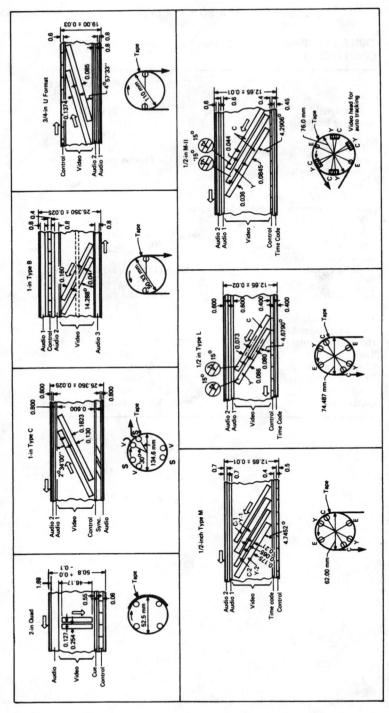

FIGURE 5.70 Head and track formats of typical broadcast video tape recorders (NTSC).

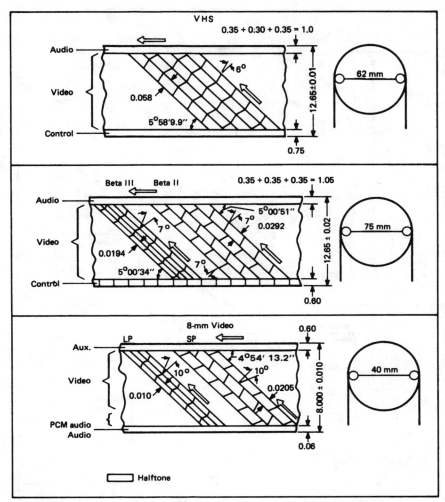

FIGURE 5.71 Head and track formats of typical home video tape recorders (NTSC).

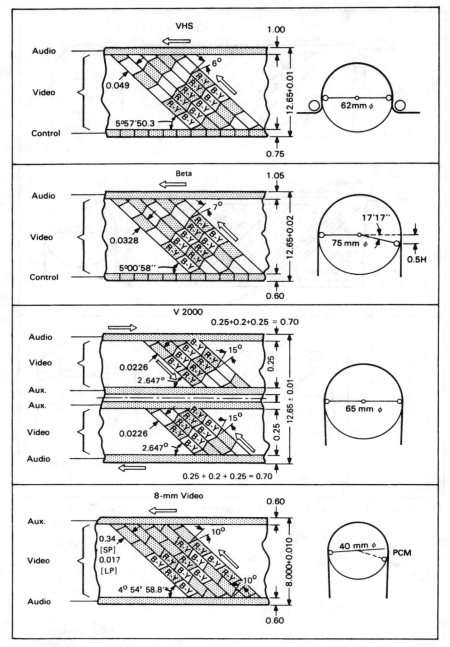

FIGURE 5.72   Head and track formats of typical home video tape recorders (PAL/SECAM).

REFERENCES

Abe, H., "Magnetic Recording of a High-Definition Television Signal," *J. SMPTE,* **90,** 192 (1981).

Abramgon, A., "A Short History of Television Recording: Part II," *J. SMPTE,* **82,** 188 (1973).

Alden, A. E., "The Development of National Standardization of the One-Inch Helical Video Tape Recording Systems," *J. SMPTE,* **86,** 952 (1977).

Amari, S., "Magnetic Recording and/or Reproducing Apparatus with Chrominance Crosstalk Elimination," U.S. Patents 4,007,482 and 4,007,484, 1977.

Anderson, C. E., "The Modulation System of the Ampex Video Tape Recorder," *J. SMPTE,* **66,** 132 (1957).

Anderson, C. E., "The Problems of Splicing and Editing Color Video Magnetic Tape," *IEEE Trans. Broadcast.,* **BC-15,** 59, (1969).

Arimura, I., and K. Sadashige, "A Broadcast-Quality Video/Audio Recording System with VHS Cassette and Head Scanning System," *J. SMPTE,* **92,** 1186 (1983).

Arimura, I., and H. Taniguchi, "A Color VTR System Using Lower-Frequency-Converted Chrominance Signal Recording" (Japanese), *Nat. Tech. Rep.,* **19,** 205 (1973).

Axon, P. E., "Electronic Recording Apparatus," *J. Telev. Soc., U.K.,* 399 (Nov., 1958).

Baldwin, J. L. E., "Digital Television Recording with Low Tape Consumption," *Intl. Broadcast. Conv. Rec.,* 133 (1978).

Bellis, F., "An Experimental Digital Television Recorder," BBC Res. Dept., Report BBC RD 1976/77, 1976.

Benson, K. B., "Video-Tape Recording Interchangeability Requirements," *J. SMPTE,* **69,** 861 (1960).

Bertram, H. N., and J. C. Mallinson, "A Theory of Eddy Current Limited Heads," *IEEE Trans. Magn.,* **MAG-12,** 713 (1976).

Camras, M., "Magnetic Transducer Head," U.S. Patent 3,079,470 (1963*a*).

Camras, M., "Experiments with Electron Scanning for Magnetic Recording and Playback of Video," *IEEE Trans. Audio,* **11,** 93 (1963*b*).

Camras, M., and R. Herr, "Duplicating Magnetic Tape by Contact Printing," *Electron.,* **22,** 78 (1949).

Chynoweth, W. R., "Ferrite Heads for Recording in the Megacycle Range," *Tele-Tech., Elec. Ind.,* 82 (Aug, 1955).

Chubachi, R., and N. Tamagawa "Characteristics and Applications of Metal Tape," *IEEE Trans. Magn.,* **MAG-20,** 45 (1984).

Cole, G. R., L. C. Bancroft, M. P. Chovinard, and J. W. McCloud, "Thermomagnetic Duplication of Chromium Dioxide Video Tape," *IEEE Trans. Magn.,* **MAG-20,** 19 (1984).

Coleman, C. H., "A New Technique for Time-Base Stabilization of Video Recorders," *IEEE Trans. Broadcast.,* **BC-17,** 29 (1971).

Croll, M. G., "A Digital Television Error-Protection Scheme Based on Waveform Estimates," BBC Res. Dept., Report BBC RD, 1978/79, 1978.

Crum, C. W., and H. W. Town, "Recent Progress in Video Tape Duplication," *J. SMPTE,* **80,** 179 (1971).

Dare, P., and R. Katsumi, "Rotating Digital Audio Tape (R-DAT): A Format Overview," *J. SMPTE,* **96,** 943 (1987).

Darnell, F. J., "Magnetization Process in Small Particles of CrO_2," *J. Appl. Phys.,* **32,** 1269 (1961).

Davidoff, F., "Digital Video Recording for Television Broadcasting," *J. SMPTE,* **84,** 552 (1975).

Dickens, J. E., and L. K. Jordan, "Thermoremanent Duplication of Magnetic Tape," *108th SMPTE Conf.,* No. 18 (1970).

Dieter, P., "Method for Transmission and/or Recording of Color Television Signals," German Patent P2629706.3, 1978.

Dolby, R. M., "Rotary-Head Switching in the Ampex Video Tape Recorder," *J. SMPTE,* **66,** 134 (1957).

Dolby, R. M., "An Audio Noise Reduction System," *J. Audio Eng. Soc.,* **15,** 4 (1967).

de Lange, H. K. A., "A Video Tape Recorder for Nonprofessional Use," *Phil. Tech. Rev.,* **26,** 186 (1965).

Duinker, S., "Durable High-Resolution Ferrite Transducer Heads Employing Bonding Glass Spacers," *Philips Res. Rep.,* **15,** 342 (1960).

Eto, Y., S. Mita, Y. Hirano, and T. Kawamura, "Experimental Digital VTR with Trilevel Recording and Fire Code Error Correction," *J. SMPTE,* **90,** 611 (1981).

Fisher, E. P. L., "Telcan," *Int. Telev. Tech. Rev.,* **4,** 238 (1963).

Fujimori, H., M. Kikuchi, Y. Obi, and T. Masumoto, "High Permeability Properties of Amorphous Co-Fe Base Alloy" (Japanese), *J. Jpn. Inst. Metals,* **41,** 111 (1977).

Fujio, T., "A Study of High-Definition TV System in the Future," *IEEE Trans. Broadcast.,* **BC-24,** 92 (1978).

Fujita, M., "Color Video Signal Recoding and Reproducing System," U.S. Patent 3,715,468, 1973.

Fujiwara, T., M. Issiki, Y. Koike, and T. Oguchi, "Recording Performances of Ba-Ferrite Coated Perpendicular Magnetic Tapes," *IEEE Trans. Magn.,* **MAG-18,** 1200 (1982).

Fujiwara, Y., T. Eguchi, and K. Ike, "Tape Selection and Mechanical Considerations for 4:2:2 DVTR," *J. SMPTE,* **93,** 818 (1984).

Geddes, W. K. E., "Dropouts in Video Tape Recording," BBC Monograph No. 57, June, 1965, p. 5.

Ginsburg, C. P., "A New Magnetic Video Recording System," *J. SMPTE,* **65,** 302 (1956).

Ginsburg, C. P., "Contact Duplication of Quadruplex Video Tapes," *J. SMPTE,* **79,** 43 (1970).

Godall, W., "Television by Pulse Code Modulation," *Bell Syst. Tech. J.,* **30,** 33 (1951).

Goldberg, A., "PCM Encoded NTSC Color Television Subjective Test," *J. SMPTE,* **82,** 649 (1973).

Harris, A., "Time-Base Errors and Their Correction in Magnetic Television Recorders," *J. SMPTE,* **70,** 489 (1961).

Hashimoto, Y., and T. Eguchi, "One-Inch Digital VTR" (Japanese), Tech. Group on Magnetic Recording, IECE Jpn. Tech. Rep. MR79–42, 1980.

Hayashi, K., "Research and Development on High-Definition Television in Japan," *J. SMPTE,* **90,** 3 (1981).

Heitmann, J., "Digital Video Recording: New Result in Channel Coding and Error Protection," *J. SMPTE,* **93,** 140 (1984).

Heitman, J. K. F., "Development of Component Digital VTRs and the Potential of the D-1 Format," *J. SMPTE,* **97,** 126 (1988).

Hendershot, W. B., "Thermal Contact Duplication of Video Tape," *Proc. Int. Broadcast. Conf. (London),* 204 (1970).

Herr, R., "Duplication of Magnetic Tape Recording by Contact Printing," *Tele-Tech.,* **8,** 28 (1949).

Hirota, A., "Recording and Reproducing Method of Color Video Signal," Japanese Patent 56–9073, 1981.

Hirota, K., M. Sugimura, and E. Hirota, "Hot Pressed Ferrites for Magnetic Recording Heads," *Ind. Eng. Chem. Prod. Res. Dev.,* **23,** 323 (1984).

Hitotsumachi, S., "VHS HiFi VTR" (Japanese), *J. Inst. Telev. Eng. Jpn.,* **37,** 1009 (1983).

Hokkyo, J., and N. Ito, "Theoretical Analysis of the Process of Contact Printing of Magnetic Recording," *Proc. Third Hungarian Conf. on Mag. Rec. (Budapest)*, 2 (1970).

IEC Standard, Publication 766, *Helical-Scan Video-Recording Cartridge and Reel-to-Reel System (EIA-J Type I) Using 12.70 mm Magnetic Tape*, 1983.

Iijima, T., and H. Hanafusa, "Plasma Polymerized Protective Film for Magnetic Recording Thin Film Tape" (Japanese), *J. IECE Jpn.*, **J67-C**, 88 (1984).

Iijima, S., K. Fujii, H. Sugaya, and M. Kano, "Pleasing the Consumer While Playing to Win," *IEEE Spectrum*, **14**, 45 (1977).

International Electrotechnical Commission, "Helical-Scan Video Tape Cassette System Using 8 mm Magnetic Tape," IEC Publication 843, 1987.

Ishida, J., "Television Signal Codes" (Japanese), *NHK Tech. Rep.*, **13**, 169 (1970).

Ishida, J., "Design Basis of PCM Television Transmission System" (Japanese), *Trans. IECE Jpn.*, **J54-A**, 589 (1971).

Iwasaki, S., "Perpendicular Magnetic Recording," *IEEE Trans. Magn.*, **MAG-16**, 71 (1980).

Iwasaki, S., "Perpendicular Magnetic Recording—Evolution and Future," *IEEE Trans. Magn.*, **MAG-20**, 657 (1984).

Iwasaki, S., K. Ouchi, and N. Honda, "Studies of the Perpendicular Magnetization Mode in Co-Cr Sputtered Films," *IEEE Trans. Magn.*, **MAG-16**, 1111 (1980).

Jacobs, I. S., "Magnetic Materials and Applications—A Quarter Century Overview," *J. Appl. Phys.*, **50**, 7294 (1979).

Johnson, W. R., "Reproducing Color Television Chrominance Signals," U.S. Patent 2,921,976, 1960.

Johnson, W. R., "Magnetostrictive Transducer for the Recording and Reproducing of Magnetic Information," U.S. Patent 3,053,941, 1962.

Jones, A. H., "Digtial Television Recording: A Review of Current Developments," BBC Res. Dept. Rep., BBC RD 29, 1973.

Kaminaka, N., H. Sakakma, K. Takahashi, K. Osano, and H. Hasegawa, "Co-Based Super-structured Nitride Alloy Film Characteristics and Applications for High Frequency Heads," *IEEE Trans. Magn.*, **26**, 2936 (1990).

Kanai, K., F. Kobayashi, and H. Sugaya, "Super-Narrow Track MR Head," *IEEE Trans. Magn.*, **MAG-11**, 1212 (1975).

Katayama, H., K. Yokoyama, and S. Nakagawa, "An Equalizing Method of Recording Pulse Waveforms for NRZ Recording" (Japanese), *Seventh Ann. Conf. Rec. Magn. Soc. Jpn.*, **PA-14**, 25 (1975).

Katayama, H., K. Yokoyama, and S. Nakagawa, "A High Speed ATC for NRZI Recording" (Japanese), *IECE Jpn., Nat. Conv. Rec.*, 199 (1976).

Kawamata, T., Y. Mizoh, H. Ushigome, and H. Hagiwara, "Abrasivity Effect of Magnetic Recording Tape Rubbing Noise" (Japanese), *J. IECE Jpn.*, **J67-C**, 62 (1984*a*).

Kawamata, T., K. Inoue, and M. Kittaka, "Study for Wear Resistance and Abrasivity of Magnetic Recording Tape" (Japanese), *J. IECE Jpn.*, **J67-C**, 227 (1984*b*).

Kawasaki, M., and S. Higuchi, "Alloy Powders for Magnetic Recording Tape," *IEEE Trans. Magn.*, **MAG-8**, 430 (1972).

Kazama, K., and H. Itoh, "Automatic Storage and Retrieval of Videotaped Programs," *J. SMPTE*, **88**, 221 (1979).

Kihara, N., "Magnetic Recording and Reproducing System," U.S. Patent 3, 188, 385, 1965; Japanese Patent 450,256 (Appl. June 21, 1961).

Kihara, N., "Compact Type VTR" (Japanese), *J. Inst. Telev. Eng. Jpn*, **17**, 667 (1963).

Kihara, N., and Y. Odagiri, "Slow-Motion Magnetic Sheet Videocorder and Its Applications," *J. SMPTE*, **84**, 789 (1975).

Kihara, N., F. Kohno, and Y. Ishigaki, "Development of a New System of Cassette Type Consumer VTR," *IEEE Trans. Consum. Electron.*, **22**, 1 (1976).

Kihara, N., K. Nakamura, E. Saito, and M. Kambara, "The Electronic Still Camera: A New Conception in Photography," *IEEE Intl. Conf. Consum. Electron.*, 325 (June, 1982).

Kihara, N., Y. Odagiri, and T. Sato, "High-Speed Video Replication System Using Contact Printing," *IEEE Intl. Conf. Consum. Electron.*, 72 (1983).

Kimura, T., N. Kobayashi, H. Fujiwara, Y. Shiroishi, M. Kudo, and T. Iimura, "Rubbing Noise of Mn-Zn Ferrite Single Crystal for Magnetic Heads," *Summaries Intl. Conf. Ferrites,* 138 (1980).

Kirk, D., "Technology: Philips Video Compact Cassette," *Video,* **8,** 12 (1979).

Kobayashi, F., and H. Sugaya, "Computer Simulation of Contact Printing Process," *IEEE Trans. Magn.,* **MAG-7,** 528 (1971*a*).

Kobayashi, F., and H. Sugaya, "Theoretical Analysis of Contact Printing on Magnetic Tape," *IEEE Trans. Magn.,* **MAG-7,** 244 (1971*b*).

Kobayashi, H., and D. T. Tang, "Application of Partial Response Channel Coding to Magnetic Recording Systems," *IBM J. Res. Dev.,* **14,** 368 (1970).

Kobayashi, T., M. Kubota, H. Satoh, T. Kumura, K. Yamauchi, and S. Takahashi, "A Tilted Sendust-Sputtered Ferrite Video Head," *IEEE Trans. Magn.,* **MAG-21,** 1536 (1985).

Kono, T., "Beta HiFi VTR" (Japanese), *J. Inst. Telev. Eng. Jpn.,* **37,** 1014 (1983).

Kornei, O., "Magnetic Head Has Megacycle Range," *Electronics,* 172 (Nov. 1956).

Maesawa, Y., M. Takao, H. Hibino, M. Odagiri, and K. Shinohara, "Metal Thin Film Video Tape by Vacuum Deposition," *Fourth Intl. Conf. Video Data Processing,* 54 (1982).

Makino, Y., K. Aso, S. Uedaira, S. Eto, M. Hiyakawa, K. Hotai, and Y. Ochiai, "Amorphous Alloys for Magnetic Head," *Proc. Third Intl. Conf. Ferrites,* 699 (1980).

Mallinson, J. C., "The Next Decade in Magnetic Recording," *IEEE Trans. Magn.,* **MAG-21,** 1217 (1985).

Mallinson, J. C., and J. Miller, "Optimal Codes for Digital Magnetic Recording," *Radio Electron. Eng.,* **47** 172 (1977).

Mallinson, J. C., H. N. Bertram, and C. W. Steele, "A Theory of Contact Printing," *IEEE Trans. Magn.,* **MAG-7,** 524 (1971).

Marzocchi, L., "Electromagnetic Sound Recording," U.S. Patent 2,245, 286, 1941.

Masterson, E. E., "Magnetic Recording of High Frequency Signals," U.S. Patent 2,773,120, 1956.

Matsumoto, H., and T. Yamamoto, "New Alloy 'Sendust' and Magnetic and Electric Properties of Fe-Si-Al Base Alloy," *J. Jpn. Inst. Metals,* **1,** 127 (1937).

Matsuura, K., K. Oyamada, and T. Yazaki, "Amorphous Video Head for High Coercive Tape," *IEEE Trans. Magn.,* **MAG-19,** 1623 (1983).

Mehrgardt, S., "Digital Processing in Video Tape Recorders," *IEEE Intl. Conf. Consum. Electron. Dig. Tech. Papers,* **IX,** 132 (1985).

Mizushima, M., "Mn-Zn Single Crystal Ferrite as a Video Head Material," *IEEE Trans., Magn.,* **MAG-7,** 342 (1971).

Mohri, K., Y. Yumde, M. Umemura, Y. Noro, and S. Watatani, "A New Concept of a Handy Video Recording Camera," *IEEE G-CE Spring Conf.,* **CE-27,** 3 (1981).

Morio. M., Y. Matsumoto, Y. Machinda, Y. Kubota, and N. Kihara, "Development of an Extremely Small Video Tape Recorder," *IEEE Trans. Consum. Electron.,* **CE-27,** 331 (1981).

Morizono, M., H. Yoshida, and Y. Hashimoto, "Digital Video Recording—Some Experiments and Future Consideration," *J. SMPTE,* **89,** 658 (1980).

Mueller-Ernesti, R., German Patent 910,602, 1941.

Mullin, J. T., "Video Magnetic Tape Recorder," *Tele-Tech., Electron. Ind.,* **13,** 77 (1954).

Nagai, K., Japanese Patent 318,961, 1961.

Nakagawa, S., "A Constitution of Concatenated Code for Digital VTR" (Japanese), ITE Jpn., Tech. Report VR 32–3, (1978).

Nakagawa, S., and K. Yokoyama, "A Design Method of Linear Density and Track Density for Maximizing Area Density in Digital Videotape Recorder" (Japanese), *Trans. IECE Jpn.,* **J 64-C,** 386 (1981).

Nakagawa, S., K. Yokoyama, and H. Katayama, "A Study on Detection Methods of NRZ Recording," *IEEE Trans. Magn.,* **MAG-16,** 104 (1980).

Nakano, K., H. Moriwaki, T. Takahashi, K. Akagiri, and M. Morio, "New 8-Bit PCM Audio Recording Technique Using an Extension of the Video Track," *IEEE Intl. Conf. Consum. Electron.,* 241 (1982).

Nelson, A. M,. "Double Transfer Curie Point and Magnetic Bias Tape Copy System," U.S. Patent 3,496,304, 1970.

Ninomiya, Y., Y. Otsuka, Y. Izumi, S. Gohshi, and Y. Iwadate, "A HDTV Broadcasting System Utilizing a Bandwidth Compression Technique-MUSE," *IEEE Trans. Broadcast.,* **BC-33,** 130 (1987).

Nomura, T., and K. Yokoyama, "Thermomagnetic Video Recording," *IEEE Trans. Magn.,* **MAG-15,** 1932 (1979).

Numakura, T., "Color Video Signal Magnetic Recording Equipment," Japanese Patent 49–44535, 1974.

Okamura, S., "Magnetic Recording Processing Equipment," Japanese Utility Patent S39–23924, 1964.

Olson, H. F., W. D. Houghton, A. R. Morgan, J. Zenel, M. Artzt, J. G. Woodward, and J. T. Fisher, "A System for Recording and Reproducing TV Signals," *RCA Rev.,* **15,** 3 (1954).

Olson, H. F., W. D. Houghton, A. R. Morgan, M. Artzt, J. A. Zenel, and J. G. Woodward, "A Magnetic Tape System for Recording and Reproducing Standard FCC Color Television Signals," *RCA Rev.,* **17,** 330 (1956).

Peters, C. J., "A Magnetically Scanned Magnetic Tape Transducer," *IEEE Trans. Elec. Comput.,* 196 (1964).

Pritchard, D. H., and J. J. Gibson, "Worldwide Color Television Standards," *J. SMPTE,* **89,** 111 (1980).

Potgeisser, J. A. L., and J. Koorneef, "Wear of Magnetic Heads," *Proc. Conf. Video and Data Rec.,* 203 (1973).

Reed, I. S., and G. Solomon, "Polynomial Codes over Certain Finite Fields," *J. Soc. Ind. Appl. Math.,* **8,** 300 (1960).

Reeves, A. H., French Patents 833,929, 1937; 837,921, 1937, and 852,183, 1938. U.S. Patent 2,272,070, 1942.

Remley, F. M., "Digital Television Tape Recording: A Report of Progress Toward a Standard," *J. SMPTE,* **94,** 914 (1985).

Reimers, U. H., W. H. Zappen, and H. F. Zettl, "KCF I—Using the Leading Edge of Technology in a Small Broadcast Camera," *J. SMPTE,* **94,** 573 (1985).

Ryan, D. M., "Mechanical Design Considerations for Helical-Scan Video Tape Recorders," *J. SMPTE,* **87,** 767 (1978).

Sadashige, K., "An Overview of Longitudinal Video Recording Technology," *J. SMPTE,* **89,** 501 (1980).

Sakakima, H., K. Osano, K. Ihara, and M. Satomi, "Multilayered Films of Nitride Alloys as Magnetic Head Materials," *J. Magn. Magn. Mater.,* **93,** 349 (1991).

Sanderson, H. J., "Method of Controlling the Position of a Write or Read Head and a Device for Carrying out the Method," U.S. Patent 4,297,733, 1981.

Sato, S., K. Takeuchi, and M. Yoshida, "Recording Video Camera in the Beta Format," *IEEE Trans. Consum. Electron.,* **CE-29,** 365 (1983).

Sawazaki, N., "Magnetic Recording Apparatus," Japanese Patent S34–171, 1955.

Sawazaki, N., M. Yagi, M. Iwasaki, G. Inada, and T. Tamaoki, "A New Video-Tape Recording System," *J. SMPTE,* **69,** 868 (1960).

Sawazaki, N., H. Tsukamoto, M. Imamura, and T. Fujiwara, "Endless Tape Fixed Head VTR," *IEEE Trans. Magn.*, **MAG-15,** 1564 (1979).

Schüller, E., "Magnetische Aufzeichnung und Wiedergabe von Fernsehbildern," German Patent 927,999, 1954.

Sekimoto, K., M. Matsui, and I. Obata, "M-II Format VTR," *Sixth Conf. Video, Audio & Data Recording,* 121 (1986).

Shannon, C. E., "A Mathematical Theory of Communication," *Bell Syst. Tech. J.,* **27,** 379 (1948).

Shibaya, H., and I. Fukuda, "The Effect of the B_s of Recording Head Cores on the Magnetization of High Coercivity Media," *IEEE Trans. Magn.,* **MAG-13,** 1005 (1977).

Shimada, Y., "Cobalt Amorphous Magnetic Materials Produced by Sputtering," *J. Jpn. Inst. Metals,* **22,** 11 (1983).

Shinohara, K., H. Yoshida, M. Odagiri, and A. Tomago, "Columnar Structure and Some Properties of Metal-Evaporated Tape," *IEEE Trans. Magn.,* **MAG-20,** 824 (1984).

Shiraishi, Y., and A. Hirota, "Magnetic Recording at Video Cassette Recorder for Home Use," *IEEE Trans. Magn.,* **MAG-14,** 318 (1978).

Snyder, R. H., "Ampex's New Video Tape Recorder," *Tele-Tech., Electron. Ind.,* **15,** 72 (1956).

Stanton, J. A., and M. J. Stanton, "Video Recording: A History," *J. SMPTE,* **96,** 253 (1987).

Sugaya, H., "Some Problems of Metallic Magnetic Material at High Frequency" (Japanese), *J. Inst. Telev. Eng. Jpn.,* **18,** 722 (1964).

Sugaya, H., "Newly Developed Hot-Pressed Ferrite Head," *IEEE Trans. Magn.,* **MAG-4,** 295 (1968).

Sugaya, H., "Magnetic Tapes for Contact Duplication by Anhysteretic and Thermal Transfer Methods," *AIP Conf. Proc.,* **10,** 1086 (1973).

Sugaya, H., "Recent Advances in Video Tape Recording," *IEEE Trans. Magn.,* **MAG-14,** 632 (1978).

Sugaya, H., "Home Video Tape Recording and Its Future Prospects," *IERE Proc.,* **54,** 75 (1982).

Sugaya, H., "Video Tape Recorder and Its Future Prospects," *J. Appl. Magn.,* **8,** 305 (1984).

Sugaya, H., "Mechatronics and the Development of the Video Tape Recorder," *ASLE Special Pub.,* **SP-19,** 64 (1985).

Sugaya, H., "The Video Tape Recorder: Its Evolution and the Present State of the Art of VTR Technology," *J. SMPTE,* **95,** 301, (March, 1986).

Sugaya, H., "The Past Quarter-Century and the Next Decade of Video Tape Recording," *J. SMPTE,* **101,** 10 (1992).

Sugaya, H., T. Nakagawa, and T. Arai, "Re-Recording in Overwrite Recording," *IEEE Trans. Magn.,* **29,** 4080 (1993).

Sugaya, H., and F. Kobayashi, "Theoretical Analysis of Contact Printing on Magnetic Tape," *IEEE Trans. Magn.,* **MAG-7,** 244 (1971*a*).

Sugaya, H., and F. Kobayashi, "Computer Simulation of Contact Printing," *IEEE Trans. Magn.,* **MAG-7,** 528 (1971*b*).

Sugaya, H., and A. Tomago, "Metal Evaporated Tape," *Symp. Magn. Media, Mfg. Methods, Hawaii,* **C-2,** 1 (1983).

Sugaya, H., F. Kobayashi, and M. Ono, "Magnetic Tape Duplication by Contact Printing at Short Wavelengths," *IEEE Trans. Magn.,* **MAG-5,** 437 (1969).

Sugaya, H., M. Deguchi, H. Taniguchi, and T. Yonezawa, "Standard Alignment Tape Recorder for EIA-J Type I Video Tape Recorder," *J. SMPTE,* **83,** 901 (1974).

Sugaya, H., F. Kobayashi, and M. Ono, Japanese Utility Patent S54-6346, 1979.

Sugimoto, M., "Crystal Growth of Manganese Zinc Ferrite," *J. Appl. Phys. (Jpn.),* **5,** 557 (1966).

Suzuki, K., E. Kimura, and K. Yokoyama, "Magnetic Recording Apparatus," Japanese Patent 480,366 (1979).

Swoboda, T. J., P. Arthur, Jr., N. L. Cox, J. N. Ingraham, A. L. Oppegard, and S. Sadler, "Synthesis and Properties of Ferromagnetic Chromium Oxide," *J. Appl. Phys.*, **32**, 374 (1961).

Tajiri, H., S. Tanaka, I Sato, M. Yagi, and N. Sawazaki, "Color Video Tape Recorder for Home Use," *J. SMPTE*, **77**, 727 (1968).

Takahashi, K., K. Ihara, S. Muraoka, E. Sawai, and N. Kaminaka, "A High Performance Video Head with Co Based Alloy Laminated Films," *Dig. Intermag. Conf.* 1987, **EB-08** (1987).

Takama, E., and M. Ito, "New Mn-Zn Ferrite Fabricated by Hot Isostatic Pressing," *IEEE Trans. Magn.*, **MAG-15**, 1958 (1979).

Tanimura, H., Y. Fujiwara, and T. E. Mechrens, "A Second Generation Type-C One-Inch VTR," *J. SMPTE*, **92**, 1274 (1983).

Tjaden, D. L. A., and A. M. A. Rijchaert, "Theory of Anhysteretic Contact Duplication," *IEEE Trans. Magn.*, **MAG-7**, 532 (1971).

Tomita, Y., "Two-Head Color Video Tape Recorder" (Japanese), *J. Inst. Telev. Eng. (Jpn.)*, **15**, 22 (1961).

Torii, M., "New Process to Make Huge Spinel Single Crystal Ferrite," *IEEE Trans. Magn.*, **MAG-15**, 873 (1979).

Torii, M., U, Kihara, and I. Maeda, "On the Rubbing Noise of Mn-Zn Ferrite Single Crystal," *Proc. Int. Conf. Ferrites*, 01AB2–4, 137 (1980).

Umeki, S., S. Saitoh, and Y. Imaoka, "A New High Coercive Magnetic Particle for Recording Tape," *IEEE Trans. Magn.*, **MAG-10**, 655 (1974).

Van den Berg, R., "The Design of A Machine for High-Speed Duplication of Video Records," *105th Tech. Conf.*, *SMPTE*, **78**, 709 (1969).

Waring, P. K., "CrO_2-Based Thermomagnetic Information Storage and Retrieval System," *J. Appl. Phys.*, **42**, 1763 (1971).

Woodward, J. G., "Stress Demagnetization in Videotapes," *IEEE Trans. Magn.*, **MAG-18**, 1812 (1982).

Yasuda, I., Y. Yoshisato, Y. Kawai, K. Koyama, and T. Yazaki, "Ultra-High-Density Recording with Sendust Video Head and High Coercive Tape," *IEEE Trans. Magn.*, **MAG-17**, 3114 (1981).

Yokoyama, K., "Basic Studies of Video Tape Recorder Design" (Japanese), *NHK Tech. J.*, **21**, 4 (1969).

Yokoyama, K., and H. Habutsu, "PCM-VTR and Editing" (Japanese), *J. Inst. Tel. Engr. Jpn.*, **32**, 843 (1976).

Yokoyama, K., and S. Nakagawa, "Trends of Research on Digital VTR" (Japanese), *J. Inst. Tel. Engr. Jpn.*, **32**, 819 (1978).

Yokoyama, K., and S. Nakagawa, "An Experimental Channel Coding for Digital Videotape Recorder," *12th Intl. Tel. Symp. Record*, 251 (1981).

Yokoyama, K., S. Nakagawa, H. Shibaya, and H. Katayama, "PCM Video Recording Using a Rotating Magnetic Sheet," NHK Labs. Note, No. 221, 1977.

Yokoyama, K., S. Nakagawa, and H. Katayama, "Experimental PCM-VTR," NHK Labs. Note, No. 236, 1979*a*.

Yokoyama, K., S. Nakagawa, and H. Katayama, "Trial Production of Experimental PCM VTR" (Japanese), *IECE Jpn. Tech. Rep.*, MR 79–8 (1979*b*).

Yokoyama, K., S. Nakagawa, and H. Katayama, "An Experimental Digital Videotape Recorder," *J. SMPTE*, **89**, 173 (1980).

Yoshida, H., and T. Eguchi, "Digital Video Recording Based on the Proposed Format from Sony," *J. SMPTE*, **92**, 562 (1983).

Zahn, H., "The BCN System for Magnetic Recording of Television Programs," *J. SMPTE*, **88**, 823 (1979).

CHAPTER 6
DIGITAL VIDEO RECORDING

Chojuro Yamamitsu

Matsushita Electric Industrial Company, Osaka, Japan

6.1 BACKGROUND

The NTSC television system has been in use in the United States since 1954. As the television networks expanded, the handling of time differences between the east and the west of the American continent emerged as a serious problem. In 1956, Ampex Corporation announced a transverse rotating-head video tape recorder (VTR) using 2-in-wide tape, which had the capability of recording enough FM bandwidth for broadcast-quality color television signals. This innovation solved the program delay problem described above, and revolutionized television production and television in general.

Later, although several analog video tape recorders (Type B, Type C) were introduced and marketed, they had several drawbacks as discussed in Chap. 5. Ideally, to solve these problems, a digital video tape recorder was required. Digital recorder research and development began in the early 1970s. The main problems were how to increase the recording density or, alternatively, decrease tape consumption, and how to reduce cost.

With the advance of digital signal processing, including modulation and error-correction techniques, tape and head improvements, and large-scale integration (LSI) manufacturing technologies, the first component digital video recorder (D-1) was introduced and has been marketed since 1987. The cost of this machine was high. Later, several other digital video recorders (D-2, D-3, etc.) were introduced. This chapter outlines the historical development of the digital video recorder, and describes the important key techniques used and their implementation in practical machines.

6.2 DIGITAL VERSUS ANALOG RECORDING

6.2.1 Video Recording by Digital Means

All analog video tape recorders record the video signal by means of frequency modulation. The analog information is converted to differences in distance between

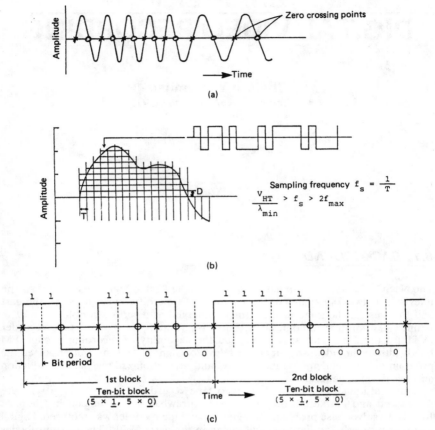

FIGURE 6.1 Typical example of FM signal and digital signal (*a*) FM signal (*b*) analog-to-digital conversion by PCM (*c*) 8-10 group coded signal.

the zero-crossing points of the FM signal (Fig. 6.1*a*). The most commonly used coding method in digital video recording is pulse-code modulation (PCM). In this coding method, the distance between the zero-crossing points is a discrete value that is an integer multiple of a time called the bit period (Fig. 6.1*c*). To encode the video signal into a digital format, the analog signal is sliced into time segments which have a duration T and an amplitude D (Fig. 6.1*b*). The discrete amplitude values are then encoded into a digital binary format. These processes are known as sampling, quantizing, and coding. With regard to quantization, a value of 2^8, or 256 levels (8 bits), is considered sufficient for broadcast quality.

6.2.2   Noise Spectrum

In analog FM recording the tape noise converts in the demodulated signal into "triangulation noise," which is proportional to the frequency as shown in Fig. 6.2.

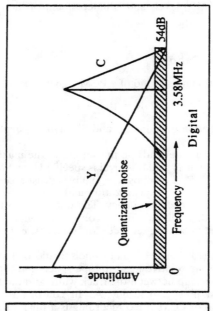

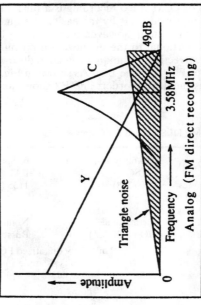

FIGURE 6.2 Noise spectrum of FM signal and PCM signal.

6.3

In digital recording the tape noise normally has no effect on the detected signal; the only noise of significance is the so-called quantization noise, which is a function of the number of quantization levels and is independent of the modulating (analog) signal frequency.

6.2.3 Signal-to-Noise Ratio

The signal-to-quantization noise ratio of a PCM signal is defined as

$$\text{SNR} = 10.8 + 6n \tag{6.1}$$

where, n is the quantization bit number, and the signal is expressed peak-to-peak and the noise rms.

The signal-to-noise ratio depends on the setting of the maximum video level to the analog-to-digital converter and this level is specified by a SMPTE standard (see Table 6.1). The actual SNR of composite signal broadcast recorders (D-2 and D-3) is 54 dB, corresponding to 8-bit quantization and a sampling frequency equal to $4\,f_{sc}$, where f_{sc} is the subcarrier frequency. The quantization levels for white and black are selected so that the full 100% color bar signal can be digitized. By comparison, the SNR of an analog recorder for broadcast use (Type C) is 48–50 dB (Fig. 6.3).

It has been established that the signal-to-noise ratio of FM video recording is closely proportional to the relative head-to-tape speed and the square root of the track width. The relationship between the track width and the tape consumption is proportional as shown in Fig. 6.4, line A. In contrast to this, the signal-to-quantization noise ratio of PCM video recording is a function of the bit rate (Eq. 6.1). The SNR can be improved 6 dB by increasing the quantization bit number from 8-bit to 9-bit. The data content, however, increases only by a factor of 9/8. The tape consumption is proportional to the quantization bit number and can be improved by using error-correction techniques which reduce the sensitivity of the digital data to tape noise (Fig. 6.4, line B1). As shown in Fig. 6.4, the straight line A represents a broadcast analog recorder; line B2 shows an experimental digital

TABLE 6.1 SMPTE Standard for Composite Coding

Parameter	525/60 systems	625/50 systems
Coded signal	NTSC	PAL
Number of samples per line (active)	910 (768)	1135 (948)
Sampling frequency	$4f_{sc}$ (14.3 MHz)	$4f_{sc}$ (17.7 MHz)
Sampling structure	Orthogonal	Nonorthogonal
Sampling phase	I/Q (123°/ 33°)	Burst (135°/ 225°)
Form of coding	Uniformly quantized PCM 8 bits / sample	
White level	200	211
Blanking level	60	64
Sync tip level	4	1
Digital interface	Parallel: SMPTE 244M, IEC 1179 Serial: SMPTE 259M	

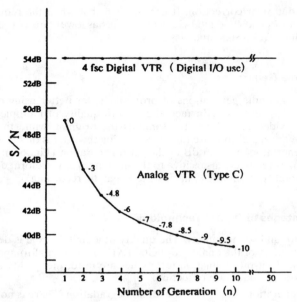

FIGURE 6.3 S/N of multiple generation.

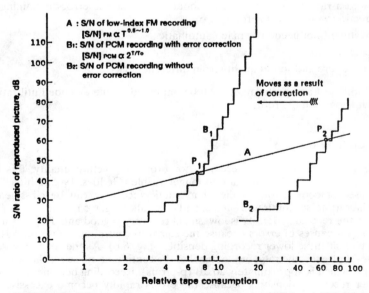

FIGURE 6.4 Comparison of tape consumption using PCM and FM video recording.

recorder without error correction. It can be seen that when the required SNR is above the points P_1 and P_2, digital video recording has lower tape consumption than analog recording (Yokoyama and Nakagawa, 1978).

6.2.4 Multiple Generation

The quality of multiple generations of programs is far better using digital rather than analog video recorders. In fact, the picture quality of multiple generations using a digital video recorder is the same as the original, while the cumulative degradation of the signal-to-noise ratio in an analog recorder is theoretically 3 dB at the second generation, and 4.5 dB at the third generation (Fig. 6.3). In addition, PCM recording is relatively insensitive to the influences of waveform distortion and time-base instability, phenomena intrinsic to magnetic recording.

6.2.5 Advantages of Digital Technology

a) High picture and sound quality. The quality of a digital signal is determined by the performances of the analog-to-digital (ADC) and digital-to-analog converters (DAC). If bit-rate reduction techniques are used, the quality also depends on the amount of data rate reduction.

b) Multiple generations of programs with no degradation. There is no degradation if a digital interface is used. Even in a consumer digital video recorder or other recorders using bit-rate reduction, the quality remains unchanged as long as the signals are copied in an unchanged digital domain.

c) Freedom from dropouts. For example, an experimental digital video recorder showed a raw block error rate of about 10^{-4} while the errors remaining after correction were almost zero.

d) Adjustment not needed or made automatic.

e) Greater reliability.

f) Same picture and sound quality from different decks.

In addition, cost and performance will be improved by the extended utilization of LSI technologies in the future.

6.2.6 Code Errors

A code error rate of 10^{-7} is necessary for broadcast picture quality; this is the threshold level at which errors are no longer visible (Geddes, 1965; Ishida, 1971). The causes of code errors in digital magnetic recording can be classified into discontinuous noise, continuous noise, and crosstalk (Fig. 6.5).

When the recording density is low, signal recovery is good and dropouts are the predominant causes of errors because the signal-to-continuous-noise ratio is sufficiently high at these lower recording densities (Fig. 6.6). As the recording density increases, however, the ratio of the signal to the continuous noise reaches its threshold value, which is approximately 20 dB (p-p/rms). Recording becomes impractical at higher recording densities because the errors rapidly become excessive. To a certain extent, errors can be corrected by using error-correction codes. However, to compensate for errors related to continuous noise, the recording density must be increased to accommodate the error-correction data which, in turn, increases the

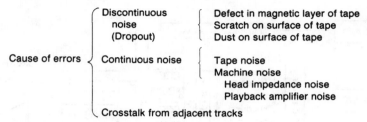

FIGURE 6.5 Causes of errors in digital magnetic recorders.

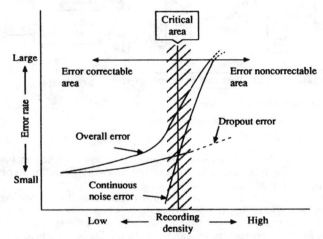

FIGURE 6.6 General relationship between error rate and recording density.

error rate. Thus there may be no net improvement. With account taken of this inherent increase in error rate, the practical limit for recording density is considered to be the point where the threshold value of the signal-to-continuous-noise ratio is as illustrated in Fig. 6.6 (Yokoyama and Nakagawa, 1978).

The signal-to-equipment-noise ratio is also important, and it is necessary to achieve a minimum ratio of 20 dB (p-p/rms). In practice, an additional marginal allowance of approximately 15 dB is required to allow for such additional factors as dropouts, pulse interference, miss-tracking, clock jitter, output level fluctuations, crosstalk from adjacent tracks, and tape wear. Thus, a signal-to-equipment-noise ratio of approximately 35 dB is necessary at least.

6.3 DIGITAL VIDEO SIGNAL PROCESSING

6.3.1 Basic Structure of a Digital Video Tape Recorder

Figure 6.7 shows the basic structure of a digital video recorder. The servo system and mechanism are not shown in the picture, because they are the same as those of

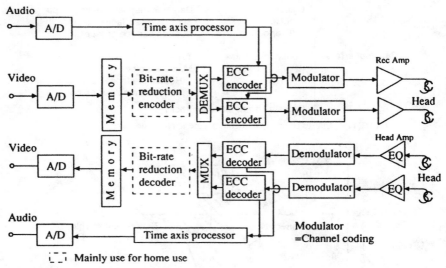

FIGURE 6.7 Block diagram of digital tape recorders.

an analog recorder. Bit-rate reduction technology (shown dashed in Fig. 6.7) has been used mainly for consumer applications but its use is spreading to professional broadcast application as well.

An analog video signal is converted into digital data by an analog-to-digital converter (ADC). Normally, the quantization is 8 bits. The PCM signal from the ADC is fed to a time-base compressing memory to insert the sync pattern, together with parities for error correction and identification (ID) codes which are needed in playback for depacketizing the bit-stream. The time-base compressed audio data is added here as well and the timing of the PCM signal is set to match the rotary-head system. Data shuffling is also carried out in this memory to conceal possible uncorrected errors, specifically longer burst errors beyond the error correction capability of the system. The shuffling moves the positions of adjacent data samples (or blocks) within a TV field or frame to positions spaced well apart on the tape in the recording mode. The shuffling is implemented within the range of a minimum editing unit (for example: one field).

When data-rate reductions are used, it has the effect of minimizing the redundancy existing in the video signal. The bit-rate-reduced video data is generally divided into n parallel channels ($n = 2$ in Fig. 6.7) in order to reduce the recordable bit rate. Then the outer parities, which can correct burst errors, are added. At the same time, multichannel audio signals are converted into digital audio data. Then the audio data are mixed and compressed along the time axes. The audio data are also shuffled and the outer parities are added to the mixed audio data. After this, the inner parities, which can correct random errors, are added to the bit-rate-reduced video data and the mixed audio data, respectively. At this time the sync pattern and IDs are included. Finally, the digital data are converted in the modulator into recording data, which have suitable recording and reproducing characteristics (channel coding).

During playback, the output signal from the heads is equalized to compensate for the deteriorated (amplitude and phase distortion) playback signal (Katayama et al., 1975). For this purpose, an automatic threshold controller (Katayama et al., 1976) or a quantized feedback equalizer may be used (Waldhauer, 1974; Wood et al., 1978; Huber, 1983; Osawa et al., 1983). After equalization, a bit-stream is generated by a discriminator and, at the same time, the clock signal is regenerated from the playback data. In the playback mode, the output signal is extracted by a process opposite to that used in the recording mode, including the reinsertion of the horizontal and vertical blanking signals and the synchronizing signals which is done in the digital domain. The jitter of the reproduced signal is absorbed by either a time-base corrector or a time-base extending memory. Such a memory can also be used for features such as jog-shuttle which enables picture search at variable speeds.

6.3.2 Coding of Color Television Systems

Both composite and component coding are used. Composite coding means that color television signals (NTSC, PAL), in which the luminance signal Y and the chrominance signal C are interleaved in the frequency domain, are directly digitized (Fig. 6.2). In component coding, the luminance signal Y and both color difference signals R − Y and B − Y are independently converted into a digital format. The important factors of coding are the sampling frequency and the quantization bit number, because these quantities define the amount of data to be recorded on tape.

To eliminate the alias components, the Nyquist theory requires that the sampling frequency f_s has to be at least twice the maximum frequency f_m of the video signal.

$$f_s > 2f_m \tag{6.2}$$

The pulse-amplitude-modulation (PAM) signal can be considered as the product of an input video signal and a sampling pulse signal (Fig. 6.8). The spectrum of a PAM signal includes the spectrum of the input signal. The original video signal can be reproduced by a low pass filter (interpolation filter) in the decoding process (Fig. 6.9). Ringing occurs if sharp cut-off, low pass filters (pre-filter and interpolation filter) are used. In practice, the sampling frequency f_s is selected to be higher than the Nyquist criterion demands, and typically

$$f_s > 2.5f_m \tag{6.3}$$

It is also desirable that the sampling-pulse width is as narrow as possible so as not to degrade the high-frequency response of the original signal.

To minimize the visibility of the moiré beat effect between the sampling and the color subcarrier frequencies, the sampling frequency should be an integer multiple of the subcarrier frequency, f_{sc}. At the early stages of development, both $2f_{sc}$ and $3f_{sc}$ and 8-bit quantization composite coding systems were used in almost all experimental digital video recorders. The $3f_{sc}$ sampling frequency was, in general, found to be preferable for both NTSC and PAL systems (Godall, 1951; Ishida, 1970; Goldberg, 1973). This leads to a data rate of 86 Mb/s for NTSC and 105 Mb/s for PAL. Under these conditions, the bandwidth is high enough for broadcast use, but the signal processing is complex for editing, picture quality adjustment, montage, and mixing because the $3f_{sc}$ sampling structure is not orthogonal.

With advances in high-density recording, a sampling frequency of four times the color subcarrier frequency $4f_{sc}$ became possible. The sampling points are orthogonal and are located in a vertical line (between lines and frames) in the television image.

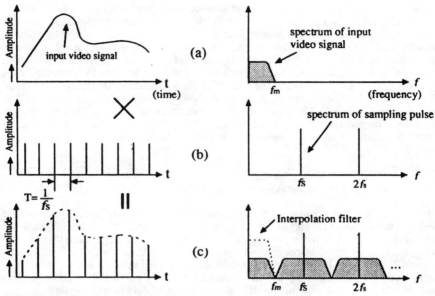

FIGURE 6.8   Sampling process of coding.

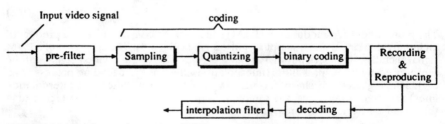

FIGURE 6.9   Fundamental structure of PCM recording system.

Signal processing using this sampling structure is easier. In 1978, composite coding parameters for the NTSC system were proposed by the SMPTE (Table 6.1). The $4f_{sc}$ sampling frequency was adopted for commercial composite digital VTRs (D-2 and D-3). The proposed quantizing rate was 8 bits.

Conversion between the NTSC, PAL, and SECAM standards is of vital importance. To facilitate such conversion, a component coding system was proposed in which the luminance signal Y and two color difference signals, $R - Y$ and $B - Y$, are individually coded, and a common sampling frequency for all these systems was standardized by Comité Consultatif International de Radio Communication (CCIR) in 1982 (Table 6.2). This component coding standard is based upon a sampling frequency of 13.5 MHz for the Y signal and 6.75 MHz (one-half of the Y signal frequency) for both the $R - Y$ and $B - Y$ signals. This sampling ratio is called 4:2:2. The selected 13.5 MHz sampling frequency is six times 2.25 MHz, which is the lowest common multiple of the two horizontal line frequencies of the 525/60 and 625/50

TABLE 6.2 Encoding Parameters (4:2:2) of Digital Television (Rec 601)

Parameters		525/60 systems	625/50 systems
Number of samples	Y:	858 (720)	864 (720)
per line (active)	R−Y, B−Y:	429 (360)	432 (360)
Sampling	Y:	13.5 MHz	
frequency†	R−Y: B−Y:	6.75 MHz,	
Sampling		Orthogonal	
structure			
Form of coding		Uniformly quantized PCM,	
		8 bits/sample, for Y, R−Y and B−Y	
Correspondence	Scale:	1 ~ 254	
between video	Y:	Quantization levels 220	
signal levels and		black level: 16	
quantization levels		white level: 235	
	R−Y :	Quantization levels 225	
	B−Y	zero signal level: 128	

†Sampling frequency synchronizes with horizontal sync signal.

systems. The quantization is based on 8 bits per sample and the total bit rate is 216 Mb/s. Signal processing is much easier than in composite coding.

In professional digital video recorders (D-1 component VTR, D-2 and D-3 composite VTRs), the quantizer has 256 levels based on 8 bits per sample. In recent years, it has become clear that a quantizer accuracy of more than 9 bits is required to avoid visible degradation of picture quality resulting from repeated A/D and D/A conversions. An accuracy of 10 bits is also desired for signal processing with digital gamma correction in a camera. In 1994, Matsushita introduced a half-inch 4:2:2 (D-5) component video recorder that can record 10-bit component data on the same tape as used in the D-3 recorders.

The total bit rate is given by

$$n f_s \qquad (6.4)$$

where f_s is the sampling frequency, and n is the quantization bit number.

The required bandwidth of an analog recorder using FM recording for broadcast use (Type C) is approximately 15 MHz (white level 10 MHz, upper side band 15 MHz), whereas digital recording requires approximately 86 MHz for a composite 4 f_{sc}, 8-bit application. Although the maximum frequency of digital data is 57.5 MHz (right side of Table 6.3), the required bandwidth of digital recording is typically 1.5 times higher than the maximum frequency. To conclude, the bandwidth required for digital recording is several times that of analog recording for consumer use (5–6 MHz). Therefore, at the early stages of the development, high-density recording to reduce tape consumption was the main goal of research for both broadcast and consumer use. More recently, and especially for consumer applications, the bit-rate reduction techniques have become a major subject of digital recording studies.

6.3.3 Error Correction and Concealment

Error correction is essential for digital video recorders because the picture quality from a digital recorder depends on the correctness of the playback data. In the

TABLE 6.3 Total Bit Rate and Bandwidth of Composite and Component Coding

	Coding		Bit rate (Mb/s)	T_{min}bandwidth (MHz)
	Sampling	Quantizing		
Composite	$4f_{sc}$	8 bits	115	57.5
(NTSC)	$3f_{sc}$	8 bits	86	43
Component	4:2:2	8 bits	216	108
(Y, R−Y, B−Y)	4:1:1	8 bits	162	81
	3:1:0	8 bits	108	54

†f_{sc}: subcarrier frequency 3.58 MHz (NTSC).
Note: The necessary recording bandwidth is different from channel coding. In practice, approximately 1.5 times the bandwidth (T_{min}) is needed.

1970s, there were many announcements of experimental digital VTRs (see Table 6.6, in the Appendix). Some of them included both error correction and error concealment and some others had only error concealment (IBA, 1978; Bosh, 1979; Sony, 1979). Error correction means that errors which occurred during the playback process are corrected completely. Error correction codes which have been proposed thus far include the following:

1. Hamming (63, 56) code (Yokoyama et al., 1977)
2. Concatenated code, formulated on erasure correction (Yokoyama et al., 1979*a*)
3. Single-erasure correction code (Hashimoto et al., 1980)
4. Fire code (Eto et al., 1981)
5. Reed-Solomon code (Reed and Solomon, 1960)

It has been established through many studies that both error correction and error concealment are necessary for a digital video recorder. As as result, all digital video recorders available on the professional market, and experimental digital VTRs designed for consumer use, include without exception both error correction and error concealment functions. The most commonly used error correction method is the Reed-Solomon code.

There are three reasons why the Reed-Solomon product code has been used for error correction in a digital video recorder. First, a number of errors equal to or less than one-half the number of parities added, or the same number of errors as the number of parities, can be corrected by erasure correction. A Reed-Solomon code is effective for both random errors and burst errors. Second, a Reed-Solomon code is faster than other methods, such as the BCH code, due to the use of word-based calculations. Third, in many digital video recorders, modulation is performed byte-by-byte using 8-8 code or 8-10 code and so on. Playback errors propagate over a complete byte, so that a Reed-Solomon code that has a code word for a byte is well suited for a digital VTR.

The larger the size of a product code, the longer the length of a correctable burst error, although the size of the product code should fall within the minimum editing unit (a field or a frame). The redundancy for the error correction codes is 16–20% of the total data. It is designed not to exceed the amount of data in the horizontal and vertical blanking intervals. In general, an inner code word (horizontal parity) is utilized to correct random errors and an outer code word (vertical parity) is used to correct burst errors. Only the inner error-correction code words are applied during slow and search modes.

The technology of error concealment makes use of the correlation and redundancy that exists in video signals. Typically a picture element has almost the same value as its neighboring elements. Therefore, remaining errors that have not been corrected are concealed to be invisible by making use of this correlation. The following processes have been used for error concealment. An uncorrected error is replaced (a) with a value equal to the average of data on the previous horizontal line and data on the next horizontal line, (b) with the value of a picture element at the same position on the previous field or on the previous frame or, (c) with a value calculated from the neighboring picture elements.

6.3.4 Modulation and Detection

Modulation that converts the source data to channel data plays an important role in high-density recording; it matches the signal characteristics to the recording channel. The important parameters for a modulation code are the minimum and maximum durations between flux changes (T_{min} and T_{max}), the detection window (T_w), and the dc component.

The shorter the wavelength recorded on the tape, the lower the playback level, and the poorer the SNR. Furthermore, the nonlinear characteristics of both tape and heads cause an increase of intersymbol interference, and this makes the peak-shift of the playback signal worse. To avoid peak-shift problems, a large T_{min} is desirable. The more flux changes there are on the tape, the easier it is to recover the clock. Additionally, a smaller T_{max} also reduces the crosstalk. Small T_{max} and large T_{min} result in concentration of the frequency spectrum in a narrower range.

The detection window T_w is the duration required for discriminating the playback signal to the value of a bit. The window includes an allowance for variation of phase in the playback signal caused by jitter in the mechanical system, and peak-shift plus jitter due to the reduced SNR in high-density recording. Therefore it is important, that T_w is as wide as possible, taking into consideration that more jitter can be accepted in a digital video recorder for consumer use. The quantity T_w is an important factor in the design of digital recorders.

Due to ac coupling, it is impossible to pass the dc component through a rotary transformer and a ring head which are key components of a video magnetic recorder. Therefore a dc-free code is required for magnetic recording. A dc-free code can be defined as a code for which the digital sum variation (DSV) of the total channel code words after concatenation of these words does not become infinite. DSV is calculated as a summation of code word digital sums (CDSs). The CDS is defined as a difference between the numbers of 1's and 0's of the channel code word. There are two types of dc free codes: one uses only channel code words for which CDS is zero; the other uses not only channel code words for which CDS is zero but also channel code words for which CDSs are not zero. In addition to a dc-free code, it is expected that errors in one channel code word will not propagate to another channel code word and that the modulation code has capabilites of error detection and/or error correction.

In the case of azimuth recording, which does not use a guard band between tracks on tape, a modulation code that causes little crosstalk and enables overwrite for editing is important. Along with this, a wider T_w is also an important factor, especially for a digital video recorder for consumer use which has more jitter in its mechanical system. Modulation codes used in early digital VTRs are listed below.

1. 8-10 block code (Baldwin, 1978; Morizono et al., 1980)
2. Scrambled NRZ (S-NRZ)
3. Miller squared code (M^2) (Mallinson and Miller, 1977)
4. Scrambled and interleaved NRZI code (S-I-NRZI) (Kobayashi and Tang, 1970; Yokoyama and Nakagawa, 1981)
5. Tri-level code with partial response process (Eto et al., 1981)
6. New 8-14 block code (Uehara, 1989, 1990)
7. NRZ code with adapted spectral energy (NRZ-ASE) (Heitmann, 1984)
8. 8-9 block code (Kameyama et al., 1973; Mita et al., 1985; Itoi et al., 1988)

Figure 6.10 shows the power spectrum of typical modulation codes. The 8-10 block code converts an 8-bit word into a 10-bit channel word by using a lookup table. The 10-bit words used have been selected from the available 1024 (2^{10}) words. In all, there are $_{10}C_5 = 252$ channel code words which have the same number of 1's and 0's. These channel code words belong to a group of CDS = 0 and make a dc-free code. Although such a modulation code using only those 252 channel code words would cause no practical problems, it is also possible to assign enough channel code words to cover all 256 words of the 8-bit system. The code used for digital audio tape (DAT) is an example of this.

An 8-10 code has the following parameters: $T_w = 0.8T$, $T_{min} = 0.8T$, and $T_{max} = 4.0T$, where T is the duration of a bit before modulation. These parameters have been selected for magnetic recording as explained above, although T_{min} is narrower than T by 20% which means that the recording density becomes 20% higher than the original. The 8-10 block codes were used in many experimental digital video recorders for both professional and consumer applications. There are reports which explain how an 8-10 block code is capable of detecting errors in channel code words by using the redundancy of the code (Yamamitsu et al., 1987), and about using an 8-10 block code for generating pilot signals for servo control (Borgers et al., 1988).

A scrambled non return to zero (S-NRZ) code was designed to reduce the dc effect when the same binary value continues by adding an M-sequence (random data for scrambling) to the input data sequence. A S-NRZ has still a rather strong dc component. However, integration detection is conventionally used for the playback data, and low-frequency components lost during the recording and playback processes can be recovered using feedback compensation. A S-NRZ code has the advantages of a long detection window, $T_w = T$, and a high SNR, but the disadvantage of causing a large amount of crosstalk. This shortcoming means also that overwriting the data is difficult. For these reasons the D-1 digital video recorder, which utilizes the code, has flying erase heads and a guard band of 5 μm between the recorded tracks.

The Miller squared (M^2) code has a coding rule whereby the transition between binary values at the center of a bit cell occurs only when the input is 1 and the transition between binary values at the border of two bit cells occurs only when the input is 0. Also, if an even number of 1's continues after the last 0 of the input, the last transition between binary values caused by the last 1 of the input will be omitted. This coding rule leads to a dc-free code. The Miller squared code parameters are $T_{min} = T$, $T_w = 0.5T$, and $T_{max} = 3T$, and this code has an easy self-locking characteristic. The maximum distance of error propagation is 3 bits. The code has no dc component and

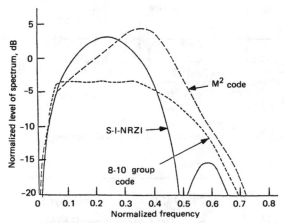

FIGURE 6.10   Power spectrum of channel codings.

few low-frequency components so that it can be easily overwritten. These are the main reasons why M^2 was selected as a modulation code for the professional D-2 digital video recorder.

A S-I-NRZI code is a modified NRZ code using scrambling and precoding processes. The so-called interleaved NRZI (I-NRZI) code is a precoded sequence of NRZ data. The precoder is shown in Fig. 6.11. Class IV partial response (Kretzmer, 1966) is very popular in the communication field; it is a detection means for S-I-NRZI, and is expressed as PR $(1, 0, -1)$. This detection process, as shown in Fig. 6.11, is defined as an addition of a playback signal to the 1 T-delayed signal. Although there are three levels after the discrimination, translating -1 back to 1 recovers the original data sequence. The precoding process and the PR $(1, 0, -1)$ detection prevent error propagation. PR $(1, 0, -1)$ detection decreases the power spectrum especially at dc and at around the Nyquist frequency. This suppression reduces noise so that the signal-to-noise ratio can be improved. Crosstalk noise from adjacent tracks is also suppressed. Class IV partial response does not require the recorded component at all to reconstruct the binary sequence from the playback signal. This means that the loss of the dc component in the rotary transformer has no effect on the reconstruction of the signal. This feature is the most valuable merit of this approach. Overwrites are also possible when this code is used (Yamamitsu, 1992).

Figure 6.12 shows the characteristics of overwrite. The results were obtained by recording the original signal using a 0.5 μm wavelength followed by an overwrite using another signal with a slightly greater wavelength. Measurements of the remaining level of the original signal after the ovewrite show that a recording current that is 3 to 4 dB higher than the optimum current gives an acceptable performance. A S-NRZI code was reported for broadcast use (Yokoyama and Nakagawa, 1981) and another S-NRZI code is used for a digital video recorder for consumer applications. There are other approaches which report having a better bit error rate using PR $(1, 0, -1)$ combined with a Viterbi decoder (Yamamitsu et al., 1989; Kanota et al., 1990).

Another new code (8-14) converts the 8-bit data word into a channel word of 14 bits in NRZ format. This code limits the number of bits with the same binary value

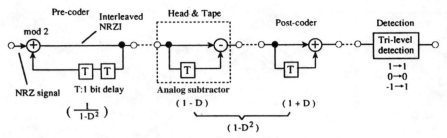

FIGURE 6.11   Explanation of interleaved NRZI and partial response.

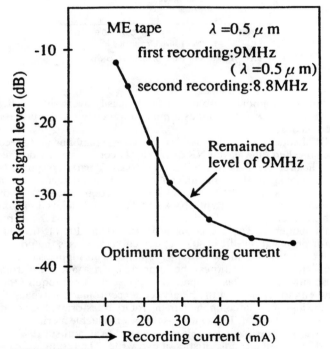

FIGURE 6.12   Example for characteristics of overwrite.

to more components. The minimum wavelength of the 8-14 code is 1.14 (8/7) times as long as M^2 and the effective bandwidth of the code is 0.875 (7/8) times as wide as M^2. The 8-14 code has superior high-frequency characteristics compared with M^2 and it is used as the modulation code in the D-3 digital recorder for professional broadcast use. This code is dc-free and allows overwrites.

Figure 6.13 shows modulation codes and their eye patterns. Recently both 16 QAM and 32 QAM (Quadrature-Amplitude Modulation) have been studied as modulation codes for a digital video recorder (Kobayashi et al., 1989).

Methods	Application	Eye pattern
Scrambled NRZ (S-NRZ)	D-1 Component DVTR	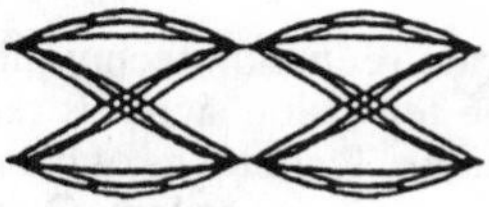
Scramble-interleaved NRZI (S-I-NRZI)	Proposed 1/4" Consumer DVTR	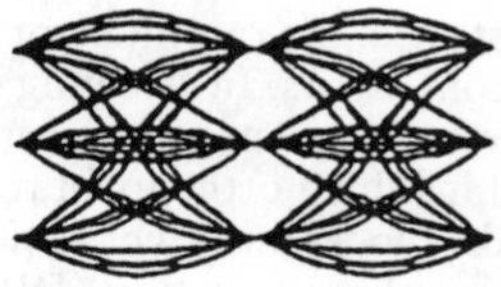
8-10 code	DAT	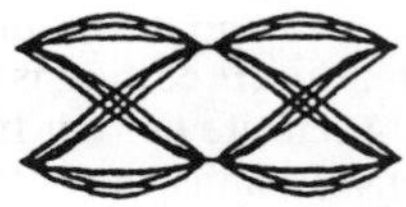
8-9 code		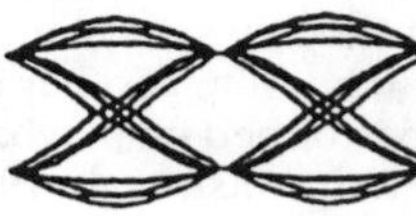
8-8 code	D-1 DVTR As pre-coding	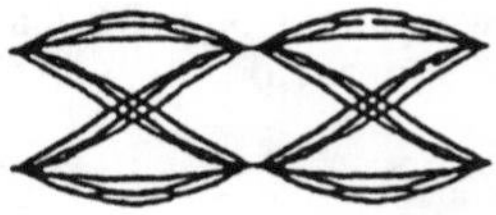
M^2 code	D-2 (19 mm) Composite DVTR	
8-14 code	D-3 (1/2") Composite DVTR	

FIGURE 6.13 Application and eye pattern of channel codings.

6.3.5 Bit-Rate Reduction

Bit-rate reduction techniques allow longer recordings because the data redundancy in the television signal is reduced using correlations in the spatial and/or temporal domains. Techniques of bit-rate reduction have been evaluated mainly for consumer digital video recorders. One of the most important items for bit-rate reduction is to preserve high picture quality. This has to be maintained in normal playback, slow (jog), and search (shuttle) modes. Small error propagation is also required. In the worst case, the raw bit error rate of video recorders will probably be around 10^{-4} for random errors. In selecting the coding method small error propagation is required, because dropouts can cause burst errors. To accomplish this, a coding technique is used in which orthogonal transformation of a block confines the error propagation within blocks into which the picture frame is divided. In the case of differential pulse-code modulation (DPCM), which causes larger error propagation, the algorithm should be designed to make the string length short. Finally, to avoid large error propagation, strong error-correction codes have been adopted. Lately most of the research and development work has concentrated on the first item.

When insert editing is considered, the length of the edited unit becomes important. If accurate field or frame editing is required, intra-field or intra-frame coding, respectively, must be selected. Single-frame editing ability may be important for consumer use and one-field editing ability is required for broadcast use.

Special effects (slow motion, stills and quick search modes), require that video heads travel across several tracks, and the signal envelope has a triangular shape. Therefore only small continuous bursts of data are obtained, and the next burst of data can be from another field. One proposed method which enables special effects to be performed on playback is where bit-rate reduction is completed in sync block units (Yamamitsu et al., 1991). Other special methods and proposals are still needed.

In summary, several bit-rate compression systems have been developed, including sub-Nyquist sampling, Hadamard transform, DPCM, discrete cosine transform (DCT), and adaptive dynamic range coding (ADRC). At present, the combination of two-dimensional DCT and variable length coding (VLC) is the most commonly used approach.

6.4 HIGH-DENSITY RECORDING

The force behind the development of high-density recording is the requirement to reduce the tape consumption to a level that makes a consumer digital video recorder practical. The development of a consumer digital VTR has been actively pursued since 1985, while the basic work on professional digital VTRs was begun in the mid-1970s.

Reduction of tape consumption can be achieved by making the minimum wavelength shorter, the track pitch narrower, and the tape thinner. These are the three important factors. Areal packing density, which is here defined as the area used to record one bit, is the basic criterion for high-density recording. The areal packing density of analog recorders has had a trend of improving tenfold in ten years, and digital recordings today have twenty to thirty times the capability they had ten years ago. The packing density of a real commercial product lags behind the laboratory model by several years (Fig. 6.14). In research laboratories, the packing density of professional digital recording (Yokoyama et al., 1979b) reached the level of a broadcast analog video recorder (Type C), and the packing density of digital recording for

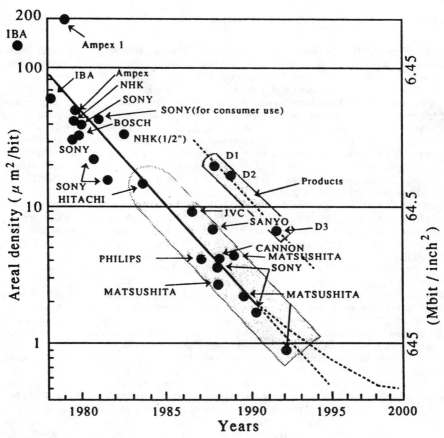

FIGURE 6.14 Development of areal density.

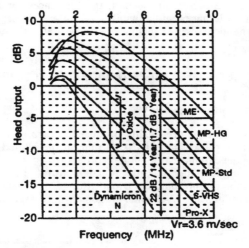

FIGURE 6.15 Tape characteristics.

consumer use (Yamamitsu et al., 1987) achieved the density of a conventional
analog VTR (VHS 6-hour mode). It has been reported that 12-hour recording time
has been realized using metal evaporated (ME) tape of 10 μm thickness.

Now it is clear that the density of digital recording is higher than that of analog
recording. The highest density reported is 1.35 μm^2/bit (track pitch 5.5 μm, wavelength 0.5 μm) using ME tape which had 4 dB improvement in C/N (Kanota et al.,
1990). The best result earlier was 2.4 μm^2/bit (track pitch 6.8 μm) using 10 μm ME
tape, allowing a 3-hour recording to be achieved using an 8 mm cassette (Yamamitsu et al., 1989). In addition to these published results, an experimental result
was reported indicating that 0.95 μm^2/bit had been realized (Kobayashi et al.,
1989). The shortest wavelength reported is 0.47 μm (Yamamitsu et al., 1988).

Improved oxide (H$_c$ = 850 Oe), metal powder MP tape (H$_c$ = 1500–1600 Oe),
and conventional ME tape (H$_c$ =1200–1700 Oe) are currently in use. A comparison
between ME and MP tapes is shown in Fig 6.15. The improvement in the performance of tape has been progressing by about 1 to 1.7 dB per year. In general, the
size of the particles of magnetic material have been made smaller and the surface of
the tape has been made smoother over the years, and this trend will continue in the
future. The smaller the particles the fewer the random errors, and the smoother the
surface the fewer the number of burst errors.

Regarding magnetic heads, the head material and construction that are suitable
for metal tape have been widely investigated. Combination heads of ferrite and
Sendust (TSS, MIG), and heads using amorphous materials have been important
recent introductions. The amorphous head has a problem in that it cannot fully
magnetize a tape which has a coercivity larger than 1500 Oe.

It seems that the minimum wavelength will be 0.3–0.4 μm. The carrier-to-noise
ratio is generally a function of wavelength (CNR$\propto\lambda^{1-1.5}$), since the shorter the
wavelength the more serious are the space losses between the head and the tape.
On the other hand, it seems that the minimum track pitch will be about 3 μm for
helical systems. Because the signal-to-noise ratio is generally proportional to the
square root of the track pitch (SNR $\propto t_p^{0.5}$), reducing the track pitch has a less
serious effect on the error rate than reducing the wavelength. In reference to the
points mentioned above, several technologies are considered important for future
development: In the first place, the carrier-to-noise ratio and the output from the
tape and head must be increased. Second, the tolerances for head shaping and
mounting, and the tolerances and runability of the mechanism must all be improved. Lastly, dynamic tracking using piezo electric materials must be introduced.

6.5 DEVELOPMENT OF A DIGITAL VIDEO RECORDER

6.5.1 Broadcast Digital Recorder[†]

Since the degradation of picture quality produced by analog recorders appeared
worse in Europe (using PAL and SECAM) than in the United States and Japan
(using NTSC), the development of digital recorders was started earlier in Europe.
Thus, the first digital video tape recorder was demonstrated by the British Broadcasting Corporation at an International Broadcasting Convention (IBC) in 1974. It
utilized a data recorder with 42-channel stationary-head system. The tape speed

[†]The early history of the development of digital video recorders is summarized in the Appendix, Table
6.6.

was 120 in/s, the data rate per channel was 2.6 Mb/s, the sampling frequency was $2f_{sc}$, and a subsampling technique was adopted. The tape width was 1 in and the recording time was 8 min.

In 1975, the Centre Communication d'Études de Télédiffusion et Télécommunications (CCETT) reported a digital video recorder (a modified Ampex Data Recorder FR-2000A) which also used a stationary-head system. This experimental model adopted DPCM coding of the Y, U, V signals decoded from SECAM and had 28 linear tracks on 1-in wide tape. The recording time was 13 min.

At the 13th annual SMPTE television conference in February 1979, Ampex demonstrated a digital video recorder based on a 2-in transversal machine (AVR-3) using 8 video heads. The track pitch was 5 mil and the guard band was 2.5 mil. The tracks for analog audio signals were arranged on the upper edge of the tape, and the tracks for time code and control signals were on the lower edge of the tape. The digital signals were recorded on the video tracks. Sixteen lines of digital video data were recorded on each transverse track. The digital video signal was recorded with 2 channels using a data rate of 43 Mb/s for each channel (Lemoine et al., 1979).

At about the same time, Bosch-Fernseh reported a modified 1-inch Type B video recorder that had a higher drum rotation speed and one-half of the normal tape speed. The track pitch was selected as 50 μm to achieve a higher recording density.

Also in 1979, NHK reported a digital video recorder based on a 1-inch Type C machine (Yokoyama et al., 1979b). In this model, the tape speed was 24.4 cm/s (standard for Type C recorders), and three video heads were used together with one-third of the regular track pitch. This development proved that the recording density of a digital video recorder could be the same as that for the corresponding analog machine.

In the same year, Sony reported a digital recorder based on a 1-in Type C machine (Steele, 1979). It also used three heads, and a track pitch one-third of normal. Two of the heads were used for video recording and one head for audio recording. The video signal was quantized to 8 bits with a sampling frequency equal to $3f_{sc}$. After performing error-correction coding and 8-10 modulation, the recording bit rate became 115 Mb/s. In this machine a recording rate per channel of 57.5 Mb/s was realized. The bit error rate of this system reached $10^{-5} - 10^{-6}$. With this error rate, the picture quality could be made acceptable using 16–17% redundancy for error-correction codes.

Sony reported another digital recorder system in Montreux in 1979. This machine had a video quantizer using 8 bits, a sampling frequency of $2f_{sc}$, a data rate of 80 Mb/s, and the format included 8 channels of audio data using 11.9 Mb/s. This was the first experimental model that recorded both video and audio data simultaneously. At the same time, Sony reported their experiments on interchangeability, and multiple copying characteristics which caused negligible deterioration of the picture after 50 generations.

After various discussions, a digital studio television coding system, specifying sampling frequency and encoding parameters, was recommended as the world standard at the 1982 general meeting of CCIR (see Table 6.2). Later, at the 1986 general meeting of CCIR, a component digital video recording system (4:2:2) based on this digital studio standard was confirmed as the standard for D-1 (Rec 657) and put into practical use. The D-1 video recorder was suitable for digital picture processing because of the high picture quality resulting from the use of component signals, but its high cost restricted its use mainly to production houses.

The television signals and their distribution in broadcasting stations are based on composite signals, therefore a composite digital video recorder was strongly desired. So in 1986 Ampex and Sony proposed jointly to SMPTE a format for a composite digital video recorder (Enberg et al., 1987). This format was confirmed as the D-2 format and has been available since 1988. Somewhat later, NHK and Matsushita introduced a 0.5-in composite digital VTR (Arimura et al., 1988). This format was proposed to SMPTE and confirmed as the D-3 format in 1993, and it has been in the marketplace since 1991.

6.5.2 Consumer Digital Recorder[†]

The development of a consumer digital video recorder was started in the latter half of the 1970s. The main elements were bit-reduction techniques with minor degradation of the picture quality, and high-density recording techniques taking into consideration the efficiency of the tape, head, modulation, detection and error correction.

In 1980, Sony reported the first experimental VTR using twice the drum rotation speed of the 0.5-inch β system. The recorded video data rate was 28.6 Mb/s. An NTSC signal was encoded using an intra-field sub-Nyquist sampling frequency of $2 f_{sc}$. The samples were divided into the sum and difference components between two lines. Each component was coded into 4 bits using a DPCM technique in which the prediction value was the previous sample for the sum component and two samples earlier for the difference component. The recording time was one hour (Yoshioka et al., 1980). In 1985, Hitachi used a VHS cassette and MP tape. The data rate was 86 Mb/s utilizing $3f_{sc}$, and 8-bit sampling was used. The recording time was one hour (Mita et al., 1983, 1985).

In 1986, Matsushita demonstrated a digital video recorder using a VHS cassette and ME tape. An NTSC signal was encoded using an inter-field sub-Nyquist sampling frequency of $2f_{sc}$. An 8th-order Hadamard transform coding with 4×2 pixel blocks was utilized, and the average bit rate was 4.5 bit/pixel. The recording time was two hours. This experimental recorder was the first one using the same drum rotation as a regular VHS machine (Yamamitsu et al., 1986).

Also in 1986, JVC developed a VHS cassette-based recorder. A bit-rate reduction system using intra-field sub-Nyquist sampling and two dimensional DPCM was used. The recording time was 2 hours (Hirota et al., 1986).

In 1986 Philips introduced a digital video recorder based on their V-2000 consumer recorder. A PAL signal was encoded using intra-field sub-Nyquist sampling. A two-dimensional DPCM or Hadamard transform was performed. The prediction value in DPCM was obtained from 9 pixels. Each differential value was coded into 3 bits using one encoder for small differential values and another encoder for large values. The use of two encoders decreased the error propagation. The Hadamard transform was performed for 4×4 pixel blocks (Driessen et al., 1986).

In 1987, Matsushita introduced a vector quantization system, which modified the experimental model which they had reported in 1986. This code improved the degradation of oblique lines and sharp edges in the picture. Metal-evaporated tape of 10 μm thickness was used in a VHS cassette. A recording time of 12 hours was realized using a 9.7 μm track pitch. A modified 8-10 code was adopted to improve error detection performance (Yamamitsu et al., 1987).

Also, in 1987 Sanyo developed a recorder using a VHS cassette and MP tape. An NTSC signal was encoded using $3f_{sc}$ and 8-bit sampling. The recording time was 2 hours (Nishikawa et al., 1987).

In the same year, Sony used an 8 mm cassette and ME tape of 10 μm thickness.

[†]The historical development of consumer digital tape recorders is summarized in the Appendix, Tables 6.7a, b.

The 3:1:0 component signal was coded by "adaptive dynamic range coding" that divided a picture into four pixel blocks, and assigned 0 to 4 bits to each block depending on the dynamic range. The recording time was 80 minutes (Kondo et al., 1987).

In 1988, Matsushita used an 8 mm cassette and ME tape of 10 μm thickness and, for the first time, used the same drum rotation speed as the analog 8 mm system. The bit-rate reduction technique was the same as the one used in the 1987 model. Scrambled NRZI was selected for channel coding and Class IV partial response was used. The recording time was one hour (Yamamitsu et al., 1988).

Also in 1988 Philips used an 8 mm cassette and MP tape. The 3:1:0 component signal was divided into 8 × 8 pixel blocks and coded using DCT technique, and the Huffman coding for variable length coding was adopted (Borgers et al., 1988).

Separately, Thomson used an 8 mm ME tape of 10 μm thickness and a special mechanism called the "matrix scan recording" that drove the drum rotation and an up/down movement to record parallel tracks on the tape. DCT and VLC were adopted for bit-rate reduction. Intra-frame DCT (8 × 8) or intra-field DCT (4 × 8 × 2) was selected based on the motion detection (Platte et al., 1988).

In 1988 NEC developed a system using a β cassette and MP tape. The component signal was divided into 8 × 8 pixel blocks and each block was coded using an optimized predictive code which was selected from seven kinds of prediction codes to minimize the degradation. The input data rate was reduced to 30 Mb/s. The 8-9 code was used as channel code (Itoi et al., 1988).

In 1989, Matsushita reported a 3-hour recording model using an 8 mm cassette and ME tape. The areal density was 2.39 μm^2/bit with 6.8 μm track pitch. A 4:1:1 input video signal was adopted to increase the bandwidth. The input data rate was lowered to 19 Mb/s by intra-field 8 × 8 DCT and VLC. This model was the first one used for experimental still, slow, and search modes with and without dynamic track following (DTF). The audio signals were recorded digitally using 48 kHz, 16 bits, and 2 channels (Yamamitsu et al., 1989).

In 1990, Sony reached a high recording density ($w = 5.5 \mu$m , $\lambda = 0.5 \mu$m) on an 8 mm cassette using advanced ME tape. The 3:1:0 video signal was coded by an adaptive dynamic range coding (ADRC) algorithm (Kanota et al., 1990). Additionally, Canon reported a high-definition (HD) base-band recorder using 1/2-in MP tape with a recording length of 90 minutes. The HD signal was encoded using sub-Nyquist sampling and DPCM coding (Kashida et al., 1987).

More recently, a consumer digital video recorder for NTSC, PAL, and SECAM systems was proposed as a standard by ten companies in July 1993. It was introduced by Matsushita and Sony in the marketplace in 1995.

6.6 EXAMPLES OF DIGITAL VIDEO RECORDERS

6.6.1 Broadcast Video Recorders

There are three formats for recording our current television signal standards: D-1, D-2, and D-3. The recorded patterns on the tape are shown in Fig. 6.16. Sync block, helical-track structures, and specifications are summarized in the Appendix, Table 6.8 and Fig 6.22. There is a separate format for high definition (HD) television signals.

6.6.1.1 D-1 Video Recorder. This format is known as "4:2:2 component digital VTR." The luminance signal is sampled at a clock rate of 13.5 MHz, while the color

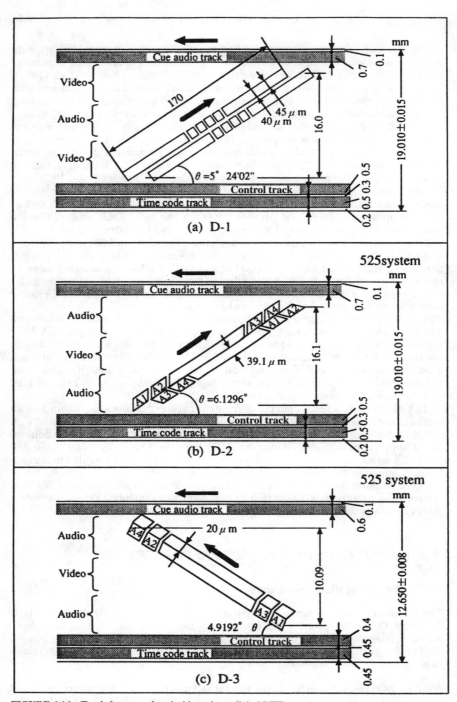

FIGURE 6.16 Track formats of typical broadcast digital VTRs.

difference signals, $R - Y$ and $B - Y$, are sampled at 6.75 MHz. This video recorder is the first one in the world that can operate on both 525/60 and 625/50 TV standards. Each active TV line has 720 samples for the luminance signal, while 360 samples for each line are used for the two color difference signals. The number of active lines is 250 lines for the 525/60 standard, and 300 lines for the 625/50 standard. Each of four audio channels is sampled at 48 kHz and quantized to 20 bits (CCIR 646). The audio data are recorded twice for redundancy in the center of track, where "dropouts" are few. Oxide tape (850 Oe) and ferrite heads are used for this VTR, with a head width of 40 μm, and a track width of 45 μm. A flying erase head is required for editing. The picture is horizontally divided into five parts and data shuffling is performed in each part. Preamble and postamble data is included in each audio and video sector to make clock recovery stable.

6.6.1.2 D-2 Video Recorder. This format is known as "composite digital VTR." Recorded video data are 768(948) samples per line and 255(304) lines per field in the 525/60 (625/50) systems, respectively. The same three sizes of cassettes are used as for D-1, but a different tape is used, namely MP with a coercivity of 1500 Oe. Each of four audio channels is sampled at 48 kHz and quantized using 20 bits (CCIR 646). The audio data are recorded twice on the video track at both edges of the tape. Azimuth recording is employed without guard band, and the track width is 39.1 μm. An erase head is not essential, although recent models do use one. The picture is divided into three parts and data shuffling is performed in each part. For the NTSC system, the audio sampling frequency of 48 kHz cannot be directly synchronized with the video field frequency, because the latter is 60 kHz/1.001. Therefore five consecutive fields are used as one unit, and 801 audio samples are recorded in each of four fields while 800 audio samples are recorded in the fifth field. The same process has been introduced in the D-3 recorders. This process can be compared with the D-1 system, in which five consecutive frames are used as one unit, and 1602 audio samples are recorded in four frames and 1600 audio samples are recorded in the fifth frame.

6.6.1.3 D-3 Video Recorder. In this format, the recorded data are the same as for the D-2 recorder. The format was originally created to make a digital camcorder using 0.5-in tape and small cassettes. The area packing density is about 2.4 times higher than that of D-2 and volume packing density is about 3 times higher than D-2. Each of the four audio signals is sampled at 48 kHz and quantized to 20 bits (CCIR 646). The audio data are recorded at both edges of the tape. The data are not duplicated but the power of error correction is increased by increasing the parity data. Metal powder tape (1600 Oe) of 11 μm thickness is used. The video shuffling area is enlarged to one field, which is the largest possible area considering field editing capability, and this feature improves the error correction and concealment performance. A new technique to improve editing and compatibility performances for narrow track widths of 20 μm was introduced. This was done by creating a guard band which is maintained for editing points only, as shown in Fig. 6.17 (Nakayama et al., 1992).

6.6.2 Requirements for a Consumer Digital Video Recorder

The most important requirement is for high picture and audio quality, superior to that of a conventional analog video recorder. For video sampling, 4:1:1/4:2:0 or an even higher rate is required to maintain the video bandwidth. For the audio signal,

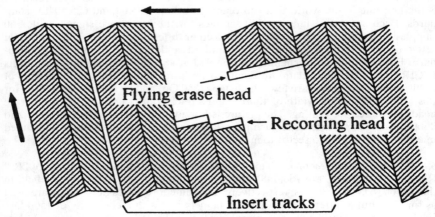

FIGURE 6.17   Flying erase performance for edit-point guard band.

at least 2 channels with 48 kHz sampling and 16-bit quantizing are needed. An extension to 4-channel recording with some kind of special processing has also been demanded.

Extension to "movie," "personal," and "table" types of applications must be possible. A recording time of 1 or 2 hours is needed for a high-quality movie recorder, whereas 3 or 4 hours is necessary for a table-top recorder. In the future, the size, power consumption, and weight of a movie recorder must be superior to the conventional analog models.

Extension to record new television standards will also be required. These include recording 16:9 wide screen TV, ED-TV, MAC, MUSE/HD-MAC.

Independent editing between video and audio, and independent edits between audio channels should be possible. Also, an edit accuracy of one frame will be required, because the distinction between professional and consumer use will eventually disappear.

Finally, longer playing time will be required. This will necessitate the use of narrower track widths and a higher ratio of bit-rate reduction.

6.6.3 Proposed Consumer Digital Video Recorder

The basic specifications of a digital video recorder for consumer use were presented in July 1993. This proposed VTR has two types of cassette on which a standard component video signal can be recorded for one hour, and for 4.5 hours, respectively. The tape is 6.35 mm-wide ME, the track width is 10 μm, and the minimum wavelength is 0.488 μm (Table 6.4). This level of high-density recording, in combination with bit-rate reduction of the video data down to 25 Mb/s, enables the long recording times to be obtained in a small cassette. Other parameters of this proposed standard are shown in Table 6.5.

6.6.3.1 Tape Pattern.   This new digital video recorder is based on the CCIR Rec. 601 data format (See Table 6.2). As illustrated in Fig. 6.18, there are 10 tracks for one video frame in the 525/60 standard or 12 tracks for one frame in the 625/50 standard. The recorder has a drum diameter of 21.7 mm and the rotational speed is 9000 rpm. Single channel and azimuth recording without guard band are used. The audio signals can be recoded in two ways: (a) 48 kHz sampling with 16-bit quantizing in 2 channels, and (b) 32 kHz sampling with 12-bit quantizing in 4 channels. One burst of audio data is independently located in each track. For the 525/60 system, one channel of (a) is recorded in the first 5 tracks of the frame while the other channel is recorded in the following 5 tracks of the same frame. For the 625/50 system, one channel of (a) is recorded in the first 6 tracks of the same frame (see Fig. 6.18). In case (a), the audio is recorded in two pairs of channels in a similar manner.

TABLE 6.4 Specification of Cassette and Tape of a Proposed Consumer Digital Video Recorder

	Standard cassette	Small cassette
Recording time	4.5 hours	1 hour
Cassette size (mm)	125 × 78 × 14.6	66 × 48 × 12.2
Tape length (m)	311	71.4
Tape thickness (μm)	7	
Track pitch (μm)	10	
Minimum wave length (μm)	0.488	
Azimuth angle (°)	$\pm$ 20°	
Linear density	104 kb/in	
Area density	2.65 Mb/in^2	
Tape	ME or equivalent tape	
Tape consumption	0.43 m^2/hour	

TABLE 6.5 Specification of Signal Processing of a Proposed Consumer Digital Video Recorder

Video input	Y:	13.5 MHz	(8 bits)
	R − Y, B − Y:	6.75 MHz	(8 bits)
Audio input	2ch-mode:	48, 44.1, 32 kHz	(16 bits)
	4ch-mode:	32 kHz	(12 bits)
ECC	Video: Reed-Solomon product code		
	$\quad$ inner (85, 77) on GF (2^8)		
	$\quad$ outer (149, 138) on GF (2^8)		
	Audio: Reed-Solomon product code		
	$\quad$ inner (85, 77) on GF (2^8)		
	$\quad$ outer (14, 9) on GF (2^8)		
	Subcode: (14, 10) Reed-Solomon code		
Modulation	24/25		
	(Scramble-interleaved NRZI)		
Data rate	Video: $\quad$ 24.95 Mb/s		
	Audio: $\quad$ 1.56 Mb/s		
	Others: $\quad$ 0.81 Mb/s		
Recording data rate	41.85 Mb/s		
Number of tracks per frame	10 tracks / frame (525/60)		
	12 tracks / frame (625/50)		

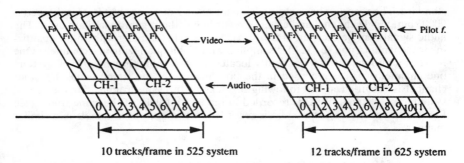

10 tracks/frame in 525 system   12 tracks/frame in 625 system

Remark : Numbers of tracks per HD frame are double of SD's

FIGURE 6.18   Track format of a proposed consumer digital VTR.

6.6.3.2   Bit-Rate Reduction.   The 4:2:2 sampled signal is reduced to 4:1:1 for the 525/60 standard and to 4:2:0 for the 625/50 standard. With the 625/50 standard, the line sequential construction seems to be acceptable, and the 4:2:0 reduction has been adopted for both MAC and HD-MAC systems. However, in the case of the 525 line standard viewed with a large TV monitor, the line sequential construction for the chrominance signals is not acceptable, and for this reason it was not adopted for the 525/60 system.

The method used for bit-rate reduction is shown in Fig. 6.19*a–i*. The compression of the frame data is divided into 8×8 DCT blocks as shown at (*a*), while the number of DCT blocks is shown at (*b*). A macro block consists of four DCT blocks for the luminance signal and two DCT blocks for each chrominance signal as indicated at (*c*). A shuffling technique based on macro blocks was adopted to improve the picture quality, although the variable-length codes are limited within this small size. This technique was selected in consideration of both error propagation and to allow special effect playback modes. In general, random shuffling is better for the normal play mode, and local shuffling is more suitable for providing special effect play modes (see (*d*)). After DCT and weighting as indicated at (*e*), the dc coefficient is transmitted as 9 bits and the ac coefficients are coded after adaptive quantization. The amount of data for the ac coefficients is controlled by a feed-forward technique to maintain a fixed amount for each group of 30 DCT blocks. The quantization is applied as follows: each DCT block is classified into one of four classes according to the maximum of the absolute value of an ac coefficient in a DCT block (see (*f*)). The ac coefficients are divided into four areas (see (*h*)) and the optimum quantizer among the sixteen possibilities from combination of classes and areas is selected by calculating the data amount for each quantizer (see (*g*)). The quantization step sizes use only the power of two to make the hardware less complex. Each ac coefficient after quantization has 10 bits, 1 bit for sign and 9 bits for absolute value. Both the class number and the quantizer number are transmitted.

A simple motion detection technique is adopted to select the intra-frame DCT mode in the normal case, and the intra-field DCT mode in special cases involving motion. The information of these DCT modes is transmitted with the data.

The variable length codes for the ac coefficients of each DCT block are transmitted in order, from the lower frequency components to the higher frequency components. The variable length codes use modified two-dimensional Huffman codes. A sync block includes all or the major part of the compressed data of the macro block. The order of sync blocks is rearranged into one frame period to record (see (*i*)).

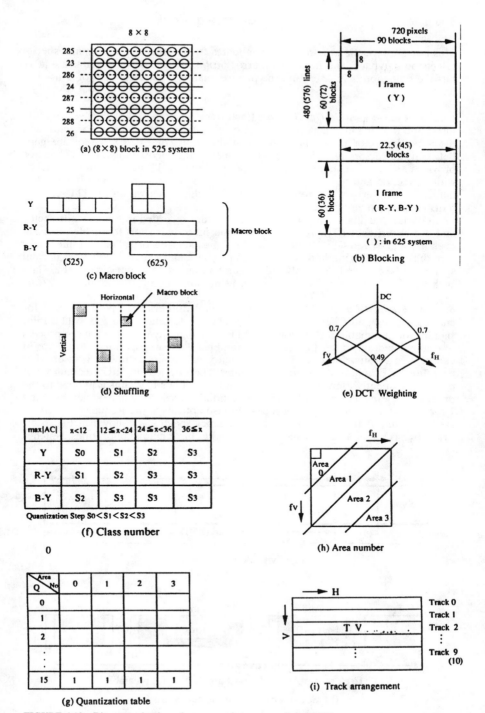

FIGURE 6.19   Bit-rate reduction of a proposed consumer digital VTR.

6.29

This bit-rate reduction method accommodates frame accurate editing, and special effects on playback, and it has small error propagation. The video data rate after bit-rate reduction is 25 Mb/s and the picture quality is good enough for consumer use.

6.6.3.3 Contents within One Track.   Each track is composed of four sectors: the insert and tracking information (ITI) sector, the audio sector, the video sector, and the subcode sector in the head scanning direction (Fig. 6.20). There are gaps between the sectors in order to establish independent editability. The ITI sector provides information about the starting point of the track, the position in the track width direction and so forth. During editing, the ITI is not erased and it is used to detect tracking errors. Therefore, the level of pilot signal within the ITI sector is 6 dB higher than elsewhere on the track.

Important auxiliary data such as time code are recorded in the subcode sector and it is re-writeable. The block length of the subcode is short to enable playback even in a high-speed search mode. And the same data is recorded on multiple tracks (sectors). Using this method of high speed playback and search at 200 times normal speed can be realized. Not only video data and audio data, but also various data such as Tele-Text data, can be recorded using both the video and audio sectors.

6.6.3.4 Channel Coding (Modulation).   Scrambled-interleaved NRZI is used for channel coding and Class IV partial response for detection (see Fig. 6.11). Pilot signals, for automatic track following (ATF), are digitally generated in the process of channel coding. In this process, the scrambled data are partitioned to groups of consecutive 24 bits, and one bit (0 or 1) that is called an "extra bit" is inserted at each border of adjacent partitioned groups. The interleaved NRZI coding takes place subsequently. Because transformation from 24 bits to 25 bits is applied to the process of coding, it is called "24/25 modulation." By selecting one bit among 0 and 1 for the extra bit, not only pilot tones but also notches in the frequency spectrum are generated at frequencies f_1 or f_2. Frequency spectra are shown in Fig. 6.21. Track F_0 has no pilot tone, while tracks F_1 and F_2 have unique pilot tones. Notches

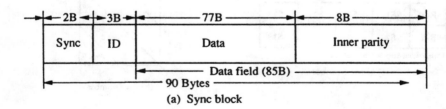

(a) Sync block

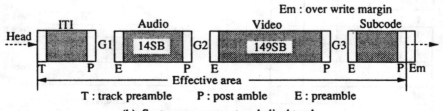

(b) Sector arrangement on helical track

FIGURE 6.20   Sync block and helical track structure of a proposed consumer digital VTR.

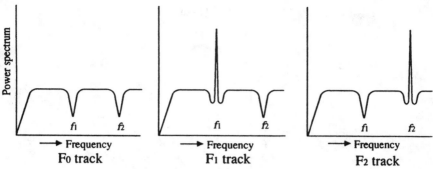

FIGURE 6.21   Spectrum of digital pilots by 24–25 modulation.

are generated in order to achieve high-quality tracking error information. Tracks are in the order of F_0, F_1, F_0, F_2, F_0, F_1 . . . in the longitudinal direction of the tape (see Fig. 6.18).

6.6.3.5   Digital Interface.   The recorder has a digital interface I/O for multiplexed bit-reduced video, audio data, and other auxiliary information. Using this interface, copying without degradation of picture quality can be performed. It will be possible to use this interface for communicating with other digital television broadcast standards and with digital data in general.

6.7   FUTURE PROSPECTS

In the broadcast field, it can be expected that small and lightweight video recorders using ME tape will be developed for both conventional and high-definition television systems. Bit-rate reduction will be introduced for 525/60 and 625/50 standards, and bit-rate reduction will also be used to develop high-definition video recorders based upon the D-1, D-2, and D-3 configurations.

In the consumer digital field, it is expected that longer playing times will be provided using a higher-bit rate reduction ratio and/or a narrower track width (5–6 μm), and products will become readily available that can handle NTSC, PAL, and SECAM standards. Also VTRs will be developed to meet new standards, such as the high-definition digital broadcasting standard (ATV) in the USA. The proposed consumer recorder already described can record at 25 Mb/s bit rate which is higher than the 19 Mb/s proposed for the US HDTV standard. A high-definition, baseband video recorder could also be based on the proposed consumer digital recorder, but would require doubling the bit rate (50 Mb/s), doubling the tape speed, and doubling the number of video heads.

Finally, the proposed VTR could be extended to data storage and multimedia applications with the capability of recording 40–50 GB of data.

APPENDIX

Relevant historical developments and technical data are summarized in Tables 6.6, 6.7a, 6.7b, and 6.8, and in Fig. 6.22.

APPENDIX TABLE 6.6 Historical Development of Experimental Digital Video Recorders for Broadcast Use

Year	Source	Encoding parameters	Mechanism	Relative speed Tape speed	Density Bit rate	Time (min)	Modulation	ECC A	ECC B
1974	BBC	$2f_{sc}$ PAL 8 bits	1″42 tracks fixed head	3.04 m/s	20 Kbpi 109 Mb/s	8	MFM	○	
1975	CCETT	Y, U V (SECAM) Component 8 bits	1″28 tracks fixed head	3.43 m/s	21.2 Kbpi 50 Mb/s	13	?	○	
1976–8 (IBC)	IBA	$2f_{sc}$ PAL 8 bits	1″ type B 2″ heads	47.4 m/s (9.6 in/s)	42.86 Kbpi 80 Mb/s	90	8-10		○
1979 (SMPTE)	Ampex	$3f_{sc}$ NTSC 8 bits	2″ transverse 8 heads	40.6 m/s (15 in/s)	27 Kbpi 86 Mb/s	90	M^2		○
1979	NHK	$3f_{sc}$ NTSC 8 bits	1″ type C Para-3 tracks	25.6 m/s (9.6 in/s)	34.5 Kbpi 104 Mb/s	90	I-NRZI PR (1,0,−1)	○	○
1979 (NAB)	Sony	$3f_{sc}$ NTSC 8 bits	1″ type C Para-3 tracks V-2, A-1	25.6 m/s (9.6 in/s)	57.5 Kbpi 115 Mb/s	90	8-10	○	○

Year	Company	Format	Head configuration	Tape speed	Density			With
1979 (Montreux)	Ampex	$4f_{sc}$ PAL 8 bits	2" transverse 8 heads Para-2 tracks	53.3 m/s (6.6 in/s)	33 Kbpi 135 Mb/s	200	M^2	O
1979 (Montreux)	Bosch	$2f_{sc}$ PAL 8 bits	1" type B 2 heads	47.4 m/s (4.8 in/s)	42.3 Kbpi 80 Mb/s	180	8-10	O
1979 (Montreux)	Sony	$2f_{sc}$ PAL 8 bits	1" type C Para-3 tracks V-2, A-1	21.39 m/s (9.4 in/s)	47.5 Kbpi 80 Mb/s	90	8-10	O O
1980	Sony	$4f_{sc}$ NTSC 8 bits	1" type C 4 heads (4ch)			180		
1980	IBA	Component 8 bits 12:4:4	1" type B			—		
1980	Sony	Component 8 bits 12:4:4	1" type C 4 heads (4ch)			90		

Notes: A: correction   B: concealment   O: with.

6.33

APPENDIX TABLE 6.7a Development of Experimental Digital Video Recorders for Consumer Use

	Sony	Matsushita	JVC	Philips	Hitachi	Sanyo	Cannon (HDTV)
Announcement Publication	1987.10	1987.6	1986.4	1986.6	1985.2	1987.10	1987.10
Tape width, Drum rotation (rpm) Diameter, Head, Channel number, Relative speed (m/s)	8mm, 3600, 40φ 1CH×2 7.5	1/2", 1800, 62φ 2CH×2 5.8	1/2", 3600, 62φ 2CH×2 11.6	1/2", 1500, 65φ 2CH×2 5.08	1/2", 5400, 62φ 2CH×2 17.4	1/2", 3600 2CH×2 11.6	1/2", 3600, 62φ 3CH×2 11.6
Tape speed (mm/s)	21.5	11.0	33.35	—	133	50.0	33.35
Track pitch (μm)	15	9.7	15	11	40	21.6	15
Minimum wave length (μm)	0.5	0.57	1.3	0.84	0.72	0.64	0.5
Linear density (kb/inch)	102	89	32	60	71	75	102
Areal density ($\mu\,m^2/b$)	3.8	2.8	9.4	4.6	14.4	6.9	3.8
Tape material	Metal Evaporated (H_c = 1150 Oe)	Metal Evaporated	Metal Oxide	CrO_2	Metal Powder (H_c = 1300 Oe)	Metal powder (H_c = 1500 Oe)	Metal powder
Video coding	Component 3:1:0 8 bit LSQ	Composite ($4f_{sc}$) 8 bit	Composite ($4f_{sc}$) 7 bit	Composite ($4f_{sc}$) 7 bit PAL	Composite ($3f_{sc}$) & Component 2: 2/1 : 2/1 8 bit	Composite ($3f_{sc}$) 6 bit	Component *1 8 bit LSQ

Input data rate (Mb/s)	108	115	100	142	86	64.4	648
Bit rate reduction	Adaptive Dynamic range coding Motion adaptive frame decimation	Field offset subsampling Hadarmard transformation (2 × 4) + VQ 4.5 bit	Field offset subsampling DPCM (2-dimensional prediction) 4 bit	Intrafield subsampling DPCM (2-dimentional prediction) 3 bit including Hadarmard transformation	—	—	Field offset subsampling DPCM (1-dimensional prediction) 4 bit
Video bit rate (Mb/s)	25	25	22	22	68	52	112
Recording rate (Mb/s)	30	40	35.7	24	96	68.5	138
Modulation	Scrambled NRZ	Modified 8–10	8–10	NRZI	8–9	Scrambled NRZ	NRZI
Detection	Partial response	Integrated detection	—	Partial response	Integrated detection	Integrated detection	Integrated detection
Error correction code	—	Reed-Solomon Error detection by 8–10	Reed-Solomon	Simple Reed-Solomon	Hamming fire/ b-adjacent	Reed-Solomon	Reed-Solomon
Audio (sampling quantizing channel, others)	No recording	No recording	No recording	No recording	No recording	44.1 kHz, 14 bit 2 Channel	No recording
Recording time (min)	80	720	120	480	30 (60)	120	90 *2
Remark	Tape thickness 10 μm	Tape thickness 10 μm					*1 Y : 64.8 MHz (4:1:0) *2 T – 160

APPENDIX TABLE 6.7b Development of Experimental Digital Video Recorders for Consumer Use

Announcement Publication	Matsushita 1986.3	Matsushita 1988.6	Sony 1980.12	Philips 1988.6	Thomson 1988.6	Matsushita 1989.6	Sony 1990.6
Tape width, Drum rotation (rpm) Diameter, Head, Channel Relative number, speed (m/s)	1/2", 1800, 62φ, 2CH×2, 5.8	8mm, 1800, 40φ, 2CH×2, 3.75	1/2", 3600, 74.5φ, 1CH×2, 14	8mm, 4500, 40φ, 2CH×1, 9.4	8mm, Special 23φ mechanical matrix scan, 1CH, -	8mm, 4500, 1CH×2, 9.4	8mm, 9000, 2CH×1, 7.8
Tape speed (mm/s)	33.35	28.6	40.0	-	-	11.8	-
Track pitch (μm)	29	20.5	30	11	10	6.8	5.5
Minimum wave length (μm)	0.57	0.47	1.0	0.68	0.7	0.69	0.49
Linear density (kb/in)	71	109	52	59.8	58.1	73	103
Areal density (μm^2/b)	8.3	4.8	14.3	4.8	4.5	2.39	1.35
Tape material	Metal oxide	Metal evaporated	CrO_2	Metal powder	Metal powder	Metal evaporated	Improved metal evaporated
Video coding	Composite ($4f_{sc}$) 8 bit	Composite ($4f_{sc}$) 8 bit	Composite ($4f_{sc}$) 7 bit	Component 3:1:0 8 bit LSQ	Component 3:1:0 8 bit LSQ	Component 4:1:1	Component 3:1:0 LSQ
Input data rate (Mb/s)	115	115	100	108	108	162	108

Bit rate reduction	Field offset subsampling Hadamard transformation 4.5 bit	Field offset subsampling Hadamard transformation (2 × 4) + VQ 4.5 bit	Intrafield subsampling (2HPALE) Sum/Diff DPCM (1-dimensional prediction) 4 bit	Block 8 × 8 Intra frame DCT VLC	Block 8 × 8 (4 × 8) × 2 Motion adaptive intrafield Intraframe DCT	block 8 × 8 Intra field DCT VLC	Adaptive Dynamic range coding (ADRC)
Video bit rate (Mb/s)	25	25	22	19	12.4	19	25
Recording rate (Mb/s)	40	32	28.6	26.0	19.4*	27	31.56
Modulation	Improved 8–10	Interleaved NRZI	Scrambled NRZI	Improved 8–10	Improved 8–10	Interleaved NRZI	M Scrambled NRZ
Detection	Integrated detection	Partial response	Integrated detection	Integrated detection	Integrated detection	Partial response (1, 0, −1)	Partial response (1, 0, −1)
Error correction code	Chain code (Inner, outer)	Reed-Solomon	Chain code (Inner, outer)	Reed-Solomon	Reed-Solomon	Reed-Solomon	Reed-Solomon
Audio (sampling quatizing channel, others)	No recording	No recording	Recorded with video	No recording	Recording with compression (256 kb/s)	48 kHz, 16 bit 2-Channel	—
Recording time (min)	120	60	60*1	105	210	180	—
Remark		Tape thickness 10 μm	*L-500 Cassette		*presumed		including presumed value

6.37

APPENDIX TABLE 6.8 Comparative Specification of Broadcast Digital Video Recorders

Items	D-1	D-2	D-3
Tapewidth (mm)	19.01	19.01	12.7
Drum rotation (rpm),	9000	5400 (6000)	5400 (6000)
Drum diameter & Head construction & wrap angle (degree)	75φ, 270°	96.4φ, 178.2°, 27.4 (30.5)	76φ, 178.1°, 21.4 (23.8)
Channel relative number speed (m/s)	2CH×2, 35.0 m/s	2CH×2	2CH×2
Tape speed (mm/s)	286.6 (286.9)	131.7	83.88
Track pitch (μm)	45 (Head width 40)	39.1 (35.2)	20 (18)
Minimum wave length (μm)	0.9	0.854 (0.79)	0.77 (0.71)
Linear density (bit/in)	56K	59K (64.3K)	75K (82K)
Areal density (μm^2/bit)	18	16.7 (13.9)	6.8 (5.6)
Tape consumption (m^2/hr)	19.61	9.01	3.82
Azimuth angle (°)	0	± 15	± 20
Tape	Improved Oxide $H_c \geq 850$ Oe	Metal—Powder $H_c \geq 1500$ Oe	$H_c \geq 1600$ Oe
Video encoding	Component (4:2:2) 8 bits Rec-601	Composite ($4f_{sc}$) 8 bits SMPTE	
Video input data rate (b/s)	216 M	115M	(142 M)
<Effective amount (b/s)>	<167M>	<94 M>	<115 M>

6.38

	227 M	127 M (153M)	125M (152M)
Recording data rate (b/s)			
Modulation	Scrambled NRZ	M²	Optimal 8–14
Detection	Integrated	Integrated	Integrated
ECC (inner × outer)		Reed-Solomon Product Code	
NTSC Video	RS(64,60) ×RS(32,30)	RS(93,85) / RS(95,87) ×RS(68,64) ×RS(12, 8)	RS(95,87) / RS(136,128) ×RS(16, 8)
NTSC Audio	outer ×RS(10,7)		
PAL Video	Same as above	RS(86,78) / RS(84,76) ×RS(83,79) ×RS(12, 8)	RS(86,78) / RS(166,158) ×RS(16, 8)
PAL Audio	outer		
Audio		48 KHz, 20 bit, 4 channel	
Recording time (min.)	S 11 13 M 34 41 L 76 94	32 94 208	64 125 245
Size (mm)	S 172×109×33 M 254×150×33 L 366×206×33		161×98×25 212×124×25 296×167×25
Thickness (µm)	16 13	13	11
Digital interface	CCIR 656 (Video) CCIR 647 (Audio)	SMPTE 244M, IEC 1179, SMPTE 259M	
VTR standard	CCIR 657	SMPTE 245 M~248M 226M	SMPTE 263M, 264M, 265M

NOTE: ( ) Value of PAL standard. S: small; M: middle; L: large

6.39

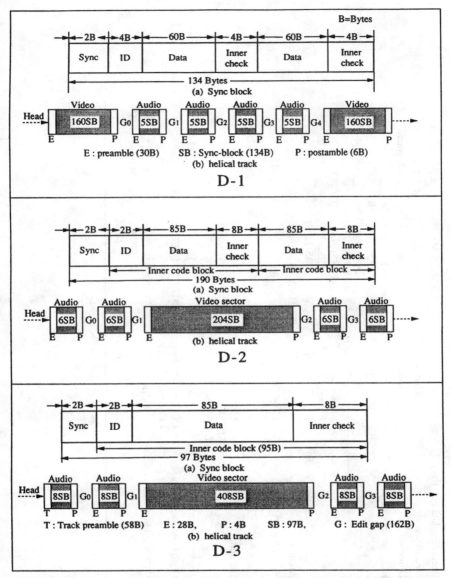

FIGURE 6.22   Sync block and helical-track structures of typical broadcast digital VTRs.

REFERENCES

Arimura, I., J. Hamalainen, M. Matsui, and C. Yamamitsu, "Feasibility of New Broadcast Digital VTR," *130th SMPTE Technical Conference,* No. 142 (1988).

Baldwin, J. L. E., "Digital Television Recording with Low Tape Consumption," *Intl. Broadcast. Conv. Rec.,* 133 (1978).

Baldwin, J. L. E., "Digital Television Recording–History and Background," *J. SMPTE,* **95,** 1206 (1986).

Borgers, S. M. C., W. A. L. Heijnemans, E. de Niet, and P. H. N. de With, "An Experimental Digital VCR with 40 mm Drum, Single Actuator and DCT-based Bit-Rate Reduction," *IEEE Trans. Consum. Electron.,* **CE-34,** 597 (1988).

Driessen, L. M. H. E., W. A. L. Heijnemans, E. de Niet, J. H. Peters, and A. M. A. Rijckaert, "An Experimental Digital Video Recording System," *IEEE Trans. Consum. Electron.,* **CE-32** (1986).

Enberg, E. et al., "The Composite Digital Format and Its Applications," *J. SMPTE,* **96,** 934 (1987).

Eto, Y., S. Mita, Y. Hirano, and T. Kawamura, "Experimental Digital VTR with Trilevel Recording and Fire Code Error Correction," *J. SMPTE,* **90,** 611 (1981).

Fujiwara, Y., T. Eguchi, and K. Ike, "Tape Selection and Mechanical Considerations for 4:2:2 DVTR," *J. SMPTE,* **93,** 818 (1984).

Geddes, W. K. E., "Dropouts in Video Tape Recording," BBC Monograph No. 57, 5, 1965.

Godall, W., "Television by Pulse Code Modulation," *Bell Syst. Tech. J.,* **30,** 33 (1951).

Goldberg, A., "PCM Encoded NTSC Color Television Subjective Test," *J. SMPTE,* **82,** 649 (1973).

Hashimoto, Y., and T. Eguchi, "One-Inch Digital VTR" (Japanese), Tech. Group on Magnetic Recording, *IECE Jpn. Tech. Rep.,* **MR79-42** (1980).

Heitmann, J., "Digital Video Recording: New Result in Channel Coding and Error Protection," *J. SMPTE,* **93,** 140 (1984).

Hirota, A., S. Hirano, and S. Higurashi, "Picture Coding for Home VTR," *Picture Coding Symposium,* **8,** 12 (1986).

Hopkins, "Progress Report on Digital Video Standards," *J. SMPTE,* **87,** 391 (1978).

Huber, W. D., "Simultaneous and Orthogonally Interactive Clock Recovery DC Null Equalization in High Density Magnetic Recording," *IEEE Trans. Magn.,* **MAG-19,** 1716 (1983).

Ishida, J., "Television Signal Codes" (Japanese), *NHK Tech. Rep.,* **13,** 169 (1970).

Ishida, J., "Design Basis of PCM Television Transmission System" (Japanese), *Trans. IECE Jpn.,* **J54-A,** 589 (1971).

Itoi, S., S. Hirata, R. Kawanaka, K. Tagami, K. Ohshima, S. Obara, and M. Ashibe, "An Experiment of Half Inch Consumer Digital VTR" (Japanese), *ITEJ Tech. Rep.,* **12,** 25 (1988).

Kameyama, et al., "Study of High Density Magnetic Drum Equipment" (Japanese), *IEICE Tech. Rep.,* **MR73-24** (1973).

Kanota, K., H. Inoue, A. Uetake, M. Kawaguchi, K. Chiba, and Y. Kubota, "A High Density Recording Technology for Digital VCRs," *IEEE Trans. Consum. Electron.,* **CE-36,** 540 (1990).

Kashida, M., S. Yamashita, Y. Ishii, M. Shimokoriyama, and A. Shikakura, "An Experimental High Definition Digital Video Recorder" (Japanese), *ITEJ Tech. Rep.,* **11,** 37 (1987).

Katayama, H., K. Yokoyama, and S. Nakagawa, "An Equalizing Method of Recording Pulse Waveforms for NRZ Recording" (Japanese), *Seventh Ann. Conf. Rec. Magn. Soc. Jpn.,* **PA-14,** 25 (1975).

Katayama, H., K. Yokoyama, and S. Nakagawa, "A High Speed ATC For NRZI Recording" (Japanese), *IECE Jpn., Nat. Conv. Rec.,* 199 (1976).

Kobayashi, H., and D. T. Tang, "Application of Partial Response Channel Coding to Magnetic Recording Systems," *IBM J. Res. Dev.,* **14,** 368 (1970).

Kobayashi, M., H. Ohta, E. Nakatsu, H. Shimazaki, and Y. Nagaoka, "A Study of Multilevel Signal Recording for Digital VCR" (Japanese), *ITEJ Tech. Rep.,* **13,** 1 (1989).

Kondo, T., N. Shirota, and K. Kanota, "Adaptive Dynamic Range Coding Scheme for Future Consumer Digital VTR" (Japanese), *ITEJ Tech. Rep.,* **11,** 19 (1987).

Kretzmer, E. R., "Generalization of a Technique for Binary Data Transmission," *IEEE Trans. Commun.,* **COM-14,** 67 (1966).

Lemoine, M., and J. Dierman, "Digital Video Recording–A Progress Report, Digital Video," *SMPTE,* **2,** 139 (1979).

Mallinson, J. C., and J. Miller, "Optimal Codes for Digital Magnetic Recording," *Radio Electron. Eng.,* **47,** 172 (1977).

Mee, C. D., and E. D. Daniel, "Magnetic Recording," Vol. III, *Video Audio and Instrumentation Recording,* Chap. 2, 1988.

Mita, S., et al., "Digital Recording Techniques Using 1/2″ Tape" (Japanese), *IEICE Jpn. Tech. Rep.,* **MR-83-9** (1983).

Mita, S., M. Izumita, and N. Doi, "Digital Video Recording Techniques Using 1/2″ Metal Particle Tape" (Japanese), *ITEJ Tech. Rep.,* **TEBS 106-3** (1985).

Morizono, M., H. Yoshida, and Y. Hashimoto, "Digital Video Recording—Some Experiments and Future Consideration," *J. SMPTE,* **89,** 658 (1980).

Nakagawa, S., "A Constitution of Concatenated Code for Digital VTR" (Japanese), *ITEJ Tech. Rep.,* **VR32-3** (1978).

Nakayama, T., Y. Oba, S. Togashi, and K. Sekimoto, "Editing Interchangeability of the Narrow Track Digital VTR" (Japanese), *J. ITEJ,* **46,** 1278 (1992).

NHK (Japan Broadcasting Corporation), "New Format Composite Digital VTR Using 1/2″ Tape," EBU MAGNUM/MUN/90 (1990).

Nishikawa, Y., N. Takayama, M. Nakashima, K. Sato, T. Matsumoto, and M. Mori, "On a Digital Recording System Using 1/2″ VTR" (Japanese), *ITEJ Tech. Rep.,* **11,** 25 (1987).

Osawa, H., Y. Okamoto, and S. Tazaki, "Fundamental Studies on Quantized Feedback for NRZ Recording" (Japanese), *IEICE Jpn. Tech. Rep.,* **MR82-37,** 1 (1983).

Platte, H-J., W. Keesen, and D. Uhde, "Matrix Scan Recording, A New Alternative to Helical Scan Recording On Videotape," *IEEE Trans. Consum. Electron.,* **CE-34,** 606 (1988).

Reed, I. S., and G. Solomon, "Polynomial Codes over Certain Finite Fields," *J. Soc. Ind. Appl. Math.,* **8,** 300 (1960).

Steele, H., "An Experimental Digital Video Recorder on a One-Inch Type C Format Machine–A Progress Report," *11th Intl. Symp. Montreux,* **IV B-3** (1979).

Uehara, T., T. Nakamura, H. Minaguchi, H. Shibaya, T. Sekiguchi, and Y. Oba, "A New 8-14 Modulation and Its Application to a Small Format VTR," *SMPTE Tech. Conf.* (1989).

Uehara, T., T. Nakamura, H. Minaguchi, H. Shibaya, T. Sekiguchi, and Y. Oba, "A New 8-14 Modulation and Its Application to a Small Format VTR" (Japanese), *ITEJ Tech. Rep. VIR90-19,* **14,** 49 (1990).

Waldhauer, F. D., "Quantized Feedback in an Experimental 280 Mb/s Digital Repeater for Coaxial Transmission," *IEEE Trans. Commum.,* **COM-22,** 1 (1974).

Wood, R. W., and R. W. Donalson, "Decision Feedback Equalization of the DC Null in High Density Digital Magnetic Recording," *IEEE Trans. Magn.,* **MAG-14,** 218 (1978).

Yamamitsu, C., K. Suesada, I. Ogura, and A. Iketani, "High Density Recording and Bit Rate Reduction for a 2-Hour Digital VTR," *IERE, Sixth Intl. Conf. on Video and Data Record.,* 113 (1986).

Yamamitsu, C., A. Ide, and T. Juri, "An Experimental Digital VTR Capable of 12-Hour Recording," *IEEE Trans. Consum. Electron.,* **CE-33,** 240 (1987).

Yamamitsu, C., A. Ide, A. Iketani, and T. Juri, "An Experimental Study on Bit Rate Reduction and High Density Recording for a Home-Use Digital VTR," *IEEE Trans. Consum. Electron.,* **CE-34,** 588 (1988).

Yamamitsu, C., A. Ide, A. Iketani, and T. Juri, "A Study on High Density Recording for a Home-Use Digital VTR" (Japanese), *ITEJ Tech. Rep.,* **12,** 25 (1988).

Yamamitsu, C., A. Ide, A. Iketani, T. Juri, S. Kadono, C. Matsumi, K. Matsushita, and H. Mizuki, "An Experimental Digital VTR Capable of 12-Hour Recording," *IEEE Trans. Consum. Electron.,* **CE-35,** 450 (1989).

Yamamitsu, C., A. Ide, M. Nishino, T. Juri, and H. Ohtaka, "A Study on Trick Plays for Digital VCR," *IEEE Trans. Consum. Electron.,* **CE-37,** 261 (1991).

Yamamitsu, C., "Trend of Magnetic Recording Technology–Consumer VTR" (Japanese), *J. ITEJ,* **46,** 1222 (1992).

Yokoyama, K., and S. Nakagawa, "Trends of Research on Digital VTR" (Japanese), *J. Inst. Tel. Engr. Jpn.,* **32,** 819 (1978).

Yokoyama, K., and S. Nakagawa, "An Experimental Channel Coding for Digital Videotape Recorder," *12th Intl. Tel. Symp. Record.,* 251 (1981).

Yokoyama, K., S. Nakagawa, H. Shibaya, and H. Katayama, "PCM Video Recording Using a Rotating Magnetic Sheet," NHK Labs. Note, No. 221 (1977).

Yokoyama, K., S. Nakagawa, and H. Katayama, "Experimental PCM-VTR," NHK Labs. Note, No. 236 (1979*a*).

Yokoyama, K., S. Nakagawa, and H. Katayama, "Trial Production of Experimental PCM VTR" (Japanese), *IECE Jpn. Tech. Rep.,* **MR79-8** (1979*b*).

Yokoyama, K., S. Nakagawa, and H. Katayama, "An Experimental Digital Videotape Recorder," *J. SMPTE,* **89,** 173 (1980).

Yoshioka, H., T. Takahashi, T. Fukuda, Y. Machida, and M. Morio, "28.6 Mbps NTSC Signal Digital Magnetic Recording Report" (Japanese), *ITEJ Tech. Rep.,* **VR42-2,** 81 (1980).

CHAPTER 7
ANALOG AUDIO RECORDING

Eric D. Daniel

Redwood City, California

7.1 AUDIO RECORDING PRINCIPLES

7.1.1 Characteristics of Audio Signals

In the recording and reproduction of audible sounds the final arbiter of quality is the human ear. It is therefore fitting that the subject of audio recording be introduced by a brief review of some of the more important aspects of psychoacoustics.

The human ear responds to sounds covering a range of frequencies extending from 20 Hz to 20 kHz. Relative to the signals discussed in other chapters, the highest frequency is modest, but the bandwidth, measured in octaves (10), is large. The range of intensities that can be detected is also large, the ratio between the loudest (threshold of feeling) and the softest (threshold of hearing) intensities being about one billion to one, or 120 dB. The smallest detectable sound is in fact comparable to the thermal energy of the molecules of air.

Different sounds of interest do not occupy the same space in the intensity-frequency plane and may not require equal treatment to give satisfactory electro-acoustic reproduction. The spaces occupied by speech and music are compared with the boundaries of hearing in the highly simplified diagram of Fig. 7.1. In the case of speech, the main components related to intelligibility are centered around 2 kHz, but most of the energy lies below 1 kHz. To reproduce every nuance of a speaker's voice requires a large bandwidth and a high signal-to-noise ratio. Merely to reproduce intelligible speech (e.g., a telephone) demands much less, and to provide maximum intelligibility with minimum power (e.g., a hearing aid) calls for a carefully restricted bandwidth and compression of the dynamic range.

Musical sounds approach all reaches of the audible spectrum, and the dynamic range between the loudest and softest passages of a symphony orchestra can be 70 dB or more. The power is not evenly distributed over the spectrum but tends to drop off at the low and at the high frequencies to an extent that is highly dependent on the particular musical instruments and composition (Sivian et al., 1931; McKnight, 1959). There is really no average power spectrum but only a set of individual spectra that may exhibit the low-frequency power of a pipe organ at one extreme and the substantial high-frequency energy of metal percussion at the other.

A listener possesses definite opinions about which sounds are wanted or un-

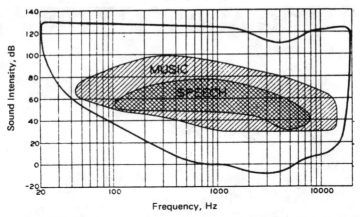

FIGURE 7.1 Simple representation of the frequency and intensity ranges of music and speech. The solid line indicates the boundaries of normal hearing (*Olsen, 1957*).

wanted and can detect one in the presence of the other with a high degree of discrimination. On the one hand, it is possible to recognize speech in the presence of a higher level of noise. On the other hand, the enjoyment of listening to music may be marred by the presence of a level of noise which, although low enough to be masked by the louder passages, is clearly evident in quiet intervals. A critical listener is also disturbed by the presence of small components of sound introduced by nonlinear distortion of the signal amplitude. Here components that are in a harmonic relationship to the signal may be less offensive than components introduced by intermodulation of the contents of a complex signal, although the latter are not necessarily dissonant (Langevin, 1963). Generally, intermodulation and harmonic distortion components are related, and it is common to specify nonlinear distortion in terms of the more easily measured harmonic components produced when a single-frequency signal is recorded.

The human ear is less sensitive to distortions of signal phase within a channel, but phase linearity has to be maintained within certain limits, otherwise the subjective impression of transients is impaired (Preis, 1983). Also, phase is critically important with respect to the directional properties of normal hearing. The fact that a sound arrives at each ear at a different time (and with a different intensity) allows the source to be located in space. More generally, the listener is aware, not only of the sound emanating straight from a source, but of secondary sounds arriving from other directions after reflections, and multiple reflections, from the boundaries of the room.

Finally, the quality of musical reproduction is degraded by the introduction of unnatural amplitude modulation caused by variations in tape sensitivity or frequency modulation caused by variations in tape speed. Subjectively, the sidebands of amplitude modulation can be perceived as noise components around the signal which detract from its clarity. Frequency modulation can be particularly disturbing, especially when listening to a musical instrument that should have little or no vibrato, such as a clarinet or a piano.

Ideally, a high-performance audio recorder must be capable of reproducing sound quality that is indistinguishable from the live performance. From the foregoing, the requirements for approaching this ideal fall into three categories. First, the recorder must match the frequency response of the ear and the dynamic range of a wide variety of music. Second, all unwanted signals, such as additive noise, modulation noise, print-through, and distortion components, must be inaudible or masked by wanted signals. Third, at least two (stereophonic) channels must be provided and their individual and mutual phase integrity maintained so as to simulate binaural effects and the associated sensations of direction, depth, and reverberation.

7.1.2 Historical Development

In 1897, Valdemar Poulsen applied for a patent using the properties of a permanent magnet, in the form of a steel wire, as a means of recording. His work achieved considerable acclaim. Working models of his "telegraphone" were exhibited and numerous, mostly short-lived, companies were set up to exploit his concept. Unfortunately, successful commercial realization could not occur until electronic amplification was developed in the 1920s. The Marconi-Stille equipment produced in the early thirties used steel tape and heads with staggered poles on either side of the tape, and was among the first magnetic recorders to achieve commercial success. Early work in the United States focused on using various compositions of stainless-steel wire as the magnetic medium, an approach that was doomed to be of limited performance.

The greatest practical advance in the early years of magnetic recording was the development of the Magnetophone in Germany in the 1930s and 40s. This equipment had all the essential features of a modern audio tape recorder: coated particulate plastic tape; gapped ring heads; separate erase, record, and reproduce heads; and a capstan and pinch-roller drive. Above all, in the higher-performance Magnetophones, ac bias was used in place of dc bias to produce dramatic improvements in linearity and background noise.

The introduction of ac bias was the most significant step forward in audio magnetic recording technology. The concept of using ac bias was not new but had been invented and patented in the United States by Carlson and Carpenter in 1927 and the basic magnetic process involved was described even earlier (Steinhaus and Gumlich, 1915). However, the concept languished in obscurity for many years, and the Magnetophone recorders were the first in which ac bias was applied in a practical, well-engineered fashion.

The 1950s saw a rapid increase in audio tape recording activities in Europe, the United States, and Japan. Inexpensive consumer recorders were manufactured, and more sophisticated equipment, mirroring the Magnetophone, was built to satisfy the growing interest on the part of the broadcasting organizations and recording studios. Theoretical studies of magnetic recording, previously neglected, were undertaken, and many of the fundamental principles were established (Wallace, 1951; Westmijze, 1953).

Technical innovations were few; progress occurred more by incremental improvements, particularly in the composition and dimensional precision of tapes and heads. Such improvements led to increased audio performance and reduced tape speed and, eventually, to convenient tape packaging such as the "compact cassette" introduced by Philips in 1963. The development of multitrack heads had naturally made magnetic recording a convenient vehicle for implementing stereo recording, an important step towards providing realistic sound reproduction. Studio recorders were subsequently developed with many more than two-channel capability to provide additional flexibility in mixing and to facilitate the production of special effects. Meanwhile, improvements were made in that key index of audio performance, signal-to-noise, ratio, not only by means of better media, heads, and electronics but by introducing electronic noise-reduction techniques.

Incremental advances in ac-biased recording will continue to be made. There are, however, alternative routes to achieving higher levels of audio recording performance, for example, the use of modulation schemes to replace the linear recording approach. The use of modulation techniques received scant attention until the seventies. Since then, momentum has increased rapidly, with emphasis on the development of digitally encoded audio recording as a means of reducing or eliminating many of the limitations inherent in ac-biased recording. Digital audio was first applied to professional studio recorders and became available indirectly to the consumer in the form of phonograph disks produced using digitally recorded master tapes. Later, several developments took place in rapid succession. Full digital recordings were commercially produced in the form of factory-recorded, play-only, nonmagnetic optical disks (*compact discs* or *CDs*) produced, again, using digitally recorded master tapes. Home video tape recorders were introduced which used FM or digital technique to incorporate the audio signal into the video track; they provide a recording capability comparable in quality to that of a CD. Finally, efforts were accelerated to produce dedicated digital audio recorders for home as well as studio use using multitrack and data compression techniques. A detailed discussion of digital audio recording technology as applied to magnetic recording is given in Chap. 8.

7.2 RECORDING WITH AC BIAS

7.2.1 Principles of Design and Operation

7.2.1.1 Recording Components. The essential components of an audio tape recorder are shown diagrammatically in Fig. 7.2. During recording, the tape is moved at constant speed successively over the erase head, which removes any previous recording; the record head, where a new program is recorded; and the reproduce head, which provides a delayed reproduction of the program for monitoring purposes.

The signal to be recorded is fed to the record head via an amplifier and equalizer, and the reproduced signal is amplified, integrated, and subjected to more equalization before being sent to the output terminals. Integration is required to compensate for the fact that an inductive reproducing head responds to the derivative of the recorded flux. The primary function of the pre- and postrecording equalizers is to correct for losses that occur in the recording and reproducing processes at short wavelengths, so that the frequency response of the recorder is flat up to the desired highest frequency (shortest wavelength).

An ac-bias current is added to the signal current in the head to linearize the otherwise highly nonlinear, hysteretic recording process. The bias current is considerably greater than the largest signal current. As discussed later, its precise magnitude is critical to all aspects of recording: sensitivity, frequency response, distortion, noise, permanence, and erasability. The frequency of the bias is not critical provided it is several times higher than the highest signal frequency: frequencies of 100 to 240 kHz are typical.

The erasing process not only must eradicate previous recordings but must leave

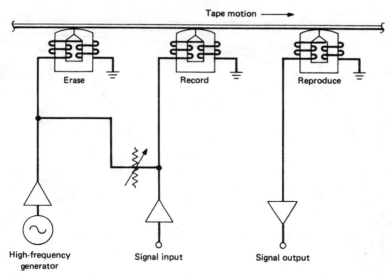

FIGURE 7.2 Block diagram of the components of an ac-biased audio tape recorder using separate erase, record, and reproduce heads.

the tape in a condition of lowest possible noise. This dictates the use of ac erasure, the head being commonly fed from the same source as the bias. It is essential that the bias and erase-current waveforms be symmetrical. Introducing a small degree of asymmetry is equivalent to adding direct current, or permanently magnetizing a head, either of which can cause a substantial increase in noise.

The heads are of ring construction, with gap lengths suited to their function. The erase-head gap length is made large, often several times the coating thickness, to assist in providing a strong erasing field throughout the whole coating. Sometimes multiple gaps are used for reasons that are discussed later. The record-head gap is typically made comparable to the coating thickness, mainly to optimize efficiency and facilitate driving the head. The reproduce head gap is made small enough to avoid significant gap loss at the shortest wavelength of interest.

7.2.1.2 *Linearity of the Recording Process.*

The physical mechanism underlying the linearizing effect of ac bias is analogous to a modified form of anhysteresis and has been discussed in detail in *Magnetic Recording Technology,* Chap. 2. It will, however, be useful to review some of the principles of ac-biased recording here in order to support the discussions of audio recording that follow.

Without bias, the relationship between remanent magnetization M_r and recording signal field H follows an S-shaped curve of the type shown dashed in Fig. 7.3. The use of an optimal amount of ac bias, equivalent to the use of a peak bias field approximately equal to the coercivity, promotes a relationship between anhysteretic magnetization M_{ar} and field H of the type shown by the full-line curve. The curve is initially straight, but the linear region is limited, and if the signal field is too high, the curve departs from linearity and distortion occurs. The data from a wide variety of longitudinally oriented particulate coatings are practically identical when normalized as shown in Fig. 7.4*a*, implying that all such tapes have the same distortion characteris-

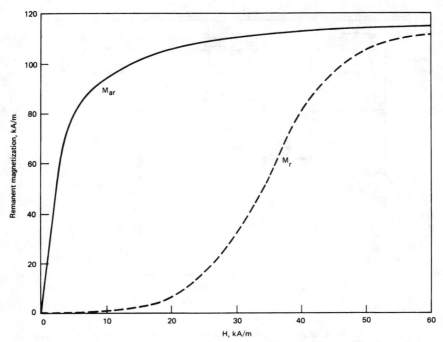

FIGURE 7.3 Anhysteretic magnetization M_{ar} as a function of signal field H for optimal bias field. The ordinary remanent magnetization curve M_r is shown dashed.

tics (Köster, 1975). The extent of this distortion can be calculated by expressing the data by the best-fitting, odd-order power series and computing the harmonic content produced when a sinusoidal field is applied. Below a reduced field of $h = 2$, the data can be represented quite accurately by three terms:

$$m_{ar} = 0.5691h - 0.756h^3 + 0.0065h^5 \qquad (7.1)$$

Calculations of long-wavelength output and third-harmonic distortion based on assuming a universal anhysteretic curve are shown in Fig. 7.4*b*. Data on the same wide range of oriented particulate coatings are contained within the shaded area, indicating good agreement between theory and experiment (Köster, 1975). The output corresponding to 3 percent third-harmonic distortion (an upper limit commonly used for audio recording) is about 6 dB below the maximum output, corresponding to a magnetization of $M_{ar} = 0.5M_s$. In practice, signal peaks may go 2 to 3 dB higher.

At the shorter wavelengths, the departure from linearity takes a different form. The transfer function of the recording process no longer follows the M_{ar} versus H curve but goes through a maximum, then falls rapidly at higher signal currents. Distortion, measured in terms of intermodulation products (harmonics are outside the pass band), does increase at higher currents. But the significant form of distortion is *compression,* a departure from linearity without a concomitant production of distortion components.

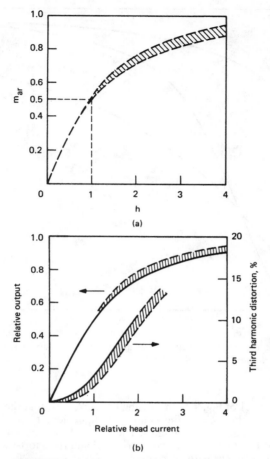

FIGURE 7.4   (*a*) The normalized anhysteretic magnetization versus signal field curve. The shaded area contains all
the data from a wide variety of longitudinally oriented
particulate media, including pure and cobalt-modified
iron oxides, chromium dioxide, and metal. (*Köster, 1975*).
(*b*) Relative output and third-harmonic distortion versus
signal current. The shaded areas contain data from the
same media as in (*a*); the full lines represent calculations
based on a universal curve (*Köster, 1975*).

7.2.1.3 Bias Adjustment.   So far, it has been assumed that the bias field can
always be adjusted to the optimal value, but this ignores the fact that the field
decreases with distance from the head. In practice the bias field is optimal only for
one elementary layer of the coating; layers above and below will be either over- or
underbiased. Adjusting the bias current so that the correctly biased layer is at the
surface is equivalent to setting the bias for maximum short-wavelength output; the
rest of the coating is underbiased and suffers increased nonlinearity of the type

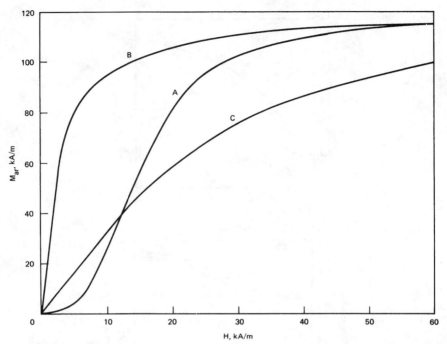

FIGURE 7.5 Modified anhysteresis curves showing the effects of curve (*A*) underbiasing, curve (*B*) optimally biasing, and curve (*C*) overbiasing.

illustrated by curve *A* of Fig. 7.5. Increasing the current so that the correctly biased layer moves to the bottom of the coating is equivalent to setting the bias for minimum distortion at long wavelengths. The surface layers carrying the bulk of the useful short-wavelength recording are overbiased and the short-wavelength output is decreased in accordance with curve *C* of Fig. 7.5.

Setting the value of bias is therefore a compromise between achieving optimum results at short and long wavelengths. The difficulty of the decision can be gained from Fig. 7.6*a*, which shows the variation of signal output with bias at a number of different wavelengths, and from Fig. 7.6*b*, which shows the variation of long-wavelength distortion with bias. Adjusting the bias for optimum short wavelengths leaves the long wavelengths underbiased and with high distortion; but using the bias best suited for long-wavelength performance causes substantial losses in short-wavelength output.

The minimum in the distortion curve can be explained on the following basis (Westmijze, 1953; Fujiwara, 1979). The coefficients of the third-and fifth-order coefficients in the power series representing the underbiased curve *B* of Fig. 7.5 are of opposite sign. This produces a null in the calculated third harmonic at a certain signal field strength. In like fashion, it is possible to set the bias and signal fields to produce a minimum in the net harmonic content of the whole coating. The minimum is too critical to be used as an operating point; its existence can be more

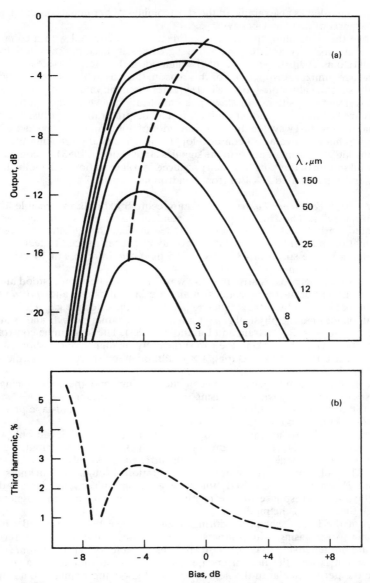

FIGURE 7.6 Typical curves showing (*a*) reproduced output versus bias current at different wavelengths and (*b*) third-harmonic distortion versus bias at a long wavelength.

properly regarded as an example of the shortcomings of harmonic content in revealing all aspects of nonlinear behavior.

Above the maximum, the decrease in distortion is coupled with a comparable decrease in sensitivity, and the long-wavelength linearity becomes substantially independent of bias. Adjusting the bias on the high side is therefore the safest policy with respect to minimizing distortion. For this reason, the bias in high-speed applications is usually set to a value equal to, or a little greater than, the value that gives maximum long-wavelength sensitivity. In slow-speed applications, where the shortest wavelengths are critically dependent on bias, it may be preferable to adjust the bias to overbias the shortest wavelength by a given amount, for example to produce a 2- or 3-dB loss. Schemes have also been developed for dynamically reducing the ac bias when the high-frequency energy in the signal is large (Jensen, 1983). A commercially successful system of this kind has been produced in collaboration with Dolby Laboratories, and is designated HX Pro (for "headroom extension").

7.2.1.4 High-Frequency Losses.

An audio recorder exhibits appreciable losses at high frequencies. The true frequency-dependent losses are small, such as those associated with losses in the cores of the heads. The significant losses are wavelength-dependent and increase in severity as the tape speed is decreased. For example, at a tape speed of 48 mm/s (1.875 in/s), the total loss at 15 kHz (wavelength of 3.2 μm) can approach 30 dB.

Short-wavelength losses arise in many ways. The ones best understood and most easily quantified occur on reproduction and are known as *gap* and *spacing losses*. The gap loss is given by $(\lambda/\pi g_{\text{eff}}) \sin(\pi g_{\text{eff}}/\lambda)$ where the effective gap g_{eff} is some 14 percent longer than the physical gap g for a tape permeability $\mu = 1$, and as much as 19% higher for $\mu = 2$ (Bertram and Lindholm, 1982). The loss can be controlled to an acceptable value by making the gap sufficiently smaller than the shortest wavelength (the loss is less than 2 dB for $g/\lambda \times \frac{1}{3}$), although too short a gap sacrifices head efficiency.

The loss caused by spacing between the medium and the reproducing head increases exponentially with decreasing wavelength, according to exp $(-2\pi d/\lambda)$ or $54.6d/\lambda$ in dB. Smooth head and tape surfaces and adequate head-tape pressure in the vicinity of the gap are essential to minimize spacing loss.

Even in the ideal case, perfect contact with the head is achieved only for the nearest elementary layer of a medium of finite thickness; the contributions to the output from layers beneath the surface will suffer progressively increasing spacing losses. The net effect, corresponding to integration through the thickness of the medium, is commonly misnamed "thickness loss," and ultimately give a 6 decibel per octave fall in response for the highly artificial case of uniform magnetization through the depth of the medium.

Two of the losses that occur during recording have been described earlier in relation to overbiasing and compression. Generally, these and other recording losses are not amenable to the precise analyses possible for reproduction. A major complication is that the field from the head rotates, so that the direction turns toward the perpendicular in the near layers. To a good approximation, however, it can be assumed that the efficiency of the bias field is independent of its direction and depends only on its *resultant* magnitude (Eldridge and Daniel, 1962; Tjaden and Leyten, 1963). Therefore, in the simplest case, recording takes place along a contour of constant resultant bias field approximately equal to the coercivity (Bertram, 1974). An element of medium acquires a magnetization proportional to the signal field at the point where the element crosses the critical bias-field contour. The longitudinal field (and magnetization) along the contour becomes vanishingly

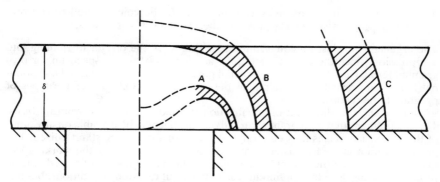

FIGURE 7.7 Diagrammatic representation of recording zones corresponding to zone (*A*) underbiasing, zone (*B*) optimal biasing for long wavelengths, and zone (*C*) overbiasing. The full lines are contours of constant resultant bias field strength (*Eldridge and Daniel, 1962*).

small toward the head surface, and this results in a predicted thickness loss that approaches 12 decibel per octave at short wavelengths, as opposed to the 6 decibel per octave deduced for uniform magnetization (or purely perpendicular magnetization). Particulate tapes, well-oriented along their length, give a response in keeping with the 12 decibel per octave prediction (Bertram, 1975).

Further losses in recording sensitivity arise because the particles of a coating do not possess the same critical switching field. Instead, there is a distribution of critical fields, associated with the switching-field distribution defined in *Magnetic Recording Technology,* Chap. 3. Consequently, recording does not take place along a single bias contour but over a zone bounded by contours equal to the highest and lowest particle switching fields. Losses occur when the length of the zone becomes comparable with the wavelength. In the simplest example of a rectangular distribution of critical fields, the zones are as depicted in Fig. 7.7, and it is apparent that the zone length, and hence the loss, increases as bias is increased. Generally, media with narrow switching-field distributions will give superior performance (Köster, 1981).

Demagnetization losses, once thought to be of major significance, are probably negligible down to wavelengths of 2 μm—comparable to the shortest wavelengths used in conventional forms of ac-biased recording (Bertram and Niedermeyer, 1982). This conclusion assumes that intimate contact is maintained between heads and tape so that demagnetizing fields are minimized by the "keeping" action of the high-permeability head core.

7.2.1.5 Equalization. As mentioned briefly above, audio recorders use pre-equalization before recording and postequalization after reproduction to correct for losses at high frequencies (short wavelengths) and to provide an overall flat frequency response over the working bandwidth. In considering how best to allot the total requirement between pre-and postequalization, there are several factors which favor preequalization:

1. Postequalization increases the reproduced noise, whereas preequalization does not.

2. The power spectrum of much musical program material falls at high frequencies, allowing headroom for preequalization.

3. Losses in recording sensitivity can, in principle, be compensated for by pre-equalization without penalty provided the signal level is not excessive.

The arguments against preequalization rest mainly on the danger of running into compression, since there is no such thing as a universal power spectrum for program material. Certain programs, or small portions of them, may exceed any nominal limits, and usually the equipment designer has no control over the types of program to be recorded.

In practice, the allotment of equalizations is made on a rather arbitrary basis. The requirement that a program recorded on one machine be playable on any other of the same class makes it essential that the postequalization be standardized. The preequalization is then adjusted to provide a flat response over the working frequency range, using the particular tape-head combination that will be used. Such a procedure cannot produce optimum results under all recording conditions, but it is the basis for the various standards described in subsequent sections.

7.2.1.6 Noise and Interference

Types of Noise.   The fundamental characteristics of noise in magnetic recording are discussed in *Magnetic Recording Technology,* Chap. 7. The purpose is to expand on those aspects that are specifically pertinent to audio recording.

Spectra of the major types of noise of interest are shown in Fig. 7.8 for a low-speed (48-mm/s) equalized system. The bottom full-line curve shows the noise that results when a tape is reproduced after being erased using a bulk eraser operating at power-supply frequency. The *bulk-erased* noise is associated directly with the particles of the coating (or the micromagnetic structure of a deposited film). When ac bias is applied in the absence of signal, the noise increases by about 3 dB in the midband. This *bias noise* is the background noise that is heard in the quiet passages of a recorded program. Also, there are modulation noises that are a function of the

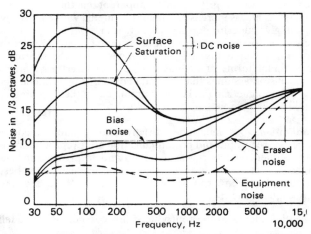

FIGURE 7.8   Noise spectra of a low-speed (47.6 mm/s or 1.875 in/s) audio recorder. The various types of noise are explained in the text (*Daniel, 1972*).

recorded signal. The simplest is the *dc noise* that occurs when direct current is fed to the recording head. When the current is sufficient to saturate the tape, the noise increases by about 10 dB at the longer wavelengths. This increase is attributed to nonuniform distribution of particles within the coating. At a lower value of direct current, the long-wavelength noise peaks to a level that may be as much as 20 dB above the bulk-erased noise. The resulting *surface noise* is attributed to variations in head-to-tape spacing caused by asperities on the tape surface.

Head and electronics noise are of concern only at the very shortest wavelengths reached in slow-speed recording. Interference effects are usually not of significance in audio equipment, with the important exception of *print-through*, the transfer of signal between adjacent layers in a stored reel of tape. Print-through is discussed in some detail in Sec. 7.2.1.7.

The audible perception of noise depends strongly upon the frequency content, bearing an inverse relationship to the low-level, equal-loudness contours of the ear (Fletcher-Munson curves). In effect, the sensitivity of the ear to low-level sounds is deficient at low-frequencies, peaks around 3 to 4 kHz, and falls off at higher frequencies. For this reason, measurements of audio background noise are often made using a weighting network that purports to take these psychoacoustic effects into account.

Bulk-Erased Noise. The simplest model of a recording medium is one which contains noninteracting, single-domain, acicular particles. Theoretically, the signal-to-noise power ratio at short wavelengths is then given by

$$\frac{S}{N} = \text{const. } w\, \frac{p}{\bar{v}}\, F(\theta)\, \frac{1}{1 + (\sigma/\bar{v})^2}\, \frac{1}{k\, dk} \tag{7.2}$$

where w = track width
p = volume packing (the volume-fraction of coating occupied by particles)
$\bar{v}$ = mean of the particle-size distribution
σ = standard deviation of the particle-size distribution
$F(\theta)$ = particle-orientation factor

and the noise comes from a narrow band of wave numbers from k to $k + dk$ (Daniel, 1972).

The various factors in Eq. (7.2) have important implications with respect to the design of audio recorders and media:

1. The power ratio is proportional to the track width; halving the track width will cause a 3-dB reduction in signal-to-noise ratio.

2. For best results, the coating should contain the maximum possible content of magnetic material of the smallest possible particle size.

3. The particle orientation factor varies from $\frac{3}{8}$ for random orientation to 1 for perfect particle alignment. There is thus a potential improvement of 4.3 dB to be gained from particle orientation.

4. The signal-to-noise will be impaired by a distribution in particle size. The lognormal type of distribution found in conventional oxide particles, such as that illustrated in Fig. 7.9 (Daniel, 1960), gives values of $\sigma/\bar{v}$ of between 1 and 1.5, or the signal-to-noise ratio is 3 to 5 dB lower than it would be with particles of uniform size.

Bias Noise. As already mentioned, the noise from a bulk-erased tape increases when it is moved over a recording head energized with ac bias. On poorly designed

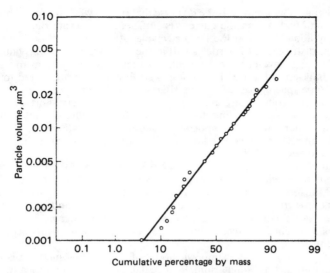

FIGURE 7.9 The size distribution of acicular ferric oxide particles. The cumulative percentage, by weight, of particles with less than a given volume is plotted on a normal probability scale versus particle volume on a logarithmic scale. The data were obtained from examination of electron photomicrographs and confirmed by sedimentation tests.

or maintained equipment, a part of this increase may be caused by an effective direct current component arising from bias waveform asymmetry or a magnetized head. The remaining part is the true bias noise and has its origin in the reaction of the bias field upon the tape. Bias noise can be explained qualitatively (Ragle and Smaller, 1965) and quantitatively (Daniel, 1972) in terms of a re-recording of noise flux. In effect, the image of the noise that appears in the core of the record head gets anhysteretically recorded back into the tape, for a net doubling (3-dB increase) of noise flux power. The process, which has been confirmed by bulk-erasure experiments, is analogous to that of contact printing (Chap. 5), which has been analyzed in considerable detail (e.g., Tjaden and Rijckaert, 1971). Thus, referring back to Fig. 7.8, the decrease of the bias-noise increment at long wavelengths can be attributed to the inability of a medium of finite thickness to collect all the available flux, while the decrease at short wavelengths can be explained by head-tape spacing. An important conclusion is that the bias-noise increment is essentially independent of the magnetic constituents of a medium.

DC Noise.   As shown in Fig. 7.8, a direct current of saturation value in the record head causes the noise level of a particulate coating to increase by 10 dB or so at the longer wavelengths. This increase occurs because deficiencies in milling and coating give rise to particle-rich regions (clumps) and particle-poor regions (voids). Such inhomogeneities cause the noise to increase with bulk magnetization because, in simple terms, a magnetized clump (or a void surrounded by magnetized material) acts like a large noise source. The phenomenon of dc noise means that background noise is sensitive to any residual magnetization in the heads and to the presence of even harmonics in the bias current. The latter cause an asymmetry of waveform that is exactly equivalent, as far as the tape is concerned, to adding a direct current to the bias.

The dc-noise behavior of deposited-film media is very different from that of particulate media. Most films show little or no increase of noise above the ac-erased level upon applying a saturating direct current, presumably because the disposition of the noise sources obeys Poisson's statistics.

Surface Noise. The maximum dc noise does not occur when tape saturation is achieved but at a somewhat lower value of direct current. As shown by the topmost curve of Fig. 7.8, the additional surface noise is confined to very long wavelengths and is associated with variations in head-to-tape spacing caused by asperities protruding from the tape surface (Eldridge, 1964; Daniel, 1964). The wavelength at which the maximum noise occurs depends primarily upon the stiffness of the tape, which, in turn, depends mainly upon base film thickness. The size and frequency of occurrence of asperities depend upon the quality of particle dispersion and surface treatment, such as calendering, associated with the manufacture of the media.

Modulation Noise. DC noise is also a measure of the multiplicative modulation noise that occurs when an audio signal is recorded. In the frequency domain, transpositions of the dc-noise spectrum appear as modulation sidebands in relatively close proximity to the signal frequency. In the time domain, dc noise shows up as relatively slow variations in the signal envelope, the extreme excursions of which may be classified as *dropouts*. Either domain can be used as a basis for carrying out specific modulation-noise measurements. Subjectively, the effect of modulation noise is to impair the clarity of the reproduced signal, particularly when the signal is a sustained and relatively pure note (e.g., from a flute).

The modulation noise from particulate media generally decreases slightly with signal frequency. The noise from film media, however, often increases markedly with signal frequency.

7.2.1.7 Print-Through

Basic Phenomenon. Print-through is a form of interference that is uniquely offensive in audio recording. Therefore it is treated here in some detail. The effect arises when the recorded magnetization M of one layer of a tape stored in a reel creates a field H that magnetizes adjacent layers. In the case of an isolated signal of short duration, the audible effect is a series of "echoes" of logarithmically ascending strength which precedes the signal itself (the *preprints*), followed by a series of echoes of logarithmically descending strength which follows the signal (the *postprints*).

The relative level of the prints increases with the time of storage, exhibiting, in the simplest cases, a logarithmic relationship. The prints also tend to increase logarithmically with the temperature of the storage environment. For storage times of a few hours or more, the printing process is essentially linear and can be written in the form

$$M_p = \frac{\chi_p H_p}{\mu_0} \qquad (7.3)$$

where χ_p the print susceptibility, is an increasing function of time and temperature. As the signal wavelength shortens, the magnitude of H_p increases, reaches a maximum at a wavelength of λ_m, then decreases exponentially as shown in Fig. 7.10. The

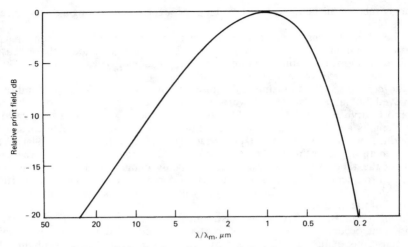

FIGURE 7.10   Theoretical print-through as a function of the reduced wavelength, λ/λ_m. The wavelength for maximum print is given by $\lambda_m = 2\pi t$, where t is total tape thickness (coating plus base film).

wavelength for maximum print field, and printed magnetization, is given approximately by

$$\lambda_m = 2\pi t \tag{7.4}$$

where $t = \delta + b$ is the total tape thickness (Daniel and Axon, 1950). Typically, the maximum field can be as high as 2.4 kA/m (30 Oe) and is reached at relatively long wavelengths in the range 75 to 300 μm.

The maximum print-to-signal ratio is given approximately by (Bertram et al., 1980)

$$p_m = \text{const.} \; \frac{\chi_p \delta/b}{1 + \delta/b} \tag{7.5}$$

This equation implies that it is desirable not only to minimize print susceptibility (see below) but also to have as thin a magnetic layer and as thick a base film as possible within the constraints of a given recorder configuration.

Ratio of Pre- to Postprints.   As mentioned earlier, the prints form two series, one that precedes, and another that follows, the signal. The relative magnitudes of these series are generally not the same. Larger prints come from the *B* layers, in which the coating faces the base film of the recorded signal layer, than from the *A* layers, lying on the side of the signal layer (see Fig. 7.11). This inequality has its origin in the fact that the print field, and hence the printed magnetization, has both longitudinal and perpendicular components which are 90 degrees out of phase. On one side of the coating the contributions these components make to the external flux add, while on the other side they subtract. This phenomenon is illustrated in Fig. 7.11. Theoretically, the ratio of the print series should be given by an expression of the type

$$\frac{_n p_b}{_n p_a} = \frac{|\chi_y - \chi_x|}{|\chi_y + \chi_x|} \tag{7.6}$$

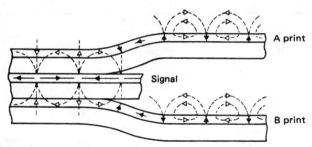

FIGURE 7.11 Diagrammatic representation of the difference between A and B prints. The components of printed magnetization give rise to external fields which add for B prints but subtract for A prints (*Daniel, 1972*).

where n indicates the order of the print, and χ_x and χ_y are the effective susceptibilities in the longitudinal and perpendicular directions (Daniel, 1972; Mallinson, 1973). If the coating were isotropic and self-demagnetization effects were negligible, the external flux from the second side would be zero. In practice, unoriented pure oxide tapes can give a print series ratio of 12 dB or more, whereas the same tapes well-oriented give ratios of as low as 3 dB. The important thing is to minimize the worst print-through of the two series, which usually implies maximizing the anisotropy.

Simulated magnetometer measurements indicate that, with many materials, the print susceptibility, as well as the initial reversible susceptibility (which governs the extent of the self-demagnetization), is greater at right angles to the direction of orientation. In cobalt-modified coatings, this situation, in conjunction with demagnetization in the perpendicular direction, can lead to a surprisingly high print-series ratio of about 15 dB, even for well-oriented tapes.

Physical Mechanisms. In media made from pure materials, for example gamma ferric oxide, print-through propensity is associated with a tendency for some particles to exhibit superparamagnetic behavior. Such behavior occurs when the thermal energy kT, during storage at absolute temperature T, becomes comparable to the anisotropy energy $v\mu_0 M_s H_0$ of a particle. Here v is the particle volume, M_s is the saturation magnetization of the material, and H_0 is the particle switching field. The probability that a particle will switch in a given time is governed by a time constant proportional to

$$\exp\,(v\mu_0 M_s H_0/2kT) \tag{7.7}$$

In the presence of a polarizing field, such as the print field, the particles will tend to be switched in the direction of this field. If all the particles had the same time constant, switching would occur at a simple logarithmic rate with time and with temperature. In fact, the assembly of particles in a coating will have a distribution of time constants governed by the distributions in particle volume, anisotropy, and—most important—interaction field. The rate of switching will therefore be according to a summation of logarithmic rates. These conclusions are in accord with the observed increases of print-through with time and temperature in the case of pure oxide media.

In media made using cobalt-modified oxides, an additional mechanism may exist and is often dominant. This mechanism is associated with the migration of Co^{2+} ions within the crystal lattice and is accelerated by increasing temperature.

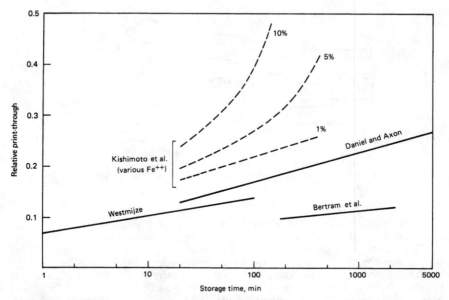

FIGURE 7.12 Print-through versus storage time. The full-line curves are for pure gamma ferric oxide (*Daniel and Axon, 1950; Westmijze, 1953; Bertram et al., 1980*), the dashed curves are for cobalt-modified berthollide iron oxides of various amounts of Fe^{2+}, expressed in atom percent (*Kishimoto et al., 1979*).

The print-through from such effects is minimized when the cobalt ions reside primarily at the surface (adsorbed) as opposed to being distributed throughout the body of the particles (doped). A low divalent-iron content (low cation vacancy concentration) is also a key factor in minimizing print-through from this cause.

Some examples of print-through versus time for various oxides are shown in Fig. 7.12. The increase of print-through with time is approximately logarithmic for the pure iron oxides. The cobalt-doped oxides show a print-through which rises more rapidly with time and exhibits a strong dependence on divalent iron content (Kishimoto et al., 1979).

7.2.1.8 *Erasure.* The function of erasure is twofold: first, to reduce any previously recorded signals to an imperceptible level; second, to leave the tape with a noise level that is at least as low as that of the bias noise. The second requirement is easily met using a properly designed and maintained head and well-balanced ac current source. Meeting the first requirement poses some problems in both head and tape design.

The simplest erase head is a ring head, similar to a record head but with a longer gap, often five or more times the thickness of the magnetic medium. When ac bias is used, the ease of erasure is essentially independent of signal level, and depends primarily on the bias level, since it is the bias that dominates the extent to which the medium is magnetized during recording. Erasure does, however, depend on wavelength in that a short-wavelength signal is inherently easier to erase than a long-wavelength one, in part because the internal demagnetizing field favors erasure. A complication arises when the leakage field from unerased portions of tape is anhysteretically recorded by the decaying field from the erase head. This re-recording effect can cause some major undulations in a partially erased signal spectrum (McKnight, 1963). The use of double-gapped erase heads and a sufficiently high erase field is the practical solution to the re-recording problem (Sawada and Yamada, 1985).

There are also some time effects associated with erasure. In particular, the ease with which a signal can be erased diminishes with the time for which the recorded signal is stored, a phenomenon related to the *viscous remanent magnetization* studied by geophysicists (e.g., Dunlop and Stirling, 1977). The erasure effect is a function of the type of magnetic material used in the media. Pure gamma ferric oxides or chromium dioxides show negligible erasure time effects, but certain types of modified iron oxides can become more difficult to erase after prolonged storage. As in the case of print-through, the worst offenders are cobalt-doped iron oxides with high vacancy (Fe^{2+}) content, and with the Co^{2+} ions uniformly distributed throughout the body of the particles. During storage, an annealing process occurs under the influence of the recorded signal magnetization and its associated internal field. The induced anisotropy created by the annealing process leads to magnetically "hard" regions that conform to the pattern of the recorded magnetization. When the stored signal is bulk erased, the signal may appear to have been removed. Upon subsequently running the tape over a record head energized with bias, the signal may magically return, in the worst case to a level of some 20 dB above the noise.

7.2.2 Open-Reel Recorders

7.2.2.1 Tape Transport. The layout of a simple open-reel audio tape transport is shown in Fig. 7.13. The constant-speed drive usually consists of a hysteresis synchronous motor turning a capstan against which the tape is held with a compliant pinch roller. Speed fluctuations, or flutter, must be kept below the level of perception, which places stringent demands upon the accuracy of all the drive elements. Separate reel motors are usually provided to power the fast-forward and rewind modes and furnish hold-back torque during all operating modes. Tape guiding is provided by a combination of fixed (flanged) and rotating (sometimes crowned) members. Rotating pulleys, fixed or on a sprung arm, also serve to mechanically isolate the reels from the head path and to dampen any tendency of the tape to go into longitudinal oscillation and produce audible squeal.

Professional transports may employ some of the techniques developed for instrumentation recorders, such as closed-loop drive, a differential dual-capstan drive, or a servo-controlled drive. Large diameter capstans that drive the tape without compliant pinch rollers have also been used. Servo-controlled drives are the favored approach in modern transports.

Open-reel audio recorders usually operate at speeds ranging from 95 mm/s (3.75 in/s) on consumer equipment to 760 mm/s (30 in/s) on professional equipment. Corresponding tape widths range from 6.3 mm (0.25 in) to 50 mm (2.0 in).

7.2.2.2 Open-Reel Heads. The construction of open-reel heads follows the traditional gapped-ring type of design. Record, reproduce, and erase heads differ mainly in the length of their gaps, which are chosen, using the guidelines outlined in an

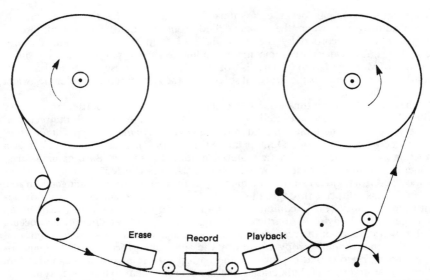

FIGURE 7.13 Typical configuration of an open-reel recorder, showing the mechanical layout and disposition of heads. The arrows on the supply and take-up reels indicate the direction in which torque is applied.

earlier section, to suit the coating thicknesses and shortest wavelengths of interest. Core losses over the audible frequency range can be held to small values using either laminated alloy or ferrite. The relatively low coercivity media generally used in open-reel recording do not place difficult demands upon the saturation characteristics of the core. The choice of core material is therefore governed mainly by such factors as the attainable mechanical and magnetic integrity of the surface and gap edges. Generally, laminated metal cores are preferred; Permalloy is used in the simplest cases, Alfenol or an equivalent is used if head wear is of particular concern. Erase heads with double gaps are often used to avoid the re-recording phenomenon discussed under erasure in Sec. 7.2.1.

It is convenient and often practical for bias and erase currents to have the same frequency, typically about 100 kHz. In professional equipment, erase efficiency is increased and biasing enhanced by making the erase frequency a subharmonic of the bias frequency; frequencies of 80 kHz and 240 kHz are commonly used.

7.2.2.3 Track Configuration and Equalization.   A two-track stereo system is used in the simplest types of quarter-inch professional tape recorders. In consumer equipment, a four-track system is still in limited use in which two tracks are used for stereo recording in one direction, and the remaining two tracks for the reverse direction. Studio recorders use wider tapes and many more tracks to accomplish the complex editing, mixing, and special effects used in modern recording studios. The widest tapes are 50 mm (2.9 in) and can accommodate 16 tracks of width 1.8 mm. This can be extended to 24 tracks of width 1.1 mm for a sacrifice of 2.4 dB in signal-to-noise ratio.

Standard postequalizations consist of integration plus linear functions of frequency that are specified in terms of the time constant of the equivalent RC circuit.

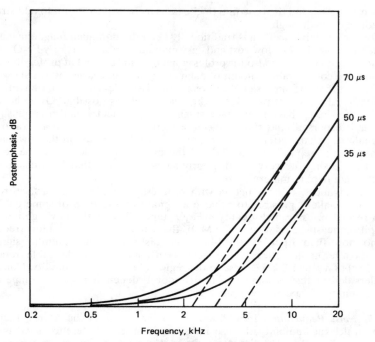

FIGURE 7.14 One-quarter-inch recorder standards: high-frequency equalization curves corresponding to 35 μs (International Electrotechnical Commission, 38 cm/s), 50 μs (National Association of Broadcasters, 38 and 19 cm/s), and 70 μs (IEC, 19 cm/s).

The more important national and international standards for high-frequency emphasis at various tape speeds are shown in Fig. 7.14. (These curves follow from the standards set down by the various international organizations in terms of tape flux.). At 15 kHz, the emphasis ranges from 10.7 to 16.5 dB. These levels of postequalization are insufficient to compensate for all the losses in the record and reproduce processes, and preequalization is used to accommodate the balance and achieve an overall flat response. Some of the standards still call for a deemphasis at low frequencies, a dubious practice that had its origin in reducing power-frequency interference, or *hum*.

The standards are implemented on a worldwide basis through the use of calibration tapes (McKnight, 1969). Calibration tapes are available which not only facilitate the accurate adjustment of frequency response but enable this to be done in terms of the absolute value of the (short-circuit) recorded flux per unit of track width in Webers per meter (Wb/m). Head azimuth alignment is another important function of standard tapes.

7.2.2.4 Open-Reel Media. Coated oxide media are universally used for open-reel recording. For consumer use, coatings of 5 to 7 μm are made on a polyester-base film of 25 μm—less for longer playing reels. For professional use, the coating is often increased to 10 μm or more to enhance the maximum output level (MOL) at long wavelengths, and the base film thickness is increased to 38 μm to add strength and reduce print-through.

Pure gamma ferric oxide has traditionally been the dominant magnetic material for open-reel media. The low cost and easy manufacturability make γ-Fe_2O_3 attractive for consumer use and also for professional use, since a reel of professional tape can contain a considerable amount of magnetic material. Earlier, it was shown that the key to achieving high signal-to-noise ratio is to develop media having well-oriented, small, uniform particles packed as densely as possible. Over the years, particles of γ-Fe_2O_3 have been made smaller, more acicular, and more easily oriented and dispersed, and the predictable increases in signal-to-noise ratio have been realized. Also, better control of particle-size distribution in the raw material and in coating preparation has allowed the average particle size to be reduced without increasing the very small, poorly shaped fraction that is associated with print-through in pure materials.

These advances, in conjunction with progress in coating and surface-treating technology, make it possible to achieve a signal-to-noise ratio of some 60 dB on studio recorders using high quality γ-Fe_2O_3 tapes. This is the unweighted, wide-band ratio, measured relative to the MOL that can be obtained at a low frequency with no more than 3 percent third-harmonic distortion. The minimum signal-to-print ratio after modest storage approaches 60 dB at a rather undesirable frequency ($\lambda_m = 2\pi t$) of about 1.2 kHz, close to the region of maximum audibility. Consumer recorders deliver results some 5 to 10 dB poorer, depending upon the tape speed and the quality of tape and equipment.

7.2.2.5 *Noise Reduction.*

In addition to reducing noise at the source, there are ways in which the audibility of noise and some forms of interference, such as print-through, can be reduced by signal processing. Early schemes used signal processing devices on reproduction only and had the disadvantage of modifying the signal as well as reducing noise. Later schemes use the *compandor* concept. This involves precompression and complementary postexpansion of the signal, with the goal of leaving the signal unaltered while reducing noise. In practice, this goal is difficult to achieve, and the first compandor systems produced a variety of unpleasant side effects related to poor input-output tracking, sensitivity to gain errors, transient problems, and audible "breathing" of the signal-modulated noise.

These problems are largely avoided in the professional noise-reduction system illustrated in Figs. 7.15 and 7.16 (Dolby, 1967). In this system, designated "A-type," signal is operated on by subtracting or adding a small differential component, rather than subjecting the whole signal to the hazards of passage through a variable-gain channel. In other words, as shown in Fig. 7.15, the higher-level signals are transmitted unchanged. Another advantage, shown in the figure, is that the compression and expansion are obtained by using identical differential networks: compression is produced by adding the differential component, expansion by subtracting it. Finally, signal modulation of the noise is made inaudible by splitting the differential component into four frequency bands and relying upon the masking effect of signals of amplitude appreciably higher than the compression thresholds in given portions of the spectrum. The filters employed are 80 Hz low-pass, 80 Hz to 3 kHz band-pass, 3 kHz high-pass, and 9 kHz high-pass. More recent systems (designated *SR* for *spectral recording*) use sliding filters controlled by the spectral content of the signal. A noise reduction of 10 dB is delivered, with negligible degradation of the signal and imperceptible signal-modulated noise effects. The system is the one most widely used in professional recording and has become the standard for the exchange of nondigital master tapes. Other noise-reduction sys-

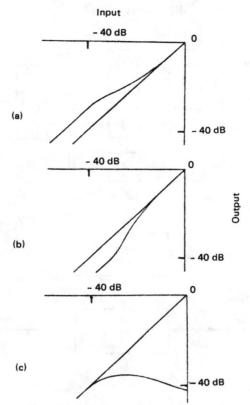

FIGURE 7.15 Transfer characteristics of a professional noise-reduction system. (*a*) Compression before recording; (*b*) complementary expansion after reproducing; (*c*) the differential component that is added to the signal to give the compression characteristic (*Dolby, 1967*).

tems have been developed (e.g., DBX, Telcon) but have not achieved the same acceptance as the Dolby system.

In all the noise-reduction systems of the compandor type, the control of signal level on recording and reproduction is critical. This requirement further emphasizes the importance of having the means of absolute calibration, via standard tapes, in audio recording.

7.2.3 Compact-Cassette Recorders

7.2.3.1 Mechanical Aspects. The compact cassette was introduced in the early 1960s as a convenient way of making portable, low-performance tape recorders. The cassette rapidly became accepted as the worldwide standard, and during the

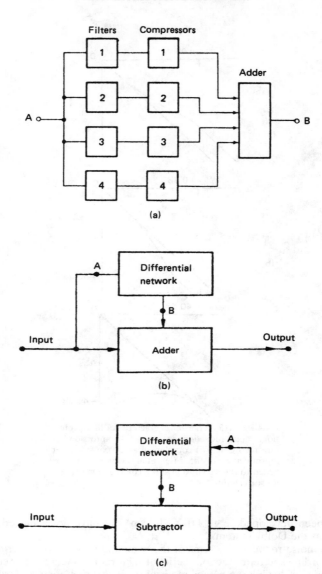

FIGURE 7.16 Block diagrams of a professional noise-reduction system showing how the same multichannel differential network (*a*) is used to form the record processor (*b*) and the reproduce processor (*c*) by connecting the network in additive or subtractive modes (*Dolby, 1967*).

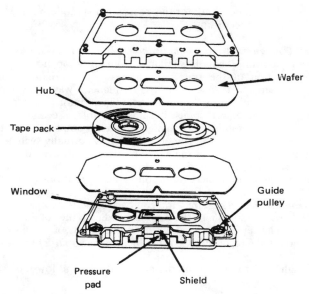

FIGURE 7.17 Compact-cassette configuration.

1970s, the performance was progressively improved to the point that cassette recorders became highly competitive with higher-performance, but less convenient, open reel recording configurations. By 1980, the compact cassette had become the dominant tape format for home use and had displaced the eight-track, endless loop cartridge for automobile use.

The principal features of the compact cassette are shown in Fig. 7.17. The cassette contains two flangeless tape reels that are driven by external, splined drive shafts, helped by low-friction liners on either side of the tape packs. Narrow tape, of width 3.8 mm (0.15 in), is fed from one reel to the other via two rotating, flanged rollers, one at each of the two upper corners. The length of tape between the two rollers is accessible at three main points: the two outermost ones given access to the capstan (inserted through the hole in the case) and pinch rollers for either direction of tape travel at the standard speed of 48 mm/s (1.875 in/s). The central opening, which contains a magnetic screen and pressure-pad assembly, provides head access. Mechanical registration with the drive relies upon the engagement of certain keying points and reference planes in the cassette body. Dependence upon plastic parts to provide this critical registration function is the intrinsic shortcoming of the compact cassette.

7.2.3.2 *Cassette Heads.* Originally, the cassette was designed to use a single record-reproduce head inserted through the central opening. Now, most cassette recorders use separate record and reproduce heads. The reproduce head is always positioned centrally to take advantage of the pressure pad and screen. The record head either contacts the tape through one of the smaller openings, or is integrated into the reproduce-head structure. Both metal and ferrite (including single-crystal) head cores have been used; but metal cores are required to accommodate high-coercivity iron-particle tapes, and, for this reason, most modern drives incorporate metal heads, at least for recording.

7.2.3.3 Track Configuration and Equalization. Four tracks are used, providing two-way stereo recording. This is similar to four-track open-reel recording, although the disposition of the tracks is different. The original standard post-equalization of the compact cassette at high frequencies was equivalent to an RC network of time constant 120 μs. When cassette tapes (initially chromium dioxide) with improved high-frequency response became available, a second standard, corresponding to 70 μs, was established. The high-frequency emphases dictated by these standards are shown in Fig. 7.18. The equalization is normally switched automatically with the bias requirement of the medium, which is described in Sec. 7.2.3.4. As in open-reel recording, standard cassettes are produced that facilitate the interchange of recordings and enable calibration to be carried out in absolute terms.

7.2.3.4 Cassette Media. The tapes for compact cassettes come mainly in three sizes, C60, C90, and C120, where the numbers indicate the total two-way playing time in minutes. The tapes differ mainly in the thickness of the base film, which ranges from a nominal 6 to 12 μm. Coating thickness is about 5 μm—rather less on the C120.

To obtain high performance using the narrow tracks and low tape speed of the

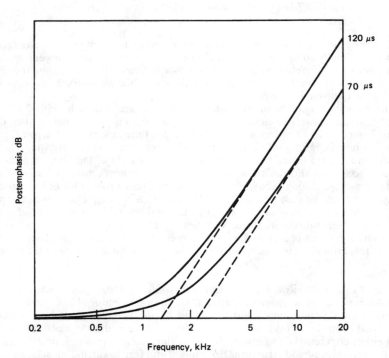

FIGURE 7.18 Compact-cassette standards: high-frequency equalizations corresponding to 120 μs (type I tape) and 70 μs (type II and IV tapes).

compact cassette format demands a great deal from the magnetic medium, and improvements in media have been the main instrument for enhancing performance over the years. Every means of increasing signal-to-noise ratio has been implemented: smaller, more uniform particles, improved dispersion and orientation, and higher particle packing density within the coating. This has resulted in cassette media which, in terms of many magnetic properties such as squareness, orientation ratio, and remanence, are superior to all other particulate media.

Cassette media have usually been the first to exploit new magnetic materials offering potential improvements in signal output, particularly at high densities. The innovative approach began with chromium dioxide in 1970 (Naumann and Daniel, 1971). Subsequently, progressively improved versions of cobalt-modified iron oxides were developed, and passivated iron particles were added to the list in the 1980s. Deposited-metal-film media are a later introduction. Media have also been developed in which a thin outer layer of higher coercivity is coated over an inner layer with the result that the bias is more uniform between short and long wavelengths. This configuration is particularly efficacious if the outer layer is metallic (particulate or film).

All these developments have involved significant changes in machine design, particularly in terms of the bias (and erase) fields necessary to match coercivity. The latter has risen from some 28 kA/m (350 Oe) for gamma ferric oxide, to 50 kA/m (650 Oe) for chromium dioxide and cobalt-modified oxides, to 80 kA/m (1000 Oe) for iron particles. All three types of media are in use, and equipment is usually provided with a switch to select between type I (normal bias), type II (high bias), and type IV (metal bias). Dual-coated media (originally designated "type III") now fit into one of the other categories. As a rule, the same switch automatically selects the equalization. The 70-μs equalization is used for chromium dioxide, cobalt-modified iron oxide, and iron-particle media. Compared with the 120-μs, the 70-μs equalization raises the higher frequencies by some 5 dB less, giving a corresponding benefit in high-frequency noise level. This difference puts normal-bias media at an unfair disadvantage with respect to the other media and does not take into account the significant improvements that have been made in gamma ferric oxide over the years.

The unweighted signal-to-noise ratio provided by a high-quality cassette recorder is in the region of 50 dB. The signal-to-print ratio after a few days storage is typically between 40 and 50 dB, depending upon the base film thickness and the type of magnetic material. The minimum ratio occurs at a frequency of about 600 Hz, more favorable from considerations of audibility than for open-reel tapes. Also, the way in which the tape is wound on a cassette (coating outside) means that the postprints are greater than the preprints—a more natural and often a less easily detectable sequence than in open-reel recording.

7.2.3.5 Noise Reduction. A major challenge in gaining broad acceptance for the compact cassette has been to improve the signal-to-noise ratio, and Sec. 7.2.3.4 outlined what can be done by working with the media. A complementary approach is to introduce an inexpensive and effective means of electronic noise reduction. A system designed specifically for this purpose was introduced in 1970 (Dolby, 1970). This system, called the "B-type," was derived from the professional A-type described earlier. It uses a single-channel approach, but the differential networks contain a variable high-pass filter having a cutoff frequency (around 2 kHz) that moves upward as the level flowing through the differential path increases. The effect is to boost low-level, high-frequency signals by 10 dB on record and attenuate them by the same amount on reproduce, for a net noise reduction of 10 dB. A more ambitious system, designated the C-type, was introduced in 1980 for use on advanced consumer recorders (Dolby, 1983). In simple terms, the C-type uses two B-type stages in series, one with its nonlinear operating range just above the other, to give a net noise reduction of 20 dB. The system also incorporates "spectral skewing" methods to reduce two related defects inherent in the B-type approach: midband modulation effects and high-frequency saturation tendencies (Dolby, 1987). In 1989, an S-type system was introduced (Cossette, 1990; Gundry and Hull, 1990), modeled upon the professional SR system, which provides a noise reduction of 24 dB. Like the C-type, the S-type is aimed at the high end of the cassette recorder market; but the S-type has the advantage over the C-type of producing acceptable sound quality when used to play recordings made on equipment using B-type or no noise reduction at all. This attribute is also held by the original B-type system.

Extensive use of the Dolby systems by the major manufacturers has done much to establish the cassette recorder as the dominant form of tape recorder for the home.

7.2.3.6 High-Speed Duplication.

7.2.3.6 High-Speed Duplication.   AC-biased magnetic recording can be made to handle frequencies one or two orders of magnitude greater than the highest audio frequency (see Chap. 9). This means that, unlike video programs, audio programs can be duplicated at speeds many times greater than the recording speed. Such high-speed duplication is used for all formats, including open-reel, where large numbers of duplicates are required. But by far the largest application is in duplicating musical programs on cassettes for the mass consumer market.

For duplication onto cassette tapes, the typical procedure is to record a duplicating master at, say 190 mm/s (7.5 in/s) using the B-type of pre-record noise reduction. The master tape is then reproduced at up to 64 times the recording speed and recorded on a series of slave machines running cassette tape at 64 times the normal speed, or 3 m/s (120 in/s). Convenience dictates that duplication takes place in both the normal or reverse time sequence, so that the master tape need not be rewound. In order to make this possible, the equipment is equalized to have the necessary phase response. A bias frequency on the order of 1 MHz is used during recording.

REFERENCES

Bertram, H. N., "Long Wavelength AC Bias Recording Theory," *IEEE Trans. Magn.*, **MAG-10,** 1039 (1974).

Bertram, H. N., "Wavelength Response in AC Biased Recording," *IEEE Trans. Magn.*, **MAG-11,** 1176 (1975).

Bertram, H. N., and D. Lindholm, "Dependence of Reproduce Gap Null on Medium Permeability and Spacing," *IEEE Trans. Magn.*, **MAG-18,** 893 (1982).

Bertram, H. N., M. Stafford, and D. Mills, "The Print-Through Phenomenon," *J. Audio Eng. Soc.*, **28,** 690 (1980).

Bertram, H. N., and R. Niedermeyer, "The Effect of Spacing on Demagnetization in Magnetic Recording," *IEEE Trans. Magn.*, **MAG-18,** 1206 (1982).

Cossette, S., "A New Analog Recording Process for Use with Consumer Recording Formats," *89th Conv. Audio Eng. Soc.*, Preprint No. 3004 (1990).

Daniel E. D., "A Basic Study of Tape Noise," Ampex Res. Rep., **AE-1** (1960).

Daniel, E. D., "A Preliminary Analysis of Surface-Induced Tape Noise," *IEEE Trans. Commun. Electron.*, **83,** 250 (1964).

Daniel, E. D., "Tape Noise in Audio Recording," *J. Audio Eng. Soc.,* **20,** 92 (1972).

Daniel, E. D., and P. E. Axon, "Accidental Printing in Magnetic Recording," *BBC Quarterly,* **5,** 7 (1950).

Dolby, R. M., "A 20 dB Audio Noise Reduction System for Consumer Applications," *J. Audio Eng. Soc.,* **31,** 98 (1983).

Dolby, R. M., "An Audio Noise Reduction System," *J. Audio Eng. Soc.,* **15,** 383 (1967).

Dolby, R. M., "A Noise Reduction System for Consumer Applications," *Conv. Audio Eng. Soc.,* Paper No. M-6, New York (1970).

Dolby, R. M., "The Spectral Recording Process," *J. Audio Eng. Soc.,* **35,** 99 (1987).

Dunlop, D., and J. Stirling, "Hard Viscous Remanent Magnetization in Fine Grain Hematite," *Geophys. Research Letters,* **4,** 163 (1977).

Eldridge, D. F., "DC and Moduation Noise in Magnetic Tape," *IEEE Trans. Commun. Electron.,* **83,** 585 (1964).

Eldridge, D. F., and E. D. Daniel, "New Approaches to AC-Biased Recording," *IRE Trans. Audio,* **AU-10,** 72 (1962).

Fujiwara, T., "Nonlinear Distortion in Long Wavelength AC Bias Recording," *IEEE Trans. Magn.,* **MAG-15,** 894 (1979).

Gundry, K., and J. Hull, "Introducing Dolby S-Type Noise Reduction," *Audio Mag.,* June (1990).

Jensen, S. J., "Recording with Feedback-Controlled Effective Bias," *J. Audio Eng. Soc.,* **31,** 729 (1983).

Kishimoto, M., T. Sueyoshi, S. Kotaoka, K. Wakai, and M. Amemiya, "Chronological Changes in Coercivity and Printing Effect of Cobalt-Substituted Iron Oxides," *J. Japan. Soc. Powder and Powder Metallurgy,* **26,** 49 (1979).

Köster, E., "A Contribution to Anhysteretic Remanence and AC Bias Recording," *IEEE Trans. Magn.,* **MAG-11,** 1185 (1975).

Köster, E., H. Jakusch, and U. Kullmann, "Switching Field Distribution and AC Bias Recording Parameters," *IEEE Trans. Magn.,* **MAG-17,** 2250 (1981).

Langevin, Robert Z., "Intermodulation Distortion in Tape Recording," *J. Audio Eng. Soc.,* **11,** 270 (1963).

Mallinson, J. C., "One-Sided Fluxes: A Magnetic Cusiosity?" *IEEE Trans. Magn.,* **MAG-9,** 678 (1973).

McKnight, J. G., "The Distribution of Peak Energy in Recorded Music," *J. Audio Eng. Soc.,* **7,** 65 (1959).

McKnight, J. G., "Erasure of Magnetic Tape," *J. Audio Eng. Soc.,* **11,** 223 (1963).

McKnight, J. G., "Flux and Flux-Frequency Measurements in Magnetic Recording," *J. SMPTE,* **78,** 457 (1969).

Mee, C. D., and E. D. Daniel (eds.), *Magnetic Recording Technology,* McGraw Hill, New York, 1996.

Naumann, K. E., and E. D. Daniel, "Audio Cassette Chromium Dioxide Tape," *J. Audio Eng. Soc.,* **19,** 822 (1971).

Olsen, H. F., *Acoustical Engineering.* Van Nostrand, New York, 1957.

Preis, D., "Phase Distortion and Phase Equalization in Audio Signal Processing," *J. Audio Eng. Soc.,* **30,** 774 (1983).

Ragle, H. U., and P. Smaller, "An Investigation of High-Frequency Bias-Induced Noise," *IEEE Trans. Magn.,* **MAG-1,** 105 (1965).

Sawada, T., and K. Yamada, "AC Erase Head for Cassette Recorder," *IEEE Trans. Magn.,* **MAG-21,** 2104 (1985).

Sivian, L. J., H. K. Dunn, and S. D. White, "Absolute Amplitudes and Spectra of Certain Musical Instruments and Orchestras," *J. Acoust. Soc. Amer.* **2,** 330 (1931).

Steinhaus, von W., and E. Gumlich, "Ideale d. h. hysteresefreie Magnetisierung," *Verh. Dtsch. Phys. Ges.,* **17,** 309 (1915).

Tjaden, D. L. A., and J. Leyten, "A 5000; 1 Scale Model of the Magnetic Recording Process," *Philips Tech. Rev.,* **25,** 319 (1963).

Tjaden, D. L. A., and A. M. A. Rijckaert, "Theory of Anhysteretic Contact Duplication," *IEEE Trans. Magn.,* **MAG-7,** 532 (1971).

Wallace, R. L., "The Reproduction of Magnetically Recorded Signals," *Bell Syst. Tech. J.,* **30,** 1145 (1951).

Westmijze, W. K., "Studies in Magnetic Recording," *Philips Res. Rep.,* **8,** 344 (1953).

CHAPTER 8
DIGITAL AUDIO RECORDING

John R. Watkinson
Watkinson International Communications, Reading, England

8.1 INTRODUCTION

The digital audio recorder has recently undergone rapid development. In the early 1980s the digital audio recorder was an expensive and cumbersome device which was waiting to become cost effective. Today it is ousting analog audio recording in virtually all applications by a combination of low first cost, low running cost, and high reliability. The sound quality is taken for granted. Like all magnetic recorders, the digital audio recorder has benefited from improved media and head design and from improvements in channel coding and error-correction technology. The use of complex coding schemes has only been possible because of parallel developments in large-scale integration (LSI) which has also resulted in related developments such as accurate convertors and compression chip sets.

In principle a digital audio recorder is a data recorder which is adapted to handle analog signals which have been pulse code modulated (Reeves, 1942]. Figure 8.1 shows how PCM works. The time axis is represented in a discrete, or stepwise manner and the waveform is carried by measurement at regular intervals. This process is called sampling and the frequency with which samples are taken is called the sampling rate or sampling frequency F_s. The samples are then expressed as the nearest value on a discrete scale of integers which can be recorded as twos complement binary numbers.

There are two main reasons for the current popularity of digital audio recording, although it is not possible to say which is the more important, as it will depend on one's standpoint.

a) The quality of reproduction from a well-engineered digital audio recorder is independent of the medium.

b) The conversion of audio to the digital domain allows processing opportunities which were denied to analog signals.

Someone who is interested only in sound quality will judge the former the most relevant. The recorder and its error-correction strategy are simply a data store and, in the absence of any compression stage, the sound quality depends only on the quality of the conversion processes. If good quality convertors can be obtained, all

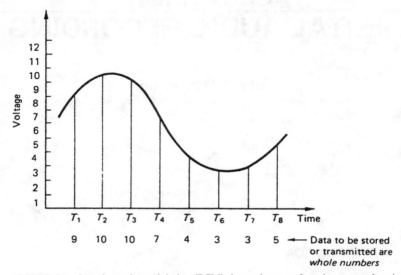

FIGURE 8.1   In pulse code modulation (PCM) the analog waveform is measured periodically at the sampling rate. The voltage (represented here by the height) of each sample is then described by a whole number. The whole numbers are stored or transmitted rather than the waveform itself.

of the shortcomings of analog recording can be eliminated to great advantage. Wow, flutter, particulate noise, print-through, dropouts, modulation noise, high-frequency compression, azimuth error, interchannel phase errors are all eliminated from the reproduced audio. When a digital recording is copied, the same numbers appear on the copy: it is not a dub, it is a clone. If the copy is indistinguishable from the original, there has been no generation loss.

The importance of convertor performance to the audio recording application is such that much recent work has been done which deserves prominence here. This is appropriate since the magnetics, the channel coding and error correction principles used are common to all data recorders and detailed treatments can be found in other chapters of this book.

In the real world everything has a cost, and one of the greatest strengths of digital technology is low cost. If copying causes no quality loss, recorders need only be adequate on the first generation whose quality is then maintained. There is no need for the great size and extravagant tape consumption of professional analog recorders which must perform far better than necessary in order to withstand generation loss. When the information to be recorded is discrete numbers, it can be packed densely on the medium without quality loss. Should some bits be in error because of noise or dropout, error correction can restore the original value. Digital recordings take up less space than analog recordings for the same or better quality. Tape costs are far less and storage costs are reduced.

Once audio is in the digital domain, it becomes data, and as such is indistinguishable from any other type of data. Systems and techniques developed in other industries for other purposes can be used for audio. Computer equipment is available at low cost because the volume of production is far greater than that of professional audio equipment. Exabyte data cassettes are used for compact disc mastering. Magnetic and magnetooptical disk drives and memories developed for computers can be put to use in audio products. A word processor adapted to handle audio samples becomes a workstation. There seems to be little point in waiting for a tape to wind when a disk head can access data in milliseconds. The difficulty of locating the edit point and the irrevocable nature of tape-cut editing are hardly worth considering when the edit point can be located by viewing the audio waveform on a screen or by listening at any speed to audio from a memory. The edit can be simulated and trimmed to sample accuracy before it is made permanent. Now that suitable LSI components are available, digital audio recorders are becoming available which use compression or source coding. The human hearing system comprises not only the physical organs, but processes also take place within the brain. We do not perceive every detail of the sound entering our ears. Auditory masking is a process which selects only the dominant frequencies from the spectrum applied to the ear. Compression takes advantage of this process to reduce the amount of data needed to carry sound of a given subjective quality by mimicking the operation of the hearing mechanism.

Reduction to around one quarter or one fifth of the PCM data rate can be virtually inaudible on high-quality compression systems, because the error between the original and the reproduced waveforms can be effectively masked. Greater compression factors inevitably result in quality loss which may be acceptable for certain applications, such as speech, but not for quality music reproduction.

The use of compression in recording applications is extremely powerful. The playing time of the medium is extended in proportion to the compression factor. In the case of tapes, the access time is improved because the length of tape needed for a given recording is reduced and so it can be rewound more quickly.

In the digital compact cassette (DCC) 4:1 compression is used on the audio data prior to recording. This means that the same tape speed as for analog cassettes can be used without needing excessively short wavelengths or narrow tracks on the tape. As a result, conventional chromium dioxide cassette tape can be used instead of the more expensive metal tape. The transport design is less critical and more contamination can be tolerated.

In workstations designed for audio and video editing, the source material is stored on Winchester disks for rapid access. Today's disk drives cannot offer sufficient storage capacity to give realistic playing times without the use of compression although this will not always be true. When a workstation is used for off-line editing, a high compression factor can be used and artifacts may be audible. This is of no consequence because the compressed sound is heard only by the editor who uses it to make an edit decision list (EDL) which is no more than a list of actions and the time codes at which they occur. The original uncompressed material is then conformed to the EDL to obtain a high-quality edited work. When on-line editing is being performed, the output of the workstation is the finished product and a lower compression factor must be used.

There are numerous proprietary compression units, and each needs the appropriate decoder to return to PCM. The combination of a compressor and a decoder is called a *codec*. The performance of a codec is usually tested on a single pass, as would be the case in a single generation recording in a consumer recorder. The same performance is not necessarily obtained if codecs are cascaded, particularly if they are of different types. If an equalization step is performed on audio which has been through a compression codec, artifacts may be raised above the masking threshold. As a result, compression may not be suitable for the recording of original material prior to post production.

8.2 CONVERSION

The input to a convertor is a continuous-time, continuous-voltage waveform, and this is changed into a discrete-time, discrete-voltage format by a combination of sampling and quantizing. These two processes are totally independent and can be performed in either order and discussed quite separately. Figure 8.2*a* shows an analog sampler preceding a quantizer, whereas Fig. 8.2*b* shows an asynchronous quantizer preceding a digital sampler. Ideally, both will give the same results; in practice each has different advantages and suffers from different deficiencies. Both approaches are found in real equipment.

Audio sampling must be regular, because the process of timebase correction prior to conversion back to analog assumes a regular original process. The sampling

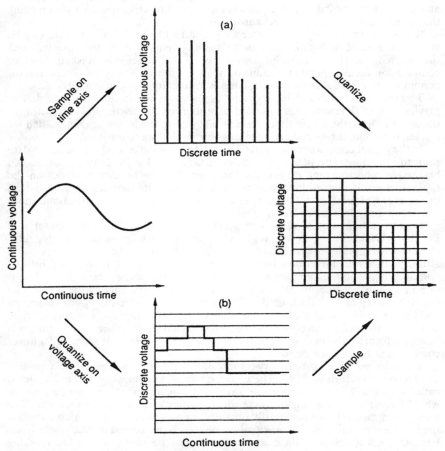

FIGURE 8.2 Since sampling and quantizing are orthogonal the sequence is unimportant. See Sec. 8.2 for details.

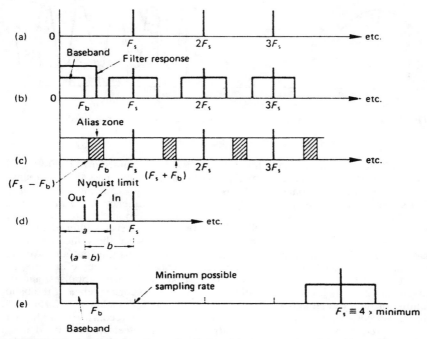

FIGURE 8.3 (*a*) Spectrum of sampling pulses (*b*) spectrum of samples (*c*) aliasing due to sideband overlap (*d*) beat frequency generation (*e*) oversampling.

process originates with a pulse train which is shown in Fig. 8.3*a* to be of constant amplitude and period. The audio waveform amplitude modulates the pulse train and produces sidebands or images above and below each harmonic of the sampling rate as shown in Fig. 8.3*b*. The sampled signal can be returned to the continuous-time domain simply by passing it into a low-pass reconstruction filter having a frequency response which prevents the images from passing. If an input is supplied having an excessive bandwidth for the sampling rate in use, the sidebands will overlap, (Fig. 8.3*c*) and the result is aliasing, where certain output frequencies are not the same as their input frequencies but instead become difference frequencies (Fig. 8.3*b*). Aliasing cannot occur when the input frequency is equal to or less than half the sampling rate, and this leads to the most fundamental rule of sampling, namely that the sampling rate must be at least twice the input bandwidth. Sampling theory is usually attributed to Shannon (Shannon, 1948) who applied it to information theory at around the same time as Kotelnikov in Russia. Nevertheless, the sampling rule is often referred to as Nyquist's theorem.

While aliasing has been described above in the frequency domain, it can be described equally well in the time domain. In Fig. 8.4*a* the sampling rate is obviously adequate to describe the waveform, but in Fig. 8.4*b* the rate is inadequate and aliasing has occurred. In a practical system it is necessary to have a low-pass, or anti-aliasing filter at the input to prevent frequencies of more than half the sampling rate from reaching the sampling stage as well as a reconstruction filter at the output.

If ideal low-pass anti-aliasing and anti-image filters are assumed, having a verti-

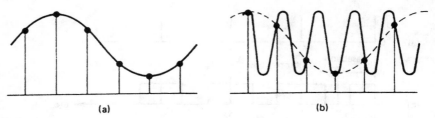

FIGURE 8.4   (*a*) Adequate sampling rate (*b*) inadequate sampling rate causing aliasing.

cal cut-off slope at half the sampling rate, the ideal spectrum shown in Fig. 8.5*a* is obtained. The impulse response of a phase linear ideal low-pass filter is a sinx/x waveform in the time domain, and this is shown in Fig. 8.5*b*. Such a waveform passes through zero volts periodically. If the cut-off frequency of the filter is one-half of the sampling rate, the impulse passes through zero at the sites of all other samples. It can be seen from Fig. 8.5*c* that at the output of such a filter, the voltage at the center of a sample is due to that sample alone, since the value of all other samples is zero at that instant. In other words the continuous-time output waveform must join up the tops of the input samples. In between the sample instants, the output of the filter is the sum of the contributions from many impulses, and the waveform smoothly joins the tops of the samples. It is a consequence of the band-limiting of the original anti-aliasing filter that the filtered analog waveform could only travel between the sample points in one way. As the reconstruction filter has the same frequency response, the reconstructed output waveform must be identical to the original band-limited waveform prior to sampling. It follows that sampling need not be audible. A rigorous mathematical proof of reconstruction can be found in Betts, 1970. Analog "brick-wall" filters are difficult to implement because for quality audio applications they must be phase-linear. In all modern digital audio recorders the steep analog filter has been avoided by the use of oversampling.

Sampling theory is only the beginning of the process which must be followed to arrive at a suitable sampling rate. The finite slope of realizable filters will compel designers to raise the sampling rate. For consumer products, the lower the sampling rate the better, since the cost of the medium is directly proportional to the sampling rate: thus sampling rates near to twice 20 kHz are to be expected. For professional products, there is a need to operate at variable speed for pitch correction. When the speed of a digital recorder is reduced, the offtape sampling rate falls and, with a minimal sampling rate, the first image frequency can become low enough to pass the reconstruction filter. If the sampling frequency is raised without changing the response of the filters, the speed can be reduced without this problem.

Early digital audio recorders used standard analog video recorders which were adapted to store audio samples by creating a pseudo-video waveform which could convey binary as black and white levels (Ishida et al., 1979). The sampling rate of such a system is constrained to relate simply to the field rate and field structure of the television standard used, so that an integer number of samples can be stored on each usable TV line in the field. Such a recording can be made on a monochrome recorder, and these recordings are made in two standards, 525 lines at 60 Hz and 625 lines at 50 Hz. Thus it is necessary to find a frequency which is a common multiple of the two and which is also suitable for use as a sampling rate. In 60 Hz video, there are 35 blanked lines, leaving 490 lines per frame, or 245 lines per field for samples. If three samples are stored per line, the sampling rate becomes 60 ×

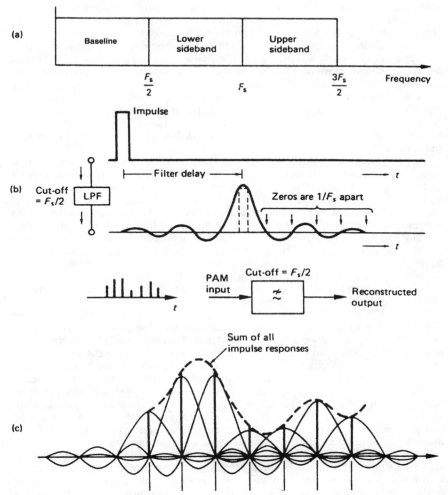

FIGURE 8.5 (*a*) Ideal spectrum if "brickwall" filter used (*b*) impulse response of ideal filter (*c*) convolution of impulse response and pulse train reconstructs waveform.

$245 \times 3 = 44.1$ kHz. In 50 Hz video, there are 37 lines of blanking, leaving 588 active lines per frame, or 294 per field, so the same sampling rate is given by $50 \times 294 \times 3 = 44.1$ kHz.

The sampling rate of 44.1 kHz came to be that of the compact disc. Even though CD has no video circuitry, the first equipment used to make CD masters was based on the U-matic VCR and this determined the sampling rate. Although video-based digital audio recorders are now obsolete, the sampling rate has become well established and is supported by many recording formats including DAT and MiniDisc.

For landlines to FM stereo broadcast transmitters having a 15 kHz audio bandwidth, the sampling rate of 32 kHz is more than adequate, and has been in use for some time in the United Kingdom and Japan. This frequency is also in use in the NICAM 728 stereo TV sound system and in digital audio broadcasting (DAB). It is also used for the Sony non-tracking (NT) format mini-cassette. The professional sampling rate of 48 kHz was proposed as having a simple relationship to 32 kHz and being far enough above 40 kHz for variable-speed operation. The currently available digital video tape recorder (DVTR) formats offer only 48 kHz audio sampling. A number of formats can operate at more than one sampling rate. Digital audio tape (DAT), digital compact cassette (DCC) and digital audio stationary head (DASH) formats are specified for all three rates, although not all available hardware implements every possibility. Most hard-disk workstations will operate at a range of rates.

Figure 8.6*a* shows that the effect of clock jitter on a sloping waveform is that samples are taken at the wrong times. A subsequent timebase correction stage prior to the DAC will remove the jitter, and the result is shown in Fig. 8.6*b*. The magnitude of the unwanted signal is proportional to the slope of the audio waveform and so the amount of jitter which can be tolerated falls at 6 dB per octave. As the resolution of the system is increased by the use of longer sample wordlengths, tolerance to jitter is further reduced. The nature of the unwanted signal depends on the spectrum of the jitter. If the jitter is random, the effect is noise-like and relatively benign unless the amplitude is excessive. Figure 8.7 shows the effect of differing amounts of random jitter with respect to the noise floor of various wordlengths. Note that even small amounts of jitter can degrade a 20 bit convertor to the performance of a good 16-bit unit.

Although it has been documented for many years (Watkinson, 1989), attention to control of clock jitter is not as great in actual hardware as it might be. Lack of jitter control accounts for much of the slight audible differences between convertors reproducing the same data. A well-engineered convertor should substantially reject jitter on an external clock and should sound the same when reproducing the same data irrespective of the source of the data. A remote convertor which sounds different when reproducing, for example, the same recording via the digital outputs of a variety of players is simply not well engineered and should be rejected. Similarly if the effect of changing the type of digital cable feeding the convertor can be heard, the unit is defective. Unfortunately many consumer external DACs fall into this category, because the steps outlined above have not been taken.

Figure 8.8*a* shows that the process of quantizing divides the voltage range up into quantizing intervals Q. In digital audio the quantizing intervals are made as identical as possible so that the binary numbers which result are truly proportional to the original analog voltage. The digital equivalents of mixing and gain changing can then be performed by adding and multiplying sample values. If the quantizing intervals are unequal this cannot be done. When all quantizing intervals are the same, the term uniform quantizing is used.

The quantizer will locate the quantizing interval bracketing the input and, in what may be considered a separate step, the quantizing interval is then allocated a code value which is almost universally a twos complement binary number. The information sent is the number of the quantizing interval in which the input voltage lay. Where that voltage lay within the interval is not conveyed, and this mechanism puts a limit on the accuracy of the quantizer. When the number of the quantizing interval is converted back to the analog domain, it will result in a voltage at the centre of the quantizing interval as this minimizes the magnitude of the error between input and output. The number range is limited by the wordlength of the

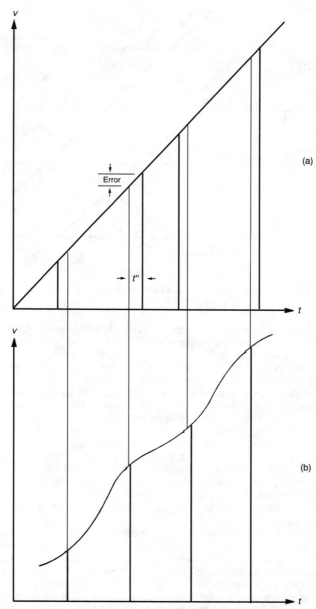

FIGURE 8.6 (*a*) Samples taken at the wrong time due to jitter are subsequently timebase corrected (*b*) noise resulting from clock jitter.

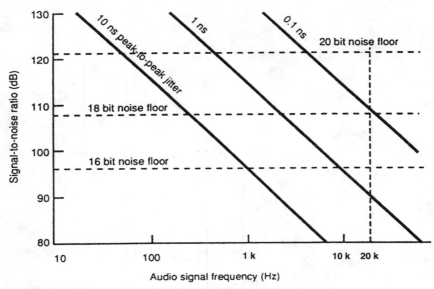

FIGURE 8.7   Effects of sample clock jitter as a function of signal frequency.

binary numbers used. In a 16-bit system, 65,536 different quantizing intervals exist, although the ones at the extreme ends of the range have no outer boundary.

The transfer function for an ideal quantizer followed by an ideal DAC is also shown in Fig. 8.8. A transfer function is simply a graph of the output with respect to the input. In audio, when the term linearity is used, this generally means the straightness of the transfer function. Linearity is a goal in audio, yet it will be seen that an ideal quantizer is anything but linear. Figure 8.8*b* shows that the transfer function is somewhat like a staircase, and zero volts analog, corresponding to all zeros digital, or muting, is half way up a quantizing interval. This is the so-called mid-tread quantizer which is universally used in audio.

Quantizing causes a voltage error in the audio sample which is given by the difference between the actual staircase transfer function and the ideal straight line. This is shown in Fig. 8.8*d* to be a sawtooth-like function which is periodic in Q. The amplitude cannot exceed $\pm$ 1/2 Q peak-to-peak unless the input is so large that clipping occurs. If a very small input signal remains within one quantizing interval, the quantizing error is the signal.

As the transfer function is nonlinear, ideal quantizing can cause distortion. As a result practical digital audio devices deliberately use non-ideal quantizers to achieve linearity. The quantizing error of an ideal quantizer is a complex function, and it has been researched in great depth (Widrow, 1961; Lipshitz, 1992; Maher, 1992). Here the characteristics of an ideal quantizer will only be pursued far enough to convince the reader that such a device cannot be used in quality audio applications.

As the magnitude of the quantizing error is limited, its effect can be minimized by making the signal larger. This will require more quantizing intervals and more bits to express them. The number of quantizing intervals multiplied by their size gives the quantizing range of the convertor. A signal outside the range will be

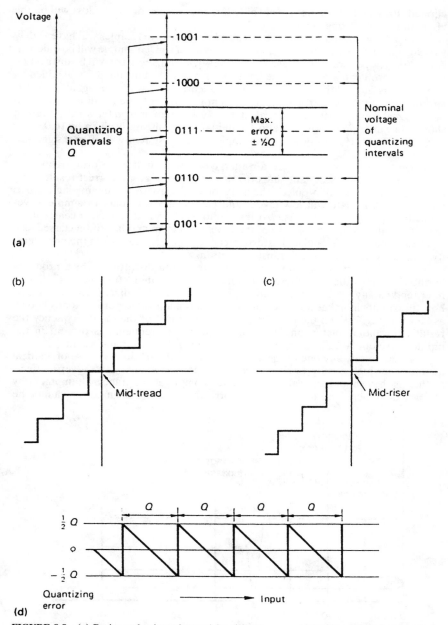

FIGURE 8.8 (a) Basic mechanism of quantizing (b) common mid-tread quantizer has a code for zero volts analog (c) uncommon mid-riser quantizer (d) quantizing error cannot exceed ± 1/2 Q.

clipped. Provided that clipping is avoided, the larger the signal the less will be the effect of the quantizing error.

Where the input signal is large and complex, successive samples will have widely varying numerical values and the quantizing error on a given sample will be independent of that on others. In this case the size of the quantizing error will be distributed with equal probability between the limits. In this case the unwanted signal added by quantizing is an additive broadband noise uncorrelated with the signal, and it is appropriate in this case to call it quantizing noise. Under these conditions, a meaningful signal-to-noise ratio can be calculated. In a system using n bit words, it can be shown that the signal-to-noise ratio for the large signal case is given by $(6.02\,n + 1.76)$ dB (Betts, 1970). By way of example, a 16-bit system will offer a signal-to-noise ratio of 98 dB.

While the above result is true for a large complex input waveform, treatments which then assume that quantizing error is always noise give incorrect results. The expression above is valid only if the probability density of the quantizing error is uniform. Unfortunately at low levels, and particularly with pure or simple waveforms this is simply not the case. At low audio levels, quantizing error ceases to be random, and becomes a function of the input waveform and has to be classed as a distortion rather than a noise. Distortion can also be predicted from the nonlinearity, or staircase nature, of the transfer function.

The nonlinearity of the transfer function results in distortion, which produces harmonics. Unfortunately these harmonics are generated after the anti-aliasing filter, and so any which exceed half the sampling rate will alias. Figure 8.9 shows how this results in anharmonic distortion which is audible as spurious tones known as "birdsinging." When the sampling rate is a multiple of the input frequency the result is harmonic distortion. When more than one frequency is present in the input, intermodulation distortion occurs, which is known as granulation.

Needless to say, any one of the above effects would preclude the use of an ideal quantizer for high-quality work. There is little point in studying the adverse effects further as they should and can be eliminated completely in practical equipment by the use of dither. The importance of correctly dithering a quantizer cannot be

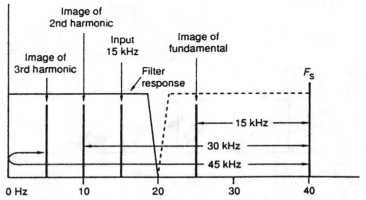

FIGURE 8.9 Quantizing distortion occurs after the anti-aliasing filter. Thus distortion products will beat or fold back to produce anharmonics as shown here. Second and third harmonics of 15 kHz produce aliased products at 10 kHz and 5 kHz.

emphasized enough, since failure to dither irrevocably distorts the converted signal, and no process can subsequently remove that distortion. The signal-to-noise ratio derived above has no relevance to practical audio applications because it will be modified by the dither and by any noise shaping used.

At high signal levels, quantizing error is effectively noise. As the audio level falls, the quantizing error of an ideal quantizer becomes more strongly correlated with the signal and the result is distortion. If the quantizing error can be de-correlated from the input in some way, the system can remain linear but noisy. Dither performs the job of decorrelation by making the action of the quantizer unpredictable and gives the system a noise floor like an analog system.

All practical digital audio recorders use nonsubtractive dither where the dither signal is added prior to quantization and no attempt is made to remove it at the DAC (Vanderkooy and Lipshitz, 1984). The introduction of dither prior to a conventional quantizer inevitably causes a slight reduction in the signal-to-noise ratio attainable, but this reduction is a small price to pay for the elimination of nonlinearities. The technique of noise shaping in conjunction with dither can overcome this restriction. The ideal (noiseless) quantizer has fixed quantizing intervals and must always produce the same quantizing error from the same signal. The addition of dither means that successive samples effectively find the quantizing intervals in different places on the voltage scale. The quantizing error becomes a function of the dither, rather than a predictable function of the input signal. The quantizing error is not eliminated, but the subjectively unacceptable distortion is converted into a broadband noise which is more benign to the ear.

Some alternative ways of looking at dither are shown in Fig. 8.10. Consider the situation where a low level input signal is changing slowly within a quantizing interval. Without dither, the same numerical code is the output for a number of sample periods, and the variations within the interval are lost. Dither has the effect of forcing the quantizer to switch between two or more states. The higher the voltage of the input signal within a given interval, the more probable it becomes that the output code will take on the next higher value. The lower the input voltage within the interval, the more probable it becomes that the output code will take the next lower value. The dither has resulted in a form of duty cycle modulation, and the resolution of the system has been extended indefinitely instead of being limited by the size of the steps. Dither can also be understood by considering what it does to the transfer function of the quantizer. This is normally a perfect staircase, but in the presence of dither it is smeared horizontally until with a certain amplitude the average transfer function becomes straight.

A conventional analog-to-digital subsystem is shown in Fig. 8.11. Following the anti-aliasing filter there will be a sampling process. Many ADCs will need a finite time to operate, whereas an instantaneous sample must be taken from the input. The solution is to use a track/hold circuit. Following sampling the sample voltage is quantized. The number of the quantized level is then converted to a binary code, typically twos complement. The general principle of a quantizer is that different quantized voltages are compared with the unknown analog input until the closest quantized voltage is found. The code corresponding to this becomes the output. The comparisons can be made in turn with the minimal amount of hardware, or simultaneously.

The purpose of a digital-to-analog convertor is to take numerical values and reproduce the continuous waveform that they represent. Figure 8.12 shows the major elements of a conventional conversion subsystem. The jitter in the clock needs to be removed with a voltage controlled oscillator (VCO) or voltage controlled crystal oscillator (VCXO). Sample values are buffered in a latch and fed to

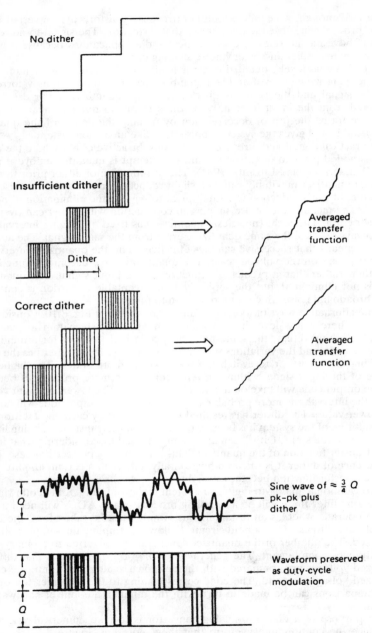

FIGURE 8.10 Wideband dither of the appropriate level linearizes the transfer function to produce noise instead of distortion. One view is that the frequent switching allows level to be preserved as duty cycle information.

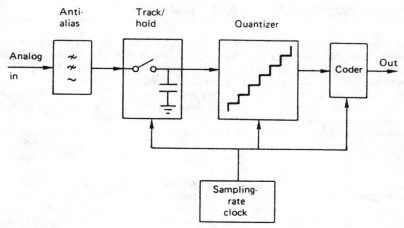

FIGURE 8.11 A conventional analog to digital subsystem. Following the anti-aliasing filter there is a sampling process, which may include a track/hold circuit. Following quantizing, the number of the quantized level is then converted to a binary code, typically twos complement.

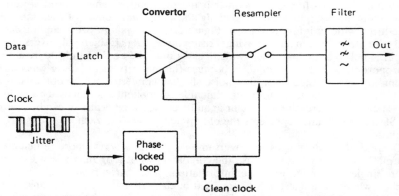

FIGURE 8.12 The components of a conventional convertor. A jitter-free clock drives the voltage conversion, output of which may be resampled prior to reconstruction.

the convertor element which operates on each cycle of the clean clock. The output is then a voltage proportional to the number for at least a part of the sample period. A resampling stage may be found next, in order to remove switching transients or to allow the use of a convertor which takes a substantial part of the sample period to operate. The resampled waveform is then presented to a reconstruction filter which rejects frequencies above the audio band.

In practice these simple approaches to conversion are no longer used in digital audio recorders. They are difficult to implement with 16-bit accuracy because of component tolerances, and provision of a longer wordlength is impossible. A further problem is the provision of steep-cut, yet phase-linear, analog filters.

8.3 OVERSAMPLING AND NOISE SHAPING

Oversampling means using a sampling rate which is greater (generally substantially greater) than the Nyquist rate. Neither sampling theory nor quantizing theory require oversampling to be used to obtain a given signal quality, but Nyquist rate conversion places extremely high demands on component accuracy when a convertor is implemented. Oversampling allows a given signal quality to be reached without requiring very close tolerance components. The advantages of oversampling are better realized when it is used in conjunction with noise shaping. Thus in practice the two processes are generally used together and the terms are often seen used in the loose sense as if they were synonymous. For a detailed and quantitative analysis of oversampling having exhaustive references the serious reader is referred to Hauser (Hauser, 1991).

Figure 8.13 shows the main advantages of oversampling. In Fig. 8.13a it will be seen that the use of a sampling rate considerably above the Nyquist rate allows the anti-aliasing and reconstruction filters to be realized with a much more gentle cut-off slope. There is then less likelihood of phase linearity and ripple problems in the audio passband. Figure 8.13b shows that information in an analog signal is two dimensional and can be depicted as an area which is the product of bandwidth and the linearly expressed signal-to-noise ratio. The figure also shows that the same amount of information can be conveyed down a channel with a SNR of half as much (6 dB less) if the bandwidth is doubled, and with 12 dB less SNR if the bandwidth is quadrupled, and so forth, provided that the modulation scheme used is perfect. Thus raising the sampling rate potentially allows the wordlength of each sample to be reduced without information loss. Figure 8.13c shows that oversampling can be used with a class of convertor having a rising noise floor. If the highly oversampled output is fed to a low-pass filter which passes only the audio band, the result is a disproportionate reduction in noise because the majority of the noise was outside the audio band. A high resolution noise shaping convertor can be obtained using this technology without requiring unattainable component tolerances. This technology is becoming increasingly popular in audio conversion because it can be realized in LSI at low cost and represents the only practical way of reaching 18- and 20-bit resolution.

Despite the advantages of oversampling, it is always more efficient, in information-capacity terms, to use the combinations of long binary words than to record single bits for every piece of information. The greatest recording efficiency is reached when the longest words are used at the slowest rate which must be the Nyquist rate. As a result, oversampling is confined to convertor technology where it gives specific advantages in implementation.

Figure 8.14 shows a digital audio tape recorder using oversampling convertors. The ADC runs at n times the Nyquist rate, but once in the digital domain the rate needs to be reduced in a type of digital filter called a decimator. The output of this is conventional Nyquist rate PCM, according to the tape format, which is then recorded. On replay the sampling rate is raised once more in a further type of digital filter called an interpolator. The system now has the best of both worlds: using oversampling in the convertors overcomes the shortcomings of analog anti-aliasing and reconstruction filters and the wordlength of the convertor elements is reduced making them easier to construct; the recording is made with Nyquist rate PCM which minimizes tape consumption.

Oversampling is a method of overcoming practical implementation problems by replacing a single critical element or bottleneck by a number of elements whose overall performance is what counts. As Hauser properly observed, oversampling

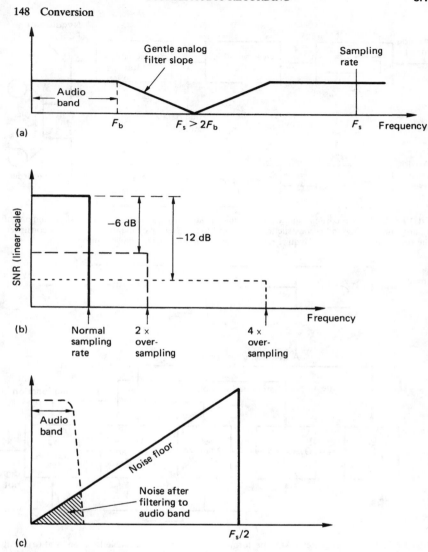

FIGURE 8.13 Oversampling has a number of advantages. At (*a*) it allows the slope of analog filters to be relaxed. At (*b*) it allows the resolution of convertors to be extended. At (*c*) a noise-shaped convertor allows a disproportionate improvement in resolution.

tends to overlap the operations which are quite distinct in a conventional convertor. Figure 8.15*a* shows that it is possible to construct an ADC of predictable performance by a taking a suitable anti-aliasing filter, a sampler, a dither source and a quantizer and assembling them like building bricks. The bricks are effectively in series and so the performance of each stage can limit the overall performance. In contrast Fig. 8.15*b* shows that, with oversampling, the overlap of operations allows

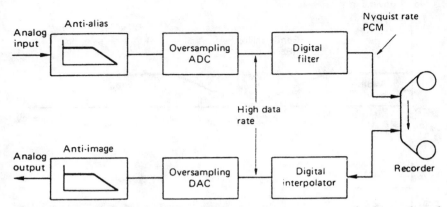

FIGURE 8.14   A recorder using oversampling in the convertors overcomes the shortcomings of analog anti-aliasing and reconstruction filters and the convertor elements are easier to construct; the recording is made with Nyquist rate PCM which minimizes tape consumption.

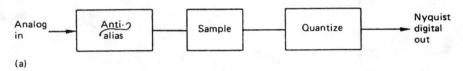

(a)

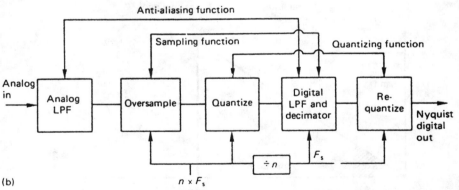

(b)

FIGURE 8.15   A conventional ADC performs each step in an identifiable location as at (*a*). With oversampling, many of the steps are distributed as shown in (*b*).

different processes to augment one another allowing a synergy which is absent in the conventional approach.

If the oversampling factor is n, the analog input must be bandwidth limited to $nF_s/2$ by the analog anti-aliasing filter. This unit need only have flat frequency response and phase linearity within the audio band. Analog dither of an amplitude compatible with the quantizing interval size is added prior to sampling at nF_s and quantizing. This dither may be outside the audio frequency band.

Next, the anti-aliasing function is completed in the digital domain by a low-pass filter which cuts off at $F_s/2$. Using an appropriate architecture this filter can be absolutely phase linear and implemented to arbitrary accuracy. The filter can be considered to be the demodulator of Fig. 8.13 where the SNR improves as the bandwidth is reduced. The wordlength can be expected to increase. The multiplications taking place within the filter extend the wordlength considerably more than the bandwidth reduction alone would indicate. The analog filter serves only to prevent aliasing into the audio band at the oversampling rate; the audio spectrum is determined with greater precision by the digital filter.

With the audio information spectrum now Nyquist limited, the sampling process is completed when the rate is reduced in the decimator. One sample in n is retained. The excess wordlength extension due to the anti-aliasing filter arithmetic must then be removed. Digital dither is added, completing the dither process, and the quantizing process is completed by requantizing the dithered samples to the appropriate wordlength which will be greater than the wordlength of the first quantizer. Alternatively noise shaping may be employed as will be described later.

Figure 8.16a shows the building brick approach of a conventional DAC. The Nyquist rate samples are converted to analog voltages and then a steep-cut analog low pass filter is needed to reject the sidebands of the sampled spectrum. Figure 8.16b shows the oversampling approach. The sampling rate is raised in an interpolator which contains a low-pass filter which restricts the baseband spectrum to the audio bandwidth shown. A large frequency gap now exists between the baseband and the lower sideband. The multiplications in the interpolator extend the wordlength considerably and this must be reduced within the capacity of the DAC element by the addition of digital dither prior to requantizing. Again, noise shaping may be used as an alternative.

Oversampling permits the use of a convertor element of shorter wordlength but requires higher speed, suggesting the use of a flash convertor. Figure 8.17 shows

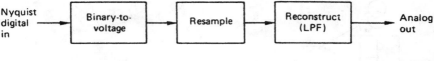

(a)

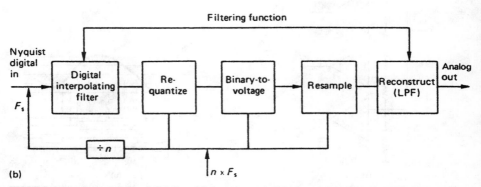

(b)

FIGURE 8.16 A conventional DAC at (a) is compared with the oversampling implementation at (b).

that the threshold voltage of every quantizing interval is provided by a resistor chain which is fed by a reference voltage. This reference voltage can be varied to determine the sensitivity of the input. There is one voltage comparator connected to every reference voltage, and the other input of all of these is connected to the analog input. A comparator can be considered to be a one-bit ADC. The input voltage determines how many of the comparators will have a true output. One comparator is necessary for each quantizing interval; thus, for example, in an 8-bit system there will be 255 binary comparator outputs, and it is necessary to use a priority encoder to convert these to a binary code. Note that the quantizing stage is asynchronous; comparators change state as and when the variations in the input waveform result in a reference voltage being crossed. Sampling takes place when the comparator outputs are clocked into a subsequent latch. This is an example of quantizing before sampling as was illustrated in Fig. 8.2. Although the device is simple in principle, it contains a lot of circuitry and can only be practicably implemented on a chip. Because computation of all bits is performed simultaneously no track/hold circuit is required, and droop is eliminated. Figure 8.17 shows a flash convertor chip. Note the resistor ladder and the comparators followed by the priority encoder. The most significant bit (MSB) can be selectively inverted so that the device can be used either in offset binary or twos complement mode.

The sigma differential pulse code modulation (DPCM) converter shown in Fig. 8.18 is advantageous for oversampled audio conversion. The current digital sample from the quantizer, which is implemented with a flash convertor, is converted back to analog in the embedded DAC. The DAC output differs from the ADC input by the quantizing error. The DAC output is subtracted from the analog input to produce an error which is integrated to drive the quantizer in such a way that the

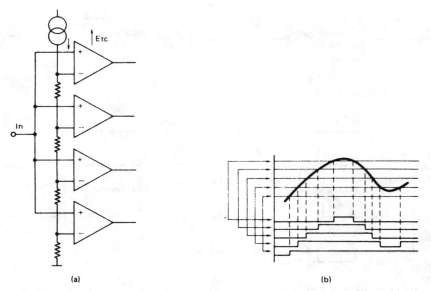

(a)   (b)

FIGURE 8.17 In the flash convertor each interval has its own comparator (*a*) resulting in waveforms at (*b*). Typical flash convertor structure (Courtesy TRW) is shown at (*c*).

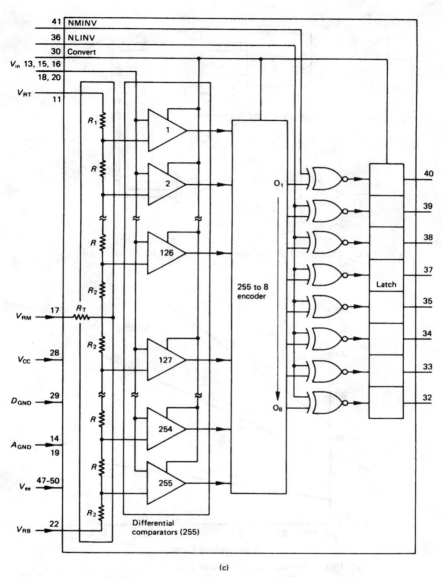

FIGURE 8.17 (*Continued*)

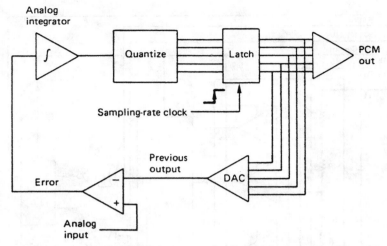

FIGURE 8.18   The Sigma DPCM convertor. See Sec. 8.3 for further details.

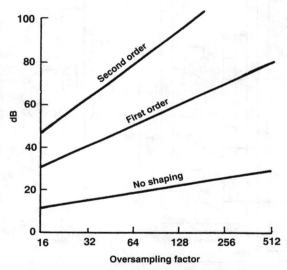

FIGURE 8.19   The enhancement of SNR possible with various filter orders and oversampling factors in noise-shaping convertors.

error is reduced. With a constant input voltage the average error will be zero because the loop gain is infinite at dc. If the average error is zero, the mean or average of the DAC outputs must be equal to the analog input. The instantaneous output will deviate from the average in what is called an idling pattern. The presence of the integrator in the error feedback loop makes the loop gain fall with rising frequency. With the feedback falling at 6 dB per octave, the noise floor will rise at 6 dB per octave.

A greater improvement in dynamic range can be obtained if the integrator is supplanted to realize a higher order filter (Adams, 1985). The filter is in the feedback loop and so the noise will have the opposite response to the filter and will therefore rise more steeply to allow a greater SNR enhancement after decimation. Figure 8.19 shows the theoretical SNR enhancement possible for various loop filter orders and oversampling factors. A further advantage of high-order loop filters is that the quantizing noise can be decorrelated from the signal, making conventional dither unnecessary. High-order loop filters were at one time thought to be impossible to stabilize, but this is no longer the case, although care is necessary.

8.4 DIGITAL AUDIO RECORDING

As the sound quality is independent of the medium in digital audio, the type of recorder will be chosen for other attributes such as speed, economy or interchangeability (Watkinson, 1994). Open-reel tape is prone to contamination and this restricts the recording density. The only open-reel format now available is the DASH format which offers 24 tracks on 1/2 inch tape running at 30 in/s using bulk ferrite heads, or 48 tracks on the same tape using thin-film heads. This old format is primitive by modern standards (it uses parity for error correction) but survives in a niche market where simultaneous recording of a large number of audio channels is required. A stereo version of DASH failed because it could not compete with DAT for size and economy, nor with disk-based workstations for speed.

Tape will always be cheap to manufacture, and will remain in use for as long as there is an economic advantage, but in cassettes to allow protection and automated handling. Stationary-head tape transports are best used with MR heads which have a noise advantage at low data rates, whereas rotary head transports use inductive heads. The rotary-head recorder has reached a high degree of refinement. Examples include DAT, a stereo 16-bit cassette, the non-tracking (NT) format which uses compression to allow a cassette the size of a postage stamp. A number of semi-professional recorders use VHS or 8 mm VCR mechanics with digital circuitry, and record eight independent audio channels by dividing the slant tracks into sectors like a disk. These can be synchronized to record an arbitrary number of channels and developments of these machines will ultimately replace open-reel recording.

The Winchester disk is used extensively for audio because it combines rapid access with high capacity. Disk-based file servers are used to record centrally all of the commercials needed by a radio station. Workstations based on Winchester disks suffer from the time taken to copy data in and out of the disks, and this problem has been tackled by incorporating exchangeable magnetooptic disks to which the Winchester disks can transfer at faster than real time.

The MiniDisc is a magnetooptic recorder using approximately 5:1 compression. In order to make the machine portable, a large buffer memory is provided and the drive transfers data incrementally faster than real time. If the pickup is knocked offtrack by an external shock, the buffer can sustain audio transfer until repositioning can take place. Compression helps reduce the size of the buffer needed.

8.5 TIME COMPRESSION

When samples are converted, the ADC must run at a constant clock rate and output an unbroken stream of samples. Time compression allows the sample stream to be broken into blocks for convenient handling.

Figure 8.20 shows an ADC feeding a pair of RAMs. As soon as the first RAM is full, the ADC output is switched to the input of the other RAM so that there is no loss of data. The first RAM can then be read at a higher clock rate than the sampling rate. As a result, the data are read in less than real time, and the output from the system pauses until the second RAM is full. Instead of being an unbroken stream, which is difficult to handle, the samples are now arranged in blocks with convenient pauses in between them. In these pauses a rotary head recorder might switch heads; a hard disk might move to another track. The use of time compression is universal in digital audio recording because it allows time for synchronizing patterns, subcode, and error correction words to be recorded. In digital-video recorders, both audio and video data are time compressed so that they can share the same heads and tape tracks. Subsequently, any time compression can be reversed by time expansion. Samples are written into a RAM at the clock rate extracted from the replay head, but read out at the standard sampling rate. In most recorders, the time expansion stage is combined with the timebase correction stage so that speed variations in the medium can be eliminated at the same time.

The transfer of samples between digital audio devices in real time is possible only if both use a common sampling rate and are synchronized. A digital audio recorder must be able to synchronize to the sampling rate of a digital input in order to record the samples. It is frequently necessary for such a recorder to play back locked to an external sampling rate reference so that the recorder can be connected to, for example, a digital mixer.

Figure 8.21 shows how the external reference locking process works. The timebase expansion is controlled by the external reference. This becomes the read clock for the RAM and so determines the rate at which the RAM address changes. In the case of a digital tape deck, the write clock for the RAM would be proportional to the tape speed. If the tape is going too fast, the write address will catch up with the read address in the memory, whereas if the tape is going too slowly the read address will catch up with the write address. The read address is subtracted from the write address and the difference is used to control the tape speed. Thus if the tape speed is too high, the memory will fill faster than it is being emptied, and the address difference will grow larger than normal. This slows down the tape. The same technique can be used with a magnetooptical disk.

Thus in a digital recorder the speed of the medium is constantly changing to keep the data rate correct. In multitrack recorders, the various tracks can be synchronized to sample accuracy so that no timing errors can exist between the tracks. If more tracks are required, extra transports can be slaved to the first to the same degree of accuracy. In stereo recorders image shift due to phase errors is eliminated. In order to replay without a reference, perhaps to provide an analog output, a digital recorder generates a sampling clock locally by means of a crystal oscillator. Provision is made on professional machines to switch between internal and external references.

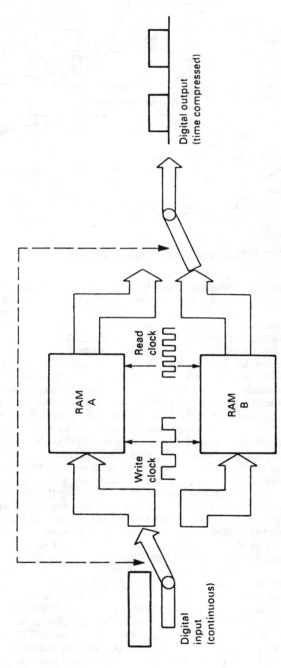

FIGURE 8.20 In time compression, RAM readout speed is greater than write speed. Practical system needs two RAM pages for continuous operation.

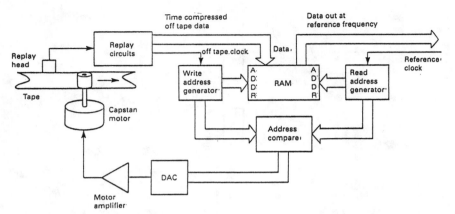

FIGURE 8.21   In reference locking, the contents of the time base corrector RAM are assessed in order to control the speed of the medium. This is done by comparing the read and write addresses.

8.6   *ERROR CORRECTION AND CONCEALMENT*

The audibility of a bit error depends upon which bit of the sample is involved. If the least significant bit (LSB) of one sample was in error in a loud passage of music, the effect would be totally masked. Conversely, if the MSB of one sample was in error in a quiet passage, no one could fail to notice the resulting loud transient. Clearly a means is needed to render errors from the medium inaudible.

The size of the error which can be corrected is proportional to the amount of redundancy and, within this limit, the samples are returned to exactly their original value. Consequently corrected errors are inaudible. If the amount of error exceeds the amount of redundancy, correction is not possible and, in order to allow graceful degradation, concealment will be used. Concealment is a process whereby the value of a missing sample is estimated from those nearby. The estimated sample value is not necessarily exactly the same as the original and so, under some circumstances, concealment can be audible, especially if it is frequent. However, in a well-designed system, concealments occur with negligible frequency unless there is an actual fault or problem. The use of concealment is probably the main difference between the error strategy of a digital audio recorder and that of a computer data recorder.

Concealment is made possible by rearranging or shuffling the sample sequence prior to recording. This is shown in Fig. 8.22 where odd-numbered samples are separated from even-numbered samples prior to recording. The odd and even sets of samples may be recorded in different places, so that an uncorrectable burst error only affects one set. On replay, the samples are recombined into their natural sequence, in which the error causes every other sample to be lost. The waveform is now described half as often, but can still be reproduced although with some loss of accuracy. Almost all digital audio recorders use such an odd/even shuffle for concealment.

In high-density recorders, more data are lost in a given sized dropout. Adding redundancy equal to the size of a dropout to every code is inefficient and, instead, interleaving is used. Figure 8.23 shows that, in block interleaving, words are reordered within blocks which are themselves in the correct order. This approach is attractive for rotary-head recorders, such as DAT, because the scanning process naturally divides the tape up into blocks. The block interleave is achieved by writing samples into a memory in sequential address locations from a counter, and

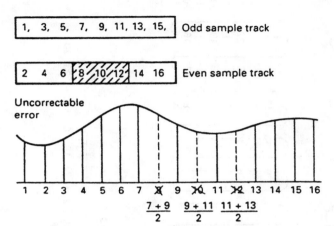

FIGURE 8.22 Odd and even samples are recorded in different locations to allow interpolation in the event of an uncorrectable error.

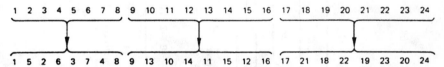

FIGURE 8.23 In block interleaving, data are scrambled within blocks which are themselves correctly ordered.

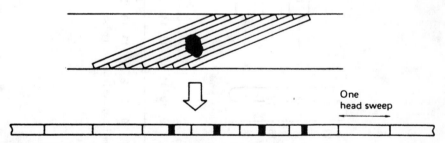

FIGURE 8.24 In helical scan a form of mechanical interleaving takes place.

reading the memory with nonsequential addresses from a sequencer. The effect is to convert a one-dimensional sequence of samples into a two-dimensional structure having rows and columns. Rotary-head recorders naturally interleave spatially on the tape. Figure 8.24 shows that a single large tape defect becomes a series of small defects owing to the geometry of helical scanning.

The alternative to block interleaving is convolutional interleaving where the interleave process is endless. In Fig. 8.25 symbols are assembled into short blocks

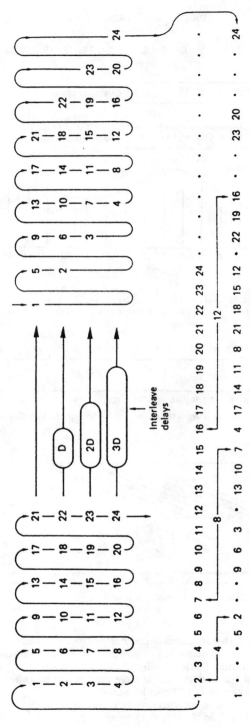

FIGURE 8.25 Convolutional interleave is obtained by shearing a column structure.

8.28

and then delayed by an amount proportional to the position in the block. The delays have the effect of shearing the symbols so that columns on the left side of the diagram become diagonals on the right. When the columns on the right are read, the convolutional interleave is obtained. Convolutional interleave works well with stationary-head recorders where there is no natural track break, and with optical and magnetooptical digital audio disks where the track is a continuous spiral. Convolutional interleave has the advantage of requiring less memory to implement than a block code. This is because a block code requires the entire block to be written into the memory before it can be read, whereas a convolutional code requires only enough memory to produce the required delays. Now that RAM is relatively inexpensive, convolutional interleave is less popular.

In the presence of burst errors alone, the system of interleaving works very well, but it is known that in most practical channels there are also uncorrelated errors of a few bits due to noise. Figure 8.26 shows an interleaving system where a dropout-induced burst error has occurred which is at the maximum correctable size. All three code words involved are working at their limit of one symbol. A random error due to noise in the vicinity of a burst error will cause the correction power of the code to be exceeded. Thus a random error of a single bit causes a further entire symbol to fail. This is a weakness of an interleave designed solely to handle dropout-induced bursts. Practical high-density equipment must address the problem of noise-induced or random errors and burst errors occurring at the same time. This is done by forming code words both before and after the interleave process. In block interleaving, this results in a product code, whereas in the case of convolutional interleave the result is called cross interleaving (Doi et al., 1979).

Figure 8.27 shows that in a product code the redundancy calculated first and checked last is called the outer code, and the redundancy calculated second and checked first is called the inner code. The inner code is generally formed along tracks on the medium although, if group coding is used, a further interleave may be required to prevent a defect on a group boundary corrupting two symbols in the same inner code. Random errors due to noise are corrected by the inner code and do not impair the burst correcting power of the outer code. Burst errors are declared uncorrectable by the inner code which flags the bad samples on the way into

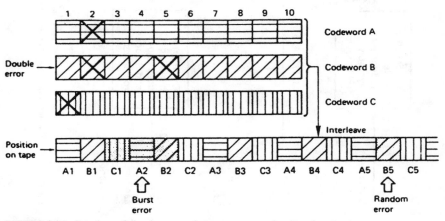

FIGURE 8.26 Interleave fails when a random error occurs close to a burst.

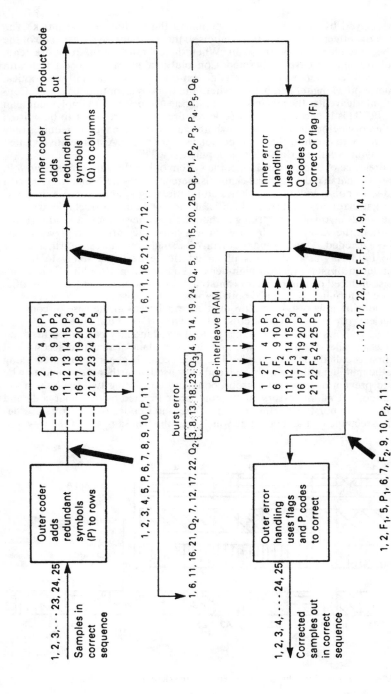

FIGURE 8.27 Product code generation and checking. See text.

the de-interleave memory. The outer code reads the error flags in order to correct the flagged symbols by erasure. As it does not have to compute the error locations, the outer code needs half as much redundancy for the same correction power. Thus the inner code redundancy does not raise the code overhead. The combination of code words with interleaving in several dimensions yields an error-protection strategy which is truly synergistic, in that the end result is more powerful than the sum of the parts. Needless to say, the technique is used extensively in modern formats such as RDAT and DCC. Reed-Solomon coding is now universally used in digital audio recorders because it is efficient and can handle erasure flags easily. An alternative to the product block code is the convolutional cross interleave. In this system, the data are formed into an endless array and the code words are produced on columns and diagonals. The MiniDisc and DASH formats use such a system. The original advantage of the cross interleave is that it needed less memory than a product code. This advantage is no longer significant now that memory prices have fallen so much. Cross interleave has the disadvantage that editing is more complicated.

The interleave, de-interleave, time compression, and timebase correction processes cause delay and this is evident in the time taken before audio emerges after starting a digital machine. Confidence replay takes place later than the distance between record and replay heads would indicate. In DASH format recorders, confidence replay is about one-tenth of a second behind the input. Synchronous recording requires additional heads which are displaced along the tape path to overcome the effect of the delays.

The presence of an error correction system means that the audio quality is independent of the tape/head quality within limits. There is no point in trying to assess the health of a machine by listening to it, as this will not reveal whether the error rate is normal or within a whisker of failure. The only useful procedure is to monitor the frequency with which errors are being corrected, and to compare it with normal figures. Professional digital audio equipment should have an error rate display.

8.7 DIGITAL AUDIO FORMATS

The hard-disk recorder stores data on concentric tracks which it accesses by moving the head radially and, while the head is moving, it cannot transfer data. Using time compression, a hard-disk drive can be made into an audio recorder with the addition of a certain amount of memory. Figure 8.28 shows the principle. The instantaneous data rate of the disk drive is far in excess of the sampling rate at the convertor, and so a large time compression factor can be used. The disk drive can read a block of data from disk, and place it in the timebase corrector in a fraction of the real time the block represents in the audio waveform. As the timebase corrector steadily advances through the memory, the disk drive has time to move the heads to another track before the memory runs out of data. When there is sufficient space in the memory for another block, the drive is commanded to read, and fills up the space. Although the data transfer at the medium is highly discontinuous, the buffer memory provides an unbroken stream of samples to the DAC and so continuous audio is obtained.

Recording is performed by using the memory to assemble samples until the contents of one disk block is available. This block is then transferred to disk at a high data rate. The drive can then reposition the head before the next block is available in memory. An advantage of hard disks is that access to the audio is much

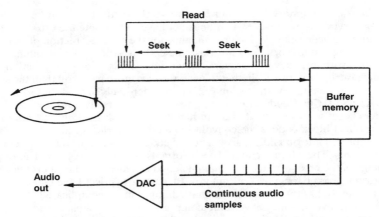

FIGURE 8.28   In a hard disk recorder, a large capacity memory is used as a buffer or timebase corrector between the convertors and the disk. The memory allows the convertors to run constantly despite the interruptions in disk transfer caused by the head moving between tracks.

quicker than with tape, as all of the data are available within the time taken to move the head.

The use of compression allows the recording time of a disk to be extended considerably. This technique is often used in plug-in circuit boards which are used to convert a personal computer into a digital audio recorder. Audio data are stored nonsequentially so that recording can still take place on a checkerboarded disk. This is easily done by time compressing the audio data into blocks which are equal in size to time code frames. The directory system of the disk links the time code frame numbers to the disk physical addresses. Thus any recording can be played simply by supplying timecode. If the timecode has come from a VTR or telecine, the audio on the hard disk will remain synchronized even if the videotape or film is shuttled. Thus disk-based recorders are popular in post production for making the soundtracks of films and television programs.

8.7.1   An Open Reel Digital Recorder

Figure 8.29 shows the block diagram of a stationary-head machine. Analog inputs are converted to the digital domain by convertors, and there must be one convertor for each audio channel to be recorded. Unlike an analog machine, there is not necessarily one tape track per audio channel. In stereo machines the two channels of audio samples may be distributed over a number of tracks in order to reduce the tape speed and extend the playing time.

The samples from the convertor are separated into odd and even for concealment purposes, and usually one set of samples is delayed with respect to the other before recording. The continuous stream of samples from the convertor is broken into blocks by time compression prior to recording. Time compression allows the insertion of edit gaps, addresses, and redundancy into the data stream. An interleaving process is also necessary to re-order the samples prior to recording. The subsequent de-interleaving breaks up the effects of burst errors on replay.

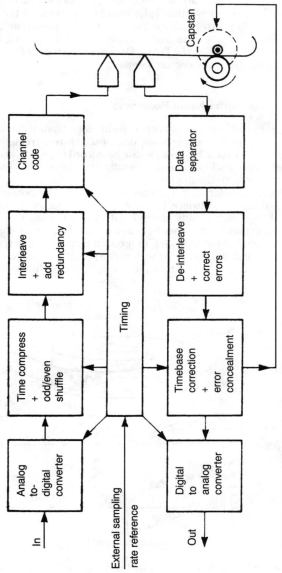

FIGURE 8.29 Stationary head recorder. See Sec. 8.7.1.

The result of the processes so far is still raw data, and these will need to be channel coded before they can be recorded on the medium. On replay a data separator reverses the channel coding to give the original raw data with the addition of some errors. Following de-interleave, the errors are reduced in size and are more readily correctable. The memory required for de-interleave may double as the timebase correction memory, so that variations in the speed of the tape are rendered undetectible. Any errors which are beyond the power of the correction system will be concealed after the odd–even shift is reversed. An analog output emerges following conversion in the DAC. On replay the tape is driven at whatever speed is necessary to obtain the correct sampling rate.

8.7.2 Rotary-Head Digital Audio Recorders

Rotary-head digital audio recorders borrow technology from video recorders. Rotary heads have a number of advantages, one of which is extremely high packing density (the number of data bits which can be recorded in a given space). In a digital audio recorder, packing density directly translates into the playing time available for a given size of the medium.

In a rotary-head recorder, the heads are mounted in a revolving drum and the tape is wrapped around the surface of the drum in a helix as can be seen in Fig. 8.30. The helical tape path results in the heads traversing the tape in a series of diagonal or slanting tracks. The space between the tracks is controlled not by head design but by the speed of the tape and, in modern recorders, this space is reduced to zero by the use of azimuth recording with corresponding improvement in packing density (Hitomi and Taki, 1986). The added complexity of the rotating heads and

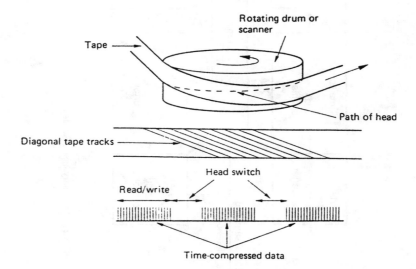

FIGURE 8.30 In a rotary-head recorder, the helical-tape path around a rotating head results in a series of diagonal or slanting tracks across the tape. Time compression is used to create gaps in the recorded data which coincide with the switching between tracks.

the circuitry necessary to control them is offset by the improvement in density. The discontinuous tracks of the rotary head recorder are naturally compatible with time compressed data. As Fig. 8.30 illustrates, the audio samples are time compressed into blocks each of which can be contained in one slant track. In a machine such as DAT there are two heads mounted on opposite sides of the drum. One rotation of the drum lays down two tracks. Effective concealment can be had by recording odd-numbered samples on one track of the pair and even-numbered samples on the other.

A rotary-head recorder contains the same basic steps as any digital audio recorder. The record side needs ADCs, time compression, the addition of redundancy for error correction, and channel coding. On replay the channel coding is reversed by the data separator, errors are broken up by the de-interleave process and corrected or concealed, and the time compression and any fluctuations from the transport are removed by timebase correction. The corrected, time stable, samples are then fed to the DAC.

In DAT the tracks are just 13 μm wide and an area-divided, track-following, system is used in which tones on the tape tracks are decoded to drive the capstan. The NT format has no tracking mechanism at all on replay. Instead, the rotary head runs at several times normal speed, crossing slant tracks and picking up sync blocks nonsequentially. These are assembled in RAM using header IDs. Any blocks which are not recovered are treated as dropouts and corrected.

8.7.3 Digital Compact Cassette

Digital compact cassette (DCC) is a consumer digital audio recorder using data reduction [Lokhoff, 1991]. Although the convertors at either end of the machine work with PCM data, these are not directly recorded, but are reduced to one quarter of their normal rate by perceptive source coding. This allows a reasonable tape consumption similar to that achieved by a rotary head recorder.

Figure 8.31 shows that DCC uses stationary heads in a conventional tape transport which can also play analog cassettes. Data are distributed over eight parallel tracks which occupy half the width of the tape. At the end of the tape the head rotates and plays the other eight tracks in reverse. Unlike the compact cassette, the DCC cassette cannot be turned over, and so all transports must be able to reverse play. The advantage of the conventional approach with linear tracks is that tape

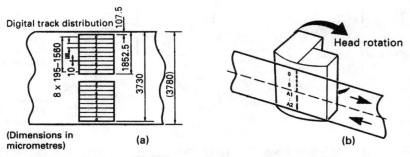

FIGURE 8.31 DCC uses nine tracks on each "side" of the tape. For compatibility with analog cassettes the head can be rotated 180° to bring into action conventional heads.

duplication can be carried out at high speed. Owing to the low frequencies recorded, DCC has to use magnetoresistive heads for playback which are more complex than conventional inductive heads, and have only recently become economic as manufacturing techniques have been developed. Such heads cannot record so separate inductive record heads must be furnished.

8.7.4 MiniDisc

MiniDisc is a system which uses a hybrid pickup as shown in Fig. 8.32. The system can play magnetooptic disks, or prerecorded phase-contrast disks, which are optically identical to the compact disc. Recordable MiniDiscs make the recording as flux patterns in a magnetic layer. However, the disks needs to be pre-grooved so that the tracking systems can operate. The grooves have the same pitch as a CD or a prerecorded MD, but the tracks are the same width as the laser spot (about 1.1 μm). The grooves are not a perfect spiral, but have a sinusoidal waviness at a fixed wavelength. Like CD, MD uses constant track linear velocity, not constant speed of rotation. When recording on a blank disk, the recorder needs to know how fast to turn the spindle to get the correct track speed. The wavy grooves are followed by the tracking servo and the frequency of the tracking error is proportional to the disk speed. The recorder simply turns the spindle at a speed which makes the grooves wave at the correct frequency. The groove frequency is 75 Hz, the same as the data sector rate, so that a zero crossing in the groove signal can also be used to indicate where to start recording. The grooves are particularly important when checkerboarded recording is being replayed. On a constant linear velocity (CLV) disk, every seek to a new track radius results in a different track speed. The wavy grooves allow the track velocity to be corrected as soon as a new track is reached.

There are two ways in which magnetooptic (MO) disks can be written. Figure 8.33*a* shows the first system, in which the intensity of laser is modulated with the

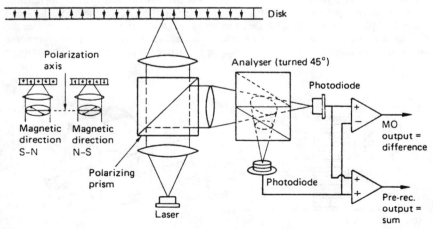

FIGURE 8.32 A pickup suitable for the replay of magnetooptic disks must respond to very small rotations of the plane of polarization.

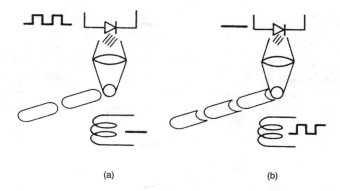

FIGURE 8.33 (*a*) High data rate MO disks modulate the laser keeping the applied field constant; (*b*) at lower rates the laser can run continuously and the field is modulated.

waveform to be recorded. Consider the disk to be initially magnetized along its axis of rotation with the north pole upwards. The disk is then rotated in a field of the opposite sense, produced by a steady current flowing in a coil. This field is weaker than the room temperature coercivity of the medium and will therefore have no effect. A laser beam is focused on the medium as it turns, and a pulse from the laser will momentarily heat a very small area of the medium above its Curie temperature, whereby this area will take on a reversed flux due to the presence of the field coils. This reversed-flux direction will be retained indefinitely as the medium cools.

Alternatively the waveform to be recorded modulates the magnetic field from the coils as shown in Fig. 8.33*b*. In this approach, the laser is operating continuously in order to raise the track beneath the beam above the Curie temperature, but the magnetization recorded is determined by the current in the coil at the instant the track cools.

As shown in Fig. 8.33, laser modulation and magnetic field modulation (MFM) leave different patterns on the disk. In laser modulation the recorded area is a convolution of the beam diameter and the pulse duration, whereas in MFM the recording is made at the trailing edge of the beam and has crescent-shaped transitions. Magnetic field modulation is used in the recordable MiniDisc for a number of reasons. First, no laser modulator is required and the same optical assembly can be used for phase change and magnetooptic disks. Second, the spot size is determined by the requirement to play prerecorded phase change disks (compact discs) in which the beam must straddle the tracks to obtain an interference effect. MFM allows a higher recording density with the necessary large size of spot. The main drawback of MFM is that the coil inductance limits the bit rate. This is not a problem in a digital audio disk but precludes use in computer disks where throughput is a performance criterion.

Although 5:1 compression is used, the MiniDisc uses the same channel coding (EFM) and error correction strategy (cross-interleaved Reed-Solomon) as the compact disk. As described earlier, the cross-interleave is convolutional and buffer zones are required in recordable disks to allow editing. Figure 8.34 shows that the buffer zone allows one convolution to finish before another begins.

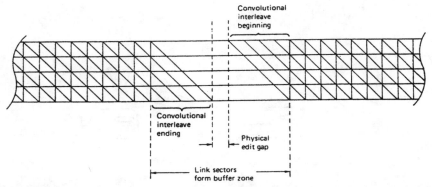

Figure 8.34   The convolutional interleave of CD is retained in MD, but buffer zones are needed to allow the convolution to finish before a new one begins, otherwise editing is impossible.

REFERENCES

Adams, R. W., "Design and Implementation of an Audio 18-bit A/D Convertor Using Oversampling Techniques," *77th Conv. Audio Eng. Soc.*, Hamburg, Germany, Preprint 2182 (1985).

Betts, J. A., *Signal Processing Modulation and Noise,* Hodder and Stoughton Ltd., Sevenoaks, England, 1970.

Doi, T. T., K. Odata, G. Fukuda, and S. Furukawa, "Crossinterleave Code for Error Correction of Digital Audio Systems," *J. Audio Eng. Soc.,* **27**, 1028 (1979).

Hauser, M. W., "Principles of Oversampling A/D Conversion," *J. Audio Eng. Soc.,* **39**, 3 (1991).

Hitomi, A., and T. Taki, "Servo Technology of R-DAT," *IEEE Trans. Consum. Electron.,* **CE-32**, 425 (1986).

Ishida, Y., S. Nishi, S. Kunii, T. Satoh, and K. Uetake, "A PCM Digital Audio Processor for Home Use VTRs," *64th Conv. Audio Eng. Soc.,* New York, preprint 1528 (1979).

Lipshitz, S. P., R. A. Wannamaker, and J. Vanderkooy, "Quantization and Dither: A Theoretical Survey," *J. Audio Eng. Soc.,* **40**, 355 (1992).

Lokhoff, G. C. P., "DCC: Digital Compact Cassette," *IEEE Trans. Consum. Electron.,* **CE-37**, 702 (1991).

Maher, R. C., "On the Nature of Granulated Noise in Uniform Quantization Systems," *J. Audio Eng. Soc.,* **40**, 12 (1992).

Reeves, A. H., "Electric Signalling System," Feb. 3, 1942, U.S. Patent 2,272,070.

Shannon, C. E. "A Mathematical Theory of Communication," *Bell Syst. Tech. J.,* **27**, 379 (1948).

Vanderkooy, J., and S. P. Lipshitz, "Resolution Below the Least Significant Bit in Digital Systems with Dither," *J. Audio Eng. Soc.,* **32**, 106 (1984).

Watkinson, J. R., *The Art of Digital Audio,* Focal Press, Boston; Oxford, England, 1989.

Watkinson, J. R., *The Art of Data Recording,* Focal Press, Boston; Oxford, England, 1994.

Widrow, B., "Statistical Analysis of Amplitude Quantized Sampled-Data Systems," *Trans. AIEE, Part II,* **79**, 555 (1961).

CHAPTER 9
INSTRUMENTATION RECORDING

James U. Lemke
San Diego, California

Instrumentation recording covers the broad field of data recording in which analog or encoded information is stored in other than standard audio, video, or computer formats. In the United States, the practice traces its origins to the early 1950s when flight-test programs required capacities and rates beyond those possible with oscillographic recorders, and the national security effort required ever-increasing surveillance bandwidths. The earliest instrumentation recorders were adapted from professional audio machines to accommodate frequency modulation (FM) and other higher-than-audio-frequency electronics. The bandwidth of the audio reproducing heads was increased by replacing the center conductor of the coaxial head cables with fine piano wire, thereby reducing the parallel capacity and raising the resonant frequency. In time, the audio-equipment manufacturers developed recorders specifically for the requirements of the instrumentation users, and standards evolved such as those of the Interrange Instrumentation Group (IRIG) (see Appendix).

Although some instrumentation recording is done on disks, the dominant formats utilize tapes. Fixed-head recorders are usually multitrack and use wide tapes, typically ½ or 1 in, although some are as wide as 2 in. Tapes are wound on precision reels having aluminum hubs and flanges and can have lengths exceeding 3000 m.

Rotary-head machines allow the highest areal packing density and are now primarily of the helical-scan configuration similar to those used for professional video recording. Early rotary-head machines for wide bandwidth analog signals were adapted from transverse-scan broadcast video recorders, with signal processing to provide time alignment of the signal overlap where it was interrupted at the end of one head scan and the beginning of another. Rotary-head machines today use high-density digital recording and the interruption is easily accommodated by digital buffering.

Various modes of recording are used for instrumentation, depending upon the type of data to be stored. Pulse-code modulation (PCM) is becoming the dominant technique for telemetry, satellite downlink, and laboratory measurements, in many cases replacing FM recording. Base-band linear recording with ac bias is done in two modes: constant-flux recording for maximum information capacity per track, and constant noise-power-ratio (NPR) recording for surveillance signals where the minimum intermodulation plus additive noise is needed across a wide band. NPR is described in more detail below.

Instrumentation recorders differ from other recorders in a number of ways but markedly so in the method of optimizing the record current and in equalizing the reproduce signals. In analog machines, the record head and reproduce head are separate structures, and each is optimized for its function. The ac bias level is optimized at band-edge—the highest signal frequency of interest—to obtain the maximum bandwidth. Audio recorders also use separate record and reproduce heads but have their bias current optimized for maximum low-frequency dynamic range. Bulk erasure is commonly used in instrumentation recording since the necessity for overwriting is seldom encountered, although some high-density digital recording machines exhibit excellent overwrite characteristics. Linear densities up to 3000 fr/mm (a wavelength of $0.67\mu m$) are achieved with partial-penetration recording of the relatively thick magnetic tape coating. Small record gaps of fractions of a micron create little phase shift during the recording process and, although not common in multitrack recorders, are increasingly being used as their benefits become better understood. Phase equalizers are used to remove much of the linear peak shift during reproduction. The tapes utilize high-coercivity, small-particle oxides and are calendered to a high finish to reduce modulation noise and spacing loss. Tape speeds can be very high, with multitrack recorders having the capability of storing data at gigabits per second. Burst-efficient error-detection and correction codes such as the Reed-Solomon code, are used to correct errors down to 10^{-9}–10^{-10}.

The dominant mode of instrumentation recording has become digital as it has in many other applications. Unlike general purpose computer recording where multiple re-writes are allowed to achieve the specified error rate of 10^{-14}, or better, or digital audio where concealment of certain errors is allowed, instrumentation recording must do the best it can on the first pass. Frequently the information being recorded is a continuous block of data from a unique experiment, or clandestinely gathered surveillance information, neither of which offers the luxury of a re-try. The usual error rate on one-pass, high-density recorders is typically about 10^{-9}–10^{-10} with the most sophisticated, multilayer error correction codes. Raw-bit errors for narrow-track, high-density instrumentation recorders are typically about 5×10^{-6} initially but degrade to about 1×10^{-5}. End of life for a tape is usually when the raw-bit error rate exceeds 1×10^{-4}. The errors are predominantly burst errors, but error histograms must be run for each recorder/tape design to ensure that the single-bit errors do not swamp the Reed-Solomon code where each error event, single-bit or long burst, is treated equally.

Historically, instrumentation recording has been at the cutting edge of high-density information storage technology. The compelling need for recording ever greater bandwidths and the availability of research funds to support that need has resulted in many innovations in instrumentation recording that have filtered down to commercial applications. An example of that effect can be found in modulation codes pioneered by the instrumentation industry. Partial response Class IV (PR IV) codes were first used in an Ampex high-density recorder many years before its commercial introduction and recent ubiquity. The function of this very powerful code will be described in Sec. 9.3.5.

9.1   HEADS AND TAPES

9.1.1   Interface

The shortest wavelengths employed by instrumentation recorders are extremely small; therefore, special care must be taken to ensure intimate contact between the gap region of the head and the surface of the tape coating. At 3000 fr/mm, for example, a spacing between the reproducing head and the tape of only $0.67\,\mu\text{m}$ will produce an attenuation of the signal of almost 55 dB. This comes from the reproducing spacing-loss law (Wallace, 1951).

$$\frac{E_d}{E_0} = 20 \log e^{-2\pi d/\lambda} \tag{9.1}$$

where E_d/E_0 is the output voltage ratio at spacings of d and zero at wave-length λ. Equation (9.1) is frequently given in the form $54.6d/\lambda$ dB. An empirical record loss factor has been found to be about $45d/\lambda$ dB (Bertram and Niedermeyer, 1982). This leads to a total loss of about $100d/\lambda$ dB when the same head is used for writing and reading.

The effective depth of recording can be found by integrating the contribution from strata distances y from the head and finding that depth δ_{eff} that contributes 90 percent of the reproduce signal. For a recording uniform in depth, the solution

$$\int_0^{\delta_{\text{eff}}} e^{-2\pi y/\lambda}dy = 0.9$$

gives

$$\delta_{\text{eff}} \approx \frac{\lambda}{e} \tag{9.2}$$

Equation (9.2) points out the necessity for maintaining a magnetically dense, smooth surface on the tape. At a density of 3000 fr/mm, 90 percent of the signal comes from a layer that is only 0.25 μm thick—about half the wavelength of visible light.

Tape speeds are relatively high on many instrumentation recorders; therefore, it is frequently a challenge to maintain head-tape contact in view of the likelihood of an entrapped-air film. As a head wears, its radius of contact increases, which exacerbates this problem. Such "tape flying" is evident from observing the envelope of the reproduced-signal amplitude for instability. Although some forms of frictional polymers can form on the head surface and considerably increase head life, without being thick enough to affect output, head buildups are generally detrimental and must be removed for acceptable performance.

The impossibility of consistently achieving the near-perfection in the head-tape interface that is required for high-density recording has led the instrumentation field to use very powerful interleaved error-detection and correction codes. The strategy in instrumentation recording is to accept long bursts of errors as the penalty for using a very high-density channel and then to correct the errors to the degree desired. Philosophically, this has been in contrast to the field of computer recording, where relatively low linear densities required little error correction.

9.1.2 Heads

Single-track heads for rotary recorders are fabricated in very much the same way as video heads. The optical gap lengths are in the range of 0.3 to 1.0 μm. Typically, the cores are made from single-crystal or hot-pressed manganese-zinc ferrite with sputtered ceramic or glass gaps and the poles assembled by glass bonding. When high-coercivity tapes are used, metal-in-gap (MIG) heads prevent head-pole-tip saturation during recording. MIG heads have ferrite cores with high-saturation metal films sputtered onto the pole faces and apex region. Frequently the ferrite-metal interface is nonparallel to the gap faces to prevent interferences between the main gap and spurious interface gaps. Track widths are controlled by notching the cores in the region of the gap prior to glass bonding. Usually the same head is used for recording and reproducing. Such heads are used on channels with relatively narrowband modulation schemes, and as a consequence, their pole faces need not be very long. The small cores result in fairly high efficiency at frequencies of up to 100 MHz. The ferrite materials must be lapped with great care and the glass bonding done under tight process control to ensure good gap definition. Aside from these considerations, the heads are relatively easy to make and, being single-track, are free from crosstalk, gap alignment, and many other problems encountered with multitrack heads.

Multitrack heads have record gap lengths of from 0.3 to 2.0 μm, reproduce gap lengths of from 0.2 to 0.5 μm, and are fabricated in halves from machined half-brackets into which the individual prewound core halves are bonded. The brackets may be made from a nonmagnetic metal such as aluminum or from a nonmagnetic ferrite in the case of the all-ferrite head. Frequently, a tip plate containing thin metal-alloy poles is bonded to the ferrite cores in such a way as to cap the cores and thereby serve as the contact surface of the head. This creates a hybrid structure with the bulk of the magnetic circuit made up of low-loss ferrite but with the gap region, where the flux density is highest, composed of thin poles of hard, high-saturation-magnetization alloy. The alloy tips may be laminated to decrease their eddy-current losses and are usually made from a soft magnetic material such as aluminum-silicon-iron.

Shields between the tracks are inserted into slots provided for them, after the two half-brackets have been gapped with a sputtered or evaporated gap material, or they are bonded into the half-brackets before gapping in the case of all-ferrite heads. Both types of heads require precise fabrication of diverse materials to submicron tolerances over dimensions that may exceed 50 mm in some heads.

The tolerances associated with track width, track position, gap length, gap scatter, gap depth, and electrical parametrics are all difficult to control; one of the most critical tolerances relates to individual head gap azimuth and the relative azimuth track-to-track. The equation relating azimuth misalignment loss L (in dB) to track width w, wavelength λ, and misalignment angle β is

$$L = 20 \log \frac{\sin[(\pi w \tan \beta)/\lambda]}{(\pi w \tan \beta)/\lambda} \qquad (9.3)$$

For a high-density, 28-track instrumentation head operating at a wave-length of 0.67 μm and a track width of 457 μm, an azimuth misalignment scatter track-to-track of 2 minutes of arc will result in a 14-dB difference in signal level between tracks if the overall azimuth alignment is optimized for one track. Since azimuth scatter exists in both record and reproduce heads, and tapes must be interchangeable between recorders, tolerances of 1 minute of arc must be maintained to keep the azimuth loss to less than 2.5 dB in the worst case. Metal heads that are bonded together by epoxy resins are more susceptible to this problem than are the all-ferrite heads.

Head designs are, of necessity, compromises between core size, inductive crosstalk, efficiency, gap depth (head life), turns, and resonance frequency. The problem is lessened somewhat when the record and reproduce heads are separate and their designs may be optimized separately. Asymmetries are often designed into the head pole-tip shapes to create compensating long-wavelength response bumps caused by the outer dimensions of the head. With care, useful response over 12 octaves can be achieved.

9.1.3 Tapes

Instrumentation tapes are in many respects similar to video tapes; they differ primarily in their width, length, packaging (reel), and in the smaller amount (or absence) of abrasive material formulated into the binder system for controlled head cleaning. Abrasivity is a property of major concern in selecting an instrumentation tape, since multitrack heads are very expensive and may have an allowable wear depth of only 10 or 12 μm. Usually, head manufacturers will warrant head life for a limited number of hours with only a few specific types of tape.

Low-density tapes use conventional gamma ferric oxide of about 28 kA/m (350 Oe) coercivity, but most high-density tapes use very small particles of cobalt-modified gamma ferric oxide of about 52 kA/m (650 Oe) coercivity. A matte finish back coating containing a conductive material is usually used to prevent electro-static buildup and to facilitate tracking and uniform winding onto the reels. The very long lengths of some tapes—sometimes exceeding 3000 m—necessitate con-trolled winding tensions to obtain a stable pack that can be accelerated to high angular rates on a tape transport without cinching or blocking and that can also be shipped without damage. Tight tolerances are maintained on slitting dimensions, surface finish, and, in the case of high-density digital recording tapes, dropouts.

Acicular tape particles are oriented along the longitudinal axis of the tape during manufacture, but the process is imperfect and most tapes will support components of magnetization perpendicular to the tape plane that are 30 percent, or more, of the saturation magnetization. This affects the equalization requirements, as will be seen later.

Since the trend toward adaptation of commercial helical-scan recorders to instru-mentation application, instrumentation tapes have become identical to commercial video tapes with additional quality control screening. Hence, metal particle and high-coercivity oxide tapes are the current norm.

9.2 RECORDING MODES

9.2.1 The Channel

In the usual communication-theory sense, a transfer function does not exist for direct recording without bias. The hysteretic properties of the tape cause the input-output function to be double-valued; in fact, even the shapes of the response and group-delay curves are dependent upon the input-signal amplitude. Furthermore, the noise of the channel is signal-dependent. Figure 9.1 shows a family of constant-

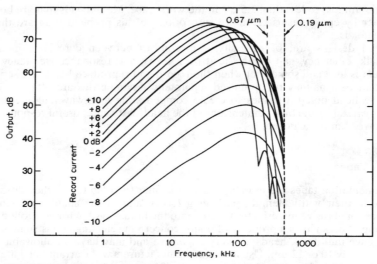

FIGURE 9.1   Constant-current response curves. A level of 0 dB represents the maximum output at $\lambda = 0.67$ μm. (Tape speed: 19 cm/s; gaps = 0.25 μm.)

current response curves with the 0 dB curve obtained by maximizing the output of 0.67-μm wavelength. An increase in record current of 10 dB reduces the bandwidth of the channel by almost two-thirds and causes a phase shift of π radians beyond the null in the response curve. For binary signals, this channel is usable since it has been found that a class of preemphasis exists that allows a detectable invariant during reproduction—the zero crossing (Mallinson and Steele, 1969). The proper preemphasis is that which allows the record-head flux at the gap to reach the tape-saturating level within each bit cell. This mode of recording is used for pulse-code-modulation (PCM) signals.

9.2.2   AC-Biased Recording

The channel can be linearized by employing ac bias in which a high-frequency current (typically four, or more, times the band-edge frequency) is added to the signal current during recording. The bias current is much larger than the signal current and is adjusted to yield the maximum signal-to-noise ratio during reproduction. For most instrumentation tapes, the bias level is about 2 dB over the level giving maximum output at band-edge. The resulting transfer function is linear over about 30 percent of the dynamic range of the channel for a 1 percent distortion level. The recording sensitivity of the channel is increased by the use of bias when the signal currents are only about 10 percent of the bias current. The transfer function is actually a member of a family of transfer functions determined by the bias level. High bias currents restrict the bandwidth of the channel but permit high signal levels for a given linearity. In high-density recorders, high signal-to-noise ratio at long wavelengths is sacrificed for bandwidth by the use of a relatively low bias current.

The channel is set up by recording a low-level signal at constant flux (head losses equalized) with the bias optimized at band-edge frequency. The maximum record level for linear operation is found by adjusting the record current to yield 1 percent third-harmonic distortion of a signal selected to be one-tenth the band-edge frequency. The reproduce channel is then equalized for flat response and the wideband signal-to-noise ratio measured. The bias is increased slightly, after which the record level for 1 percent distortion is reset, the channel reequalized, and the signal-to-noise ratio again measured. By this process, the proper bias for maximum signal-to-noise ratio is found. The constant-current channel is commonly used for telemetry recording, but it exhibits a nonflat signal-to-noise ratio with a maximum at midband. Another approach to setting up the linear channel results in a flat signal-to-noise ratio and a flat response. This technique is called flat noise-power-ratio recording and will be discussed in Sec. 9.3.

9.2.3 Frequency-Modulation Recording

Frequency-modulation recording was originally developed for telemetry channels where dc response, linearity, and low intermodulation were primary considerations. A relatively large modulation index is used for enhanced signal-to-noise ratio since this ratio increases with the square of the modulation index. In some cases, pilot tones are demodulated from spare channels to allow first-order correction of flutter-induced noise. Frequency modulation is used primarily for the recording of laboratory data when great accuracy is not required but dc response is necessary. Most other applications have been replaced with pulse-code-modulation (PCM) recording.

9.2.4 Pulse-Code Modulation Recording

The bulk of instrumentation recording, including that done on multitrack recorders, uses the binary mode without bias. Rotary-head recorders employ this technique exclusively and have achieved areal densities greater than 10^5 bits per square millimeter. Many different modulation codes are used in PCM, including run-length-limited (RLL) codes such as the (2, 7) code widely used in computer storage, and the modified duobinary code, also known as Class IV partial response.

Instrumentation recording has pioneered the area of very high linear densities where the channel is dominated by burst errors. In multitrack records it was convenient to interleave the data across the tape width to reduce burst error lengths, since the tracks were statistically independent with regard to dropouts. It is now very common to use Reed-Solomon parallel-interleaved codes for multitrack recorders and such codes in serial interleave for rotary-head instrumentation applications. Raw bit-error rates of 10^{-4} are corrected to 10^{-9}–10^{-10} with low overhead.

9.2.5 Vector Field Recording

Considerable evidence exists for the proposition that recording on conventional particulate media involves both longitudinal and perpendicular components of magnetization. The vector nature of the magnetization is detectable in instrumentation recording where small record gaps and relatively low write currents are used, but it also can be seen in the erasure process when an erase head is used. Prominent resonances in erasure as a function of erase-head field have been known for some

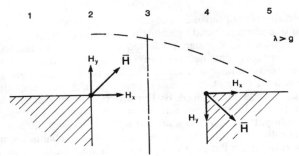

FIGURE 9.2   Record-head field vectors at gap edges.

time (McKnight, 1963) but were not susceptible to analysis with a longitudinal-recording model alone. The inclusion of the perpendicular component is necessary to create interference, the source of the resonances.

The field from a write head is vector in nature and may be broken down into longitudinal and perpendicular components as shown in Fig. 9.2. The peak field at the gap edges has values H_y and H_x as shown. Although the resultant fields are at $\pm 45°$ at the corners, they are always orthogonal and rotate to 0° and 90° a small distance from the gap edges at the head surface. The magnetic coating of the tape consists of acicular particles, each with a preferred axis of magnetization. The particles are imperfectly oriented so that a significant population has axes canted toward the perpendicular direction. Magnetization measurements on typical tapes reveal about a 30 percent perpendicular magnetization component when the proper demagnetization compensation is taken into account.

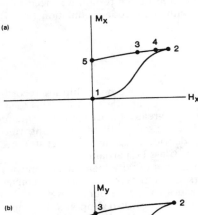

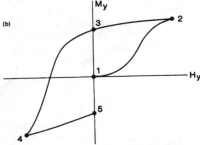

FIGURE 9.3 Remanent magnetizations near the medium surface, M_x and M_y, induced by (a) the left gap edge and (b) the right gap edge. (See Fig. 9.2 for points 1 through 5.)

It is instructive to consider the field history of an initially unmagnetized particle ensemble near the surface of the tape as it traverses the gap region, as shown in Fig. 9.3. Five regions are indicated: (1) far from the left gap edge, (2) the left gap edge, (3) the gap centerline, (4) the right gap edge, and (5) far from the right gap edge. Considering a wavelength that is long relative to the gap length, the M-H curves are shown for the longitudinal field component and the perpendicular field component. The longitudinal field component is unidirectional, decreasing only slightly at the gap centerline near the head surface. Consequently, the longitudinal magnetization is established by the peak longitudinal field at the left gap edge. The perpendicular magnetization, established by the peak perpendicular field, is created at the right gap edge. Thus the perpendicular and longitudinal magnetizations are separated by a distance approximately equal to the record-head gap length. This leads naturally to interference effects, as will be shown.

The vector fields emanating from a magnetized region of the recording medium are different for longitudinal magnetizations and perpendicular magnetizations, as shown in Fig 9.4. Both types of magnetization generate longitudinal and perpendicular external fields that are related to each other as Hilbert transform pairs (defined below). Ideally, ring heads respond only to the longitudinal external fields from either longitudinal magnetizations or perpendicular magnetizations (similarly, pole heads respond only to perpendicular external fields).

The longitudinal-only sensitivity of the ring head derives from the fact that, in a high-efficiency head, the core reluctance is small relative to the gap reluctance, and consequently, most of the magnetomotive force from the external field appears across the gap. The head is equivalent, therefore, to a thin rectangular coil outlining the gap face and lying with its plane in the plane of the gap. Such a coil is insensitive to perpendicular external fields since they do not link the coil, whereas the longitudinal external fields do. A ring head thus senses an even function of external-field intensity ($\cos kx$) from the longitudinal magnetization and an odd function ($-\sin kx$) from the perpendicular magnetization (see Fig. 9.4).

The Hilbert transform of a function is obtained by the convolution of that function with $-1/\pi t$

$$\hat{e}_L(t) = -\frac{1}{\pi t} * e_p(t)$$

$$= \frac{1}{\pi} \int_{-\infty}^{+\infty} \frac{e_p(t)}{t' - t} \, dt' \qquad (9.4)$$

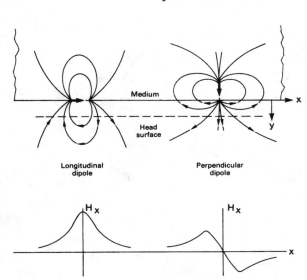

FIGURE 9.4   Idealized longitudinal field from dipoles rotated $\pi/2$.

The Hilbert transform of a function is also equivalent to its Fourier transform with fixed coefficients but with each component rotated by $-\pi/2$.

If separate longitudinal and perpendicular sinusoidal magnetizations were recorded by the same gap edge and, therefore, at the same site in the recording medium, the reproduce head flux would be of the form $(A \cos kx - B \sin kx)$, where A and B are the relative magnitudes of the longitudinal and perpendicular fields, respectively. If, however, the components are separated in the direction of tape travel by a distance equal to the gap length, as described above, constructive or destructive interference will result as a function of wavelength. In fact, the optimum record gap length is $\lambda/4$ for maximum signal-to-noise ratio, where λ is the wavelength at band-edge (Lemke, 1982). That is the spacing that puts the cosine function recorded at the leading edge of the record-head gap in phase with the $-$sine function recorded at the trailing gap edge. The effect is very pronounced at low recording intensities, as encountered in partial-penetration recording, but less so at higher recording intensities where some of the leading-edge magnetization is altered by the intense trailing-edge field.

As noted above, erasure with an erase head exhibits characteristics that are explainable only though the employment of both magnetization vectors. Figure 9.5 shows the obvious presence of re-recording of a signal with marked resonances during the process of erasure (McKnight, 1963). For the particular recording conditions reported, certain frequencies (2100 Hz, 5000 Hz, and 8000 Hz) exhibit a high degree of erasure that peaks at a critical erase current and diminishes at higher

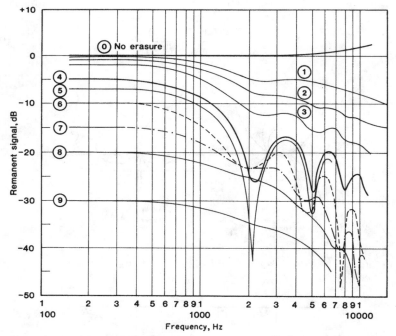

FIGURE 9.5   AC erasure. Erasure ac current increasing from 0 to 9 (*McKnight, 1963*).

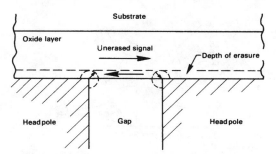

FIGURE 9.6 Re-recording by overwriting, without ac erasure.

currents. This is due to re-recording the original signal out of phase at the peaks, with the erase field serving as a bias field. The wavelengths at which resonance occurs are unaffected by erase current and are related to the dimensions of the head gap and the recorded signal.

The source of the re-recorded signal field is the unerased layer that lies deeper in the coating than the depth of penetration of the erase field. The erase field erases a stratum on the surface of the tape and then serves as a bias field for the underlying layers that then function as a signal source. As can be seen schematically in Fig. 9.6, the surface layer is magnetized in a sense opposite to that of its source. It is tempting to argue that the out-of-phase flux from the surface layer that is in close proximity to the read head is weak and cancels the contribution of flux from the deeper unerased layer. That is, in fact, the mechanism of overwrite in unbiased recording with thick media using partial-penetration recording, where the peak in overwrite occurs at a wavelength dependent upon the overwriting current. However, such a model fails to account for the fixed critical wavelengths that are independent of the erasure field magnitude and for the multiple peaks shown in Fig. 9.5.

In Fig. 9.2, the vector fields from the gap edges at ±45° angles are orthogonal and generate Hilbert-transform-pair magnetizations in the same way that was considered earlier. At low fields near the surface of the head, the field lines are concentrated at the gap edges, as shown in Fig. 9.7, and two distinct erasure zones exist having orthogonal peak field directions. The layer of recording that is not erased by the two zones has an external field that links the erase head. The erase head acts as a very large-gap reproduce head in that flux circulates in its core from the recorded tape, but it also acts as a record head in the biased mode with two zones of recording. The magnetization thus recorded can have a large magnitude since the flux is concentrated at the gap corners and the anhysteretic process has a susceptibility of typically about 3. At wavelengths that are long relative to the erase-head gap length, the flux in the core causes a re-recording that is in phase with the unerased signal, and at the wavelength equal to the gap length, no flux links the core. At wavelengths less than the erase-head gap length, the flux in the core can have a reversed polarity and cause gap-edge signals to be recorded that oppose the originating signal, and interference occurs. At wavelengths such that

$$g = \frac{3\lambda}{4} , \frac{7\lambda}{4} , \frac{11\lambda}{4} , \cdots$$

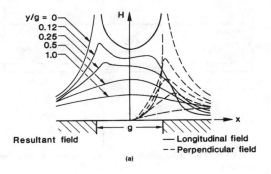

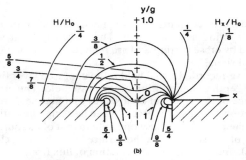

FIGURE 9.7   Fields in the vicinity of the recording gap. (*a*) Field distribution; (*b*) contours of equal field strength (*Duinker, 1957*).

the two Hilbert component signals are in destructive interference, as seen in Fig. 9.8, and a null in the response results. This is, in effect, the condition of zero re-recording and, therefore, the condition of maximum erasure. The erasure peaks will occur at wavelengths such that

$$\lambda_n = \frac{4g}{4n - 1} \tag{9.5}$$

where n is an integer. In the McKnight reference (1963), the tape speed was 38.1 cm/s, the gap of the erase head was 133 μm (108 μm of mica and two 12.7-μm glue lines), and the critical frequencies were 2100 Hz, 5000 Hz, and 8000 Hz. The first three values of n give frequencies of 2142 Hz, 5000 Hz, and 7857 Hz, in very good agreement with the experimental results. Thus, the erasure process gives evidence of the importance of both longitudinal and perpendicular components in analyzing the operation of a recording channel.

The simultaneous presence of phase-separated Hilbert transform pairs in instrumentation recording has a significant impact on a number of performance characteristics of the recording channel. It affects the shape of the response curve in constant-current recording, and it is a free parameter that can be used to increase the band-edge signal-to-noise ratio. It poses a problem, however, in equalizing

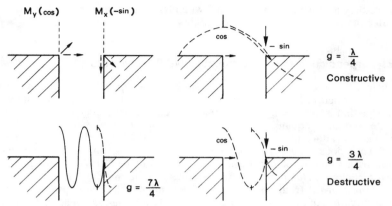

FIGURE 9.8 Constructive and destructive interferences from Hilbert pairs of magnetization.

linear channels, as will be discussed in Sec. 9.3, and in analyzing the spectral response of a channel using a single-transition magnetization change and Fourier analysis. The perpendicular components are masked by demagnetization of the semi-infinite magnetization pattern of the single transition, with the result that the channel does not follow the model at short wavelengths where the perpendicular demagnetization is much reduced. The analysis problem can be obviated by employing a triplet or missing-pulse response rather than a single transition.

9.3 EQUALIZATION AND SIGNAL-TO-NOISE RATIO

9.3.1 Head Losses

Record-head loss refers to the reduction in available flux at the gap as a function of frequency for constant-current head excitation. According to the reciprocity principle, reproduce heads suffer the same loss in sensitivity as they would as record heads. These losses are readily measured and are compensated for by preequalization and postequalization.

Reproduce losses are measured by recording a tape at low speed with two frequencies, band-edge and one-half band-edge, and then reproducing it at speeds that are doubled over many octaves. With each speed-doubling, the one-half-band-edge signal reproduces at the frequency of the former band-edge signal and should exhibit no frequency losses. Losses that do appear are due to misalignment at the higher speed or, more usually, to spacing loss induced by the tape flying. The head loss is the residual loss after correction for misalignment and spacing loss at each frequency. Record-head losses are measured similarly—by reproducing at a fixed low speed and doubling the record speed over the same range.

Typical instrumentation multitrack heads with ferrite cores and metal tips exhibit about 3 dB of loss at 2 MHz and about 10 dB at 10 MHz. Although bias currents are about 10 times the signal current, the bias-induced increase in recording sensitivity is only about a factor of 3 when head losses are accounted for; this is the value of typical anhysteretic susceptibility for oxide media.

9.3.2 Perpendicular and Longitudinal Field Components

A constant-flux recording results in a response that typically rises somewhat less than 6 dB per octave to peak, where it then rolls off in an ever-increasing slope to a band-edge that is usually chosen such that the peak-to-band-edge loss is less than 20 dB. The frequency equalization of this response to one that is flat is not difficult, but it does introduce phase shift that must be removed. The classical equation for reproduction does not contain a phase-shift term since it assumes a constant magnetization as a function of depth into the tape (Wallace, 1951). Real recordings, however, generate a leading phase with frequency that must also be equalized. The leading phase arises from the wavelength-dependent effective depth of recording and the curvature of the recording field produced by a ring-type head. The shortest-wavelength signals reside on the surface of the tape, whereas the centroid of the longer-wavelength signals is deeper and, therefore, retarded.

A channel equalized for phase and amplitude yields an unexpected square-wave response, as seen in Fig. 9.9. The rounding of the trailing edge is not derivable from the band-limited Fourier components of the square-wave but, rather, is due to the Hilbert transform components, discussed earlier, that are generated by the perpendicular magnetization. The effect of the Hilbert transform is to rotate each Fourier component through $\pi/2$ while keeping the coefficients unchanged. A Fourier sine expansion of a square wave (Fig. 9.10a) will lead to a Hilbert expansion in cosine terms (Fig. 9.10b) if each component is rotated by $\pi/2$. If the Hilbert terms are weighted by 30 percent of the Fourier terms and the components are band-limited, a waveform results that is similar to Fig. 9.9.

In some instrumentation recorders, the effect of the perpendicular component is compensated somewhat by differentiating the signal, inverting it, and adding it to the original signal to compensate for the unwanted trailing-edge droop. This technique works well at only one frequency but gives acceptable results over a modest range of frequencies. A channel equalized in this way can be misleading when its phase response is judged from its square-wave waveform. The phase response of the channel is actually highly distorted to accommodate at one square-wave frequency the Fourier and Hilbert components that cannot, in general, be equalized simultaneously to give a square wave at all frequencies. A properly equalized channel yields a waveform as in Fig. 9.9.

The existence of both longitudinal and perpendicular magnetization components also results in a modification to the response curve that affects equalization (Lemke, 1982). Interferences between the leading and trailing edges of the record-head gap change the shape of the response curve and are responsible for the fact that the unequalized response initially rises at 5.5 dB per octave, rather than the 6 dB per octave expected from simple theory.

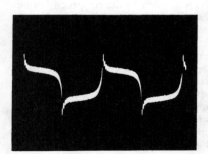

FIGURE 9.9 Square waves showing in-phase Fourier and Hilbert components with properly phase equalized channel and conventional tape ($M_y/M_x \approx 0.4$).

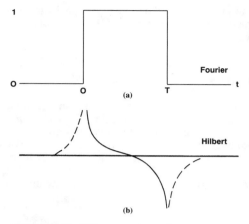

FIGURE 9.10 Hilbert transform of a square wave.

9.3.3 Multiplicative Noises

The dominant sources of noise in most instrumentation channels are multiplicative rather than additive. Multiplicative noise is caused by coating inhomogeneities, variations in spacing and azimuth loss, and variations in time-base error (flutter). Multiplicative errors are more important to instrumentation recording than to computer recording owing to the much shorter wavelengths typically used in the instrumentation field. Also error-concealment techniques cannot be used, as they are in audio or video recording.

Modulation noise derives its name from the fact that it is evident only in the presence of a signal and appears as a modulation of that signal. It exists in few recording systems, photographic film being the primary other medium that exhibits the effect. Its existence complicates the analysis of a channel since information theory assumes that signal and noise are independent functions, an assumption which is grossly incorrect for a magnetic recording channel.

Modulation noise has two sources associated with the magnetic coating: bulk inhomogeneities and surface finish (including asperities). The bulk inhomogeneities can be controlled somewhat through the use of dispersants and careful milling of the magnetic dispersion prior to coating. The spectrum of this kind of modulation noise is predominantly long-wavelength. The surface-induced noise is much more difficult to control and has a severe effect on signals at short wavelengths where the highest information density resides. As noted in Eq. (9.2), 90 percent of the signal is contributed by a thin layer of depth λ/e. For a 0.67μm wavelength, 90 percent of the signal resides in a layer of thickness corresponding to the wavelength of ultraviolet light. Even the best optical surfaces, if achievable on the tape surface, would have measurable modulation noise that would have to be considered in designing an error-detection and error-correction method.

Magnetic recording at wavelengths usual in instrumentation recorders represents an unusual channel from a communication-theory point of view. As system design is currently practiced, the channels enjoy an embarrassment of riches in average signal-to-noise ratio but suffer from the worst-case modulation-noise limit. Much more must be done to push the instrumentation-channel density further to an additive-noise limit, and a portion of the increased capacity should then be spent to implement error-detection and error-correction codes tailored to the peculiarities of instrumentation recording.

9.3.4 Noise-Power Ratio

The noise-power ratio (NPR) is a critical measurement in telephone systems since it measures not only the thermal noise in a channel but also all of the intermodulation components present from other channels. It was adapted to instrumentation recording for use in surveillance recorders which are required to detect weak signals in the presence of strong signals over a wide bandwidth. Equal probability of error per root-Hertz is achieved by making the NPR constant over the channel bandwidth. The resultant channel satisfies the Shannon equation in its simplest form

$$C = 2B\log_2(1 + \text{SNR}) \tag{9.6}$$

where C = information capacity in bits per second
$\quad B$ = bandwidth of the channel
$\quad \text{SNR}$ = the signal-to-noise ratio.

Flat noise-power ratio in magnetic recording is achieved solely through pre-emphasis and is an iterative process. It is measured by recording white noise in a biased channel that has a frequency-selectable, narrow-notch filter. During reproduction, a narrower-band selective voltmeter is used to measure the thermal noise and the intermodulation products that have been created in the band from all of the noise sources outside the band. The ratio of the noise signal in the vicinity of the notch to the noise in the notch is the noise-power ratio at that frequency (Fig. 9.11).

Preemphasis at band-edge to levels above the record current that causes 1 percent third-harmonic distortion, will result in a greater signal-to-noise ratio at band-edge, but the harmonics of that signal, although not reproducible, will intermodulate with in-band frequencies and lower the signal-to-noise ratio at midband. Some loss at midband can be tolerated, since that is the region of maximum signal-to-noise ratio, but too much band-edge preemphasis must be avoided. At low frequencies, considerable preemphasis is possible since the intermodulation products are also of low frequency and do not affect the higher frequencies. By moving the selective filters across the band and iterating the adjustments in bias and preemphasis, it is possible to equalize a channel optimally. It is also possible, in principle, by this technique to adapt the signal-to-noise ratio (including intermodulation products) of a channel to match closely the optimum channel-response curve for a particular code. The transfer characteristics of a flat-noise-power-ratio channel, relating noise-power ratio to input signal level, is given (Tant, 1974) by

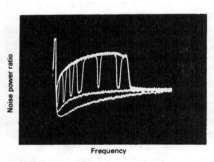

FIGURE 9.11 Flat noise-power ratio showing multiple notches. The NPR is constant for all frequencies independent of any subsequent postequalization for flat response.

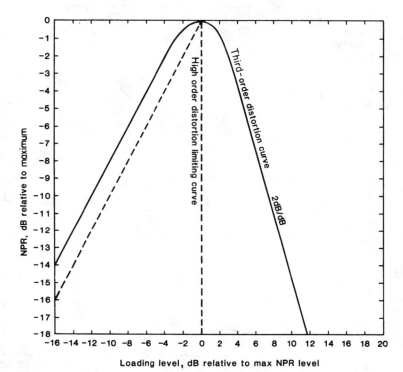

FIGURE 9.12 Noise-power ratio for third-order distortion is an instrumentation tape channel.

$$NPR = 10 \log \frac{P}{P_0} - 10 \log \left[\left(\frac{P}{P_0} \right)^\gamma + (\gamma{-}1) \right] + \log \gamma \qquad (9.7)$$

where P_0 = power at the maximum value
   P = relative power
   γ = order of distortion

The value of γ is 3 for magnetic recording which is dominated by third-order harmonic distortion. As shown in Fig. 9.12, the noise-power ratio rises 1 dB for each decibel of input below the maximum and falls 2 dB per decibel of input above the maximum, as can be seen in the equations below.

Linear region: $(P/P_0)^\gamma \ll (\gamma - 1)$

$$NPR = 10 \log \frac{P}{P_0} + 10 \log \frac{\gamma}{\gamma - 1} \qquad (9.8)$$

Nonlinear region: $(P/P_0)^\gamma \gg (\gamma - 1)$

$$NPR = 10 \log \gamma - (\gamma - 1) \, 10 \log \frac{P}{P_0} \qquad (9.9)$$

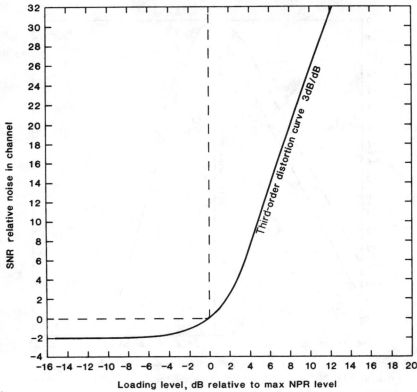

FIGURE 9.13 Signal-to-noise ratio for third-order distortion in an instrumentation tape channel.

The signal-to-noise ratio relative to that at the maximum for the linear and nonlinear regions, respectively, is

$$\text{SNR} = -10 \log \frac{\gamma}{\gamma - 1} \tag{9.10}$$

and

$$\text{SNR} = \gamma \left[10 \log \frac{P}{P_0} \right] - 10 \log \gamma \tag{9.11}$$

In the linear region, the signal-to-noise ratio is unaffected by adjacent channels and is limited only by thermal noise. Above the maximum noise-power ratio, however, the signal-to-noise ratio deteriorates 3 dB for each decibel of input. At the maximum, the thermal-noise power is twice the intermodulation power. Figure 9.13 shows input-output curves for signal-to-noise ratio.

A typical preemphasis curve for flat noise-power ratio is shown in Fig. 9.14. It is interesting to note that much of the total equalization is in the record channel, in contrast to constant-flux recording where it is all in the reproduce channel. For flat noise-power-ratio recording, the reproduce channel is equalized only to facilitate detection of the signal.

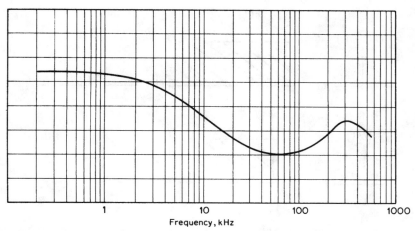

FIGURE 9.14 Flat noise-power-ratio preemphasis curve for a record gap length of 0.25 μm (300 kHz; 19 cm/s). Ordinate scale is 10 dB per step.

9.3.5 High-Density Digital Recording with PR-IV

Many modulation codes have been used in instrumentation recording to increase the recording efficiency over that possible with straight NRZ. Various run-length-limited and charge-constrained codes have also been employed to accommodate rotary transformers and other channel demands. The most efficient modulation codes have been partial response, Class IV, the so-called $1\text{-}D^2$ code, and its variants, EPR, E^2PR, and so forth. The importance of partial response signaling is so great that it is appropriate to describe the technique in some detail. The method used is derived from communication theory since it illuminates very well the elementary functions occurring in PR IV that tend to be somewhat obscured by the usual $1\text{-}D^2$ formalism (Lemke, 1989).

In PR IV recording, the record signal is conventional NRZ signaling, the read channel is equalized to a sine response, and the output is detected as three levels: $+2$, 0, and -2 that correspond to bit states of 1, 0, and 1, respectively.

Important features of PR IV signaling are that there is no signal energy at zero frequency (this reduces channel crosstalk); there is no energy at the bit rate, the other zero of the sine response; and intersymbol interference is greatly reduced relative to normal signaling.

An impulse function, $\delta(t - t')$ has a Fourier transform that is a complex number, $e^{ikt'}$, in frequency space, i.e., it contains all frequencies of equal amplitude initially in phase at time t'. If the frequency space is bandlimited to a bandwidth of B, the Fourier transform of that spectrum is a sinc function with nulls at $1/2B$, $1/B$ and so forth. The addition of a second impulse at time T results in two overlapping sinc functions that result in intersymbol interference, ISI (see Fig. 9.15).

The analysis that follows will consider impulses for clarity in explaining the PR IV code with a positive impulse corresponding to a 1 and a negative impulse corresponding to a 0. It is important to note, however, that the actual signaling is performed not with impulses but with conventional NRZ current in the record head. This simplification is possible since the Fourier transform of a rectangular function, $\Pi(t)$, corre-

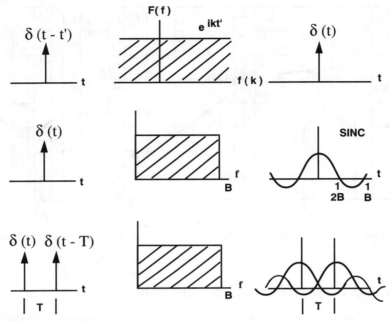

FIGURE 9.15 The Fourier transform of single and double impulses in a broadband and bandlimited channel. A further transform yields an impulse, sinc function, and interfering sinc functions, respectively.

sponding to NRZ recording, is a sinc function and the Fourier transform of a bandlimited impulse function is also a sinc function (Bracewell, 1978).

Consider now two impulses spaced at $\pm T/2$. Their Fourier transform is the sum of two complex numbers:

$$e^{ikT/2} + e^{-ikT/2} = \cos kT/2 + i \sin kT/2 + \cos kT/2 - i \sin kT/2$$
$$= 2 \cos kT/2$$

Figure 9.16 shows the impulses and the spectrum. Note that the first null is at $k = \pi/T$; the spectrum may be bandlimited to that frequency.

By reversing the polarity of one of the impulses, a sine spectrum results:

$$e^{ikT/2} - e^{ikT/2} = \cos kT/2 + i \sin kT/2 - \cos kT/2 + i \sin kT/2$$
$$= 2 i \sin kT/2$$

Figure 9.17 shows those impulses and spectrum. The first null is at $k = 2\pi/T$. The spectrum has desirable characteristics for magnetic recording in that there is no energy at zero frequency and a null exists at the bit rate, but the spectrum is twice as broad as with the like-polarity impulses. This is easily rectified by doubling the spacing between the impulses to achieve a bit rate at $k = \pi/T$ as shown in Fig. 9.18.

It is interesting to note at this point that an impulse of energy into a channel with a bandlimited cosine response at $1/2T$ will result in two sinc functions T apart that add as one broad pulse with their tails tending to cancel each other (low ISI). This is called duobinary signaling, or PR-I.

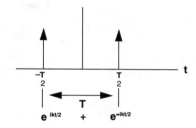

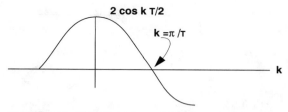

FIGURE 9.16 The frequency spectrum of two like-polarity impulses T apart.

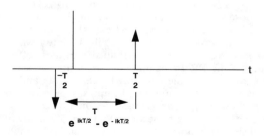

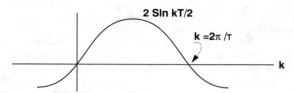

FIGURE 9.17 The frequency spectrum of two opposite polarity impulses T apart. Note that the spectrum to the first null is twice that in Figure 9.16.

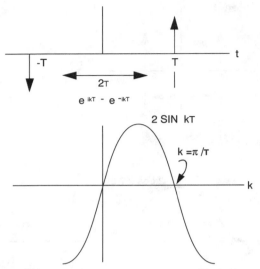

FIGURE 9.18 Opposite polarity impulses $2T$ apart have their first null in frequency spectrum at the same frequency as like impulses T apart (Fig. 9.16).

An impulse of energy in a sine channel bandlimited to $1/2T$ results in two sinc functions $2T$ apart whose tails also tend to cancel for the same reduced ISI. The resulting dipulse is the basis for the description "partial response"; the signal resulting from a signaling event is received only partially at time t with the rest of the information arriving at time $t + T$. Figure 9.19 illustrates these effects.

The dipulse nature of the PR IV channel causes some signals to add with the result that the information is contained in three levels: $+ 2$, 0, and $- 2$. Figure 9.20 shows a bit stream, corresponding numbered impulses (and the equivalent NRZ current waveform), and the output sum of the sinc functions.

It is desirable to do a pre-coding to accommodate the $2T$ delay in the signaling. This is easily accomplished with an Exclusive-Or gate and two single period delays (the origin of the $1\text{-}D^2$ nomenclature). In Fig. 9.21 it is assumed that 2 zeroes are initially loaded into the two delays. The output at C will appear at B after two periods as shown by the transfer arrows. Binary code C is written as a NRZ current in the record head. The resultant double-pulses create the levels ± 2 and 0, as shown, that demodulate into A', the original bit stream.

In order to create the necessary sine response, filters are usually used in the passband of the recorder to carve out a sine response. It is interesting to note, however, that a Wallace channel is already a sine channel and suitable for PR IV signaling by using the gap null to form the sine response. Figure 9.22 shows the desired channel response, $\sin(\pi g/\lambda)$, with the gap-null defining bandedge, $g = \lambda$, and the dominant terms of the Wallace equation. Figure 9.23 shows the normalized response of a VHS-type magnetic recording channel with a 0.5 μm record/reproduce gap adjusted for constant current recording at a low current so that $\delta_{50} = 0.11\ \lambda$. Considering only the thickness and gap aperture terms of the Wallace equation (neglecting spacing loss), it is seen that the channel is already PR IV

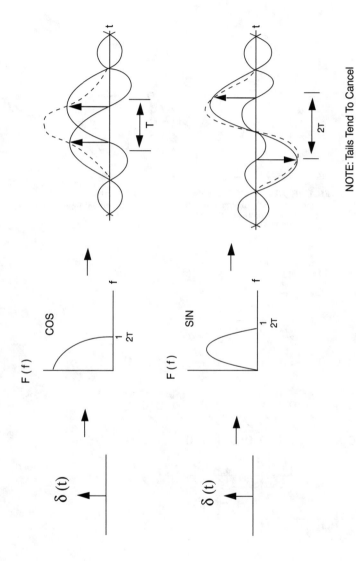

FIGURE 9.19 An impulse of energy in a bandlimited cosine channel or bandlimited sine channel yields dual sinc functions whose tails tend to cancel (reduced ISO). Note the T and $2T$ delays.

NOTE: Tails Tend To Cancel

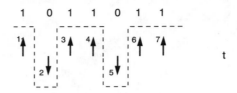

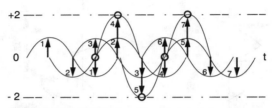

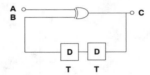

FIGURE 9.20 PR IV signaling. Each impulse creates a
second reversed polarity impulse $2T$ later. NRZ signaling
causes 2 sinc functions $2T$ apart that add for levels of ± 2
and 0.

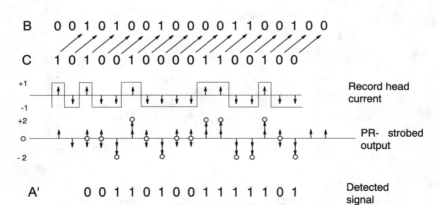

FIGURE 9.21 Precoding with an Exclusive-Or chip and two delays of T each. A is the input
data stream, C is the encoded data stream that is used to create the NRZ current in the write
head, and A' is the detected data.

PR IV

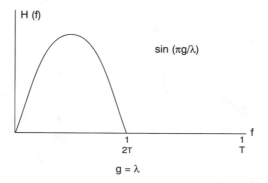

$$\frac{a\,(1 - e^{-2\pi\delta/\lambda})\sin\,(\pi g/\lambda)/(\pi g/\lambda)e^{-2\pi d/\lambda}}{\sin\,(\pi g/\lambda)}$$

FIGURE 9.22   The desired transfer function $H(f)$ for a PR IV channel with the gap null as part of the equalizer (g = null wavelength = the bit cell length). The Wallace dominant terms are the equalizer.

equalized without any additional equalization. Figure 9.24*a* shows the eye pattern of that recorder which has been recorded with a NRZ data stream at 100,000 bits/inch using only the gap-null for the equalizer. The detected three levels are also shown in Fig. 9.24*b*.

Many advantages accrue from such a method.

1. With adequate SNR, the signalling rate may be up to twice the frequency at which the head playback-gap null occurs. That is, rather than operating the channel up to a frequency where the signal has dropped to 3 dB below the peak, for instance, as is done in most digital recording, the bandwidth is almost doubled by going out to signal extinction at the gap null. Alternatively, the required equalization may be obtained by rolling off the channel response before the gap null, particularly if signal-to-noise considerations dictate the use of a playback gap smaller than the Nyquist-rate wavelength.

2. Adjacent-track crosstalk, which is a major source of error in high-track-density recorders, is very much reduced by the sine response that is zero at zero frequency.

3. The channel matches the recording response very well with zero response at zero frequency and at the bit rate. Equalization involves compensating only for the spacing loss.

4. Although SNR is theoretically lost through three-level detection as compared to peak detection, there is a net gain in effective SNR by avoiding differentiation for peak detection and by the reduction of long-wavelength crosstalk.

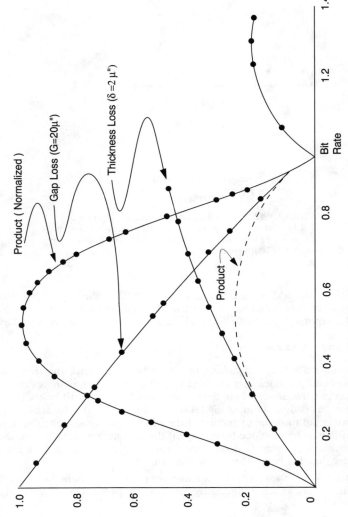

FIGURE 9.23 The normalized product of the gap loss and thickness loss terms of the Wallace equation at 100,000 bits/inch using a 20 μinch playback head gap as the equalizer.

9.26

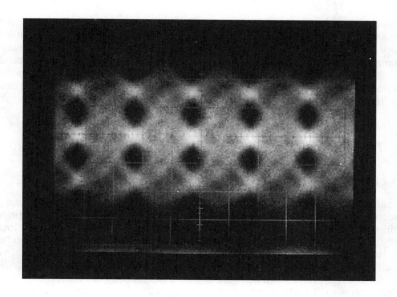

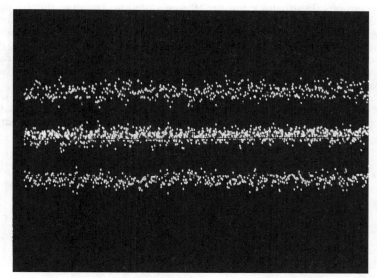

FIGURE 9.24 (*a*) Eye patterns and (*b*) detected three levels for a VHS recorder at 100,000 bits/inch.

The method of detection described for the PR IV channel involves extracting the clock and strobing the waveform into a three level slicing detector. Frequently the density sought is so high that more sophisticated lattice detectors are necessary to accommodate the low signal-to-noise ratio. Viterbi detectors are commonly used in such situations. With a reasonable number of gates it is possible to approach the 3 dB improvement in effective signal-to-noise ratio such maximum likelihood detectors offer.

9.4 TAPE TRANSPORT

9.4.1 Fixed Heads

The earliest instrumentation tape-transport designs adapted from professional audio recorders were replaced with new transport concepts to meet the more stringent requirements of data recording. Although many formats have been tried in the quest for error-free tape transport, all of them are flawed to various degrees. Unfortunately, the uniform transport of an elastic medium such as tape is a very difficult task, and no format is as free from disturbances as would be desired. Some of the formats that have been built are shown schematically in Fig. 9.25.

The professional audio configuration of Fig. 9.25a isolates the head area from the take-up-reel disturbances, but the tension variations from the supply reel are magnified since the tension at the input to the capstan (and, therefore, at the last head) is increased by the wrap around the heads. The friction at the head-tape interfaces, μ, increases the tape tension over a combined head-wrap angle of θ by a factor of exp $(\mu\theta)$. For typical wrap angles of $10°$ per head and a friction coefficient of 0.2, the input-reel tension disturbances are increased by about 15 percent across the head stack.

Several other configurations employed in instrumentation recorders are shown in Fig. 9.25b, c, d, and e. Figure 9.25b shows the closed-loop approach that was developed as an attempt to isolate the heads from reel disturbances by clamping the

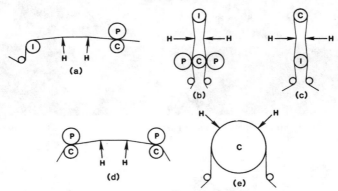

FIGURE 9.25 Several common tape-drive configurations. All of them transmit input-reel flutter disturbances to the head region. (C = capstan; H = head; I = idler; P = pinch roller.)

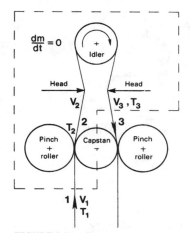

FIGURE 9.26   Closed-loop tape-drive configuration. Mass flow into the dashed region equals the mass flow out of the region.

tape to the capstan surface by two pinch rollers. Variations of this approach used a stepped capstan and pinch rollers to establish a fixed-tension differential. Figure 9.25c has no pinch rollers, since the capstan has a large wrap angle. The free idler is coated with a high-friction layer so that there is no slippage between it and the tape after the tape is at speed.

Figure 9.25d shows a two-capstan drive with differential speed between the two capstans to maintain tension at the heads. Usually, pinch rollers are used to prevent tape slippage. Figure 9.25e shows a typical capstan arrangement designed to permit high-speed servoing of the tape speed for time-base error correction. Frequently the tape is lifted off the vacuum capstan locally to permit improved head-to-tape contact relative to what is possible with the head urged against tape in contact with the capstan surface. Various devices for achieving compliance have been interposed between the capstan-head region and the reels, including vacuum columns and moving arms. Frequently the reel speed is servoed from the compliance structure to maintain constant tape tension. The introduction of compliance is only partially effective in preventing reel disturbances from entering the head area.

The operation of a tape transport may be analyzed simply by utilizing the conservation of mass in considering the flow of tape into and out of imaginary closed regions of the transport. For example, consider the dashed-line boundary in Fig. 9.26. The mass flow into region 1 must equal the mass flow out of region 3. Other regions can be placed in the tape path, and a series of simultaneous equations can be arrived at for complete analysis of the tape motion.

Defining a modulus of strain per unit length and tension as $\Omega = \Delta L/LT$, the density per unit length of tape relative to the initial density ρ_0 is

$$\rho = \frac{\rho_0}{1 + \Omega T} \tag{9.12}$$

The tape velocity entering the capstan at region 1 has the capstan velocity of V_1 and the rate of mass flow into the region is

$$\frac{dm}{dt_1} = \frac{V_1 \rho_0}{1 + \Omega T_1} \tag{9.13}$$

Similarly, the mass flow out of region 3 is

$$\frac{dm}{dt_3} = \frac{V_3 \rho_0}{1 + \Omega T_3} \tag{9.14}$$

Since the two tape paths are driven by the same capstan surface, $V_1 = V_3$ and $T_3 = T_1$. Thus, the tension inside the closed loop is governed by the input tension outside the loop and is, in fact, exactly equal to T_1, including any disturbances on that

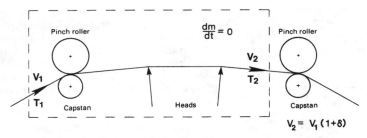

FIGURE 9.27   Dual capstan drive configuration.

tension. The differential tape length that has been created by $T_1 + \Delta T_1$ in the immediate vicinity of the input side of the capstan is clamped to the capstan by static friction generated by the pinch roller and is transported to region 2, where it is released into a new tension environment. A transition from static friction to dynamic friction occurs between the tape and the capstan surface at region 2 as the pinch-roller force is reduced. This can excite longitudinal vibrations in the tape that appear in the form of high-frequency flutter.

All tape-drive configurations experience flutter at the head sites from outside stimuli independently of the method of capstan drive, unless the tape tension is forced to go to zero just prior to the input capstan that precedes the head site. Some configurations are worse than others. Consider the design shown in Fig. 9.27. The output capstan is designed to a surface velocity slightly higher (by a factor δ) than that of the input capstan; this establishes tape tension in the head region. The two regions are when the symbols V_1, T_1, and V_2, T_2 appear in Fig. 9.27, and the velocities in these regions are related by $V_2 = V_1(1 + \delta)$. The mass flow through the dashed region requires that

$$\frac{V_1 \rho_0}{1 + \Omega T_1} = \frac{V_1(1 + \delta)\rho_0}{1 + \Omega T_2} \tag{9.15}$$

For a given tape, the tension in region 2, ignoring tension losses from wrap angle across the heads, is dependent upon the input tension T_1 and the capstan speed differential.

$$T_2 = \frac{\delta}{\Omega} + T_1(1 + \delta) \tag{9.16}$$

Since T_1 contains fluctuating terms from reel disturbances, it is desirable to keep the input tension low and derive most of the tension in the head-region from the term δ/Ω.

$$\frac{\delta}{\Omega} \gg T_1(1 + \delta) \tag{9.17}$$

Although the reel disturbances are amplified by the factor $(1 + \delta)$, they can be very much reduced by using the dual capstan configuration.

Ideally, tape tension into the input capstan would be zero, however it is possible

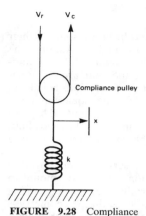

V_r V_c

Compliance pulley

x

k

FIGURE 9.28 Compliance model.

to limit somewhat the disturbances that are transmitted by the input tension by using compliant arms or vacuum columns. The action of the compliance can be seen from examining a simple pulley and tape arrangement, as shown in Fig. 9.28. The massless pulley is attached to a spring with force constant k that exerts a tension in the tape at a position x of $kx/2$. The tape is assumed to be delivered to the pulley from the reel at an average velocity V_r and removed from the pulley by the capstan at a fixed velocity V_c equal to V_r. A small sinusoidal velocity component in V_r would cause a peak change in the length of tape of

$$\Delta L = \int_0^{T/4} \Delta V_r \cos \omega t \, dt = \frac{\Delta V_r}{\omega} \qquad (9.18)$$

The mechanical advantage is 2, therefore $\Delta L = 2 \, \Delta x$ and

$$\Delta T = \frac{\Delta V_r k}{4\omega} \qquad (9.19)$$

The disturbances are, therefore, reduced by a small spring constant k and are largest at low frequencies, decreasing at 6 dB per octave. In practice, the inertia of the compliant arm permits disturbances at frequencies above several tens of hertz to pass unattenuated by the compliance. Also, the compliant device is usually a rotating arm with mechanical advantage much less than shown in Fig. 9.28.

Frequently, the position of compliant arms or tape positions in vacuum columns are used to servo the supply and take-up reel speeds to achieve constant tape tension, particularly on the supply side. Except for the lowest-frequency components that can be handled by the servo bandwidth, some of the reel disturbances still get through since the vacuum column has an effective spring constant associated with its loop-position servo.

Vacuum columns serve a very useful function in edge-guiding tape; this function is unrelated to their role in tape tensioning. During manufacture, all tapes are slit from wide webs by rotary knives. The tapes exhibit a small weave related to the circumference (typically 20 cm) of the knives. If the column is tapered to encourage the tape to ride on one edge, and if the length of tape in the column exceeds twice the knife circumference, the tape in the column, which is folded and relatively stiff, will ride continuously on the two peaks of the slitting weave. Reproducible tracking to several microns, as evidenced by output envelope, can be maintained between transports of the same type using this technique.

Low-frequency disturbances that enter the head region can be removed through servoing the speed of a low-inertia capstan with a reference signal on the tape. On sophisticated transports, such servos are used to reduce the time-base error (TBE) to the order of 10 ns. The time-base error is the time integral of the velocity flutter and is often of more interest than is the instantaneous velocity of the tape. Most high-frequency disturbances contribute little to the time-base error but can cause signal errors by modulating signals with unwanted sidebands. So-called scrape flutter is induced by abrupt large tension transitions, as noted above, and by friction at fixed surfaces such as the heads.

9.4.2 Rotary Heads

The primary advantage of rotary-head transports over fixed-head transports is their greater areal information packing density. For tape-noise-limited systems, the signal-to-noise ratio is reduced 3 dB for each track-width halving, but the bandwidth is doubled since two tracks can be accommodated in the same area. The net gain is 3 dB in information-handling capacity each time the trackwidth is halved. Rotary head transports currently handle well over 2×10^5 bits per square millimeter, and are theoretically capable of densities well beyond optical limits. They are restricted by the bandwidth they can handle in one track. Bandwidths beyond about 300 Mb/s per track are difficult to achieve and will probably require multiple rotary heads.

Typically, two servos (and sometimes a third—a tension servo) are employed to synchronize the linear tape advance and the head position in its rotary mount to ensure that the tracks are positioned on the tape in a reproducible, nonoverlapping pattern that can be duplicated during reproduce. The basic head-tape geometry is very similar to the video formats, and, in fact, many of the rotary-head instrumentation transports have been adapted from professional video recorders.

APPENDIX

The frequent need to exchange data tapes and reproduce data on disparate recorders has led to strong standards activities in instrumentation recording. The primary source of such standards for multitrack recorders has been the Telemetry Group of the Range Commanders Council (RCC). The RCC membership includes the U.S. Army White Sands Missile Range, Pacific Missile Test Center, Eastern Space and Missile Center, Naval Weapons Center, Air Force Flight Test Center, Kwajalein Missile Range, Western Space and Missile Center, Air Force Satellite Control Facility, Atlantic Fleet Weapons Training Facility, Tactical Fighter Weapons Center, U.S. Army Yuma Proving Ground, Naval Air Test Center, and U.S. Army Electronic Proving Ground. Associate members include many other DoD agencies, NASA, and government contractors such as Aerospace Corporation and Sandia National Laboratories.

A technical committee of the RCC, the Interrange Instrumentation Group (IRIG), has published standard documents (IRIG, Ref.) relevant to instrumentation recording: IRIG 106-86, *Telemetry Standards* (chaps. 6, 7, and 8) and RCC Document 118-79, *Test Methods for Telemetry Systems and Subsystems* (vol. III, Test Methods for Recorder/Reproducer Systems and Magnetic Tape).[†] A revision of the Test Methods document will be numbered 118-89.

It is expected that the standards committees will specify formats for signal preambles for use in automatic adjustment of recorder and reproducer parameters for direct and FM recording.

Rotary recorders are also being considered by the Recorders and Reproducers Committee of the Telemetry Group with standards expected ultimately to encompass other-agency standards for the so called large-format recorders as well as the small-format recorders based on consumer video recorders. Two current rotary standards for large-format machines are MIL-STD-2179 and ANSI ID-1 in addition

---

[†]Available from National Defense Logistics Agency, Attn: FDRA, Cameron Station, Alexandria, VA 22304-6145.

to SMPTE standards. In general, the small-format machines are used in the 20 Mb/s and below range, whereas the large-format machines can operate at rates of multi-hundreds of megabits per second.

REFERENCES

Bertram, H. N., and R. Niedermeyer, "The Effect of Spacing in Magnetic Recording," *IEEE Trans. Magn.,* **MAG-18,** 1206 (1982).

Bracewell, Ronald N., *The Fourier Transform and its Applications,* McGraw-Hill, New York, 1978.

Duinker, S., Tijdsch. ned. Radiogenoot., **22,** 29–48 (1957).

EMI engineering staff, *Modern Instrumentation Recording,* EMI Technology, London, England, 1978.

Howard, J. A., and L. N. Ferguson, "Magnetic Recording Handbook," Hewlett Packard Application Note 89, Palo Alto, CA, 1970.

Kretzmer, E. R., "Generalization of a Technique for Binary Communication," IEEE Trans. Commun., **14,** 67 (1966).

Lemke, J. U., "Ferrite Transducers," *Ann. N. Y. Acad. Sci.,* **189,** 171 (1972).

Lemke, J. U., "An Isotropic Particulate Magnetic Medium with Additive Hilbert and Fourier Field Components," *J. Appl. Phys.,* **53,** 2561 (1982).

Lemke, J. U., "Magnetic Recording of Digital Audio," *Proc. AES, 7th Intl. Conf.,* 21–27 (1989).

Mallinson, J. C., and C. W. Steele, "Theory of Superposition in Tape Recording," *IEEE Trans. Magn.,* **MAG-5,** 886 (1969).

McKelvey, J. P., "General Kinematics of Winding Processes," *Am. J. Phys.,* **53,** 1156 (1985).

McKnight, J. G., "Erasure of Magnetic Tape," *J. Audio Eng. Soc.,* **11,** 223 (1963).

NASA, *High Density Digital Recording,* NASA Reference Publication, 1111, Washington, D.C., 1985.

Star, J., "Specifying Phase Response and Envelope Delay in an Instrumentation Tape Recorder," *Telemetry J.,* **5,** 17 (1970).

Tant, M. J., *The White Noise Book,* White Crescent Press, Luton, England, 1974.

Wallace, R. L., "The Reproduction of Magnetically Recorded Signals," *Bell Syst. Tech. J.,* **30,** 1145 (1951).

CHAPTER 10
SIGNAL AND ERROR-CONTROL CODING

Arvind M. Patel
IBM Corporation, San Jose, California

10.1 INTRODUCTION

A magnetic recording channel is designed to accept data for storage and deliver the same on demand at a later time, with reasonable access time and without errors. These data may be in the form of fixed- or variable-length records corresponding to user-identified blocks which can be updated or redefined at any time. In a typical magnetic recording channel, the incoming data are first encoded with an error-correction code with a well-defined data format. The data format is designed to fit the requirements imposed by the device architecture, and the error-correction code is designed to protect the data against commonly encountered error modes. A second encoder then converts data into an analog signal in accordance with a waveform encoding technique or a modulation code. This code is designed to fit the requirements of the magnetic recording channel for high packing density and error-free detection of the recorded data.

Error-control coding and modulation techniques have played a significant role in the design and development of digital magnetic recording products. The trend towards higher densities and data rates has presented continuing demands for innovations and improvements in signal coding and error-control techniques. The ability to operate at a lower signal-to-noise ratio and to tolerate an increased number of correctable errors has become part of the design strategy. As a result, the cost of storage is reduced significantly through defect tolerance and higher yield in manufacturing, while very high data integrity, as seen by the user, has been provided.

In this chapter, we present summary results on signal encoding techniques and the theory of error-correction coding in relation to the requirements of digital magnetic recording channels. We also present examples of the modulation codes and error-correction schemes used in various magnetic tape and disk products. The chapter is not meant to be a survey of all the coding results used in magnetic recording. However, it will present a variety of results and help the reader to gain a sufficient hold on many useful concepts without requiring a background in the mathematical development of the theory.

10.2   SIGNAL-CODING METHODS

Binary information is recorded on magnetic media as magnetic transitions in the form of a coded binary waveform. For example, a 1 and a 0 of the binary data can be identified by an up and a down level in the waveform, respectively. This mapping of the waveform is known as the *non-return-to-zero* (NRZ) data-encoding method. Alternatively, a 1 and a 0 of the binary data may be represented by a presence and an absence of a transition in the binary waveform, respectively. This mapping of the waveform is known as the *modified non-return-to-zero* (NRZI) data-encoding method. In digital magnetic recording, each magnetic transition on the medium generates a corresponding electric pulse in the readback signal. This pulse is detected as a positive or negative peak in the waveform by means of the well-known peak-detection channel. An error in detecting this pulse will result in a 1-bit error in NRZI-coded data. In contrast, the same error will propagate indefinitely in NRZ-coded data since a transition in the NRZ waveform represents a switch from a string of 1s to a string of 0s, or vice versa. Thus, NRZI is the commonly accepted encoding method in digital magnetic recording.

The principal drawback of NRZI is that long strings of 0s are recorded as long periods with no magnetic transitions, and hence no pulses in the readback signal; the read clock can lose synchronization during these periods. Furthermore, circuits with dc response are required for signal processing and data detection. The NRZI method is also subject to a more subtle difficulty. At high densities, the readback pulses produced by a string of consecutive 1s tend to interfere with one another. When such a string of 1s is preceded or followed by a string of consecutive 0s, this interference is asymmetrical, causing the first or last few pulses to have larger amplitudes; thus the baseline appears to drift. A similar shift can arise from a string of consecutive 0s if the dc response of the electronic circuitry is less than adequate. Interference also causes the pulses to seem to slide into the signal-free zone occupied by the 0s, creating a displacement in time of the pulse peaks. This peak shift can be a significant fraction of the nominal time between bits. These problems have led to a variety of coding modifications being made to the basic NRZI method, as shown in Fig. 10.1.

Phase encoding (PE) was devised to alleviate some of these problems. It is used on $\frac{1}{2}$-in tapes recorded at 1600 bits per inch. In PE, a 1 corresponds to an up-going transition and a 0 to a down-going transition at the center of the bit cell. Where two or more 1s or 0s occur in succession, extra transitions are inserted at the bit-cell boundaries. The resulting waveform is self-clocking and has no dc component, since the waveform in each bit cell has up (positive) and down (negative) signal levels of equal duration. However, PE requires twice the transition density of the NRZI method for a random data pattern. Thus recording efficiency is poor.

Frequency modulation (FM) has transitions at every bit-cell boundary. FM is similar to PE in all waveform properties, although the 1 and 0 correspond to a presence or absence of a transition rather than to an up or down transition at the center of the corresponding bit cell. In certain applications, FM has been supplanted by delay modulation, or MFM, which provides enough clocking transitions without doubling the transition density. In MFM, as in FM, a 1 and a 0 correspond to the presence and absence, respectively, of a transition in the center of the corresponding bit cell. Additional transitions at the cell boundaries occur only between bit cells that contain consecutive 0s. This method retains an adequate minimum rate of transitions for clock synchronization without exceeding the maxi-

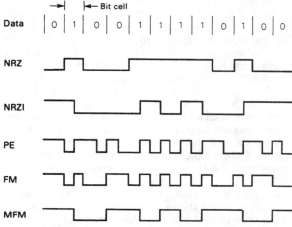

Figure 10.1 Waveform encoding methods in early products.

mum transition density of NRZI. A disadvantage is the dc component, with indefinitely large accumulated dc charge for some data patterns, such as 0110110110. . . .

Modified forms of NRZI include synchronized NRZI (NRZI-S) and group-coded recording (GCR). In these methods, the data stream is precoded by adding bits to break up long strings of 0s. In NRZI-S, a 1 extends each 8-bit group to 9 bits and establishes a synchronization transition. In GCR, each 4-bit group is mapped into 5 bits using a fixed assignment that guarantees that the coded data stream never contains more than two consecutive 0s. The detection process for both methods is the same as that for NRZI, but maximum transition density is necessarily higher. These methods marked the beginning of precoding the binary data with run-length-limiting codes for desired properties in the resultant waveform. These run-length-limiting codes are also called *modulation codes*.

10.3 MODULATION CODES

A modulation code for magnetic recording is a one-to-one mapping of binary data into a constrained binary sequence which is then recorded on the magnetic recording medium in the form of an NRZI waveform. In this waveform, the maximum and minimum spaces between consecutive transitions correspond to the maximum and minimum run lengths of 0s between two consecutive 1s in the corresponding binary sequence. Thus, the modulation codes for magnetic recording fall into the class of run-length-limited (RLL) codes. These codes are characterized by the parameters (d, k) where d represents the minimum and k represents the maximum number of 0s between two consecutive 1s in the coded sequence (Franaszek, 1970). The parameter d controls the highest transition density and the resulting intersymbol interference. The parameter k controls the lowest transition density and ensures adequate frequency of transitions for synchronization of a read clock. The parameter k is also useful in limiting the amount of delay in detection of the readback data;

in particular, in the maximum-likelihood process where detection of any readback pulse is delayed until confirmation from the following pulse of opposite polarity.

The run-length constraints, however, are not the only consideration if the channel uses ac-coupling network elements in processing the read-write signals. For example, in a rotary-head system, the head is coupled through a transformer. In that case, a dc component in the waveform results in a nonzero average value of the amplitude and causes charge accumulation at the ac-coupling element. A constraint on the maximum accumulated charge is an effective means of reducing the signal distortion caused by the ac-coupling network element. In the case of a binary coded sequence, the accumulated charge increases or decreases by one unit at each digit depending on an up or down level, respectively, in the corresponding waveform. A run-length-limiting code with charge constraint is characterized by the parameters $(d, k; c)$ where d and k are the previously described run-length constraints, and the accumulated charge at any digit position in the coded sequence is bounded by $\pm c$ units (Patel, 1975).

If, on average, x data bits are mapped into y binary digits in the coded sequence $(y \geq x)$, the ratio x/y is called the *rate of the code*. A run-length-limiting code is completely described by its rate and the code parameters, written as "$x/y\ (d, k)$" code, or "$x/y\ (d, k; c)$" code. The following are some of the important characteristics of these codes.

1. *Density ratio.* A higher value of d provides greater separation between consecutive transitions in the recorded waveform, although with some trade-off in the rate of the code. The ratio of the data density versus the highest density of recorded transitions is a measure of recording efficiency and is called the *density ratio* (DR) given by:

$$\text{DR} = \frac{\text{data density}}{\text{transitions density}} = \frac{x}{y}(d + 1)$$

2. *Detection window.* The read waveform is processed through the channel where the presence or absence of a transition within each signaling element is detected using a variable-frequency clock. The available time for detection, called the *detection window,* is determined by the width of the signaling element in terms of the data bit cell. This is completely determined by the rate of the code.

$$\text{Detection window} = \frac{x}{y} \text{ (width of the data bit cell)}$$

3. *Maximum/minimum pulse width ratio.* The ratio of maximum pulse width to minimum pulse width is related to the resolution or uniformity in the resulting read waveform and the corresponding peak-shift problem when a series of long-wavelength pulses follow a short-wavelength pulse or vice versa. This ratio is also related to the worst-case crosstalk between two adjacent tracks, which occurs when long-wavelength pulses in one track produce interference into short-wavelength pulses in the next track, or vice versa. This ratio is given by:

$$\frac{\text{Maximum pulse width}}{\text{Minimum pulse width}} = \frac{k + 1}{d + 1}$$

The rate x/y of the code is bounded above by the information capacity of the constrained sequences (Shannon, 1948). The information capacity of the unconstrained binary sequences is 1 bit per digit, and that of constrained sequences is

TABLE 10.1 Information Capacity of Coded Sequences

Parameters				
d	k	c	Capacity $\geq$ rate	Density ratio
0	3	$\cdots$	$0.947 > \frac{8}{9}$	8/9
1	3	$\cdots$	$0.552 > \frac{1}{2}$	1
1	3	3	$0.500 = \frac{1}{2}$	1
1	6	$\cdots$	$0.669 > \frac{2}{3}$	4/3
1	7	$\cdots$	$0.679 > \frac{2}{3}$	4/3
1	7	10	$0.668 > \frac{2}{3}$	4/3
2	7	$\cdots$	$0.517 > \frac{1}{2}$	3/2
2	7	8	$0.501 > \frac{1}{2}$	3/2
2	8	7	$0.503 > \frac{1}{2}$	3/2
3	7	$\cdots$	$0.406 > \frac{2}{5}$	8/5
4	9	$\cdots$	$0.362 > \frac{1}{3}$	5/3
5	17	$\cdots$	$0.337 > \frac{1}{3}$	2

necessarily less than 1 bit per digit. This capacity is a strong function of the constraints and can be determined for any given (d, k) or $(d, k; c)$ parameters. Table 10.1 lists the capacities and possible rates corresponding to some (d, k) and $(d, k; c)$ parameters (Franaszek, 1970; Patel, 1975). Figure 10.2 provides an insight into the interrelation of various code parameters; the figure shows that the density ratio progressively increases with larger values of the parameter d, although the capacity decreases. It also shows how the density ratio is affected as one allows a wider range of pulse widths. The ratio $(k + 1)/(d + 1)$ determines this range and is strongly related to the amount of peak shift of adjacent transitions, crosstalk between adjacent tracks at high linear and track densities, and overwrite noise. The maximum rate and density ratio are not always realizable with a practical algorithm in all (d, k) codes. A good algorithm realizes a rate that is close to the information capacity of the constrained sequences, uses a simple implementation, and avoids the propagation of errors in the decoding process.

Codes with a fixed wordlength can be developed through an exhaustive search of code words which can be catenated without violating the desired constraints. A look-up table may be used; however, in some cases a comprehensive word assignment can be obtained to create logic equations for encoding and decoding, as is the case with an $\frac{8}{9}$ (0, 3) block code (Patel, 1985a). Sometimes a design with variable-length code words provides shorter word lengths with reduced error propagation, as occurs with the $\frac{1}{2}$ (2, 7) code (Franaszek, 1972). Low-rate codes can be designed by creating isomorphic state diagrams (Patel, 1975) to represent the constrained and unconstrained sequences. In general, this provides an iterative algorithm with some look-ahead or look-back requirements, or both, as occurs with a $\frac{1}{2}$ (1, 3; 3) code, otherwise known as *zero modulation code*. Zero modulation also provides a case study of a code with infinite look-ahead; one in which the rate approaches the information capacity of the sequences, and yet the error propagation remains zero. When the look-ahead requirement is finite and reasonable, the isomorphism of the state diagrams can be obtained easily through a step-by-step procedure (Adler et al., 1983).

Many different modulation codes are in use in various magnetic tape and disk

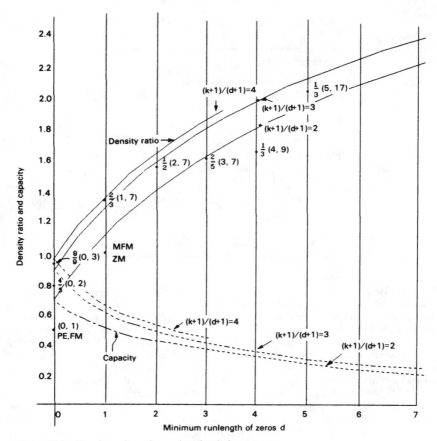

Figure 10.2   Density ratio and capacity of coded sequences.

products. These codes are the result of a steady evolution of waveform design along with that of the high-performance magnetic recording channel including the clocking and signal-detection process. In modern machines, the choice of code parameters involves trade-offs (MacKintosh, 1980) between the various properties of a code and the characteristics of a particular device. Table 10.2 lists these codes with their parameters. The earlier data-encoding methods NRZI-S, PE, FM, and MFM are also identified in this table with (d, k) parameters in order to put them in perspective. GCR is a $\frac{4}{5}$ $(0, 2)$ block code used in tape machines recording at 250 bits per millimeter (6250 bits per inch) in 9-track standard data format. This code is replaced by a new, more efficient $\frac{8}{9}$ $(0, 3)$ block code in the newest tape subsystem. Zero modulation (ZM) was specifically designed for a mass storage system which uses a rotary head and requires dc-free waveform. ZM is a $\frac{1}{2}$ $(1, 3; 3)$ code with an iterative algorithm and a strong error-detection capability. High-performance disk files have shown preference for codes with higher density ratios, such as the $\frac{1}{2}$ $(2, 7)$ code with variable-length code words, and the $\frac{2}{3}$ $(1, 7)$ code. The modulation codes for the PRML channel will be discussed in Sec. 10.4.

TABLE 10.2 Modulation Codes Used in Magnetic Recording Products

Code	RLL d, k	Rate	Range of pulse widths in waveform†	PW ratio (max/min)	Density ratio	Detection window	Max DC charge	Usage
NRZI	0, ∞	1	*(graphical)*	∞	1	1	∞	800 bpi tape
NRZI-S	0, 8	8/9	*(graphical)*	9	0.89	0.89	∞	13xx disk
PE	0, 1	1/2	*(graphical)*	2	0.5	0.5	T	24xx tape
MFM (Miller)	1, 3	1/2	*(graphical)*	2	1	0.5	∞	23xx disk
GCR	0, 2	4/5	*(graphical)*	3	0.8	0.8	∞	33xx disk
8/9	0, 3	8/9	*(graphical)*	4	0.89	0.89	∞	3420 tape
ZM	1, 3	1/2	*(graphical)*	2	1	0.5	3T/2	3480 tape
Miller[2]	1, 5	1/2	*(graphical)*	3	1	0.5	3T/2	3850 MSS
3PM	2, 11	1/2	*(graphical)*	4	1.5	0.5	∞	ISS-8470
2, 7	2, 7	1/2	*(graphical)*	2.67	1.5	0.5	∞	3370-80 disk
1, 7	1, 7	2/3	*(graphical)*	4	1.33	0.67	∞	3390 disk

(Range of pulse widths column scale: 0.5T, T, 2T, 3, 4, 5, 6, 7, 8, 9)

†The left-hand vertical bar denotes the pulse width of the clock.

10.7

10.3.1   The $\frac{8}{9}$ (0, 3) Code

Recent tape-storage subsystems record data at a density of 24,000 bits per inch in an 18-track data format on $\frac{1}{2}$-in tape using the $\frac{8}{9}$ (0, 3) group code. It is a one-to-one mapping of the set of all 8-digit binary sequences (data bytes) onto a set of 9-digit binary code words as given in Table 10.3 (Patel, 1985a). The coded binary sequence corresponding to any sequence of data bytes possesses the following two properties: (1) The run lengths of consecutive 0s between any two 1s are limited to zero, one, two, and three only; thus it is called $\frac{8}{9}$ (0, 3) code. (2) The pattern $S = 100010001$ is not a code word and also does not occur anywhere in the coded sequence with original or shifted code-word boundaries; thus S can be used as a synchronization pattern at selected positions in the data stream to identify format boundaries.

The code-word assignment of Table 10.3 provides simple and inexpensive encoder and decoder logic. The encoder logic for the mapping is derived using four functions, M, N, R, and S. These are the controlling functions which identify the subsets in the mapping depending on the types of partitions in the code-word assignment. Any 9-bit code word W is partitioned into three parts: W_1 of four digits, a connecting digit C, and W_2 of four digits.

$$W = [W_1], C, [W_2]$$

Any 8-bit data group is partitioned into two parts; V_1 of four digits and V_2 of four digits.

$$V = [V_1], [V_2]$$

The function M represents the subset in the mapping where the partitions W_1 and W_2 are the same as V_1 and V_2, respectively. The connecting digit C is 1, and there are 154 code words in this subset. Function N represents the subset in the mapping where the partition W_1 is a special identifying pattern for V_1 and the partition W_2 is the same as V_2. The connecting digit C is 0, and there are 20 code words in this subset. Function R represents the subset in the mapping where the partition W_1 is a special identifying pattern for V_2 and the partition W_2 is the same as V_1. The connecting digit C is 0, and there are 50 code words in this subset. Function S represents the subset in the mapping where partitions W_1 and W_2 both are special identifying patterns for V_1 and V_2, respectively. The connecting digit C is 0, and there are 32 code words in this subset.

The functions M, N, R, and S are generated by logic expressions describing the corresponding subsets in the mapping. Each digit of the 9-bit code word corresponding to an 8-bit data byte is then obtained using logic expressions involving M, N, R, and S. The decoder logic is derived in the same manner, using the partitioning functions M, N, R, and S in reverse.

Let $[X_1, X_2, X_3, X_4, X_5, X_6, X_7, X_8]$ and $[P_1, P_2, P_3, P_4, P_5, P_6, P_7, P_8, P_9]$ denote the 8-bit data byte and the corresponding 9-bit coded pattern, respectively. The encoder and decoder functions are given by the binary logic equations shown in Tables 10.4 and 10.5, respectively. The decoder logic also includes an error-checking function E which checks for an invalid pattern in place of a code word. Each code word also possesses opposite parity relation with the corresponding data byte; this can be used as a diagnostic check for the encoder and decoder hardware.

10.3.2   Zero Modulation: $\frac{1}{2}$ (1, 3; 3) Code

Zero modulation (ZM) (Patel, 1975) features waveforms with zero dc component. It was created especially for a rotary-head storage system (IBM 3850). The read-

TABLE 10.3 The $\frac{8}{9}$ (0, 3) Modulation Code†

X	P	X	P	X	P	X	P
00000000	011001011	01000000	010001011	10000000	111001011	11000000	110001011
00000001	011001001	01000001	010001001	10000001	111001001	11000001	110001001
00000010	001001101	01000010	010010010	10000010	100010010	11000010	110010010
00000011	101100011	01000011	010010011	10000011	100010011	11000011	110010011
00000100	011001010	01000100	010001010	10000100	111001010	11000100	110001010
00000101	101100101	01000101	010010101	10000101	100010101	11000101	110010101
00000110	101100110	01000110	010010110	10000110	100010110	11000110	110010110
00000111	101100111	01000111	010010111	10000111	100010111	11000111	110010111
00001000	011001111	01001000	010001111	10001000	111001111	11001000	110001111
00001001	101101001	01001001	010011001	10001001	100011001	11001001	110011001
00001010	101101010	01001010	010011010	10001010	100011010	11001010	110011010
00001011	101101011	01001011	010011011	10001011	100011011	11001011	110011011
00001100	011001110	01001100	010001110	10001100	111001110	11001100	110001110
00001101	101101101	01001101	010011101	10001101	100011101	11001101	110011101
00001110	101101110	01001110	010011110	10001110	100011110	11001110	110011110
00001111	101101111	01001111	010011111	10001111	100011111	11001111	110011111
00010000	001001011	01010000	011100101	10010000	011101001	11010000	011101101
00010001	001001001	01010001	001100101	10010001	001101001	11010001	001101101
00010010	011001101	01010010	010110010	10010010	100110010	11010010	110110010
00010011	100100011	01010011	010110011	10010011	100110011	11010011	110110011
00010100	001001010	01010100	010100101	10010100	010101001	11010100	010101101
00010101	100100101	01010101	010110101	10010101	100110101	11010101	110110101
00010110	100100110	01010110	010110110	10010110	100110110	11010110	110110110
00010111	100100111	01010111	010110111	10010111	100110111	11010111	110110111
00011000	001001111	01011000	111100101	10011000	111101001	11011000	111101101
00011001	100101001	01011001	010111001	10011001	100111001	11011001	110111001
00011010	100101010	01011010	010111010	10011010	100111010	11011010	110111010
00011011	100101011	01011011	010111011	10011011	100111011	11011011	110111011
00011100	001001110	01011100	110100101	10011100	110101001	11011100	110101101
00011101	100101101	01011101	010111101	10011101	100111101	11011101	110111101
00011110	100101110	01011110	010111110	10011110	100111110	11011110	110111110
00011111	100101111	01011111	010111111	10011111	100111111	11011111	110111111
00100000	101001011	01100000	011100110	10100000	011101010	11100000	011101110
00100001	101001001	01100001	001100110	10100001	001101010	11100001	001101110
00100010	001010010	01100010	011010010	10100010	101010010	11100010	111010010
00100011	001010011	01100011	011010011	10100011	101010011	11100011	111010011
00100100	101001010	01100100	010100110	10100100	010101010	11100100	010101110
00100101	001010101	01100101	011010101	10100101	101010101	11100101	111010101
00100110	001010110	01100110	011010110	10100110	101010110	11100110	111010110
00100111	001010111	01100111	011010111	10100111	101010111	11100111	111010111
00101000	101001111	01101000	111100110	10101000	111101010	11101000	111101110
00101001	001011001	01101001	011011001	10101001	101011001	11101001	111011001
00101010	001011010	01101010	011011010	10101010	101011010	11101010	111011010
00101011	001011011	01101011	011011011	10101011	101011011	11101011	111011011
00101100	101001110	01101100	110100110	10101100	110101010	11101100	110101110
00101101	001011101	01101101	011011101	10101101	101011101	11101101	111011101
00101110	001011110	01101110	011011110	10101110	101011110	11101110	111011110
00101111	001011111	01101111	011011111	10101111	101011111	11101111	111011111
00110000	011100011	01110000	011100111	10110000	011101011	11110000	011101111
00110001	001100011	01110001	001100111	10110001	001101011	11110001	001101111
00110010	001110010	01110010	011110010	10110010	101110010	11110010	111110010
00110011	001110011	01110011	011110011	10110011	101110011	11110011	111110011
00110100	010100011	01110100	010100111	10110100	010101011	11110100	010101111
00110101	001110101	01110101	011110101	10110101	101110101	11110101	111110101
00110110	001110110	01110110	011110110	10110110	101110110	11110110	111110110
00110111	001110111	01110111	011110111	10110111	101110111	11110111	111110111
00111000	111100011	01111000	111100111	10111000	111101011	11111000	111101111
00111001	001111001	01111001	011111001	10111001	101111001	11111001	111111001
00111010	001111010	01111010	011111010	10111010	101111010	11111010	111111010
00111011	001111011	01111011	011111011	10111011	101111011	11111011	111111011
00111100	110100011	01111100	110100111	10111100	110101011	11111100	110101111
00111101	001111101	01111101	011111101	10111101	101111101	11111101	111111101
00111110	001111110	01111110	011111110	10111110	101111110	11111110	111111110
00111111	001111111	01111111	011111111	10111111	101111111	11111111	111111111

†Synchronization pattern: 100010001; X = data byte; P = code word.

TABLE 10.4   The Encoder Function: $\frac{8}{9}$ (0, 3) Code

$$[X_1, X_2, X_3, X_4, X_5, X_6, X_7, X_8] \rightarrow [P_1, P_2, P_3, P_4, P_5, P_6, P_7, P_8, P_9]$$
8-digit data byte $\rightarrow$ 9-digit code word

$M = AH$ where $A = X_1 + X_2 + X_3$

$N = \overline{A}G$ $H = (X_5 + X_6 + X_7)(X_7 + X_8)$

$R = B\overline{H}$ $B = (X_1 + X_2)(X_3 + X_4) + X_3 X_4$

$S = \overline{A}\overline{G} + \overline{B}\overline{H}$ $G = (X_5 + X_6)(X_7 + X_8) + X_7 X_8$

$P_1 = X_1 M + N + X_5 R + (X_1 + X_3) S$

$P_2 = X_2 M + \overline{X}_7 \overline{X}_8 R + \overline{X}_3 (\overline{X}_4 \oplus X_7) S$

$P_3 = X_3 M + \overline{X}_4 N + \overline{X}_6 \overline{X}_7 R + \overline{X}_2 S$

$P_4 = X_4 M + N + R$

$P_5 = M$

$P_6 = X_5 M + X_5 N + X_1 R + S$

$P_7 = X_6 M + X_6 N + X_2 R + [(X_3 \oplus X_5) + X_7] S$

$P_8 = X_7 M + X_7 N + X_3 R + \overline{X}_7 \overline{X}_8 S$

$P_9 = X_8 M + X_8 N + X_4 R + \overline{X}_6 S$

TABLE 10.5   The Decoder Function: $\frac{8}{9}$ (0, 3) Code

$$[P_1, P_2, P_3, P_4, P_5, P_6, P_7, P_8, P_9] \rightarrow [X_1, X_2, X_3, X_4, X_5, X_6, X_7, X_8]$$
9-digit code word $\rightarrow$ 8-digit data byte

$M = P_5$

$N = P_1 \overline{P}_2 P_4 \overline{P}_5$

$R = (\overline{P}_1 + P_2) P_4 \overline{P}_5$

$S = \overline{P}_4 \overline{P}_5$

$X_1 = P_1 P_5 + P_6 R + P_1 P_2 S$

$X_2 = P_2 P_5 + P_7 R + \overline{P}_3 S$

$X_3 = P_3 P_5 + P_8 R + P_1 \overline{P}_2 S$

$X_4 = P_4 P_5 + \overline{P}_3 N + P_9 R + \overline{P}_1 (\overline{P}_2 \oplus P_7 \overline{P}_8) S$

$X_5 = P_6 P_5 + P_6 N + P_1 R + (P_1 \overline{P}_1 \overline{P}_2 \oplus P_7) P_8 S$

$X_6 = P_7 P_5 + P_7 N + \overline{P}_3 R + \overline{P}_9 S$

$X_7 = P_8 P_5 + P_8 N + \overline{P}_1 P_7 \overline{P}_8 S$

$X_8 = P_9 P_5 + P_9 N + \overline{P}_2 R + (P_1 + \overline{P}_7)\overline{P}_8 S$

Error check

$E = \overline{P}_1 \overline{P}_2 \overline{P}_3 + \overline{P}_2 \overline{P}_3 \overline{P}_4 \overline{P}_5 + \overline{P}_4 \overline{P}_5 \overline{P}_6 + \overline{P}_5 \overline{P}_6 \overline{P}_7 \overline{P}_9 + \overline{P}_6 \overline{P}_7 \overline{P}_8$
$+ \overline{P}_8 \overline{P}_9 + \overline{P}_3 \overline{P}_4 \overline{P}_5 \overline{P}_7 \overline{P}_8 + P_1 \overline{P}_4 \overline{P}_5 \overline{P}_8 (P_2 \oplus \overline{P}_7)$

Synchronization pattern

$P_1 \overline{P}_2 \overline{P}_3 \overline{P}_4 P_5 \overline{P}_6 \overline{P}_7 \overline{P}_8 P_9$

write signal in this type system is transmitted to a rotary transducer by coupling through a transformer whose primary and secondary coils are in continuous relative motion.

In the coded ZM binary sequence, any two consecutive 1s are separated by at least one and at the most three 0s. This sequence is converted into a waveform using a transition for a 1 and no transition for a 0 in the binary sequence. Consequently, the narrowest pulse in the ZM waveform spans two digits in the coded sequence, thus keeping the ratio of the data density to the highest-recorded transition density close to 1. Similarly, the widest pulse spans four digits, thus limiting the range of different pulse widths. In the ZM waveform, the accumulated dc charge value always remains within ± 3 units, and it always returns to a zero value at specific boundaries.

The stringent coding constraints of ZM also provide a powerful check on errors in decoding the read data. In particular, the commonly encountered bit-shift errors in magnetic recording are always detected by the bound of ± 3 units on the accumulated change.

The ZM algorithm maps every data bit sequentially into two binary digits. The mapping is described in terms of a data bit to be encoded, one preceding data bit, and the two coded digits corresponding to the preceding data bit and in terms of two parity functions that look ahead and back relative to the bit being encoded. Look-ahead parity $P(A)$ is the count, modulo 2, of 1s in the data stream, beginning with the data bit being encoded and counting forward to the next 0 bit; look-back parity $P(B)$ is the count, modulo 2, of all 0s in the data stream from its beginning up to the present bit. For example, in the data sequence 01011110, with bit positions considered from left to right, $P(A) = 1$ at the second, fifth, and seventh bits and $P(B) = 1$ at the first, second, and eighth bits.

The encoding and decoding rules are expressed in the form of binary logic functions. The encoding function is

$$a_0 = \bar{d}_0 \bar{d}_{-1} + d_0 \bar{d}_{-1} \overline{P(A)} P(B) + d_{-1} \bar{a}_{-1} \bar{b}_{-1} \tag{10.1}$$

$$b_0 = d_0 [P(A)\bar{d}_{-1} + \overline{P(B)} + b_{-1}] \tag{10.2}$$

and the decoding function is

$$d_0 = b_0 + a_0 \bar{a}_1 \bar{b}_1 + a_0 a_{-1} \bar{b}_{-1} \tag{10.3}$$

where the symbol d represents a data bit; a and b represent coded digits; and subscripts -1, 0, and 1 signify preceding, current, and succeeding bits, respectively. For convenience, the nonexistent bit preceding the first data bit is assumed to be 1 and its look-back parity is 0; the nonexistent bit following the last bit is 0. Figure 10.3 shows a typical data sequence encoded into ZM waveform.

Look-back *parity* $P(B)$ can be obtained by updating a 1-bit storage cell for every 0 in the data as data bits are encoded. Look-ahead parity $P(A)$ depends on the length of a string of 1s in the succeeding data sequence. When the algorithm imposes no limit on the length of this string, the computation of $P(A)$ requires an encoder with infinite memory. In order to limit the amount of memory, a parity is inserted at the end of every section of f data bits, which makes $P(B)$ equal to 0 at position $f + 1$ at the end of each section. When $P(B)$ is 0, the encoding functions no longer depend on $P(A)$. Thus, $P(A)$ has no effect on ZM mapping at the boundary of every section of $f + 1$ bits in the data sequence with parity bits, and the computation of $P(A)$ at any data bit need not extend farther than f bits. Then $P(A)$ is given by the binary logic function of the data stored in f bits of memory

$$P(A) = d_0\bar{d}_1 + d_0d_2\bar{d}_3 + d_0d_2d_4\bar{d}_5 + \cdots \\ + d_0d_2d_4\cdots d_{t-4}\bar{d}_{t-3} + d_0d_2d_4\cdots d_{t-4}d_{t-2}$$ (10.4)

where $t = f$ if f is even and $t = f - 1$ if f is odd.

The encoding process is delayed by f bit periods in a continuous stream of data for computing $P(A)$, but the decoding errors in ZM do not propagate, and the decoding process always terminates at the section boundary.

In the particular rotary-head system under discussion, the value of f is 128. A known unique pattern is inserted at the end of each section and is used as a synchronization pattern. This pattern is

$$S = 01000100101000101000101001.$$

The waveform corresponding to S satisfies the ZM pulse-width constraints. It has zero dc component, but does not satisfy the ± 3 charge constraint. The pattern S contains the sequence 00101000101000, which is the shortest among those that never occur in the valid ZM pattern in its original or shifted position. Thus, when the synchronization is lost, the sequence S can still be identified from the shifted data, which then reestablishes the synchronization.

The reverse of the waveform corresponding to S also makes a good synchronization mark. This distinction may be used to mark the beginning of the data in a segment by means of the reverse sync waveform in contrast with the regular sync waveform at the end of each section.

One interesting property of the ZM-coded waveform is read-backward symmetry. A properly terminated ZM waveform, when read backward, is a ZM waveform corresponding to the same data in reverse. In particular, when a parity bit is appended to the data to make $P(B)$ equal to 0 at the end, the encoding process terminates the dc charge value at zero at the end of the corresponding waveform. Such a waveform, which has a zero dc component, can be decoded forward or backward by means of the ZM decoding algorithm.

The zero-modulation algorithm is unique in that it achieves a rate that comes arbitrarily close to the channel capacity with corresponding increase in look-ahead, as was promised by the Shannon theorem. Other codes with relaxed parameters, such as $\frac{1}{2}$ (1, 4; 3), called *modified zero modulation* (Ouchi, 1976), and $\frac{1}{2}$ (1, 5; 3), called *Miller squared code* (Miller, 1977), are also available for waveforms with zero dc component and with a very small amount of look-ahead.

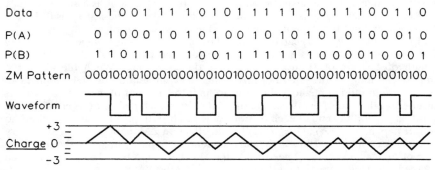

Data   0 1 0 0 1 1 1 1 0 1 0 1 1 1 1 1 1 0 1 1 1 0 0 1 1 0

P(A)   0 1 0 0 0 1 0 1 0 1 0 0 1 0 1 0 1 0 1 0 1 0 0 0 1 0

P(B)   1 1 0 1 1 1 1 1 0 0 1 1 1 1 1 1 1 0 0 0 0 1 0 0 0 1

ZM Pattern   0001001010001000100100100010001000100101010010010100

Figure 10.3   Encoded ZM waveform.

10.3.3   The $\frac{1}{2}$ (2, 7) Code

The $\frac{1}{2}$ (2, 7) code (Franaszek, 1972) is used in high-performance disk files (such as IBM 3370, 3375, and 3380). It has variable-length codewords. The main advantage this code offers is that the minimum spacing between transitions is three clock periods, as compared to only two for MFM with the same clock and detection window. There are two encoded bits corresponding to each data bit. Thus the detection window is one-half the bit cell, and recorded-transitions density is lower by a factor of 1.5. The mapping of variable-length code words is given in Table 10.6.

The encoding of the data can be done by partitioning the data sequence into two-, three-, and four-bit partitions to match the entries in the code table and then mapping them into corresponding code words. The decoding process is similar but in reverse. An equivalent but more convenient iterative algorithm for this code is also available (Eggenberger et al., 1978). For this purpose, let d_i denote the ith data bit and a_i and b_i denote the corresponding two encoded digits. The preceding and following data bits are indicated by the subscripts $i - 1$ and $i + 1$, respectively, and $i = 0$ indicates the digits in process. The encoding equations use an intermediate variable p_i which provides the necessary look-back and look-ahead to determine the word boundaries. The equations are given by

$$a_0 = \bar{d}_0 d_1 \bar{d}_2 \bar{p}_{-2} + d_0 d_1 \bar{p}_{-2} \tag{10.5}$$

$$b_0 = \bar{d}_1 p_{-1} \tag{10.6}$$

where

$$p_0 = \bar{d}_0 d_1 + d_0 d_1 \bar{p}_{-1} + \bar{d}_0 \bar{d}_1 \bar{d}_2 \bar{p}_{-1} \bar{p}_{-2} \tag{10.7}$$

The value $p_0 = 1$ indicates that d_2 is the last digit of the word. The decoding equation is independent of the word boundaries and is given by

$$d_0 = a_{-1} + a_0 \bar{b}_1 + b_0 (a_{-2} + b_{-2}) \tag{10.8}$$

The sequential encoding and decoding process can be initialized and terminated by means of a known preamble and postamble of 0 values. As can be seen from the decoding equation, any error in a coded bit may cause a decoding error in up to two following data bits, the current data bit, and up to one preceding data bit. Thus, the error propagation is limited to four consecutive data bits. Another code used, $\frac{1}{2}$ (2, 11), is called the *three-position modulation* (3 PM) code (Jacoby, 1977); it has

TABLE 10.6   Code Table for $\frac{1}{2}$ (2, 7) Code

Data	Code word
10	0100
11	1000
000	000100
010	100100
011	001000
0010	00100100
0011	00001000

similar parameters (see Table 10.2) and fixed word length. This design also requires look-ahead and look-back in encoding.

10.3.4   The $\frac{2}{3}$ (1, 7) Code

It is known that $(d, k) = (1, 6)$ sequences have the information capacity of 0.669 bits per symbol; however, a practical encoding and decoding algorithm for a rate $\frac{2}{3}$ code is not available. The known algorithm (Horiguchi and Morita, 1976) is unattractive in terms of complexity and error propagation. A code with the next best set of constraints is $\frac{2}{3}$ (1, 7), which is available in various forms. Here we present the code that is used in a particular magnetic disk product (Jacoby and Kost, 1984). In this code, the minimum spacing between transitions is two clock periods as in MFM; however, the clock period and the detection window are two-thirds of a bit cell, as compared to one-half of a bit cell in MFM. The recorded-transitions density is lower by a factor of $(2 \times \frac{2}{3}) = 1.33$, the density ratio.

The mapping rules are described in Tables 10.7 and 10.8 by means of a basic code table and a substitution table. The basic encoding table shows a mapping for the four 2-bit data words. When the data are encoded according to the basic encoding table, some catenations of 3-bit code words violate the $d = 1$ constraint. Whenever that happens, an appropriate substitution is made, using double-word entries from the substitution table, that removes the violations. In decoding the 3-bit partitions, the cases in which the substitution was made during encoding will be identified using look-ahead or look-back. Then all words can be decoded without ambiguity.

Here we create a new more convenient iterative algorithm for this code, in which the encoding and decoding rules are expressed in the form of binary logic equations. In these equations the symbols a, b represent a 2-bit data word; the

TABLE 10.7   Basic Encoding Table for $\frac{2}{3}$ (1, 7) Code

Data	Code
00	101
01	100
10	001
11	010

TABLE 10.8   Substitution Encoding Table for $\frac{2}{3}$ (1, 7) Code

Data	Code
00.00	101.000
00.01	100.000
10.00	001.000
10.01	010.000

symbols x, y, z represent a corresponding 3-digit code word; and subscripts -1, 0, and 1 signify preceding, current, and succeeding bits, respectively. The encoding function is given by

$$x_0 = \bar{a}_0 \bar{b}_0 \bar{z}_{-1} + \bar{a}_0 b_0 (b_{-1} + \bar{x}_{-1} \bar{y}_{-1}) \tag{10.9}$$

$$y_0 = a_0 (b_0 + \bar{a}_1 b_1) \tag{10.10}$$

$$z_0 = \bar{b}_0 (a_1 + \bar{b}_1)(a_0 + \bar{z}_{-1}) \tag{10.11}$$

and the decoding function is given by

$$a_0 = \bar{x}_0 (y_0 + z_0) \tag{10.12}$$

$$b_0 = \bar{x}_0 \bar{y}_0 \bar{z}_0 \bar{z}_{-1} + (x_0 + y_0)(x_1 + y_1 + z_1)\bar{z}_0 \tag{10.13}$$

The sequential encoding or decoding operation processes groups of two data bits and three coded bits at each cycle. For convenience, the nonexistent preceding bits at the first cycle and following bits at the last cycle are assumed to be zero. As can be seen from the decoding equations, any error in a coded bit may cause a decoding error in the preceding b bit, the current a and b bits, and the following b bit. Thus, the error propagation is limited to five consecutive data bits.

This concludes the discussion of data encoding methods and modulation codes. When these codes are used in recording and reading the data at high data rates, the detection window is a very important parameter. For example, at the data rate of 6 MB/s, the detection window for a half-rate code is 10.4 ns. Thus lower rate codes with larger value of d provide an increasingly difficult trade-off between the detection window and the density ratio in applications with very high density and data rates.

10.4 MODULATION CODES FOR THE PRML CHANNEL

IBM has been leading the way toward use of the partial-response (PR) channel and maximum-likelihood (ML) detection process in high-performance disk files. In a PRML channel, the readback pulses from adjacent transitions are allowed to interfere with each other in a predetermined manner (commonly known as PR-Class 4 signaling). Thus, there is no need to avoid inter-symbol interference by coding with a d constraint, i.e., d can be zero in PR Class 4 signaling. The read signal with known amount of inter-symbol interference is sampled at data rate and the data that the samples represent are interpreted by means of the Viterbi maximum-likelihood detection process. The ML process anticipates and unravels the inter-symbol interference and minimizes the probability of error in interpreting the sampled data. One of the features of PR4 signaling is that the sequence of the samples of the read signal can be de-multiplexed into odd-indexed and even-indexed subsequences and each subsequence can be processed by an independent ML detector at half the data rate. Thus a code for the PRML channel needs an additional constraint k_1 limiting the maximum number of sequential zeros in each of the two interleaved subsequences of the data sequence and is characterized by parameters $(d, k/k_1)$ where d and k represent the usual limits on the minimum and maximum number of sequential zeros in the overall sequence of NRZI data. The parameter k_1 adequately limits the detector complexity and delay in ML processing of the two interleaved subsequences of data. The $\frac{8}{9}$ rate (0, 4/4) code is a widely used code in PRML channels now offered by many vendors. The $\frac{8}{9}$ rate (0, 3/6) code and the $\frac{16}{17}$ rate (0, 6/6) code are other interesting codes among the known and available codes for the PRML channel.

10.4.1 The $\frac{8}{9}$ Rate (0, 4/4) PRML Code

The $\frac{8}{9}$ rate (0, 4/4) code was designed for use in IBM's PRML channel and was first used in the IBM 9336 disk product shipped in the year 1991. It is now widely used in PRML channels offered by many vendors. The smallest values of the parameters k and k_1 for which fixed-block 8-bit to 9-bit mappings exist, are (0, 4/4) and (0, 3/6) codes (Eggenberger and Patel, 1987). With one byte look-ahead, a pseudo fixed-block mapping can be obtained for a (0, 3/5) code (Marcus, Patel, and Siegel, 1988).

Let P denote a 9-digit code word in the (0, 4/4) PRML code where

$$P = [P_1, P_2, P_3, P_4, P_5, P_6, P_7, P_8, P_9] \tag{10.14}$$

The constraint $k = 4$ in the overall coded sequence can be realized by eliminating 9-digit sequences with runlength of three zeros at either end or runlength of five zeros within. This constraint is described by the following boolean equation:

$$\begin{gathered}(P_1 + P_2 + P_3)\,(P_2 + P_3 + P_4 + P_5 + P_6)\,(P_3 + P_4 + P_5 + P_6 + P_7) \\ (P_4 + P_5 + P_6 + P_7 + P_8)\,(P_7 + P_8 + P_9) = 1\end{gathered} \tag{10.15}$$

Similarly, the constraint $k_1 = 4$ in the sequence of all-odd digit positions and that in the sequence of all-even digit positions are described by (10.16) and (10.17), respectively.

$$(P_1 + P_3 + P_5)\,(P_5 + P_7 + P_9) = 1 \tag{10.16}$$

$$(P_2 + P_4 + P_6)\,(P_4 + P_6 + P_8) = 1 \tag{10.17}$$

There are 279 valid 9-digit binary sequences that satisfy Eqs. (10.15), (10.16), and (10.17). Out of these 279 sequences, 256 are chosen and carefully assigned one-to-one to the 256 8-bit binary data sequences. Table 10.9 presents the code with this assignment. Next, we present the logic for encoder and decoder implementation of this code.

An 8-bit binary byte X and its assigned 9-digit code word P are given by

$$X = [X_1, X_2, X_3, X_4, X_5, X_6, X_7, X_8] \tag{10.18}$$

$$P = [P_1, P_2, P_3, P_4, P_5, P_6, P_7, P_8, P_9] \tag{10.19}$$

The main partition in making the assignment is the set of data bytes in which the first and last four bits of the 8-bit data sequence X can be mapped without change into first and last four digits respectively of the 9-digit code word P. The middle digit (5th position) of the 9-digit code word in this partition is always 1. There are 163 words in this partition (set M), which can be identified by the function M given by

$$M = (X_1 + X_2 + X_3)\,(X_4 + X_5)\,(X_6 + X_7 + X_8) + X_2 X_7 \tag{10.20}$$

TABLE 10.9 The (0, 4/4) Code Word Assignments

$X \leftrightarrow P$		$X \leftrightarrow P$		$X \leftrightarrow P$		$X \leftrightarrow P$	
00000000	011101110	01000000	111101110	10000000	10010111 0	11000000	100001110
00000001	011101001	01000001	111101001	10000001	10010100 1	11000001	100001001
00000010	011101111	01000010	010010010	10000010	10010111 1	11000010	110010010
00000011	011100001	01000011	010010011	10000011	10010000 1	11000011	110010011
00000100	011101100	01000100	111101100	10000100	10010110 0	11000100	100001100
00000101	011101101	01000101	111101101	10000101	10010110 1	11000101	100001101
00000110	011100100	01000110	010010110	10000110	10010010 0	11000110	110010110
00000111	011100101	01000111	010010111	10000111	10010010 1	11000111	110010111
00001000	011101011	01001000	111101011	10001000	10010101 1	11001000	100001011
00001001	011001001	01001001	010011001	10001001	10011001 1	11001001	110011001
00001010	011000111	01001010	010011010	10001010	10001101 0	11001010	110011010
00001011	011001011	01001011	010011011	10001011	10001101 1	11001011	110011011
00001100	011001100	01001100	010011100	10001100	10001110 0	11001100	110011100
00001101	011001101	01001101	010011101	10001101	10001110 1	11001101	110011101
00001110	011001110	01001110	010011110	10001110	10001111 0	11001110	110011110
00001111	011001111	01001111	010011111	10001111	10001111 1	11001111	110011111
00010000	110101110	01010000	111000110	10010000	10010011 0	11010000	110100110
00010001	110101001	01010001	010110001	10010001	10011000 1	11010001	110110001
00010010	110101111	01010010	010110010	10010010	10011001 0	11010010	110110010
00010011	110100001	01010011	010110011	10010011	10011001 1	11010011	110110011
00010100	110101100	01010100	010110100	10010100	10011010 0	11010100	110110100
00010101	110101101	01010101	010110101	10010101	10011010 1	11010101	110110101
00010110	110100100	01010110	010110110	10010110	10011011 0	11010110	110110110
00010111	110100101	01010111	010110111	10010111	10011011 1	11010111	110110111
00011000	110101011	01011000	111000011	10011000	10010001 1	11011000	110100011
00011001	110001011	01011001	010111001	10011001	10011100 1	11011001	110111001
00011010	110000111	01011010	010111010	10011010	10011101 0	11011010	110111010
00011011	110001011	01011011	010111011	10011011	10011101 1	11011011	110111011
00011100	110001100	01011100	010111100	10011100	10011110 0	11011100	110111100
00011101	110001101	01011101	010111101	10011101	10011110 1	11011101	110111101
00011110	110001110	01011110	010111110	10011110	10011111 0	11011110	110111110
00011111	110001111	01011111	010111111	10011111	10011111 1	11011111	110111111
00100000	001101110	01100000	001001110	10100000	10110111 0	11100000	101001110
00100001	001101001	01100001	001001001	10100001	10110100 1	11100001	101001001
00100010	001101111	01100010	010010010	10100010	10110111 1	11100010	111010010
00100011	001100001	01100011	011010011	10100011	10110000 1	11100011	111010011
00100100	001101100	01100100	001001100	10100100	10110110 0	11100100	101001100
00100101	001101101	01100101	001001101	10100101	10110110 1	11100101	101001101
00100110	001100100	01100110	011010110	10100110	10110010 0	11100110	111010110
00100111	001100101	01100111	011010111	10100111	10110010 1	11100111	111010111
00101000	001101011	01101000	001001011	10101000	10110101 1	11101000	101001011
00101001	001011001	01101001	011011001	10101001	10101001 1	11101001	111011001
00101010	001011010	01101010	011011010	10101010	10101101 0	11101010	111011010
00101011	001011011	01101011	011011011	10101011	10101101 1	11101011	111011011
00101100	001011100	01101100	011011100	10101100	10101110 0	11101100	111011100
00101101	001011101	01101101	011011101	10101101	10101110 1	11101101	111011101
00101110	001011110	01101110	011011110	10101110	10101111 0	11101110	111011110
00101111	001011111	01101111	011011111	10101111	10101111 1	11101111	111011111
00110000	001100110	01110000	011100110	10110000	10110011 0	11110000	111100110
00110001	001110001	01110001	011100001	10110001	10111000 1	11110001	111110001
00110010	001110010	01110010	011110010	10110010	10111001 0	11110010	111110010
00110011	001110011	01110011	011110011	10110011	10111001 1	11110011	111110011
00110100	001110100	01110100	011110100	10110100	10111010 0	11110100	111110100
00110101	001110101	01110101	011110101	10110101	10111010 1	11110101	111110101
00110110	001110110	01110110	011110110	10110110	10111011 0	11110110	111110110
00110111	001110111	01110111	011110111	10110111	10111011 1	11110111	111110111
00111000	001111000	01111000	011100011	10111000	10100001 1	11111000	111100011
00111001	001111001	01111001	011111001	10111001	10111100 1	11111001	111111001
00111010	001111010	01111010	011111010	10111010	10111101 0	11111010	111111010
00111011	001111011	01111011	011111011	10111011	10111101 1	11111011	111111011
00111100	001111100	01111100	011111100	10111100	10111110 0	11111100	111111100
00111101	001111101	01111101	011111101	10111101	10111110 1	11111101	111111101
00111110	001111110	01111110	011111110	10111110	10111111 0	11111110	111111110
00111111	001111111	01111111	011111111	10111111	10111111 1	11111111	111101111

The partition M_1 consists of the data bytes in which the first four bits of P are the same as those in X. This set includes set M (163 assignments) and 12 other assignments identified by a specific structure of the first four bits in X given by the equation

$$(X_1 + X_3) \, X_4 = 1 \tag{10.21}$$

The remaining 81 assignments are divided into partitions N_1, R_1 and S_1 in consideration of exclusive structures of the first four bits in X with special rules of mapping for each set. The partitions N_1, R_1 and S_1 consist of 42, 7 and 32 assignments, respectively, and are identified by the following structures of the first four bits in X:

$$\text{For } N_1 \; \overline{M} \, (X_1 + X_3) \, \overline{X}_4 = 1 \tag{10.22}$$

$$\text{For } R_1 \; \overline{M} \, (\overline{X_1 + X_3}) \, X_2 = 1 \tag{10.23}$$

$$\text{For } S_1 \; \overline{M} \, (\overline{X_1 + X_3}) \, \overline{X}_2 = 1 \tag{10.24}$$

The code possesses read-backward symmetry. Thus, the last four bits of X map into last four bits of P in a manner that is symmetrical with the first four bits (reading backwards). Thus the sets M_2, N_2, R_2 and S_2 are counterparts of the sets M_1, N_1, R_1 and S_1, respectively, and are identified by exclusive structures of the last four bits of X given by logic equations symmetrical to those in Eqs (10.21), (10.22), (10.23) and (10.24).

One variation is added in the above design in order to avoid an all-ones coded sequence. The all-ones code word is replaced by another unused code word by changing P_5, the middle digit, to zero. Chart 10.1 presents the logic equations for the resulting encoder function.

The decoder function identifies the same partitions as those in the encoder using

CHART 10.1   (0, 4/4) PRML Code: Encoder

$$[X_1 \, X_2 \, X_3 \, X_4 \, X_5 \, X_6 \, X_7 \, X_8] \rightarrow [P_1 \, P_2 \, P_3 \, P_4 \, P_5 \, P_6 \, P_7 \, P_8 \, P_9]$$

Partitions

$$M = (X_1 + X_2 + X_3) \, (X_4 + X_5) \, (X_6 + X_7 + X_8) + X_2 \, X_7$$

$M_1 = M + (X_1 + X_3) \, X_4$	$M_2 = M + (X_8 + X_6) \, X_5$
$N_1 = \overline{M} \, (X_1 + X_3) \, \overline{X}_4$	$N_2 = \overline{M}(X_8 + X_6) \, \overline{X}_5$
$R_1 = \overline{M} \, (\overline{X_1 + X_3}) \, X_2$	$R_2 = \overline{M}(\overline{X_8 + X_6}) \, X_7$
$S_1 = \overline{M} \, (\overline{X_1 + X_3}) \, X_2$	$S_2 = \overline{M}(\overline{X_8 + X_6}) \, \overline{X}_7$

Encoding Function

$$P_1 = M_1 \, X_1 + N_1 \, X_1 + R_1 + S_1 \, X_4 \qquad\qquad \equiv X_1 + R_1 + S_1 \, X_4$$
$$P_2 = M_1 \, X_2 + R_1 + S_1$$
$$P_3 = M_1 \, X_3 + N_1 \, X_3 + R_1 + S_1 \, \overline{X}_4 \qquad\qquad \equiv X_3 + R_1 + S_1 \, \overline{X}_4$$
$$P_4 = M_1 \, X_4 + N_1 \, \overline{X}_2 + R_1 \, \overline{X}_4 + S_1(\overline{X}_5 + S_2)$$
$$P_5 = M \, (\overline{X_1 \, X_2 \, X_3 \, X_4 \, X_5 \, X_6 \, X_7 \, X_8})$$
$$P_6 = M_2 \, X_5 + N_2 \, \overline{X}_7 + R_2 \, \overline{X}_5 + S_2(\overline{X}_4 + S_1)$$
$$P_7 = M_2 \, X_6 + N_2 \, X_6 + R_2 + S_2 \, \overline{X}_5 \qquad\qquad \equiv X_6 + R_2 + S_2 \, \overline{X}_5$$
$$P_8 = M_2 \, X_7 + R_2 + S_2$$
$$P_9 = M_2 \, X_8 + N_2 \, X_8 + R_2 + S_2 \, X_5 \qquad\qquad \equiv X_8 + R_2 + S_2 \, X_5$$

---

exclusive structures of bit patterns in the 9-digit sequence P and obtains logic equations for the components of X. The decoder equations appear on Chart 10.2.

The list of unused code words appears in Table 10.10.

10.4.2 The $\frac{16}{17}$ Rate (0, 6/6) PRML Code

Another PRML code of high interest is the $\frac{16}{17}$ rate (0, 6/6) code (Patel, 1989). This is a fixed-block mapping of 2 bytes at a time with the best possible rate and smallest values of the parameters k and k_1. Recently, some suppliers are offering a PRML channel with this higher rate code.

The (0, 6/6) PRML code is a mapping of 16-bit data words into 17-bit code words. The higher rate of $\frac{16}{17}$ requires mapping of a large number of code words; 65536 words as compared to 256 in the case of rate $\frac{8}{9}$ codes. The assignment of these 65536 code words is carried out using gated partitions, each of which is built upon a specific code structure. The resultant code is implemented with very simple encoding and decoding logic.

The code structure makes use of symmetry in the code constraints with respect to the bit positions in the code words. The data word consists of two bytes, A and B, where B is denoted backward ($\hat{B}$) for read-backward symmetry in notation as:

$$\text{DATA WORD} = A, \hat{B}$$
$$= (A_1, A_2, \ldots A_7, A_8)(B_8, B_7, \ldots B_2, B_1)$$

Similarly, the code word consists of 17 bits in the form of two bytes P and Q with a catenating digit C, where Q is denoted backward ($\hat{Q}$) as shown below:

$$\text{CODE WORD} = P, C, \hat{Q}$$
$$= (P_1, P_2, \ldots P_7, P_8), C, (Q_8, Q_7, \ldots Q_2, Q_1)$$

In order to realize the (0, 6/6) constraints we choose from the set of 17-bit sequences the code words with the following properties; binary-logic equations are also given to describe these properties.

1. Not more than 3 zeros at either end of the code word.

$(P_1 + P_2 + P_3 + P_4)(Q_4 + Q_3 + Q_2 + Q_1) = 1$

2. Not more than 3 zeros in the odd positions at either end of the code word.

$(P_1 + P_3 + P_5 + P_7)(Q_7 + Q_5 + Q_3 + Q_1) = 1$

3. Not more than 3 zeros in the even positions at either end of the code word.

$(P_2 + P_4 + P_6 + P_8)(Q_8 + Q_6 + Q_4 + Q_2) = 1$

4. Not more than 6 zeros in odd positions within the code word.

$(P_3 + P_5 + P_7 + C + Q_7 + Q_5 + Q_3) = 1$

5. Not more than 6 adjacent zeros within the code word.

$(P_3 + P_4 + P_5 + P_6 + P_7 + P_8 + C)(C + Q_8 + Q_7 + Q_6 + Q_5 + Q_4 + Q_3) = 1$
$(P_4 + P_5 + P_6 + P_7 + P_8 + C + Q_8)(P_8 + C + Q_8 + Q_7 + Q_6 + Q_5 + Q_4) = 1$
$(P_5 + P_6 + P_7 + P_8 + C + Q_8 + Q_7)(P_7 + P_8 + C + Q_8 + Q_7 + Q_6 + Q_5) = 1$
$(P_6 + P_7 + P_8 + C + Q_8 + Q_7 + Q_6) = 1$

CHART 10.2 (0, 4/4) PRML Code: Decoder

$$[P_1\, P_2\, P_3\, P_4\, P_5\, P_6\, P_7\, P_8\, P_9] \rightarrow [X_1\, X_2\, X_3\, X_4\, X_5\, X_6\, X_7\, X_8]$$

Partitions

$$M = P_5 + P_1\, P_2\, P_3\, P_4\, P_6\, P_7\, P_8\, P_9$$
$$A_1 = \overline{P}_6 + \overline{P}_2 + P_4 \qquad\qquad A_2 = \overline{P}_4 + \overline{P}_8 + P_6$$
$$M_1 = M + \overline{A}_2 \qquad\qquad\qquad\quad M_2 = M + \overline{A}_1$$
$$N_1 = \overline{M}\, A_2\, \overline{P}_2 \qquad\qquad\qquad N_2 = \overline{M}\, A_1\, \overline{P}_8$$
$$R_1 = \overline{M}\, A_2\, P_2\, (P_1\, P_3) \qquad\qquad R_2 = \overline{M}\, A_1\, P_8\, (P_9\, P_7)$$
$$S_1 = \overline{M}\, A_2\, P_2\, (\overline{P_1\, P_3}) \qquad\qquad S_2 = \overline{M}\, A_1\, P_8\, (\overline{P_9\, P_7})$$

Decoding Function

$$X_1 = M_1\, P_1 + N_1\, P_1$$
$$X_2 = M_1\, P_2 + N_1\, \overline{P}_4 + R_1$$
$$X_3 = M_1\, P_3 + N_1\, P_3$$
$$X_4 = M_1\, P_4 + R_1\, \overline{P}_4 + S_1\, \overline{P}_3$$
$$X_5 = M_2\, P_6 + R_2\, \overline{P}_6 + S_2\, \overline{P}_7$$
$$X_6 = M_2\, P_7 + N_2\, P_7$$
$$X_7 = M_2\, P_8 + N_2\, \overline{P}_6 + R_2$$
$$X_8 = M_2\, P_9 + N_2\, P_9$$

TABLE 10.10 Unused Words

1.	111000111
2.	011000110
3.	011000011
4.	110000110
5.	001001111
6.	100001111
7.	101001111
8.	111100100
9.	111100001
10.	111100101
11.	001100111
12.	100100111
13.	101100111
14.	011100111
15.	110100111
16.	111100111
17.	111001100
18.	111001001
19.	111001101
20.	111001110
21.	111001011
22.	111001111
23.	111111111

From the large number of 17-bit binary sequences we need to choose 65,536 valid code words to make a one-to-one assignment to each of the 16-bit data words. This is done by creating partitions with specific code structures, each of which maps from a specific subset of 16-bit data words. The aggregate of these partitions forms the $\frac{16}{17}$ (0, 6/6) code.

The code possesses read-backward symmetry. The encoder and decoder functions are realized by very simple logic functions as presented in Charts 10.3 and 10.4, respectively. The code table is not reproduced here, simply because of its large size. The mapping, however, can be easily simulated in software to check for the uniqueness of code word assignments and for the resulting run-length constraints.

The synchronization pattern or any other special requirements are not attended in the logic equations. These can be added according to the needs of the specific application.

10.5 ERROR-CORRECTION CODING

The standard $\frac{1}{2}$-in 9-track tape drives have progressively increased their dependence on error detection and correction coding in order to achieve higher densities and data rates. The development of error-correction coding (ECC) in tape-storage drives is summarized in Table 10.11. In earlier tape machines, a vertical byte-parity check (VRC) and a longitudinal track-parity check (LRC) were used. Later, as the density was increased to 31.5 bits per millimeter (800 bits per inch), a cyclic redundancy check (CRC) byte was added (Brown and Sellers, 1970) at the end of the record to provide one-track error correction on rereading of the record. Subsequently, the recording tape with 250 bits per millimeter (6250 bits per inch) used a powerful scheme, called optimal rectangular code (ORC), with a byte-processing algorithm which provided on-the-fly correction of up to two erased tracks (Patel and Hong, 1974). All these tape products used parallel-track format and provided correction of track erasures. The mass storage system with a single-element rotary head used a single-track data format and provided correction of long sections of data (Patel, 1980a). The latest 18-track machines use a new code called *adaptive-cross-parity* (AXP) code and provide correction of up to four erased tracks (Patel, 1985b).

Contemporary magnetic disk products use error-correction coding schemes that correct one burst of error in a variable-length block of up to one full track. Earlier products used the Fire code (Fire, 1959), in which processing is slow, one bit at a time. The later products used byte-oriented structures using the algebra of Reed-Solomon codes (Hodges et al., 1980). Table 10.12 presents a summary of the development of ECC in disk-storage products.

Encoding for error detection and correction consists of creating a well-defined structure on random data by introducing data-dependent redundancy. Presence of errors is detected when this structure is disturbed. Errors are corrected by making a minimum number of alterations to reestablish the structure. A good error-correction coding scheme provides this function with a reasonable amount of cost in terms of redundancy, processing time, and hardware. For this purpose, the operations in finite fields are found to be most convenient. The simplest finite field is the binary field of two elements. The sum and product operations in this field are modulo-2 sum and modulo-2 product as given by the following tables:

$$
\begin{array}{c|cc}
+ & 0\ 1 \\
\hline
0 & 0\ 1 \\
1 & 1\ 0
\end{array}
\qquad
\begin{array}{c|cc}
\times & 0\ 1 \\
\hline
0 & 0\ 0 \\
1 & 0\ 1
\end{array}
$$

CHART 10.3 $\frac{16}{17}$ (0, 6/6) Code Encoder

$$\text{DATA WORD} = [A_1, A_2, A_3, A_4, A_5, A_6, A_7, A_8, B_8, B_7, B_6, B_5, B_4, B_3, B_2, B_1]$$

$G = \bar{A}_1 \bar{A}_2 \bar{A}_3 \bar{A}_4$ $E = \bar{A}_2 \bar{A}_4 \bar{A}_6 \bar{A}_8$ $X = \bar{A}_1 \bar{A}_3 \bar{A}_5 \bar{A}_7$

$H = \bar{B}_1 \bar{B}_2 \bar{B}_3 \bar{B}_4$ $F = \bar{B}_2 \bar{B}_4 \bar{B}_6 \bar{B}_8$ $Y = \bar{B}_1 \bar{B}_3 \bar{B}_5 \bar{B}_7$

$g = \bar{X} \bar{Y} G$ $M = \bar{X} \bar{Y} \bar{G} \bar{H}$ $e = M E$

$h = \bar{X} \bar{Y} H$ $d = A_7 + B_7$ $f = M F$

$P_1 = A_1 + X B_4 + g B_4$

$P_2 = A_2 + X + g \bar{H} B_7 + f \bar{d}$

$P_3 = A_3 + X A_2 + g A_7$

$P_4 = A_4 C + \bar{X} \bar{C} (\bar{e} + d)$

$P_5 = A_5 + X A_4$

$P_6 = A_6 + e B_4$

$P_7 = A_7 \bar{g} + X + h + (e + f) \bar{d}$

$P_8 = A_8 + e (d + B_2)$

$C = M \bar{E} \bar{F}$

$Q_8 = B_8 + f (d + A_2)$

$Q_7 = B_7 \bar{h} + Y + g + (e + f) \bar{d}$

$Q_6 = B_6 + f A_4$

$Q_5 = B_5 + Y B_4$

$Q_4 = B_4 C + \bar{Y} \bar{C} (\bar{f} + d)$

$Q_3 = B_3 + Y B_2 + h B_7$

$Q_2 = B_2 + Y + h \bar{G} A_7 + e \bar{d}$

$Q_1 = B_1 + Y A_4 + h A_4$

CHART 10.4 $\frac{16}{17}$ (0, 616) Code Decoder

$$\text{CODE WORD} = [P_1, P_2, P_3, P_4, P_5, P_6, P_7, P_8, C, Q_8, Q_7, Q_6, Q_5, Q_4, Q_3, Q_2, Q_1]$$

$S = P_4 Q_4 P_7 Q_7 C$ $X = P_2 \bar{P}_4 \bar{C}$ $g = P_4 Q_4 \bar{P}_7 \bar{C} + \bar{P}_2 \bar{Q}_2 S$

                    $Y = Q_2 \bar{Q}_4 \bar{C}$ $h = P_4 Q_4 \bar{Q}_7 \bar{C} + \bar{P}_2 \bar{Q}_2 S$

                    $e_1 = \bar{P}_2 \bar{P}_4 \bar{C}$ $e = e_1 + Q_2 S$

                    $f_1 = \bar{Q}_2 \bar{Q}_4 \bar{C}$ $f = f_1 + P_2 S$

$A_1 = P_1 (C + \bar{X} \bar{g})$

$A_2 = P_2 (C + h + \bar{X} Y) + f P_2 Q_8 + X P_3$

$A_3 = P_3 (C + \bar{X} \bar{g})$

$A_4 = P_4 C + f Q_6 + (h + Y) Q_1 + X P_5$

$A_5 = P_5 (C + \bar{X})$

$A_6 = P_6 (C + \bar{e})$

$A_7 = P_7 (C + e_1 + f_1 + \bar{X} Y) + h Q_2 + g P_3$

$A_8 = P_8 (C + \bar{e})$

$B_8 = Q_8 (C + \bar{f})$

$B_7 = Q_7 (C + e_1 + f_1 + X\bar{Y}) + g P_2 + h Q_3$

$B_6 = Q_6 (C + \bar{f})$

$B_5 = Q_5 (C + \bar{Y})$

$B_4 = Q_4 C + e P_6 + (g + X) P_1 + Y Q_5$

$B_3 = Q_3 (C + \bar{Y} \bar{h})$

$B_2 = Q_2 (C + g + X \bar{Y}) + e Q_2 P_8 + Y Q_3$

$B_1 = Q_1 (C + \bar{Y} \bar{h})$

TABLE 10.11   Error-Correction Coding in Tape Drives

Year	IBM product	Density, b/mm	No. of tracks	Data code	ECC capability
1953–8	72X	4–22	9	NRZI	Parity track and LRC
1962	729	31.5	9	NRZI	Parity track and CRC, one-track correction on reread
1966	24XX	63	9	PE	Parity track and CRC, one-track correction on-the-fly
1973	3420	250	9	GCR (0, 2)	Parity track and ORC 1 check byte/7 bytes, two-track correction on-the-fly
1975	3850 MSS	275[†]	[†]	ZM (1, 3; 3)	Interleaved subfield code, word = 15 sections, section = 16 bytes, redundancy 2 sections/15 sections, on-the-fly correction of two sections
1985	3480	880	18	(0, 3)	Multitrack correction, adaptive cross-parity code

[†]Rotary head.

TABLE 10.12   Error-Correction Coding in Disk Drives

Year ship	IBM product	Density b/mm	t/mm	Data code	ECC capability
1957	350	4	0.8	NRZI	Parity check
1962	1301	20.4	2	NRZI	CRC check
1963	1311	40	2	NRZI	Multiple error detection
1966	2314	86.6	3.9	FM	Multiple error detection
					Single-burst correction correct/detect
1971	3330	159	7.6	MFM	11 bits/22 bits
1973	3340	222	11.8	MFM	3 bits/11 bits
1976	3350	253	18.7	MFM	4 bits/10 bits
1979	3370	478	25	(2, 7)	9 bits/17 bits
1980	3375	478	31.5	(2, 7)	9 bits/17 bits
1981	3380	598	31.5	(2, 7)	17 bits/33 bits
1985	3380E	638	54.6	(2, 7)	17 bits/33 bits
1987	3380K	677	82.2	(2, 7)	Multiple-burst correction, two-level coding

For the sake of coding, binary sequences are interpreted as polynomials with binary coefficients. Modulo-2 sum and product operations on these polynomials are used in creating coding structures which are easy to implement with binary shift registers and logic hardware.

10.6   POLYNOMIAL CODE STRUCTURE

A polynomial with binary coefficients can be used to represent a sequence of binary bits. For example, message B with k information bits is represented by a polynomial $B(x)$ as follows

$$B = [b_0, b_1, b_2, \ldots, b_{k-1}] \tag{10.25}$$
$$B(x) = b_0 + b_1x + b_2x^2 + \cdots + b_{k-1}x^{k-1} \tag{10.26}$$

When we attach r check bits at the low end of this message, the resultant code word W is a sequence of $n = k + r$ bits given by

$$W = [c_0, c_1, \ldots, c_{r-1}, b_0, b_1, \ldots, b_{k-1}] \tag{10.27}$$

Let a polynomial $C(x)$ represent the r check bits

$$C(x) = c_0 + c_1x + \cdots + c_{r-1}x^{r-1} \tag{10.28}$$

Then, attaching the check bits at the low end can be simply written in polynomial form as

$$W(x) = C(x) + x^r B(x) \tag{10.29}$$

The r check bits are determined by a coding process which requires that every code word $W(x)$ is divisible by a preselected polynomial $G(x)$ with zero remainder. $G(x)$ is called the *generator polynomial* of the code. Thus we have

$$W(x) = 0 \text{ modulo } G(x) \tag{10.30}$$

Then, from Eqs. (8.18) and (8.19) we have

$$C(x) = -x^r B(x) \text{ modulo } G(x) \tag{10.31}$$

In the binary field, we can ignore the negative sign. Thus, $C(x)$ represents the r-bit remainder when one divides $x^r B(x)$ by $G(x)$. Equation (10.31) provides the means for computing r check bits for a k-bit information sequence $B(x)$ such that the resultant n-bit code word $W(x)$ is divisible by $G(x)$.

The code thus generated posseses a cyclic property: For a specific code word length n, any cyclic shift of a code word is also a code word when the high-order bit corresponding to x^n after the shift is wrapped around to the low-order bit corresponding to x^0. This code-word length n is the smallest positive integer e that satisfies the relation

$$x^e = 1 \text{ modulo } G(x) \tag{10.32}$$

Alternatively, e is the minimum number of cyclic shifts in a modulo-$G(x)$ register after which it resets to its original content. The integer e is called the *cycle length* or *exponent* of $G(x)$. The codes are called *cyclic codes*.

The code-word length may be shortened to fit the requirements of a particular application. In that case, a number of information digits at the high-order end of the code word are physically absent and are assumed to be zero in processing. We will see that the cyclic structure is very useful in mechanizing the encoding and decoding operations by means of shift registers and modulo-2 summing (exclusive-or) circuits.

On readback, the received word, denoted by $\hat{W}(x)$, may be different from $W(x)$ in some positions. Thus on computing the remainder in accordance with Eq. (10.30), we may not get a result of zero. Let $S(x)$ denote this remainder computed from $\hat{W}(x)$ as

$$S(x) = \hat{W}(x) \text{ modulo } G(x) \tag{10.33}$$

Let $E(x)$ denote the difference between the received word $\hat{W}(x)$ and the original code word $W(x)$; it represents the errors in $\hat{W}(x)$ in polynomial form

$$E(x) = \hat{W}(x) - W(x) \tag{10.34}$$

$E(x)$ is called the *error pattern* or *error polynomial*. Note that presence of an error corresponds to a one value for the coefficient of $E(x)$ in the corresponding position. From Eqs. (10.30), (10.33), and (10.34) we have

$$S(x) = E(x) \text{ modulo } G(x) \tag{10.35}$$

Thus, $S(x)$ as computed from the received word in accordance with Eq. (10.33) depends only on the errors. $S(x)$ is called the *syndrome of errors*. Absence of errors will result in a zero value for $S(x)$. A nonzero syndrome will need further interpretation in order to determine the exact nature of the errors. This process of interpreting the syndrome is called the *decoding process*.

If the generator polynomial $G(x)$ is a product of two or more polynomials, then the code word $W(x)$ must be divisible by each of the factors in order to be divisible by $G(x)$. In some applications, this fact is used to simplify the decoding process by obtaining and interpreting the separate syndromes corresponding to each of the factors of $G(x)$. The decoding process and the range of error detection and correction capability depend on the choice of the generator polynomial and other practical considerations. We will describe these in detail in the discussion of various practical applications.

As seen so far, the encoding and decoding operations in cyclic codes require computation of the remainder when a given polynomial is divided by $G(x)$. In particular, the encoding operation is given by Eq. (10.31), the syndrome generation is described by Eq. (10.33), and the decoding of the errors is an interpretation of Eq. (10.35). All these computations can be carried out easily and conveniently by means of a linear-feedback shift register.

Consider a shift register as shown in Fig. 10.4 with feedback connection according to the coefficients of a binary generator polynomial $G(x)$:

$$G(x) = g_0 x^0 + g_1 x^1 + g_2 x^2 + \cdots g_{r-1} x^{r-1} + x^r \tag{10.36}$$

where $g_i = 1$ means a connection is present and $g_i = 0$ means a connection is absent.

The binary content of the shift register is viewed as a degree-$(r - 1)$ polynomial, and the feedback connection effectively performs

$$x^r = g_0 x^0 + g_1 x^1 + g_2 x^2 + \cdots g_{r-1} x^{r-1} \text{ modulo } G(x) \tag{10.37}$$

Thus an upward-shifting operation in this shift register corresponds to multiplying the contents by x and reducing the results modulo $G(x)$.

We can use this shift register for encoding the data $B(x)$ to compute check bits $C(x)$ in accordance with Eq. (10.31). The data bits are entered at the feedback input (see Fig. 10.4), which is equivalent to premultiplying the entering digit by x^r. Each shifting operation, onwards, multiplies the content of the shift register by x. The high-order coefficient b_{k-1} of $B(x)$ is entered first, followed by $b_{k-2}, b_{k-3}, \dots$, b_1, b_0, in that order, with each successive shifting operation. The contents of the shift register at each shift successively represent

$$b_{k-1} x^r \text{ modulo } G(x)$$
$$b_{k-2} x^r + b_{k-1} x^{r+1} \text{ modulo } G(x)$$
$$\vdots$$
$$b_0 x^r + b_1 x^{r+1} + \cdots b_{k-1} x^{r+k-1} \text{ modulo } G(x)$$

Thus the final content, at the end of k shifts, is the check polynomial $C(x)$ as defined in Eq.(10.31). The encoding progresses in synchronism with bit-by-bit transmission of the k data bits. After k shifting operations, the check bits are ready in the shift register and may be shifted out during the following r shifts. The feedback connections of the shift register are disabled during these last r shift cycles.

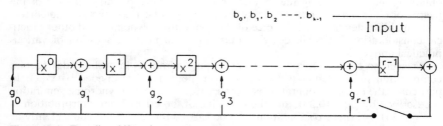

Figure 10.4   Encoding shift register.

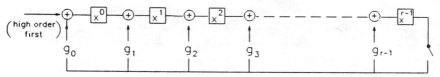

Figure 10.5   Shift register for syndrome generation.

On readback, we can use a similar shift register to process the received word $\hat{W}(x)$ for generation of the syndrome $S(x)$ in accordance with Eq. (10.33). In this case the entire received word (including check bits) is entered at the x^0 position of the shift register, as shown in Fig. 10.5. The high-order digit is entered first, followed by other digits in succession. When the last digit is entered, the content of the shift register is the syndrome $S(x)$ as defined in Eq. (10.33).

A nonzero value of $S(x)$ indicates the presence of errors in accordance with Eq. (10.35). Since $S(x)$ is the remainder, there are many error polynomials $E(x)$ which will satisfy Eq. (10.35). Here, an assumption will be made regarding the most likely error patterns, such as single error, single-burst error of smallest length, etc. In fact, code design will specify the range of most likely error patterns that will provide a unique solution to Eq. (10.35). These are called *correctable error patterns*. Various techniques are used to process the syndrome $S(x)$ to arrive at a correctable error position and determine its error pattern. We will examine some of these techniques in the discussion of various practical applications.

10.6.1   Cyclic Codes for Error Detection

One of the most widely used binary cyclic codes is called the *cyclic redundancy check* (CRC); it is used for detection of errors in transmission and storage of serial data. Any polynomial with long cycle length can be used as a generator for CRC. The error-detection capability is largely determined by the degree r of $G(x)$ or the number of CRC bits (Brown and Peterson, 1961). In particular, any single-burst error of length r or less is detected. Also, the fraction of undetected single-burst errors of length $r + 1$ is $1/2^{r-1}$ and that of length greater than $r + 1$ is $1/2^r$. For example, the commonly used 16-bit CRC has a cycle length of $2^{15} - 1$ and has the generator

$$G(x) = 1 + x^2 + x^{15} + x^{16} = (1 + x)(1 + x^2 + x^{15})$$

It will provide detection of all single-burst errors of length 16 or less and detect better than 99.998 percent of all other burst errors in a binary record of any length up to 32,767 bits. A linear-feedback shift register for this generator is shown in Fig. 10.6. This is essentially the only hardware needed for encoding and decoding variable-length binary records for error detection. The CRC character is generated by serially shifting the binary information in the feedback shift register as it is transmitted. The CRC character is then transmitted at the end of the information sequence. On readback, the received sequence is processed in the same manner. The generated CRC character is compared with the received check character for detection of any errors in the received message.

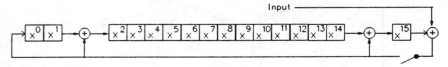

Figure 10.6 Serial CRC register.

10.6.2 Interleaving Cyclic Codes

A burst error can be effectively handled by spreading its effect over many code words. This is easily done by physically interleaving m code words to create an m-times-longer message. The interleaving operation can be viewed as arranging m code words of the original code into m rows of a rectangular block and then sending the digits column by column. The resulting code is an m-way interleaved code. A burst error of length m or less will affect at the most one digit in each of the m code words in the interleaved code. Thus if the original code corrects single-bit errors, then the m-way interleaved code corrects single-burst errors of length m or less.

The interleaving can be accomplished simply by replacing each binary storage element of the encoding shift register with m binary storage elements connected in tandem. The feedback connections are not changed. In fact, if the original code is a cyclic code then the interleaved code is also a cyclic code. If the generator of the original code is a degree-r polynomial $G(x)$, then the generator of the interleaved code is a degree-mr polynomial $G(x^m)$. The decoding process for the interleaved code follows from the decoding of the original code. Interleaving is illustrated later in various applications of error-correction coding in magnetic recording products.

10.6.3 Fire Code

The Fire code (Fire, 1959) is commonly used in magnetic disk products for detection and correction of single-burst errors in variable-length records. This is a cyclic code with generator polynomial of the form

$$G(x) = (x^c + 1)G_1(x) \qquad (10.38)$$

where the factor $G_1(x)$ determines the position of the error, and the factor $(x^c + 1)$ relates to the pattern of the error burst. A Fire code is capable of correcting a burst error of length b when $c \geq 2b - 1$. Simultaneous detection of a longer burst of length up to d bits can be included in the capability when $c \geq b + d - 1$. The polynomial $G_1(x)$ must be of degree $m \geq b$. The full length of the code words is determined by the cycle length of $G(x)$ which is the least common multiple of the number c and the cycle length of $G_1(x)$.

The encoding of a Fire code is carried out with a shift register connected for modulo $G(x)$ operation in accordance with Eq. (10.31) as described previously. The syndrome of error in the Fire code is computed as two separate remainders $S_0(x)$ and $S_1(x)$ corresponding to the two factors $(x^c + 1)$ and $G_1(x)$ of the generator $G(x)$. Thus in place of syndrome Eq. (10.33) we have two equations

$$S_0(x) = \hat{W}(x) \text{ modulo } (x^c + 1) \qquad (10.39)$$

$$S_1(x) = \hat{W}(x) \text{ modulo } G_1(x) \qquad (10.40)$$

Similarly, the error pattern of Eq. (10.35) will be written in the form of two equations

$$S_0(x) = E(x) \text{ modulo } (x^c + 1) \tag{10.41}$$
$$S_1(x) = E(x) \text{ modulo } G_1(x) \tag{10.42}$$

The most likely and correctable error pattern is a burst of length b or less. Hence, we can express the error polynomial $E(x)$ more specifically as an error burst at location p as follows

$$E(x) = x^P E_b(x) \tag{10.43}$$

where $E_b(x)$ is a degree-$(b - 1)$ polynomial representing a b-bit burst, and p is the location of the low-order bit of this burst in the error polynomial $E(x)$. All other unspecified coefficients in $E(x)$ are zero. From Eqs. (10.41), (10.42), and (10.43) we get

$$S_0(x) = x^P E_b(x) \text{ modulo } (x^c + 1 \tag{10.44}$$
$$S_1(x) = x^P E_b(x) \text{ modulo } G_1(x) \tag{10.45}$$

Since n is the cycle length of $G(x)$, we can use Eq. (10.32) and rewrite Eq. (10.44) and (10.45) as

$$x^{n-P}S_0(x) = E_b(x) \text{ modulo } (x^c + 1) \tag{10.46}$$
$$x^{n-P}S_1(x) = E_b(x) \text{ modulo } G_1(x) \tag{10.47}$$

Now we can describe the decoder hardware and algorithm. The hardware consists of two shift registers SR_0 and SR_1 similar to the one shown in Fig. 10.5. A shifting operation in SR_0 and SR_1 multiplies the contents in each by x modulo $(x^c + 1)$ and x modulo $G_1(x)$, respectively. These registers are used to compute syndromes $S_0(x)$ and $S_1(x)$ from the received code word $\hat{W}(x)$ in accordance with Eqs. (10.39) and (10.40), respectively. The computed syndromes are then decoded by means of the same two shift registers by a method called the *error-trapping technique* (Peterson, 1961).

Notice from Eqs. (10.46) and (10.47) that, after $(n - p)$ shifts of registers SR_0 and SR_1, the original contents $S_0(x)$ and $S_1(x)$ will both reduce to the burst error $E_b(x)$. Uniqueness of the burst pattern is assured, since SR_0 merely circulates the pattern and $c \geq 2b - 1$ (see Fig. 10.7). Since p is unknown, we will have to examine the contents after each shifting operation. The exact error pattern is recognized from the fact that the contents of SR_0 and SR_1 must be equal, and the contents of SR_0 may be a b-bit burst in the low-order (b) bit positions; the high-order $(c - b)$ bit

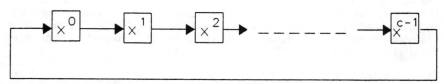

Figure 10.7   Shift register SR_0; multiplication by x modulo $(x^c + 1)$.

positions must be zero. When these two requirements are satisfied we have captured the error pattern. Since n is known, the number of shifts $(n - p)$ determines the position of the burst, starting with its low-order bit.

In some applications, when the cycle length n is large and the practical length of any code word is relatively short, one may use backward-shifting registers in which a shifting operation amounts to multiplication of the contents by x^{-1} modulo $x^c + 1$ and x^{-1} modulo $G_1(x)$ respectively. In that case p instead of $n - p$ shifting operations will be required, since

$$x^{n-p} = x^{-p} \text{ modulo } G(x) \qquad (10.48)$$

Later we will see an application of Fire codes in magnetic disk products, which include a design modification that further reduces the number of shifting operations. Fire codes are limited in their capability to the correction of only one burst, and the bit-by-bit processing is relatively slow. Thus Fire codes will remain popular in low-data-rate applications where error correction can be deferred until the end of a variable-length record. In contrast, the codes in extended binary fields, in particular, the Reed-Solomon codes (Reed and Solomon, 1960) provide more flexibility in terms of capability options and fast byte-parallel processing.

10.7 CODE STRUCTURES IN EXTENDED BINARY FIELDS

The binary base field can be extended to a finite field of 2^m elements, also known as the Galois field GF(2^m) in which the field elements are represented by m-bit binary bytes. As an example, we will consider the Galois field GF(2^8) in which the 256 distinct elements are represented by the 256 eight-bit bytes. Each element can be written as an eight-bit column vector A or a polynomial $A(x)$ with eight binary coefficients as follows

$$A = \begin{bmatrix} a_0 \\ a_1 \\ a_2 \\ a_3 \\ a_4 \\ a_5 \\ a_6 \\ a_7 \end{bmatrix} \qquad (10.49)$$

$$A(x) = a_0 + a_1 x + a_2 x^2 + a_3 x^3 + a_4 x^4 + a_5 x^5 + a_6 x^6 + a_7 x^7 \qquad (10.50)$$

The sum and product of the elements in GF(2^8) are computed as the modulo-2 sum and product of the corresponding polynomials with the results reduced modulo $P(x)$, where $P(x)$ is a prime polynomial of degree 8. (A polynomial is prime if it cannot be factored into two or more polynomials of lower degrees. It is also called an *irreducible polynomial*.) Thus the sum and product of two field elements $A(x)$ and $B(x)$ are defined as

$$\text{Sum} = A(x) + B(x) \text{ modulo } P(x) \qquad (10.51)$$

$$\text{Product} = A(x) \times B(x) \text{ modulo } P(x) \qquad (10.52)$$

Since $P(x)$ is a degree-8 polynomial, the result of the reduction modulo $P(x)$ is always a polynomial of degree less than 8, thus an element of the field. Furthermore, $P(x)$ is irreducible, which ensures that the result of the sum or product of field elements is always a unique field element. The 0 element of this field is the byte with $b_i = 0$ for all i; the 1 element is the byte with $b_i = 1$ for $i = 0$ and $b_i = 0$ for all other values of i. The sum and product of the elements of an extended binary field can be implemented in hardware using binary ex-or gates. This is illustrated for the elements of $GF(2^8)$ in the Appendix Sec. 10.A.6.

The field operations can be expressed in a more convenient form as the matrix-sum and matrix-product operations using the companion matrix T of the polynomial $P(x)$. The companion matrix T is defined in terms of the coefficients of $P(x)$ as

$$T = \begin{bmatrix} 0 & 0 & 0 & 0 & 0 & 0 & 0 & p_0 \\ 1 & 0 & 0 & 0 & 0 & 0 & 0 & p_1 \\ 0 & 1 & 0 & 0 & 0 & 0 & 0 & p_2 \\ 0 & 0 & 1 & 0 & 0 & 0 & 0 & p_3 \\ 0 & 0 & 0 & 1 & 0 & 0 & 0 & p_4 \\ 0 & 0 & 0 & 0 & 1 & 0 & 0 & p_5 \\ 0 & 0 & 0 & 0 & 0 & 1 & 0 & p_6 \\ 0 & 0 & 0 & 0 & 0 & 0 & 1 & p_7 \end{bmatrix} \tag{10.53}$$

where $P(x)$ is given by

$$P(x) = p_0 + p_1 x + p_2 x^2 + p_3 x^3 + p_4 x^4 + p_5 x^5 + p_6 x^6 + p_7 x^7 + x^8 \tag{10.54}$$

For any field element $A(x)$ we can compute a corresponding 8×8 matrix T_A by substituting $x = T$ in Eq. (10.50). Thus T_A is given by

$$[T_A] = a_0[I] + a_1[T] + a_2[T^2] + \cdots + a_7[T^7] \tag{10.55}$$

where T^i denotes T multiplied by itself i times, I is the 8×8 identity matrix, and all results are reduced modulo 2. Now the sum and product of field elements $A(x)$ and $B(x)$ can be computed through modulo-2 matrix expressions

$$[\text{sum}] = [A] + [B] \tag{10.56}$$

and $$[\text{product}] = [T_A][B] \tag{10.57}$$

where A and B are vector forms of $A(x)$ and $B(x)$ respectively and T_A is the matrix given by Eq. (10.55). The operations defined by the polynomial equations, Eqs. (10.51) and (10.52), and those defined by the matrix equations, Eqs. (10.56) and (10.57), are equivalent. This follows from the fact that the vector multiplication by the matrix T is equivalent to the polynomial multiplication by x modulo $P(x)$.

If the 8-bit field element expressed as x modulo $P(x)$ is denoted by α, then the field element expressed by x^i modulo $P(x)$ is α^i, the element α multiplied by itself i times. The corresponding matrix T^i is the matrix T multiplied by itself i times. A shift-upward operation (without new input) in a modulo-$P(x)$ shift register is equivalent to multiplying the contents, an 8-bit vector, by the matrix T. This shift register is similar to the one shown in Fig. 10.5 for modulo-$G(x)$ computations. If e is the minimum number of shift-upward operations after which the shift register resets to its original contents, then e is called the *cycle length* of the shift register. It is the smallest positive integer such that

$$x^e \text{ modulo } P(x) = x^0 \tag{10.58}$$

Thus, the 8-bit field elements α^i expressed as x^i modulo $P(x)$ for $i = 0, 1, 2, \ldots$, $e - 1$ are distinct nonzero elements of $GF(2^8)$. The corresponding matrices T^i for $i = 0, 1, 2, \ldots, e - 1$ are also distinct, and $T^e = T^0 = I$ where I is an 8×8 identity matrix.

Now the 8-bit column vectors in the companion matrix T of Eq. (10.53) can be identified as the elements of $GF(2^8)$ as follows

$$T = [\alpha, \alpha^2, \alpha^3, \alpha^4, \alpha^5, \alpha^6, \alpha^7, \alpha^8] \tag{10.59}$$

Since
$$[T][\alpha^i] = [\alpha^{i+1}] \tag{10.60}$$

we can obtain T^2, T^3, $\ldots$ iteratively and it follows that the matrix T^i is given by

$$T^i = [\alpha^i, \alpha^{i+1}, \alpha^{i+2}, \alpha^{i+3}, \alpha^{i+4}, \alpha^{i+5}, \alpha^{i+6}, \alpha^{i+7}] \tag{10.61}$$

Table 10.13 lists all the irreducible polynomials of degree 8 and their cycle lengths. The reciprocal of each of the listed polynomials is also an irreducible polynomial with the same cycle length.

The maximum cycle length for a degree-8 polynomial is $(2^8 - 1)$. A polynomial with maximum cycle length is called a *primitive polynomial*. A primitive polynomial is necessarily an irreducible polynomial (but not vice versa). When $P(x)$ is a degree-8 primitive polynomial, we have $e = 255$, and hence all 255 nonzero 8-bit field elements can be expressed as remainders x^i modulo $P(x)$ for $i = 0, 1, 2, \ldots, 254$. In that case, the element α, expressed as x modulo $P(x)$, is called a *primitive element*. Any nonzero 8-bit field element $A(x)$ and corresponding matrix T_A can be expressed as α^i and T^i, respectively, for some specific value i, where $0 \le i \le 254$. This unique integer i can be regarded as the logarithm to the base α of the field element $A(x)$. (For the case of field operations that use a nonprimitive polynomial $P(x)$, the element α expressed as x modulo $P(x)$ is not primitive; thus the base for the logarithm will have

TABLE 10.13 Irreducible Polynomials of Degree 8

				Coefficients					
	p_0	p_1	p_2	p_3	p_4	p_5	p_6	p_7	p_8	Cycle
No.	p_8	p_7	p_6	p_5	p_4	p_3	p_2	p_1	p_0	length
1	1	0	0	0	1	1	1	0	1	255
2	1	0	1	1	1	0	1	1	1	85
3	1	1	1	1	1	0	0	1	1	51
4	1	0	1	1	0	1	0	0	1	255
5	1	1	0	1	1	1	1	0	1	85
6	1	1	1	1	0	0	1	1	1	255
7	1	0	0	1	0	1	0	1	1	255
8	1	1	1	0	1	0	1	1	1	17
9	1	0	1	1	0	0	1	0	1	255
10	1	1	0	0	0	1	0	1	1	85
11	1	0	1	1	0	0	0	1	1	255
12	1	0	0	0	1	1	0	1	1	51
13	1	0	0	1	1	1	1	1	1	85
14	1	0	1	0	1	1	1	1	1	255
15	1	1	1	0	0	0	0	1	1	255
16	1	0	0	1	1	1	0	0	1	17

to be some element other than α. Any finite field has at least one primitive element. Any two finite fields with the same number of elements are isomorphic. The one-to-one correspondence of this isomorphism is established through the one-to-one correspondence between the primitive elements of the two fields.)

Now we are ready to describe some practical coding schemes based on the operations in GF(2^m). These codes are often referred to as *byte-correcting* or *symbol-correcting codes*. Since modern data-processing machines almost always use bytes in their data flow it is altogether fitting that operations in GF(2^m), and concepts in coding theory which use the byte as a basic element for processing, provide a more convenient and efficient method of processing errors.

10.7.1 Reed-Solomon Codes

Now, we extend the concepts of cyclic codes to the codes in an extended binary field GF(2^m), where a field element is represented by an m-bit binary byte. A polynomial with coefficients in GF(2^m) can be used to represent a sequence of bytes. In fact, all processing of these polynomials is done byte-parallel using the sum and product operations defined in the extension field GR(2^m). This may look overwhelmingly complex now, but it turns out to be simple, convenient, and efficient. In this system, the generator $G(x)$, the information sequence $B(x)$, the remainder $C(x)$, and the code word $W(x)$ are all polynomials whose coefficients are elements in GF(2^m). In other words, the information symbols, the check symbols, and the errors in these codes are in the form of m-bit bytes. Among these, the Reed-Solomon codes (Reed and Solomon, 1960) are of particular interest. They are convenient in implementation and most efficient in code capability.

The Reed-Solomon codes are cyclic codes with symbols in GF(q). In particular, we use 8-bit binary bytes as symbols in GF(2^8). In these codes, r check bytes provide correction of t error bytes and u erasure bytes, when $r \geq 2t + u$. (An erasure byte is an erroneous byte with known location.)

The degree-r generator polynomial of this code is given by

$$G(x) = (x - \alpha^0)(x - \alpha^1)(x - \alpha^2) \cdots (x - \alpha^{r-1}) \qquad (10.62)$$

where α is any element of GF(2^8). The main characteristic[†] of this $G(x)$ is that the roots $\alpha^0, \alpha^1, \alpha^2, \ldots, \alpha^{r-1}$ are the r consecutive powers of an element of GF(2^8). A full-length code word will have n symbols, where n, the cycle length of $G(x)$, is the least integer for which $\alpha^n = \alpha^0$. When α is the primitive element of GF(2^8) then n has the largest value ($2^8 - 1$). The actual length may be shorter or variable from $r + 1$ up to n.

The generator polynomial $G(x)$ is used in computing the check bytes in a manner analogous to that used in binary cyclic codes. In particular, on multiplying out the factors in Eq. (10.62), we can rewrite $G(x)$ in the form of Eq. (10.36) with coefficients g_i in GF(2^8)

$$G(x) = g_0 x^0 + g_1 x^1 + g_2 x^2 + \cdots + g_{r-1} x^{r-1} + x^r$$

Then the encoding shift register is similar in form to that shown in Fig. 10.4, although here we process bytes instead of bits. All lines in the data flow are 8 bits in parallel, each x^i storage device holds 8 bits, and the feedback connections require

---

[†] $G(x) = (x - \alpha^a)(x - \alpha^{a+1}) \cdots (x - \alpha^{a + r-1})$ provides the most general definition, where a is any integer. However, a nonzero value of a can be viewed as a constant scale factor. Specific choice of a, in some cases, provides symmetry or other useful structure.

multiplication by the field element g_i in GF(2^8). This process is illustrated in an application in Sec. 10.9.

Next, we examine the coding relations implied by the roots of the generator polynomial. By definition of cyclic codes, a code word $W(x)$ is divisible by $G(x)$. Thus with an appropriate quotient polynomial $Q(x)$ we can write

$$W(x) = Q(x)G(x) \tag{10.63}$$

From Eq. (10.62) we see that

$$G(x) = 0 \qquad \text{at } x = \alpha^0, \alpha^1, \alpha^2, \dots, \alpha^{r-1} \tag{10.64}$$

Substituting this in Eq. (10.63) we have

$$W(x) = 0 \qquad \text{at } x = \alpha^0, \alpha^1, \alpha^2, \dots, \alpha^{r-1} \tag{10.65}$$

The code word polynomial $W(x)$ can be written as

$$W(x) = B_0 + B_1 x + B_2 x^2 + \cdots + B_{n-1} x^{n-1} \tag{10.66}$$

where $B_0, B_1, \dots, B_{r-1}$ represent the r check bytes, and $B_r, B_{r+1}, \dots, B_{n-1}$ represent the k data bytes. From Eqs. (10.65) and (10.66) we obtain the coding rule corresponding to each of the r roots of the generator polynomial by substituting $x = \alpha^j$

$$B_0 + B_1 \alpha^j + B_1 \alpha^{2j} + \cdots + B^{n-1} \alpha^{(n-1)j} = 0$$

$$\text{for } j = 0, 1, 2, \dots, r - 1. \tag{10.67}$$

The product of field elements B and α^i can be expressed as the modulo-2 matrix product $T^i B$, where T is the companion matrix corresponding to α and B is an 8-digit column vector. Thus the coding relations of Eq. (10.67) can be expressed as the modulo-2 matrix equations

$$B_0 \oplus B_1 \oplus B_2 \oplus \cdots \oplus B_{n-1} = 0$$

$$B_0 \oplus TB_1 \oplus T^2 B_2 \oplus \cdots \oplus T^{n-1} B_{n-1} = 0 \tag{10.68}$$

$$B_0 \oplus T^2 B_1 \oplus T^4 B_2 \oplus \cdots \oplus T^{2(n-1)} B_{n-1} = 0$$

$$B_0 \oplus T^j B_1 \oplus T^{2j} B_2 \oplus \cdots \oplus T^{(n-1)j} B_{n-1} = 0 \qquad j < r$$

The coding relations of Eq. (10.68) represent r simultaneous equations in GF(2^m) that each code word must satisfy. The r unknown check bytes can be determined by solving these equations; however, this is not necessary. Instead, we will use a shift-register circuit in GF(2^m) to obtain the r check bytes analogous to r check bits for the binary cyclic codes in GF(2). On the other hand, the coding relations of Eq. (10.68) are very useful at the receiver end, where they can be easily checked and used for detection and correction of errors.

Reed-Solomon codes provide correction of t errors and u erasures with r check bytes, when $r \geq 2t + u$. Among these, the 1-byte-correcting Reed-Solomon code with two-way or three-way interleaving provides an interesting alternative to a Fire code for burst-error correction in magnetic-recording disk products. In two-way interleaving, we can correct one byte in each of the two phases of interleaving; thus any two adjacent bytes in the interleaved codeword are correctable. Any burst of length $(m + 1)$ bits or less is always confined to two adjacent m-bit bytes and hence is correctable by this code. Three-way interleaving allows correction of three adjacent m-bit bytes and hence any burst of length $(2m + 1)$ bits or less will be correctable. In magnetic-recording tape products, up to 16-way interleaving has been used for correction of long bursts in rotary-head systems. The byte processing in Reed-Solomon codes is fast and convenient, in contrast to the slow bit-by-bit processing in Fire codes. Furthermore, Reed-Solomon codes provide other options, such as correction of multiple-byte or multiple-burst errors with a reasonable amount of redundancy and cost of decoding.

A complete on-the-fly decoder for correction of multiple byte errors with Reed-Solomon codes is described in the Appendix (Patel, 1986). Decoder equations and architecture are presented in which the location of each error is computed in a cyclic order and the value of that error is determined simultaneously without explicit information regarding the unknown locations of other errors. As a result, one can begin delivery of the decoded data symbols, one at a time, in synchrony with each cycle of the decoding process, regardless of the number of errors in the code word. This decoder structure is well suited for large-scale integration in the chip design with pipelined data flow; compared to any decoder with comparable correction capability, it will provide delivery of the data with the minimum access time.

The code for nine-track tape systems with 6250 bits per inch (IBM 3420) is based on the decoding equations of the single-byte-correcting Reed-Solomon code. It uses 8-bit bytes as symbols in a code word with two check symbols and seven-data symbols. The code words are in the form of an eight-by-nine rectangle with two orthogonal sides as check bits. This code, called *optimal rectangular code*, possesses orthogonal symmetry around one of the diagonals of the eight-by-eight square block formed by eight horizontal bytes along or eight vertical bytes across eight tracks; the ninth track is a parity track providing the byte-parity check on all recorded bytes. This diagonal symmetry is an artifact of algebra that allows a tapelike data format for encoding and a Reed-Solomon structure for decoding rectangular code words that exhibit a geometric relationship with the errors along the tracks. The code provides correction of up to two erased tracks or one unknown track in error. Further details on this code may be found in the reference (Patel and Hong, 1974).

The error-recovery scheme for the rotary-head mass storage system (Patel, 1980a) is also based on the single-byte-correcting Reed-Solomon code. In Sec. 10.9, we present the implementation of this scheme, illustrating the encoding process and the procedures for on-the-fly correction of a single-byte error and two byte erasures.

In digital audio and video recording systems, it has been demonstrated that error-control coding can be cost-effective in consumer products. One code, used in the compact-disk digital audio player, is a two-dimensional arrangement of the Reed-Solomon code with an extensive amount of interleaving (Carasso and Nakajima, 1982; Doi, 1984). It is called the *cross interleave Reed-Solomon code* (CIRC) and is designed for correction of long burst errors. It also provides interpolation of the audio signal for the detected, but uncorrectable, longer bursts of error. This interpolation of the signal, called *error concealment,* is an effective compromise solution for very long errors in audio and video applications. Error concealment is not useful for computer data.

10.8 TWO-LEVEL CODING ARCHITECTURE

In this section, a coding architecture is presented that facilitates correction of multiple bursts of error in each record in a typical disk storage application. This architecture embodies a code such as Reed-Solomon code in a two-level arrange-

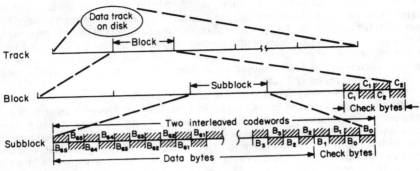

Figure 10.8 Two-level coding data format.

ment which offers high coding efficiency with a fast decoding strategy that closely matches the requirements of on-line correction of multiple-burst errors. The first-level capability in the two-level coding arrangement is designed for a specific reliability performance, so that an average disk file will not be required to utilize the second-level capability in its routine daily operations. The second-level capability is the "reserve" capability which will be frequently invoked in case of a "weaker" device or a "failing" device in which the soft error rate is substantially above the average. An application of Reed-Solomon code and two-level coding in a high-performance disk file (IBM 3380K) is described in Sec. 10.12.

The data format in the two-level coding scheme (Patel, 1987) is designed around a two-level architecture consisting of subblocks within a block as shown in Fig. 10.8. Each subblock consists of m data bytes and r_1 check bytes. The subblock is a code word from a code with minimum Hamming distance[†][†] of d_1 symbol units and the symbols (bytes) are elements of Galois field (GF(2^b)). Each block consists of n subblocks and r_2 check bytes which are shared by all its subblocks. The data part of the block-level code is viewed as modulo-2 superposition of n subblock code words. The r_2 check bytes (either independently or along with the superpositioned r_1 check bytes of all subblocks) provide a minimum Hamming distance of d_2 (over one subblock) at the block level where $d_2 > d_1$. The code words of both levels may be interleaved in order to provide correction for burst errors or clustered multisymbol errors.

The decoding process provides correction of up to t_1 errors and detection of up to $t_1 + c$ errors in each subblock, where $d_1 = 2t_1 + c + 1$. If the number of errors in a subblock exceeds the error-correcting capability at the first level, such errors are either left uncorrected or are miscorrected. If all errors were confined to one subblock, the block level code will provide correction of up to t_2 errors, where $d_2 \geq 2t_2 + 1$. However, many combinations of errors in multiple subblocks, including t_2 errors not confined to one subblock, are also correctable, as claimed in the following theorem.

[††]The Hamming distance between two code words is defined as the number of positions in which their symbols are unequal. The minimum Hamming distance between all pairs of code words of a code is a design parameter that specifies its error detection and correction capability. The r check bytes in the design of a Reed-Solomon code provide a minimum Hamming distance of $r + 1$ symbol units.

Theorem 1: Let d_1 and d_2 denote the minimum Hamming distance in the subblock-level code and block-level code respectively, where $d_1 = 2t_1 + c + 1$ and $d_2 \geq 2t_2 + 1$. This two-level coding scheme provides correction of t_2 errors anywhere in the block, provided $t_2 \leq 2t_1 + c$. In particular, it provides correction of a errors in the subblock with most errors, up to b errors in each of the other subblocks, and y errors in the block-check bytes, where a, b, and y are any nonnegative integers such that $a + y \leq t_2$, $b \leq t_1$, and $a + b \leq 2t_1 + c$.

The set of parameters t_2, t_1, and c defines a two-level scheme. Let (a, b) denote an error combination consisting of a errors in one subblock and up to b errors in each of the other subblocks in a block where $a \geq b$. The errors in the block-level check bytes may be considered as part of a errors in the subblock that is corrected at the second level. Then Theorem 1 defines the (a, b) combinations corrected at each level. The (a, b) combinations corrected at the first level are defined by all values $a \leq t_1$ and $b = a$. The (a, b) combinations corrected at the second level are defined by all values a such that $t_1 < a \leq t_1 + c$ with $b = t_1$, and $t_1 + c < a \leq t_2$ with $b = 2t_1 + c - a$.

Before presenting the proof of the theorem, we present a simple decoding strategy for the two-level coding scheme, which provides correction of all error combinations specified in the theorem. It is assumed that syndromes at each level are decoded for (up to) a fixed number of errors using minimum-distance decoding which finds a code word that differs from the received word in the fewest possible positions. The overall decoding process for the two-level code then follows the steps given below:

Step 1. Compute and decode the syndromes for each subblock for up to t_1 errors. If a subblock is uncorrectable or if the number of decoded errors is larger than that in any of the previously decoded subblocks, then update the contents of a buffer memory. (The buffer holds the error information and the subblock number for a subblock which is either uncorrectable or requires correction of the greatest number of errors.)

Step 2. Compute the block-level syndrome set $\{S\}$ from the received data, including all subblock level error corrections. If $\{S\} \neq 0$ or if a subblock had uncorrectable errors at the first level, then second-level processing is required. The subblock f is identified by the information in the buffer memory as an uncorrected subblock or a subblock with greatest number of corrected symbols.

Step 3. Modify the block-level syndrome set $\{S\}$ as follows:

$$\{S'\} \leftarrow \{S\} - \{S_f\}$$

where $\{S_f\}$ is the contribution to the block level syndromes due to the error corrections in the subblock f. If subblock f was left uncorrected in Step 1, then $\{S_f\} = 0$. The error information for computation of $\{S_f\}$ is available in the buffer memory.

Step 4. Use the modified syndrome set $\{S'\}$ of Step 3 and decode for up to t_2 errors in subblock f, including the block level check bytes. If the errors are found uncorrectable, then there are too many errors.

Step 5. Remove, if any, the subblock level corrections in subblock f. Enter the block level corrections in subblock f and the block level check bytes.

Step 2 of the above decoding procedure detects and identifies the subblock with more than t_1 errors uniquely. This is the key to the proof of the theorem.

Proof of Theorem 1. We assume that the subblock with most errors ($i = f$) contains up to $t_1 + c + x$ errors; each of the other subblocks ($i \neq f$) contains up to $t_1 - x$ errors and block check bytes contain y errors. The subblock number f and the nonnegative integers x and y are not known.

When $x = 0$ all errors at the subblock level are corrected or detected properly since they are all within the capability of the subblock code. If a subblock f has more than t_1 errors, it will be identified by the first-level decoder as an uncorrectable subblock. When $x > 0$ consider the subblock with $(t_1 + c + x)$ errors. Since the minimum Hamming distance d_1 is $2t_1 + c + 1$, the nearest code word must differ from the received word in at least $(2t_1 + c + 1) - (t_1 + c + x)$ positions. Thus, the first level decoder may miscorrect the subblock f by introducing additional errors in at least $t_1 - x + 1$ positions and as many as t_1 positions. Alternatively, the decoder may find subblock f uncorrectable if its Hamming distance from the nearest code word is greater than t_1. In contrast, the first-level decoder will correct $t_1 - x$ or fewer positions in each of the other subblocks, all of which will be corrected properly.

At the block level, the syndrome set $\{S\}$ is computed from the received data which include all subblock level error corrections. The set $\{S\}$ is, then, the block level syndrome set for all errors still present in the block, that is in subblock f and the block-check bytes. These are at most $t_2 + t_1$ errors which include $(t_1 + c + x) + y$ original errors and up to t_1 miscorrections. Since the minimum Hamming distance $d_2 (\geq 2t_2 + 1)$ exceeds $t_2 + t_1$, the corresponding syndromes $\{S\}$ must be nonzero. Thus the uncorrected or miscorrected errors in the block will be detected at the block level in Step 2 of the decoding procedure. The subblock f, with $t_1 + c + x$ errors is uniquely identified in Step 2 from the fact that (it was declared uncorrectable or) the number of corrections in subblock f exceeds those in any of the other subblocks by at least 1. If all subblocks were corrected properly at the subblock level, then the value of f is of no consequence at the block level.

Let $\{S_f\}$ denote the block-level syndromes due to the error patterns introduced by the decoder in subblock f. We can remove these error patterns from subblock f and their contribution $\{S_f\}$ from the syndromes $\{S\}$. Thus, the set $\{S\} - \{S_f\}$ represents the syndromes for the original $t_1 + c + x$ errors in subblock f and y errors in the block-level check bytes. The syndromes $\{S\}$ and $\{S_f\}$ are all known quantities. The block-level decoding of $\{S\} - \{S_f\}$ for t_2 errors will, then, provide proper correction of all remaining errors. This completes the proof of the theorem.

From a practical viewpoint, a given decoding process can be considered on-the-fly if it meets the following test, namely: the error correction on the previously received subblock is completed before the last byte of the next subblock is received. The processing will require a one-subblock delay (Patel, 1986). Thus, on-the-fly decoding is possible if and only if the subblock decoding time is smaller than or equal to the subblock read time. The criterion for on-the-fly decoding can be given as:

$$\frac{\text{subblock decoding time}}{\text{subblock size}} \times \text{data rate} < 1$$

Another important consideration is the above-cited one-subblock delay in decoding for errors. This delay directly affects the most important performance parameter of the disk file—namely, the access time. Thus it is desirable to partition the block into subblocks with corresponding short subblock delay.

The two-level scheme provides a fast decoding strategy that closely matches the requirements of on-the-fly correction of errors in a very flexible data format. The subblock level has the smaller block delay and provides very fast correction of most of the errors commonly encountered in an average disk file. The second level, on a larger block size, provides detection and correction of additional errors that may be encountered in a weaker device. The block-level decoding may be relatively slow and may include the conventional head-shift and reread functions. This design makes the most use of the available redundancy and provides substantial match to the error-correction requirements of future disk files.

10.8.1. Error-Rate Performance of Two-level Coding Schemes

The basic error event is a "byte-in-error." A burst error may cause correlated errors in adjacent bytes; however, sufficient interleaving is assumed to effectively randomize these errors. With appropriate interleaving, all bytes are assumed equally likely to be in error as seen by the coding scheme. In disk files, major defects in the media are avoided by means of surface analysis test and defect-skipping strategy. The error-correction code is expected to provide coverage for errors caused by noise and small defects that cannot be identified easily in the surface analysis test. These errors are usually two to four bits long. Typically two-way or three-way byte interleaving of the code words is adequate in disk-file applications, which will also allow for small amounts of error propagation in the encoding and detection process.

Let p denote the probability of the basic error event—a byte-in-error. For a given value of p, the probability of any combination of multiple errors in a subblock and a block can be then calculated using binomial and multinomial expressions. The total probability of no-error and correctable-error combinations at the first level of decoding will then lead to the uncorrectable (or miscorrected) error rate at the first level. Similarly, the total probability of no-error or correctable-error combinations at the second level of decoding will lead to the uncorrected (or miscorrected) error rate at the second level.

Let $P_{SB}(t)$ denote the probability that t bytes are in error in a subblock of N bytes. Then $P_{SB}(t)$ can be computed from p as

$$P_{SB}(t) = \binom{N}{t} p^t (1 - p)^{N-t}$$

Next, we compute the probability $P_B (\le t_1)$ of up to t_1 errors in each of the n subblocks of a block. This is the probability of no-error and all correctable-error combinations at the first-level decoding.

$$P_B (\le t_1) = \left[\sum_{t=0}^{t_1} P_{SB}(t) \right]^n$$

Next, we compute the probability $P_B (a, b)$ of the event with a errors in one subblock and up to b errors in all the other subblocks in a block where $b < a$. This is the probability of an additional combination (a, b) of errors corrected at the second level. This probability is given by

$$P_B (a, b) = n P_{SB} (a) \left[\sum_{t=0}^{b} P_{SB}(t) \right]^{n-1} \qquad \text{for } b < a$$

Now it is easy to compute the total probability of no-error and correctable-error combinations at the first and second level by combining probabilities of mutually exclusive error combinations covered by both levels of decoding. Let $P_T(t_2, t_1; c)$ denote this probability for a scheme characterized by parameters t_2, t_1, and c. Then we write the total probability as

$$P_T(t_2, t_1; c) = P_B(\leq t_1) + \sum_{\{(a,b)\}} P_B(a, b)$$

where $\{(a, b)\}$ represents the set of all (a, b) combinations correctable at the second level, namely, all values of a such that $t_1 < a \leq t_1 + c$ with $b = t_1$ and $t_1 + c < a \leq t_2$ with $b = 2t_1 + c - a$. From the above three equations, we can express $P_T(t_2, t_1; c)$ as

$$P_T(t_2, t_1; c) = \left[\sum_{t=0}^{t_1} P_{SB}(t) \right]^n + \sum_{a=t_1+1}^{t_1+c} nP_{SB}(a) \left[\sum_{t=0}^{t_1} P_{SB}(t) \right]^{n-1}$$

$$+ \sum_{a=t_1+c+1}^{t_2} nP_{SB}(a) \left[\sum_{t=0}^{2t_1+c-a} P_{SB}(t) \right]^{n-1}.$$

Now we can compute the probability PU_B of uncorrectable error in a block, after first level correction.

$$PU_B(\leq t_1) = 1 - P_B(\leq t_1)$$

and the total probability PU_T of an uncorrectable error for the two-level scheme as

$$PU_T(t_2, t_1; c) = 1 - P_T(t_2, t_1; c)$$

The average number of bytes transferred per uncorrectable error event at the first and second levels can be computed from the error probabilities PU_B and PU_T respectively, as follows:

$$\text{Bytes per uncorrectable error at first level} = \frac{n \times N}{PU_B}$$

$$\text{Bytes per uncorrectable error at second level} = \frac{n \times N}{PU_T}$$

In Fig. 10.9 we plot the results of these computations for some typical examples. The line marked $t_1 = 3$ represents the performance of a conventional one-level coding scheme with correction of three errors in every 250-byte (sub)block. The next four lines represent the two-level coding arrangements consisting of 40 subblocks in a block and $(t_2, t_1; c) = (4, 3; 0), (5, 3; 0), (5, 3; 1)$ and $(6, 3; 1)$ showing successive and substantial improvements in error-rate performance provided by the small amount of additional shared redundancy at the second level over $t_1 = 3$ at the first level. Also plotted, for comparison, is the performance of a conventional one-level coding scheme with correction of six errors ($t_1 = 6$) in every 250-byte (sub)block.

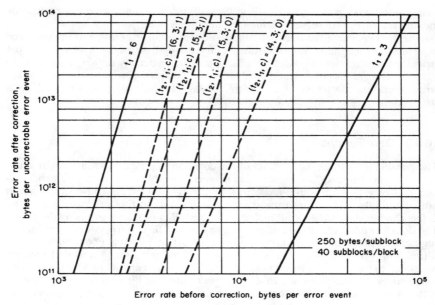

Figure 10.9   Error-rate performance of two-level coding schemes.

10.9   ERROR-RECOVERY SCHEME FOR A ROTARY-HEAD TAPE STORAGE SYSTEM

The error-recovery scheme to be described here illustrates various important concepts in coding to obtain specific features (Patel, 1980a). The basic building block of the scheme is a 15-byte code word of a single-byte-correcting Reed-Solomon code. The scheme demonstrates (1) the power of interleaving code words for long-burst correction; (2) how the use of subfields in a field provides interesting relationships of bit errors, byte errors, and burst errors and also provides economies in implementation; and (3) how a modulation code and an error-correction code can work together to enhance the error-correction capability. It is used in the IBM 3850 mass storage system.

This mass storage system consists of an array of data cartridges about 4.8 cm (1.9 in) in diameter and 5.9 cm (3.5 in) long, with a capacity of 50 million characters each. Each cartridge contains magnetic tape 6.9 cm (2.7 in) wide and 19.5 m (64 ft) long on which data are organized in cylinders analogous to those of a disk file; data can be transferred to the disk file one cylinder at a time. Up to 4720 cartridges are stored in hexagonal compartments in a honeycomblike apparatus that includes a mechanism for fetching cartridges from the compartments in order to read data and to write data on them and for replacing them back into the compartments.

Instead of the multitrack fixed head used in conventional tape machines, a rotary read-write head is used in this mass storage system. The rotary head creates short slanted stripes across the tape instead of long tracks along the tape. The tape follows a helical path around a mandrel and is stepped in position from one slanted stripe to the next over a circular slit in the mandrel which houses the continuously moving read-write transducer element of the rotary head.

The data are recorded as coded binary sequences corresponding to the presence or absence of magnetic flux transitions in fixed-length stripes at a density of 26.4 stripes per centimeter (67 stripes per inch) and linear density ranging from 1356 to 2712 flux transitions per centimeter (3444 to 6888 flux transitions per inch). A read-write operation always involves the processing of whole stripes, with each data stripe containing exactly 4096 net data bytes after decoding.

10.9.1 Data Format

The parallel multitrack data format of the conventional tape machines is not available. Instead, the data are organized in resynchronizable sections in order to facilitate recovery from mixed-mode errors involving 1-bit errors caused by random noise, multiple 2-bit errors caused by bit shift, and clusters of errors caused by defects and dust particles—this includes the capability of resynchronizing the clock. The data format of the stripe is illustrated in Fig. 10.10. The stripe is divided into 20 segments. The segments are appended to each other, forming a continuous waveform; however, each segment is a separate entity and can be decoded without reference to the data in other segments. Each segment consists of 13 data sections followed by 2 check sections. In a write operation, the bit values for the 2 check sections are computed in accordance with an error-correction code by processing

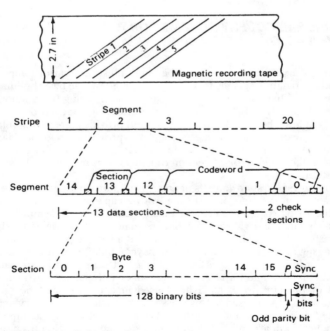

Figure 10.10 Stripe data format.

the 13 data sections as they are being recorded. The computed check sections are then appended to the 13 data sections, thus completing a segment.

Each section is 129 bits long and consists of 16 bytes of binary information with an overall odd-parity bit. This sequence of 129 bits is encoded into a 258-digit, zero-modulation waveform followed by a known unique synchronization signal (see Sec. 10.3 for details on ZM). The odd-parity bit serves the dual purpose of checking data errors and of limiting the memory requirement in ZM. The sections are appended to one another to form a continuous ZM waveform. Thus, each section is protected by the synchronization signal at both of its ends. This allows resynchronization of the decoding clock at the beginning and at the end of each section, in the event of a long error causing loss of synchronization.

The data format for the error-correction code is designed around the resynchronizable sections. The 16 bytes in each section belong to 16 different code words, as shown in Fig. 10.11. Each code word consists of 15 bytes—one from each of the 15 sections in a segment. Let k be the index for the code words and j be the index for the sections in a segment, where $0 \leq k \leq 15$ and $0 \leq j \leq 14$. Then B_{jk} denotes the byte in position k in section j. The group of bytes B_{0k}, B_{1k}, B_{2k}, ..., B_{14k} is recorded in position k of the sections 0, 1, 2, ..., 14, respectively, and form the kth code word W_k. Thus, the 16 code words are interleaved in the data format of 15 sections in a segment. This interleaving of the code words facilitates correction of mixed-mode errors. When a defect or dust particle affects up to 2 full sections, the resultant error is recoverable by correcting the corresponding 2 bytes in each of the 16 code words. On the other hand, many combinations of multiple 1-bit and 2-bit errors in a segment are also recoverable, since each code word can detect and correct any one of its bytes. Any stripe with a defect length of more than 128 bits is demarked by the write operation. Every write operation is followed by a readback check. Every demarked stripe is bypassed by the read operation.

Excluding the 2 error-checking sections in each segment, the 20 segments in a stripe provide a net recording space for a data stream of 4160 bytes (Fig. 10.12). The first 2 bytes in this data stream are reserved for stripe identification. This is followed by a block of 4096 bytes of data, 60 bytes of filler 0s, and 2 bytes of cyclic

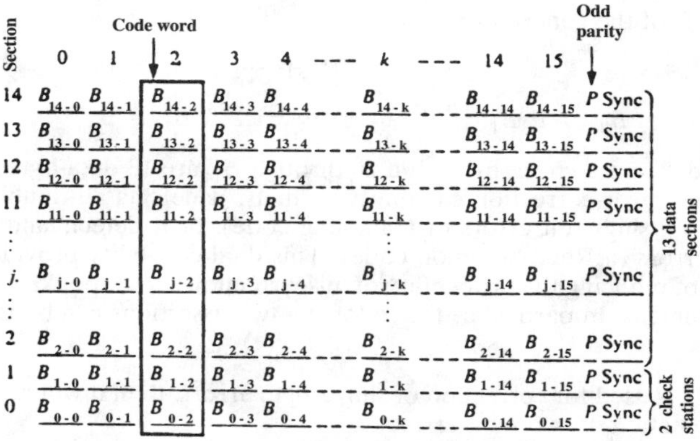

Figure 10.11 A segment: 15 sections formed with 16 interleaved code words.

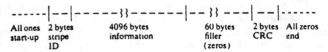

Figure 10.12 Data stream of 4160 bytes in a stripe.

redundancy check (CRC) code. The 2-byte CRC code provides an overall check for the data integrity of the stripe, including errors caused by malfunctions in the data-flow hardware and error-correction process. The read operation is retried both with and without a change in the read-amplifier gain setting when an uncorrectable error is encountered in any code word or when a miscorrected error is detected by the CRC at the end of the stripe.

10.9.2 Error-Correction Code

As just described, the error-recovery scheme is designed around the concept of resynchronizable sections. The basic building block of this scheme is a 15-byte code word of a single-byte-correcting Reed-Solomon code. The generator polynomial of this code is given by

$$G(x) = (x - \beta^0)(x - \beta^1) \tag{10.69}$$

where β is an element of $GF(2^8)$ and is also a primitive element of a 16-element subfield of $GF(2^8)$. In particular

$$\beta = \alpha^\lambda \tag{10.70}$$

where α is a primitive element of $GF(2^8)$ and $\lambda = 68$ (λ must be a multiple of 17 and a prime to 15). The elements β, β^2, β^3, . . . , β^{15} are distinct nonzero elements of a 16-element subfield of $GF(2^8)$, and $\beta^{15} = \beta^0$. The sum and product of these elements are closed in the sense that the result is always one of the elements of the subfield. It will be seen later that these properties of the subfield elements facilitate implementation of the decoder and save hardware and decoding time.

As seen in the set of Eq. (10.68), the two coding relations corresponding to the roots β^0 and β^1 of the generator polynomial can be written as

$$B_0 \oplus B_1 \oplus B_2 \oplus \cdots \oplus B_{14} = 0 \tag{10.71}$$

$$B_0 \oplus T^\lambda B_1 \oplus T^{2\lambda} B_2 \oplus \cdots \oplus T^{14\lambda} B_{14} = 0 \tag{10.72}$$

where B_0 and B_1 are 2 check bytes and B_3 through B_{14} are 13 data bytes. This code possesses dual error-correction capability; namely, it detects all double-bit errors and corrects all single-bit errors (a Hamming code), or it detects and corrects all single-byte errors (a Reed-Solomon code). This dual capability provides an effective method of reducing the probability of miscorrections in a tapelike, mixed-mode error environment. In particular, the following two assertions can be made (Patel, 1980a):

1. If the code is used for correction of single-byte errors, then it will not miscorrect any combination of two 1-bit errors.
2. If the code is used for correction of single-bit errors, then it will not miscorrect any combination of one byte error with a 1-bit error in another byte.

In the particular application under discussion, the code is used for correction of single-byte errors in the absence of error pointers. In this mode, the code exhibits a high level of protection against miscorrection of noise-induced bit errors in more than one byte. In the presence of error pointers, the code corrects two erroneous bytes. Another feature of this error recovery scheme is the zero-modulation encoding and its dual-function role. Zero modulation ensures the absence of a dc component in the recording signal and also provides very reliable error-detection pointers.

In a read operation, each section is read through the ZM decoding algorithm, which also checks for errors through stringent run-length and dc-charge constraints. Error-free ZM patterns possess run lengths of at least one and at most three 0s between two 1s, and the dc-charge value is always constrained within ±3 units. Thus, two consecutive 1s or four consecutive 0s indicate an error. The dc charge can be monitored with an up-down counter which increments for every digit position recorded with a positive level and decrements in a similar manner when the level is negative; it signals an error if the total exceeds ±3 at any time. The charge value must also be zero at the end of the section, before the synchronization pattern. These checks and the odd parity at the end of each section detect most errors, including the 2-bit errors caused by bit shift and the dropout and synchronization errors caused by defects and dust particles. The errors in ZM decoding do not propagate, and the decoding process always terminates at a section boundary. Thus, the presence of an error is usually detected by the ZM error-detection circuits in the vicinity of the error within the same section. The resynchronization signal at the beginning and at the end of each section provides or confirms the proper phase of the ZM double-frequency clock, thereby rendering each section independent in error modes.

All detected errors are reported to the decoder of the error-correction code for error recovery. Errors in up to two full sections in a segment can be recovered by means of this error-correction code; this includes the longest error in a worst-case situation in which the defect coincides with a section boundary and affects two adjacent sections. A wide variety of shorter multiple errors are also detected and corrected by the same error-correction code.

Encoding Process.   The generator polynomial of Eq. (10.69) can be rewritten as

$$G(x) = x^2 + (1 + \alpha^\lambda)x + \alpha^\lambda \tag{10.73}$$

The encoding can be performed by a shift register network built for modulo $G(x)$ operations. Figure 10.13 shows a block diagram of this shift register, which can be

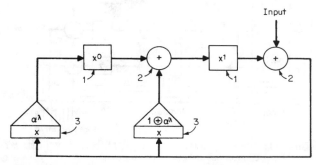

Figure 10.13   Block diagram of encoding network.

constructed from the conventional binary network elements. The sum of any field elements β_1 and β_2, represented by eight-digit binary vectors B_1 and B_2, can be accomplished by the modulo-2 matrix sum of B_1 and B_2. The multiplication of any field element β by the elements α^λ and $1 \oplus \alpha^\lambda$ can be accomplished by the modulo-2 matrix multiplications $T^\lambda B$ and $[I \oplus T^\lambda]B$, respectively, where the eight-digit binary vector B represents β, and matrix T is given by

$$T = \begin{bmatrix} 0\,0\,0\,0\,0\,0\,0\,1 \\ 1\,0\,0\,0\,0\,0\,0\,1 \\ 0\,1\,0\,0\,0\,0\,0\,0 \\ 0\,0\,1\,0\,0\,0\,0\,1 \\ 0\,0\,0\,1\,0\,0\,0\,0 \\ 0\,0\,0\,0\,1\,0\,0\,1 \\ 0\,0\,0\,0\,0\,1\,0\,0 \\ 0\,0\,0\,0\,0\,0\,1\,0 \end{bmatrix} \qquad (10.74)$$

The resulting encoding network is, in fact, an eight-channel binary shift register, as shown in Fig. 10.14, in which each storage element of Fig. 10.13 is replaced by

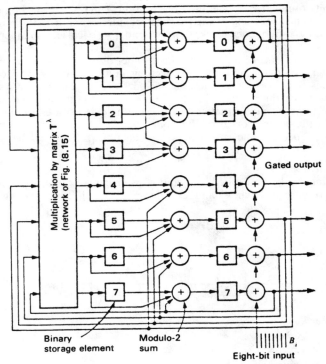

Figure 10.14   Encoding shift register $G(x) = T^\lambda \oplus (1 \oplus T^\lambda)x \oplus X^2$. All feedback connections are gated open for output.

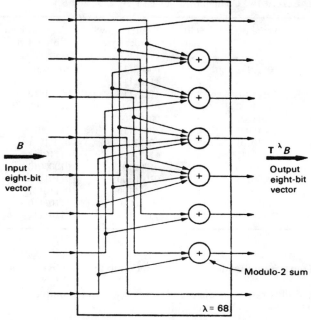

Figure 10.15 Network for multiplication by T^λ.

eight binary storage elements, and the modulo-2 matrix multiplication or addition is realized by means of a set of binary modulo-2 gates (XOR circuits). Figure 10.15 shows separately a network of modulo-2 gates for multiplication of any 8-bit vector with the matrix T^λ.

The matrix T^λ for $\lambda = 68$ can be computed from T and is given by

$$T^{68} = \begin{bmatrix} 0&0&0&0&1&0&0&0 \\ 1&0&0&0&1&1&0&0 \\ 0&1&0&0&0&1&1&0 \\ 0&0&1&0&1&0&1&1 \\ 1&0&0&1&0&1&0&1 \\ 0&1&0&0&0&0&1&0 \\ 0&0&1&0&0&0&0&1 \\ 0&0&0&1&0&0&0&0 \end{bmatrix} \qquad (10.75)$$

The 15-byte code word W consists of 2 check bytes B_0 and B_1 and 13 data bytes B_2, $B_3, \ldots, B_{14}$. The check bytes B_0 and B_1 are computed by processing the data bytes $B_2, B_3, B_4, \ldots, B_{14}$ in the encoding shift register of Fig. 10.14. Initially, the storage elements of the shift register are all set to zero. The ordered sequence of data bytes $B_{14}, B_{13}, B_{12}, \ldots, B_2$ is entered into the shift register in 13 successive shifts, as 8-bit parallel vector inputs. At the end of this operation, the shift register contains the check bytes B_1 and B_0 in its high- and low-order positions, respectively. Then B_1 and

TABLE 10.14 Computation of Check Bytes B_0 and B_1

	Write data input	Shift count	Contents low-order byte	Contents high-order byte
B_{14}	10010111	1	00000111	10010000
B_{13}	11101000	2	11101111	10010000
B_{12}	10101010	3	11111111	00101010
B_{11}	11111000	4	01010001	01111100
B_{10}	11011001	5	00101000	11011100
B_9	10010001	6	10000110	11100011
B_8	00010101	7	00101011	01011011
B_7	01111111	8	01111010	01110101
B_6	00000000	9	01001101	01000010
B_5	00100111	10	01000100	01101100
B_4	10000001	11	11011100	01110101
B_3	01010101	12	00010010	11101110
B_2	10111110	13	$\boxed{00101101 = B_0}$	$\boxed{01101111 = B_1}$

B_0 are gated out without feedback and appended to the data bytes to form a 15-byte code word.

Table 10.14 illustrates this encoding process with an example showing the contents of the shift register after each shift.

10.9.3 Syndromes of Error

The read data are checked for errors by means of the coding equations, Eqs. (10.71) and (10.72). All 16 code words of a segment are stored in a temporary storage pending any correction of errors. The decoding process is carried out by applying the decoding algorithm to each of the 16 code words independently. The algorithm will correct any 1 byte in an unknown position or any 2 bytes in indicated positions in each of the 16 code words. Let $\hat{B}_0$, $\hat{B}_1$, $\hat{B}_2$, . . . , $\hat{B}_{14}$ denote the read bytes corresponding to the written bytes B_0, B_1, B_2, . . . , B_{14}, respectively. Let S_0 and S_1 denote the results of computations when the read byte values are substituted in place of the written byte values in the left-hand side of Eqs. (10.71) and (10.72). If the read code word is error-free, then S_0 and S_1 both will be zero, as seen from these equations; however, a nonzero value in S_0 or S_1 indicates that one or more read bytes are in error. The 8-bit vectors S_0 and S_1 are called *syndromes of error* and are given by

$$S_0 = \hat{B}_0 \oplus \hat{B}_1 \oplus \hat{B}_2 \oplus \cdots \oplus \hat{B}_{14} \tag{10.76}$$

and

$$S_1 = \hat{B}_0 \oplus T\hat{B}_1 \oplus T^{2\lambda}\hat{B}_2 \oplus \cdots \oplus T^{14\lambda}\hat{B}_{14} \tag{10.77}$$

The syndrome vectors S_0 and S_1 can be computed by means of two separate 8-bit shift registers SR_0 and SR_1, respectively. These shift registers are shown in Fig. 10.16. The shifting operation in SR_0 and SR_1 corresponds to multiplying the content vector by the matrix I and by the matrix T^λ, respectively. Initially, the registers are set to contain zeros. The ordered sequence of read bytes $\hat{B}_{14}$, $\hat{B}_{13}$, $\hat{B}_{12}$, . . . , $\hat{B}_1$, $\hat{B}_0$ is entered into both registers, SR_0 and SR_1, in 15 successive shifting operations, with

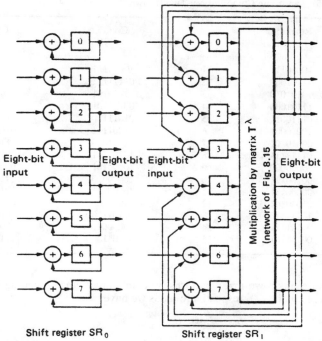

Figure 10.16 Decoding shift registers. All feedback connections are gated open and multiplication by T^{λ} is bypassed for output.

$\hat{B}_{14}$ entering first. As a result, SR_0 contains the syndrome S_0, and SR_1 contains the syndrome S_1. Table 10.15 illustrates the syndrome generation process with an example showing the contents of the two shift registers after each shift.

10.9.4 Correction of Two Bytes

When the erroneous sections are indicated by ZM detection, this information is passed on to the decoder in the form of error pointers. Let i and j denote the position values of the two erroneous bytes in a code word, where $i < j$. The symbols E_i and E_j are used to represent the unknown error patterns in bytes B_i and B_j, respectively, so that

$$\hat{B}_i = B_i \oplus E_i \qquad (10.78)$$

and

$$B_j = B_j \oplus E_j \qquad (10.79)$$

When the indices i and j are known, the unknown error patterns E_i and E_j can be determined by processing the syndromes S_0 and S_1, provided all other bytes are error-free. The syndrome equations, Eqs. (10.76) and (10.77), can be reduced in

TABLE 10.15　Syndrome Computation: Two Known Bytes in Error

	Read data input	Shift count	Contents of SR_0	Contents of SR_1
B_{14}	10010111	1	10010111	10010111
B_{13}	11101000	2	01111111	11101111
B_{12}	10101010	3	11010101	01000010
B_{11}	11111000	4	00101101	11101000
B_{10}	01110011	5	01011110	11011101
B_9	10010001	6	11001111	01010110
B_8	00010101	7	11011010	01100100
B_7	01111111	8	10100101	00100001
B_6	00000000	9	10100101	00001000
B_5	00100111	10	10000010	11110111
B_4	00000111	11	10000101	00110110
B_3	01010101	12	11010000	00010010
B_2	10111110	13	01101110	00010010
B_1	01101111	14	00000001	10000011
B_0	00101101	15	$\boxed{00101100 = S_0}$	$\boxed{11100111 = S_1}$

terms of these unknown error patterns by combining with the coding equations, Eqs. (10.71) and (10.72), respectively. Thus we have

$$S_0 = E_i \oplus E_j \tag{10.80}$$

and
$$S_1 = T^{i\lambda} E_i \oplus T^{j\lambda} E_j \tag{10.81}$$

Since i and j are known, the two simultaneous equations, Eqs. (10.80) and (10.81), may be solved for the two unknown variables E_i and E_j to obtain

$$E_j = [I \oplus T^{(j-i)\lambda}]^{-1}[S_0 \oplus T^{-i\lambda}S_1] \tag{10.82}$$

and

$$E_i = S_0 \oplus E_j \tag{10.83}$$

Equations (10.82) and (10.83) may be implemented with simple hardware. For this, the closure property and the multiplicative inverse of the subfield elements, which were discussed before, are used. In particular, we note that

$$T^{p\lambda} = T^{-i\lambda} \tag{10.84}$$

and

$$T^{q\lambda} = [I \oplus T^{(j-i)\lambda}]^{-1} \tag{10.85}$$

where p and q depend only on the known values of i and j. The parameters p and q are precalculated for all possible values of i and j and are given in Tables 10.16 and 10.17, respectively.

Thus the decoding equations, Eqs. (10.82) and (10.83), can be rewritten into simpler form as

$$E_j = T^{q\lambda}[S_0 \oplus T^{p\lambda} S_1] \tag{10.86}$$

and

$$E_i = S_0 \oplus E_j \qquad (10.87)$$

the decoder then consists of the following four simple steps:

Step 1. Multiply S_1 by the matrix $T^{p\lambda}$

Step 2. Add S_0 to the result of step 1

Step 3. Multiply the result of step 2 by $T^{q\lambda}$

Step 4. Add S_0 to the result of step 3

Table 10.18 illustrates this syndrome-decoding process with an example showing the results at each of the four steps.

The multiplication by $T^{p\lambda}$ and $T^{q\lambda}$ of steps 1 and 3 can be performed by means of the shift register SR_1 of Fig. 10.16 with p and q shifting operations, respectively. The addition of S_0 of steps 2 and 4 can be accomplished by entering the vector S_0 into SR_1 at the time of the last shifting operation of the previous step. The results of steps 3 and 4 provide the correction patterns E_i and E_j for bytes $\hat{B}_i$, and $\hat{B}_j$, respectively. When only one byte is in error, as indicated by pointer i, and the second pointer value j is undefined, the syndrome processing still determines E_i and

TABLE 10.16 Parameter p as a Function of i

i	0	1	2	3	4	5	6	7	8	9	10	11	12	13	14
p	15	14	13	12	11	10	9	8	7	6	5	4	3	2	1

TABLE 10.17 Parameter q as a Function of $(j - i)$

$j - i$	1	2	3	4	5	6	7	8	9	10	11	12	13	14	†
q	3	6	11	12	5	7	2	9	13	10	1	14	8	4	0

†j is undefined, and error pattern E_j is zero.

TABLE 10.18 Syndrome Processing for Two Erroneous Bytes

Step	Operation	Contents of SR_1
1	Shift $SR_1 \, p = 11$ times	10111110
2	Add contents of SR_0 to SR_1	10010010
3	Shift $SR_1 \, q = 7$ times	$10101010 = E_j$
4	Add contents of SR_0 to SR_1	$10000110 = E_i$
	$\hat{B}_i = 00000111$	$\hat{B}_j = 10101010$
	$E_i = 10000110$	$E_j = 10101010$
Corrected	$B_i = 10000001$	Corrected $B_j = 11011001$

E_j, in which E_j must result in a zero value. A nonzero value of E_j in this case indicates an uncorrectable error in one or more unknown byte positions.

10.9.5   Detection and Correction of One Byte

Through violations of one or more ZM constraints, almost all errors are detected. However, if any error escapes this detection, the decoder may encounter a code word with nonzero syndromes and absence of error pointers. In this case the syndromes are processed for detection and correction of a 1-byte error. Here the decoder determines the index i of the erroneous byte and the corresponding error pattern E_i. When all other bytes are error-free, the syndrome equations, Eqs. (10.76) and (10.77), in view of the coding equations, Eqs. (10.71) and (10.72), reduce to

$$S_0 = E_i \tag{10.88}$$

and

$$S_1 = T^{i\lambda} E_i \tag{10.89}$$

Thus, the error pattern E_i is determined by the syndrome S_0. Also, from Eqs. (10.88) and (10.89) we have

$$T^{-i\lambda} S_1 = S_0 \tag{10.90}$$

that is,

$$T^{(15-i)\lambda} S_1 = S_0 \tag{10.91}$$

Once again, using the shift register SR_1 of Fig. 10.16, the index i can be determined. With S_1 as the initial content, SR_1 is shifted and its contents are compared

TABLE 10.19   Syndrome Computation: One Byte in Error

	Read data input	Shift count	Contents of SR_0	Contents of SR_1
$\hat{B}_{14}$	10010111	1	10010111	10010111
$\hat{B}_{13}$	11101000	2	01111111	11101111
$\hat{B}_{12}$	10101010	3	11010101	01000010
$\hat{B}_{11}$	11111000	4	00101101	11101000
$\hat{B}_{10}$	01110011	5	01011110	11011101
$\hat{B}_9$	10010001	6	11001111	01010110
$\hat{B}_8$	00010101	7	11011010	01100100
$\hat{B}_7$	01111111	8	10100101	00100001
$\hat{B}_6$	00000000	9	10100101	00001000
$\hat{B}_5$	00100111	10	10000010	11110111
$\hat{B}_4$	00000111	11	10000101	00110110
$\hat{B}_3$	01010101	12	11010000	00010010
$\hat{B}_2$	10111110	13	01101110	10000011
$\hat{B}_1$	01101111	14	00000001	00001001
$\hat{B}_0$	00101101	15	$\boxed{10101010 = S_0}$	$\boxed{01001101 = S_1}$

TABLE 10.20 Syndrome Processing for One Erroneous Byte

Shift count	Contents of SR_0	Contents of SR_1	Equal
15	10101010	01001101	No
14	10101010	10000110	No
13	10101010	00010100	No
12	10101010	01100001	No
11	10101010	00101100	No
10	10101010	10101010	Yes

Erroneous byte position = 10

$$\hat{B}_{10} = \quad 01110011$$
$$\text{Error} = \quad \underline{10101010} \quad \text{(contents of } SR_0)$$
$$\text{Corrected } B_{10} = \quad 11011001$$

with S_0 while counting down from 15 with each shift. When the contents do compare with S_0, the count indicates the index i of the erroneous byte. If the contents do not compare with S_0 even when the counter reaches zero, then this indicates the presence of two or more erroneous bytes. Tables 10.19 and 10.20 illustrate the syndrome computation and syndrome decoding processes for the case of one byte in error.

10.10 CODING IN AN 18-TRACK TAPE-STORAGE SUBSYSTEM

A recent tape-storage subsystem (IBM 3480) introduced a tape cartridge with an 18-track data format which uses a new coding scheme called the *adaptive cross-parity code* (AXP) (Patel, 1985b). In this scheme, the 18 tracks are divided into two interleaved sets of 9 tracks, and each set consists of 7 data tracks and 2 check tracks. The number of check tracks, thus, are in the same proportion as that in a prior 9-track scheme; however, by adaptive use of the checks in the two interleaved sets, the new scheme corrects up to 3 erased tracks in any one set of 9 tracks and up to 4 erased tracks in the two sets together.

The coding structure is based on the concept of interacting vertical and cross parity checks. The vertical parity checks are applied independently to each of the two sets of tracks; the cross parity checks extend over both the sets, providing adaptive usage of redundancy. The decoding procedure is iterative and uses parity equations which involve only one unknown variable at a time. The resulting implementation is simple and inexpensive.

During the iterative error-correction process, the decoder identifies an approaching new erroneous track and corrects up to two erroneous tracks in the two sets together. The third erroneous track in one set and the fourth erroneous track of the two sets together are corrected on-the-fly or on reread when they are identified as erasures by external means.

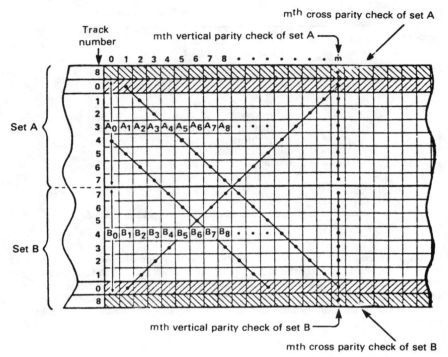

Figure 10.17 Data format; adaptive cross parity code; 18 tracks grouped into two sets.

10.10.1 Encoding Equations

As shown in Fig. 10.17, 18 parallel tracks are recorded along the tape. The tracks are grouped into two sets. Set A consists of any 9 parallel tracks and set B consists of the remaining 9 parallel tracks. In Fig. 10.17 the two sets are shown side by side with a symmetrically ordered arrangement of the tracks. This is done for convenience in describing the code. In actual practice, however, the tracks from two sets are interleaved and may be arranged in any other order.

Let $A_m(t)$ and $B_m(t)$ denote the mth bit in the track t of set A and set B, respectively. The track number t takes on values from 0 to 8 in each set. The bit position m takes on values from 0 to M. Tracks labeled 0 and 8 in each set are check tracks.

Each check bit in track 0 of set A provides a cross parity check along the diagonal with positive slope, involving bits from both sets, as seen in Fig. 10.17. The mth cross parity check of set A is given by the encoding equation

$$A_m(0) = \sum_{t=1}^{7} A_{m-t}(t) \oplus \sum_{t=0}^{7} B_{m-15+t}(t) \tag{10.92}$$

where the circle superimposed on the summation symbol indicates modulo-2 sum.

Each check bit in the track 0 of set B provides a cross parity check along the diagonal with negative slope, involving bits from both sets, as seen in Fig. 10.17. The mth cross parity check of set B is given by the encoding equation

$$B_m(0) = \sum_{t=1}^{7} B_{m-t}(t) \oplus \sum_{t=0}^{7} A_{m-15+t}(t) \qquad (10.93)$$

Eqs. (10.92) and (10.93) can be rewritten in a more convenient symmetrical form as

$$\sum_{t=0}^{7} [A_{m-t}(t) \oplus B_{m-15+t}(t)] = 0 \qquad (10.94)$$

$$\sum_{t=0}^{7} [B_{m-t}(t) \oplus A_{m-15+t}(t)] = 0 \qquad (10.95)$$

At the beginning of the record, computations of the cross-parity-check bits for positions 0 to 15 involve data-bit values from void positions (with negative position numbers). For convenience, these data-bit values will be considered to have zero binary value. At the end of the record, in order to provide diagonal checks to all bits in each track, the zero check track in each set will be extended 15 positions. The check bits on the extended positions also involve some data-bit values from void positions which will be assumed to have zero binary value.

Each check bit in the eighth track of set A is a vertical parity check over the bits of the same position number m in set A. The mth vertical parity check of set A is given by the equation

$$\sum_{t=0}^{8} A_m(t) = 0 \qquad (10.96)$$

Similarly, the mth vertical parity check of set B is given by the equation

$$\sum_{t=0}^{8} B_m(t) = 0 \qquad (10.97)$$

10.10.2 Error Syndromes

Let $\hat{A}_m(t)$ and $\hat{B}_m(t)$ denote the bit values corresponding to $A_m(t)$ and $B_m(t)$, respectively, as they are read from the tape. These read-back bits may be corrupted by errors. The result of the parity checks of Eqs. (10.94), (10.95), (10.96), and (10.97) applied to the read-back data is called the *syndrome of error*. A nonzero syndrome is a clear indication of the presence of an error.

The mth cross parity check of set A yields the syndrome

$$Sd_m^a = \sum_{t=0}^{7} \hat{A}_{m-t}(t) \oplus \hat{B}_{m-15+t}(t) \qquad (10.98)$$

The mth cross parity check of set B yields the syndrome

$$Sd_m^b = \sum_{t=0}^{7} \hat{B}_{m-t}(t) \oplus \hat{A}_{m-15+t}(t) \tag{10.99}$$

The mth vertical check for set A yields the syndrome

$$Sv_m^a = \sum_{t=0}^{8} \hat{A}_m(t) \tag{10.100}$$

The mth vertical check for set B yields the syndrome

$$Sv_m^b = \sum_{t=0}^{8} \hat{B}_m(t) \tag{10.101}$$

The modulo-2 difference between the read $\hat{A}_m(t)$ and the written $A_m(t)$ is called the *error pattern* $e_m^a(t)$ in the mth position of track t of set A.

Therefore, for set A we have

$$e_m^a(t) = \hat{A}_m(t) \oplus A_m(t) \tag{10.102}$$

Similarly, for set B

$$e_m^b(t) = \hat{B}_m(t) \oplus B_m(t) \tag{10.103}$$

Now if we compare the coding equations, Eqs. (10.94), (10.95), (10.96) and (10.97), with the corresponding syndrome equations, Eqs. (10.98), (10.99), (10.100) and (10.101), respectively, and substitute $e_m^a(t)$ and $e_m^b(t)$ from Eqs. (10.102) and (10.103), we get

$$Sd_m^a = \sum_{t=0}^{7} e_{m-t}^a(t) \oplus e_{m-15+t}^b(t) \tag{10.104}$$

$$Sd_m^b = \sum_{t=0}^{7} e_{m-t}^b(t) \oplus e_{m-15+t}^a(t) \tag{10.105}$$

$$Sv_m^a = \sum_{t=0}^{8} e_m^a(t) \tag{10.106}$$

$$Sv_m^b = \sum_{t=0}^{8} e_m^b(t) \tag{10.107}$$

Many different types of errors can be corrected by processing these syndromes. In tapes the predominant errors are track errors caused by large-size defects in the magnetic medium. The erroneous track may be identified by detecting loss of signal, excessive phase error, inadmissible recording pattern, or any other similar external pointer. In the absence of such external pointers, the erroneous track can be identified by processing the syndromes. We will show that any one of the following combinations of track errors can be corrected by processing the syndromes.

1. Up to three known erroneous tracks in one set *and* up to one known erroneous track in the other set

2. Up to two known or one unknown erroneous track in each of the two sets
3. Up to one known *and* one unknown erroneous track in one set, *and* up to one known erroneous track in the other set

10.10.3 Correction of Errors in Known Erroneous Tracks

Errors confined to three known tracks in set A are correctable if set B is error-free or has only one known track in error. The erroneous tracks are indicated by track-error pointers i, j, k in set A and y in set B. If y is undefined, then set B is assumed to be error-free.

For convenience in decoding, i is the lowest and k is the highest track index among the erroneous tracks from track number 0 to 7. Track j is the remaining erroneous track so that either $(i < j < k)$ or $(j = 8$ and $i < k)$. Since set B has only one known track in error, the vertical-parity-check syndromes Sv_m^b yield the error patterns for this track. On elimination of the known zero-error patterns corresponding to the error-free tracks, Eq. 10.40 can be rewritten as

$$Sv_m^b = e_m^b(y) \tag{10.108}$$

Assume that all errors are corrected up to byte $m - 1$ and the syndrome equations are adjusted for all corrected error patterns. Then, as shown in Fig. 10.18, the error patterns for the mth position of track i, j, and k of set A can be determined from the syndromes Sd_{m+i}^a, Sd_{m+15-k}^b, and Sv_m^a. We can write the equations for these syndromes from Eqs. (10.104), (10.105), and (10.106).

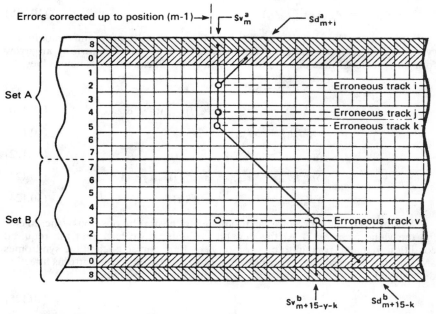

Figure 10.18 Three-track correction in set A.

On eliminating the known zero-error patterns corresponding to the error-free tracks and the corrected error patterns up to position $m - 1$ in each track, these equations can be written as

$$Sd^a_{m+i} = e^a_m(i) \tag{10.109}$$

$$Sd^b_{m+15-k} = \begin{cases} e^a_m(k) \oplus e^b_{m+15-y-k}(y) & \text{if } y < 8 \\ e^a_m(k) & \text{if } y = 8 \text{ or set } B \text{ is error-free} \end{cases} \tag{10.110}$$

$$Sv^a_m = e^a_m(i) \oplus e^a_m(j) \oplus e^a_m(k) \tag{10.111}$$

From Eq. (10.108), we have

$$Sv^b_{m+15-y-k} = e^b_{m+15-y-k}(y) \tag{10.112}$$

If $Sv^b_{m+15-y-k}$ in Eq. (10.112) is nonzero for some $0 \le y \le 7$ and y is unknown, then set B must be processed first to identify the unknown track in error.

Equations (10.109) to (10.112) yield the error patterns

$$e^a_m(i) = Sd^a_{m+i} \tag{10.113}$$

$$e^a_m(k) = \begin{cases} Sd^b_{m+15-k} \oplus Sv^b_{m+15-y-k} & \text{if } y < 8 \\ Sd^b_{m+15-k} & \text{if } y = 8 \text{ or set } B \text{ is error-free} \end{cases} \tag{10.114}$$

$$e^a_m(j) = Sv^a_m \oplus e^a_m(i) \oplus e^a_m(k) \tag{10.115}$$

The mth bits in tracks i, j, and k are then corrected, using these error patterns as

$$A_m(i) = \hat{A}_m(i) \oplus e^a_m(i) \tag{10.116}$$

$$A_m(j) = \hat{A}_m(j) \oplus e^a_m(j) \tag{10.117}$$

$$A_m(k) = \hat{A}_m(k) \oplus e^a_m(k) \tag{10.118}$$

Before proceeding for the correction of the next position, we must modify the syndromes affected by these corrections. The modification is shown by an arrow from the previous value of a syndrome (with its modification) to its new value

$$Sd^a_{m+i} \leftarrow Sd^a_{m+i} \oplus e^a_m(i) \tag{10.119}$$

$$Sd^a_{m+j} \leftarrow Sd^a_{m+j} \oplus e^a_m(j) \qquad \text{if } j < 8 \tag{10.120}$$

$$Sd^a_{m+k} \leftarrow Sd^a_{m+k} \oplus e^a_m(k) \tag{10.121}$$

$$Sd^b_{m+15-i} \leftarrow Sd^b_{m+15-i} \oplus e^a_m(i) \tag{10.122}$$

$$Sd^b_{m+15-j} \leftarrow Sd^b_{m+15-j} \oplus e^a_m(j) \quad \text{if } j < 8 \tag{10.123}$$

$$Sd^b_{m+15-k} \leftarrow Sd^b_{m+15-k} \oplus e^a_m(k) \tag{10.124}$$

Now the decoding procedure can be applied to the next bit position by incrementing the value of m by 1. At the new bit position m, we have met the required condition that all errors up to bit position $m - 1$ are corrected, and the syndromes are adjusted for corrected error patterns. In particular, all error patterns affecting the syndrome value Sd^a_{m-1} are corrected. Consequently, we expect that

$$Sd^a_{m-1} = 0 \tag{10.125}$$

A nonzero value of Sd_{m-1}^a indicates the presence of uncorrected errors. This provides a partial check on the uncorrectable multitrack errors that are beyond the correction capability of the code.

Errors in two known tracks in set A can be corrected if set B has at the most one unknown or two known tracks in error. The erroneous tracks in set A are indicated by track-error pointers i and j, where $i < j$. The error patterns $e_m^a(i)$ and $e_m^a(j)$ for the tracks i and j can be calculated from the local syndromes Sd_{m+i}^a and Sv_m^a as seen from Eqs. (10.113) and (10.115).

Errors confined to only one known track in set A can be corrected by means of only the vertical-parity-check syndrome Sv_m^a of set A. Since the check Sv_m^a ranges over set A only, this correction capability is not affected by the error conditions in set B. The erroneous track in set A is indicated by a track-error pointer j, and the error pattern $e_m^a(j)$ for the known erroneous track j is obtained from Eq. (10.115).

10.10.4   Generation of Track-Error Pointers

10.10.4.1   *Pointer to First Erroneous Track in Set A.*   Errors confined to only one unknown track in set A can be detected and corrected if set B has, at most, one unknown or two known tracks in error. It is assumed that errors in all tracks in set B are corrected up to bit position $m - 1$, and that the syndrome values are adjusted for all corrected error patterns. When all tracks in set A are error-free, the parity-check syndromes Sv_m^a and Sd_{m-i}^a are equal to zero for $0 < i < 7$. When any of these syndromes is found to be nonzero, it is an indication that an error is present in at least one of the tracks in the vicinity—that is, within the next seven bit positions. Assuming that only one erroneous track is affecting the syndromes, the index of the erroneous track can be determined by examining syndromes Sd_{m+7}^a and Sv_m^a as the bit-position value m progresses. The following assertion characterizes the generation of the first track-error pointer in set A:

Assertion 1:   Let m_1 and m_2 denote the lowest values of bit positions such that

$$Sd_{m+i}^a \neq 0 \qquad \text{for } m = m_1 \text{ and } i = 7 \qquad (10.126)$$

$$Sv_m^a \neq 0 \qquad \text{for } m = m_2 \qquad (10.127)$$

Then track q is in error at bit position m_2 and the track index q is given by

$$q = \begin{cases} 7 - (m_2 - m_1) & \text{if } m_1 > m_2 \\ 8 & \text{otherwise} \end{cases} \qquad (10.128)$$

The proof of assertion 1 follows from the geometric considerations depicted in Fig. 10.19. In the case when m_2 is greater than or equal to m_1, if the resulting value q is smaller than zero, then the syndromes are affected by two or more unknown erroneous tracks and the errors are uncorrectable. In the special case where m_1 is not captured, even when the bit position value exceeds m_2, the error is in the vertical-parity-check track. The process can be implemented using a running counter with the iterative operation, counting down from the value 7.

Once we have the index value of the erroneous track, the errors can be corrected by applying the procedure for correction of one track with track-error pointer, as discussed previously.

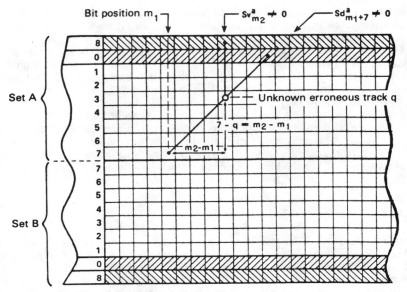

Figure 10.19   Generation of pointer to first erroneous track.

10.10.4.2   *Pointer to Second Erroneous Track in Set A.*   Consider the case when set
A is being corrected for errors in a known erroneous track, and another unknown
track in set A begins to be affected by errors. This second unknown erroneous track
can be detected, and both erroneous tracks of set A can be corrected provided that
set B has, at the most, one known track in error.

For simplicity, first consider the case when tracks 0 to 7 in set B are error-free.
Later it will be easy to see how the equations can be modified to include the effect
of a known erroneous track in set B. Let p denote the known erroneous track in set
A, and assume that, so far, all remaining tracks in set A are error-free. Also assume
that all errors are corrected up to bit position $m - 1$ and the syndrome values are
adjusted for all corrected error patterns.

First consider the case where p is not the vertical-parity track, that is, $p \neq 8$. The
error pattern of the mth position of the track p affects the syndromes Sd^b_{m+p},
Sd^b_{m+15-p}, and Sv^a_m. In the absence of errors in any other tracks

$$Sd^a_{m+p} = Sd^b_{m+15-p} = Sv^a_m = e^a_m(p) \qquad (10.129)$$

However, as any one of the other tracks begins to be affected by an error, the
syndrome relationship of Eq. (10.129) will no longer hold. We can make the following assertion by observing the effect of the new erroneous track on this relationship:

Assertion 2:   Let p denote the known erroneous track where $p \neq 8$. Let m_1 and
m_2 denote the lowest bit positions such that

$$Sd^a_{m+1} \neq Sv^a_m \qquad \text{for } m = m_1 \text{ and } i = p \qquad (10.130)$$

$$Sd^b_{m+15-k} \neq Sv^a_m \qquad \text{for } m = m_2 \text{ and } k = p \qquad (10.131)$$

Then the track q is in error starting at the bit position m that is the greater of m_1 and m_2; and q is given by

$$q = \begin{cases} p - (m_2 - m_1) & \text{if } m_2 \neq m_1 \\ 8 & \text{if } m_2 = m_1 \end{cases} \tag{10.132}$$

The proof of assertion 2 follows from the geometric considerations depicted in Fig. 10.20, which considers the case when m_2 is greater than m_1. Note in this case that if the resulting value q is smaller than 0, the syndromes are being affected by two or more unknown erroneous tracks and the errors are uncorrectable. Similarly, in the case when m_2 is smaller than m_1, if the resulting value q is greater than 7, the unknown erroneous track is in set B and will be detected and corrected later by the decoder in set B. In the case when m_2 is equal to m_1, the erroneous track q is in the vertical-parity-check track of set A. The process can be implemented using a running counter with the iterative operation, counting up or down from the value p depending upon the relationship between m_2 and m_1.

Next consider the case where the first unknown erroneous track is the vertical-parity-check track in set A, that is, $p = 8$. The error pattern of the mth position in track p in this case affects the syndrome Sv_m^a only. In the absence of errors in any other track in set A or set B, the cross parity syndromes must all be zero. However, as any other track in set A begins to be affected by an error, the cross parity syndromes will no longer be zero as the bit position value m is incremented. We make the following assertion:

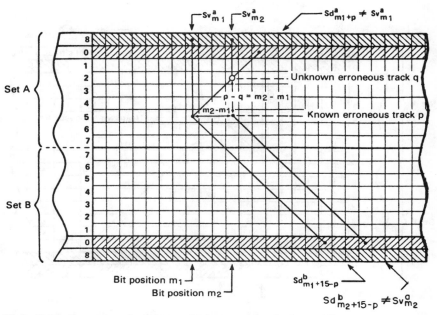

Figure 10.20 Generation of pointer to second erroneous track when $p \neq 8$.

Assertion 3:   Let p denote the known erroneous track where $p = 8$. Let m_1 and m_2 denote the lowest bit positions such that

$$Sd^a_{m+i} \neq 0 \qquad \text{for } m = m_1 \text{ and } i = 7 \tag{10.133}$$

$$Sd^b_{m+15-k} \neq 0 \qquad \text{for } m = m_2 \text{ and } k = 7 - (m_2 - m_1) \tag{10.134}$$

Then track q is in error beginning at bit position m_2, and the index q is given by

$$q = k \tag{10.135}$$

The proof of assertion 3 follows from the geometric considerations depicted in Fig. 10.21. Note that if the resulting value of q is smaller than zero, the syndromes are affected by two or more unknown erroneous tracks and the errors are uncorrectable. The process can be implemented using a running counter with the iterative operation, counting down from the value 7.

Now we show the modification for the more general case when set B has, at the most, one track in error. Let y be the erroneous track in set B. The error patterns for this track are all known from the vertical-parity-check syndrome Sv^b_m of set B. If $y \neq 8$, then these error patterns also affect the values of cross-parity-check syndromes Sd^b_m. In order to account for the effect of these error patterns, we use the adjusted value $Sd^b_m \oplus Sv^b_{m-y}$ in place of Sd^b_m for any required value of m. In particular, in assertions 2 and 3, the syndrome Sd^b_{m+15-k} from set B is replaced by a composite syndrome SB where

$$SB = \begin{cases} Sd^b_{m+15-k} \oplus Sv^b_{m+15-y-k} & \text{if } y < 8 \\ Sd^b_{m+15-k} & \text{if } y = 8 \text{ or set } B \text{ is error-free} \end{cases} \tag{10.136}$$

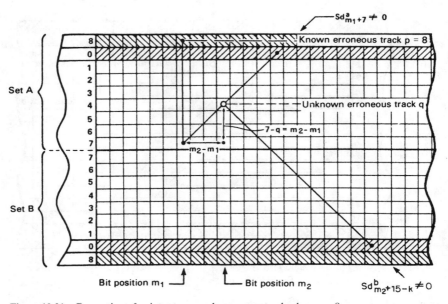

Figure 10.21   Generation of pointer to second erroneous track when $p = 8$.

TABLE 10.21   Corresponding Variables in Set A and Set B

Set A	A_m	Sd_m^a	Sv_m^a	SA	i	j	k	e_m^a
Set B	B_m	Sd_m^b	Sv_m^b	SB	x	y	z	e_m^b

If $Sv_{m+15-y-k}^b$ is nonzero for some $0 \le y \le 7$ and y is unknown, then set B must be processed first to identify the unknown track in error. The count value $q > 7$ in assertion 2 indicates this condition.

It is interesting to note that the syndromes used in the generation of track error pointers, namely Sd_{m+i}^a, SB, and Sv_m^a, are the same in form as those used in Eqs. (10.113), (10.114), and (10.115) for correction of errors. Thus, with appropriate values for the variables i and k, the same hardware can be used to generate syndromes for both processes.

The coding rules possess a built-in mirror-image symmetry around set A and set B. In particular, the encoding and decoding equations for set B can be obtained from those of set A by substitution of corresponding variables in set B, as shown in Table 10.21.

10.10.5   Implementation of the Decoding Process

The decoding process consists of two distinct functions: (1) the detection and identification of the erroneous tracks, and (2) the correction of errors in known erroneous tracks. The internal pointer generator identifies the first erroneous track in both sets and subsequently identifies a second erroneous track in one of the two sets. Additional erroneous tracks may be detected and identified by external signals which usually require some form of analog sensing of the playback conditions of the data recorded on the various tracks. This includes detection of loss of read signal, excessive phase error, inadmissible recording code patterns, or any other similar external indicators.

Once an internal or external track-error pointer is generated, it may be kept on for the entire remaining length of the record. Similarly, any track-error pointer may be turned off at an appropriate bit position in a record if the error patterns corresponding to the indicated track turn out to be zero consistently for a significant length of the record, thus confirming that the track is error free. This allows replacement of the track-error pointer if and when some other track becomes erroneous, particularly in the case of long records.

It may be noted that the errors in a new erroneous track begin to affect the decoding process as much as 15 bit positions ahead of the actual error. Thus the beginning of each new external track-error pointer must be extended 15 bit positions earlier by means of a pointer look-ahead function. For the same reason, in the case of internal generation of track-error pointers, the beginning of two erroneous tracks cannot always be detected successfully if they occur in the vicinity of each other.

The error correction is done at the mth bit position which progresses from the zero value to the last bit position, of value M, in a recurring manner. In order to compute error patterns at the mth bit position, one requires the syndrome values ranging from bit-position m up to $m + 15$. Furthermore, it is necessary that all syndrome values be modified to account for the corrected error patterns prior to position m. The decoding process progresses in synchronism with the incoming read data characters. The actual correction of each received data character is delayed by 15 character positions.

10.11 SINGLE-BURST CORRECTION IN MAGNETIC DISK STORAGE

The earlier disk storage products used either a simple parity check or a cyclic redundancy check (CRC) at the end of the record for the purpose of detection of errors. In these products, rereading was the only means of error recovery. Single-burst-error correction was introduced in disk drives from the year 1971 onward, with a Fire code, with a modified Fire code and finally with interleaved codes based on Reed-Solomon algebra. Rereading is still an important part of the error-recovery procedure in all these products. The code is designed to provide good error-detection capability, and error correction is limited to only one burst of error in a record which may be as long as the entire track.

10.11.1 Error Control in Disk Products Using Fire Codes

Fire codes have been used in disk drives introduced in the 1970s. The IBM 3340 and 3350 compatible disk storage products use a Fire code with the following generator polynomial

$$G(x) = (x^{13} + 1)(x^{35} + x^{23} + x^8 + x^2 + 1) \tag{10.137}$$

The degree of $G(x)$ is 48, and the cycle length is $13 \times (2^{35} - 1)$. Thus the code requires 6 check bytes at the end of very long code words. It is capable of correcting one burst of error up to 7 bits long. It can be used to correct any burst of length b bits or less while providing detection of a longer burst of length up to d bits if $b + d - 1 \leq 13$. In a 1973 disk file (IBM 3340), for instance, the parameters b and d are chosen to be 3 and 11, and in a later development (IBM 3350) they are 4 and 10, respectively. The cycle length of $13 \times (2^{35} - 1)$ far exceeds the length of any records in these disk products. Thus any practical record with 6 check bytes at the end forms a much-shortened variable-length code word. The encoding of this code word can be carried out by means of a 48-bit modulo-$G(x)$ shift register, as discussed before. The decoding can be done using the error-trapping technique. This requires two shift registers: one, connected for modulo $(x^{13} + 1)$, determines the pattern of the error burst; the other, connected for modulo $(x^{35} + x^{23} + x^8 + x^2 + 1)$, determines the location of the error burst. Since the cycle length of the second polynomial is very long, backward shifting operations will save time in decoding. This decoding method was also presented earlier in the section on Fire codes.

10.11.2 Modified Fire Codes

Some disk products (e.g., IBM 3330) use a modified Fire code (Chien, 1969) where the modification is intended to reduce the number of shifting operations required in the decoding process. The error location, in this code, is determined by means of several short-cycle-length polynomials instead of one long-cycle-length polynomial. The generator polynomial of this code is given by

$$G(x) = G_0(x)G_1(x)G_2(x)G_3(x) \tag{10.138}$$

where
$$G_0(x) = x^{22} + 1 \tag{10.139}$$

$$G_1(x) = x^{11} + x^7 + x^6 + x + 1 \tag{10.140}$$

$$G_2(x) = \begin{matrix} x^{12} + x^{11} + x^{10} + x^9 + x^8 + x^7 + x^6 \\ + x^5 + x^4 + x^3 + x^2 + x + 1 \end{matrix} \tag{10.141}$$

$$G_3(x) = x^{11} + x^9 + x^7 + x^6 + x^5 + x + 1 \tag{10.142}$$

The degree of $G(x)$ is $22 + 11 + 12 + 11 = 56$. Hence the code requires 7 check bytes with maximum code-word length given by the cycle length of $G(x)$. The cycle lengths of $G_0(x)$, $G_1(x)$, $G_2(x)$, and $G_3(x)$ are 22, 89, 13, and 23, respectively. The cycle length of $G(x)$ is the least common multiple of these numbers, which is the product $22 \times 89 \times 13 \times 23 = 585,442$. The code is used for correcting any single burst of length up to 11 bits. Furthermore, it is claimed that it simultaneously detects any single burst of length up to 22 bits and most of the commonly encountered multiple random errors.

The encoding of this code requires a 56-bit shift register connected according to the composite polynomial $G(x)$, and the encoding process is the bit-by-bit shift-register processing in cyclic codes. The decoding is carried out with four shift registers SR_0, SR_1, SR_2, and SR_3 in which the feedback connections are in accordance with the polynomials $G_0(x)$, $G_1(x)$, $G_2(x)$, and $G_3(x)$, respectively.

In accordance with Eq. (10.43) the error pattern is an 11-bit error burst at position p represented by the polynomial

$$E(x) = x^p E_{11}(x) \tag{10.143}$$

The syndromes of error S_0, S_1, S_2, and S_3 are computed as four separate remainders using the four decoding shift registers. As in Eqs. (10.44) and (10.45), these syndromes can be expressed as

$$S_0(x) = x^p E_{11}(x) \text{ modulo } (x^{22} + 1) \tag{10.144}$$

$$S_1(x) = x^p E_{11}(x) \text{ modulo } G_1(x) \tag{10.145}$$

$$S_2(x) = x^p E_{11}(x) \text{ modulo } G_2(x) \tag{10.146}$$

$$S_3(x) = x^p E_{11}(x) \text{ modulo } G_3(x) \tag{10.147}$$

The decoding operation proceeds as follows: If all four syndromes are zero, then it is concluded that the word contains no error. If some but not all syndromes are zero, then an uncorrectable multiple-burst error is detected which will require rereading of the data. If all four syndromes are nonzero, then they will be processed in their respective shift registers in order to determine the error pattern and location.

The error pattern is trapped as usual by shifting the syndrome S_0 in the SR_0 register until the 11 high-order stages of the 22-stage register contain zeros; thus the burst is trapped in the 11 low-order stages of SR_0. Then the other syndromes are shifted in their respective registers until the contents in each match the error pattern captured in SR_0. Let C_0, C_1, C_2 and C_3 denote the number of shifts required with shift registers SR_0, SR_1, SR_2, and SR_3 in the above process of capturing the error pattern.

Each shift register has a short cycle length (the number of shifts after which it resets to its original content). Thus the error pattern must be captured within the cycle length of each register, otherwise the error is uncorrectable. Thus $C_0 < 22$, $C_1 < 89$, $C_2 < 13$, and $C_3 < 23$. The actual location p of error in the code word satisfies the following simultaneous congruence relations

$$(n - p) \equiv C_0 \text{ modulo } 22 \equiv C_1 \text{ modulo } 89 \equiv C_2 \text{ modulo } 13 \equiv C_3 \text{ modulo } 23$$

The integer $n - p$ may be computed through the Chinese remainder theorem as follows: Find four integers $A_0, A_1, A_2,$ and A_3 such that

$$\left(\frac{n}{22}\right)A_0 + \left(\frac{n}{89}\right)A_1 + \left(\frac{n}{13}\right)A_2 + \left(\frac{n}{23}\right)A_3 = 1 \text{ modulo } n$$

where n is $22 \times 89 \times 13 \times 23$. Then $n - p$ is given by

$$n - p = \left(\frac{n}{22}\right)A_0 C_0 + \left(\frac{n}{89}\right)A_1 C_1 + \left(\frac{n}{13}\right)A_2 C_2$$

$$+ \left(\frac{n}{23}\right)A_3 C_3 \text{ modulo } n \tag{10.148}$$

The constants A_0, A_1, A_2, and A_3 are predetermined as 17, 11, 7, and 13, respectively. Thus $n - p$ and then p can be easily computed using the above equation.

Thus the decoding process consists of the following steps when the syndromes S_0, S_1, S_2, and S_3 are all nonzero:

Step 1. Capture error pattern and determine C_0, C_1, C_2, and C_3

Step 2. Compute $M = 452{,}387 \, C_0 + 72{,}358 \, C_1 + 315{,}238 \, C_2 + 330{,}902 \, C_3$

Step 3. Divide M by 585,442 and find remainder m

Step 4. Subtract m from 585,442 to obtain position value p

Thus, the fast decoding of Fire code is possible only when a facility for arithmetic operations is readily available. In particular, four multiplications, three additions, one division, and one subtraction are required in order to determine the position value p from the shift counts C_0, C_1, C_2, and C_3 of the shift registers. The number of shifting operations is limited to less than 22 shifts for the error pattern and less than 89 shifts for the error location.

The later disk drives (such as IBM 3370, 3375, and 3380) use byte-oriented processing with single-byte-correcting Reed-Solomon codes and two-way or three-way interleaving. The encoding and decoding processes in these applications are similar to those already described for the various tape products.

10.12 MULTIBURST CORRECTION IN MAGNETIC DISK STORAGE

The high-performance disk storage products are required to maintain or improve their high standards of reliability and availability performance in spite of the in-

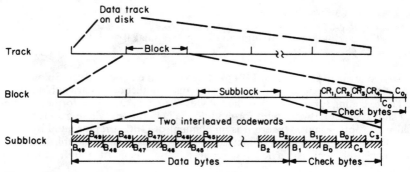

Figure 10.22   Data format.

creased storage density and data delivery rate in the later models. A relatively greater number of soft errors, including multiburst errors are required to be processed very fast. A two-level coding architecture is often used (see Sec. 10.8) in which the first-level capability is designed to provide a specific reliability performance with on-the-fly processing. The second-level capability is the "reserve" error protection that increases the availability performance by providing additional error correction in the case of a weaker device or a failing device.

In this section, we describe one application of the two-level coding architecture that is currently in use in the IBM 3380J and 3380K disk files. In these files, the data format of a disk track is designed around Reed-Solomon code and a two-level coding arrangement consisting of subblocks within a block.

The data are stored in the form of user-defined variable-length blocks (records). Each block is partitioned into fixed-length subblocks, except that the last subblock may be shorter with fewer user bytes or may include pad bytes. Each subblock (except the last) consists of 96 user bytes and six first-level check bytes in the form of two interleaved code words. At the end of the block, six additional check bytes are appended, two of which are used for second-level error correction and the remaining four are used for an overall data-integrity check after correction of the errors at both levels. The data format is shown in Fig. 10.22.

The basic error event in the 3380J and 3380K files is a burst error that may affect up to two adjacent bytes. The two-way interleaved two-level code of Fig. 10.22 provides correction of at least one error event in each subblock and up to two error events in any one of the many subblocks of a variable-length block.

The coding equations are created in terms of symbols in $GF(2^8)$. These symbols are represented by 8-bit binary bytes. A subblock consists of two interleaved words of a primary code. The primary code word consists of three check bytes denoted by B_0, B_1 and C_3; and m data bytes denoted by B_2, B_3, ... B_{m+1}, which satisfy the following modulo-2 matrix equations

$$B_0 \oplus TB_1 \oplus T^2 B_2 \oplus \cdots \oplus T^{m+1} B_{m+1} = 0 \qquad (10.149)$$

$$B_0 \oplus T^2 B_1 \oplus T^4 B_2 \oplus \cdots \oplus T^{2(m+1)} B_{m+1} = 0 \qquad (10.150)$$

$$B_0 \oplus T^3 B_1 \oplus T^6 B_2 \oplus \cdots \oplus T^{3(m+1)} B_{m+1} = C_3 \qquad (10.151)$$

where $\oplus$ signifies modulo-2 sum

B_i = an 8-bit column vector
$i = 0, 1, \ldots, m + 1 \leq 2^8 - 2$
T = companion matrix of primitive polynomial $1 + x^3 + x^5 + x^7 + x^8$
$m = 48$

The code given by Eqs. (10.149) to (10.151) is an extended Reed-Solomon code providing one-symbol correction and two-symbol detection in each subblock.

The encoding for the first two check bytes B_0 and B_1 can be performed by means of a shift-register network built for modulo-$g(x)$ operations where $g(x)$ is a polynomial with roots α and α^2 where α is an element of GF(2^8) represented by an 8-bit byte, that is the first column of matrix T. The computation of the third check byte C_3 in each subblock is carried out separately by means of a shift register with multiplier T^3.

The block consists of any number of subblocks, say n, with one additional check byte denoted by C_0 at the end. This check byte is the modulo-2 sum of all subblock bytes excluding C_3 and accumulated over all subblocks as specified by the following modulo-2 matrix equation:

$$C_0 = \sum_{\text{subbk}=1}^{n} \left(\sum_{i=0}^{m+1} B_i \right)_{\text{subbk}} \qquad (10.152)$$

The above described primary code words are two-way interleaved. Thus, there are six check bytes at the end of each subblock and two check bytes at the end of the block that provide the desired error-correction capability. The remaining four check bytes at the end of the block are for data-integrity check over the corrected data stream. This error-detection part of the second-level code is described in Sec. 10.12.3.

It is readily seen that $n = 1$, Eqs. (10.149) to (10.152) together represent a code that is an extended Reed-Solomon code for correction of two symbol errors. In case of n greater than 1, the block-level code word can be viewed as modulo-2 superposition of n subblock code words. Two symbol errors in this superpositioned code word are correctable.

Suppose that a block consisting of n subblocks encounters multiple symbols in error. If these errors are located in separate subblocks, then each error will be corrected as a single-symbol error in the corresponding subblock, and the block-level error syndromes will vanish by the corrected error patterns. If one of the subblocks had two symbols in error, then the subblock-level processing will detect these errors and correct all others as single-symbol errors. At the block level, the subblock-level syndromes, together with block-level syndromes, will be reprocessed for the correction of the subblock with two symbols in error. If any subblock had more than two symbols in error, or if two or more subblocks had multiple symbols in error, then these errors cannot be corrected.

10.12.1   Decoding Process: First Level

Let $\hat{B}_i$ and $\hat{C}_3$ denote the read bytes corresponding to the written bytes B_i and C_3 respectively. The syndromes of error at the subblock level are denoted by S_1, S_2, and S_3, corresponding to the coding equations (10.149), (10.150), and (10.151), respectively, and are given by:

$$S_1 = \hat{B}_0 \oplus T\hat{B}_1 \oplus T^2\hat{B}_2 \oplus \cdots \oplus T^{m+1}\hat{B}_{m+1} \tag{10.153}$$

$$S_2 = \hat{B}_0 \oplus T^2\,\hat{B}_1 \oplus T^4\,\hat{B}_2 \oplus \cdots \oplus T^{2(m+1)}\hat{B}_{m+1} \tag{10.154}$$

$$S_3 = \hat{B}_0 \oplus T^3\,\hat{B}_1 \oplus T^6\,\hat{B}_2 \oplus \cdots \oplus T^{3(m+1)}\hat{B}_{m+1} \oplus \hat{C}_3 \tag{10.155}$$

A nonzero value of S_1, S_2 or S_3 indicates presence of an error. Suppose the subblock has only one byte in error. Let x and E_x denote the error location and error pattern respectively. That is,

$$\hat{B}_i = \begin{cases} B_x \oplus E_x & \text{for } i = x \\ B_i & \text{for } i \neq x \end{cases} \tag{10.156}$$

Then in view of Eqs. (10.149) to (10.151) and (10.153) to (10.156), the syndromes reduce to:

$$S_1 = T^x\,E_x \tag{10.157}$$

$$S_2 = T^{2x}\,E_x \tag{10.158}$$

$$S_3 = T^{3x}\,E_x \tag{10.159}$$

Thus the decoding equation is given by:

$$E_x = T^{-x}S_1 = T^{-2x}S_2 = T^{-3x}S_3 \qquad \text{if } B_x \text{ is in error} \tag{10.160}$$

Note that a one-byte error in check byte C_3 affects the syndrome S_3 only. In that case the decoding equation is given by:

$$0 = S_1 = S_2 \neq S_3 \qquad \text{if } C_3 \text{ is in error}$$

The decoding can be accomplished by means of three shift registers, with T^{-1}, T^{-2}, and T^{-3} multiplier circuits. With S_1, S_2, and S_3 as initial contents, the three registers are shifted and the contents are compared after each shifting operation until they are equal. The resultant number of shifts determines x, and the final content in each register is the error pattern E_2. The byte $\hat{B}_x$ is then corrected as $\hat{B}_x \oplus E_x$.

The hardware implementation of the decoding function described above is shown in Fig. 10.23. The syndromes S_1, S_2, and S_3 are entered into appropriate shift registers at clock zero. Each clock cycle generates a shifting operation of the decoding shift registers, creates a zero or nonzero error pattern for the corresponding byte position, and delivers a corrected data byte. After $m + 1$ clock cycles, if none of the bytes received a correction (indicated by latch L_1 off) and S_1 and S_2 both are not 0 (indicated by latch L_1 on), then the decoder declares an uncorrected subblock error by turning on the UE signal. When UE signal is on, the uncorrected subblock is flagged and the original syndromes S_1, S_2, and S_3 are passed on to the block level for two-error correction.

Note that the corrected bytes in the decoder of Fig. 10.23 are delivered in a reverse order compared to that in the encoder. If desirable, this reversal can be eliminated by modifying the decoder as follows. Substitute $(m + 1) - \bar{x}$ for x in Eq. (10.160) and rewrite it as

$$E_{(m+1)-\bar{x}} = T^{\bar{x}}\,[T^{-(m+1)}S_1] = T^{2\bar{x}}\,[T^{-2(m+1)}S_2] \tag{10.161}$$

$$= T^{3\bar{x}}\,[T^{-3(m+1)}S_3]$$

In this equation, $\bar{x}$ represents the number of shifts, and $\bar{x} = 0, 1, 2, \ldots, m, m + 1$ corresponds to the byte-position values $x = m + 1, m, m - 1, \ldots, 1, 0$, thereby

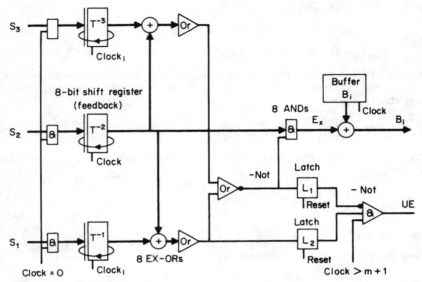

Figure 10.23   First-level decoder.

canceling the reversal of the byte order. To accomplish this, the decoder hardware in Fig. 10.23 must be modified in accordance with Eq. (10.161) as follows:

1. The shift-register multipliers T^{-1}, T^{-2}, and T^{-3} in Fig. 10.23 must be replaced by the multipliers T, T^2, and T^3, respectively.
2. The syndromes S_1, S_2, and S_3 must be premultiplied by $T^{-(m+1)}$, $T^{-2(m+1)}$, and $T^{-3(m+1)}$, respectively, before being entered into the respective shift registers. Note that when $m + 1 = 255$, this premultiplication is not required since $T^{255} = I$.

In general, the circuits for premultiplication by $T^{-(m+1)}$, $T^{-2(m+1)}$, and $T^{-3(m+1)}$ depend on the value of m, and each circuit requires a small number of EX-OR gates.

With these modifications, the decoder delivers the corrected bytes in the same order as they were processed by the encoder, starting with B_{m+1} and ending with B_0.

10.12.2   Decoding Process: Second Level

The syndrome of error at the block level is denoted by S_0 corresponding to the coding equation (10.152) and is given by:

$$S_0 = \hat{C}_0 \oplus \sum_{\text{subbk}} \left(\sum_i \hat{B}_i \right)_{\text{subbk}} \tag{10.162}$$

This syndrome is computed as modulo-2 sum of the (first-level-corrected) read bytes excluding the check bytes $\hat{C}_3$ for all subblocks and including the block-level check byte $\hat{C}_0$.

If each subblock in a block encounters, at the most, one byte in error, they will be all corrected by the first-level processing. In the absence of any uncorrected error, the second-level syndrome S_0 will be zero. However, if one of the subblocks encounters two bytes in error, then the first-level processing for that subblock will give an uncorrectable-error (UE) signal and pass on the syndromes S_1, S_2, and S_3 to the second level for further processing. Let y and z denote the locations and E_y and E_z denote the corresponding patterns for the uncorrected two errors. Then the second-level syndrome equation (10.162) for S_0 and the first-level syndrome equations (10.153), (10.154), and (10.155) for S_1, S_2, and S_3 will reduce to the following relations in terms of the error locations y and z and the patterns E_y and E_z for the two errors.

$$S_0 = E_y \oplus E_z \qquad (10.163)$$

$$S_1 = T^y E_y \oplus T^z E_z \qquad (10.164)$$

$$S_2 = T^{2y} E_y \oplus T^{2z} E_z \qquad (10.165)$$

$$S_3 = T^{3y} E_y \oplus T^{3z} E_2 \qquad (10.166)$$

Next, we proceed to decode the combined set of subblock and block-level syndromes for two-symbol errors. First we obtain the 8-digit vectors P, Q, and R, which are functions of the syndromes S_0, S_1, S_2, and S_3, as given by:

$$P = (S_2 \otimes S_2) \oplus (S_3 \otimes S_1) \qquad (10.167)$$

$$Q = (S_2 \otimes S_1) \oplus (S_3 \otimes S_0) \qquad (10.168)$$

$$R = (S_0 \otimes S_2) \oplus (S_1 \otimes S_1) \qquad (10.169)$$

where $\otimes$ denotes the product operation of the field elements in $GF(2^8)$, and the field elements are represented by binary 8-digit vectors.

We note here that P, Q, and R are necessarily nonzero when there are two bytes in error and both are in one of the subblocks. In contrast, when the check byte C_0 or C_3 is among the two erroneous bytes, this is indicated by $P = R = 0$. The decoder uses the computed values of P, Q, and R to solve the error locator equation

$$T^{-2i}P + T^{-i}Q + R = 0 \qquad (10.170)$$

in which the two unique solutions $i = x$ and $i = y$ represent the two error locations and the corresponding error value is given by

$$E_i = \frac{R}{T^{2i}S_0 \oplus S_i} \qquad (10.171)$$

The error-location values y and z can be obtained by means of three shift registers with matrix multipliers T^0, T^{-1}, T^{-2}. Initially, the shift register with the T^{-2} multiplier is loaded with vector P, that with the T^{-1} multiplier is loaded with vector Q, and that with the T^0 multiplier is loaded with R. After each shift, the sum of contents of the three shift registers is examined for all-zero value. For the two erroneous bytes, there will be exactly two shift count values, y and z, at which the sum of the contents of the three shift registers will equal zero value.

The hardware implementation of this two-symbol decoding function is shown in Fig. 10.24. The computation of P, Q, and R is accomplished through combinatorial logic circuits, each of which requires 140 two-input EX-OR gates and 128

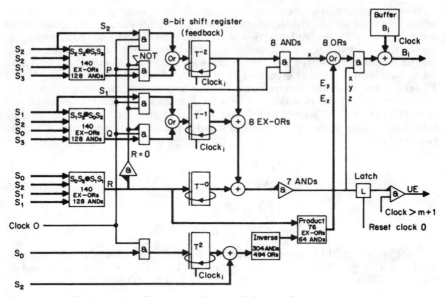

Figure 10.24 Syndrome decoding: one- and two-symbol correction.

AND gates. The computed values are entered into appropriate shift registers at clock zero (0).

Each clock cycle generates a shifting operation of the decoding shift registers, creates a zero or nonzero error pattern for the corresponding byte, and delivers a corrected data byte. Generation of the error pattern includes computation of the algebraic inverse of a field element, and the product of two elements. The hard-wired logic for the algebraic inverse requires 304 AND gates and 494 OR gates; and for the product of two elements, 76 EX-OR gates and 64 AND gates.

When the value of R is zero, the decoder identifies this as a special case and processes the syndromes S_2 and S_1 in place of P and Q, respectively; and corrects a one-symbol error in the subblock bytes. The case of $P = 0$ also corresponds to a one-symbol error in the subblock bytes; however, this does not require special processing. After $m + 1$ clock cycles, if none of the bytes received a correction (zero or nonzero pattern), then the decoder declares an uncorrected-error (UE) signal.

Here again, the corrected bytes in the decoder of Fig. 10.24 are delivered in a reverse order compared to that in the encoders. This reversal may be removed by modifying the decoder in the same manner as was done for the decoder of Fig. 10.23. We substitute $(m + 1) - j$ for i in the decoding equations (10.160) and (10.161), and rewrite them as

$$T^{2j} [T^{-2(m+1)}P] \oplus T^j [T^{-(m+1)}Q] \oplus R = 0 \tag{10.172}$$

$$E_{(m+1)-j} = R/(T^{-2j} [T^{2(m+1)} S_0] \oplus S_2) \tag{10.173}$$

In these equations, j represents the number of shifts, and $j = 0, 1, 2, \ldots, m, m + 1$ corresponds to the byte-position values $i = m + 1, m, m - 1, \ldots, 1, 0$; thereby canceling the reversal of the byte order. To accomplish this, the decoder hardware in Fig. 10.24 must be modified in accordance with the above equations (10.162) and (10.163) as follows:

1. The shift register multipliers T^{-2}, T^{-1}, and T^2 in Fig. 10.24 must be replaced by the multipliers T^2, T, and T^{-2}, respectively.
2. The variables P (or S_2), Q (or S_1), and S_0 must be premultiplied by $T^{-2(m+1)}$, $T^{-(m+1)}$, and $T^{2(m+1)}$, respectively, before being entered into the respective shift registers. Note that when $m + 1 = 255$, this premultiplication is not required since $T^{255} = I$. In general, the circuits for premultiplication by $T^{-2(m+1)}$, $T^{-(m+1)}$, and $T^{2(m+1)}$ depend on the value of m, and each circuit requires a small number of EX-OR gates.

With these modifications, the decoder delivers the corrected bytes in the same order as they were processed by the encoder, starting with B_{m+1} and ending with B_0.

10.12.3   Data Integrity Check

The two-level code in the IBM 3380J and 3380K disk files includes four additional check bytes at the second level (Fig. 10.22). These check bytes provide a strong data-integrity check over the corrected data stream. Each of these four check bytes are applied to both code words disregarding the two-way interleaving. They are denoted as CRC checks and are given by

$$\mathrm{CRC}_1 = \sum_i T^{-i} D_i \qquad (10.174)$$

$$\mathrm{CRC}_2 = \sum_i T^{-2i} Z_i \qquad (10.175)$$

$$\mathrm{CRC}_3 = \sum_i T^{-3i} D_i \qquad (10.176)$$

$$\mathrm{CRC}_4 = \sum_i T^{-4i} Z_i \qquad (10.177)$$

where matrix T^{-i}, and the sequences $\{D_i\}$ and $\{Z_i\}$ are defined as follows:

The *matrix* T is the companion matrix of the primitive polynomial $1 + x^3 + x^5 + x^7 + x^8$. Different powers of the same T are used to create all CRC as well as error-correction functions. It provides a computational convenience when second-level correction requires recomputation of the CRC check in software. In particular, the software will be able to use the same tables for computation of Galois field operations.

The *byte-sequence* $\{D_i\}$ consists of all bytes in a record excluding the second-level check bytes. The byte sequence $\{Z_i\}$ consists of the same except it also excludes two check bytes corresponding to the last two byte positions of each *normal-*

length subblock. The first-level check bytes in these sequences (and the corresponding error patterns) may be replaced by null bytes (all-zeros) in CRC calculations. This will eliminate the need for correcting errors in the check bytes.

The *sequence* $\{Z_i\}$ is offset from the sequence $\{D_i\}$ by two bytes at the end of each subblock. With 255 as the exponent for T^{-1} and T^{-2}, this offset arrangement provides an effective CRC cycle length of $255 \times 256 = 65280$ bytes in sequence $\{D_i\}$ and $255 \times 254 = 64770$ bytes in sequence $\{Z_i\}$. This means that two identical detectable error patterns will not cancel each other in both types of CRC checks in any record of up to 255 subblocks of data.

In the readback process, the CRC syndromes are generated on-the-fly along with the error-correction syndromes as the data are received using shift registers with premultipliers T^{-1}, T^{-2}, T^{-3}, and T^{-4}. Furthermore, CRC syndromes will be adjusted for the first-level error correction in hardware and later for the second-level error correction in software. The equations for the four CRC syndromes S_{-1}, S_{-2}, S_{-3}, and S_{-4} are:

$$S_{-1} = \hat{C}RC_1 \oplus \sum_i T^{-i}\hat{D}_i \oplus \sum_i T^{-i}E_1(D_i) \oplus \sum_i T^{-i}E_2(D_i) \quad (10.178)$$

$$S_{-2} = \hat{C}RC_2 \oplus \sum_i T^{-2i}\hat{Z}_i \oplus \sum_i T^{-2i}E_1(Z_i) \oplus \sum_i T^{-2i}E_1(Z_i) \quad (10.179)$$

$$S_{-3} = \hat{C}RC_3 \oplus \sum_i T^{-3i}\hat{D}_i \oplus \sum_i T^{-3i}E_1(D_i) \oplus \sum_i T^{-3i}E_2(D_i) \quad (10.180)$$

$$S_{-4} = \hat{C}RC_4 \oplus \sum_i T^{-4i}\hat{Z}_i \oplus \sum_i T^{-4i}E_1(Z_i) \oplus \sum_i T^{-4i}E_2(Z_i) \quad (10.181)$$

where the symbol ˆ indicates readback bytes, $E_1(D_i)$ and $E_1(Z_i)$ represent the first-level error-correction patterns and $E_2(D_i)$ and $E_2(Z_i)$ represent the second-level error-correction patterns corresponding to the recorded bytes D_i and Z_i, respectively. The error patterns corresponding to the check bytes will be replaced by null bytes.

The data sequence $\{D_i\}$ and the corresponding sequence of error-correction patterns $\{E_1(D_i)\}$ appear at the input and output of the first-level decoder, respectively, with exactly one subblock delay. If second-level error correction is required, then the error patterns $\{E_2(D_i)\}$ will be available later through software decoding at the second level.

If the first-level decoder includes a subblock buffer and on-the-fly error correction, then first-level CRC syndromes can be computed from the corrected data which is the combined sequence $\{D_i \oplus E_1(D_i)\}$. However, if the first-level error correction is deferred, then the first-level CRC syndromes may be computed by combining separate computations with $\{D_i\}$ and $\{E_1(D_i)\}$ sequences.

The second-level error correction, if any, will involve one of the subblocks and up to four error bytes. The byte count i in sequence $\{D_i\}$ for each of the four error bytes will be determined from the error-location numbers. Then the terms $T^{-3i}E_2(D_i)$ for each error can be computed using the antilog tables.

$$T^{-3i} E_2(D_i) = \log_\alpha^{-1} \{[\log_\alpha E_2(D_i) - 3i] \text{ modulo } 255\} \qquad (10.182)$$

This leads to the second-level CRC check corresponding to the syndromes S_{-1} and S_{-3}. The byte count i in sequence $\{Z_i\}$ for each of the four errors will also be determined and the computations for syndromes S_{-2} and S_{-4} will be done in a similar manner. These final values of CRC syndromes must be zero if no errors are present.

The four CRC bytes in two-level code provide error detection for protection against miscorrections of excessive errors. However, any errors in CRC bytes will tend to create unnecessary reread operations with undue performance penalty. In order to avoid this, one nonzero CRC check on $\{D_i\}$ sequence and one on $\{Z_i\}$ sequence may be ignored whenever errors are not corrected at the second level. All nonzero CRC checks may be ignored whenever errors are not corrected at either level. Alternatively, the CRC check bytes may be placed within the last subblock so that the two-level correction is also applicable to the CRC bytes.

APPENDIX   ON-THE-FLY DECODER FOR MULTIPLE BYTE ERRORS

10.A.1   Reed-Solomon Codes

The Reed-Solomon codes (Reed and Solomon, 1960) are a subclass of the general class of Bose-Chaudhuri codes (Bose and Ray-Chaudhuri, 1960) (BCH Codes) with symbols in GF(q). The generator polynomial of a BCH code is defined in terms of its roots in an extension field. These roots, in turn, provide specific error detection and correction capability of the code. In a Reed-Solomon code r check bytes provide correction of t error bytes and u erasure bytes, when $r \geq 2t + u$. (An erasure byte is an erroneous byte with known location.) The degree-r generator polynomial of this code is given by

$$G(x) = (x - \alpha^a)(x - \alpha^{a+1})(x - \alpha^{a+2}) \cdots (x - \alpha^{a+r-1}) \qquad (10.183)$$

where α is any element of GF(2^m) and a is any integer. The main characteristic of this $G(x)$ is that the roots, $\alpha^a, \alpha^{a+1}, \alpha^{a+2}, \ldots, \alpha^{a+r-1}$ are the r consecutive powers of an element of GF(2^m). A full-length code word will have n symbols, where n is the least integer for which $\alpha^n = \alpha^0$. The actual length may be shorter or variable from $r + 1$ up to n.

In order to formulate the decoding process, we examine the coding relations implied by the roots of the generator polynomial. By definition of cyclic codes, the generator polynomial $G(x)$ is one of the factors of the code word polynomial $W(x)$. Thus with an appropriate multiplier polynomial $Q(x)$, we can write

$$W(x) = Q(x)G(x) \qquad (10.184)$$

From Eq. (10.183), we see that

$$G(x) = 0 \qquad \text{at } x = \alpha^a, \alpha^{a+1}, \alpha^{a+2}, \cdots, \alpha^{a+r-1} \qquad (10.185)$$

Substituting this in Eq. (10.184), we have

$$W(x) = 0 \qquad \text{at } x = \alpha^a, \alpha^{a+1}, \alpha^{a+2}, \cdots, \alpha^{a+r-1} \qquad (10.186)$$

The code word polynomial $W(x)$ in terms of information bytes and check bytes can be written as

$$W(x) = B_0 + B_1 x + B_2 x^2 + \cdots + B_{n-1} x^{n-1} \qquad (10.187)$$

where $B_0, B_1, \ldots B_{r-1}$ represent the r check bytes, and $B_r, B_r + 1, \ldots \ldots, B_{n-1}$ represent the k data bytes. From Eqs. (10.186) and (10.187), we obtain the coding relations corresponding to the r roots of the generator polynomial by substituting $x = \alpha^a, \alpha^{a+1}, \alpha^{a+2}, \ldots, \alpha^{a+r-1}$.

$$\sum_{i=0}^{n-1} B_i (\alpha^{a+j})^i = 0 \qquad \text{for } j = 0, 1, 2, \ldots, r-1 \qquad (10.188)$$

The common factor α^a in all the roots of the generator polynomial can be viewed as a scale-up factor in all equations. The r coding relations, with a equal to zero, can be written as

$$\sum_{i=0}^{n-1} \alpha^{ji} B_i = 0 \qquad \text{for } j = 0, 1, 2, \ldots, (r-1) \qquad (10.189)$$

where $B_0, B_1, B_2, \ldots, B_{n-1}$ are the n symbols of the code word.

In the readback process, the corresponding syndromes S_j can be computed from the received code word as

$$S_j = \sum_{i=0}^{n-1} \alpha^{ji} \hat{B}_i \qquad \text{for } j = 0, 1, 2, \ldots, r-1 \qquad (10.190)$$

where $\hat{B}_i$ represents the received symbol corresponding to B_i.

Let v denote the actual number of symbols in error in a given code word. The error values are $E_i = (\hat{B}_i - B_i)$, where i represents an error-location value from a set of different error locations given by $\{I\} = \{i_1, i_2, \ldots, iv\}$. The relationship between the syndromes and the errors are then given by

$$S_j = \sum_{i \in \{I\}} \alpha^{ji} E_i \qquad \text{for } j = 0, 1, 2, \ldots, r-1 \qquad (10.191)$$

Any nonzero value of a syndrome indicates the presence of errors. The decoder processes these syndromes to determine the locations and values of the errors. A set of $2t$ consecutive syndromes is sufficient to determine the locations of t errors. If the locations were known, then a set of only t consecutive syndromes is sufficient to determine the values of t erasures (errors with known locations).

10.A.2 On-the-Fly Decoder

Since the original works of Reed and Solomon (1960), and Bose and Chaudhuri (1960), the decoding problem has been studied by many. Peterson (1960) and Gorenstein and Zierler (1961) provided the basic key to the solution of the decoding problem through the concept of the error-locator polynomial. The coefficients of the error-locator polynomial are computed by solving a set of linear equations.

Berlekamp (1965) and Massey (1965) provided an iterative method for computing the coefficients of the error-locator polynomial. The roots of the error-locator polynomial represent the locations of the symbol in error. Chien (1964) suggested a simple mechanized method for searching these roots, using a cyclic trial-and-error procedure. Forney (1965) provided simplifications in computations of the error values in the case of the codes with nonbinary symbols. The iterative method of Berlekamp and Massey provided yet another way of computing the error values.

Here we present decoder equations and architecture in which the location and value of each error are computed in a cyclic order without explicit information regarding the locations of other errors which are yet to be determined. This method expands the *Chien search* function (which normally finds only the error locations in a cyclic manner) into a complete mechanization of the error-correcting procedure. As a result, we can begin delivery of the decoded data symbols, one at a time, in synchrony with each cycle of the Chien search. Thus, access time is not impacted by the time required for the computation of the locations and values of *all* errors.

In this method, the hardware is highly simplified. In particular, the result of the Chien search need not be stored, and one set of hardware computes the locations and values of all errors and corrects them at the appropriate cycle *during* the Chien search. The method includes other specific improvements in the design and implementation of the on-the-fly decoder, as listed below:

1. All division operations are eliminated from the computations of the error-locator equation.

2. Lemmas 1, 2, and 3 provide a convenient closed-form expression for error values. This new expression requires a smaller total number of operations and only one division operation in on-the-fly computation of the error values.

3. The special cases of fewer errors are processed through a single set of hardware as a routine procedure.

4. The decoding equations, as well as the decoder design, possess a nested form of architecture which allows processing of fewer syndromes for fewer errors. Thus, the same hardware (LSI chip or chips) can be used in various applications with varying reductions in redundancy.

These improvements, with the new on-the-fly error-correction architecture, make the decoder implementation highly structured and well suited for LSI chip design with pipelined data flow.

10.A.3   Equation for Error Locations

Consider the polynomial with roots at α^i, where $i \in \{I\}$. This is called the error-locator polynomial, and is defined as

$$\prod_{i \in \{I\}} (1 - a^{-i}x) = \sum_{m=0}^{r} \sigma_m x_m = \sum_{m=0}^{t} \sigma_m x^m \qquad (10.192)$$

In the case of erasures, the coefficient α^{-i} in each factor of the locator polynomial is known. Thus, the coefficients σ_m can easily be computed. In the case of errors, the coefficients σ_m can be determined from the syndromes. For a given received word, the decoder will proceed to determine σ_m as if there were t roots in the locator polynomial. If the actual number of errors v is less than t, this will result in σ_m being zero for all $m > v$.

Substituting $x = \alpha^i$ in Eq. (10.192), we get

$$\sum_{m=0}^{t} \sigma_m \alpha^{mi} = 0 \qquad \text{for } i \in \{I\} \tag{10.193}$$

Using Eqs. (10.191) and (10.193), it is easy to verify that the syndromes S_j and the coefficients σ_m of the error-locator polynomial satisfy the following set of relationships:

$$\sum_{m=0}^{t} \sigma_m S_{m+k} = 0 \qquad \text{for } k = 0, 1, \ldots, (t-1) \tag{10.194}$$

The set of equations (10.194) can be rewritten in matrix notation as

$$\begin{bmatrix} S_0 & S_1 & \cdots & S_t \\ S_1 & S_2 & \cdots & S_{t+1} \\ \cdot & \cdot & \cdots & \cdot \\ \cdot & \cdot & \cdots & \cdot \\ \cdot & \cdot & \cdots & \cdot \\ S_{t-1} & S_t & \cdots & S_{2t-1} \end{bmatrix} \begin{bmatrix} \sigma_0 \\ \sigma_1 \\ \cdot \\ \cdot \\ \cdot \\ \sigma_{t-1} \\ \sigma_1 \end{bmatrix} = 0 \tag{10.195}$$

Let M denote the t-by-$(t+1)$ syndrome matrix on the left side of Eq. (10.195). Let M_t denote the square matrix obtained by eliminating the last column in matrix M. If M_t is nonsingular, then the above set of equations can be solved, using Cramer's rule, to obtain

$$\frac{\sigma_m}{\sigma_t} = \frac{\Delta_{tm}}{\Delta_{tt}} \qquad \text{for } m = 0, 1, \ldots, t-1 \tag{10.196}$$

where Δ_{tt} is the nonzero determinant of matrix M_t, and Δ_{tm} denotes the determinant of the matrix obtained by replacing the mth column in the matrix M_t with the negative of the last column of the matrix M for each $m = 0, 1, \ldots, t-1$.

If matrix M_t is singular, that is, Δ_{tt} is zero, then the set of equations (10.184) is a dependent set. It can be shown that in the case of fewer than t errors, $\Delta_{tt} = \Delta_{tm} = 0$ for all m. Conversely, simultaneous occurrence of $\Delta_{tt} = 0$ and $\Delta_{tm} \neq 0$ indicates more than t errors. Thus when Δ_{tt} is zero, we assume fewer than t errors (and check for $\Delta_{tm} = 0$ for all m). In that case, σ_t is zero. We can delete σ_t and the last row and the last column of the syndrome matrix in Eq. (10.195). The resulting matrix equation corresponds to that for $t-1$ errors. This process is repeated, if necessary, so that the final matrix equation corresponds to that for v errors and M_v is nonsingular. Then we need the set of determinants Δ_{vm}, where $m = 0, 1, \ldots, v$.

It can easily be seen that Δ_{vm} for $v = t - 1$ is a cofactor of Δ_{tt} corresponding to column $m - 1$ and row t in matrix M_t. We can express Δ_{tt} in terms of these cofactors:

$$\Delta_{tt} = \sum_{m=0}^{t-1} S_{t-1+m} \Delta_{(t-1)m} \tag{10.197}$$

Thus, the values Δ_{vm} for $v = t - 1$ need not require separate computations. They are available as byproducts of the computation for Δ_{tt}. In fact, Δ_{vm} for subsequent smaller values of v are all available as byproducts of the computation for Δ_{tt} through the hierarchical relationships of lower-order cofactors.

Thus, in the case of fewer errors, the decoder finds $\Delta_{tt} = 0$ and automatically backtracks through prior computations to the correct value of v, and uses the previously computed cofactors Δ_{vm}. This is illustrated later through hardware implementation of the case $t = 3$.

To accommodate the special cases of all fewer errors, we replace Eq. (10.196) by a more convenient general form.

$$\frac{\sigma_m}{\sigma_v} = \frac{\Delta_m}{\Delta_v} \qquad \text{for } m = 0, 1, 2, \ldots, t \qquad (10.198)$$

where v is determined from the fact that $\Delta_{mm} = 0$ for all $m > v$ and $\Delta_{mm} \neq 0$ for $m = v$. Then Δ_m is defined with the new notation as

$$\Delta_m = \begin{cases} \Delta_{mm} & \text{for } m > v \\ \Delta_{vm} & \text{for } m \le v \end{cases} \qquad (10.199)$$

Since $\sigma_0 = 1$ we can determine σ_m for all values of m, using Eq. (10.198). However, we will see that the coefficients σ_m are not needed in the entire decoding process. To this end, we obtain a modified error-locator equation from Eqs. (10.193) and (10.198) as given by:

$$\sum_{m=0}^{t} \Delta_m \alpha^{mi} = 0 \qquad \text{for } i \in \{I\} \qquad (10.200)$$

The error-location values $i \in \{I\}$ are the set of v unique values of i which satisfy Eq. (10.200).

10.A.4 Expression for Error Values

The error-locator polynomial, as defined by Eq. (10.193), has v roots corresponding to v error-location values. Now consider a polynomial which has all roots of the error-locator polynomial except one corresponding to the location value $i = j$. This polynomial is defined as

$$\prod_{\substack{i \in (I) \\ i \neq j}} (1 - \alpha^{-1}x) = \sum_{m=0}^{v-1} \sigma_{j,m}x^m = \sum_{m=0}^{t-1} \sigma_{j,m}x^m \qquad (10.201)$$

When the actual number of error locations v is less than t, the coefficients σ_j, m are zero for $m = v, \ldots, t - 1$. This is done to allow processing of any value of v through the same set of hardware.

Substituting $x = \alpha^i$ in Eq. (10.191), we get

$$\sum_{m=0}^{t-1} \sigma_{j,m}\alpha^{mi} = 0 \qquad \text{for } i \in \{I\}, \, i \neq j \qquad (10.202)$$

Now, taking a hint from Eq. (10.184), we examine a similar expression involving the syndromes and the coefficients σ_j, m of the new polynomial. Using Eq. (10.181), we substitute for the syndrome S_m and get

$$\sum_{m=0}^{t-1} \sigma_{j,m} S_m = \sum_{m=0}^{t-1} \sigma_{j,m} \sum_{i \in (I)} \alpha^{mi} E_i \qquad (10.203)$$

Interchanging the order of summing parameters m and i in Eq. (10.193) we get

$$\sum_{m=0}^{t-1} \sigma_{j,m} S_m = \sum_{i \in \{I\}} E_i \sum_{m=0}^{t-1} \sigma_{j,m} \alpha^{mi} \qquad (10.204)$$

Now, using Eqs. (10.192) and (10.194), we obtain

$$\sum_{m=0}^{t-1} \sigma_{j,m} S_m = E_j \sum_{m=0}^{t-1} \sigma_{j,m} \alpha^{mj} \qquad (10.205)$$

Thus, we have an expression for the error values

$$E_j = \frac{\displaystyle\sum_{m=0}^{t-1} \sigma_{j,m} S_m}{\displaystyle\sum_{m=0}^{t-1} \sigma_{j,m} \alpha^{mj}} \qquad (10.206)$$

This expression for error values is well known. Notice that with a known error-locator polynomial and the error-location value j, explicit values of other error locations are not required in computing the coefficients σ_j, m. Thus, we can eliminate σ_j, m and reduce expression (10.206) further to obtain a more convenient form for on-the-fly processing. To this end, we prove Lemmas 1, 2, and 3 which follow.

In Lemma 1, we obtain a relation which expresses the coefficients σ_j, m in terms of the known coefficients σ_k of the error-locator polynomial.

Lemma 1

$$\sum_{k=0}^{m} \sigma_k \alpha^{kj} = \sigma_{j,m} \alpha^{mj} \qquad \text{for } 0 \le m < t \qquad (10.207)$$

Proof:
From the definition of polynomials in Eqs. (10.192) and (10.201) we have

$$\sum_{m=0}^{t} \sigma_m x^m = (1 - \alpha^{-j} x) \sum_{m=0}^{t-1} \sigma_{j,m} x^m \qquad (10.208)$$

Comparing the coefficients of each term in the polynomials on the two sides of Eq. (10.208), we obtain

$$\sigma_m = \begin{cases} \sigma_{j,m} - \sigma_{j,m-1} \alpha^{-j} & \text{for } 0 < m < t \\ \sigma_{j,m} & \text{for } m = 0 \end{cases} \qquad (10.209)$$

Using Eq. (10.209), we can substitute for σ_k, where $k \le m < t$, and obtain

$$\sum_{k=0}^{m} \sigma_k \alpha^{kj} = \sigma_{j,0} + \sum_{k=1}^{m} (\sigma_{j,k}\alpha^{kj} - \sigma_{j,k-1}\alpha^{(k-1)j}) \tag{10.210}$$

On eliminating the canceling terms from Eq. (10.210), we get

$$\sum_{k=0}^{m} \sigma_k \alpha^{kj} = \sigma_{j,m}\alpha^{mj} \qquad \text{for } 0 \le m < t \tag{10.211}$$

This completes the proof of Lemma 1.

Next, we rewrite the denominator of the expression in Eq. (10.206), using the result of Lemma 1.

Lemma 2

$$\sum_{m=0}^{t-1} \sigma_{j,m}\alpha^{mj} = \sum_{k=0}^{t} - k\sigma_k\alpha^{kj} \tag{10.212}$$

Proof: Using Lemma 1, we first obtain

$$\sum_{m=0}^{t-1} \sigma_{j,m}\alpha^{mj} = \sum_{m=0}^{t-1} \sum_{k=0}^{m} \sigma_k\alpha^{kj} \tag{10.213}$$

Collecting all terms with the same values of k in Eq. (10.213), we then get

$$\sum_{m=0}^{t-1} \sigma_{j,m}\alpha^{mj} = \sum_{k=0}^{t-1} (t-k)\sigma_k\alpha^{kj} \tag{10.214}$$

Using Eq. (10.183), we can rewrite Eq. (10.214) as

$$\sum_{m=0}^{t-1} \sigma_{j,m}\alpha^{mj} = -t\sigma_t\alpha^{tj} + \sum_{k=0}^{t-1} -k\sigma_k\alpha^{kj} \tag{10.215}$$

which is the same as Eq. (10.212). This completes the proof of Lemma 2.

Now, we again use the result of Lemma 1, and obtain a more convenient expression for the numerator in Eq. (10.206) in the following lemma.

Lemma 3

$$\sum_{m=0}^{t-1} \sigma_{j,m}S_m = \sum_{m=0}^{t-1} \xi_m\alpha^{-mj} \tag{10.216}$$

where

$$\xi_m = \sum_{i=0}^{t-1-m} \sigma_i S_{m+i} \tag{10.217}$$

Proof: Using Lemma 1, we can express $\sigma_{j,m}$ in terms of σ_k, obtaining

$$\sum_{m=0}^{t-1} \sigma_{j,m}S_m = \sum_{m=0}^{t-1} S_m\alpha^{-mj} \sum_{k=0}^{m} \sigma_k\alpha^{kj} \tag{10.218}$$

Substituting $m - h$ for k on the right-hand side of Eq. (10.218), we get

$$\sum_{m=0}^{t-1} \sigma_{j,m} S_m = \sum_{m=0}^{t-1} S_m \sum_{h=0}^{m} \sigma_{m-h} \alpha^{-hj} \tag{10.219}$$

Now, interchanging the order of summing parameters m and h in Eq. (10.219) gives

$$\sum_{m=0}^{t-1} \sigma_{j,m} S_m = \sum_{h=0}^{t-1} \alpha^{-hj} \sum_{m=h}^{t-1} \sigma_{m-h} S_m \tag{10.220}$$

Substituting $k + h$ for m in Eq. (10.220), we have

$$\sum_{m=0}^{t-1} \sigma_{j,m} S_m = \sum_{h=0}^{t-1} \alpha^{-hj} \sum_{k}^{t-1-h} \sigma_k S_{k+h} \tag{10.221}$$

This completes the proof of Lemma 3.

The computation of ξ_m for $m = 0$ to $t - 1$ in Eq. (10.217) of Lemma 3 requires $t(t + 1)/2$ multiplications of the type $\sigma_i S_{m+1}$. The number of multiplications can be reduced in the case of ξ_m for $m < (t - 1)/2$ by using Eq. (10.194) which yields the following alternate expression:

$$\xi_m = \sum_{i=t-m}^{t} -\sigma_i S_{m+i} \tag{10.222}$$

Equation (10.217) requires the syndromes $S_0, S_1, \ldots, S_t-1$, and Eq. (10.222) requires the syndromes $S_t, S_{t+1}, \ldots, S_{2t-1}$. When we use Eq. (10.217) for $m \geq (t - 1)/2$ and Eq. (10.222) for $m < (t - 1)/2$, the number of multiplications required is the minimum and is equal to the integer closest to $(t + 1)^2/4$.

Note that Eq. (10.217) does not satisfy the requirement that the same hardware process the case of fewer errors with fewer syndromes, since the high-order terms do not vanish automatically. Furthermore, Eq. (10.222) cannot be used if the decoder is designed for t erasures where the syndromes $S_t, S_{t+1}, \ldots, S_{2t-1}$ may not be available. The following corollary of Lemma 3 provides an alternate equivalent expression which removes the difficulty mentioned above.

Corollary

$$\sum_{m=0}^{t-1} \sigma_{j,m} S_m = \alpha^{-\mu j} \sum_{m=0}^{t-1} \beta_m \alpha^{mj} \tag{10.223}$$

where $0 \leq \mu < t$ and the coefficients β_m are given by

$$\beta_m = \begin{cases} \displaystyle\sum_{k=0}^{m} \sigma_k S_{k-m+\mu} & \text{for } m \leq \mu \\[4mm] \displaystyle\sum_{k=m+1}^{t} -\sigma_k S_{k-m+\mu} & \text{for } m > \mu \end{cases} \tag{10.224}$$

Proof: Using the result for Eq. (10.193), we can rewrite the terms with $m > \mu$ in the right-hand side of Eq. (10.208) as follows:

$$\sum_{m=0}^{t-1} \sigma_{j,m} S_m = \sum_{m=0}^{\mu} S_m \alpha^{-mj} \sum_{k=0}^{m} \sigma_k \alpha^{kj} + \sum_{m=\mu+1}^{t-1} S_m \alpha^{-mj} \sum_{k=m+1}^{t} -\sigma_k \alpha^{kj} \tag{10.225}$$

The proof of the corollary, then, follows steps similar to those in Eqs. (10.219) to (10.211) of Lemma 3. First, substitute $m - h$ for k, and rewrite the right-hand side of Eq. (10.22) with m and h as summing parameters. Then, interchange the order of summing parameters m and h. Next, substitute $k + h$ for m, and rewrite the right-hand side with h and k as summing parameters. Finally, substitute $\mu - m$ for h. This completes the proof of the corollary.

The important feature of the expression in the corollary is that the high-order terms vanish automatically in the case of fewer errors, and the resultant computation involves a reduced set of syndromes S_0 $S_1, \ldots, S_{v-1}$, where v is the actual number of errors or erasures, and $\mu < v \leq t$.

The number of multiplications in computing β_m of Eq. (10.224) depends on the choice of μ. The minimum number of multiplications is, again, the integer closest to $(t + 1)^2/4$ when $\mu = \mu$, where μ is the largest integer under $(t - 1)/2$.

The same hardware can also be used in applications with a smaller set of available syndromes $S_0, S_1, \ldots, S_{\tau-1}$ and up to τ errors or erasures, provided that $\mu < \tau \leq t$. From this point of view, a lower value of μ is desirable. The choice of $\mu = 0$ offers the maximum flexibility in terms of the applicability of the same hardware for processing fewer errors with fewer syndromes. The number of multiplications required in computing β_m in Eq. (10.224) with $\mu = 0$ is $(t^2 - t + 2)/2$, which is not the lowest value possible, but it is still lower than the maximum value required in Lemma 3.

In view of the above observations, we will use the expression in the corollary of Lemma 3 for decoder implementation. For large values of t, it is advisable to use $\mu = \mu$ for greatest economy in hardware. In the case of small values of t, $\mu = 0$ provides greater flexibility in adapting other smaller values of t later without modifying the already fabricated hardware.

Now, we can rewrite Eq. (10.206), using the results of Lemma 2 and the corollary of Lemma 3. As a result, any error value E_i can be expressed as

$$E_i = \alpha^{-\mu i} \frac{\sum\limits_{m=0}^{t-1} \beta_m \alpha^{mi}}{\sum\limits_{m=0}^{t} - m\sigma_m \alpha^{mi}} \tag{10.226}$$

where

$$\beta_m = \begin{cases} \sum\limits_{k=0}^{m} \sigma_k S_{k-m+\mu} & \text{for } m \leq \mu \\ \sum\limits_{k=m+1}^{t} -\sigma_k S_{k-m+\mu} & \text{for } m > \mu \end{cases} \tag{10.227}$$

In view of Eq. (10.198), the coefficients σ_m can be eliminated to obtain error values in terms of Δ_m, as follows.

$$E_i = \alpha^{\mu i} \frac{\sum\limits_{m=0}^{t-1} \phi_m \alpha^{mi}}{\sum\limits_{m=0}^{t} -m\Delta \alpha^{mi}} \tag{10.228}$$

where

$$\phi_m = \begin{cases} \sum\limits_{k=0}^{m} \Delta_k S_{k-m+\mu} & \text{for } m \leq \mu \\ \sum\limits_{k=m+1}^{t} -\Delta_k S_{k-m+\mu} & \text{for } m > \mu \end{cases} \tag{10.229}$$

In the case of the binary base field, the denominator of Eq. (10.228) further simplifies since the terms with even values of $m(m = 0 \mod 2)$ vanish. The resultant expression for E_i for the binary base field is

$$E_i = \alpha^{-\mu i} \frac{\sum_{m=0}^{t-1} \phi_m \alpha^{mi}}{\sum_{m=0}^{t} \Delta_m \alpha^{mi}} \tag{10.230}$$

where
$$\phi_m = \begin{cases} \sum_{k=0}^{m} \Delta_k S_{k-m+\mu} & \text{for } m \le \mu \\ \sum_{k=m+1}^{t} -\Delta_k S_{k-m+\mu} & \text{for } m > \mu \end{cases} \tag{10.231}$$

Note that the computation for the denominator in Eq. (10.230) is already available as the sum of all odd (or even) terms in the computations of Eq. (10.200). For each value of i, the numerator can be computed and multiplied by the inverse of the denominator in synchrony with the search for error locations. The resultant E_i is used for correcting the outgoing ith symbol $\hat{B}_i$ whenever the error-locator equation (10.200) is satisfied.

10.A.5 Decoder Implementation

Figure 10.25 is a block diagram of the on-the-fly decoder. The decoding process is continuous in an uninterrupted stream of data arriving in the form of a chain of n-symbol code words. The decoder computes syndromes for the incoming code word as it decodes and corrects errors in the (previously received) outgoing code word.

Each clock cycle corresponds to an input of one data symbol of the incoming code word concurrent with an output of one corrected data symbol of the outgoing code word. A buffer holds at least n symbols of the uncorrected data between the incoming and outgoing symbols.

We use the three-error-correcting Reed-Solomon code in GF(2^8) as an example of special interest for application in computer products. Six check symbols correspond to the six roots α^0, α^1, α^2, α^3, α^4, α^5 of the generator polynomial. The corresponding syndromes are denoted by S_0, S_1, S_3, S_4, and S_5, respectively. These syndromes are computed from the received word in the conventional manner in accordance with Eq. (10.190). The implementation for this step is well known, using EX-OR circuits and shift registers. Here, we present the hardware implementation for the remaining

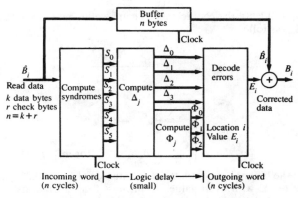

Figure 10.25 Decoder block diagram.

steps of the decoding procedure, using the equations developed in the previous sections.

1. *Computation of coefficients.* For the three-error case, the matrix in Eq. (10.195) for the coefficients σ_m of the error-locator polynomial can be written as:

$$\begin{bmatrix} S_0 & S_1 & S_2 \\ S_1 & S_2 & S_3 \\ S_2 & S_3 & S_4 \end{bmatrix} \begin{bmatrix} \sigma_0 \\ \alpha_1 \\ \sigma_2 \end{bmatrix} = \sigma_3 \begin{bmatrix} S_3 \\ S_4 \\ S_5 \end{bmatrix} \qquad (10.232)$$

The corresponding determinants Δ_{33}, Δ_{32}, Δ_{31}, Δ_{30} of Eq. (10.196) are given by the following expressions, where $\oplus$ denotes the modulo-2 vector sum of 8-bit bytes:

$$\Delta_{33} = S_2(S_1S_3 \oplus S_2S_2) \oplus S_3(S_0S_3 \oplus S_1S_2) \oplus S_4(S_1S_1 \oplus S_2S_0) \quad (10.233)$$

$$\Delta_{32} = S_3(S_1S_3 \oplus S_2S_2) \oplus S_4(S_0S_3 \oplus S_1S_2) \oplus S_5(S_1S_1 \oplus S_2S_0) \quad (10.234)$$

$$\Delta_{31} = S_0(S_4S_4 \oplus S_3S_5) \oplus S_1(S_3S_4 \oplus S_2S_5) \oplus S_2(S_3S_3 \oplus S_2S_4) \quad (10.235)$$

$$\Delta_{30} = S_1(S_4S_4 \oplus S_3S_5) \oplus S_2(S_3S_4 \oplus S_2S_5) \oplus S_3(S_3S_3 \oplus S_2S_4) \quad (10.236)$$

These four expressions can be implemented through combinational logic circuits as shown in Fig. 10.26. These circuits require 24 product operations and 14 sum operations in $GF(2^8)$. A typical product operation in $GF(2^8)$ requires, at the most, 73 EX-OR gates and 64 AND gates. A sum operation in $GF(2^8)$ is a modulo-2 vector sum which requires 8 EX-OR gates. The hardware of Fig. 10.26 can be further reduced, if desired, by time-sharing some of the repetitive functions.

The determinants Δ_{22}, Δ_{21}, and Δ_{20} for the two-error case are cofactors in the expression (10.223) for Δ_{33}, as was expressed in Eq. (10.197) for the general case of t errors. These cofactors are:

$$\Delta_{22} = S_1S_1 \oplus S_2S_0 \qquad (10.237)$$

$$\Delta_{21} = S_0S_3 \oplus S_1S_2 \qquad (10.238)$$

$$\Delta_{20} = S_1S_3 \oplus S_2S_2 \qquad (10.239)$$

In Fig. 10.26, the computations for Δ_{22}, Δ_{21}, and Δ_{20} are shown as the interim in the expression (10.227) for Δ_{22}, which are readily available syndromes:

$$\Delta_{11} = S_0 \qquad (10.240)$$

$$\Delta_{10} = S_1 \qquad (10.241)$$

Figure 10.27 shows the hardware implementation of Eq. (10.199), where the decoder identifies the correct number v of errors, and selects appropriate values for Δ_m. When Δ_{33} is nonzero, the parameters Δ_3, Δ_2, Δ_1, and Δ_0 take the values Δ_{33}, Δ_{32}, Δ_{31}, and Δ_{30}, respectively. When Δ_{33} is zero, then Δ_2, Δ_1, and Δ_0 take the values Δ_{22}, Δ_{21}, and Δ_{20}, respectively, which corresponds to the syndrome equations for two symbol errors. Similarly, if Δ_{22} is also zero, then Δ_1 and Δ_0 take the values Δ_{11} and Δ_{10}, respectively, which correspond to the syndrome equations for one symbol error. Thus, Fig. 10.27 produces the appropriate values of the coefficients Δ_3 Δ_2, Δ_1, Δ_0 for the error-locator equation (10.200), rewritten for the case of $t = 3$ as

$$\Delta_3\alpha^{3i} \oplus \Delta_2\alpha^{2i} \oplus \Delta_1\alpha^i \oplus \Delta_0 = 0 \qquad \text{for } i \in \{I\} \qquad (10.242)$$

Figure 10.28 provides a check for consistency of the coefficients in the case of fewer than three errors. In particular, when $\Delta_{33} = 0$, we must have $\Delta_{32} = \Delta_{31} = \Delta_{30} = 0$. Also, when $\Delta_{33} = \Delta_{22} = 0$, we must have $\Delta_{21} = \Delta_{20} = 0$, and when $\Delta_{33} = \Delta_{22} = \Delta_{11} = 0$, we must have $\Delta_{10} = 0$. Violation of any of these conditions implies the presence of

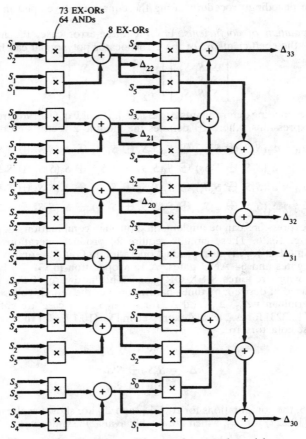

Figure 10.26 Coefficients of the error-locator polynomial.

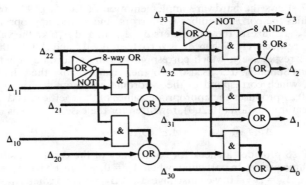

Figure 10.27 Selection of coefficients for correct numbers of errors.

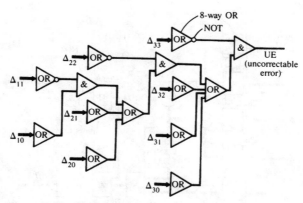

Figure 10.28 Check for consistency of coefficients.

more than three errors, resulting in an uncorrectable-error (UE) signal at the output of the circuit in Fig. 10.28. With some additional hardware (not shown in Fig. 10.28), we can obtain v as a two-digit binary number $a_1 a_0$. This number is the largest value of m for which $\Delta_{mm} \neq 0$ ($1 \leq m \leq 3$), and is given by the following logic functions:

$$a_1 = (\Delta_{33} \neq 0) \text{ OR } (\Delta_{22} \neq 0) \tag{10.243}$$

$$a_0 = (\Delta_{33} \neq 0) \text{ OR } [(\Delta_{22} \neq 0) \text{ AND } (\Delta_{11} \neq 0)] \tag{10.244}$$

This value of v will be used by the decoder in Figs. 10.30 and 10.31, shown later.

Next, we show the hardware implementation for obtaining the values of coefficients ϕ_m in the numerator of the error-value equation (10.230). For the case of three errors, Eq. (10.231) with $\mu = 0$ can be rewritten for ϕ_0, ϕ_1, and ϕ_2 as follows:

$$\phi_0 = \Delta_0 S_0 \tag{10.245}$$

$$\phi_1 = \Delta_2 S_1 \oplus \Delta_3 S_2 \tag{10.246}$$

$$\phi_2 = \Delta_3 S_1 \tag{10.247}$$

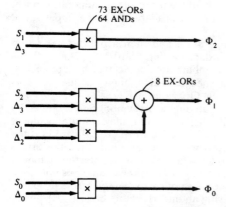

Figure 10.29 Coefficients for the error-value expression.

Figure 10.29 shows the implementation of Eqs. (10.245), (10.246), and (10.247), which requires four product operations and one sum operation in GF(2^8). The error-value equation (10.230), for the case of three errors, can be rewritten as

$$E_i = \frac{\phi_2 \alpha^{2i} \oplus \phi_1 \alpha^i \oplus \phi_0}{\Delta_3 \alpha^{3i} \oplus \Delta_1 \alpha^i} \tag{10.248}$$

2. *On-the-fly correction.* Figure 10.30 shows the mechanized shift-register circuits for determining error locations and error values in accordance with Eqs. (10.242) and (10.248), respectively. The computed values of the coefficients Δ_3, Δ_2, Δ_1, Δ_0 and ϕ_2, ϕ_1, ϕ_0 are entered into appropriate shift registers at clock zero.

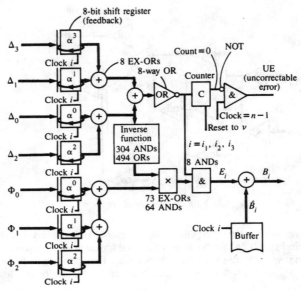

Figure 10.30 Cyclic decoder circuit.

Each clock cycle generates a shifting operation of these registers. A shifting operation multiplies the contents of each register by a specific constant, namely α^3 α^2, and α in the case of the registers for Δ_3, Δ_2, and Δ_1, respectively; and α^2 and α in the case of the registers for ϕ_2 and ϕ_1, respectively. Multiplication by a constant requires a small number of EX-OR gates.

At the ith clock cycle $(0 \le i < n)$, the upper set of summing circuits in Fig. 10.30 at the output of the shift registers are presented with all the terms of Eq. (10.242). If the sum is zero, then Eq. (10.242) is satisfied and we have captured the error location. Similarly, at the ith clock cycle, the lower set of summing circuits at the output of the shift registers are presented with all the terms of the numerator in Eq. (10.248). The denominator for (10.248) is already available from the upper set of summing circuits.

Subsequent networks for an inverse operation and then a product operation compute the error value E_i for each i in accordance with Eq. (10.248). The algebraic inverse in GF(2^8) can be obtained through combinational logic, which maps each 8-digit binary sequence into its inverse—a specific 8-digit binary sequence. This requires, at the most, 304 AND gates and 494 OR gates.

When the error location is captured, the outgoing word symbol $\hat{B}_i$ is modified by E_i through the output sum network. For all other values of i, the computed value of E_i is ignored. When all bytes B_0 through $_{n-1}$ of the code word are delivered (at the final clock cycle $n - 1$), if v error locations were not captured, then the errors exceed the correction capability of the decoder. This condition is detected by means of a counter which counts down from a preset value of v. If the count does not reach zero at the final clock cycle, then the decoder has not corrected the errors properly. The decoder indicates this condition by giving an uncorrectable-error (UE) signal.

3. *Delivery order of corrected bytes.* The corrected bytes in the decoder of Fig.

10.30 are delivered in the order $B_0, B_1, B_2, \ldots, B_{n-1}$. This is the reverse order compared to that in the encoding operation since the check bytes correspond to the low-order positions. The reversal can easily be removed by introducing a reversal relationship between clock cycle count j and byte location number i. We substitute $n - j$ for i in the decoding equations (10.242) and (10.248), and rewrite them as

$$(\Delta_3 \alpha^{3n})\alpha^{-3j} \oplus (\Delta_2 \alpha^{2n})\alpha^{-2j} \oplus (\Delta_1 \alpha^n)\alpha^{-j} \oplus \Delta_0 = 0 \qquad (10.249)$$

$$E_{(n-j)} = \frac{(\phi_2 \alpha^{2n})\alpha^{-2j} \oplus (\phi_1 \alpha^n)\alpha^{-j} \oplus \phi_0}{(\Delta_3 \alpha^{3n})\alpha^{-3j} \oplus (\Delta_1 \alpha^n)\alpha^{-j}} \qquad (10.250)$$

In these equations, j represents the clock cycle count where $j = 1$ to n, successively, correspond to the byte-position values $i = n - 1$ to 0. This provides delivery of bytes in the order $B_n - 1, \ldots, B_1, B_0$, which is the same order as that in the encoding process.

To accomplish the above-mentioned modifications, the following changes will be made in the decoder hardware of Fig. 10.30: (1) The shift-register multipliers α^3, α^2, and α are replaced by α^{-3}, α^{-2}, and α^{-1}, respectively; (2) The coefficients Δ_3, Δ_2, and Δ_1 are premultiplied by α^{3n}, α^{2n}, and α^n, respectively, and the coefficients ϕ_2 and ϕ_1 are premultiplied by α^{2n} and α^n, respectively.

In the case of shortened code, the premultiplication circuits depend on the value of n, and each circuit requires a small number of EX-OR gates. In the case of full-length code, α^{mn} is unity for all values of m, hence these premultiplication circuits are not needed. The decoder, with the above two modifications, appears in Fig. 10.31.

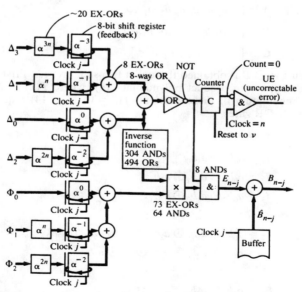

Figure 10.31 Modified cyclic decoder circuit.

10.A.6 Operations in Extended Binary Fields

The binary base field can be extended to a finite field of 2^m elements, also known as the Galois field $GF(2^m)$ in which the field elements are represented by m-bit binary bytes. As an example, we will consider the Galois field $GF(2^8)$ in which the 256 distinct elements are represented by the 256 eight-bit bytes. Each element can be written as a polynomial $A(x)$ with eight binary coefficients as follows

$$A(x) = a_0 + a_1x + a_2x^2 + a_3x^3 + a_4x^4 + a_5x^5 + a_6x^6 + a_7x^7$$

The zero element of this field is the byte A with $a_i = 0$ for all i; the 1 element is the byte A with $a_i = 1$ for $i = 0$ and $a_i = 0$ for all other values of i. The sum and product of any two elements in this field are computed as the modulo-2 sum and product of the corresponding polynomials with the results reduced modulo $P(x)$, where $P(x)$ is a prime polynomial of degree 8. (A polynomial is prime if it cannot be factored into two or more polynomials of lower degrees. It is also called an irreducible polynomial.) Thus the sum and product of two field elements $A(x)$ and $B(x)$ are defined as

$$\text{Sum} = A(x) + B(x) \text{ modulo } P(x)$$

$$\text{Product} = A(X) \times B(x) \text{ modulo } P(x)$$

Since $P(x)$ is a degree-8 polynomial, the result of the reduction modulo $P(x)$ is always a polynomial of degree less than 8, thus an element of the field. Furthermore, $P(x)$ is irreducible, which ensures that the result of the sum or product of field elements is always a unique field element.

Figure 10.32 represents the estimated hardware for implementing the product function in $GF(2^8)$. A, B, and C are elements of $GF(2^8)$, and are represented by 8-bit byte binary vectors, where $C = A \otimes B$.

$$A = [a_7, a_6, a_5, a_4, a_3, a_2, a_1, a_0]$$

$$B = [b_7, b_6, b_5, b_4, b_3, b_2, b_1, b_0]$$

$$C = [c_7, c_6, c_5, c_4, c_3, c_2, c_1, c_0]$$

The product $A \otimes B$ is obtained through a two-step process. First, we compute the coefficients f_i of the product polynomial $F(x)$, where $F(x) = F(A) \times F(B)$ modulo-2. Computation of the coefficients $f_i(i = 0, \ldots, 14)$ requires 64 AND gates and 49 EX-OR gates.

$$f_0 = a_0b_0$$

$$f_1 = a_0b_1 \oplus a_1b_0$$

$$f_2 = a_0b_2 \oplus a_1b_1 \oplus a_2b_0$$

$$f_3 = a_0b_3 \oplus a_1b_2 \oplus a_2b_1 \oplus a_3b_0$$

$$\vdots \quad \vdots \quad \vdots \quad \vdots \quad \vdots$$

$$f_7 = a_0b_7 \oplus a_1b_6 \oplus a_2b_5 \oplus \cdots \oplus a_6b_1 \oplus a_7b_0$$

$$f_8 = a_1b_7 \oplus a_2b_6 \oplus a_3b_5 \oplus \cdots \oplus a_7b_1$$

$$\vdots \quad \vdots \quad \vdots$$

$$f_{13} = a_6b_7 \oplus a_7b_6$$

$$f_{14} = a_7b_7$$

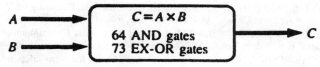

Figure 10.32 Product function.

Next, we reduce the polynomial F modulo $p(x)$, where $p(x)$ is a primitive binary polynomial of degree 8. We use $p(x) = x^8 + x^4 + x^3 x^2 + 1$. The reduction of f_i modulo $p(x)$ requires, at the most, 24 EX-OR gates.

$$C_0 = f_0 \oplus f_8 \oplus f_{12} \oplus f_{13} \oplus f_{14}$$
$$C_1 = f_1 \oplus f_9 \oplus f_{13} \oplus f_{14}$$
$$C_2 = f_2 \oplus f_8 \oplus f_{10} \oplus f_{12} \oplus f_{13}$$
$$C_3 = f_3 \oplus f_8 \oplus f_9 \oplus f_{11} \oplus f_{12}$$
$$C_4 = f_4 \oplus f_8 \oplus f_9 \oplus f_{10} \oplus f_{14}$$
$$C_5 = f_5 \oplus f_9 \oplus f_{10} \oplus f_{11}$$
$$C_6 = f_6 \oplus f_{10} \oplus f_{11} \oplus f_{12}$$
$$C_7 = f_7 \oplus f_{11} \oplus f_{12} \oplus f_{13}$$

The logic for the entire product function requires one level of AND circuits and five levels of EX-OR circuits, which in turn require 64 AND gates and a maximum of 73 EX-OR gates. Note that when one of the multiplicands, say A, is a known constant, then the expression for each component C_i of C will reduce to EX-OR of selected components of the second multiplicand, namely B. The resultant product function requires no AND gates and only a small number of EX-OR gates (maximum 25), depending on the constant A.

REFERENCES

Adler, R. L., D. Coppersmith, and M. Hassner, "Algorithms for Sliding Block Codes," *IEEE Trans. Info. Theory,* **IT-29,** 5 (1983).

Berlekamp, E. R., "On Decoding Binary Bose-Chaudhuri-Hocquenghem Codes," *IEEE Trans. Info. Theory,* **IT-11,** 577 (1965).

Bose, R. C., and D. K. Ray-Chaudhuri, "On a Class of Error-Correcting Binary Group Codes," *Info. Control,* **3,** 68 (1960).

Brown, D. T., and W. W. Peterson, "Cyclic Codes for Error Detection," *Proc. IRE,* **49,** 228 (1961).

Brown, D. T., and F. F. Sellers, Jr., "Error Correction for IBM 800-bit-per-inch Magnetic Tape," *IBM J. Res. Dev.,* **14,** 384 (1970).

Carasso, M., and H. Nakajima, "What is the Compact Disk Digital Audio System?" *IEEE Int. Conf. on Consum. Electron. Digest of Tech. Papers,* 138 (1982).

Chien, R. T., "Cyclic Decoding Procedures for the Bose-Chaudhuri-Hocquenghem Codes," *IEEE Trans. Info. Theory,* **IT-10,** 357 (1964).

Chien, R. T., "Burst-Correction Codes with High-Speed Decoding," *IEEE Trans. Info. Theory,* **IT-1,** 109 (1969).

Doi, T. T., "Error Correction in the Compact Disk System" *Audio,* **24,** April (1984).

Eggenberger, J. S., and P. Hodges, "Sequential Encoding and Decoding of Variable Word Length, Fixed Rate Data Codes," U.S. Patent 4,115,768, (1978).

Eggenberger, J. S., and A. M. Patel, "Method and Apparatus for Implementing Optimal PRML Codes," U.S. Patent No. 4,707,681 (1987).

Fire, P., "A Class of Multiple-Error-Correcting Binary Codes for Non-Independent Errors," Sylvania Report RSL-E-2, Sylvania Reconnaissance Systems Lab., Mountain View, Calif., 1959.

Forney, Jr., G. D., "On Decoding BCH Codes," *IEEE Trans. Info. Theory,* **IT-11,** 549 (1965).

Franaszek, P. A., "Sequence-State Methods of Run-Length-Limited Coding," *IBM J. Res. Dev.,* **14,** 376 (1970).

Franaszek, P. A., "Run-Length-Limited Variable Length Coding with Error Propagation Limitation," U.S. Patent 3,689,899 (1972).

Gorenstein, D. C., and N. Zierler, "A Class of Error-Correcting Codes in p^m Symbols," *J. Soc. Indus. Appl. Math.,* **9,** 207 (1961).

Hocquenghem, A., "Codes Correcteurs d'Erreurs," *Chiffres (Paris)* **2,** 147 (1959).

Hodges, P., W. J. Schaeuble, and P. L. Shaffer, "Error Correcting System for Serial-by-Byte-Data," U.S. Patent 4,185,269 (1980).

Horiguchi, T., and K. Morita, "An Optimization of Modulation Codes in Digital Recording," *IEEE Trans. Magn.,* **MAG-12,** 740 (1976).

Jacoby, G. V., "A New Look-Ahead Code for Increased Data Density," *IEEE Trans. Magn.,* **MAG-13,** 1202 (1977).

Jacoby, G. V., and R. Kost, "Binary Two-Thirds Rate Code with Full Look-Ahead," *IEEE Trans. Magn.,* **MAG-20,** 709 (1984).

MacKintosh, N. D., "The Choice of a Recording Code," *Radio Electron. Eng,* **50,** 177 (1980).

Marcus, B. H., A. M. Patel, and P. H. Siegel, "Method and Apparatus for Implementing a PRML Code," U.S. Patent No. 4,786,890 (1988).

Massey, J. L., "Step-by-Step Decoding of the Bose-Chaudhuri-Hocquenghem Codes," *IEEE Trans. Info. Theory,* **IT-11,** 580–585 (1965).

Miller, J. W., U.S. Patent 3,108,261 (1963).

Miller, J. W., U.S. Patent 4,027,335 (1977).

Ouchi, N. K., "Apparatus for Encoding and Decoding Binary Data in a Modified Zero Modulation Data Code," U.S. Patent 3,995,264 (1976).

Patel, A. M., "Zero Modulation Encoding in Magnetic Recording," *IBM J. Res. Dev.,* **19,** 366 (1975).

Patel, A. M., "Error-Recovery Scheme for the IBM 3850 Mass Storage System," *IBM J. Res. Dev.,* **24,** 32 (1980a).

Patel, A. M., "Multitrack Error Correction with Cross-Parity-Check Coding." U.S. Patent 4,205,324 (1980b).

Patel, A. M., "Improved Encoder and Decoder for a Byte-Oriented (0, 3) § Code," *IBM Tech. Disclosure Bull.,* **28,** 1938 (1985a).

Patel, A. M., "Adaptive Cross-Parity Code for High-Density Magnetic Tape Subsystem," *IBM J. Res. Dev.,* **29,** 546 (1985b).

Patel, A. M., U.S. Patent 4,525,838 (1985c).

Patel, A. M., "On-the-Fly Decoder for Multiple Byte Errors," *IBM J. Res. Dev.,* **39,** 259 (1986).

Patel, A. M., U.S. Patent 4,706,250 (1987).

Patel, A. M., "Rate 16/17 (0, 6/6) Code," *IBM Tech. Disclosure Bull.* **38,** 8 (1989).

Patel, A. M., and S. J. Hong, "Optimal Rectangular Code for High-Density Magnetic Tapes," *IBM J. Res. Dev.,* **18,** 579 (1974).

Peterson, W. W., "Encoding and Error-Correction Procedures for the Bose-Chaudhuri Codes," *IEEE Trans. Info. Theory,* **6,** 459 (1960).

Peterson, W. W., *Error Correcting Codes,* MIT Press, Cambridge, Mass., 1961.

Prusinkiewicz, P., and S. Budkowski, "A Double-Track Error-Correction Code for Magnetic Tape," *IEEE Trans. Computers,* 642 (1976).

Reed, I. S., and G. Solomon, "Polynomial Codes over Certain Finite Fields," *J. Siam.,* **8,** 300 (1960).

Shannon, C. E., "A Mathematical Theory of Communication," *Bell Syst. Tech. J.,* **27,** 379 (1948).

Wolf, J. K., "Adding Two Information Symbols to Certain Nonbinary BCH Codes, and Some Applications," *Bell Systems Tech. J.,* **48,** 2408 (1969).

APPENDIX
CONVERSION TABLE

Units for Magnetic Properites

Quantity	Symbol	Gaussian & cgs emu†	Conversion factor C‡	SI§
Magnetic flux density, magnetic induction	B	gauss (G)	10^{-4}	tesla (T), Wb/m^2
Magnetic flux	Φ	maxwell (Mx), G·cm^2	10^{-8}	weber (Wb)
Magnetic potential difference, magnetomotive force	U	gilbert (Gb)	$10/4\pi$	ampere (A)
Magnetic field strength, magnetizing force	H	oersted (Oe)	$10^3/4\pi$	A/m
Magnetization	M	emu/cm^3	10^3	A/m
Specific saturation magnetization	σ	emu/g	1	A·m^2/kg
Magnetic moment	m	emu	10^{-3}	A·m^2
Susceptibility	χ	dimensionless	4π	dimensionless
Permeability of vacuum	μ_o	dimensionless	$4\pi \times 10^{-7}$	Wb/(A·m)
Permeability	μ	dimensionless	$4\pi \times 10^{-7} = \mu_o$	Wb/(A·m)
Demagnetization factor	N	dimensionless	$1/4\pi$	dimensionless

†Gaussian units and cgs emu are the same for magnetic properties. The defining relation is $B = H + 4\pi M$.

‡Multiply a number in Gaussian units by C to convert it to SI.

§SI (Système International d'Unités) has been adopted by the National Bureau of Standards and is based on the definition $B = \mu_o(H + M)$.

INDEX

Italic page numbers indicate where defining or detailed descriptions are given.

2-19-97